T0322055

Research Anthology on Social Media Advertising and Building Consumer Relationships

Information Resources Management Association
USA

Volume II

Published in the United States of America by
    IGI Global
    Business Science Reference (an imprint of IGI Global)
    701 E. Chocolate Avenue
    Hershey PA, USA 17033
    Tel: 717-533-8845
    Fax: 717-533-8661
    E-mail: cust@igi-global.com
    Web site: http://www.igi-global.com

Library of Congress Cataloging-in-Publication Data

Names: Information Resources Management Association, editor.
Title: Research anthology on social media advertising and building consumer
  relationships / Information Resources Management Association, editor.
Description: Hershey, PA : Business Science Reference, [2022] | Includes
  bibliographical references and index. | Summary: "This edited research
  book considers best practices and strategies of utilizing social media
  successfully throughout various business fields to promote products,
  build relationships, and maintain relevancy by discussing common
  pitfalls and challenges companies face as they attempt to create a name
  for themselves in the online world"-- Provided by publisher.
Identifiers: LCCN 2022015784 (print) | LCCN 2022015785 (ebook) | ISBN
  9781668462874 (hardcover) | ISBN 9781668462881 (ebook)
Subjects: LCSH: Internet advertising. | Internet marketing. | Social
  media--Economic aspects. | Customer relations.
Classification: LCC HF6146.I58 .R47 2022 (print) | LCC HF6146.I58 (ebook)
  | DDC 659.14/4--dc23/eng/20220407
LC record available at https://lccn.loc.gov/2022015784
LC ebook record available at https://lccn.loc.gov/2022015785

British Cataloguing in Publication Data
A Cataloguing in Publication record for this book is available from the British Library.

For electronic access to this publication, please contact: eresources@igi-global.com.

List of Contributors

Table of Contents

Volume II

Section 3
Tools and Technologies

Section 4
Utilization and Applications

Volume IV

Section 6
Managerial Impact

Section 7
Critical Issues and Challenges

Preface

Social media has become a key tool that businesses must utilize in all areas of their practices to build relationships with their customer base and promote their products and services. Through social media, businesses have access to a global customer base of which they can reach, interact with, and develop their brand. This technology is no longer optimal as those who do not take advantage of the many benefits it offers continue to struggle with outdated practices. In order for a business to flourish, further study on the advantages social media provides in the areas of marketing and developing consumer relationships is required.

Staying informed of the most up-to-date research trends and findings is of the utmost importance. That is why IGI Global is pleased to offer this four-volume reference collection of reprinted IGI Global book chapters and journal articles that have been handpicked by senior editorial staff. This collection will shed light on critical issues related to the trends, techniques, and uses of various applications by providing both broad and detailed perspectives on cutting-edge theories and developments. This collection is designed to act as a single reference source on conceptual, methodological, technical, and managerial issues, as well as to provide insight into emerging trends and future opportunities within the field.

The *Research Anthology on Social Media Advertising and Building Consumer Relationships is* organized into seven distinct sections that provide comprehensive coverage of important topics. The sections are:

1. Fundamental Concepts and Theories;
2. Development and Design Methodologies;
3. Tools and Technologies;
4. Utilization and Applications;
5. Organizational and Social Implications;
6. Managerial Impact; and
7. Critical Issues and Challenges.

The following paragraphs provide a summary of what to expect from this invaluable reference tool.

Section 1, "Fundamental Concepts and Theories," serves as a foundation for this extensive reference tool by addressing crucial theories essential to understanding the best practice of social media utilization for business processes. The first chapter of this section, "Social Media for Business Purposes: Objectives Pursued and Satisfaction in the Results," by Prof. Aitziber Nunez-Zabaleta of UPV EHU, Leioa, Spain, analyzes the specific work tasks that 302 professional workers from the Basque region in Spain perform on social media (SM) for attaining their objectives, together with the work satisfaction they gain. The final chapter of this section, "How Social Commerce Characteristics Influence Consumers'

Online Impulsive Buying Behavior in Emerging Markets," by Prof. Vu Minh Ngo of Van Lang University, Vietnam and Profs. Nguyen Cao Lien Phuoc and Quyen Phu Thi Phan of University of Economics, The University of Danang, Vietnam, investigates the role of social commerce characteristics in shaping consumers' online impulsive buying behavior. The study's outcomes offer useful insights to both academicians and practitioners.

Section 2, "Development and Design Methodologies," presents in-depth coverage of the design and development of advertising strategies on social media based on consumer buying behavior. The first chapter of this section, "Effects of Social Media Marketing Strategies on Consumers Behavior," by Profs. Shamsher Singh and Deepali Saluja of Banarsidas Chandiwala Institute of Professional Studies, India, investigates how social media affects the decision-making process of consumers and the impacts of various marketing strategies used by firms on social media. The study employs the survey method to collect primary data from 200 customers who have been regularly using social media. Factor analysis and ANOVA has been used to gain insights in the study. The selected respondents are assumed to represent the population in the urban areas of Delhi. The final chapter of this section, "Social Media Advertisements and Buying Behaviour: A Study of Indian Working Women," by Prof. Yuvika Gupta of IMS Unison University, India and Prof. Samik Shome of Institute of Management, Nirma University, India, identifies the factors that are influencing the working women purchase behaviour. It explains that demographic variables such as age and income of working women do play a significant role in online purchases. The key contribution of this paper is to provide the corporate houses an assessment of the extent to which the working women in India are influenced by social media in their online buying behavior.

Section 3, "Tools and Technologies," explores the various tools and technologies used in advertising through social media from implementation to analytics. The first chapter of this section, "Social Media as a Marketing Tool," by Prof. Rajeshwari Krishnamurthy of Great Lakes Institute of Management, India, discusses how social media can be used as a marketing tool. Right from describing the various forms of social media, it touches upon the different methods by which social media are engaged with by a marketer. The tasks of creating awareness, generating interest, encouraging action, resulting in purchase, and doing brand advocacy are all covered. The final chapter of this section, "Paradigms of Public Relations in an Age of Digitalization: Social Media Analytics in the UAE," by Prof. Badreya Al-Jenaibi of The United Arab Emirates University, UAE, explores the uses of social media in public relations (PR) departments in the United Arab Emirates (UAE). It seeks to lay the basis for understanding the place of social media in the UAE and to contribute to the analysis of the issue of social change in the PR offices. The chapter assesses the state of PR in the UAE in relation to global media and highlights needs in this area for both public and private enterprises. Presenting interview data taken from a cross section of 40 organizations throughout the UAE, it addresses perceptions of benefits, challenges, public acceptance, and future strategies of social media in relation to global SM as whole. It finds that barriers to the use and acceptance of SM in PR have mostly been lifted.

Section 4, "Utilization and Applications," describes how advertising and marketing strategies are used and applied in social media. The first chapter of this section, "Maturity Profiles of Organizations for Social Media," by Prof. Edyta Abramek of University of Economics in Katowice, Poland, analyzes case studies of selected organizations in terms of their achievements in the use of social media. The profiling method applied in the study facilitated evaluating the model of the selected organization. The final chapter of this section, "Social Media in Micro-Enterprises: Exploring Adoption in the Indonesian Retail Sector," by Profs. Savanid Vatanasakdakul and Chadi Aoun of Carnegie Mellon University, Doha, Qatar and Prof. Yuniarti Hidayah Suyoso Putra of Macquarie University, North Ryde, Australia, proposes a research model derived from the Unified Theory of Acceptance and the Use of Technology and extended by integrating the task-technology-fit framework, along with price value propositions.

Section 5, "Organizational and Social Implications," includes chapters discussing the impact of social media advertising on both the companies and on the consumers. The first chapter of this section, "Firm's Competitive Growth in the Social Media Age," by Prof. Nermeen Atef Ahmed Hegazy of Cairo University, Egypt, explains social media as a strategic marketing tool which can be used by firms to help gain competitive advantage. It further discusses the techniques applied to social media advertising for firms. The final chapter of this section, "Social Media Marketing and Brand Loyalty Among Online Shoppers in Anambra State, Nigeria: Mediating Effect of Brand Awareness," by Profs. Ebuka Christian Ezenwafor, Adeola A. Ayodele, and Chukwudi Ireneus Nwaizugbo of Nnamdi Azikiwe University, Akwa, Nigeria, examines the mediating effect of brand awareness on social media marketing and brand loyalty among online shoppers in a typical emerging market.

Section 6, "Managerial Impact," covers the internal and external impacts of social media on companies. The first chapter of this section, "Social Media and E-Commerce: A Study on Motivations for Sharing Content From E-Commerce Websites," by Prof. Beatriz Casais of School of Economics and Management, University of Minho, Portugal & IPAM Porto, Portugal and Prof. Tiago Da Costa of Faculty of Economics, University of Porto, Portugal, uncovers which motivations serve as a background for individuals sharing intentions of e-commerce content. The final chapter of this section, "Social Media, Online Brand Communities, and Customer Engagement in the Fashion Industry," by Prof. Guida Helal of American University of Beirut, Lebanon, focuses on theoretical and managerial implications. This chapter considers the influence social media brand communities and social identity may have on a fashion brand.

Section 7, "Critical Issues and Challenges," presents coverage of academic and research perspectives on challenges to using social media as a tool for advertising. The first chapter of this section, "Consumption in the Digital Age: A Research on Social Media Influencers," by Prof. Eda Turanci of Ankara Haci Bayram Veli University, Turkey, examines the relationship between influencers and consumption. The final chapter of this section, "An Empirical Study on Determining the Effectiveness of Social Media Advertising: A Case on Indian Millennials," by Profs. Taanika Arora and Bhawna Agarwal of Amity College of Commerce and Finance, Amity University, India, proposes a conceptual model based on social media advertising, which examines the impact of some identified antecedents such as entertainment, informativeness, credibility, incentives, pre-purchase search motivation, and social escapism motivation on attitude towards social media advertising and further see the impact on purchase intention.

Although the primary organization of the contents in this multi-volume work is based on its seven sections, offering a progression of coverage of the important concepts, methodologies, technologies, applications, social issues, and emerging trends, the reader can also identify specific contents by utilizing the extensive indexing system listed at the end of each volume. As a comprehensive collection of research on the latest findings related to consumer relationships on social media, the *Research Anthology on Social Media Advertising and Building Consumer Relationships* provides managers, business owners, entrepreneurs, researchers, scholars, academicians, practitioners, instructors, and students with a complete understanding of the applications and impacts of social media as a tool for advertising and building brand image. Given the vast number of issues concerning usage, failure, success, strategies, and applications of social media in modern business strategies and processes, the *Research Anthology on Social Media Advertising and Building Consumer Relationships* encompasses the most pertinent research on the applications, impacts, uses, and strategies of social media advertising.

Chapter 28
The Discount Effect in Food and Beverage Advertising and Instagram's Likes Power:
An Experimental Study

Nilton Gomes Furtado
https://orcid.org/0000-0002-6372-4693
University of Aveiro, Portugal

Julia Vasconcelos Furtado
https://orcid.org/0000-0002-4335-6272
University of Aveiro, Portugal

Pedro H. Drudi
Anhembi Morumbi University, Brazil

Rafael de Vasconcelos Silva
University of Aveiro, Portugal

Lauro César Vieira Filho
University of Aveiro, Portugal

ABSTRACT

This study aims to understand the effect of evident sales promotion on the number of likes on Instagram. Due to the rising use of social media to communicate with the market and the promotion of products to guests, few academic investigations have been made in this area. Most technology research in the hospitality industry has focused on technology in service and production areas of operations or the use of web-based marketing for tourism operations and travel agents. The two most effective sales offer patterns were used in a 2×2 experiment, with the intention of finding out if a large amount of likes on Instagram influences the purchase intention of the product offered. Four randomized questionnaires were distributed among 4 university groups, obtaining 923 respondents. To validate the hypotheses the study proceeded with the descriptive technique and analysis of variances (ANOVA).

DOI: 10.4018/978-1-6684-6287-4.ch028

INTRODUCTION

The food and beverage industry is a critical component of the Brazilian economy, even when facing a period of economic recession in 2016, with a decrease of -3.75% on revenues in 2015 (Brazilian Association of Bars and Restaurants - ABRASEL), this sector contributed with approximately 10.1% of the Brazilian Gross Domestic Product (ABIA, 2017). On the other hand, bar's and restaurants' segment found that at least 32.9% of Brazilians have some kind of meal outside - not home cooking - on a daily basis. IFB's (Food Service Brazil Institute) recent studies indicates that 64% of sales are from small and medium-sized establishments.

The industry's competitiveness makes the use of discount advertisement something common among companies, as means to attract consumer's attention (Aureliano-Silva, Strehlau, & Strehlau, 2017). Discounts are effective in selling products directly to consumer. It is widely used and can be presented in several formats, such as in percentage or monetary value (Aureliano-Silva, Brandão, Strehlau, Pimenta, & Pimenta, 2015); offering a second product as a gift at the purchase of the product on sale, is reported as well in some cases. Such offers have already been used in retail for years, leading to academic research on the matter (Santini, Lübeck, & Hoffmann, 2015). However, over the past two decades there had been an increase in the use of digital media and social networks for marketing purposes, such as the sale/discount advertising (Needles & Thompson, 2013).

Due to food and beverage industry size and relevance, it is essential to understand how to use components of foodservice operations and technology to increase effectiveness in several business aspects such as marketing, recruitment, training, guest service, and global operations. With increasing availability and use of technology and social media, social networking platforms had become a new media to be used by restaurants and other service organizations (DiPietro, Crews, Gustafson, & Strick, 2012; Kaplan & Haenlein, 2009). Social media can be used in many ways, including content, social networking websites or blogs (Facebook and Twitter), and collaborative projects. Social media can be understood as "[i]nternet applications that help consumers share insights, experiences and perspectives" (Kaplan & Haenlein, 2009).

The social media is defined as a web-based service that allows individuals to build a public network or public profile within a delimited system; create a list of other users with whom they share a connection and view/cross its own list of connections, as well as those made by others within the system (Boyd & Ellison, 2008). These platforms allow people to find others with similar interests and to share those interests through the Internet. The survey by the Global Web Index found that the Brazilian public spent about 40 minutes online every day, in 2015, making Brazil the third country in the world (only behind Thailand and Saudi Arabia) in the use of smartphone on the internet (Bayindir & Kavanagh, 2018).

The smartphones' use as a means of access to social media continues to increase, and small and medium-sized companies, especially in bars and restaurants industry, have little advertising and marketing strategy, once only the big corporations actually invest in advertising and branding. Social media like Facebook, MySpace, Twitter, LinkedIn and others can be used by the industry to recruit staff, advertise and solicit guest feedback (Furtado & Oliveira, 2016).

The current study aims to understand the discount effect on consumer's opinion/decision, when it is advertised with the number of likes on Instagram. Due to the recent advent of social media use to communicate with market and clients, few academic investigations in this field have been held. Most studies on technology in hospitality industry has focused on technology in service and production operations areas, or in the web-based marketing use for tourism operations and travel agents (DiPietro et al., 2012;

Furtado, Canto, Oliveira, & Moretti, 2017; Gregory, Wang, & DiPietro, 2010; Lovelock & Gummesson, 2004). The two most effective promotion patterns were used in a 2×2 experiment, aiming to find out if a large number of likes on Instagram influences on intended purchase of the product being promoted.

The present chapter is divided in:

1. Theoretical reference on sales promotions.
2. Theoretical reference on advertising techniques.
3. Method and control procedures.
4. Experimental data analysis.
5. Conclusion.

SALES PROMOTIONS

Several studies have shown the use of discounts as a marketing tool to consumer's attraction and influencing purchase intention (Aureliano-Silva et al., 2017; Santini et al., 2015). The relationship between price and purchase intention is directly linked to two factors: product quality and price aversion (Oliveira, 2007). In Price Search strategy, the buyer chooses the most expensive product to avoid the risk of buying a low-quality product. In Price Aversion strategy, on the other hand, the buyer opts for a cheaper product in order to avoid the risk of making great purchase sacrifice. By relating the assertion to pricing in promotions, it can be understood that the price presentation in promotions can be related to consumer's behavior and purchase intention (Aureliano-Silva et al., 2017; Kukanja, Gomezelj Omerzel, & Kodrič, 2017; Namin, 2017): The use of dollar signs or any other element referring to the payment will be less effective to the purchase intention. However, according Aureliano-Silva et al. (2015), when using the discount in currency, the relation with purchase intention is greater.

Another attribute used in promotional actions is the use of discount by percentage. Based on the research carried out by (Medeiros, Gosling, Alves, & Vera, 2015) discounts up to 25% are effective in influencing purchase intention. Above this value, the product's perception of quality is affected, leading the consumer to characterize the product as 'low quality'. The work of Aureliano-Silva et al. (2015) shows a lower purchase intention when a percentage discount is used, when compared to monetary discount. Furthermore, when the attributes of the product are omitted such as the discount value, it can lead to a negative interpretation by the consumer over the product's discount, particularly due to the connection to the need of payment (Aureliano-Silva et al., 2015; Santini et al., 2015). However, such research had been carried out on products from different industries, demanding a check on the results in food and beverage industry, and the study indicates only the consumer's purchase intention, as well as the quality and value perceptions of the product, not measuring the attractiveness of the discount in percentage when compared to the currency discount. Thus, hypotheses 1, 2, and 3 were created:

H1: The currency discount will lead to greater purchase intention, when compared to percentage discount.
H2: The influence of the higher number of likes on the sales with a monetary discount of 7 Reais (BRL), will have greater attractiveness than the same offer with lower number of likes.
H3: The influence of the highest number of likes on the 20% discount offer will be more attractive than the same offer with lower number of likes.

It is also common to offer free items in addition to the product offered. Such offers may be in the form of a bonus-pack, popularly used as an example, in the lightweight format buy 2 pay 1 (Twenge, Campbell, Hoffman, & Lance, 2010) or freebie items, which are products other than the one sold but offered as a prize for the purchase of the product. Bokunewicz and Shulman (2017) present the effectiveness of freebie items in fast-food industry on purchase intention and in offer attractiveness', considering that the product offered as a gift should not be much higher value nor much lower than the currency discount, which would cause consumer mistrust (Ha, 2015).

ADVERTISING TECHNIQUES

Instagram is a photo and video sharing site with followers and friends, and even links to other social networks such as Facebook and Twitter. It is no longer a secondary social network, and it should be part of the marketing planning of any Business to Consumer (B2C) company (Nobre & Silva, 2014). It is even estimated that about 67% of the world's top brands are using Instagram, reaching over 100 million active users on the network (Nuno, 2018).

Social media marketing strategy is useful in market and academics resources (Nobre & Faria, 2017; Nobre & Silva, 2014). Social media with Facebook and Instagram should be used by companies, small and middle business. (Nobre & Silva, 2014; Soares, Pinho, & Nobre, 2012) The influence of the social media show that it can be used as a new method to increase the number of clients, and to bring consumers closer to the company.

There is an increased use of social media for advertising and feedback (Singh, Sarfaraz, Sarfaraz, & Jenab, 2015). Beyond that, it influences increased or decreased revenue management. Furthermore, this phenomenon has lowered the product lifecycle at restaurants, that in order to make profit, must opt for technology that responds to changing customer requirements - both implicit and explicit, efficiently and profitably (Furtado, Pereira, Pereira, & Moreira, 2019; Furtado & Cunha, 2017; Furtado, Furtado, Vieira, & Cunha, 2019).

The social media use brings satisfaction to the customer, and in some cases, may be able to generate loyalty to a restaurant (Furtado & Cunha, 2017; Furtado et al., 2019; Helena Nobre & Silva, 2014; Soares et al., 2012). However, this factor is not fundamental to generate loyalty, while dining experience, environment and other factors directly influence customers loyalty in catering.

We have to pay special attention to gender, since its influence on social media participation stands out, showing that the attitude of technology usage may have a relation to this demographic variable (Venkatesh, Morris et al., 2003).

Based on these studies, Hypothesis 4 and 5 were elaborated:

H4: The gender influence in purchase intention of product with greater number of likes.
H5: The gender influence in purchase intention of products that presents monetary discount value on percentage.

METHOD AND CONTROL PROCEDURES

The survey used questionnaires as data collection procedure, with the purpose of collecting data within the subjects to generate the information necessary to verify and attain the study objectives.

The sample was composed of undergraduate and graduate students from four universities: two public and two private universities, located in the city of São Paulo (BRAZIL). Four randomized questionnaires were distributed to four groups from each university, that obtained 923 respondents.

The survey presented one advertisement with seven questions, being two demographics and five questions about purchase intention related to the picture presented and the perception of the number of likes. Following are figures of each survey. The figure 1 shows the variations of the picture used at the surveys, there were 4 variations - each one had a promotion type (percentage or monetary discount) and number of likes - 20% discount with lower likes, 7 reais discount with lower likes, 20% discount with higher likes and discount of 7 reais with higher number of likes.

Figure 1. Survey promotions images

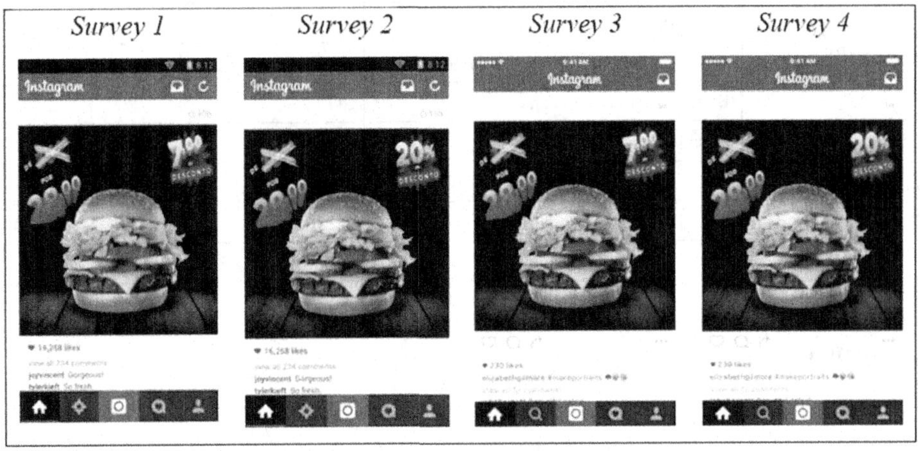

As a research technique, a convenience sample had been used, a common technique in which one chooses a population sample that is accessible. Therefore, subjects involved in the research were chosen because of their availability, not through statistical criteria. In general, convenience sample allows greater operational accessibility and lower sample costs, however, those results may be limited in providing general statements with statistical accuracy regarding population sample.

EXPERIMENTAL DATA ANALYSIS

In the first questionnaire, the lower number of likes was analyzed when compared to the monetary discount of 7 Reais (BRL) presented in the advertisement. There were 137 respondents, in which 62 (45.3%) were male and 75 (54.7%) female, with an average age of 25 years. The second questionnaire evaluated the influence of the lower number of likes compared to the percentage discount (20%) in the advertisement. There were 139 respondents participating, being 42 (30.2%) males, 92 (66.2%) females and 5 (3.6) chose not to declare their gender, with a mean age of 23 years. Moreover, a third questionnaire was elaborated, to evaluate the influence of the higher number of likes compared to the monetary discount of 7 Reais (BRL) presented in the advertisement. There were 295 respondents, being 131 (44.6%) male, 161 (54.8%) female and 2 (0.7) preferred did not declare their gender, with a mean age of 28 years. Finally, with the fourth questionnaire, we established the criterion of 20% discount with a higher number of likes in the ad. There were 342 respondents, which 142 (41.6%) were male, 194 (56.9%) female and 5 (1,5) preferred did not declare their gender, with mean age of 23 years.

In order to validate the hypotheses, we proceed with descriptive technique and analysis of variances (ANOVA). $P < 0.05$ was used as a parameter of significance (Hair, 2010; Hair, Black, Babin, & Anderson, 2014). The statistical software SPSS version 24 was used for statistical analysis.

Table 1. Test of Homogeneity of Variance

		Levene' Statistics	df1	df2	*Sig.*
Purchase intention with monetary discount of 7 Reais (BRL)	Based on mean	,555	2	136	*,575*
	Based on median	,515	2	136	*,599*
	Based on median and with df adjusted	,515	2	135,944	*,599*
	Based on trimmed mean	,472	2	136	*,625*
Purchase Intention with 20% percentage discount	Based on mean	1,599	2	136	*,206*
	Based on median	1,136	2	136	*,324*
	Based on median and with df adjusted	1,136	2	135,640	*,324*
	Based on trimmed mean	1,537	2	136	*,219*

Table 2. Test ANOVA

		Between Groups				In Groups	Total
		Combined	Linear Term				
			Inconsiderate	Considerate	Desviation		
Purchase intention with monetary discount of 7 Reais (BRL)	Sum of Squares	11,726	1,732	2,175	9,552	434,921	446,647
	Df	2	1	1	1	136	138
	Mean Square	5,863	1,732	2,175	9,552	3,198	
	Z	1,833	,542	,680	2,987		
	Sig.	,164	,463	,411	,086		
Purchase Intention with 20% percentage discount	Sum of Squares	,701	,559	,048	,653	343,745	344,446
	Df	2	1	1	1	136	138
	Mean Square	,350	,559	,048	,653	2,528	
	Z	,139	,221	,019	,258		
	Sig.	*,871*	*,639*	*,890*	*,612*		

The Variance Homogeneity Test (table 1) showed that the purchase intention with monetary discount of 7 Reais (BRL) presented an average significance of p-value (sig 0.575), while the purchase intention discount with 20% percentage discount, obtained a significance mean p-value (sig 0.206), showing that the monetary discount value is more representative than the percentage value.

The ANOVA results presented on table 2 above, determined that there is a statistically significant difference (z = 0.680, p = 0.411) between the monetary discount and the percentage discount variables (z = 0.019, p = 0890). The following are the results of the TukeyScheffePost-Hoc test (table 3), which indicates the presence or absence of a statistically significant difference in the number of Likes at an individual level and gender difference.

Table 3. Multiple comparisons

	Gender		Mean Difference (I-J)	Std. Error	Sig.	95% Confidence Interval	
						Lower Bound	Upper Bound
Purchase intention with monetary discount of 7 Reais (BRL)	Female	Male	,553	,333	,224	-,24	1,34
		Not to declare	-,604	,821	,743	-2,55	1,34
	Male	Female	-,553	,333	,224	-1,34	,24
		Not to declare	-1,157	,846	,361	-3,16	,85
	Not to declare	Female	,604	,821	,743	-1,34	2,55
		Male	1,157	,846	,361	-,85	3,16
Purchase Intention with 20% percentage discount	Female	Male	-,052	,296	,983	-,75	,65
		Not to declare	,343	,730	,885	-1,39	2,07
	Male	Female	,052	,296	,983	-,65	,75
		Not to declare	,395	,752	,859	-1,39	2,18
	Not to declare	Female	-,343	,730	,885	-2,07	1,39
		Male	-,395	,752	,859	-2,18	1,39

Although the ANOVA test had indicated the presence of a statistically significant difference (p = 463) in number of likes between the two categories (monetary and percentage), the TukeyScheffePost-Hoc test did not statistically identify any significant differences at individual level.

The results of TukeyScheffePost-Hoc test on table 3 also indicate that no homogeneous subset is present at a statistically significant combined level (p = .164) between the two variables, analyzing that H1 - The currency promotion will have greater purchase intention, compared to the promotion in percentage, is supported.

Through the multiple comparisons' observation, it shows the influence of gender in the purchase of the product with greater monetary discount to the percentage with the male gender significance (p = 0.224), while the female gender has (p = 983). There was no significance related to those who do not declare the gender x female (p = 885), do not declare gender x male (0.361). Those comparisons sustain the H5 - Gender influence in the intention to purchase products that presents monetary discount value.

Table 4. Descriptive analysis

		N	Mean	Std. Error	Error	95% Confidence Interval	
						Lower Bound	Upper Bound
Purchase intention with monetary discount of 7 Reais (BRL) (higher number of likes)	Female	62	2,85	1,782	,226	2,40	3,31
	Male	75	3,17	1,804	,208	2,76	3,59
	Total	137	3,03	1,794	,153	2,73	3,33
Purchase Intention with 20% percentage discount (higher number of likes)	Female	62	2,60	1,541	,196	2,21	2,99
	Male	75	2,48	1,630	,188	2,10	2,86
	Total	137	2,53	1,586	,136	2,26	2,80
Purchase intention with monetary discount of 7 Reais (BRL) (lower number of likes)	Female	62	1,53	,503	,064	1,40	1,66
	Male	75	1,55	,501	,058	1,43	1,66
	Total	137	1,54	,500	,043	1,46	1,62
Purchase Intention with 20% percentage discount (lower number of likes)	Female	62	1,53	,503	,064	1,40	1,66
	Male	75	1,60	,493	,057	1,49	1,71
	Total	137	1,57	,497	,042	1,49	1,65

The descriptive statistics on table 4 also indicate an average value of 2.85 (95% confidence interval: lower bound of 2.40 upper bound of 3.31) in purchase intention with monetary discount of 7 Reais (BRL) (greater number of likes) males. Also, mean value of 3.17 (95% confidence interval: lower bound of 2.76 upper bound of 3.59) in purchase intention with a monetary discount of 7 Reais (BRL) (greater number of likes) female, with a standard deviation of 1,782 males and the deviation standard 1,804. Therefore, the statistics sustains hypothesis H3 - The influence of gender in the intention to buy the product with a greater number of likes.

Then, a One-Way ANOVA test was performed to test the hypothesis and to identify the presence or absence of a statistically significant difference in the content level of likes on Instagram among the four categories: purchase intention with monetary discount of 7 Reais (BRL) (higher number of likes), purchase intention with 20% discount (higher number of likes), purchase intention with monetary discount of 7 Reais (BRL) (lower number of likes) and purchase intention with 20% discount (lower number of likes).

Following the contextual variables: number of likes, purchase intention, money discount and percentage discount, hypothesis H2 - The influence of the higher number of likes on the promotional discounted money - had been tested using the One-Way ANOVA test to identify the presence of differences statistically between categories.

The ANOVA results presented at table 5 above, can determine that there is a statistically significant difference (z = 1,070, p = 0.303) between the monetary discount variables with the higher number of likes and discount with percentage with the higher number of likes (z = 0.183, p = 0.670). Among the variables with the lower number of likes, purchase intention with monetary discount of 7 Reais (lower number of likes), the significance was (z = 0.028, p = 0.867), and also purchase intention with 20% percentage discount (lower number of likes) its significance was (z = 0.629, p = 0.429).

The presence of statistically significant results in the One-Way ANOVA (p = 0.867) in the purchase intention with monetary discount with greater number of likes, as presented above, indicates that H2 is supported when related to the level of likes contained in Instagram's posts. That is the case, the results are statistically significant, since the results are more sporadic due to the homogeneity of the group of students.

To support H2, the results should indicate a higher level of likes in the monetary promotion when compared to the lower number of likes in the monetary discount, so these variables could be statistically significant.

Table 5. ANOVA

		Sum of Squares	df	Mean Square	Z	Sig.
Purchase intention with monetary discount of 7 Reais (BRL) (greater number of likes)	Between Groups	3,443	1	3,443	1,070	,303
	Within groups	434,440	135	3,218		
	Total	437,883	136			
Purchase Intention with 20% percentage discount (greater number of likes)	Between Groups	,463	1	,463	,183	,670
	Within groups	341,639	135	2,531		
	Total	342,102	136			
Purchase intention with monetary discount of 7 Reais (BRL) (a smaller number of likes)	Between Groups	,007	1	,007	,028	,867
	Within groups	34,022	135	,252		
	Total	34,029	136			
Purchase Intention with 20% percentage discount (a smaller number of likes)	Between Groups	,156	1	,156	,629	,429
	Within groups	33,435	135	,248		
	Total	*33,591*	*136*			

CONCLUSION

The role of emotions in a marketing and consumer decision-making context has been highlighted by several authors, in many contexts (Israeli, Lee, & Karpinski, 2017; Campbell, 2013; Leung, Bai, & Stahura, 2015). The reference to emotion was also presented when related to purchases of products (goods) and services (Berry, Zeithaml, & Parasuraman, 1990; Campbell, 2013; Soares et al., 2012). In a more specific sense of service, (Becker, Nobre, & Kanabar, 2013; Nogueira Tomas, Pierre Meschgrahw, & Lúcia Chicarelli Alcantara, 2012; Soares et al., 2012) leverage the intimate and intangible nature of services as a means of highlighting why emotion may be a particular influence on the services' purchase.

It had been shown that the presence of the attributes of higher likes influences the consumer and the presence of discount in percentage is significant. The correspondence between the 4 questionnaires with the ads was considered in the heterogeneous groups of students (Ha, 2015; Souza et al., 2015), supporting H2 hypotheses - The influence of the greater number of likes on the offer with monetary discount of 7 Reais, will have greater attractiveness than the same offer with less number of likes; H3 - The influence of the greater number of likes in an offer with a 20% discount will have greater attractiveness than the same offer with less number of likes; and H4 - The influence of gender in the intention to buy the product with greater number of likes.

The promotional images production only performs in a sense of creating forms of action that brands and platforms modulate and calibrate openly (Brandau, 2010; Furtado & Oliveira, 2016). Brands' efforts to experiment with mobile media imaging machines, our bodies, and cultural spaces draw attention to the need to critically examine how modes of participatory, discursive, and algorithmic control are interrelated (Frazer & Merrilees, 2012; Joachimsthaler & Aaker, 1997; Singh & Pattanayak, 2016). The hypothesis H1 - The promotion in currency will present greater intention to buy, compared to promotion in percentage, was supported, and it is important to understand how companies can improve their communication and marketing for the consumer, and if the social environment plays a role in the success. The effectiveness of social media marketing is difficult to derive, because the amount of advertising that an ad or business can receive on the Internet can depend heavily on word of mouth (Campbell, 2013; Soares et al., 2012).

As mobile social media like Instagram become more algorithmic, an important issue concerns the images produced under the trademark hashtags or promotions can influence how gender norms are reproduced in mobile social media (Aureliano-Silva et al., 2015, 2017; Berta, 2009). Supporting, therefore, hypothesis H5 - The influence of gender in the intention to buy products that presents value of monetary discount to the percentage.

In future works, it would be interesting to analyze how the algorithms recognize the performance of gender norms as associated patterns. The analysis of how brands reinforce, and exploit gender norms needs to take into account the interdependence between the discursive and algorithmic aspects of mobile social media platforms.

REFERENCES

ABIA. (2017). Números do setor de alimentos e bebidas, Brasil, 2017. Retrieved from https://www.abia.org.br/vsn/anexos/faturamento2017.pdf

Aureliano-Silva, L., Brandão, M. M., Strehlau, S., Pimenta, R. F., & Pimenta, R. F. (2015). O efeito do formato de apresentação de desconto em ambiente crowding: Um estudo experimental. *RACE - Revista de Administração Contabilidade e Economia*, *14*(2), 653. doi:10.18593/race.v14i2.6735

Aureliano-Silva, L., Strehlau, S., & Strehlau, V. (2017). Please! Wrap this gift for me: The brands effect with different promotional frames. *ICTACT Journal on Management Studies*, *3*(1), 452–456. doi:10.21917/ijms.2017.0061

Bayindir, N., & Kavanagh, D. (2018). *Global Web Index - Social*. Retrieved from www.globalwebindex.com

Becker, K., Nobre, H., & Kanabar, V. (2013). Monitoring and protecting company and brand reputation on social networks: When sites are not enough. *Global Business and Economics Review*, *15*(2/3), 293. doi:10.1504/GBER.2013.053075

Berry, L. L., Zeithaml, V. A., & Parasuraman, A. (1990). Five Imperatives for Improving Service Quality. *Sloan Management Review*, *31*(4), 29–38. Retrieved from https://search.proquest.com/openview/8b3a8e9fbf82128a35d092cf3a81003f/1?pq-origsite=gscholar&cbl=26142

Berta, D. (2009). Brands say employees atwitter for social sites. *Nation's Restaurant News, 43*(15), 1+14.

Bokunewicz, J. F., & Shulman, J. (2017). Influencer identification in Twitter networks of destination marketing organizations. *Journal of Hospitality and Tourism Technology, 8*(2), 205–219. doi:10.1108/JHTT-09-2016-0057

Boyd, M. D., & Ellison, B. N. (2008). Social Network Sites: Definition, History, and Scholarship. *Journal of Computer-Mediated Communication, 13*(3), 210–230. doi:10.1111/j.1083-6101.2007.00393.x

Brandau, M. (2010). *Chipotle, McD sign on with Facebook Deals.* Nation's Restaurant News.

Campbell, A. (2013). Word-of-Mouth Communication and Percolation in Social Networks. *The American Economic Review, 103*(6), 2466–2498. doi:10.1257/aer.103.6.2466

de Oliveira, S. L. I. (2007). *Desmistificando o marketing.* São Paulo: Novatec Editora.

DiPietro, R. B., Crews, T. B., Gustafson, C., & Strick, S. (2012). The Use of Social Networking Sites in the Restaurant Industry: Best Practices. *Journal of Foodservice Business Research, 15*(3), 265–284. doi:10.1080/15378020.2012.706193

Frazer, L., & Merrilees, B. (2012). Pioneering Asian Franchise Brands: Pho24 in Vietnam. *Journal of Marketing Channels, 19*(4), 295–309. doi:10.1080/1046669X.2012.700264

Furtado, J. V., Pereira, A. R., Pereira, I., & Moreira, A. C. (2019). Does Theory Really Fit Real Life Situations? In Handbook of Research on Entrepreneurship, Innovation, and Internationalization (pp. 419–438). Hershey, PA: IGI Global. doi:10.4018/978-1-5225-8479-7.ch016

Furtado, N. G., Canto, R. S., de Oliveira, S. L. I., & Moretti, S. L. A. (2017). Perceptions in the use of technology for payments: A study of customer behavior in food and beverage sector. *Ágora - Revista de Divulgação Científica, 22*(2), 4–23.

Furtado, N. G., & Cunha, R. da S. (2017). *A influência da adoção de technologia de meios de pagamentosna satisfação do consumidor: Um estudo com consumidores de restaurantes.* Universidade Anhembi Morumbi.

Furtado, N. G., & de Oliveira, S. L. I. (2016). *Expectativas e percepções no uso da tecnologia de pagamentos voltada ao cliente.* São Paulo: III - Encontro Dos Mestrados Profissionais Em Administração.

Furtado, N. G., Furtado, J. V., Vieira, L. C., & Cunha, R. da S. (2019). The influence of technologic payment adoption in satisfaction: a study with restaurant costumers. *International Journal of Business Excellence.* doi:10.1504/IJBEX.2019.10020420

Gregory, A., Wang, Y., & DiPietro, R. B. (2010). Towards a functional model of website evaluation: A case study of casual dining restaurants. *Worldwide Hospitality and Tourism Themes, 2*(1), 68–85. doi:10.1108/17554211011012603

Ha, A. (2015). An Experiment: Instagram Marketing Techniques and Their Effectiveness. *Communication Studies.* Retrieved from http://digitalcommons.calpoly.edu/comssp/185

Hair, J. F. (2010). *Multivariate data analysis.* Prentice Hall.

Hair, J. F., Black, W. C., Babin, B. J., & Anderson, R. E. (2014). *Multivariate Data Analysis* (7th ed.)., Retrieved from www.pearsoned.co.uk

Israeli, A., Lee, S. A., & Karpinski, A. C. (2017). Investigating the Dynamics and the Content of Customers' Social Media Reporting after a Restaurant Service Failure. *Journal of Hospitality Marketing & Management, 26*(6), 606–626. doi:10.1080/19368623.2017.1281193

Joachimsthaler, E., & Aaker, D. A. (1997). Building brands without mass media. *Harvard Business Review, 75*(1). PMID:10174453

Kaplan, A. M., & Haenlein, M. (2009). The fairyland of Second Life: Virtual social worlds and how to use them. *Business Horizons, 52*(6), 563–572. doi:10.1016/j.bushor.2009.07.002

Kukanja, M., Gomezelj Omerzel, D., & Kodrič, B. (2017). Ensuring restaurant quality and guests' loyalty: An integrative model based on marketing (7P) approach. *Total Quality Management & Business Excellence, 28*(13–14), 1509–1525. doi:10.1080/14783363.2016.1150172

Leung, X. Y., Bai, B., & Stahura, K. A. (2015). The Marketing Effectiveness of Social Media in the Hotel Industry: A Comparison of Facebook and Twitter. *Journal of Hospitality & Tourism Research (Washington, D.C.), 39*(2), 147–169. doi:10.1177/1096348012471381

Lovelock, C., & Gummesson, E. (2004). Whither services marketing? *Journal of Service Research, 7*(1), 20–41. doi:10.1177/1094670504266131

Medeiros, S. A. De, Gosling, M., Alves, L., & Vera, R. (2015). *Emoções em Experiências Negativas de Turismo: um estudo sobre a influência na insatisfação, 26*, 188–215.

Namin, A. (2017). Revisiting customers' perception of service quality in fast food restaurants. *Journal of Retailing and Consumer Services, 34*, 70–81. doi:10.1016/j.jretconser.2016.09.008

Needles, A., & Thompson, G. (2013). Social Media Use in the Restaurant Industry: A Work in Progress. *Center for Hospitality Research Publications, 13*(7), 6–16. Retrieved from http://scholarship.sha.cornell.edu/chrpubs/101

Nobre, H., & Faria, J. (2017). Exploring marketing strategies in architectural services: The case of the architecture firms in Portugal. *International Journal of Business Excellence, 12*(3), 273–293. doi:10.1504/IJBEX.2017.084438

Nobre, H., & Silva, D. (2014). Social Network Marketing Strategy and SME Strategy Benefits. *Journal of Transnational Management, 19*(1), 138–151. doi:10.1080/15475778.2014.904658

Nogueira Tomas, R., Pierre Meschgrahw, R., & Lúcia Chicarelli Alcantara, R. (2012). *As redes sociais e o comportamento de compra do consumidor: O reinado do & BOCA-A-BOCA & ESTÁ DE VOLTA?* doi:10.5585/remark.v11i2.2325

Nuno, M. (2018). As 6 redes sociais mais usadas do mundo. E-Konomista. Retrieved from https://www.e-konomista.pt/artigo/redes-sociais-mais-usadas/

Santini, F. O., Lübeck, R. M., & Hoffmann, C. S. (2015). Promoção de vendas: Uma análise dos fatores influenciadores da intenção de compra de um produto em desconto. *Revista Pensamento Contemporâneo Em Administração, 9*(4). doi:10.12712/rpca.v9i4.490

Singh, M., Sarfaraz, A., Sarfaraz, M., & Jenab, K. (2015). Analytical QFD model for strategic justification of advanced manufacturing technology. *International Journal of Business Excellence*, 8(1), 20–37. doi:10.1504/IJBEX.2015.065979

Singh, P. K., & Pattanayak, J. K. (2016). Study of the Relationship among the Factors of Brand Equity: A Study on Fast-food Brands. *Global Business Review*, 17(5), 1227–1239. doi:10.1177/0972150916656694

Soares, A. M., Pinho, J. C., & Nobre, H. (2012). From Social to Marketing Interactions: The Role of Social Networks. *Journal of Transnational Management*, 17(1), 45–62. doi:10.1080/15475778.2012.650085

Souza, F., De Las Casas, D., Flores, V., Youn, S., Cha, M., Quercia, D., & Almeida, V. (2015). Dawn of the selfie era: The whos, wheres, and hows of selfies on Instagram. In *COSN 2015 - Proceedings of the 2015 ACM Conference on Online Social Networks* (pp. 221–231). ACM. doi:10.1145/2817946.2817948

Twenge, J. M., Campbell, S. M., Hoffman, B. J., & Lance, C. E. (2010). Generational differences in work values: Leisure and extrinsic values increasing, social and intrinsic values decreasing. *Journal of Management*, 36(5), 1117–1142. doi:10.1177/0149206309352246

Venkatesh, V., Morris, M. G., Davis, G. B., & Davis, F. D. (2003). User acceptance of information technology: Toward a unified view. *Source: MIS Quarterly*, 27(3), 425–478. doi:10.2307/30036540

This research was previously published in the Handbook of Research on Social Media Applications for the Tourism and Hospitality Sector; pages 136-148, copyright year 2020 by Business Science Reference (an imprint of IGI Global).

Chapter 29
Social Media Advertisements and Buying Behaviour:
A Study of Indian Working Women

Yuvika Gupta

https://orcid.org/0000-0001-8284-2049

IMS Unison University, India

Samik Shome

https://orcid.org/0000-0001-8618-6763

Institute of Management, Nirma University, India

ABSTRACT

Advertising patterns are making significant shifts towards social media from their traditional format. Social media has become a norm for the majority of companies due to progressive change in the mindset of consumers. In the current scenario, working women play an important role in the purchase decision of the family. Moreover, some studies revealed that in some cases working women solely make product purchases. According to the Pew Research, women (73%) lead over men (65%) in the use of social media. The purpose of this study is to identify the factors that are influencing the working women purchase behaviour. The paper witnessed that demographic variables such as age and income of working women do play a significant role in online purchase. The key contribution of this paper is to provide the corporate houses an assessment of the extent to which the working women in India are influenced by social media in their online buying behaviour.

1. INTRODUCTION

Social media in recent times has created an avenue for decentralized communication channel and opened the door for all to have a voice across the globe. It has provided a platform to participate in a democratic fashion. It is undeniable that social media plays an important role in impacting culture, economy and peoples overall view of the world. It is a new forum that brings society to exchange idea, connect with,

DOI: 10.4018/978-1-6684-6287-4.ch029

relate to, and mobilize for a cause, seek advice, and offer guidance. The global social media users figure has reached to be 3.5 billion[1] as of October 2019. With over 460 million internet users, India is the second largest online market, behind China. It is estimated that by 2021, there will be approximately 635.8 million internet users in India[2].

As more than one-third of the global population uses social media, both corporate and consumers at the present time by means of social networking sites are desperately trying to make themselves more apparent and effective in the market[3]. It is estimated that the worldwide digital advertising will expand almost to $517 billion in 2023 from $333.3 billion in 2019[4]. As the sphere of social media keeps on revamping itself with new features, businesses need to progress with the same pace to make themselves more visible in this competitive market. Today the consumers research products and services online before making any purchase. According to ROBO Economy (2018), 82 per cent of smartphone users consult social media about the purchases they are about to make in-store and 45 per cent read reviews before making a purchase[5]. Hence, social media has made a significant impact on the concept of sell and purchase across the globe. It has not only become a new marketing channel but it has also created a new paradigm for the way in which consumers connect with brands and each other.

In line with the global technological advancements in communication, the Indian economy is also undergoing a paradigm shift in its socioeconomic and cultural structure in recent years. These changes have not only been reflected in the business scenario, but also in the attitude of the people. The country witnessed more independence in the decision-making power of women and also in their improved social and economic status. In fact, the numbers of women entrepreneurs are also increasing significantly in recent times. According to the report of Global Entrepreneurship Monitor (2017), women in India are nearly one-third more likely to start a business out of necessity than men. It is predicted that under same necessity and proper digital skills, women can do wonders in the business. As a result, the social media usage has been increasing exponentially among women. Indeed, studies revealed that in India women spend significantly more time on social networking sites than men (Sultana and Nayeem, 2015). The awareness of women consumers' cognizance during recent years also indicates a remarkable shift in the pattern of consumer buying behaviour. Researchers has identified several factors which affect females buying behaviour: need, style, rising income, concern for self, wide variety of products and multiple brands available in the market, among others (Furqan, 2018; Voorveld, et. al, 2018). The messages in different advertisements are also created strongly to attract the women consumers. The most vulnerable group who are more attracted to the message is young women. Thus, this study critically evaluates the role of social media advertisements and factors that shape consumers' buying behavior. The purpose of this study is to uncover the effects of social media advertisements on young women's buying behaviour. In order to determine the more prominent reasoning amongst a sample size, the following objectives are being observed: (i) to study the impact of positive reviews on social media advertisements on the buying behaviour of Indian working women; (ii) to examine the impact of income on their purchase behaviour; and (iii) to identify the factors that significantly influence their online purchase.

This research draws and builds on findings from an extensive primary survey and also from the various empirical and conceptual studies subject to secondary analysis. As this study explicitly examines interrelationships between social media buying behaviour and female professionals in the Indian context, it is definite that this study will contribute to the existing body of knowledge towards social networking and its influence on consumer behaviour. The organization of the paper is as follows. Section 2 provides a brief literature review. The research methodology used in the paper is discussed in Section 3. The research findings are provided in Section 4, followed by managerial implications of the study in Section 5. The concluding remarks are provided in Section 6.

2. LITERATURE REVIEW

Social media in broader term can be defined as online service with the aid of which users are empowered and enabled to not only create but also share different content (Shantanu et al., 2017). It comprises of social networking sites, online communities, user generated content, video sharing sites, online review and virtual games, where consumers can publish, or edit, generate and design content (Krishnamurthy and Dou, 2008). Indeed, online social networks have profoundly changed the transmission of information by making it incredibly easy to share and assimilate information on the internet (Akrimi and Khemakhem, 2012). Trusov et al. (2009) defined social networking sites as network of friends for social or professional interactions. A study by Bannister, et al. (2013) on tech-savvy young adults, evaluates their attitudes towards social media advertisements. It revealed that Facebook users are active site participants but unlikely to click-through advertisements to make product purchases. The continuous increase of the amount of time people spend online directly affects their behaviour in sharing and interacting on social media (Muthiah and Kannan, 2015).

Social media is widely used to assist consumers in buying decision by providing information about what, when, and where to buy products (Pate, 2013). The distinctive features of social media and its immense popularity have revolutionized businesses; they are now based on online communities for attracting new customer base (Bagozzi and Dholakia, 2002). Social media has also influenced consumer behaviour from information gathering to post purchase behavior (Mangold and Faulds, 2009). Tresna and Wijaya (2015) in their research demonstrated the relationship between social media usage and its functionalities towards brand loyalty among consumers. A study by Kaplan and Haenlein (2010) also revealed that social media helps in connecting businesses to consumers, develop relationships and promote those relationships timely and at low cost. On the theoretical front, Schivinski and Dąbrowski (2015) studied social media in the context of user-generated content (UGC) and firm generated content (FGC). They analyzed the impact of user-generated social media brand communication on brand loyalty and perceived brand quality.

Akar and Topcu (2011) examined different factors that influence consumer's attitude toward social media marketing and highlighted that consumers buying behavior is affected by the online reviews and shared shopping experiences. According to Akrimi and Khemakhem (2012), intention of recommendation on the social network is influenced by interpersonal connectivity, product involvement, social influence and attitude toward recommendation. In addition to it, Furqan (2018) also resulted that the social media marketing activities on brand's facebook page affects the customer buying decision. For purchase behavior, the evaluative component of social identity is twice as influential as the effect of cognitive dimension (Wang, 2017). Voorveld, et al. (2016), showed that consumers relied more on online channels for information when making an online purchase than when making an offline purchase. Bhatt and Bhatt (2012) in their research showed that website designing factors such as, ease/attractiveness of website, service quality of websites and web security, also influence the perceptions of consumers towards online shopping.

Dennis (2018) studied gender-wise buying behaviour in different countries and found that the differences between men and women buying behaviour are greater than the economic differences among countries. Research done by Meyers-Levy et al. (2015) suggests that advertisements can highly influence women buying behaviour along with information received from their friends. Similarly, studies by Bearden et al. (1990) and Rainne (2002) revealed women are more inclined to social influence than men. Female users are likely to copy similar types of social media posts and be more inclined to purchase goods that become known to them via, or are used personally by their favourite celebrities (Khan and Dhar, 2006; Wilcox et al., 2011; Wilcox and Stephen, 2013). On the other hand, as per Kargaonkar et al. (2006), female customers tend to perceive greater risks than males, and the perceived risks are greater for experience goods than it is for search goods. It can be said that female consumers are more worried about whether only one review is true or manipulated, so when shopping for experience goods, female consumers will read more reviews to verify the quality of products being considered. Singh (2014) concluded from the study that word of mouth from female consumer families and friends can influence decision style, as what and where to buy. Park, et al. (2009), discovered that females tend to search for significantly more kinds of information, customer reviews when shopping.

The changing role of women has been a major demographic trend over the years. The increase in the number of women joining workforce have brought about societal changes due to their change in taste and style. The changing trends of women at work and their family lifestyle and income have shown relationship between working women and their pattern of buying behaviour (Kahne, 2001). Sakkthivel and Sriram (2015) attempted to unveil the influence of social network websites in providing marketing mix and external information variables that impact women consumer buying behaviour. The study revealed that the selected variables like society, reference groups, brand reputation, place and promotion have significant impact over women consumer buying behaviour. In the same context, Roux and Maree (2016) also studied female consumers' motives for joining apparel brand communities, their engagement levels, brand attitudes and buying intentions, as well as the interrelationships amongst these elements. It posited that female consumers who are engaged in a brand community online would be likely to display favourable attitudes towards the brand.

On the other hand, consumer buying behavior refers to the selection, purchase and consumption of goods and services for the satisfaction of their wants (Ramya and Ali, 2016). Anandarajan and Sivagami (2016) proposed that consumer buying behavior is the entirety of a consumer's attitudes, preferences, intentions, and decisions pertaining to the consumer's behavior in the marketplace when purchasing a product or service. Many factors, characteristics, and specificities are combined to build up the behavior of any individual. The perception of the quality, awareness of the product and consumer opinion influences the consumer buying decision. As such, this study critically evaluates the role of advertisements and factors that shape consumers' buying behaviour.

To sum up, in today's technology driven world, social media have become an avenue where retailers can extend their marketing campaigns to a wider range of consumers. It has advanced from simply providing a platform for individuals to stay in touch with their family and friends to learn more about companies and their products. Hence, it will be interesting to study the influence of social media advertisements and buying behaviour of working women in the Indian context. The paper will also examine the potential factors that influence the buying behavior and purchase intention of women consumers.

3. RESEARCH METHODOLOGY

Questionnaire based sample analysis was the base of this study. The sample is believed to be representative of the population, but nonetheless it was a convenience sample which may be defined as 'a form of non-probabilistic or purposive sample drawn on a purely opportunistic basis from a readily accessible subgroup of the population' (Baker 1990, Welman and Kruger 2005). An extensive primary survey has been conducted through a well-structured questionnaire with the aim to get the views of women respondents about their purchase information, awareness of brands, influence of others on the purchase decision and views about the marketing of brands on the social networking websites like, Facebook and Twitter. In view of the fact that, Facebook and Twitter are among social media sites which has the maximum average number of followers (Social Marketing Report India, 2019).

The respondents were asked to rate their agreement level on a 5 point scale (5 being Strongly Agree) to capture their behaviour on social media advertising. A pilot survey of 25 respondents testing has been done in Dehradun. To check the reliability of the questionnaire, Cronbach's alpha was also calculated.

3.1. Data Collection

The survey was conducted among 200 working women between the age group of 20 to 39 years who are regularly purchasing through online portals. The figure of 200 respondents was in line with sample sizes related to young females research as expressed by Mafini et al. (2014) who cited similar sample sizes in research conducted by Bakewell and Mitchell (2004), Drake-Bridges and Burgess (2010), Durvasula, et al. (1993), Kim (2003), and Kwan, et al. (2008). In terms of spending power, they have more money to spend than consumers of the same age groups but from previous generations (Morton, 2002; Mafini, et al. 2014). The age group of 20 to 39 years is considered in research as segment of Generation Y consumers is heavily influenced by technology such as the internet and has significantly 'evolved' from previous generations thus presenting a challenge in targeting them (Valentine and Powers 2013). The data was collected from five major cities of India namely, New Delhi, Bangalore, Hyderabad, Kolkata and Mumbai with 40 respondents from each city. There is a rationale behind choosing these large metropolitan cities. Compared to the other cities of India, these five cities tallies for the largest usage of social media among women. The questionnaire was circulated through email to the target personnel.

3.2. Research Hypotheses

Based on the observations of the respondents, the study also wanted to confirm whether these responses are true for all the women purchasing online. The following hypotheses have been formulated to evaluate the applicability of these observations:

H_1: Positive reviews on social media influence purchase behaviour of Indian working women.
H_2: Income of Indian working women has positive relation with their online buying behaviour.

After compiling the data, correlation and factor analysis was done to find relationships between the identified variables a working women purchasing behaviour. Correlation is used to examine the strength of relationships between variables. Likewise, factor analysis is conducted to determine the factors influencing the purchasing behaviour of working women in India.

4. RESULTS AND DISCUSSIONS

Primarily, to check the reliability and validity of the questionnaire, Cronbach's alpha, Kaiser-Meyer-Olkin (KMO) and Bartlett test were performed. The value of 0.84 for Cronbach's alpha indicates good internal consistency of the items in the scale. Similarly, the value of KMO was 0.866 and statistically significant values for Bartlett's test for sphericity ($p < 0.05$) indicated that factor analysis is appropriate. Test is also done to check the homoscedasticity and linearity of the data (Figure 1).

Figure 1. Homoscedasticity and linearity test

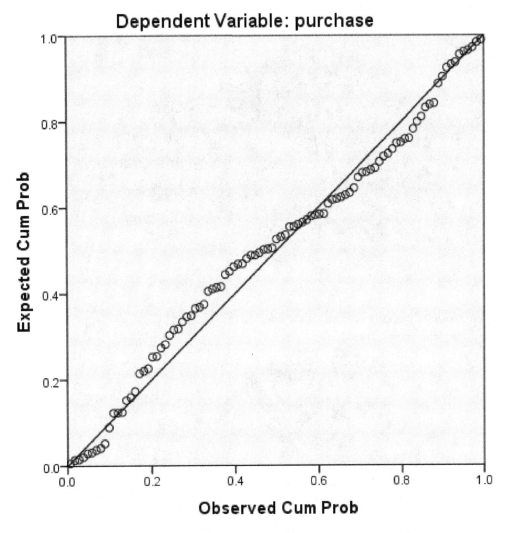

4.1. Sample Profile

The age-wise composition of the sample respondents indicates that 131 (65.5 per cent) respondents belong to the age group of 20-29 and 69 (34.5 per cent) are between 30-39 years of age. Likewise, 100 women are married, 98 are bachelor and other two are divorced. The economic parameters of the respondents are provided in figures below. The data reveals that a significant proportion of the respondents are highly qualified. In total, 150 of them are having a post-graduate degree and 13 are doctorate (Figure 1). Also, 80 per cent of the respondents are working in private job. A small proportion is also in teaching proportion (Figure 3).

Figure 2. Figure 2. Qualification of working women (respondents)

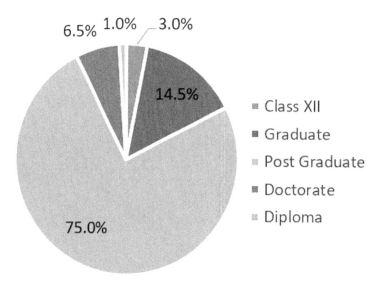

Figure 3. Profession of working women (respondents)

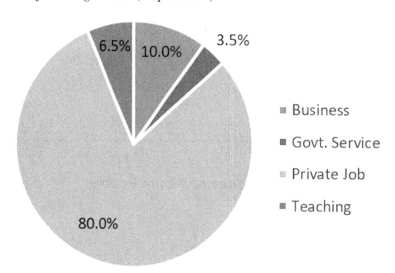

From Figure 4, it can be inferred that majority of the respondents (38 per cent) are having a monthly income between INR 20,000 to INR 40,000. Only 21.5 per cent of the entire sample is having an income of less than INR 20,000 monthly. It shows that the sample respondents are fairly from well off educated families and most likely to have the capacity to purchase online.

Figure 4. Monthly income of working women (respondents)

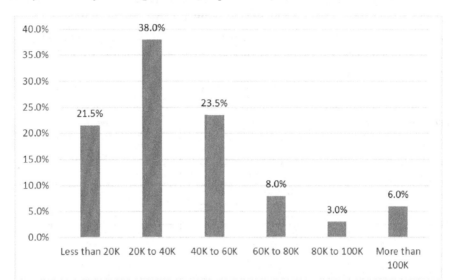

4.2. Findings of Objective 1

To examine the relationships between the likelihood of positive reviews and purchasing behaviour, the correlation between the two variables are calculated and the result is presented in Table 1. It can be clearly stated that the positive reviews on social media affect the consumer buying behavior as the correlation coefficient between positive reviews and purchase behavior is 0.475. Consumer may study the reviews due to the written by reference groups such as friends, relatives etc. but not necessary will purchase the product.

Table 1. Correlation between positive reviews and purchase intention

		Positive Reviews	**Purchase**
Positive Reviews	Pearson Correlation	1	.475**
	Sig. (2-tailed)		.000
	N	200	200
Purchase	Pearson Correlation	0.475**	1
	Sig. (2-tailed)	.000	
	N	200	200

**. Correlation is significant at the 0.01 level (2-tailed).

4.3. Findings of Objective 2

According to Jain (2016), the increase in income of any individual has a positive spin-off effect on the disposable income. This will indulge in impulse buying behavior of the person. This proposition is measured in this objective by calculating the correlation between the income level and purchasing behaviour of working women in India. The study result reveals that the income of the working women affect their buying behaviour and the first hypothesis is accepted (Table 2). However, it is found from the survey that the purchasing behaviour of the different income group women is different which is quite obvious. It can be infer that as the working women have developed as an important segment for the marketers in India, therefore, the marketers should consider them with utmost importance in buying decision process (Guha, 2013).

Table 2. Correlation between purchase intention and income of working women

		Purchase	**Income**
Purchase	Pearson Correlation	1	.470**
	Sig. (2-tailed)		.000
	N	200	200
Income	Pearson Correlation	0.470**	1
	Sig. (2-tailed)	.000	
	N	200	200

**. Correlation is significant at the 0.01 level (2-tailed)

4.4. Findings of Objective 3

One of the primary objectives of this study is to find out the factors that influence Indian working women to purchase online. The study considered various parameters including time saving, convenience, easy delivery, offers & discounts, avoid crowd, etc. as the plausible aspects to explore the various dimensions of impact of social media advertising on professional women. The respondents were asked to rate their agreement level on a 5 point scale (5 being Strongly Agree) with respect to online purchase. Table 3 shows that they are inclined to have positive opinions on all the parameters as all the ratings of average responses are more than 3 with very moderate standard deviation. Hence, the survey definitely observes lots of satisfactory effects of online purchase by Indian working women.

However, the study further tried to identify which are the major factors from the above observations (see Table 3) that influence significantly in online purchase. The study adopted Principal Component Method to extract the components. The components which exhibit more than one Eigen Value are taken as principal components. As highlighted in Table 4, the first three components whose Eigen value is greater than one (5.711, 1.930 & 1.114 respectively) together explain 62.5 per cent variations in the model, the number of principal components have been taken as three.

Table 3. Descriptive statistics of working women (respondents)

	Mean	Std. Deviation	Analysis N
Time Saving	4.42	0.652	200
Convenience	4.44	0.581	200
Easy Delivery	4.32	0.671	200
No Travel	4.45	0.591	200
Easy Accessibility	4.36	0.634	200
Easy Comparison	4.26	0.750	200
Offers & Discounts	4.37	0.745	200
Brand Availability	4.17	0.769	200
Detailed Information	4.11	0.819	200
Fewer Expensive	3.81	0.813	200
Avoid Crowd	4.07	0.914	200
Avoid Impulsive Shopping	3.73	1.007	200
Avoid Discrete Purchase	3.76	0.859	200
Easy to Find Favorite Brand	4.19	0.744	200

Table 4. Total variance explained

Component	Initial Eigenvalues			Extraction Sums of Squared Loadings			Rotation Sums of Squared Loadings		
	Total	% of Variance	Cumulative %	Total	% of Variance	Cumulative %	Total	% of Variance	Cumulative %
1	5.711	40.794	40.794	5.711	40.794	40.794	3.195	22.822	22.822
2	1.930	13.787	54.581	1.930	13.787	54.581	2.941	21.008	43.830
3	1.114	7.961	62.542	1.114	7.961	62.542	2.620	18.712	62.542
4	.787	5.624	68.166						
5	.753	5.379	73.545						
6	.701	5.008	78.553						
7	.566	4.044	82.597						
8	.522	3.730	86.327						
9	.410	2.930	89.257						
10	.349	2.494	91.751						
11	.333	2.382	94.133						
12	.308	2.203	96.336						
13	.280	2.003	98.340						
14	.232	1.660	100.000						

Extraction Method: Principal Component Analysis.

Finally, after estimating the loading of variables on each factor, a Varimax with Kaiser Normalization rotation has been performed to ensure the orthogonality between the factors. The Rotated Component Matrix, presented in Table 5, exhibit the final loading of individual variables on each identified component. Further, as per guidelines of Hair et al. (2013), the study considered 0.40 as cut off factor loading for a sample size of 200.

Table 5. Rotated Component Matrix

	Component		
	1	**2**	**3**
Avoid Impulsive Shopping	0.866		0.099
Avoid Discrete Purchase	0.831		0.113
Avoid Crowd	0.687		0.157
Fewer Expensive	0.648		0.166
Detailed Information	**0.558**	**0.548**	0.072
Easy Comparison		0.779	0.130
No Travel		**0.643**	**0.454**
Easy Accessibility		**0.636**	**0.537**
Offers & Discounts		0.605	
Brand Availability	**0.464**	**0.567**	
Easy to Find Favorite Brand	**0.423**	**0.522**	
Convenience			0.832
Time Saving			0.813
Easy Delivery			0.757

Extraction Method: Principal Component Analysis.
Rotation Method: Varimax with Kaiser Normalization.
a. Rotation converged in 6 iterations.

Five variables including *Detailed Information, No Travel, Easy Accessibility, Brand Availability & Easy find favourable brand* have to be dropped from the study as they depict cross loading on two components simultaneously. The rest of the variables are distinctly loaded on either of the three identified components. Therefore, the three factors may be acknowledged with their respective variables and the result is summarized in Table 6.

Table 6. Summary result

Factor 1	**Factor 2**	**Factor 3**
Avoid impulsive shopping	Easy comparison	Convenience
Avoid discrete purchase	Offers & Discounts	Time Saving
Avoid crowd		Easy Delivery
Fewer expensive		

Avoid impulsive shopping, Avoid discrete purchase, Avoid Crowd, Less Expensive are distinctly loaded on Factor 1 with loadings 0.866 (> 0.40), 0.831 (> 0.40), 0.687 (> 0.40) and 0.648 (> 0.40) respectively, which clearly indicate the ***economic dimension*** of the buyers. Similarly, Easy comparison with loading 0.636 (> 0.40) and Offers & Discounts with 0.605 (> 0.40) are encumbered on Factor 2 indicating the ***competitive dimension*** of the consumers. Likewise, Convenience with loading 0.832 (> 0.40), Time Saving with 0.813 (> 0.40) and Easy Delivery with 0.757 (> 0.40) are highly inclined on Factor 3 which confirms the ***convenience dimension*** of purchasers.

5. MANAGERIAL IMPLICATIONS OF THE STUDY

The study was primarily conducted to understand the impact of demographics in influencing the consumption of services over internet. As demographic factors play a vital role in figuring out the psyche of buyers in offline marketing, imbibing the same for online would be helpful to the corporate to profile potential internet buyers. It would help them to devise strategies and customize the offerings according to age, gender, occupation and income. The differential price technique could be adopted for different age, occupation and Income groups. Products/services could be customized according to gender. It could fix different pricing for different income groups such as student receives comparatively lower fare than the business man or corporate executive. Hence, it is very useful for the organizations to identify the impact of demographics. The study revealed gender and income level have significant impact on consuming different categories of services online. The study has shown the significance of demographics influence on online consumption of services in the growing Indian market. There are enormous opportunities present for online marketers to tap the potential of rapidly increasingly online market space in India. The understanding and mapping of online consumers through demographics could enable their focus better. The corporate world may take cue from the study for devising better strategies to face their face less consumes online.

6. CONCLUSION

In the present era of digitization, the social media and its influence on consumer buying behaviour deserve a closer attention from the researchers and marketers. Online consumers apart from shopping also generate online support for their peers which help in establishing trust on social media and affect their buying behaviour. Analysis of the collected data revealed that working women buying behaviour in India is influenced by the peers trust on social media sites. In this research the prime focus is on Indian working females, to analyze and evaluate their perception and behaviour towards social media advertising. Thus the research shows how social media and social factors influence trust and intention to buy through social networking sites. It was also found that social participation on social media after purchase is also one of the important elements for Indian working women for their self-esteem. A demographic variable such as age, occupation and income does play a significant role in influencing the online purchase of working women. Consequently, Indian working women who perceive higher self-concept will generally hold a high level of involvement in social media.

ACKNOWLEDGMENT

Samik Shome is the corresponding author of this paper.

REFERENCES

Abraham, L. B., Mörn, M. P., & Vollman, A. (2010). *Women on the Web: How Women are Shaping the Internet*. ComScore, Incorporated.

Akar, E., & Topcu, B. (2011). An Examination of the Factors Influencing Consumer's Attitudes towards Social Media Marketing. *Journal of Internet Commerce*, *10*(1), 35–67. doi:10.1080/15332861.2011.558456

Akrimi, Y., & Khemakhem, R. (2012). What drive Consumers to spread the word in Social Media? *Journal of Marketing Research & Case Studies*, 1–14. doi:10.5171/2012.969979

Anandarajan, S., & Sivagami, T. (2016). Consumer Purchase Decision Behaviour towards Cosmetics Marketing. *Asia Pacific Journal of Research*, *1*(317), 144–149.

Bagozzi, R. P., & Dholakia, U. M. (2002). Intentional Social Action in Virtual Communities. *Journal of Interactive Marketing*, *16*(2), 2–21. doi:10.1002/dir.10006

Bannister, A., Kiefer, J., & Nellums, J. (2013). College Students' Perceptions of and Behaviors regarding Facebook Advertising: An Exploratory Study. *The Catalyst*, *3*(1), 2. doi:10.18785/cat.0301.02

Bearden, W. O., & Rose, R. L. (1990). Attention to Social Comparison Information: An Individual Difference Factor affecting Consumer Conformity. *The Journal of Consumer Research*, *16*(4), 461–471. doi:10.1086/209231

Beig, F. A., & Khan, M. F. (2018). Impact of social media marketing on brand experience: A study of select apparel brands on Facebook. *Vision*, *22*(3), 264–275. doi:10.1177/0972262918785962

Bhatt, S., & Bhatt, A. (2012). Factors Influencing Online Shopping: An Empirical Study in Ahmedabad. *The IUP Journal of Marketing Management*, *11*(4), 51–65.

Dennis, C., Morgan, A., Wright, L. T., & Jayawardhena, C. (2010). The Influences of Social E-shopping in Enhancing Young Women's Online Shopping Behaviour. *Journal of Customer Behaviour*, *9*(2), 151–174. doi:10.1362/147539210X511353

Guha, S. (2013). The Changing Perception and Buying Behaviour of Women Consumer in Urban India. *IOSR Journal of Business and Management*, *11*(6), 34–39. doi:10.9790/487X-1163439

Hair, J. F., Black, W. C., Babin, B. J., & Anderson, R. E. (2010). *Multivariate Data Analysis* (7th ed.). New York: Macmillan.

Hajli, M. N. (2014). A Study of the Impact of Social Media on Consumers. *International Journal of Market Research*, *56*(3), 387–404. doi:10.2501/IJMR-2014-025

Jain, R. (2016). Impulse Buying Behaviour amongst Working Women with respect to the city of Ahmedabad. *International Journal of Innovative Science. Engineering & Technology*, *3*(1), 323–335.

Kahne, H. (2001). Women in Paid Work: Some Consequences and Questions for Family Income and Expenditures. *NA-Advances in Consumer Research, 8.*

Kaplan, A. M., & Haenlein, M. (2009). The Fairyland of Second Life: Virtual Social World and How to Use Them. *Business Horizons, 52*(6), 563–572. doi:10.1016/j.bushor.2009.07.002

Kaplan, A. M., & Haenlein, M. (2010). Users of the World, Unite! The Challenges and Opportunities of Social Media. *Business Horizons. Kelley School of Business, 53,* 59–68.

Kaplan, A. M., & Haenlein, M. (2011). Two Hearts in Three Quarter Time: How to Waltz the Social Media/Viral Marketing Dance. *Business Horizons, 54*(3), 253–263. doi:10.1016/j.bushor.2011.01.006

Khan, U., & Dhar, R. (2006). Licensing Effect in Consumer Choice. *JMR, Journal of Marketing Research, 43*(2), 259–266. doi:10.1509/jmkr.43.2.259

Korgaonkar, P., Silverblatt, R., & Girard, T. (2006). Online Retailing, Product Classifications, and Consumer Preferences. *Internet Research, 16*(3), 267–288. doi:10.1108/10662240610673691

Krishnamurthy, S., & Dou, W. (2008). Note from Special Issue Editors: Advertising with User-generated Content: A Framework and Research Agenda. Journal of Interactive Advertising, 8(2), 1-4.

Laroche, M., Mohammad, R. H., & Richard, M. O. (2013). To be or not to be in Social Media: How Brand Loyalty is affected by Social Media? *International Journal of Information Management, 33*(1), 76–82. doi:10.1016/j.ijinfomgt.2012.07.003

Le Roux, I., & Maree, T. (2016). Motivation, engagement, attitudes and buying intent of female Facebook users. *Acta Commercii, 16*(1), 1–11. doi:10.4102/ac.v16i1.340

Lee, E. (2013). *Impacts of Social Media on Consumer Behaviour- Decision Making Process* (Bachelor Thesis). Turku University of Applied Sciences, Finland.

Mafini, C., Dhurup, M., & Mandhlazi, L. (2014). Shopper typologies amongst a Generation Y consumer cohort and variations in terms of age in the fashion apparel market. *Acta Commercii, 14*(1), 11. doi:10.4102/ac.v14i1.209

Mangold, W. G., & Faulds, D. J. (2009). Social media: The New Hybrid Element of the Promotion Mix. *Business Horizons, 52*(4), 357–365. doi:10.1016/j.bushor.2009.03.002

Meyers-Levy, J., & Loken, B. (2015). Revisiting Gender Differences: What we Know and What Lies Ahead. *Journal of Consumer Psychology, 25*(1), 129–149. doi:10.1016/j.jcps.2014.06.003

Muthiah, S., & Kannan, K. V. (2016). A Budding Dimension Of Social Media As Marketing Communication In Hotel Industry. *Primax International Journal of Commerce and Management Research, 4*(1), 1–8.

O'Brien, C. (2011). The Emergence of the Social Media Empowered Consumer. *Irish Marketing Review. Mercury Publishers Ltd., 21*(1), 32–50.

Park, J., Yoon, Y., & Lee, B. (2009). *The Effect of Gender and Product Categories on Consumer Online Information Search.* ACR North American Advances.

Pate, S. S., & Adams, M. (2013). The Influence of Social Networking Sites on Buying Behaviours of Millennials. *Atlantic Marketing Journal*, 2(1), 7.

Prasad, S., Gupta, I. C., & Totala, N. K. (2017). Social Media Usage, Electronic Word-of-Mouth and Purchase-Decision Involvement. *Asia-Pacific Journal of Business Administration*, 9(2), 134–145. doi:10.1108/APJBA-06-2016-0063

Raacke, J., & Raacke, J. B. (2008). MySpace and Facebook: Applying the uses and gratifications theory to exploring friend-networking sites. *Cyberpsychology & Behavior*, 11(2), 169–174. doi:10.1089/cpb.2007.0056 PMID:18422409

Rainne, L. (2002). *Internet and American Life*. Washington, DC: Pew Internet and American Life Project.

Ramya, N., & Mohamed Ali, S. A. (2016). Factors affecting consumer buying behavior. *International Journal of Applied Research,* 2(10), 76-80.

Sakkthivel, A. M., Edolyi, M., & Ponraj, J. (2010). Empirical Investigation On The Impact Of Internal And External Variables That Influence Customer Loyalty, Customer Life Time Value And Consumer Switching Behaviour In A Growing Competitive Environment. *International Journal of Management Rivulet, 1*, 1–13.

Sakkthivel, A. M., & Sriram, B. (2015). Influence of Social Network Websites over Women Consumers from Islamic Religion: A Structural Equation Modelling Approach. *Journal of Internet Banking and Commerce*, 20(2).

Schivinski, B., & Dabrowski, D. (2015). The impact of brand communication on brand equity through Facebook. *Journal of Research in Interactive Marketing*, 9(1), 31–53. doi:10.1108/JRIM-02-2014-0007

Singh, J. (2014). *Impact of Internet and Social Media on Women Empowerment in India*. Social Media, Society & Social Media.

Sultana, W., & Nayeem, S. (2015). Social Media Usage Among Women: A Study in Mangalore Taluka. *National Journal on Advances in Computing and Management*, 6(2).

Tresna, L., & Wijaya, J. C. (2015). The impact of social media towards brand equity: An empirical study of Mall X. *iBuss Management, 3*(2), 7–48.

Trusov, M., Bucklin, R. E., & Pauwels, K. (2009). Effects of Word-of-Mouth versus Traditional Marketing: Findings from an Internet Social Networking Site. *Journal of Marketing*, 73(5), 90–102. doi:10.1509/jmkg.73.5.90

Valentine, D. B., & Powers, T. L. (2013). Generation Y values and lifestyle segments. *Journal of Consumer Marketing*, 30(7), 597–606. doi:10.1108/JCM-07-2013-0650

Voorveld, H. A., Noort, G. V., Muntinga, D. G., & Bronner, A. F. (2018). Engagement with Social Media and Social Media Advertising: The Differentiating Role of Platform Type. *Journal of Advertising*, 47(1), 38–54. doi:10.1080/00913367.2017.1405754

Voorveld, H. A., Smit, E. G., Neijens, P. C., & Bronner, A. F. (2016). Consumers' cross-channel use in online and offline purchases: An Analysis of Cross-Media and Cross-Channel Behaviors between Products. *Journal of Advertising Research*, *56*(4), 385–400. doi:10.2501/JAR-2016-044

Wang, T. (2017). Social identity dimensions and consumer behavior in social media. *Asia Pacific Management Review*, *22*(1), 45–51. doi:10.1016/j.apmrv.2016.10.003

Welman, J. C., Kruger, S. J., & Mitchell, B. (2005). *Research Methodology* (3rd ed.). Oxford: Oxford University Press.

Wilcox, G. B., & Kim, K. K. (2012). Multivariate Time Series use for the Measurement of Social Media Effects. *Marketing Management Journal*, *22*(2), 90–101.

Wilcox, K., & Stephen, A. T. (2013). Are Close Friends the Enemy? Online Social Networks, Self-Esteem, and Self-Control. *The Journal of Consumer Research*, *40*(1), 90–103. doi:10.1086/668794

ENDNOTES

[1] https://www.smartinsights.com/social-media-marketing/social-media-strategy/new-global-social-media-research/ accessed on December 10, 2019.

[2] https://www.tmaworld.com/our-thinking/worldwide-digital-trends-2019 accessed on November 17, 2019.

[3] https://www.businesstoday.in/current/economy-politics/india-internet-users-to-reach-627-million-this-year-report/story/325084.html accessed on December 7, 2019.

[4] https://www.emarketer.com/content/global-digital-ad-spending-2019_accessed on November 27, 2019.

[5] https://www.forbes.com/sites/johnellett/2018/02/08/new-research-shows-growing-impact-of-online-research-on-in-store-purchases/#ac4015916a0b accessed on November 18, 2019.

This research was previously published in the International Journal of Online Marketing (IJOM), 10(3); pages 48-61, copyright year 2020 by IGI Publishing (an imprint of IGI Global).

Section 3
Tools and Technologies

Chapter 30
Social Media as a Marketing Tool

Rajeshwari Krishnamurthy
Great Lakes Institute of Management, India

ABSTRACT

This chapter talks about how social media can be used as a marketing tool. Right from describing the various forms of social media, it touches upon the different methods by which social media are engaged with by a marketer. The tasks of creating awareness, generating interest, encouraging action, resulting in purchase, and doing brand advocacy are all covered. There is also a section on how the marketer can evaluate the effectiveness of these social media options both in comparison with traditional media as well as in isolation.

CHAPTER OBJECTIVES

This chapter looks at using social media in the context of it being a marketing technique. In the process, the advantages and disadvantages of this medium versus the traditional media has been discussed. Customer engagement tools for measuring effectiveness (including Return on Investment) along with evaluation methodologies for social media have been highlighted. There is a detailed example of a social medium- mobile application- its uses and challenges. Finally the chapter closes with outlining what maybe the barriers for social media adoption by organizations.

INTRODUCTION

Social media is used to refer to those media that use web based and mobile technology to use communication into an interactive dialogue. (Dewing, 2012) Also called 'consumer generated media' the objective here is to combine technology in a social forum to make it user friendly for the public. The biggest advantage here is to offer a two way interactive medium unlike the traditional media which is one way.

DOI: 10.4018/978-1-6684-6287-4.ch030

The exponential growth of social media in the last few years is indisputable. The medium has altered the way in which people communicate with one another and even do business with each other. Its true value is still being explored and it is growing by leaps and bounds. The mainstream way of doing marketing is undergoing a discontinuous change thanks to this social medium.

Figure 1. Social media aspects
Source: (Wasserman, n.d.)

The above figure describes the various aspects of social media. Starting from 'Know your customer'- which talks about understanding who is your target profile, moving onto Setting a target for the social media such as reaching so many customers or call to action, then executing a plan that takes into account different platforms and formats and finally monitoring if the results are as per expectations, 'social media' has come a long way.

Compared to this, traditional medium like television or print no longer have the same impact. For decades marketers have been struggling to increase the 'interactivity' factor in communication with the audience i.e. conventional media like Television or Radio talk to consumers in a single direction without taking inputs from them or seeking to even understand if there is adequate comprehension from the other side so that the message can be modified real time. In most cases, feedback used to come in much later that any meaningful change was almost impossible before the campaign finishes. There are also other issues like fixed costs of production that is looming large in traditional medium and takes away a significant portion of the total ad budget. Airing costs in these media is also becoming prohibitive – so much so that companies are looking for cheaper alternatives.

Consumer's comfort with internet and digital medium has also contributed to the growing popularity of the social medium. The broadband penetration in the country has been increasing, thanks to the Government initiatives as well some easy to use hardware that is making this transition easier. From business point of view also, this trend is catching up. Though the shift to making it the solo medium of marketing has not taken place, the spends in this medium is clearly on the rise.

Of course adoption of social media is not easy. There are barriers to be overcome on many fronts. Organizationally, technologically, financially and so on and so forth. There is a lot of learning to do and that is not easy. Some functions take to it more easily than others. And some others have been traditionally more familiar with social media in certain forms. For example, Human Resources department has been using on line tools for personnel selection, psychometric testing etc. But using social media for reaching out to consumers and persuading them to buy products services is a challenge that many companies are struggling with.

SOCIAL MEDIA AS A MARKETING PLATFORM

According to Web 2.0, social media is a pool of information which is designed to be interactive. Social media marketing is an activity where marketing and promotions takes place through various social media platforms. Usually a marketing plan comprise of both traditional and new media.

Figure 2. Social media as a marketing tool (Nairuthram, 2016)

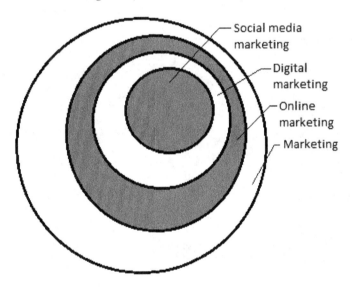

As is evident from the above Figure 2, social media is becoming the inner core of the Marketing function. Moving onto Digital and then onto online, later to Marketing as a whole, this media has come a long way in making its presence felt. Consumers always lead the way in which marketers have to communicate. The last five years have witnessed discontinuous changes in which media is consumed and technology devices used by consumers. Almost every aspect of the daily life has got disrupted, thanks to technology intervention. Mobile phones, television, air conditioners, laptops- all of them. Which necessarily means that companies need to adopt these in order to reach out to end users. This has an effect in the creative execution, media planning, acquiring media liasioning skills etc. One of the key decisions that advertising industry agency if grappling today is whether they need to branch out to become a specialist social media outfit to whether to continue to do the set of traditional agency tasks that they are used to. Always a tough choice.

Social media is an open system that enables two way interaction with consumers and works on building ongoing brand-consumer relationships, unlike in traditional advertising which helps to promote sales. Some statistics regarding social media importance to business (Nairuthram, 2016):

- There are more than 1.7 billion active Facebook users around the globe!
- Instagram (owned by Facebook) boasts half a billion users;
- Twitter acknowledges one-third of a billion – well, 317 million;
- WeChat has 806 million users.

Fundamentally, social media works because human beings are social creatures who would like to communicate and have social conversations. Social media provides a platform by facilitating discussions and forums for various cause and also helps in collecting reviews and feedbacks on various goods and services. It can also be stated as a platform to share information and develop content which can be viewed by all users. SMM for business helps to increase customer engagement and reach. A seller can track the behavior of potential customers by getting their feedback.

Figure 3. Forms of social media (Davis, 2009)

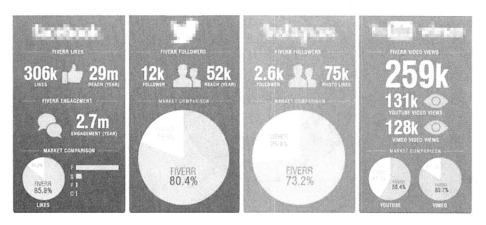

ADVANTAGES AND DISADVANTAGES OVER TRADITIONAL MEDIA

A marketing campaign usually consists of both traditional and social media, which is a part of nontraditional media. Every part of the campaign should be carefully designed to capture as much audience as possible.

The above figure shows comparative aspects between traditional medium and social medium.

First is the point on target audience. Traditional media, though it has well defined target audience, does not customize its messages across the various segments. This results in a lot of spillage or wastage. Potential customers not intended for this receive communication and in worst cases, this may end up creating displeasure among them. Whereas, social media targets customers in a personal manner and hence has higher relatability with target group. Thus this medium scores better on this aspect of target audience.

Figure 4. Pros and Cons of social media (Davis, 2009)

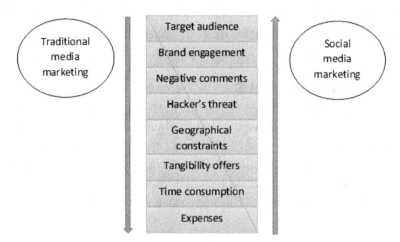

The second aspect is that of brand engagement. The capacities of both these media to engage a brand through these media is different. Traditional medium uses television, radio, print etc. to create brand values or personality. Engaging is mostly a one way process and this is a limitation. There is no opportunity for consumers to express their opinion on the brand in traditional medium. But in social media such as Facebook, twitter, blogging etc. consumers have an interactive relationship with the brand. This is useful in building a more robust brand and ends up being a more effective form of brand engagement.

Thirdly, social media allows consumers to own the brand and in the process permits negative comments. This shows the confidence of organizations. By allowing a dialogue, a sense of ownership of the brand among the consumers increases. Whereas in traditional media, there is no window for consumers to allow negative comments. While the positive side of this is that fact that the brand image does not get tarnished publicly, the down side is that the organizations never get to really understand what the consumers think of their brands (Poirier, 2013).

Social media suffers from Hacker's threat. I.e. it has the potential of its image getting modified by hackers as it is in open format. This is a serious issue. But in traditional medium, there is no such problem. The hardware is sealed and delivered tamper proof. This enables far better control of the message being disseminated by traditional media.

The next point is about geographical constraints. This is a big differentiator that results in high amount of cost efficiencies for social media. Due to the globally pervasive nature of internet, social media is able to reach out to audiences worldwide. Compared to this, traditional media has insulated reach. I.e. whether television or radio or print is able to reach consumers within defined geographical boundaries. Given this, the cost per reach of this traditional medium is far higher than social media that covers a much wider canvas.

Tangibility offers refers to the product or service offerings made available by the different media. Social media due to its inherent nature, carries along with it the ability to allow consumers to alter the offerings. Whereas traditional media is unable to do that.

Time consumption for both media is different. The average time of viewing across both these media are different. Given the costs constraints, the traditional format has fixed shorter time slots for consumption. On the other hand, social media has longer duration of consumption of communication.

The last point on expenses has been touched upon before. In terms of both fixed costs of production and media airing costs, social media scores higher over traditional media. To sum up, social media is increasingly becoming a medium of choice for many marketers due to the above list of benefits.

CUSTOMER ENGAGEMENT TOOLS

Customer engagement refers to the ability of a certain medium to be able to engage the customer across various parameters (Klaassen, 2009).

These could range from attracting attention, talk to them captivity, persuade them about a certain offering, nudge them towards a purchase decision etc. The outcome of this customer engagement aspect can therefore be measured in those terms such as conversion rates, amount of traffic etc. Some of these are shown in below Figure 5.

Figure 5. Customer engagement
Source: (Klaassen, 2009)

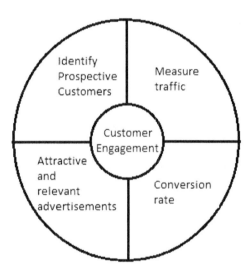

Various tools used by Social Media Marketing are media sharing sites, blogs/microblogs, social bookmarking sites, virtual/online communities, SNSs, virtual worlds etc.

To do the above, identifying prospective customers is the starting point. Figure 5 above depicts that. Customer engagement is the core of marketing but working on it does not make any sense when we do not have the right customers to follow. So our first priority should be to find our target audience and then plan our activities according to their behavior and interest (By 2016 Why 70% of Small Businesses Will Depend On Social Media Tool To Reach New Customers, 2015).

Our task gets easier when we have these customers in our network. Else we have to monitor when they are onboard. To add more value to this network, we should share relevant content and analyze their response. If the response is not favorable, then we need to look for other ways in which we could engage and convert them to prospective customers.

There should be consistent engagement of customers in social media other than posting links and creating advertisements (Media Buying, 2009). Various tools can be used to measure the traffic and also the behavior of customers. Engagement with target audience completely depends on the time spent for interaction. We spend lot of our productive time in answering the queries and getting involved in discussions to make them understand the effectiveness of our product.

Having invested considerable amount of time and monetary requirements, it is obvious that we will measure the returns. Is there any one step solution to measure ROI? To answer this, we need to define our social media goals clearly and also measure them. In this phase, it is easier to know the conversion rate of our customers. If the rate is not as expected, then we can work on changing the current activities and also adding other effective measures to drive traffic and increase the conversion rate.

SETTING GOALS IN SOCIAL MEDIA

Goals in social media can be based on web traffic, customer loyalty, conversion rate etc. Usually, a SMART (Specific Measurable Achievable Realistic Timely) technique is used to set goals in social media. Smaller measurable components are to be arrived at such as - Number of visits, clicks and shares, comments etc.-depending on which goal one is chasing.

Figure 6. Goals of social media (Bosomworth & Chaffey, 2012)

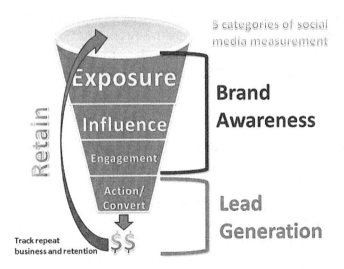

The above figure shows the various parameters on measuring social media goals.

At a very basic level, creating brand awareness can be a measure. Just launching a campaign on Facebook or twitter helps do this. Using strong influencers or networks is another way to create brand awareness. This is also done through viral marketing when a particular communication goes viral due to the storytellers in the group. Engagement is yet another way to look at brand awareness since unqualified awareness does not lead to brand recall or equity building but engagement does. Hence awareness has to view in its ability to engage the consumers through its brand communication.

Once this engagement is successful, it may result in 'lead' generation through action/ conversion. If there is a specific call to action by the social medium used, by way of clicks or visit to website etc., then that is measures at this stage. It is classified as potential customer or a prospect or a lead. Once this lead is converted successfully, he/she becomes the customer. Then the organization takes all efforts to 'retain' the customer through various means.

Traditional marketing tools may be successful in acquiring leads but are not cost effective as compared to Social media. Campaigns in Social media are designed with lot of creativity to attract the audience. Whereas in traditional media there are various limitations such as geographical constraints, expense etc. which hinders the overall performance of the campaign and may not reach most of the audience.

MEASURING RETURN ON INVESTMENT ON SOCIAL MEDIA

There are challenges in measuring social media effectiveness. Following are a few of them expressed by organizations- inability to correlate them with business outcomes, insufficient analytics or expertise, inadequate tools for measurement and heavily unreliable data.

However, it is not impossible to measure the ROI of social media. It is more important to identify the RIGHT metrics that will make this possible. Fundamentally, it is critical to understand how much money is going into social media and what is the return one is getting in terms of reach or other media aspects. For most companies, the former is easy but the latter is where organizations get jittery. Specifically, efforts need to go in which part contributes to what part of return on investment for the social media campaign. This will also allow you to understand where to improve your inputs so that the output is more efficient.

If a person ran Google AdWords campaigns and never checked how much they were paying per click, what kind of click-through-rate would they be getting or whether any of the people who clicked on the ads were actually converting, it would be a completely wasted investment. Hence it is essential to measure your ROI.

There are three steps in this:

1. Defining social media goals that require some kind of behavioral change from the point of view of the user and hence are important to be tracked. Metrics like social shares and followers are nice to track too, but they shouldn't be the main goals;
2. The second aspect is that of linking goals to specific campaigns. Each campaign has a specific objective and that has to be taken into account. Unless this context is made clear, marketers can come to wrong conclusions regarding the same;
3. Some tools that help in tracking visits from sites are Google urn builder and this information will be included in Google analytics reporting.

TRACKING THE GOALS

It is important to track the goals that one has set. This is critical and needs understanding of how to go about choosing the tools needed for various purposes. An illustration for the same has been given discussed below.

Figure 7.
Source: *How to Get Google to Instantly Index Your New Website, 2015*

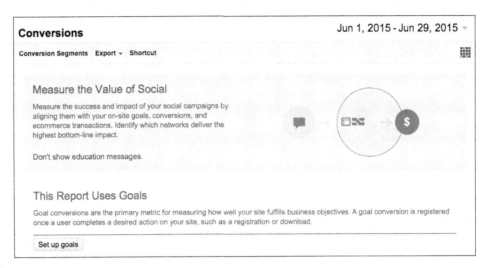

If one don't have any goals set up, there would be a prompt to create one.

Figure 8.
Source: *How to Get Google to Instantly Index Your New Website, 2015*

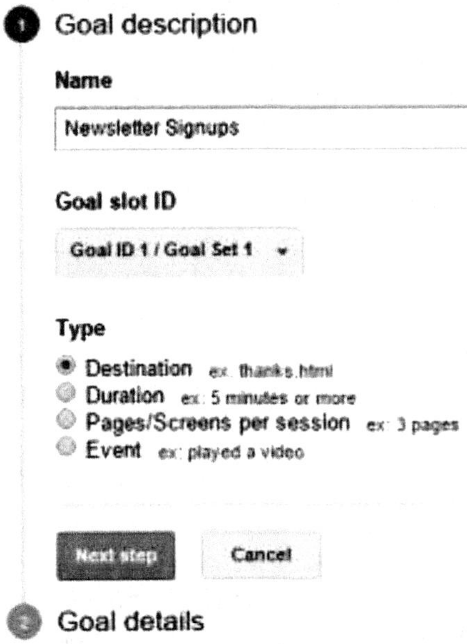

Figure 8 shows a screenshot that describes the procedure to set up a goal that has been defined earlier. For instance, if the goal was to get newsletter signups, one will have to setup a special thank you page on the site for after someone subscribes. But if the goal is to increase time on site for Twitter users by say X%, or to get traffic from Facebook to watch a video on a landing page, one could choose the appropriate goal type. In the given example, the goal can be set as a destination page.

Figure 9. Screenshot depicting goal description
Source: Nizan, 2016

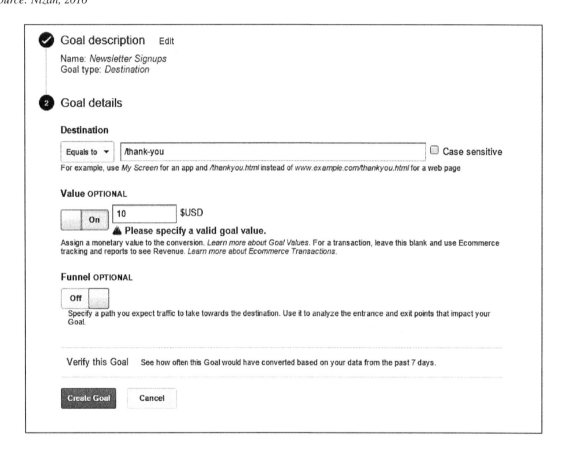

For this part, one needs to enter the actual destination URL that will trigger a conversion. One needs to ensure that this page is not indexed in Google, so that the only way for someone to land on it is by going through the email signup process.

It is essential now to attach a value to each conversation. The process of adding value to a conversation can be described as below:

1. **Lifetime Value x Conversion Rate:** Calculate the lifetime value of a customer, and multiply that by your conversion rate (average number of email subscribers who become customers) to find out what the potential value of each visit is;
2. **Average Sale:** If the goal of your campaign is to try to get sales, then you'll want to calculate your average sale amount and set that as the value. In this case, your destination page would have to be the page that shows up after a customer completes a purchase.

At the end one would be able to see the conversions and the actual amount earned from those conversions. Figure 6 shows a brief excerpt of the same.

Figure 10. Screenshot showing status of goals in various social media tools
Source: Nizan, 2016

Social Network ?	Conversions ? ↓	Conversion Value ?
		$ ( )
	% of Total: 1.49% ( )	% of Total: 1.08% ($)
1. Twitter		
2. Facebook		
3. LinkedIn		

3. **Track Your Social Media Expenses:** In order to figure out whether you're getting a positive or negative ROI for social media campaigns, you'll also have to measure how much you're spending. Here's what should be included in that number:

   a. **Man-hours:** Your time is valuable. Whether you're a solo-preneur, or you have a social media team, add up the man-hours that go into a specific social media marketing campaign over a specified period of time. Don't just use an employee's annual salary, because they're more than likely going to be working on several projects throughout the year. Measure this investment per-campaign;

   b. **Content:** Did you get a landing page written by a professional copywriter? Or maybe you outsourced status updates. These costs are easy to overlook, but they count.

   c. **Social media tools:** Using Facebook and Twitter is free, but if you're using a tool like Sprout Social or other social media management software, you need to add those costs in. Just like with the man-hours, you should calculate this on a per-campaign basis. So if your campaign lasts for one month, only add in the cost of a month of the software, not an entire year;

   d. **Ad costs:** If you're running a Promoted Tweet, Facebook Ad or boosting a Facebook post, add in that cost as well.

Once you have your expenses calculated, you'll be able to calculate your social media ROI for every campaign with this simple formula:

(Earnings – Costs) x 100 / Costs

Earnings is based on the value you calculated in the previous section. And your costs are the items listed above (man-hours, content, etc.)

You can figure out the specific ROI for each social network by segmenting your earnings and costs per social channel, and using that same formula above. After looking at the numbers, you'll be able to decide which social platforms are doing the best for your company, and focus in on those. For any social networks or campaigns that are bringing in a negative ROI, you can either try to adjust by spending less, or by making your campaigns more effective.

NON-QUANTITATIVE BENEFITS OF SOCIAL MEDIA

There are innumerable benefits of social media other than just the numbers. Word of mouth or referrals is one such. Getting influenced by peer group on a brand that they just used is a powerful way of marketing a brand. And social media enables that because of the interactive nature.

So while these types of returns are difficult to track, it's important to keep them in mind when you're going over the ROI of social media campaigns. Numbers don't always convey the full picture on what is happening to a brand campaign. Brand building is a key part of social media objective and it has to be viewed in that light.

Social Media Adoption

In recent times, social media spends have gone up across organizations. Of course, the rate of adoption among corporates have not been proportionate to the promise that the medium holds. There are some barriers that need to be unshackled before the medium moves towards it true potential. Let us see some barriers that inhibit the adoption in a corporate setup.

First the unfamiliarity of the medium by Senior Management. Many top management personnel have grown up with traditional medium like television, radio and print. They find it difficult to learn a new medium at a later age. Some of them even consider this' a waste of time'! They'd rather delegate this to the youth in the organizations.

But this approach does more harm than good. Social media has a powerful double edge implication of Ownership versus control. i.e. the more and more brands throw open brand communications and campaigns to the public, making them interactive, shareable and inviting comments, the higher the risk of the management losing control over the brand. A classic example of this would be the social media campaign that the brand Dove undertook. Titled 'real beauty', it encouraged consumers to upload pictures of themselves in candid forms, without make up, making them accept themselves the way they were. In contrast to the huge public admiration of svelte figurines and slim looks, this Dove campaign celebrated the 'inner beauty' in women. The campaign was a smash hit, rapidly increasing market shares over 25% in a few months and the brand imagery scores climbing at a healthy rate. The organization in this case, was willing to give ownership to the consumers and reaped the benefits generously.

The point is this. Social media is risky. But by not embracing it, organizations run a different risk of alienating or not participating in the potential word of mouth opportunity for their brands. Whether the companies have a social media strategy or not, consumers will continue to write/opine about various brands. Hence it is advisable for the senior management to take active interest and immerse themselves to make this happen.

This can take place broadly in two ways- through personal learnings or organizational learnings. The first one recommends that top management starts doing one of the following- blogging, begin social networks, be on twitter/ Facebook themselves, upload/watch YouTube videos etc. All these will make them hands on with social media and make them understand the fine differences between that and traditional media.

The second approach-namely organizational learning- is even more important. Many examples come to mind. Unilever makes its senior management interact/meet with the top echelons of Facebook/Google/ Twitter for some regular periods- to exchanges notes on technology and its possibilities. They also have a reverse mentoring process- wherein the top management is mentored on social media by the younger employees for several weeks. And finally, there is also a 'swapping' arrangement- where employees spend a couple of weeks in the social media organizations and vice versa. In fact one such initiative has resulted in an online campaign for the detergent brand Tide-which went digital and garnered some good reviews for the brand.

The other barrier that impedes social media adoption is the difficulty of efficacy measurement. While there are GRPs, Readership and listenership numbers available for traditional media, social media still focusses on engagement through eyeballs, click throughs etc. that don't reflect spend efficiencies holistically (Stern, 2010). And this becomes a deterrent for organizations.

Overall it can be said that organizations should use Social media not to impress people but to impact people. And work along with it to create great brands.

Purchase Decision Journey

A recent article in New York Times talked about how Amazon has become 'The Shelf Space' for shopping for consumers (Maheshwari, 2017). So much so, that if your product is not present on Amazon, then it is largely invisible to consumers. This radical departure in shopping behavior is reflective of how social media and internet are shaping marketer's strategies across brands.

Increasingly, more than three or four media are used by companies in order to lure customers. And this was referred to as 'Integrated Marketing Communications'. The question that was pertinent was 'how do I therefore allocate monies across the various media". But now the answer to that seems to be found in deciphering what is called the 'Purchase decision journey' of consumers.

Consumers typically go through a series of steps before finalizing to buy a brand. This is referred to as the Purchase decision journey that he/she undertakes (Iblasi, Bader, & Al-Qreini, 2016). Marketers would do well to map this for individual categories and products and this will dictate which medium will be suitable to perform what task. The steps are –Consideration to buy, Evaluating alternatives, decision to buy, forming relationship with the brand and finally becoming an advocate for the brand.

Let us begin with the first one- Consideration to buy. This is the first information seeking step-hence brands will do well to be present through the SEOs. In the Amazon example, it is essential to list your products on the portals to make it visible to consumers. And we need to follow the path that consumers do in order to make that happen. In some categories such as paints, it may still be the dealer network that will proceed information so there is a need to communicate to that network.

The second step is that of evaluating alternatives. This is where product reviews and feedback come in. Given the opinion that gets rapidly formed on social media for brands, companies should have a proactive blog or reviewer team that will engineer this. Amazon reviewers needs to be sensitized about the products and maybe even given a free sample to test them. And companies need to understand competitors' offering very well if they're to give a comparison of that to prospects at this stage.

The third stage is that of buying. This is where transaction ease, price and after sales service factors- all come in. How can social media be helpful here? The website of the company or the products needs to have easy navigation and on-line purchase option. Also there needs to be information on availability in that site. The payment gateways are to be geared such that they facilitate the most common banks' net banking or credit/debit cards. After sales service in terms of warranty or guarantees – need to be built into the product sale visibility. It is also at this stage that one needs emotional gratification for purchasing the brand and hence lean media such an s YouTube advertising will go a a long way in ensuring this. According to survey in the USA, advertising on lean media results in more effective return on investment for any campaign as it is better targeted and the consumers who are watching the shows are more involved unlike watching television where there tends to be more interruption.

The fourth stage of relationship building has been made easy by internet. Again real time feedback, instant consumer complaint handling or changing communication messages if not working- all these help build better messages. Also personal customization goes a long way.

Finally making customers the advocates for the brand. If the first steps are done well among set of consumers very well, the last one falls in place. Word of mouth or viral marketing is the most powerful tool for conversion. Social media through its transparency makes this more convenient.

Increasingly therefore the marketers are allocating monies across how many customers are to be addressed across which stage of the purchase decision journey instead of how much monies are given across various steps.

Table 1. Categories of social media

Communication	Collaboration
Blogs-Blogger, Blogspot,Vox	Central desktop
Aggregators-Twine,Netvibes	Social news
Diaspora-Facebook,Hi5, Linkedin	Wikimedia
Microblogs-Twitter	Document Management

Source (Marketing Stack, n.d.)

Social Media and Mobile Applications

One of the biggest impacted area through social media is the mobile application. Apps (aka applications on mobile) have redefined commerce. Since the consumer has become more mobile savvy, companies are scrounging to recruit personnel who are comfortable in this space and are constantly ready to learn and innovate.

The segment that has witnessed radical departure in their job description are the product managers and the marketers. They are learning how to build brands, create marketing campaigns and measure them- all through the usage of mobile applications.

Whether your company is digitally driven or not is irrelevant. Regardless, a product manager will either get busy integrating the front end of product development through apps or the customer transaction step-i.e. sale closure- through apps. Other processes like testing, obtaining customer feedback, tracking customer satisfaction- can also be woven through apps.

All these end up making Apps not just as a tool but a channel for growth itself. It needs to serve as a platform for communication, transactions, time management, ecommerce, etc.

Some things, therefore all product managers need to learn are:

- Doing consumer behavioral research differently;
- Gone are the days when market research was a reactive response from organizations to understand consumer needs. Now the information needs to be real time and interactive. And mobile apps are

just the right tool to enable that. This means that the research process of training of researchers, designing questions with simplicity- etc. all need to undergo a change;

- Cross functional effort on product design;
- Due to the nature of inputs from various stakeholders (customers, vendors, trade, salesforce, R and D), the speedy response needs to get translated into product designs that reflect that superior and holistic understanding. Is your product manager capable of that?
- Aesthetics as important as content.

Today the end user wants it all- form and function, ease and accuracy, instant gratification as well as long term reliability. This means that every interface with the consumer is an opportunity for brand building. The company cannot divorce the role of user interface either through a website or a Facebook page with that of a mobile app that performs a specific function. That puts pressure on the product manager to be familiar with all aspects of social media, as there is very high overlap between users of one medium and others, unlike traditional medium, where apart from the TV viewing, there was not much duplication in reach across other media.

- Evaluating media with new metrics.

The above point on social media savviness means that the product manager should know newer ways of evaluating mobile app effectiveness. What worked yesterday may not be relevant today. Can he look at rapidity of app downloads, time taken for full app navigation, volume of app based transactions, retention of apps by customers etc. as the defining measures for the mobile app performance? These will have to be stitched into his/her media plan evaluation.

These are some ways how a product managers' role is changing. Of course technically there are a lot of challenges that he needs to cope with- starting from synching with the operating system of the mobile to creating an UI for customer engagement and not treat it like a desk top.

The M-Payment

Paying through mobile- 'M Commerce' as it is popularly called, has been growing by leaps and bounds. There are more than 4 billion individuals today, using a mobile phone (Aguilar, n.d.). The mobile payments in the US alone have gone from 14% in 2014 to 39% in 2016 and is expected to reach 70% in 2017-18.All these are making the mobile payments industry and startups in this area transform to meet the growth needs.

While there are many kinds of mobile payments ranging from internet browser led (directing to a shopping cart and then receipts), PIN led (contactless technologies) and mobile wallets (storage of your payment information), it is erroneous to think that the mobile payment transactions will be limited to smartphones or tablets.

In these cases, the technology of Bluetooth plays an active part. The Bluetooth Low Energy (BLE) transfer takes place on either the consumer or merchant's device where data is stored in a mobile payment account. Example PayPal, Apple Pay, Android Pay and Samsung Pay. Here the startups would begin with a text message service, then mobile apps and finally contactless payment systems. Google is also toying with facial recognition to confirm an individual's identity.

The other majors in the customer value chain- namely the banks- such as JPMorgan Chase & Co., Bank of America Corp., Wells Fargo & Co. and U.S. Bancorp, have a created a joint venture called clear change that allows customers to transfer funds instantly to another bank account through their phones. Retailers like Wal-Mart Stores Inc. are rolling out their own products to fuel mobile payments, and also providing additional services like location and customer coupon deals.

Social media and messaging apps have also jumped into the fray. Soon through FB and Whatsapp you will be able to make payments. So these organizations will become all in one- news, entertainment and commerce- formidable giants to deal with. They will also make targeted communication to clients for promotional offers etc. much more effective.

All these will have implications in the Regulations front. This should ensure transparency and standardization of payment mechanisms in the future across the world. The trends indicate that by 2020, 90 percent of smartphone users will have made a mobile payment.

The Marketer needs to learn many things as far as the above trends go. Firstly, the buyer behavior which is an important component of any consumer study is radically shifting. So understanding these patterns across industries is a must. Secondly, brand loyalty is going to move hand in hand with mobile savviness and technology adoption for consumers. This means that brands that are not digital today have no choice but to be so in times to come, if they are to retain their customers. Also a new segment called the 'techno literate' is fast emerging as a basis on which consumers need to be targeted, regardless of other segmentation criteria of age, gender, location etc. Finally, collaboration with stakeholders is expected to reach a new high i.e. to say that to evaluate tie ups with banks on the one hand and social media on the other, as a part of the brand sales and distribution strategy is becoming a need of the hour. Accordingly competencies will need to be drawn up for the marketing team.

CONCLUSION

New age media is synonymous with social media. This is a fast growing medium and has benefited through consumer habit change and their need for instant gratifications (Rajeshwari, n.d.). The audience is getting hooked to scoail media across age, gender, geographies. Social media is tapping on the most basic insitinct of a human being which is of being social and connected. This connectivity is now a boon for the marketers as it helps in increasing the reach of the communication as well as products. It has only made it easier to identify reference groups that are virtually active and create a large contribution to the pocket of the manufacturer. This audience is connected to the social media not just through their systems but also through their mobile apps, which has made them available nearly 24x7. This has further diminished the barriers of time and geography. We are now living in a unified and highly connected society which creates one global market and global communication to the customers. "The future of social media is the future of media itself It is how people access online content *now*" said David Murphy, Founder and Editor of Mobile Marketing Daily. And it is not hard to see why.

REFERENCES

Aguilar, R. (n.d.). *Building an advocacy marketing strategy using the social media funnel*. Retrieved from REmomd: http://remomd.com/social-media/building-advocacy-marketing-strategy-using-social-media-funnel.html

Bosomworth, D., & Chaffey, D. (2012). Creating a Social Media Marketing Plan. *Smart Insights*. Retrieved from http://www.carmichaelcentre.ie/sites/default/files/Need-to-know-social-media-strategy-smart-insights_0.pdf

Buying, M. (2009, Sep 30). *Online's Slice of Ad Spending Grows Worldwide*. Retrieved from eMarketer: https://www.emarketer.com/Article/Onlines-Slice-of-Ad-Spending-Grows-Worldwide/1007298

By 2016 Why 70% of Small Businesses Will Depend On Social Media Tool To Reach New Customers. (2015, Dec 30). Retrieved from SMEJoinup: https://smejoinup.com/blog/by-2016-why-70-of-small-businesses-will-depend-on-social-media-tool-to-reach-new-customers/

Davis, A. (2009, May 13). *Banner ads drive search behaviour: study*. Retrieved from Campaign: Banner ads drive search behaviour: study.

Dewing, M. (2012). *Social Media: An Introduction*. Library of Parliment.

How to Get Google to Instantly Index Your New Website. (2015). Retrieved from Neil Patel Digital: https://neilpatel.com/blog/google-index/

Iblasi, W. N., Bader, D. M., & Al-Qreini, S. A. (2016). The Impact of Social Media as a Marketing Tool on Purchasing Decisions (Case Study on SAMSUNG for Electrical Home Appliances). *International Journal of Managerial Studies and Research, 4*(1), 14–28.

Klaassen, A. (2009, Nov 2). *The State of Search Marketing: 2009*. Retrieved from AdAge: http://adage.com/article/digital/digital-marketing-state-search-marketing-2009/140083/

Maheshwari, S. (2017, Jul 31). *As Amazon's Influence Grows, Marketers Scramble to Tailor Strategies*. Retrieved from New York Times: https://www.nytimes.com/2017/07/31/business/media/amazon-advertising.html

Marketing Stack. (n.d.). Retrieved Jan 3, 2018, from Alexa: https://try.alexa.com/marketing-stack/

Nairuthram, S. (2016, Jun 15). *Social Media Marketing*. Retrieved from Easy Walkers Digital: http://www.eazywalkers.com/social-media-marketing/

Nizan, Y. (2016, Apr 26). *LTV Calculator – The Naive method*. Retrieved from Soomla Blog: http://blog.soom.la/2016/04/ltv-calculator-naive-method.html

Poirier, S. (2013, Nov 19). *Social Media Building Blocks: The 6 Spheres Of Social Media Marketing*. Retrieved from Business to Community: https://www.business2community.com/social-media/social-media-building-blocks-6-spheres-social-media-marketing-0687662

Rajeshwari, K. (n.d.). *Why is social media adoption low?* Retrieved from BLoC: Business Line On Campus: http://www.bloncampus.com/columns/marketing-moves/why-is-the-adoption-of-social-media-low/article9937231.ece

Stern, A. (2010, Feb 3). *8 Ways to Improve Your Click Through Rate.* Retrieved from iMedia: 8 Ways to Improve Your Click Through Rate.

Wasserman, A. (n.d.). *4 Steps to a Successful Social Media Campaign.* Retrieved from Prescient Digital Media: http://www.prescientdigital.com/articles/web-2.0/4-steps-to-a-successful-social-media-campaign

This research was previously published in Application of Gaming in New Media Marketing; pages 181-201, copyright year 2019 by Business Science Reference (an imprint of IGI Global).

Chapter 31
Social Media Usage in Online Consumer Decision Process and Buying Behaviour

Lydia Andoh-Quainoo
Pentecost University College, Ghana

ABSTRACT

This chapter examines the usage of social media in predicting consumer buying process. A mixed method approach has been applied, a cross sectional survey and in-depth interviews were conducted in three universities in Ghana. The responses were collected from individuals in the age group of 18 -30. Data was analysed using Logistics Regression and Thematic analyses. The findings revealed that the social media behaviour of young consumers could significantly influence their behaviour at the pre-purchase information search and evaluation levels. The findings suggest young consumers are more likely to use social media for marketing activities such as purchasing, hence industries should redirect more activities towards this digital channel. This implies that social media is driving young consumers into e-commerce and that presents a huge opportunity for business and marketers.

INTRODUCTION

Social media has emerged as technology beyond cell phone and one of the most dynamic, interdisciplinary socially facilitated media of contemporary society (Kaplan & Haenlein, 2010; Hjorth & Hendry, 2015). Social media combines wed 2.0 and social networking technological applications to connect users to a wide range of sites such Facebook, Wechat, Instagram etc. (Wei, Huang & Zheng, 2018). Social media comprises of different digital network platforms including Social Networking Sites (SNS). SNS's are platforms where individuals are able to connect with others on sites such as Facebook, Myspace, Whatapp, Instagram, Twitter, Wechat, Snapchat, etc to share information, personal images, blogs and others (Khan, 2017; Pookulangara & Koesler, 2011). Social networking sites have become the most popular aspect of social media and it is used for social connection, for sharing of media content, for academic work and

DOI: 10.4018/978-1-6684-6287-4.ch031

searching for and buying of goods and services generated by these contents (Watulak & Whitefield, 2016). This is followed by social news sites, internet sites that feature users-posted stories. Such stories are graded based on popularity, as voted on by other users of the site or by site administrators. It's also known as Social Bookmarking sites and they include Digg, Reddit, and Scoop. Another aspect of social media is the media sharing sites which permits users to upload your photos, videos and audio to or from other sites anywhere in the world. One predominant example of social media sharing site is YouTube. com where most people share videos with others and tag them. There is also yet another form of social media referred to as blogging which is publication on the World Wide Web consisting of discrete, diary-style entries referred to as post.

Emergent usage behaviour on social media and social networking sites is growing higher among young consumers especially college students. Carter & Yeo (2016) reported that young university students both undergraduates and postgraduates on daily basis averagely use chat about 20 times especially familiar social networking sites such as Wechat, Twitter, Facebook, Whatsapp and Instagram (Khan, 2017; Whiting & Williams, 2013). Due to the prolific usage of social media, its usage in businesses is becoming growing significantly (Ioanas & Stoica, 2014). Although, Social media presents a digital media challenge to businesses and marketers in view of the fact that it is totally different from traditional media and other digital media. It portrays a dual communication channel which demonstrate superior business interaction and effective tool which offers more power to customers (Keegan & Rowley, 2017). Yet there is an increasing usage for this digital media at different levels of business processes

The important role of social media in emergent business and marketing practices cannot be over emphasized as it serves different functions in e-commerce processes including communication, brand building, market space, customer engagements, customer relationship management and market research and intelligence (Ioanas & Stoica, 2014; Song & Yoo, 2016; Zhang, 2017). Social media in recent times has taken dominance in communicating the value of products and services and creating a superior customer experiences in digital marketplace. Businesses and marketers are engaging in social media strategies to reach and engage customers in various ways such as advertising, promotion, branding, data and viral marketing, other commercial activities on social media. Social networks have become a platform for enhancing the overall marketing strategy Social Media content are used to access and generate product and services and build product referrals and responses (Dolan et al., 2015).

Customers are be able to monitor their favorite brands, post questions and make comments related to services or products on social media platforms like Facebook, Twitter, Youtube and Instagram. Businesses on the other hand have developed digital competences to connect directly with consumers, engage in business interactions and ascertain discussions about their brands through these social media platforms. Due to the usage of social media in the shopping experiences of consumers there is growing interest in social media consumer decision and buying behaviour (Ioanas & Stoica, 2014; Pookulangara & Koesler, 2011; Zhang et al., 2017)

However, there has been limited research focus on online social media and consumer decision making. Few studies have been directed at the social media decision making at managerial level. For instance, Keegan and Rowley (2017) posit that social media should be planned, implemented and evaluated at the managerial levels to ascertain the achievement of marketing objectives based on key performance indicators. Some have researches have also focused on smart phone usage online purchasing behaviour (Arif, Aslam & Ali, 2016; Byrne & Rowley, 2013). While a few have concentrated on the use of social media in the various stages of the consumer decision process (Song & Yoo, 2016). However the extent to which social media is used in daily information searching, selection and choosing products and services online is low and that provides more room for research in this aspect of social media.

This chapter therefore seeks to explore the extent to which Social media is used in consumer decision process or how it can be applied in social media purchasing behaviour by young consumers. The core contribution of this chapter is to contribute to knowledge on social media facilitated daily consumer decision and buying activities and the integration into online consumer decision process and buying behaviour.

THEORETICAL BACKGROUND

Consumer Buying Behaviour

Consumer behavior is the study of individuals, groups or organizations and the behaviour they exhibit during the selecting, securing, using of product and services to satisfy their needs . Consumer behavior can be defined as the behavior consumer's display in searching for, purchasing, using, evaluating, and disposing of products and services that they expect will satisfy their need. (Schiffman & Kanuk, 2010). It focuses on what people spend valuable resources such as money, time and energy in consumables. Consumer behaviour involves studying how people buy, what they buy, when they buy and why they buy when consumers are making purchasing decisions, the pass through the processes of recognition, (Blackwell, Miniard, & Engel, 2006). Consumer buying behaviour is influenced by two major factors. These factors are individual and environmental. The major categories of individual psychological factors affecting consumer behaviour are, consumer Knowledge, perception, learning, motivation, personality, beliefs, attitudes and life styles. The second category of factors is environmental factors. Environmental factors represent those items outside of the individual that affect individual consumer's buying behaviour process. These factors include culture, social class, reference group, family and household. The above mentioned factors are the major determinants behind the firmness of consumers to opt for a given good or service (Blackwell, Miniard, & Engel, 2006). Consumers' physical and social environment has huge influences on consumers' buying behaviour and can make a big difference in their desire and motives for product purchase.

In recent times the emergence digital media has transformed consumer buying behaviour due to the shift in retail platforms to the digital market space. Digital media consumer behaviour such as smart phone and social media behaviour has become distinct from offline buying behaviour and has emerged as online buying, significant to consumer buying and consumption behaviours. Through social media consumers have access to a global retail market both locally and far from their domestic market. This offers them a numerous opportunity to have more product information such as product offering, prices and demand for customized services (Holmes, Byrne & Rowley, 2013; Sunil, 2015). This has offered more opportunities for consumers to have access to a huge amount of information and social media has become a major channel for the supply of such information. Customers disseminate voluntarily information to one another through social media (Ioanas & Stoica, 2014; Pookulangara & Koesler, 2011). Consumers also search for a lot of information about products and services which they expect will satisfy their needs better. They also receive ratings and feedback from rated consumer experiences (Sunil, 2015) through the use of social media. Social media therefore plays a key role in the whole decision process. Consumers have a higher need for information particularly, product information. Social media has improved significantly the manner in which consumers receive information from different industries on many products and services. It has also influences the information needs; information obtained and has transformed the way consumers integrate information searching at during the various stages in the Consumer Decision Process (CDP) (Zha, 2019; Zhang, 2017).

The Consumer Decision Model

Consumer decision-making models have been widely used in consumer behavior studies especially for offline consumer behaviour. Consumer decision-making has long been of interest to researchers leading to a number of models that try to explain the stages that a consumer goes through when making a buying behavior. However, one of the most popular contemporary consumer behavior model is the Engel-Blackwell-Miniard Model which has receive constant advancement for the last four decades, improving understanding of consumer behavior theory and knowledge by (Blackwell et al., 2001)

There are three major stages involved as consumers attempt to buy before the final action of buying. These include; pre-purchase, purchase and post purchase. The cognitive decision sequence are further broken down into core seven -point model based on; problem identification, search for information search (internal and external), evaluation of alternatives, purchasing and post purchasing decision. The seven point decision process can be categorized broadly into pre-purchase, purchase and post purchase and are discussed below:

Figure 1. Consumer decision model

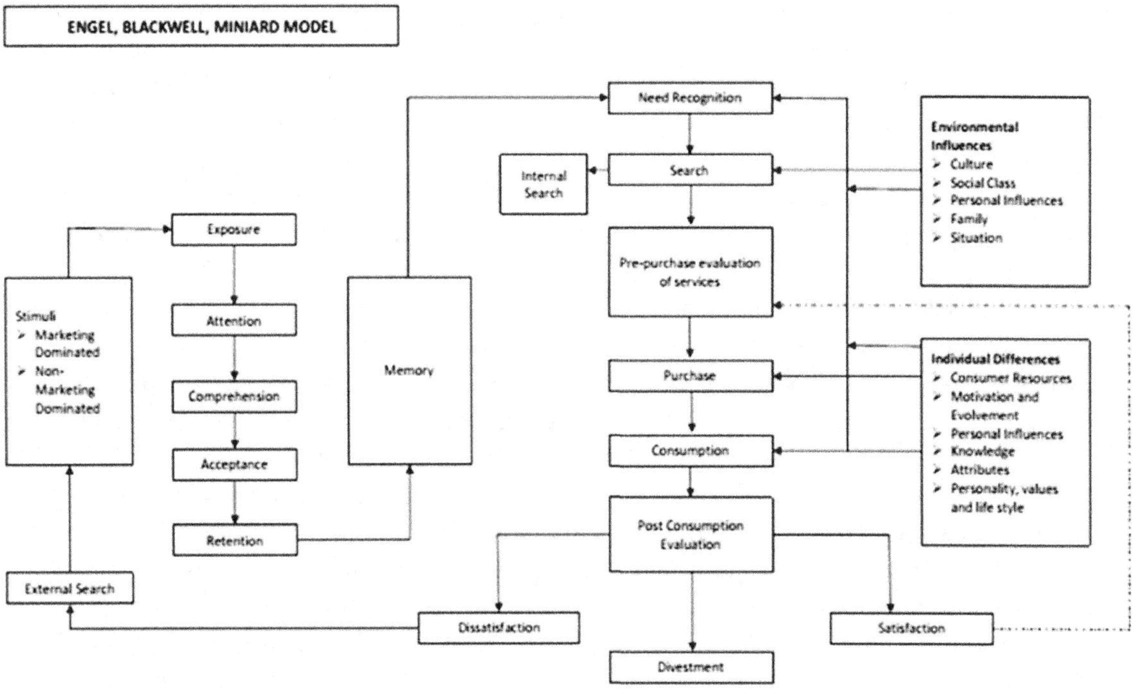

Source: Blackwell, Miniard and Engel, 2001: Rau and Samiee, 1981; Foxall, 1980.

Pre-Purchase Stage

The pre-purchase stage is considered to be a preliminary stage whereby the consumer can get know needs and make the necessary steps towards fulfillment of the need. The pre-purchase stage is where consumers recognize a need, search for information and conduct pre-purchase evaluations to decide ad select the best option of the product or service they intend to buy.

Problem recognition is the first step of consumers' buying behaviour process that may occur because consumer has an expected state desired to be attained than the current state. Problem recognition takes place whenever a consumer recognizes a significant difference and a discrepancy between the desired and the actual state of affairs, which is in sufficient magnitude to arouse and activate the buying process (Schiffman & Kanuk, 2010). Consumers' buying behaviour begins with the result of problems or a single problem. Consumers at different stages portray different behaviours before buying and this stage give them motivation to continue with other behaviours associated with their need recognition. When an individual is triggered externally, for instance, a person may see a television advertisement for a vacation, the stimuli triggers thoughts or ideas about the possibility of making a buying (Kotler and Keller 2009). Digital technologies such as Smart phone and social media has drastically changed consumer needs and have allowed for much greater customization of products, services, and promotional messages than do older marketing tools (Schiffman & Kanuk, 2010). These technological changes have been designated as one of the major factors causing changes in the market and customers behaviour.

Once a problem is recognized, consumers begin to seek pertinent information from internal and external sources about the product and services they desire. Internal search involves the consumers' memory on what is known about the product, while external search includes word of mouth, stores visit, trial and online, information, advertisements and social media. The social media environment effectively allows consumers to use such tools in buying behaviour and the Internet has become an important tool for information search.

Information search is very critical in consumer buying decision and behaviour and social media has become an important source of information in online consumer behaviour. For instance, in the Hotel Industry, it has been found that social media plays a critical role at the pre-travel stage in searching for and obtaining the relevant information. That is, social media becomes the main tool used in travel arrangement by customers before moving (Varkaris & Nuehofer, 2017).

The next step to evaluate available options from the total consideration set to the choice set of two or three products. Alternative evaluation process sets in and depending on their motives or goals of purchase; consumers establish criteria for evaluating weighing options. Based on set criteria consumers start to compare and evaluate several alternatives in terms of products features and their desires. Sometimes consumers' choices may be complex and may the consideration of alternatives best to fulfill their needs (Blythe, 2008; Schiffman & Kanuk; 2010).

Purchase Decision and Consumption

When consumers find alternatives and evaluate them based on their selection criteria, they make their choice among the alternatives by purchasing them. The choice can be influenced by the gathered information from different including mobile phone and social media (Hawkins & Mothers Baugh, 2010; Song & Yoo 2015). Purchase behaviour also include the consumption of goods and services.at the consumption stage consumers seek information on how the product or service is used.

Post Purchase Evaluation Behaviour

After the consumption, the consumer then experiences certain levels of satisfaction or dissatisfaction, and evaluates the wisdom of the choice made in selecting the alternative. Two potential outcomes are derived from this phase – satisfaction or dissonance. When consumer experiences dissonance towards the buying, the choice is 'devaluated' and the consumer begins the process of searching, obtaining information and evaluating other options for future buying decision, in which triggers new behaviour. It is a phase when the consumer decides whether or not to move from merely implementing the product to a full adaption; that is, whether to use the product repeatedly or repurchase or not. The quality of their conclusion becomes important in this stage of steps and how well the choice worked out. Consumers compare their perceptions and experiences of the product with their expectations.

With the advent of digital media such as computer, smart phone and social media, consumers are constantly online creating and sharing content with others. Such technological behaviour has also influenced the behaviour of consumers in online purchasing decisions and behaviour in this new digital market. At the post purchase stage evidence suggest that consumer experiences and satisfaction influence the word of mouth and repeat purchase in mobile and social media commerce (San-Martin et al., 2016). Once more, the process of shopping has also evolved and revolutionized since the emergence of digital media technology. Consumers search for products and services and others needs through digital means such as smartphone and social media (Sunil, 2015). It is therefore important to explore the use of social media in online consumer decision and behaviour.

The Influence of Social Media in the Online Consumer Decision Process

Consumer decision process has been migrated unto the digital media platform where there is pre-purchase, purchase and post purchase activities are displayed. In applying the consumer decision model to the digital media online buying behaviour researchers have considered the use of smart phone and social media in the different stages of the model that can be well applicable and better utilized by online consumers in order to facilitate effective online customer strategy. Others have also focused on industries and online products which yield themselves better for the application of the consumer decision model (Song &Yoo, 2015; Varkaris & Neuhofer, 2017). Findings suggest that using smart phone and social media remains relevant and significantin the online consumer decision process and buying behaviour (Holmes et al., 2013; Song &Yoo, 2015; Sunil, 2015; Varkaris & Neuhofer, 2017). Holmes et al., 2013 reported that in the UK smart phone usage remains highest with products which have higher emotional involvement. Also, there is high usage of smart phone at the pre-purchase stage where needs are recognized, information is searched and alternatives are evaluated than during actual purchase.

According to Varkaris and Neuhofer, (2017) consumer decision making using social media has not changed but it rather been adapted in the new digital system where brands on social media are observed and selected based online reviews help consumers to come up with consideration set and pre purchase evaluation. Although not much has been done on social media, evidence from some studies suggest a remarkable usage of social media in searching for and evaluating particularly at the pre purchase stages in e-commerce. In online buying process consumers use social media to identify needs, search for products and services and select product and service brands (Varkaris & Neuhofer, 2017). Other findings also suggest that using social media can be critical in pre-purchase stage when using a service and support customers in making decision for engaging in the service process (Song & Yoo, 2015; Sunil, 2013). Other reports also shows that social media benefits such as functional and monetary including convenience, and coupon all facilitate the pre purchase stage of buying particularly the pre-purchase evaluation and information search (Song & Yoo, 2015).

The Influence of Social Media in Information Search and Evaluation

Social media usage in consumer decision process remains higher at the information search level and consideration n of alternatives where they are more likely to compare brands and prices for pre-purchase evaluation, particularly, where the emotional involvement is high on the product or service in question (Byrne & Rowley, 2013; Varkaris & Neuhofer, 2017). Social media exposes consumers to new shopping related information. Zhang et al. (2017) reported that the cumulative usage of social networking sites could be positively associated with online shopping activities. This has made information generation and sharing critical at the pre-purchase information stage of consumer buying behaviour. According to Jha, (2019) social media influences information at different stages of customer's decision making particularly at the searching stage. Social media user generated information such as customer reviews creates positive perception towards online purchasing which fosters intention to buy and actual online buying. This implies that social media usage does not only foster information search but also in evaluation and actual selection.

The use of social media in service information, pre-purchase evaluation and actual buying has been high in service industries. Song and Yoo (2016) focused on the role of social media during the pre-purchase stage in hotel and restaurants and found that social media support consumer decision significantly in their selection of these services. It was reported that there is a positive relationship between function and monetary benefits obtained from social media during the pre-purchase stage. The functional benefits are mainly information search, exchange of information, past experiences from other users which monetary benefits included coupons, price rebates and special offers. This has been supported by Varkaris & Neuhofer, (2017) who also reported that in the Hospitality industry, specifically hotel search, evaluation and selection, social media plays a major role. Consumer use social media channels for comprehensive search using trip Advisor predominantly. This was followed by Facebook, Instagram, Youtube and Twitter. They use such channels to search, compare and evaluate the hotels which they have a need to use.

To this end it was necessary to examine social media use in consumer decision and buying behaviour especially at the pre-purchase stage in young consumers (Arif et al., 2016; Song & Yoo, 2015; Varkaris & Neuhofer, 2017).

Social Media Use and Information Search by Youth in Ghana

Social media usage in young people includes information gathering and sharing of content as well as interactions with friends and relatives. Social networking sites have become the most popular aspect of social media and it is used for social connection, for sharing of media content, for academic work and searching for and buying of goods and services generated by these contents (Watulak & Whitefield, 2016). In social media usage is on the ascendency in young people (Owusu-Acheaw & Larson, 2015; Yeboah & Dominic, 2014). There are only a few studies which have reported on social media behaviour of young people in Ghana. Most studies have connected the academic performances of students and social media usage behaviour. For instance, Yeboah & Dominic, (2014) reported that tertiary students spend too much time on social media which affects their concentration, and result to poor performance.

This has been supported by Owusu-Acheaw and Larson, (2015) reported that social media is quiet high in some tertiary institutions where students spend between 30 minutes to three hours on social media. It was also found that there is a direct relationship between students' academic performance and the extent of social media usage. This if not controlled students' academic performance will be influenced negatively by their social media behaviour.

Other studies have also explored the social antecedents driving social media usage behaviour. Karikari et al. (2017) reported that social media support the generation social capital and user well-being but it usage can be influenced by external social pressure. Thus young people have social pressure to connect with friends through social networking sites hence the high usage behaviour. Hence, the main social factor motivating usage behaviour in social media is the need to connect with others. This is one of the few studies from an emerging economy on social media. Still most of the studies are from developed countries and this calls for more studies in the developing world to bridge the gap. Again, with the high usage rate knowledge about its usage in social commerce is still lacking hence this study explores how psychosocial drivers for engage predict social commerce in young people.

METHODOLOGY

The study adopted a mixed method approach where both qualitative and quantitative methods were employed due the research objectives. The survey method which is a widely used data collection in measuring multiple variables and hypotheses testing was used to collect quantitative data while in-depth interviews were used for the qualitative data. The Survey method allowed for a deductive approach based on theoretical framework with empirical measurement through data analysis and interview complemented the survey data. Using both qualitative and quantitative methods added richness and details to research results which might be lacking when using just one method.

Sampling and Data Collection

The target population was young consumers from age 18-35 currently pursuing tertiary education at the various universities. They being in their prime ages from 18-35 years gave them more time to use social media and to explore its functions more because majority of them are not in employment. They are the most active users of digital media because they are the generation who has been exposed widely to mobile phone since they were born (Karikari et al., 2017). The Universities were considered to be concentrated convergence point for most young people at the prime age in the country. To ensure sample representativeness, a probability sampling specifically a two stage cluster sampling where clusters were selected purposively and respondents were also selected at random from this cluster. Three faculties were selected at random from each university and students were randomly selected for the survey. Each member of the population had an equal chance of being selected for survey. Each member of the population had an equal chance of being selected for survey. A total population of 605 was selected randomly for the study. Out of these 30 students who were considered to be active users were selected as key informants for in-depth interview as well.

Table 1. Characteristics of respondents

Variables	Frequency	Percent
Institution: U.G	201	33.3
U.C.C	222	36.8
KNUST	182	30.0
Age: 20 years & below 21-25 years 26-30 years 31-35years 36 years and above	210 252 115 25	34.8 41.7 19.0 4.2 0.3
Sex: male	292	48.3
Female	312	51.7
Frequently used S. media		
Facebook	211	34.9
Whatsapp Twitter Instagram	158 116 72	26.2 19.2 11.9

Instrument and Measures

The survey questionnaire was made of questions assessing the social demographic data such as age, gender and which type of social media they frequently used. The questionnaire also captured the use of social media in searching for products and buying . All variables were measured using a five-point Likert scale anchored from 1 to 5 and categorized into various responses ranging from (5) strongly agree to strongly disagree (0)All variables were measured using a five-point Likert scale anchored from 1 to 5 and categorized into various responses ranging from (1)strongly factors. All variables were with the acceptable range for Cronbach's Alpha .75 -.899 which suggests robust reliability levels. The qualitative data was collected with an interview guide and solicited for information on social media daily usage practices and usage in the consumer decision process. Both questionnaire and interview guide were adapted from Consumer Decision Model from (Blackwell et al., 2001 Song & Yoo, 2015; Varkaris & Neuhofer, 2017).

Data Collection and Analysis

Prior to data collection, there were preliminary visits to the selected public universities for permission from appropriate authorities through a letters. Students were contacted and invited for participation at the lecture halls. After seeking consent of students, initial briefing was also give before participation, participation was purely optional. Students were randomly selected, to respond to questions by completing the questionnaire while those selected for qualitative data were interviewed and recorded with their consent. In all 604 questionnaires were fully completed and were subjected to analysis using descriptive analyses and Logistic Regression. Data from interviews were transcribed and subjected to thematic analysis. The results are presented and discussed below;

Table 2. Integration of social media in buying decision and behavior

Buying Beh	Odds Ratio	Std. Err.	Z	P<z	[95%Conf. Interval]
S. MEDIA	2.422	.47835	4.48	0.000	1.645211 3.567495

Generally, Social media usage showed alikelihood **of (OR 2.422)** significant at **P<0.000** displaying a strong significance. This means consumers who use social media are twice likely to search for products and buy products online through their social media platform. This also further tested on specific social media platforms and it was observed that specific social media platforms differ in the extent to which they could be used in business and the buying behaviour.

Table 3. Specific social media platforms and usage in online buying process and behavior

S. Media usage &consumer decision	Odds Ratio	Std. Err	Z	P>z	95% Conf. Interval
Facebook	5.5225	1.9085	4.94	0.000	2.805277 10.8718
Youtube	4.5876	.96988	7.21	0.000	3.031344 6.942967
Instagram	2.0292	.35928	4.00	0.000	1.434301 2.87109
Twitter	.37298	.07413	-4.96	0.000	.2526371 .5506562
Whatsapp	3.6015	1.2821	3.60	0.000	1.792469 7.236347

This table compares the purposes for which people use mobile and their respective connections to using social media in buying or shopping behaviour. The table shows that there is a significant positive relationship between high users of Facebook, Instagram, Whatsapp, and Youtube in the use of social media in buying processes and behaviour as shown in the Table 2 above demonstrated by the odds ratios as follows Facebook **(OR=5.5225),** Youtube **(OR=4.5768), WhatSapp (OR=3.6015),** and Instagram **(OR=2.0292),** all significant at **(P<0.000)** with the exception of Twitter which did not show significant relationship. This means that users of Facebook use the media for buying process and decisions than the other social media platforms. This could probably be due to the time of its emergence as Facebook appears to be older than the other platform.

Daily Social Media Usage Practices of Social Media in Online Buying Behavior

Concerning daily usage lifestyle and practices, it was found that users have well integrated the mobile phone and social media into every fiber of their day's activities to the extent that the mobile phone and social is the first thing consumers wake to and say good morning to and the last activity for the day as shown in their responses;

Right from bed, I go in for my phone and I browse Facebook to see what is I missed while asleep. I update my status religiously. It makes me feel happy and belonging (ST 6).

It is my phone alarm which wakes me up and I consult it almost every 10 seconds to check my messages on social media. (ST8)

This respondent admitted how strongly attached she is to her smart phone and social media as she uses it within her daily routines all the time. In fact, it is her first priority after waking up from sleep.

Aside using social media for daily routines and coordination, some respondents believed that social media can be used for searching for products and services at the pre-purchase stage but its might not be safe for purchasing

I have not made any online purchase yet but I do go for window shopping on social media. I do not special reason I just don't feel comfortable to purchase items online (ST 4).

I use my phone in searching for products on social media and other sites such as a shoe and other cloths but I do not buy from any websites such as Tonaton (24).

I only search for information about the products (ST 22)

Some of the respondents were not comfortable probably due to security risk and other fraudulent activities reported in online buying. These make online shopping such as social media particularly challenging in some parts of Africa. The reports on security issues were something running through the thoughts of respondents.

I do buy stuff on social media with my phone. I don't do that regularly because it is quite difficult closing buying deal with a mobile phone. It's comes with its own security issues. It is complicated so I prefer doing that on a computer than on my phone (ST 17).

Yes, I do buy online but I do buy from some selective sites that I am sure about (ST5)

Despite the challenges associated with the social media buying, there are some people who still take the risk to buy from social media sites. There are those who are online buyers through their phones and social media

Yes, I do I love to buy sneakers online directly from the manufactures and I do that a lot from England. (ST 15)

I have bought items online before from websites and social media, I love to browse through jewelry shops and places where they sell ladies items (ST 13).

Yes, I bought a beauty cream based on the health benefits that I read about from the social media (ST 22).

Yes I do online purchases items via the internet and social media from time to time using my mobile phone (ST 19).

Yes I do buy items online and I can recall that I last bought a make-up set from Facebook but I prefer Facebook because in most cases you pay at the point of delivery (ST 11).

Yes I do that a lot. Especially when am in Nigeria (ST 10)

However, for some respondents they neither buy nor search for products and services with their mobile phone and their main reason is the security and trust issues in social media commerce e.g Security issues and fear of losing money. These comments below also show a knowledge and perception gap which could be addressed if m-commerce and s-commerce will succeed

I have never bought any product from social media before, to me its quit complicated (ST2).

I don't really trust these online sales. So I don't buy from them (ST 18)

I have never tried buying online because I do not have a bank account (ST 19).

I don't buy items online or social media using because I do not trust these sites (ST17).

The reasons above also suggest the some consumers have already formed some wrong perceptions about buying through the internet. However, some consumers also do not buy due to other reasons either than online security issues.

The findings revealed that general social media usage behaviour is predictor of its usage in online buying behaviour. It shows that users of social media are two times likely to use social media in buying decisions and behaviour. This means that users of social media have assimilated social media into their online buying decision process and behaviour.

These findings suggest that social media has a significant relationship with consumer buying behaviour, meaning that consumers who are dependent on social media are likely to engage in buying activities including searching for products and services and buying. If so then young people's involvement with social media can be redirected into other productive activities including business and buying. Although not many works have connected social media usage and commerce, it was very important to explore social media as a platform for marketing and business as well as engaging young consumers for business growth sustainability. This seem to be confirmed Varkaris & Neuhofer, (2017) researched on how consumers use social media in UK at the pre-purchase stage for hotel selection. The study supports the findings of this study about remarkable use of social media in search for and evaluating hotel services options before selection of choices, which hitherto was not the case in the absence of social media era. For instance, some studies in confirms that sizeable number of young people prefer searching for all the options online and the daring ones who are risk takers and have the online buying requirements such as payment systems and know-how of the procedure can buy. This seem to be social exclusion where those who lack the know-how, are risk averse and lack the digital resources are not enthused about buying from online. The findings shows that truly young consumers engage social media in their daily consumption and primary at pre-purchase stage supporting finding by Song and Yoo (2016) that the use of social media in service information, pre-purchase evaluation and actual buying has been high but not consistent with service industry per se.

The findings from the qualitative data on social media consumer decision and buying behaviour of young people throws more light on the use social media in prediction social media engagement in searching for products and services, consumer decision process and online buying behaviour. The findings indicated that there are three categories of online consumers; the majority who mostly search for products and services but buy offline, those who search products and buy and those who do not search or buy due to security threats. For most people searching for information is the safest place to be hence more and younger people search for all kinds of products online through social media and mobile phone particularly fashion and electronic products. According to the Consumer decision Model by Blackwell et al. 2001 consumers recognize a need before searching for information and then proceed to make choices in offline buying behaviour, however in online buying process it appears that need recognition can be both online and offline and more information search is conducted online before deciding to buy online or offline. This means that the Consumer Decision Model can be applied depending on the market segment, the digital media used, the product or service or even industry at stake. This confirms some of the studies in social media online behaviour suggesting that integration of social media in online decision process and buying behaviour can be high at pre purchase and evaluation stage (Blackwell et al., 2001 Song & Yoo, 2015; Jha, 2019;Varkaris & Neuhofer, 2017).

IMPLICATIONS OF THE STUDY

Social media in marketing and online buying behaviour appears to be still low, therefore Businesses and Marketers should explore the full usage of social media to target young consumers for products and services by creatively and innovatively connecting marketing communication and engagement to drive social media marketing and commerce. Young people's involvement in social media could be redirected from unhealthy behaviour on social media such too much emphasis on unacceptable relationship and wrong information or entertainment "infortainment" into other productive and responsible behaviours and activities including learning, working, commerce and buying. Social media use in commercial activities including banking, ticketing, payment of bills should be encourage at national levels just like the way the social interaction side of this digital media has been popularized.

The Consumer Decision theory as it applies in offline behaviour has been applied from pre-purchase, purchase and post –purchase. However, in online buying behavior such as m-commerce and social commerce behaviour, although digital media is well integrated it appears to be highly applied at the pre-purchase level with lower integration at purchase and at post purchase. This implies that for online consumer behaviour consumer decision and buying mostly occurs at pre-purchase with selected purchases but post purchase activities are not done offline. That means consumers use digital media to search for products and services, evaluate and d It was also found that dependence on social media has a significant relationship with commerce, meaning that consumers who are dependent on social media are likely to engage in commercial activities including searching for products and services and buying. To strengthen social media use in online consumer decision process and buying behaviour, there should be some incentives for buying online such as price rebates, and free deliveries.

Government commitment to digital business in terms of adoption and infrastructure will also be a significant driver in ensuring the growth and advancement in digital marketing. The level of commitment towards infrastructure and systems such as deliveries, payments and reduction in the risk associated with mobile commerce would all drive young people to use smartphone for online buying. The use of digital money such as mobile money should be well integrated in the economy to drive e-commerce and m-commerce.

Young people's involvement behaviour in social media should be redirected from relationship and "infotainment" into other productive activities including commerce and buying. Social media use in commercial activities including banking, ticketing, payment of bills should be encouraged at national levels just like the way the social interaction side of this digital media has been popularized.

Since pre-purchase activities are high on social media, businesses should make good use of social media platform for the influencing consumer decision process to enhance pre-purchase activities. Also innovations and applications for effective m-commerce and integration of online buying behaviour should be created to increase usage of social media in buying from the digital market. Businesses who wish to thrive in online digital markets should work on innovative ways of payment such as using mobile money and other electronic or digital means of payment since young users have a stronger propensity towards mobile commerce. If businesses and marketers could get millennial to buy online they could own them for life.

However, the study is limited to only students and other researches can also focus on the young people in general. Future research can further extend to actual commerce engagement and activities on social media and processes involved in social media buying.

CONCLUSION

There has been a phenomenon growth in social media usage in young people's new digital media usage behaviour. Consequently, younger consumers have responded to seeking some business benefits from social media. However, there has been lack of literature on social media usage and how they predict business and marketing usage. The study came to a conclusion that social media behaviour is not only concerned about usage behaviour but business and consumer buying behavior as well.

REFERENCES

Arif, I., Aslam, W., & Ali, M. (2016). Students' dependence on smartphones and its effect on purchasing behavior. *South Asian Journal of Global Business Research*, 5(2), 285–302. doi:10.1108/SAJGBR-05-2014-0031

Barger, V., Peltier, J. W., & Schultz, D. E. (2016). Social media and consumer engagement: Areview and research agenda. *Journal of Research in Interactive Marketing, 10,* 4. pp. 268-287. doi:10.1108/JRIM-06-2016-0065

Bolton, R. N., Parasuraman, A., Hoefnagels, A., Migchels, N., Kabadayi, S., Gruber, T., ... Solnet, D. (2013). Understanding Generation Y and their use of social media: A review and research agenda. *Journal of Service Management*, 24(3), 245–267. doi:10.1108/09564231311326987 doi:10.1108/09564231311326987

Buluklu, Y. (2017). Mobile games on the basis of uses and gratifications approach: A comparison of the mobile game habits of university and high school students. *The International Journal of Research into New Media Technologies*, 1–17. doi:. doi:10.1177/1354856517748159

Carter, S., & Yao, A. (2016). Mobile apps usage by Malaysian business undergraduates and postgraduates: Implications for consumer behaviour theory and marketing practice. *Internet Research, 26*(3), 733–757. doi:10.1108/IntR-10-2014-0273

Ioanăs, E., & Stoica, I. (2014). Social media and its impact on consumers behavior. *International Journal of Economic Practices and Theories, 4*(2).

Jha, B. (2019). The role of social media in communication: Empirical study of online purchasing intention of financial products. *Global Business Review.* pp. 1-17.

Kaplan, A. M., & Haenlein, M. (2010). Users of the world, unite. The challenges and lucre of social media. *Business Horizons, 53*(1), 59–68. doi:10.1016/j.bushor.2009.09.003

Karikari, S., Osei-Frimpong, K., & Owusu-Frimpong, N. (2017). Evaluating individual level antecedents and consequences on social media use in Ghana. *Technological Forecasting and Social Change, 123,* 68–78. doi:10.1016/j.techfore.2017.06.023

Keegan, B. J., & Rowley, J. (2017). Evaluation and decision making in social media marketing. *Management Decision, 55*(1), 15–31. doi:10.1108/MD-10-2015-0450

Khan, M. L. (2017). Social media engagement: What motivates user participation and consumption on YouTube? *Computers in Human Behavior, 66,* 236–247. doi:10.1016/j.chb.2016.09.024

Lim, J. (2016). Effects of social media users attitudes and perceptions of the attributes of news agency content and their intention to purchase digital subscriptions. *New Media & Society, 18*(8), 1403–1421. doi:10.1177/1461444814558669

Owusu-Acheaw, M., & Larson, A. G. (2015). The use of social media and its impact on academic performance of tertiary students: A study of Koforidua Polytechnic, Ghana. *Journal of Education and Practice, 6*(6).

Pookulangara, S., & Koesler, K. (2011). Cultural influence on consumer's usage of social networks and its impact on online purchase intentions. *Journal of Retailing and Consumer Services, 18*(4), 348-354.

Sahney, S. K. (2013). "Buyer's motivation" for online buying: an empirical case of railway eticketing in Indian context. *Journal of Asia Business Studies,* pp. 43-64, doi:. doi:10.1108/JABS-07-2011-0036

Sata, M. (2013). Factors affecting consumer buying behavior of mobile phone devices. *Mediterranean Journal of Social Sciences, 4*(12). doi:10.5901/mjss.2013.v4n12p103

Schiffman, L. G., & Kanuk, L. L. (2010). *Consumer Behaviour* (10th ed.). Prentice Hall.

Sheldon, P., & Bryant, K. (2016). Instagram: Motives for its use and relationship to narcissism and contextual age. *Computers in Human Behavior, 58,* 89–97. doi:10.1016/j.chb.2015.12.059

Song, S., & Yoo, M. (2016). The role of social media during the pre-purchasing stage. *Journal of Hospitality and Tourism Technology, 7*(1), 84–99. doi:10.1108/JHTT-11-2014-0067

Sundar, S., & Limperos, A. (2013). Uses and Grats 2.0: New gratifications for new media. *Journal of Broadcasting & Electronic Media, 57*(4), 504–525. doi:10.1080/08838151.2013.845827

Sunil, D. (2015). Trends and practices of consumers buying online and offline: An analysis of factors influencing consumer's buying. *International Journal of Commerce and Management*, *25*(4), 442–455. Doi.org/10.1108/IJCoMA-02-2013-0012 doi:10.1108/IJCoMA-02-2013-0012

Whiting, A., & Williams, D. (2013). Why people use social media: A uses and gratifications approach. *Qualitative Market Research*, *16*(4), 362–369. doi:10.1108/QMR-06-2013-0041

Zhang, Y., Trusov, M., Stephen, A. T., & Jamal, Z. (2017). Online shopping and social media: friends or foes. *Journal of Marketing*, *81*(6), 24–41. doi:10.1509/jm.14.0344

KEY TERMS AND DEFINITIONS

Consumer Buying Behavior: Consumer behavior is the study of individuals, groups or organizations and the behavior they exhibit during the selecting, securing, using of product and services to satisfy their needs.

Consumer Decision Model: Consumer decision-making models have been widely used in consumer behavior studies especially for offline consumer behavior.

Chapter 32
Micro Organization Use of Social Media for Business-to-Business Customers

Lisa S. Rufer
Rider University, USA

Rosalyn J. Rufer
https://orcid.org/0000-0003-4659-9699
Empire State College (SUNY), USA

Savita Hanspal
State University of New York at Potsdam, USA

ABSTRACT

Marketing communications have evolved on account of development of greater interaction between organizations due to the availability of new electronic media. Much has been written about the effect of these new communication channels and how they can be used to retain consumers. However little evidence has been presented to show how these channels of communication are used by smaller organizations, particularly when serving business to business customers. This research builds on earlier exploratory work of Brink and Atanassova and Clark to provide empirical evidence of the importance of social media usage for small organizations when serving business customers. However, unlike Brink, this research separates small firms from medium size organizations and focuses on the subcategory of micro organizations (fewer than 50 employees).

DOI: 10.4018/978-1-6684-6287-4.ch032

INTRODUCTION

Micro Organizations Use of Social Media for Business to Business Customers

The availability of new electronic media has had a profound impact on marketing communications that has led to the development of greater interactions between business organizations. This technology has created a marketing environment where barriers to communications have been broken due to the emergence of several options for speedy communication channels that has increased firm competition. Today, the firms must not only consider traditional media and forms of communication but also allocate their communication budgets to reach customers through the new and emerging media (Agnihotri, Dingus, Hu, & Krush, 2016). Prior to these developments, smaller organizations have had to balance their limited resources when designing their integrated communication strategies. They were unable to grow their business, increase their reach to the customers, or manage their customer relationships as they lacked the resources to hire employees on a large scale to manage these functions efficiently and effectively. E-commerce has brought about the possibility of handling many marketing and communication tasks without requiring the resources previously thought necessary. The competitive advantage of larger organizations in being able to communicate on a large scale because of their resources, appears to be compromised as the smaller organizations and businesses have started realizing the potential offered by social media and e-communication channels. With the increased use of e-channels of communication, it is proposed that the competitive gap caused by limited resources between the larger and smaller organizations has been reduced.

Micro organizations typically have the fewest resources because of their size. For the purpose of this study, micro organizations are defined as those with less than 50 employees and are typically associated with entrepreneurial organizations. A number of studies have looked at how these smallest organizations contribute to economic growth (e.g., Chovancová, Nedu, & Ogbonna, 2015; Jha & Depoo, 2017; Reddy, 2007; Toma, Grigore, & Marinescu, 2014). The ability of these micro organizations to create sustaining relationships with their business to business customers has become increasingly important in many regions of the world as a pathway to economic growth (Collins & Reutzel, 2016; Stel, 2006). Similarly, much has been written about the effect of these new communication channels and how they can be used to retain consumers. However, little evidence has been presented to show how these channels of communication are used by smaller (micro) organizations, particularly, when serving business to business customers. The research presented here, builds on the earlier exploratory work of Brink (2017) and Atanassova and Clark (2015), which provides empirical evidence on the importance of social media usage for small organizations when serving business customers. However, unlike Brink (2017), this research separates small firms from medium size organizations and focuses on the subcategory of micro organizations (less than 50 employees).

Brink (2017) states that because of the limited resources of small and medium size organizations, they have more often used social media in B2C (serving consumer markets) communications than B2B (serving business customers). This conclusion by Brink (2017), was based on findings from the literature and a case study combining small and medium size firms, without looking at the most entrepreneurial firms, the micro organizations. Brink (2017) found the digital networking media used by small and medium size enterprises (SMEs) play an important part in the performance of the organization, as defined by their ability to form sustaining relationships. These customer relationships have been shown to be critical to the performance of the firm (Battor & Battor, 2010). Furthermore, communication strategies have been shown to support these relationships when serving business customers (Tuominen, Rajala, & Moller, 2000). The empirical research, presented here, attempts to identify if there is any difference between the micro and larger organizations in the use of social media as a part of their communication strategy and how these organizations allocate resources in their promotion mix. The objective of this study attempts to answer the question not addressed by Brink (2017): whether social media may or may not be used by micro organizations to reach business customers in a way different from those organizations that are larger and employ more than 50 employees.

BACKGROUND

The landscape of marketing has changed dramatically over the past several decades. The type of communication channels used as well as the audience to which products and services are marketed has compelled organizations to change marketing communication strategies to reach their present and potential target markets and to sustain continuing customer engagement. Danaher and Dagger (2013) found that a chain of department stores were successful using digital media, in addition to traditional media options. Their study found empirical evidence that e-mail and sponsored Google searches had an influence on purchase outcomes for the consumer market. However, the focus on sales alone failed to identify the effect of building a brand relationship through social media and the long-term effect on performance. Studies such as that by Go and You (2016), found that large firms in consumer products industry sectors (e.g., IKEA and JetBlue) are likely to use social media communication channels to build consumer relationships. Not only do recent studies look primarily at the consumer market, they also report on the use of social media by medium and large firms. The important contribution from these studies is the understanding of how these organizations build sustaining relationships with their customers through a change in communication strategies.

Moreover, developments such as increased competition, technological developments, and consumer sophistication, especially with the growing technology savvy generations – or the new consumer, have contributed further to evolving communication strategies (Okazaki & Barwise, 2011). This has resulted in a shift in the funds the firms allocate to advertising in mass marketing campaigns using traditional media alone, to multi-pronged efforts for building brand communities that include social networking channels (Colliander & Dahlen, 2011). Researchers have assessed the effects of the use of multimedia at the brand level (Naik, Raman, & Winer, 2005). A topic of importance in this line of research has been the allocation of resources across media (Naik et al., 2005; Raman & Naik 2004); and the finding that the optimal design of communication programs is based largely on external, consumer driven factors (Voorveld, Neijens, & Smit, 2011). More recently, similar effects have been seen when communicating with all the organization's stakeholders, including their business customers (B2B).

The increase in market competition and advances in promotion mix enabled by electronic commerce and social media have had several implications for organizations and its customers including a change in the buyer-seller relationships (Agnihotri et al., 2016; Katona, Zubcsek, & Sarvary, 2011). The sales force and its level and quality of communications has been shown to be an important contributor to the success of the business to business transactions (Brooksbank, 1995; Schaefer & Pettijohn, 2006). However, the limited resources of micro organizations, adversely impacted their ability to build important relationships with such customers using more traditional communication strategies that were more expensive and time consuming and offered little interactivity (Atanassova & Clark, 2015).

Agnihotri et al. (2016) found empirical evidence that social media helps to expand the impact of the organization's salesforce. They concluded that social media can be used to develop relationships with B2B customers by enhancing the role of the salesforce to increase brand loyalty. Katona et al. (2011) attribute the impact of personal connection as key to diffusing information through social media. Hence, communication strategies have changed considerably as a result of the interaction between organizations and the engagement of stakeholders through electronic media. Most of the existing literature fails to differentiate between medium, small and micro organizations as part of the analysis. It can be hypothesized that if social media enhances the brand management for medium and small firms it should also enhance these relationships for micro organizations: the entrepreneurial start-ups and those with the least resources. Wamba and Carter (2014) looked at how industry sector and firm size had an influence on the use of social media by small and medium size enterprises in the B2B market. However, they failed to identify how micro organizations used these same social media tools when compared to SME. Based on the work of Katona et al. (2011), it appears that personal connections will enhance the effectiveness of social media and the interactions of the salesforce with B2B customers to build relationships, regardless of the size of the firm.

One challenge for all organizations, especially micro organizations, is how to best allocate resources on the ever-expanding social media technologies (Rufer, 2014). Due to the fact that micro organizations have a visible impact on economic growth, it is important to know how social media is used by them when serving business customers. While some of the recent studies cited above have explored whether there is a relationship between the use of social media to build relationships with the firm's customers, particularly in the consumer market (B2C); very few have studied the impact of use of social media in building B2B relationships and even fewer have focused on how micro organizations use social media. The previous studies have primarily focused on medium and larger organizations. Those that studied SME, have not differentiated between medium, small, and micro organizations or on the B2B selling situations. This study attempts to fill this gap. It defines micro organizations and explores how they use social media to reach their stakeholders and to build their B2B customer relationships. It also compares micro organizations' social media use to that of firms with more than 50 employees in order to reach their stakeholders through e-commerce channels.

FOCUS OF THE ARTICLE

This study investigated the relationship between company size with the allocation of monetary resources on social media; the use of social media or digital networks to reach different stakeholders; and differences in the use of social media and the type of industry for the business customer (B2B). To better define the relationship between size of company and the use of social media when serving business customers, the first analysis determined if the company size made a difference in social media usage. This was followed by an analysis that just looked at those just serving business customers. For this purpose, the companies were categorized into micro organizations (less than 50 employees) and larger companies that employed more than 50 employees.

METHODOLOGY

Data Collection Procedures. Data was collected via a mail survey sent to all members (1000) on the mailing list of a Chamber of Commerce in an Upstate New York county consisting of organizations that conduct business across the service, manufacturing and government sectors. Each business received an envelope with instructions, the survey, and a pre-addressed stamped return envelope. The response rate for this survey was approximately 9% (92 respondents), which has been proven to be an acceptable response rate for collecting data from businesses (Rasmussen & Thimm, 2009).

One respondent from each organization, holding the position of either the marketing manager or director, was asked to participate in the survey. The survey asked respondents to indicate the importance of Facebook, Twitter, Yelp, Four Square, Tumblr, Pinterest, Blogs, LinkedIn, Text Messaging, and Mobile Marketing in reaching the organization's stakeholders on a 1 (Very Unimportant) to 5 (Very Important) Likert-type scale. Respondents also answered questions regarding the size of their company; percentage of money allocated towards use of social media vis-à-vis other media including print, radio, television, direct mail, and personal selling; whether they served the consumer market, both consumer and business market, or only business customers; and finally, the company's industry.

HYPOTHESES

Based on previous literature, the size of the firm varied for most industries: some were large and some SME (small and medium sized enterprises). As large companies have better financial resources and larger budgets for promoting their products across different media, they are also likely to spend more on social media as compared to the micro organizations. In addition to the size of the organization, respondents were asked if they served the B2C market, B2C and B2B, or solely served the B2B market. The sample was divided into firms by size (micro and those with more than 50 employees) and then limited the study to those that served B2B customers only. The following six hypothesis were tested based on the size of the firm and their usage of social media to reach different stakeholders. This study identified firms with less than 50 employees because the current literature provides evidence for both large organizations and SME but not the micro organizations.

H1a: Larger size organizations (with more than 50 employees) allocate more money to social media out of their communication budget compared to micro organizations (with less than 50 employees).
H1b: Larger size organizations allocate more money on social media out of their communication budget compared to micro organizations, when serving business customers.

In order to identify whether the type of social media used varied by firm size, the following social media were included: Facebook, LinkedIn, Twitter, Blogs, Tumblr, Yelp, Pinterest, Short Message System (SMS), Mobile marketing, and Four Square. The second hypothesis explored whether the social media usage differed amongst large and micro organizations and whether different social media platforms were used to reach their different stakeholders. Accordingly, it was hypothesized that:

H2a: The use of social media or digital networking channels to reach different stakeholders differs for firms with larger size organizations and micro organizations.

H2b: The use of social media or digital networking channels to reach different stakeholders by B2B firms differs for firms with larger size organizations and micro organizations.

Finally, in order to determine if the use of social media differed on the basis of types of industry as found by Wamba and Carter (2014), the industries were classified into the following categories- service, manufacturing, and government agencies. It was important to study responses from different industries as they differ in their decision-making policies, procedures, communication with stakeholders, and building customer relations. It was hypothesized that:

H3a: There is a difference between the percentages of the communication budget spent on social media in different types of industries based on different sizes of the firms.
H3b: There is a difference between the percentages of the communication budget spent on social media in different types of industries based on different sizes of the B2B firms.

SOLUTIONS AND RECOMMENDATIONS

Prior to any statistical analyses to answer the research questions, descriptive statistics and correlations were calculated. In order to measure differences in social media usage, one-way ANOVA tests were used for testing Hypothesis 1a and 2a. The independent variable was the grouping based on the size of organization and the dependent variable was either money allocated towards social media (H1a) or type of social media used to reach stakeholders (H2a). Company size was used as a categorical variable and was measured in terms of the number of employees: resulting into two groups, micro organizations (less than 50 employees) and larger size organizations (greater than 50 employees). For hypothesis 3, an ANCOVA was run to examine the main effects and interaction effect of size of organization and industry on the dependent variable of the percentage spent on social media. Industry was a categorical variable that was grouped into three categories: service, manufacturing, and government agencies. As in the study by Wamba and Carter (2014) industry became the control variable and size of the organization was the independent variable. However, Wamba and Carter (2014) focused on the use of Facebook by SMEs but not on how much was spent on social media. This analysis was then replicated with only those organizations that served business customers.

Descriptive Statistics: Descriptive statistics and select frequencies for the size of the organization and the percentage of money allocated to social media were evaluated. On average companies allocated 33% of monetary resources towards social media; 31% on print advertising; 25% on Direct Mail; and 11% on TV or Radio advertising. Seventy-five percent (n = 68) of respondents reported that their company had less than 50 employees. Additionally, out of the total firms surveyed, 44% belonged to the service industry; 18% to government and approximately 38% to manufacturing. Since 75% of the firms were micro organizations, many technology startups and innovators, this could likely skew the data toward the manufacturing industry. The decision-makers here were primarily the director of the organization (n = 37) or the marketing manager (n = 33). Following the analysis of the descriptive statistics, each of the three hypotheses were tested comparing social media usage for micro organizations to that of larger firms.

Money Allocation to Social Media Usage

H1a: Larger size organizations (with more than 50 employees) allocate more money on social media out of their communication budget compared to micro organizations (with less than 50 employees).

Monetary allocation of resources towards social media was treated as a continuous variable as it was measured by the percentage of money companies were allocating towards social media usage. An independent t-test was used to compare the percentage of the promotion budget used for social media, print advertising, and direct mail for micro organizations compared to larger firms. The results of the t-test did not find significant differences between micro and larger firms for social media (t (65) = -.135, p = .89) or print advertising (t (50) = 1.69, p = .09). Descriptive analysis showed that both larger and micro organizations spent 33% of their promotion budget on social media. On the other hand, the results of the t-test revealed that the differences were significant for use of direct mail (t (59) = 1.96, p = .05). Larger organizations spent around 28% of their budget on direct mail, whereas micro organizations spent approximately 39% on direct mail.

Use of Social Media to Reach Stakeholders

H2a: The use of social media or digital networking channels to reach different stakeholders differs for larger size organizations and micro organizations.

An ANOVA analysis was conducted to examine if different types of media were used to reach specific stakeholders such as customers, employees, community, marketing channels, suppliers, and stockholders/investors by micro and larger organizations. There was no statistical evidence found that there was a significant difference between larger size firms and micro organizations when using social media as a communication vessel with channels and suppliers. However, there was evidence that when communicating with employees, larger firms were more likely to use Facebook (p = .03) than micro organizations. Furthermore, when communicating with customers, larger size organizations were more likely to use mobile marketing (p = .01) as compared to micro organizations. Lastly, micro organizations are more likely to use text messaging to reach stockholders (p = .002) and employees (p = .05) as compared to larger size organizations. These results are shown in Table 1.

Social Media Usage, Type of Industry and Micro and Larger Organizations

H3a: There is a difference between the percentages of the communication budget spent on social media in different types of industries based on different sizes of the firm.

An ANCOVA was run to test differences between different types of industries and the amount of money spent on social media. There was insufficient evidence to support this hypothesis (p = .573). Thus, when looking at the amount spent on social media, there appeared to be no difference between micro organizations and larger firms regardless of the industry in which they operate.

Table 1. Analysis of Variance between Larger and Micro Organization using different digital platforms serving all customers (consumer and business)

		Sum of Squares	df	Mean Square	F	Sig.
The use of Mobile Marketing to reach your customers	Between Groups	12.055	1	12.055	6.389	.01
	Within Groups	166.045	88	1.887		
	Total	178.100	89			
The use of Facebook to reach your employees	Between Groups	7.278	1	7.278	5.075	.02
	Within Groups	119.027	83	1.434		
	Total	126.306	84			
The use of text messaging to reach your employees	Between Groups	3.742	1	3.742	3.425	.05
	Within Groups	90.681	83	1.093		
	Total	94.424	84			
The use of text messaging to reach your shareholders	Between Groups	7.601	1	7.601	6.138	.01
	Within Groups	96.599	78	1.238		
	Total	104.200	79			

Focusing on B2B Customers

For those firms that only serve business customers, it was important to know whether there was a difference in the percentage of the integrated communication budget spent on social media between the micro organizations and larger size organizations. It was hypothesized that:

H1b: Larger size organizations allocate more money on social media out of their communication budget compared to micro organizations, when serving the business customers.

Using ANOVA, it was found that there was no significant difference between the percentage of the total communication budget spent on social media when comparing micro organizations and larger firms that serve business customers. In fact, for both micro organizations and larger firms serving B2B customers, approximately 28% spent 70% of their communication budget on social media and almost 27% spent 10% of their budget on print media. This shows that there is a shift in the importance of print advertising and social media advertising for reaching B2B customers. The three remaining questions are 1) whether this is different for the type of stakeholder being reached; 2) does the digital channel used differ when reaching B2B stakeholders; and 3) if the type of industry makes a difference in use of social media when trying to reach B2B customers.

When serving all consumers including business customers, it was found that larger organizations and micro organizations differed in using social media to reach different stakeholders except for communicating with channels and suppliers. In order to find out whether larger firms used different digital media to reach different stakeholders as compared to those used by micro organizations, when serving B2B customers, the following hypothesis was examined:

H2b: The use of social media or digital networking channels to reach different stakeholders by B2B firms differs for those with micro organizations and larger size organizations.

Using an ANOVA, it was found that there were significant differences between the use of LinkedIn to reach different stakeholders when serving business customers amongst micro organizations and larger firms (see Table 2). Micro organizations were more likely to use LinkedIn to reach their business customers compared to larger firms ($p = .001$). In the previous analysis reported by the authors, it was revealed that larger firms were likely to use mobile marketing, particularly when serving the business to consumer and a combination of consumer and business customers. However, no significant differences were found in use of mobile marketing between the larger and micro firms when serving the B2B customers ($p = .74$).

While the descriptive analysis indicated that there was no difference between larger and micro organizations when communicating with channels and suppliers, there is statistical evidence that for firms just serving B2B customers, there is a difference between larger organizations and micro firms. The statistical evidence is presented in Table 2. Larger organizations were more likely to use LinkedIn ($p = .03$) to reach their channel members and micro organizations were more likely to use twitter ($p = .05$) for those firms only serving the B2B customers. The other statistically significant finding was that instead of using text messaging to reach shareholders, B2B micro organizations were more likely to use twitter to reach shareholders ($p = .04$) compared to larger organizations.

Table 2. ANOVA for Digital Media used To Reach Different Stakeholders

		Sum of Squares	df	Mean Square	F	Sig.
Use of mobile marketing to reach your customers	Between Groups	1.027	2	.514	.292	.74
	Within Groups	151.198	86	1.758		
	Total	152.225	88			
Use of LinkedIn to reach your customers	Between Groups	21.311	2	10.656	7.143	.001
	Within Groups	128.284	86	1.492		
	Total	149.596	88			
Use of Twitter to reach channels	Between Groups	9.890	2	4.945	3.435	.03
	Within Groups	105.096	73	1.440		
	Total	114.987	75			
Use of LinkedIn to reach channels	Between Groups	9.892	2	4.946	3.039	.05
	Within Groups	118.792	73	1.627		
	Total	128.684	75			
Use of Facebook to reach your employees	Between Groups	.600	2	.300	.190	.82
	Within Groups	127.817	81	1.578		
	Total	128.417	83			
Use of Twitter to reach shareholders	Between Groups	7.747	2	3.873	3.365	.04
	Within Groups	87.469	76	1.151		
	Total	95.215	78			

In order to determine whether or not the type of industry impacts social media expenditure when comparing larger firms to micro organizations, the following hypothesis was tested:

H3b: There is a difference between the percentage of the communication budget spent on social media in different types of industries based on different sizes of the B2B firms.

Once more, an ANCOVA was used to test the hypothesis. There was insufficient evidence to support this hypothesis ($p = .729$). Thus, when looking at the amount spent on social media, there appeared to be no difference between micro organizations and larger firms that serve only business customers, regardless of the industry in which they operate.

Recommendations

Social media has become an important communication strategy for micro organizations. This may be in part because of the limited resources of micro organizations; however, the evidence showed that even for larger firms, there has been a shift from print advertising to the use of digital networking media. In fact, there was no statistical evidence that firms with more than 50 employees allocated a larger proportion of their promotional budget to social media as compared to micro organizations. Furthermore, there was no statistical evidence to support that there was a difference between organizations in different industries for the importance of social media, as found by Wamba and Carter (2014). Since this proved to not be a supported hypothesis for our data set, the recommendations are made across industries as opposed to focusing on the data for each industry. As mentioned earlier, these results may be due to the fact that 75% of our respondents were from micro organizations. The results of this study show that using social media may now transcend industry boundaries, regardless of the size of the organization or type of industry. Thus, micro organizations have effectively used social media to reach a variety of stakeholders, particularly when serving both consumers and business customers, improving their reach

Figure 1.

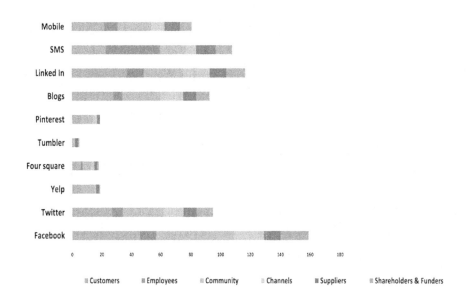

and communications. The bar chart in Figure 1 presents the number of firms indicating the importance of the use of social media to reach each stakeholder.

This study adds to the literature because it provides statistical evidence of how micro organizations that serve only B2B customers successfully use social media differently than larger organizations. Whereas no statistical evidence was found regarding any difference in how micro organizations communicate with channel members when serving either the consumer market or both the consumer and business markets, there was statistical support that micro organizations use twitter and larger organizations use LinkedIn to reach channel members. It was not that micro B2B organizations, did not use LinkedIn to reach other stakeholders; there was statististical evidence that they used LinkedIn more often to reach their business customers compared to larger firms. Liu (2018) stated that the key to B2B marketing is interpersonal relationships, thus larger firms with more resources may use more personal selling to create these relationships. This study adds additional support to earlier studies, which have reported that digital media can be used to increase the effectiveness of personal selling. It appears that this may be the reason that micro organizations, faced with limited resources, are likely to use LinkedIn to reach their B2B customers. They may also want to consider delivering messages to their channel members via LinkedIn, learning from larger firms. Micro organizations may also want to continue supporting the use of Facebook, Twitter, and mobile marketing to enhance the effectiveness of their sales force when serving B2B customers.

FUTURE RESEARCH DIRECTIONS

The limitations of this study will be used to inform future research. The first consideration is based on the little variance in the size of companies; 75% of the respondents had less than 50 employees. Thus, future research should try to encompass a more diverse company breakdown with regards to size. A second limitation of this study is that the data was collected from one county and thus the results may not be as generalizable as would be desired. Future research should focus on collecting data from different counties within the US and countries to be as generalizable as possible. Despite these limitations, this study starts to fill in gaps in how companies are utilizing social media for reaching different stakeholders, particularly for micro firms serving B2B customers. It also confirms the widespread use of social media by businesses regardless of the industry.

CONCLUSION

This empirical study adds to the body of literature by providing evidence that there is no difference between micro firms and larger organizations that serve just business to business customers in the proportion of money allocated to social media. What this does provide is statistical evidence that micro organizations can effectively use social media to reach their business customers, channels, and shareholders. Facebook, Twitter, and mobile marketing were shown to be important communication platforms across organizations to reach customers and the community, and that they were equally important for larger and micro firms, consistent with the findings of Cesaroni, and Consoli, (2015). However, this study, points to a significant use of LinkedIn by micro organizations to reach their business customers. The contributions of this empirical study confirm that the same social media strategies may be effective for larger and micro organizations in both service and manufacturing sectors and that micro organizations may want to explore different social media, leveraging their current expertise in the use of LinkedIn for reaching more of their stakeholders.

REFERENCES

Agnihotri, R., Dingus, R., Hu, M. Y., & Krush, M. T. (2016). Social media: Influencing customer satisfaction in B2B sales. *Industrial Marketing Management, 53*, 172–180. doi:10.1016/j.indmarman.2015.09.003

Atanassova, I., & Clark, L. (2015). Social media practices in SME marketing activities: A theoretical framework and research agenda. *Journal of Customer Behaviour, 14*(2), 163–168. doi:10.1362/14753 9215X14373846805824

Battor, M., & Battor, M. (2010). The impact of customer relationship management capability on innovation and performance advantages: Testing a mediated model. *Journal of Marketing Management, 26*(9-10), 842–857. doi:10.1080/02672570903498843

Brink, T. (2017). B2B SME management of antecedents to the application of social media. *Industrial Marketing Management, 64*, 57–65. doi:10.1016/j.indmarman.2017.02.007

Brooksbank, R. (1995). The new model of personal selling: Micromarketing. *Journal of Personal Selling & Sales Management, 2*, 61–66.

Cesaroni, F. M., & Consoli, D. (2015). Are small businesses really able to take advantage of social media? *Electronic Journal of Knowledge Management, 13*, 257–268.

Chovancová, M., Osakwe, C. N., & Ogbonna, B. U. (2015). Building strong customer relationships through brand orientation in small service firms: An empirical investigation. *Croatian Economic Survey, 17*, 111–138.

Colliander, J., & Dalhen, M. (2011). Following the fashionable friend: The power of social media. *Journal of Advertising Research, 51*(1), 313–320. doi:10.2501/JAR-51-1-313-320

Collins, J. D., & Reutzel, C. R. (2016). Entrepreneurial strategies for emerging markets. *The Journal of Business Strategy, 1*, 47–66.

Danaher, P. J., & Dagger, T. S. (2013). Comparing the relative effectiveness of advertising channels: A case study of a multimedia blitz campaign. *JMR, Journal of Marketing Research, 50*(4), 517–534. doi:10.1509/jmr.12.0241

Go, E., & You, K. H. (2016). But not all social media are the same: Analyzing organizations' social media usage patterns. *Telematics and Informatics, 33*(1), 176–186. doi:10.1016/j.tele.2015.06.016

Jha, R., & Tilokie, D. (2017). Role of microenterprises in recovering U.S. economy-post 2008 financial crisis. *Journal of Applied Business & Economics, 19*, 9–28.

Katona, Z., Zubcsek, P. P., & Miklos, S. (2011). Network effects and personal influences: The diffusion of an online social network. *JMR, Journal of Marketing Research*, *48*(3), 425–443. doi:10.1509/jmkr.48.3.425

Liu, Y. Y. (2018). The core business relationship built on trust and reliance. *International Journal of Organizational Innovation*, *11*, 1–9.

Naik, P. A., Raman, K., & Winer, R. (2005). Planning marketing-mix strategies in the presence of interactions. *Marketing Science*, *24*(1), 25–34. doi:10.1287/mksc.1040.0083

Okazaki, S., & Barwise, P. (2011). Has the time finally come for the medium of the future. *Journal of Advertising Research*, *51*(1), 59–71. doi:10.2501/JAR-51-1-057-071

Raman, K., & Naik, P. A. (2004). Long-term profit impact of integrated marketing communications program. *Review of Marketing Science*, *2*(1), 1–23. doi:10.2202/1546-5616.1014

Rasmussen, K. B., & Thimm, H. (2009). Fact-based understanding of business survey non-response. *Electronic Journal of Business Research Methods*, *7*, 83–92.

Reddy, M. (2007). Small business in small economies: Constraints and opportunities for growth. *Social and Economic Studies*, *1*, 304–321.

Rufer, R. (2014). Integrated marketing communication: Creating brand communities, a case study. In G. Atinc (Ed.), *Proceedings of the 74th Annual Meeting of the Academy of Management*. 10.5465/ambpp.2014.12819abstract

Schaefer, A. D., & Pettijohn, C. E. (2006). The relevance of authenticity in personal selling: Is genuineness an asset or liability? *Journal of Marketing Theory and Practice*, *1*(1), 25–35. doi:10.2753/MTP1069-6679140102

Toma, S. G., Grigore, A. M., & Marinescu, P. (2014). Economic development and entrepreneurship. *Procedia Economics and Finance*, *8*, 436–443. doi:10.1016/S2212-5671(14)00111-7

Tuominen, M., Rajala, A., & Moller, K. (2000). Intraorganizational relationships and operational performance. *Journal of Strategic Marketing*, *8*(2), 139–160. doi:10.1080/096525400346222

Van Stel, A. (2006). International Studies in Entrepreneurship Series: Vol. 13. *Empirical analysis of entrepreneurship and economic growth*. Springer. doi:10.1007/0-387-29419-8

Voorveld, H., Neijens, P. S., & Smit, E. G. (2011). Opening the black box: Understanding cross-media effects. *Journal of Marketing Communications*, *17*(2), 69–85. doi:10.1080/13527260903160460

Wamba, S. F., & Lemuria, C. (2014). Social media tools adoption and use by SMES: An empirical study. *Journal of Organizational and End User Computing*, *26*(2), 1–17. doi:10.4018/joeuc.2014040101

ADDITIONAL READING

Aaker, D. (2013). Find the shared interest: A route to community activation and brand building. *Journal of Brand Strategy*, *2*, 134–145.

Castronovo, C., & Huang, L. (2012). Social media in an alternative marketing communication model. *Journal of Marketing Development and Competitiveness*, *6*, 117–134.

Day, G. S. (2011). Closing the marketing capabilities gap. *Journal of Marketing*, *75*(4), 183–195. doi:10.1509/jmkg.75.4.183

Hur, W., Ahn, K., & Kim, M. (2011). Building brand loyalty through managing brand community commitment. *Management Decision*, *49*(7), 1194–1213. doi:10.1108/00251741111151217

Hutton, G., & Fosdick, M. (2011). The globalization of social media, consumer relationships with brands evolve in the digital space. *Journal of Advertising Research*, *51*(4), 564–570. doi:10.2501/JAR-51-4-564-570

Schultz, D. E. (2011). IMC measurement: The challenges of an interactive marketplace. *International Journal of Integrated Marketing Communications*, *3*, 7–24.

Yan, J. (2011). Social media in branding: Fulfilling a need. *Journal of Brand Management*, *18*(9), 688–696. doi:10.1057/bm.2011.19

KEY TERMS AND DEFINITIONS

ANCOVA: A statistical tool used to examine differences between three or more groups while using a continuous variable as a control variable between the groups.

ANOVA: A statistical tool used to examine differences between three or more groups.

Business-to-Business Marketing: Selling products or services to organizations that utilize these products or services for use in their products or services that they sell to their customers. As opposed to consumer marketing that sells products or services to customers that use these products or services for their own personal consumption.

Entrepreneurial Firms: Are typically characterized by small organizations that spur economic growth through innovation. These organizations are typically risk takers that identify new ways of doing business.

Micro Organizations: An organization that has less than 50 total employees.

SME: Small and medium enterprise; an organization classified as a small and medium enterprise is classified as an organization with less than either 500 or 250 employees.

Social Media: Digital networking services that provide avenues for connecting with individuals with shared interests.

This research was previously published in the Encyclopedia of Organizational Knowledge, Administration, and Technology; pages 2140-2152, copyright year 2021 by Business Science Reference (an imprint of IGI Global).

Chapter 33
Communicating and Building Destination Brands With New Media

Anita Goyal

ⓘ https://orcid.org/0000-0002-7655-8428

Indian Institute of Management, Lucknow, India

ABSTRACT

The chapter aims to discuss building destination brands with the use of brand placements, like in movies and in songs, brand communities, and storytelling through new media options. The objective is to share how these three tools using new media can help build a destination's brand awareness, brand recognition, brand associations, and brand personality. The chapter presents the meaning of new media and old media and then details the meaning and applications of brand placements, brand community, and storytelling. There is a discussion to understand how these three tools help build a destination brand by sharing information with consumers. The use of three techniques will help gain consumers' attention and may develop their attitudes in favour of destination brands to visit the destination.

INTRODUCTION

Destination branding is gaining momentum but still is in the early stages of growth (Kumar & Kaushik, 2017). Destination branding may include marketing and promotion of a country, city, religious places, or any location which may be useful and attractive to tourists for worth spending resources. Many destinations are still not popular, not well-known, and visited by a few explorers. However, these destinations may be beneficial to be explored by tourists and, in turn, be fruitful and helpful for the growth of the place (destination). Building a destination brand needs a well-designed communication strategy, such as nation branding by Malaysia and India (Kumar & Kaushik, 2017), capital branding by Australia and New Zealand (Peirce & Ritchie, 2007).

Tourism marketers can consider different media types to communicate about destination information and build a destination brand. Various media are primarily classified as traditional media and new media. Traditional media includes television, radio, newspapers, and magazines, also referred to as old media. New media relates to web-related communications and includes blogs, online social networks,

DOI: 10.4018/978-1-6684-6287-4.ch033

Wikis, social media forms (like YouTube), and virtual worlds (Friedman & Friedman, 2011). Marketers usually use both media in combination though they may consider only one form of media as per the requirement of communication objectives to target audiences. Friedman and Friedman have shared new media characteristics as 5C's, viz.; communication, collaboration, community, creativity, and convergence. New media characteristics differentiating from old media are digital, interactive, hypertextual, networked, virtual, and simulated (Thompson, 2018).

Available information to tourists helps them in decision making for holiday locations. In other words, media choice by marketers may help tourists to evaluate different stages of the decision-making process, viz, problem identification, information search, evaluation of alternatives, and purchase (Hudson & Thal, 2013). Besides helping to provide information for the first four stages, new media options also help share the post-purchase experience like writing in travel blogs, which may become useful to other travellers in destination decision-making.

Tourism-related organisations like e-travel agents, hotels, airlines, and tourism organisations like Disney communicate through new media. However, it is considered that all these are unable to utilise these media platforms. According to Divol et al. (2012), less than 1% of an average marketing budget is likely to be allocated for social media by such tourism organisations. This limited use of new media indicates a very high opportunity to work with new media platforms to build destination brands. New media provides several diverse possibilities besides being creative to reach the target tourists.

Therefore, the chapter aims to discuss building destination brands with the use of brand placements like in movies (Park & Berger, 2010) and in songs (Srivastava, 2020), brand communities (Muniz & O'Guinn, 2001), and storytelling (Ben Youssef et al., 2019) through new media options. Brand placements are ones where brand advertising is combined within a movie or song or drama. It can be assessed as indirect advertising and can work due to likeness for actors in a movie/ drama or a singer singing the song. A brand community is a group of consumers who are admirers of a brand or a specialised group of consumers and are non-geographically bound. Marketers usually bring consumers together on a social platform to get informed, interact, and share about the brand. The storytelling form of communication is a known mode for destination marketing, which can be applied explicitly to destination brand building.

Thus, the objective is to share how the three tools can help build destination brand awareness, brand recognition, brand associations, and brand personality. Brand awareness and recognition help in considering a destination for a possible holiday, and brand associations and brand personality may help in making a final choice for the destination to be visited. Thus, awareness, associations, and personality knowledge about a destination may help a traveller to evaluate a destination for making a decision whether to visit the destination or not. This chapter, thus, explores the current literature to build an introductory theme and strong knowledge foundation around the stated objective. The focus is on secondary data with relevant real applications of destination brand placements, brand community, and storytelling in new media to build destination brands. Real-life applications as case examples are cited in the chapter though the chapter does not focus on an in-depth case study.

With the above brief background, the proposed chapter will first build on the knowledge of destination branding and old (traditional) and new media followed by meaning, characteristics, applications, advantages and disadvantages of the three techniques of marketing communication, viz.; brand placements, brand community, and storytelling. The chapter will detail the application of brand placements, brand community, and storytelling in destination branding through new media. The use of three techniques will help gain consumers' attention and may build their attitudes in favour of destination brands.

BACKGROUND

The section on background shares meaning and existing literature for understanding destination marketing and branding, traditional and new media, brand placement, brand community, storytelling, brand awareness, brand associations, and brand personality.

Destination Marketing and Branding

A destination as a tourism site may attract travellers from various perspectives. Consumers may visit a place to have medical treatment (medical tourism) with the dual aspect of therapy as well as tourism (Hyder et al., 2019). Wellness tourism is also captured along health tourism but more with relaxing and rejuvenating health perspective (like related to spa, yoga, meditation). It is associated with body and mind wellness rather than an official medical treatment, as primarily indicated in medical tourism (Luo et al., 2017; Smith & Kelly, 2006). Ecotourism is defined as responsible travel to natural areas that protect the natural environment and improve local people's wellbeing. Thus, ecotourism may contribute to sustainability (Singh et al., 2007). Lehew and Wesley (2007) have identified that tourist shoppers may not be an important segment for tourist market places. However, there are destinations that are now popular as shopping destinations. Religious tourism is also popular to have spiritual tourism experience (Haq & Jackson, 2009; Sharpley & Sundaram, 2005), where India is one of the famous destinations (Urban, 2019). The elderly segment, besides people from all age groups, undertake spiritual tourism in India either yearly or at some intervals of time, viz; Chardham yatra, Vaishno Devi Darshan. Like religious tourism, sports tourism is also an example of destination tourism where a sports event can attract sports enthusiast as a tourist (Ziakas, 2020), which can happen at local, national, and international levels. The literature provides overview, understanding, and insights about various possibilities of benefit-based or factor-based tourism, which can become the basis for destination marketing and branding. For example, heritage tourism related to heritage properties or heritage-based organisations (Garrod & Fyall, 2017), rural tourism (Yin, 2020), and marine tourism (Kinseng et al., 2018). The present chapter considers positive forms of destination tourism only and not counting the ones related to negative ones like drug-based tourism (Prayag et al., 2015).

Gross et al. (2008) had studied the relationship between tourism involvement and place attachment. It was identified that factors, namely centrality to lifestyle, attraction, self-expression, food, and wine, contribute to tourism involvement, whereas place identity and place dependence are related to place attachment. Destination branding can be developed using these factors. Therefore, destination brand building is a challenging task and needs consideration of several factors to achieve the brand image and brand equity. Promotion is one such activity that is essential to build destination brands. Promotions can be done through traditional and new media, which are discussed below.

Traditional and New Media

Traditional media is also referred to as old media and includes communication through various media: television, direct snail mail, door-to-door sales, newspapers, magazines, radio (Danaher & Rossiter, 2011). On the other side, new media includes communication through mobile marketing where SMS (short message service) marketing is primarily for text messages, and wireless application protocol (WAP) is for multi-media messages. Other new media forms include emails, blogs, youtube, and other web-related communications. The literature presents the benefits, uses, pros, and cons of these various media options. Attributes of perceived intrusiveness, reliability, trustworthiness, convenience, and entertainment value are considered to evaluate and compare the old and new media options (Danaher & Rossiter, 2011). New media is indicated to be high on the dimensions of vividness, interactivity, informational context, entertaining content, and valence of comments (de Vries et al., 2012). Mobile advertising provides an opportunity to support location-based applications, for example – to identify the nearest high-rated restaurant (Grewal et al., 2020). New media applications are found in political, social, and cultural traditions in the context of the Europe-Asia region (Morris et al., 2012). However, it is studied that culture can play a role in SMS marketing acceptance. Young Koreans attitude towards SMS advertisements was more positive than their American counterparts (Muk & Chung, 2015).

New media is considered to give an added advantage to adapt to individual users' requirements rather than having a generic message to the masses (Kennedy, 2008; Muk & Chung, 2015). According to a study by Danaher and Rossiter (2011), traditional channels are assessed high on trust and reliability both in consumer and business markets, and email marketing as emailers are accepted more among business customers. On the other hand, Morimoto and Chang (2006) have indicated the potential risk of email marketing besides its popularity. One needs to use email marketing with the care that it should not be perceived as irritating and disruptive to workflow and affecting workflow because many-a-times, especially for business customers, email use is more task-oriented. In the case of direct mail messages, neutral messages and gratitude based communication was found to be more persuasive than messages related to an obligation to make a purchase.

Ayeh et al. (2012) have presented that social media plays a vital role for travellers and has cited that one in three travel purchasers access social media information. Travellers use social media as a useful source of information for purchase decision making. Social media's role is identified in buying low-cost airline services (Bigne et al., 2016). Bizirgianni and Dionysopoulou (2013) have indicated the high usage of social media by young travellers for various travel-related services and information. The study on social networking sites (SNS) shows that SNS provides travellers with satisfaction through social support and positive emotions. Thus, both new and old media can be assessed to have their advantages and disadvantages according to consumer perceptions and requirements depending upon the use time and the reason for usage.

Brand Placement

Product placement is defined as the inclusion of a product, brand, or firm in entertainment programming for promotional purposes. It can be through both audio and visual means (Meyer et al., 2016, p.531). Entertainment and automobile brands have been found in Indian movies as in-film brand placements and were identified as the most common execution-style by showing a brand's usage in movies. The volume of in-film product/brand placements in Hollywood movies was found to be higher in comparison to the Indian movies (Kureshi & Sood, 2011). Though no case study was identified in particular, many movies have destination placements. For example, among very well-likes Indian movies, San Francisco is in the movie 'Love Aaj Kal' (translated in English as 'Love Today Tomorrow'), and London in movies 'Kabhi Khushi Kabhi Gum' (translated in English as 'Sometimes Joy Sometimes Sorrow') as well as in 'Queen'. Likewise, Washington and New York were evident in the movie 'Spiderman Coming Home'.

It is studied that three placement characteristics, viz, prominence, serial positions, and plot connection had significant effects on brand recognition. It is suggested that both cognitive and emotional processing of information are required for brand recognition in the brand placement situation. Thus both emotional experiences and brand placement characteristics play an important role in brand recognition of brands placed in movies (Song et al., 2019). Chan et al. (2016) have performed an experiment to indicate that the prior information to consumers about brand placement will result in a less positive brand attitude and lower purchase intention toward the placed brand. Similarly, a less well-known placed brand also shows a less positive brand attitude and lower purchase intention for the placed brand.

Van Vaerenbergh (2017) has examined an understanding of brand name placement in song lyrics. It is identified that consumer awareness towards paid brand name placements in song lyrics positively affects consumers' brand awareness with no negative effects on brand attitudes. Further, disclosure of information, whether a paid or unpaid brand name placement, increases brand attitudes. Thus, it is evident that sharing media-related information regarding brand name placements in song lyrics will be fruitful for building positive meaning for the brand. Liu et al. (2015) have identified that the effects of product placement presentation on social media are similar to the impact of product placement in other media. It is required to maintain a synergy between the media chosen, context, and the brand placed. Further, brand placement in social media gives an advantage of longer browsing time with a possible in-depth understanding of the brand.

Destination placements in movies are identified to be successful for building tourism. United Kingdom (UK) is a pertinent example of the same. The appearance of Alnwick Castle in the area of North East England, Northumberland in the Harry Potter movie resulted in a 120% increase in visitor numbers to the Castle. It is reported that Alnwick Castle became popular world-wide due to placement in Harry Porter movie as the Hogwarts School of Witchcraft and Wizardry. A number of Bollywood movies have London as destination placement, which resulted in building London as a popular tourism destination. UK Film Council particularly worked out to target the Bollywood market for filming movies in UK (Tanskanen, 2012). New Zealand is also a movie friendly location. Tourism to New Zealand was also enhanced by the placement of its landscapes in The Lord of the Rings movie. Tourists visited the landscapes shown in the movie and explored more landscapes in New Zealand (Josiam et al., 2014).

An empirical study in the Indian context, with 670 respondents, has shown the positive impact of destination placement in movies (Josiam et al., 2014). According to the Josiam et al. (2014) study results, Indians were interested in visiting such destinations after seeing the movies with destination placements. 45.7% of the respondents wanted to visit the UK, 40.9% Switzerland, 38.2% Italy, 24.5% Spain, 16% France, and 9.7% Germany. Spanish Tourism board had observed a 32% increase in tourists from India after the Bollywood film 'Zindagi Na Milegi Dobara' (translation in English: Will not get this life again) in a Spanish backdrop.

Brand Community

Brand Community can be defined and explained as a specialised, non-geographically bound community, based on a structured set of social relationships among admirers of a brand. It is specialised because there is a branded good or service as its central focus. It is considered to be denoted by a shared consciousness, rituals and traditions, and a sense of moral responsibility. However, each of these qualities is situated within a commercial and mass-mediated ethos and has its particular expression. Brand communities are participants in the brand's more extensive social construction and play a vital role in their ultimate legacy (Muniz & O'Guinn, 2001). Community members' identification with the brand community is a central characteristic of the community (Chang et al., 2019). Through the empirical study, Chang et al.

delved deeper into how a brand community generates firm-level benefits to a company and provides a framework for understanding how a brand community offers member-level benefits for customers and explores the antecedents of community identification. It was identified that communication has a significant and positive effect on community identification. Rituals and symbols also have a significant and positive relationship with community identification and cultivate shared behaviours among members, such as specific dress codes or vernacular that reinforce community bonds (Swimberghe et al., 2018).

McAlexander, Schouten and Koenig (2002) have found that consumers and marketers jointly build communities. They explored the brand communities of Jeep and Harley Davidson through ethnographic research and discovered new ways of understanding communities. Social media outlets are effective ways of developing relationships with customers by creating brand fan pages (which are like brand communities) on social networking sites. Companies can place brand posts (with content like videos, messages, or any relevant information) on these brand fan pages. Customers can become members at these brand fan pages, become fans, and start liking/ sharing on these pages.

Facilitation of shared consumer experiences (McAlexander et al., 2002) that can be used for strengthening brand communities has been employed quite effectively in the case of the tourism sector. Chang et al. (2020) shared the example of Kauai's Hawaiian island as a brand community blog dedicated to a sole location where members promote insider information on hidden sites. The members gain veritable status only when their personal story is shared on the review.

There is very limited research in the area of destination brand communities. From one perspective, there seems to be a challenge to develop a destination brand community, especially if the scope of the destination is too narrow. In other words, for example, if the destination brand community is the Singapore community. The question arises that why a person will stick to be a member of the Singapore community? A person may travel once or twice or say thrice as a tourist but will not visit Singapore every time for tourism. The person will also like to explore other destinations to enrich her/his experience and want to see different destinations. Therefore, one needs to consider developing a broad community, say country based community. However, there are possible benefits of developing communities for both firms and travellers, besides limitations. A significant advantage will be that it will help to reduce perceived risks to visit a destination or a country [refer to Appendix on short notes about perceived risk].

There are nearly nil examples identified to see the involvement of visitors as a part of the brand community. However, there are a few examples where the destination members worked together as a community to build the destination. One of the classic examples is of the place called Juzcar, which is now popular as Smurf Village. Juzcar is located 115 kilometres from Malaga (Southern Spain) and 25 km from Ronda. It is a small village with 230 inhabitants in Serrania de Ronda. Juzcar is known as Smurf Village since 2011 when Sony Pictures painted the entire village blue for the premiere of the movie "The Smurfs 3D". After the premiere, the Juzcar people continued with the theme, blue painted village. Today the town attracts more than 80000 tourists a year around the world. They organise a number of Smurf themed events like competition, trade fairs. There are also Smurf theme based weddings. In this situation, the involvement of a place to promote the movie helped create awareness about the place, which in turn was well developed by inhabitants of the Juzcar village as Smurf community for attracting the tourists (Real, 2016).

Storytelling

One way to define the story is that storytelling is pervasive throughout life. Much information is stored, indexed, and retrieved in the form of stories. However, people may sleep while listening to lectures, but stories result in action. "People relate to each other in terms of stories – and products and brands often play both central and peripheral roles in their stories" (Woodside et al., 2008, p. 97). Thus storytelling is more involving, and one can visualise the happenings well narrated like children get involved while listening to a story and can visualise in their minds. Hsiao et al. (2013) have studied the role of storytelling on travel blogs in travellers' adoption of travel products. Blogs have been identified as an important medium to recommend travel products and influential for making travel plans. Moscardo (2020) has highlighted the role of stories in the tourism industry. Moscardo has identified three forces supporting the effect of a story in tourism. The first force is building on the experiential approach to tourism; the second is about the rise of mobile social media, user-generated content, and gamification; and the third one is Asian Wave in tourism. Stories are identified around tourists' experiences, destination promotion, and destination planning.

Laurell and Söderman (2018) have studied the role of storytelling in social media in the context of professional sports organisations. Further, literature presents a concept of 'Transmedia storytelling', which is a way to communicate multiple stories about a brand/activity in different media channels by various sources. These all stories though standalone, are integrated. Each story adds some new information and remains unique and tied together with other stories, such as Star Wars stories in films, cartoons, graphic novels, and video games. Coombs (2019) has studied the use of transmedia storytelling in the context of corporate social responsibility communication.

Storytelling is one of the emerging trends. It is also considered to be a useful tool to understand those feelings and emotions that people are not able to express explicitly. Psychologists have ways to assess the underlying perceptions through stories. Therefore, whether someone is interested in sharing a story with someone and listening to a story, marketers can gain a lot from story sharing. Stories may be used to assess destination personalities. Stories are engaging, so these will also attract consumers to read on social media.

Storytelling in destination building is in the infancy stage and thus has many studies indicating the possibilities of developing stories rather than real examples and case studies. Nonetheless, there is an exception of 'New Zealand Story' in 2003. This story was developed by Tourism New Zealand, New Zealand Trade & Enterprise, and Education New Zealand. The aim was to leverage the "New Zealand-ness" of exporting businesses through a story told in three chapters: Open Spaces, Open Hearts, and Open Minds to build the national brand. It highlighted caring for people and places with "kaitiaki", a Maori concept of custodianship, with an open and honest approach. The story played a significant role in building the world image of New Zealand (Pera, 2017).

Brand Awareness

A consumer's ability to recall and recognise a brand indicates brand awareness (Aaker, 1996). A brand is recalled when a consumer is able to identify a brand by looking at the product category, whereas a brand is recognised with a brand-related cue. Brand knowledge contributes to brand awareness. It is the stepping stone to build a brand. Marketing communications' primary objective is to let consumers know about the brand, and only then the brand image and purchase intention follow. Both traditional and new media can create brand awareness for a new brand or a less known brand.

Sms marketing is found to have a significant impact on brand awareness and the perceived quality of products (Smutkupt et al., 2012). Online Social Networks with interactive features are found effective in building brand awareness for various brands, including destinations. Brands in the hospitality industry and tourist destinations are considering using online social networks to build brand awareness. Barreda et al. (2015) has identified the positive role of social media as online social networks to build brand awareness and, in turn, generating positive word-of-mouth communication. Kim, Choe and Petrick (2018) have indicated celebrity writers' role in building brand awareness of festival destinations. Therefore, it can be assessed that new media forms help travellers to know about travel products and destination information. Destination placements in movies result in building awareness about tourist places among travellers.

Belize, a small country on the Caribbean coast of Central America, could not attract tourists. Belize is an example of building tourism through digital marketing. A video about Belize was placed on the homepage of their official tourism website. Belize channel got 612 registered users on YouTube, 16.3 million followers on Twitter, engaging more than 150,000 fans on Facebook conversations, 4500 followers on Pinterest Boards, and 4300 likes on Instagram. Belize also maintained accounts on Vine and Snapchat with 268 and 78 followers respectively in 2016. Viewer's profile was also seen on YouTube and Vimeo (Real, 2016). Thus, Belize is able to attract tourists through the use of new media.

Brand Associations

The existing knowledge base presents that brand associations have a significant role in brand building in the mind of consumers (Keller, 1993). Brand association indicates any brand knowledge about the brand in the customer's mind (Chen, 2001). A set of associations is considered the underlying value of a brand name, indicating a brand's meaning to people (Aaker, 1991). The brand associations can present both positive and negative information about the brand in the customer's mind (Emari et al., 2012). It is anything linked in memory to a brand. Thus, brand associations play a key role in developing brand equity (Christodoulides & de Chernatony, 2010).

Brand associations are broadly classified into three categories, namely, attributes, benefits, and attitudes (Keller 1993). Brand associations include usage situations, product categories, product attributes, and customer benefits (Broniarczyk & Alba, 1994). However, they do not have to be brand specific to provide the benefit (Henderson et al., 1998). Chen (2001), based on extant literature, has classified brand associations into product associations (functional attribute and non-functional attribute associations) and organisational associations (corporate ability and corporate social responsibility associations). Brand associations indicate how consumers associate with brands by keeping the brand meanings in their minds.

Vieceli and Shaw (2010) have indicated that brand and product category knowledge can be developed through advertising and other promotional methods, resulting in more brand associations, leading to building brand information. Therefore, brand associations are developed by consumers based on information gathered or received from various promotions by marketers. Consumers also learn about a brand through their own experiences while using a brand, which also results in building brand associations. It is imperative that consumers develop brand associations on their own, through the product's usage, match the associations communicated by marketers, and enhance brand meanings. The positive associations enhance brand value and brand image vis-à-vis negative associations.

New media promotions help potential tourists to develop associations with the destinations. For example, in the case of Belize, viewers on videos and other content on various new media channels were able to associate Belize with beaches, lush rainforest, ancient Mayan temples, white sandy islands, and other communicated attractions/ themes (Real, 2016). According to an empirical study, communication through destination placements in movies help tourists to associate with the highlighted places or activities or benefits in movies about the destinations like good shopping in UK and Italy; relaxation in France; nature and sceneries in UK, Spain, and Italy; and cultural sites in UK and Italy (Josiam et al., 2014).

Brand Personality

Here in this chapter, brand personality is considered in terms of the personality of a destination. Brand personality plays a significant role in the success of a brand. Brand personality is defined by Aaker (1997) as "a set of human characteristics associated with a brand". There are generally three sources of brand personality: the first one is the consumers' brand associations; the second is brand image developed by a company, and the third is about the product attributes itself. Thus, in a tourist site, the features, attractions, and unique aspects of destinations will provide a personality to the destination. The perceived personality of Las Vegas was identified along the dimensions of vibrancy, sophistication, competence, contemporary, and sincerity, which influences visitors to revisit the place (Usakli & Baloglu, 2011).

Kim and Lee (2015) have studied how a city's personality, along with a city image, can affect the revisit intention of visitors. It is identified that city personality can have a positive or negative effect depending on the constructs. It is worthy of communicating the right slogan while promoting a city as a destination to potential visitors. Similarly, Salehzadeh et al. (2016) have examined the positive influence of brand personality on the revisit intention to a tourist city in Iran. Pereira et al. (2015) have studied that golf players associate personality dimensions with golf destinations like Algrave. The personality dimensions related to Algrave were reliability, hospitality, uniqueness, and attractiveness, which were around enjoyment, distinctiveness, and friendliness. Thus golf destinations can be represented with the personality dimensions of the place. One may need to assess which personality dimensions are appropriate for a destination.

One example is New Zealand, associated with spirited, adventure, and daring personality (UKEssays, 2018). Tourists visit New Zealand for adventurous activities as they associate the place with their adventure-oriented personality. This personality of New Zealand is developed through movie placement and storytelling in digital new media. According to an empirical study, Australia is identified with the personality of sincerity more than any other personality trait (Ye, 2012). Similarly, Switzerland is identified with the romantic personality among Indians, which is an image developed through Bollywood movies (Josiam et al., 2014).

DISCUSSION

New media is primarily distinguished, being interactive and internet-based media. Nonetheless, the degree of an interactive feature differs among different forms of new media. Email advertising is comparatively less interactive than social networking sites. However, all media have a role in developing brand awareness. As mentioned, brand awareness is a primary requirement for any brand to be successful. Therefore, any destination as a brand needs consumer awareness. The meaning of brand awareness is not considered only in terms of brand recall or brand recognition but having good knowledge about the brand. The in-depth awareness and understanding are possible by being connected with the brand, which can be achieved through brand placements involving platforms like movies, storytelling, and community membership. Brand placements may create brand awareness, while storytelling and community participation will further add to the knowledge and build a destination image.

Like Paris, Switzerland, Italy, Singapore, and others, the most popular tourist destinations would have been started from zero awareness to low awareness to high awareness. Today, these destinations will be having the top of mind recall. Thus, if awareness needs to be created for a new destination with near nil visitors, then new media will be useful because today majority of the world population has access and high usage rate of internet and social networking sites. Nevertheless, only sending a message as SMS or email may not bring desired brand awareness with a high recall rate. There is a need to keep building enriching awareness with communications on youtube, SMS, email, and then moving to storytelling and community development.

With the achievement of brand awareness as the primary step to attract visitors to know about a destination, brand building's next level of achievement is enhancing brand associations. Brand associations and brand awareness are highly connected. There is simultaneous growth of brand associations in the mind of consumers with an increase in brand awareness. As travellers gain more information about any destination by understanding destination features, touristic sites, and eating joints, destination association networks increase in travellers' minds. Thus, high awareness will lead to high associations, and increased positive associations will result in the destination's liking, which may attract travellers to visit the destination. For example, the case of Belize, a small country on the Caribbean coast of Central America. Belize builds awareness and associations for the destination through new media.

Depending upon the existing literature, it will be worthwhile to communicate brand information with rich data about destination features, places to visit, and the like, which will help in developing brand associations about the destination brand. A rich set of associations will increase knowledge about the brand and, in turn, will result in connection with the brand. The required rich information about a destination that will bring involvement can be shared through storytelling. Storytelling is connected to imagination and, therefore, involves consumers with the brand. Tourists also share stories on blogs or social networking sites based on their travel experiences. Brand communities are the higher involvement medium where consumers participate and share their experiences in an interactive mode – posting a message and receiving feedback and again replying. The successful case of Juzcar as Smurf Village is a live example of developing a local destination community to attract and welcome visitors. The same has the potential to involve visitors as community members on new media. Marketers' inputs and involvement are needed to develop internet platforms where travellers can share their stories and develop communities say on Facebook or other social networking sites where travellers can be invited to become members. More associations will help travellers to contribute to discussion among brand community members. Additionally, destination placement in movies and songs will create an association of that movie and song with the destination. Whenever a person comes across that particular movie or song, it is likely to recall that destination. Suppose, during a conversation, a particular song is recalled with a destination name. It is possible that discussion may start around the destination actually triggered through the song.

Destination brand personality is another way to build destination brands. Destination personality will attract those travellers whose personality is much in line with the destination brand personality. A traveller will be more interested in visiting places that match his/her traits. For example, an adventurous personality person will be more investigating about New Zealand for adventurous activities. A shopping oriented person is likely to be more inclined to Dubai. Golf playing sportspersons will visit destinations known to have Golf playing facilities. It is foremost the one characteristic like shopping, which attracts travellers, but destination personality indicates that all requirements will be fulfilled by the destination like easy travel, convenient stay, excitement, variety of shops, variety of offers, and the like. Today, there are many destinations that may be known for a particular benefit and can be associated with human personalities but are not developed with a personality perspective. Sharing stories about destination experiences on social networking sites, within brand communities, on blogs, or presenting on youtube may reveal the destination personality which travellers can co-relate. Marketers need to work out the personality characteristics of places and show that personality dimension in communications.

Looking from the view of new media platforms: SMS advertising, a more one-way communication tool, will create brand awareness and build brand associations. Email advertising may help to build brand associations along with brand awareness. Brand placements in movies and songs or any performance will also help in brand awareness, leading to brand associations and knowledge. Brand placements can contribute to brand association depending upon the richness of information shown or shared while placing a brand in a movie, song, or drama. For example, a movie in the London setting will show various tourist sites in the background, which are likely to be registered in consumers' minds. Destination placement may also project destination personality if the same destination in different placements shows the place to be visited for the same characteristics, say for golf playing, health cure, yoga, and the like.

It can be indicated that brand placement in movies, songs, YouTube content, or any entertainment content on social media, developing destination brand communities on new interactive media, and sharing destination stories on new media platforms can play a significant role in building destination brand image. This may help to attract tourists and travellers to visit the destinations. In other words, a destination will be known with meaning and have its value proposition.

FUTURE RESEARCH DIRECTIONS

The extant literature shares the various platforms to build destination brands. However, the research is destination branding is still developing and presents ample scope to explore and gain knowledge about building and maintaining successful destination brands. Application of destination storytelling and brand community is still in the infancy stage in contrast to destination placements in movies. There is minimal availability of case studies with quantitative data considering new media applications for destination branding. Extant literature is also limited with studies sharing quantitative analysis with case studies.

There is a need to investigate what motivates travellers to write their travel stories on blogs or other social media. Even travellers like to write on which social media can be explored and accordingly can be motivated to do the needful. Further, there is yet emerging research studies in destination brand communities. Brand communities provide a wide scope to interact with travellers. It is required to study consumer behaviour towards their joining, staying ad interacting in the community. One needs to know how the interest of consumers (travellers) can be maintained within a community or are there some self-motivating factors that let consumers be a member of communities.

Again, there is a possibility to delve deeper into understanding the role of destination placements in movies or songs, or other social media. Future studies can investigate whether destination brand placements contribute to building destination personality and if yes, then how? Similarly, there is an opportunity to identify destination brand personalities because such personalities are unknown for even many known travel destinations. Researchers can identify ways to analyse destination personalities.

CONCLUSION

Destination branding is an upcoming area of study for scholars and a concern for travel marketers or organisations. It has its challenges. The destination brand is not like a physical good, which can be well investigated physically before purchase. Thus, it involves many questions before any traveller will decide to visit a destination. Often, a traveller sees a destination only once because there are many other destinations to explore in the future. In other words, a tourist may be visiting a destination once in a lifetime. Therefore, there is always a challenge to invite a flow of travellers to a destination and even attract the same visitors again and again.

This chapter presents new media as a promising medium to communicate and build destination brands through brand placements, brand communities, and storytelling. This chapter shares the extant literature with live examples and case studies as appropriate in the context of having a conceptual foundation to develop destination brands through indicated tools in new media. However, there are limited empirical studies with live examples or case studies. The existing literature is also exploring the possibilities of new media and indicated tools for destination branding. Thus, there is a need to conduct further empirical and exploratory studies to unearth the applications. There is also a need to look out for case studies from real life to understand the factors for successfully implementing the tools.

Communicating destination brands via these three forms on new media can help in building a destination brand by developing destination brand awareness, brand associations, and brand personality for long success. Brand placements in movies or songs can help in building awareness and knowledge about a destination. Destination brand communities can help make a sound purchase decision for a destination with nil or less perceived risks. Similarly, storytelling can provide information about destination features, restaurants, and tourist sites. A story can also share visitors' experiences to a destination, which will help identify a destination for a future visit. Thus, brand communities and story sharing will provide an interactive platform for actual visitors to share their experiences. In a nutshell, destination brand placements, destination brand communities, and destination personalities developed on new media will help future travellers to make sound informed decisions to visit a destination with meaning.

REFERENCES

Aaker, D. A. (1991). *Managing brand equity*. The Free Press.

Aaker, D. A. (1996). Measuring brand equity across products and markets. *California Management Review, 38*(3), 102–120. doi:10.2307/41165845

Aaker, D. A. (1997). Dimension of brand personality. *JMR, Journal of Marketing Research, 34*(3), 347–356. doi:10.1177/002224379703400304

Ayeh, J., Leung, D., Au, N., & Law, R. (2012). Perceptions and strategies of hospitality and tourism practitioners on social media: an exploratory study. In *Information and Communication Technologies in Tourism* (pp. 1–12). Springer.

Barreda, A., Bilgihan, A., Nusair, K., & Okumus, F. (2015). Generating brand awareness in Online Social Networks. *Computers in Human Behavior*, *50*, 600–609. doi:10.1016/j.chb.2015.03.023

Ben Youssef, K., Leicht, T., & Marongiu, L. (2019). Storytelling in the context of destination marketing: An analysis of conceptualisations and impact measurement. *Journal of Strategic Marketing*, *27*(8), 696–713. doi:10.1080/0965254X.2018.1464498

Bigne, E., Andreu, L., Hernandez, B., & Ruiz, C. (2016). The impact of social media and offline influences on consumer behaviour. An analysis of the low-cost airline industry. *Current Issues in Tourism*, *21*(9), 1014–1032. doi:10.1080/13683500.2015.1126236

Bizirgianni, I., & Dionysopoulou, P. (2013). The influence of tourist trends of youth tourism through social media (sm) & information and communication technologies (ICTs). *Procedia: Social and Behavioral Sciences*, *73*, 652–660. doi:10.1016/j.sbspro.2013.02.102

Broniarczyk, S. M., & Alba, J. W. (1994). The importance of the brand in brand extension. *JMR, Journal of Marketing Research*, *31*(May), 214–228. doi:10.1177/002224379403100206

Chan, F. F. Y., Petrovici, D., & Lowe, B. (2016). Antecedents of product placement effectiveness across cultures. *International Marketing Review*, *33*(1), 5–24. doi:10.1108/IMR-07-2014-0249

Chang, C., Ko, C., Huang, H., & Wang, S. (2019). Brand community identification matters: A dual value-creation routes framework. *Journal of Product and Brand Management*, *29*(3), 289–306. doi:10.1108/JPBM-02-2018-1747

Chen, A. C.-H. (2001). Using free association to examine the relationship between the characteristics of brand associations and brand equity. *Journal of Product and Brand Management*, *10*(7), 439–451. doi:10.1108/10610420110410559

Christodoulides, G., & de Chernatony, L. (2010). Consumer-based brand equity conceptualisation and measurement: A literature review. *International Journal of Market Research*, *52*(1), 43–66. doi:10.2501/S1470785310201053

Coombs, T. (2019). Transmedia storytelling: A potentially vital resource for CSR communication. *Corporate Communications*, *24*(2), 351–367. doi:10.1108/CCIJ-11-2017-0114

Danaher, P., & Rossiter, J. (2011). Comparing perceptions of marketing communication channels. *European Journal of Marketing*, *45*(1/2), 6–42. doi:10.1108/03090561111095586

de Vries, L., Gensler, S., & Leeflang, P. (2012). Popularity of brand posts on brand fan pages: An investigation of the effects of social media marketing. *Journal of Interactive Marketing*, *26*(2), 83–91. doi:10.1016/j.intmar.2012.01.003

Divol, R., Edelman, D., & Sarrazin, H. (2012). Demystifying social media. *The McKinsey Quarterly*, *66*(2). https://search.proquest.com/docview/1491805837?accountid=44542

Emari, H., Jafari, A., & Mogaddam, M. (2012). The mediatory impact of brand loyalty and brand image on brand equity. *African Journal of Business Management*, *17*(6), 5692–5701.

Friedman, L. W., & Friedman, H. H. (2011). The New Media Technologies: Overview and Research Framework. SSRN *Electronic Journal, April*. doi:10.2139/ssrn.1116771

Garrod, B., & Fyall, A. (2017). Managing heritage tourism. *Managing Heritage and Cultural Tourism Resources: Critical Essays. Volume One*, *27*(3), 151–178. doi:10.4324/9781315249933-18

Grewal, D., Bart, Y., Spann, M., & Zubcsek, P. (2016). Mobile Advertising: A Framework and Research Agenda. *Journal of Interactive Marketing*, *34*, 3–14. doi:10.1016/j.intmar.2016.03.003

Gross, M. J., Brien, C., & Brown, G. (2008). Examining the dimensions of a lifestyle tourism destination. *International Journal of Culture, Tourism and Hospitality Research*, *2*(1), 44–66. doi:10.1108/17506180810856130

Haq, F., & Jackson, J. (2009). Spiritual journey to Hajj: Australian and Pakistani experience and expectations. *Journal of Management, Spirituality & Religion*, *6*(2), 141–156. doi:10.1080/14766080902815155

Henderson, G. R., Iacobucci, D., & Calder, B. J. (1998). Brand diagnostics: Mapping branding effects using consumer associative networks. *European Journal of Operational Research*, *111*(2), 306–327. doi:10.1016/S0377-2217(98)00151-9

Hsiao, K. L., Lu, H. P., & Lan, W. C. (2013). The influence of the components of storytelling blogs on readers' travel intentions. *Internet Research*, *23*(2), 160–182. doi:10.1108/10662241311313303

Hudson, S., & Thal, K. (2013). The Impact of Social Media on the Consumer Decision Process: Implications for Tourism Marketing. *Journal of Travel & Tourism Marketing*, *30*(1-2), 156–160. doi:10.1080/10548408.2013.751276

Hyder, A., Rydback, M., Borg, E., & Osarenkhoe, A. (2019). Medical tourism in emerging markets: The role of trust, networks, and word-of-mouth. *Health Marketing Quarterly*, *36*(3), 203–219. doi:10.1080/07359683.2019.1618008 PMID:31210584

Josiam, B. M., Spears, D., Dutta, K., Pookulangara, S. A., & Kinley, T. L. (2014). "Namastey London": Bollywood movies and their impact on how Indians perceive European destinations. *Hospitality Review*, *31*(4), 2. https://digitalcommons.fiu.edu/hospitalityreview/vol31/iss4/2

Keller, K. L. (1993). Conceptualising, measuring, and managing customer-based brand equity. *Journal of Marketing*, *57*(1), 1–22. doi:10.1177/002224299305700101

Kennedy, H. (2008). New media's potential for personalisation. *Information Communication and Society*, *11*(3), 307–325. doi:10.1080/13691180802025293

Kim, H. B., & Lee, S. (2015). Impacts of city personality and image on revisit intention. *International Journal of Tourism Cities*, *1*(1), 50–69. doi:10.1108/IJTC-08-2014-0004

Kim, S., Choe, J., & Petrick, J. (2018). The effect of celebrity on brand awareness, perceived quality, brand image, brand loyalty, and destination attachment to a literary festival. *Journal of Destination Marketing & Management*, *9*, 320–329. doi:10.1016/j.jdmm.2018.03.006

Kinseng, R. A., Nasdian, F. T., Fatchiya, A., Mahmud, A., & Stanford, R. J. (2018). Marine-tourism development on a small island in Indonesia: Blessing or curse? *Asia Pacific Journal of Tourism Research*, *23*(11), 1062–1072. doi:10.1080/10941665.2018.1515781

Kumar, V., & Kaushik, A. K. (2017). Achieving destination advocacy and destination loyalty through destination brand identification. *Journal of Travel & Tourism Marketing*, *34*(9), 1247–1260. doi:10.10 80/10548408.2017.1331871

Kureshi, S., & Sood, V. (2011). In-film placement trends: A comparative study of Bollywood and Hollywood. *Journal of Indian Business Research*, *3*(4), 244–262. doi:10.1108/17554191111180591

Laurell, C., & Söderman, S. (2018). Sports, storytelling and social media: A review and conceptualisation. *International Journal of Sports Marketing & Sponsorship*, *19*(3), 338–349. doi:10.1108/IJSMS-11-2016-0084

Lehew, M. L. A., & Wesley, S. C. (2007). Tourist shoppers' satisfaction with regional shopping mall experiences. *International Journal of Culture, Tourism and Hospitality Research*, *1*(1), 82–96. doi:10.1108/17506180710729628

Liu, S. H., Chou, C. H., & Liao, H. L. (2015). An exploratory study of product placement in social media. *Internet Research*, *25*(2), 300–316. doi:10.1108/IntR-12-2013-0267

Luo, Y., Lanlung (Luke), C., Kim, E., Tang, L., & Song, S. (2017). Towards quality of life: The effects of the wellness tourism experience. *Journal of Travel & Tourism Marketing*, *35*(4), 410–424. doi:10.1 080/10548408.2017.1358236

McAlexander, J. H., Schouten, J. W., & Koenig, H. F. (2002). Building Brand Community. *Journal of Marketing*, *66*(1), 38–54. doi:10.1509/jmkg.66.1.38.18451

Meyer, J., Song, R., & Ha, K. (2016). The effect of product placements on the evaluation of movies. *European Journal of Marketing*, *50*(3–4), 530–549. doi:10.1108/EJM-12-2014-0758

Morimoto, M., & Chang, S. (2006). Consumers' attitudes toward unsolicited commercial email and postal direct mail marketing methods. *Journal of Interactive Advertising*, *7*(1), 1–11. doi:10.1080/152 52019.2006.10722121

Morris, J., Rulyova, N., & Strukov, V. (2012). Introduction: New Media in New Europe-Asia. *Europe-Asia Studies*, *64*(8), 1349–1355. doi:10.1080/09668136.2012.712271

Moscardo, G. (2020). The story turn in tourism: forces and futures. *Journal of Tourism Futures*. doi:10.1108/JTF-11-2019-0131

Muk, A., & Chung, C. (2015). Applying the technology acceptance model in a two-country study of SMS advertising. *Journal of Business Research*, *68*(1), 1–6. doi:10.1016/j.jbusres.2014.06.001

Muniz, A. M. Jr, & O'Guinn, T. C. (2001). Brand community. *The Journal of Consumer Research*, *27*(4), 412–432. doi:10.1086/319618

Park, D. J., & Berger, B. K. (2010). Brand placement in movies: The effect of film genre on viewer recognition. *Journal of Promotion Management*, *16*(4), 428–444. doi:10.1080/10496491003591261

Peirce, S., & Ritchie, B. W. (2007). National Capital Branding. *Journal of Travel & Tourism Marketing*, *22*(3-4), 67–78. doi:10.1300/J073v22n03_06

Pera, J. (2017). *New Zealand, a story-marketing destination benchmark*. Retrieved from https://envisioningtourism.com/2017/09/18/new-zealand-a-story-marketing-destination-benchmark/

Pereira, R. L. G., Correia, A., & Schutz, R. L. A. (2015). Golf destinations' brand personality: The case of the algarve. *International Journal of Culture, Tourism and Hospitality Research*, *9*(2), 133–153. doi:10.1108/IJCTHR-05-2014-0037

Prayag, G., Mura, P., Hall, M., & Fontaine, J. (2015). Drug or spirituality seekers? Consuming ayahuasca. *Annals of Tourism Research*, *52*, 175–177. doi:10.1016/j.annals.2015.03.008

Real, J. L. R. (2016). *Destination branding. A compilation of success cases*. Retrieved from https://www.ibraveproject.eu/files/manual-final.pdfU

Salehzadeh, R., Khazaei Pool, J., & Soleimani, S. (2016). Brand personality, brand equity and revisit intention: An empirical study of a tourist destination in Iran. *Tourism Review*, *71*(3), 205–218. doi:10.1108/TR-02-2016-0005

Sharpley, R., & Sundaram, P. (2005). Tourism: A sacred journey? The case of ashram tourism, India. *International Journal of Tourism Research*, *7*(3), 161–171. doi:10.1002/jtr.522

Singh, T., Slotkin, M. H., & Vamosi, A. R. (2007). Attitude towards ecotourism and environmental advocacy: Profiling the dimensions of sustainability. *Journal of Vacation Marketing*, *13*(2), 119–134. doi:10.1177/1356766707074736

Smith, M., & Kelly, C. (2006). Wellness Tourism. *Tourism Recreation Research*, *31*(1), 1–4. doi:10.1080/02508281.2006.11081241

Smutkupt, P., Krairit, D., & Ba Khang, D. (2012). Mobile marketing and consumer perceptions of brand equity. *Asia Pacific Journal of Marketing and Logistics*, *24*(4), 539–560. doi:10.1108/13555851211259016

Song, S., Chan, F. F. Y., & Wu, Y. (2019). The interaction effect of placement characteristics and emotional experiences on consumers' brand recognition. *Asia Pacific Journal of Marketing and Logistics*, *32*(6), 1269–1285. doi:10.1108/APJML-04-2019-0236

Srivastava, R. (2020). Brand Placement in a Movie Song and its Impact on Brand Equity. *Journal of Promotion Management*, *26*(2), 233–252. doi:10.1080/10496491.2019.1699627

Swimberghe, K., Darrat, M., Beal, B., & Astakhova, M. (2018). Examining a psychological sense of brand community in elderly consumers. *Journal of Business Research*, *82*, 171–178. doi:10.1016/j.jbusres.2017.09.035

Tanskansen, T. (2012). *Film Tourism: Study on how films can be used to promote tourism* (Bachelor's thesis). Laurea University of Applied Sciences, Laurea Kerava. Retrieved from https://core.ac.uk/download/pdf/38073247.pdf

Thompson, K. (2018). *Main characteristics of New Media – ReviseSociology*. https://revisesociology.com/2018/12/13/main-characteristics-new-media/

UKEssays. (2018). *Destination image and brand personality of New Zealand marketing essay*. Retrieved from https://www.ukessays.com/essays/marketing/destination-image-and-brand-personality-of-new-zealand-marketing-essay.php?vref=1

Urban, H. B. (2019). 'The Cradle of Tantra': Modern transformations of a tantric centre in Northeast India from nationalist symbol to tourist destination. *South Asia: Journal of South Asia Studies*, *42*(2), 256–277. doi:10.1080/00856401.2019.1570609

Usakli, A., & Baloglu, S. (2011). Brand personality of tourist destinations: An application of self-congruity theory. *Tourism Management*, *32*(1), 114–127. doi:10.1016/j.tourman.2010.06.006

Van Vaerenbergh, Y. (2017). Consumer reactions to paid versus unpaid brand name placement in song lyrics. *Journal of Product and Brand Management*, *26*(2), 151–158. doi:10.1108/JPBM-05-2016-1167

Vieceli, J. M. (2011). The measurement of the number, uniqueness and valence of brand associations across three product categories. *Journal of Customer Behaviour*, *10*(3), 245–269. doi:10.1362/147539211X602504

Woodside, A., Sood, S., & Miller, K. (2008). When consumers and brands talk: Storytelling theory and research in psychology and marketing. *Psychology and Marketing*, *25*(2), 97–145. doi:10.1002/mar.20203

Ye, S. (2012). The impact of destination personality dimensions on destination brand awareness and attractiveness: Australia as a case study. *Tourism (Zagreb)*, *60*(4), 397–409.

Yin, L. (2020). Forecast without historical data: Objective tourist volume forecast model for newly developed rural tourism areas of China. *Asia Pacific Journal of Tourism Research*, *25*(5), 555–571. doi:10.1080/10941665.2020.1752755

Ziakas, V. (2020). Leveraging sport events for tourism development: the event portfolio perspective. *Journal of Global Sport Management*, 1-30. doi:10.1080/24704067.2020.1731700

ADDITIONAL READING

Brennan, I., & Babin, L. (2004). Brand Placement Recognition. *Journal of Promotion Management*, *10*(1-2), 185–202. doi:10.1300/J057v10n01_13

Dieguez, T., & Conceição, O. (2020). Innovative Destination Branding: Porto. In Á. Rocha, A. Abreu, J. de Carvalho, D. Liberato, E. González, & P. Liberato (Eds.), *Advances in Tourism, Technology and Smart Systems. Smart Innovation, Systems and Technologies* (Vol. 171). Springer., doi:10.1007/978-981-15-2024-2_12

Kao, D. (2019). The impact of envy on brand preference: Brand storytelling and psychological distance as moderators. *Journal of Product and Brand Management*, *28*(4), 515–528. doi:10.1108/JPBM-08-2018-2004

Lund, N., & Kimbu, A. (2020). Applying the Hollywood scriptwriting formula to destination branding. *Current Issues in Tourism*, 1–21. doi:10.1080/13683500.2020.1739005

Peco-Torres, F., Polo-Peña, A., & Frías-Jamilena, D. (2020). Brand personality in cultural tourism through social media. *Tourism Review,* (ahead-of-print). doi:10.1108/TR-02-2019-0050

Schau, H., Muñiz, A. Jr, & Arnould, E. (2009). How Brand Community Practices Create Value. *Journal of Marketing, 73*(5), 30–51. doi:10.1509/jmkg.73.5.30

Tong, X., Su, J., & Xu, Y. (2017). Brand personality and its impact on brand trust and brand commitment: An empirical study of luxury fashion brands. *International Journal of Fashion Design. Technology and Education, 11*(2), 196–209. doi:10.1080/17543266.2017.1378732

Wheeler, F., Frost, W., & Weiler, B. (2011). Destination brand identity, values, and community: A case study from rural Victoria, Australia. *Journal of Travel & Tourism Marketing, 28*(1), 13–26. doi:10.108 0/10548408.2011.535441

KEY TERMS AND DEFINITIONS

Brand Associations: Brand association indicates any brand knowledge about the brand in the customer's mind. A brand association can be created via the association with attitudes, attributes, and benefits.

Brand Awareness: Brand awareness refers to whether consumers can recall or recognise a brand, or simply whether consumers know about a brand. Two important aspects of brand awareness are brand recognition and recall.

Brand Community: A brand community is a specialised, non-geographically bound community, based on a structured set of social relationships among admirers of a brand. It is marked by a shared consciousness, rituals and traditions, and a sense of moral responsibility.

Brand Personality: It is defined as a set of human characteristics associated with a brand. Research studies indicate a relationship between brand personality and human personality to provide meaning to brands according to human traits.

Brand Placement: Brand placement refers to the paid inclusion of branded products or brand identifiers, through audio and/or visual means, within mass media programming.

New Media: The new media is described in terms of changes in production of communicated information due to convergence of technology and media, storage (digitisation and indexing), presentation (in a video display of sorts), and distribution over telecommunication networks.

Storytelling: It is about telling about a brand in a story. The central principle of creating good brand stories is to construct indices, such as locations, decisions, actions, attitudes, difficulties, decisions or conclusions. Indices in brand stories can arouse automatic awareness, comprehension and empathy among consumers.

This research was previously published in Impact of New Media in Tourism; pages 1-20, copyright year 2021 by Business Science Reference (an imprint of IGI Global).

APPENDIX

Perceived Risk

Related to consumer behaviour, perceived risk is the risk that is perceived by a consumer while evaluating or making a purchase decision irrespective of the fact whether that risk really exists or not. There is a diferent kind of perceived risks. These are a physical risk, financial risk, social risk, time risk, and psychological risk.

Physical risk is the risk where a consumer may fear any harm to herself in physical form. For example: there is a physical risk of consuming unhealthy food because one may fell sick. Therefore, a consumer may be very careful to visit a restaurant at a destination if there is any information about unsafe food consumption. Even if the food is safe but the prevailing news will result in fear for non-consumption of food in restaurants. In an extreme situation, a traveler may postpone the visit to that particular destination.

Financial risk is the risk where a consumer may fear not getting the worth of money spent or may fear spending extra. For example: if a consumer avails a tourist pack designed by a travel agent to visit two destinations and makes a one-time payment without a detailed expense list. However, during the visit, the consumer identifies that the food expenses are not included in the package, and the information was not shared before buying the package. Such information or experience will result in financial risk of hidden costs. Sometimes, the risk is perceived because a consumer is purchasing a plan for the first time though there are no hidden costs. If a traveler is a community member, then he/she can clarify the issue within the community and negate the risk perception.

Social risk is when a consumer may fear what others will say if I buy a particular brand or product. For example: if a consumer visits a restaurant that is not considered of status within the consumer's social circle, then the consumer will fear the risk of visiting that restaurant because he/she would not like to be seen there by his/her friends.

Time risk is the risk associated with not making a decision within a particular time period. For example: there is a discount offer to buy airline tickets with a deadline. It is not known that prices will be high after the discount period or another discount scheme will come in the future. Therefore, a consumer may be under pressure to buy tickets because there is a risk of losing the opportunity of availing a discount.

Psychological risk is one when a consumer fears that he/she is making the right decision or not. Normally, when there is limited information available to make a decision, or there are many choices, one can have psychological risk because one lacks clear criteria to make a purchase decision.

Chapter 34
The Ubiquitous Role of Mobile Phones in Value Co-Creation Through Social Media Marketing

Syed Far Abid Hossain

ⓘD https://orcid.org/0000-0003-0729-1456

College of Business Administration, International University of Business Agriculture and Technology, Bangladesh

Xu Shan

Xi'an Jiaotong University, China

Abdul Qadeer

Xi'an Jiaotong University, China

ABSTRACT

The purpose of this paper is to ascertain the contemporary role of mobile phones in value co-creation through social media marketing. How mobile phones, in particular, smartphones with the help of numerous social media generate value co-creation, is the key objective of this study. A random sampling method was used to conduct a survey in different universities in China to identify the role of mobile phones in value co-creation. Findings from primary data collection indicated that mobile phones play a vital role in value co-creation because of the extensive use of social media. If value co-creation through social media marketing develops with the help of producers, suppliers and other intermediaries with the necessary technology and trust, the society, as well as customers, may enjoy a unique way of shopping. Future studies with mixed methodology and respondents who use different social media as a tool to generate value co-creation may shed light on the undiscovered phenomenon of social media marketing in the context of the mobile phone.

DOI: 10.4018/978-1-6684-6287-4.ch034

INTRODUCTION

As per recent statistics, seven out of ten people use at least one social media in the USA and 88% of companies use social media as a marketing tool (Seoexpert, 2018). It is expected that the monthly average expected social media users may reach as high as 3.02 billion by 2021 (Statista, 2019). In the contemporary arena, mobile phones, in particular, smartphones have a reciprocal connection to social media. As social media received immense popularity regardless of age, gender or generation (Hossain, Ying, and Saha, 2019); it has intentionally or unintentionally become a tool for marketing. Usually, social media is to interact with friends and family members and to get in touch in a smart way of communication such as sharing something like photos, videos or even status update. However, the use of social media has become a regular habit among human being in the twenty-first century. People who have no basic need to communicate with family members may use social media to communicate with friends or even strangers. Many people want to share their achievements, happiness, sadness, etc. with the help of social media (Liu, Wu, and Li, 2019) in order to feel relaxed. Mobile phones made this easier and more comfortable to get in touch with each other. As people carry a mobile phone and get uninterrupted internet facilities now a day, they can always be connected with social media. Although a mobile phone is a basic device to make and receive phone calls, the reality is, mobile phones are used mostly for using social media either for sending text messages, audio call, video call, and group messaging, sharing moments in various ways, etc.

BACKGROUND OF THE STUDY

Mobile phone or mobile devices are part and parcel of our life and people are getting used to operating smartphones due to its attractive features and multidimensional usage (Almunawar et al., 2018). Such a strong reciprocal relationship with a device and a human being has not been observed before. For example: if we compare other devices such as computers, television, radio or any other devices, undoubtedly, mobile phone is the device used most among people now a day and this use has a strong connection with a various social media platform. Based on geographical location, the type of social media may differ, nonetheless, the ultimate result is the strong inseparable connection between smartphones and social media. Based on the contemporary scenario, the author (s) attempted to discover the role of mobile devices in value co-creation with the help of social networking.

LITERATURE REVIEW ON SOCIAL MEDIA MARKETING AND VALUE CO-CREATION

Most literature on social media marketing to date focused on reputed companies, multinational organizations, various case studies of reputed brands, etc. In comparison, very little has been discovered about value co-creation through social media marketing or entrepreneurial activities (Khajeheian, 2013). Consumers attitude toward social media marketing has been discovered recently (Shareef et al., 2019) which indicate the strong focus of companies toward social media advertising in order to reach the customer in a more effective way. Social media marketing has proven as a well-structured content which may flexibly broaden the horizon of a company and its customer base (Prasad & Saigal, 2019). Recent research also talks about innovation in social media marketing (Pacauskas, Rajala, Westerlund, & Mäntymäki, 2018). Although this innovative marketing activities are well defined and analyzed, the unique way to conduct innovation marketing is still under the shadow. The mobile phone may be an option which can be used to conduct innovation marketing in generating value co-creation. In order to expose business activities, social commerce is discussed as an advanced tool for marketing (Schaupp & Bélanger, 2019). Also, a reciprocal attempt at social and mobile media can boost marketing communication activities (Yang, Kang, & Wang, 2019). Kasemsap (2019) investigated that with the benefit of social media, marketers can be in touch with innumerable potential customers than ever before but selecting or choosing the proper media could be the most challenging tool for strategic marketing mix activities.

Figure 1. Twitter Social Media Users Statistics

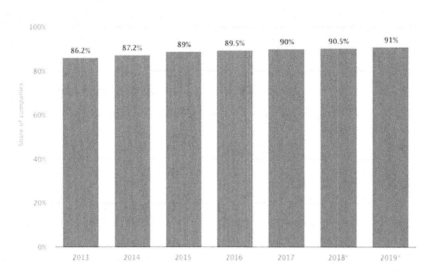

Figure 2. Most popular social networking sites. Source: Dreamgrow, (2018)

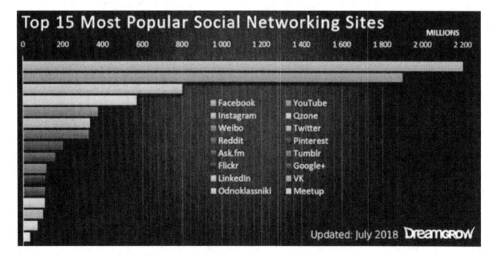

Value co-creation from a social perspective is a combination of generating value through three different stakeholders includes managers, employees, and customers (Devereux & Gallarza, 2019). As a result, a company can generate value for the customers through social media marketing using smartphones and at the same time, end users who are usually involved with other jobs may also generate value-co creation in participating social marketing activities or sometimes defined by researchers as media entrepreneurship (Khajeheian, 2013). Sharing knowledge, values, and information through social media as well as representing views and comments about a particular platform such as Facebook can furthering value co-creation (Sahni & Appiah, 2019). The reasons why people engage in social media marketing are realistic as well as a mean to earn extra money to survive. It is obvious that some people want to earn money for living and some people want to earn money for a better living. Khajeheian and Arbatani (2011) investigated a few numbers of causes why more and more people are involved with social media marketing. The main reasons are ease of entrance, less or no investment and specialized digital sector to conduct business activities. The mobile phone is working as the most suitable supporting device in this value co-creation activities for all the stakeholders involved.

MOBILE PHONES IN VALUE CO-CREATION

It might be a question why people want to buy products through the mobile phone without proper information or knowledge about it? Why people pay online to a stranger? What is the guarantee that the product will be delivered without any trouble? The only answer in this regard is "trust". Social media marketing most of the time people trust each other. Mobile phones can't create any value if there is no trust. Most people buy and sell things in a social media group. In these days people are more connected to each other so that they can trust each other (Van Huy, Thinh, Pham, & Strickler, 2019). People like to share their feelings about a particle purchase or any other activities. Many people are interested to buy products while they realize a very attractive offer.

Some people have no time to find a particular product or they don't have any time to go to shopping complexes. Some friends in the social media group are always involved with some buying and selling activities. Although it's a bit difficult to match the product one member may need, however, there are always various types of customers. For instance, in a social media group, there are 500 people consisting of women and men. If someone wants to sell cosmetics item, for example, he or she might get a response from some women in the group. In this case, the interesting thing is, group members, trust each other because they are connected for social media activities and that is why the group is formed for. Each and every group used in social media may have some particular reasons or rules, however, some people always try to enter with the permission of the admin and try to conduct some social media marketing activities. This is simply a value co-creation process with the frequent usage of mobile devices in the contemporary era. When some people are addicted to the mobile phone for only recreational activities, this concept can be a breakthrough which may generate some extra earning as well as save some people from unnecessary excessive use of mobile phones for non-productive activities (Leung & Liang, 2019).

Figure 3. Selected Social media for marketing activities
Source: Statista, (2019)

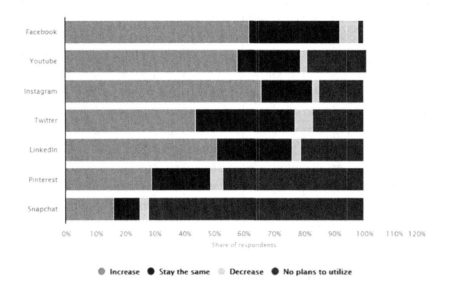

CONTEMPORARY SOCIAL MEDIA MARKETING AND OPPORTUNITIES

Hossain et al. (2019) discussed variety seeking tendency of people in various issues. Buying and selling products is sometimes not a necessity but a hobby these days. People either try to sell or buy products only for curiosity or to earn extra money apart from regular work. Case 1: Alice, a thirty-two years old woman work as a full-time English teacher in China. She is married and has a baby girl. She teaches English in the kindergarten with average income.

To earn extra money, she sells cosmetic items online. She uses WeChat as a platform to advertise products like lipsticks, facial cream, facial masks, make-ups, jewelry, etc. Alice is a little tricky in this business to choose the products. She knows which products are not highly available in the local markets. She also knows the potential buyers and their budget. Alice choose products based on these factors and always set a competitive price to attract customers. Within just one year time period, Alice received about 1200 new friends request from various sources who purchased from her and felt happy about it. Alice initially invested one thousand RMB (USD 147 approx.) to buy some items to sell. At this moment she doesn't have any specific accounts to inform that how much she earns every month, however, she confirmed that the income is getting more than her actual salary and she is planning to quit her job soon. Although this is a simple business opportunity due to less investment and low risk, to date, there is no effective legal restriction found. If the companies consider it positively, they might come up with new opportunities such as individual App, tax return to government, the identity of the sellers and so on to make this process valid and smooth.

Figure 4. Regional rate of mobile phone penetration, January 2019
Source: Statista, 2019

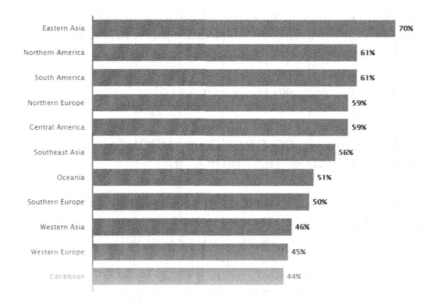

Case 2:

Bai Jie Ru is a 24 years girl. Dance is her passion and she teaches dance in a dance school. She only can work part time as the students and classes are limited. Logically the income is not satisfactory enough. Recently, she was motivated by one of her friend who only sells products online and earns a noticeable amount of money in the last few months. As she was closely connected to the parents of her students, she used social media group as a platform to sell her products. In the beginning, she decided to sell only lipsticks which are with good quality and affordable price. She received noticeable responses from the social media group. Now, she expanded the product line, created a dedicated social media group for selling products, offered a discount to members who can introduce a new customer and that is it. All are simple strategies without high investments and very low risk compared to traditional business set up.

From the cases above, one matter is evident that the parties involved in this activity are generating value for the customers (Hossain, 2019) by introducing a new product to them. On the other hand, it's a favor for the marketers to boost their selling without and additional advertising or promotional cost. Value co-creation is observed here from manufacturer to end users. However, this business set up should have a legal platform so that the society or country may also be benefited from the tax credit. If local government adopt some rules or regulations to perform online business activities then this phenomenon may change the scenario of the society where many people are jobless, deprived and struggling to survive in the society.

Social media marketing activities usually make people happy with introducing unknown products, discount, and trust. Another influencing factor at the same time to discuss here is about socio-economic development. This is such an opportunity which can be taken by anyone who really wants to involve with this activity. Mostly, the people involved with this activity, has no personal website, business identity or logo. However, some of them are renowned due to social media marketing. Social media marketing is an opportunity for new marketers who can enter the market without the risk of wasteful investment in the advertisement (Keswani, 2019) and promotional activities. Instead, if they emphasize more on social media marketing, the chance is more to become successful in the market due to the trust earned by sellers sell through social media. It is extremely difficult to make people believe about a product or service for the advertiser, marketers or even celebrities. Customers know about the promotion and advertising and do not want to trust the quality of the products easily. However, social media marketing can play a vital role to generate satisfactory sales due to the trust of the sellers.

THE FRAMEWORK OF VALUE CO-CREATION THROUGH MOBILE PHONES IN SOCIAL MEDIA MARKETING

Without opportunities and challenges, the business does not exist. Mobile phones created limitless opportunity with a new business framework. There is no doubt about the concurrent increase of mobile shopping especially with the use of social media. The contextual situation is in favor of social media marketing, however, the popularity varies based on geographical locations around the globe. As a result, numerous research conducted based on a unique country as well as a unique industry to further investigate the issue and build a favorable business model. As value co-creation through social media marketing with the help of mobile phones has not been investigated enough, a new framework is suggested here to highlight the contemporary issues, opportunities, and challenges regarding social media marketing. This framework is an indication of social media marketing with the specialized assistance of mobile devices. This framework may offer cornerstone for the decision makers as well as future researchers in the development of social media marketing in multidimensional ways which might be more effective and a strong marketing strategy in the near future. The framework is not specifically quantitative or qualitative, rather, it's a blend of both so that the intended framework can be extended in the future to discover more about the phenomenon and represent how the consumers may behave due to the changes (Solomon et al., 2012).

In the first phase of the framework, three types of antecedents are resented which are: Personal factors, social factors, and psychological factors. These antecedents with the influence of some moderating and mediating factors, represent the final opportunity of social media marketing with mobile devices as a unique idea to conduct business. The overall value co-creation process lies within the whole process. The framework consists of one moderating variable, three mediating variables and the outcome of this study which is "opportunity". The next sections will discuss these in details. In order to reach in depth of the issue, a questionnaire has been designed and conducted for this study. The questionnaire consists of different scales along with multiple choice questions and short answers. The reason behind conducting the questionnaire is to discover the real scenario of social media marketing with the help of portable devices to generate value co-creation such as advantages, barriers to start-up, flexibility, affordability, etc. The result indicates unique ideas and opportunities of social media marketing in a different way to create value in society.

The findings in this study basically based on descriptive analysis. A sample of 22 social media entrepreneurs was chosen to find out the opportunity of social media marketing with the help of mobile devices in order to generate value co-creation. The respondents are actively involved with media entrepreneurship and use a mobile phone as a mean of conducting the business process. Person administered interview was conducted to figure out the contemporary scenario of media marketing especially in the social media marketing platform and mobile devices as a tool. After conducting the full interview, the researcher utilized and coded key points in analyzing the study further. Interview finding is helpful to develop a theory with further modification from experts in order to come up with a more trustable unique theory. With the same procedure and modifications accordingly, the final framework was developed and confirmed. The overall framework which consists of four variables and nine various factors has been discussed below in details.

Figure 5. Structure of social media marketing

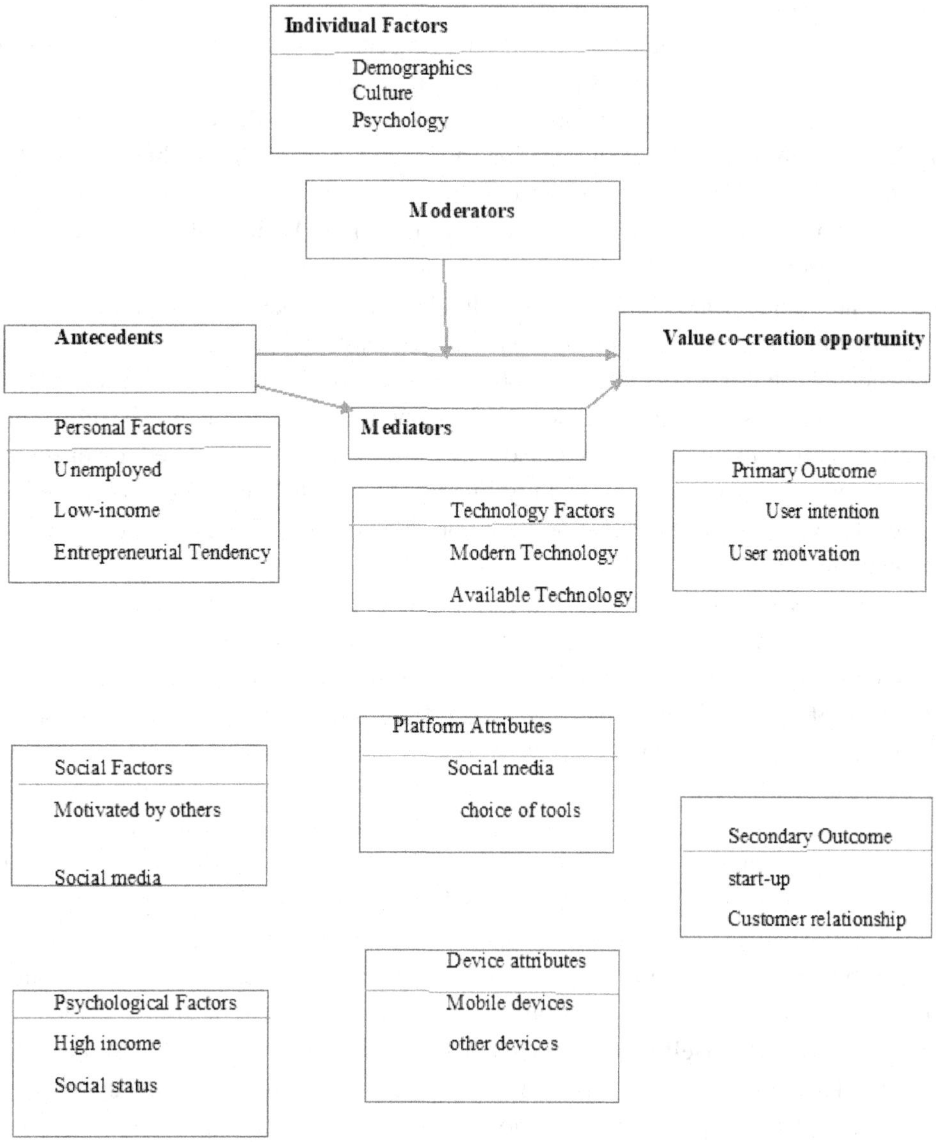

RESEARCH DESIGN

There are some moderating factors involved according to the framework shown in the study which may affect the relationship between dependent and independent variables in this study. These moderators are mostly individual factors. Firstly, the demographic information is important. For example, Age, sex, marital status, income, race, education, religion, etc. may affect to grab an opportunity to become an entrepreneur even though the facilities are available. In some developing countries, women are not allowed to even communicate with people outside the family. In this circumstance, the cultural issue as well as the psychology of people to become socialized act as a moderator and affect the relationship between dependent and independent variables.

Mediating variables act as mechanisms which can bring changes in between independent and dependent variables. The first mediator in this study is technology factors. In this era, modern technology like 5G mobile internet, internet of things, cloud services, Wi-Fi, LiFi (will be introduced soon with LED technology), VR, AR, Web-based communication in real time (WebRTC) technology are blessing for the human being. The more availability of these technologies mediates more positively to enjoy more opportunity for social media marketing and generate more value. Availability of technology is another important mediator in this regard. In some countries, technologies related to social media marketing activities are available and affordable. Even, the technology which may help to send the desired product to the customer within a short period of time is also available. In this case, the value of co-creation will be positively affected. Platform attributes is another mediator in this study. Social media is a platform for many entrepreneurs to start a new business with a low possible risk involved. Choice of tools like selecting a certain app or to be involved with so many groups in the social media world may mediate independent and dependent variables of this study. Finally, device attributes are the other mediating factor which indicates the type of mobile devices or other portable devices and their usage in social marketing activities to generate more value.

There are three antecedents represented in the framework. The first one is personal factors. The main personal cause behind motivating to be an entrepreneur is having no job or unemployment problem. People want to earn money as well as want to find a job for income, security and social status. However, the recent increase of graduates and a shortage of good jobs motivated some people to become an entrepreneur who chose social media as a marketing tool for value co-creation. Low or limited income is another personal factor which drives people to be involved with additional activities or earning source. The two cases discussed in this study are mainly based on low or limited income. In addition, some people have an entrepreneurial tendency. They are usually motivated to business and do not like to work for others. For this kind of people, social media marketing is a blessing as they can start a particular business very easily. There are some social factors which work as an antecedent in this study. This first one is motivated by other people. This happens when people are connected to each other due to sharing information on social media. Some people share it for business purpose and some people get motivated to do the same. Social media itself is also a social factor in this circumstance. Social media is the most powerful and reachable now a day and capable to generate more value for the customers with more buying and selling in various ways. There is another antecedent which is psychological factors. Some people dream to earn a lot of money and become rich. Jobs always have fixed or limited income. As a result, higher income tendency motivates people to conduct marketing activities especially with the help of mobile devices and this phenomenon is effective for more value co-creation.

THE SURVEY

The authors decided to conduct a survey among social media marketing users and entrepreneurs regardless of age, gender, and profession. In order to assume the length and the comprehensibility, a pretest among 4 participants was conducted. In order to make it flexible, the survey was then re-designed that is the authors edited, added or removed some questions. A final survey was designed and administered.

Figure 6. Perception of social media marketing

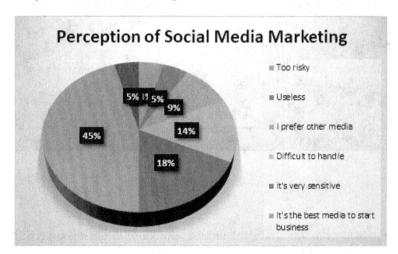

Perception of Social Media Marketing

The first question in the survey was about the perception of respondents about social media marketing. 45% of the respondents said that it's the best media to start a business however, 18% believe that it is quite sensitive due to recommender system, star rating and dissatisfaction of some buyers for unusual reasons which may affect other potential customers. 14% claimed that it's very difficult to handle if the number of customers too many and less manpower support.

Value Co-Creation

The chart above represents various ways of value co-creation in society with a specialized focus on mobile devices. According to the result shown in the diagram, customers perceived more value due to instant and continuous support from the seller. Usually, sellers are either known or highly trusted in a social media marketing group. They try their level best to keep the goodwill up to mark. In addition, respondents also focused on better customer service and trust issue. Sometimes, in terms of traditional purchase, it's comparatively more complex to reach the responsible authority. For example, Customers try to connect them via call center or customer support helpline and then they need to wait for getting the desired service. Conversely, in terms of social media marketing, customers usually enjoy the freedom of instant help and support. Although the easiest way to work independently is a crucial concern in this research, the author has received comparatively low feedback in terms of value co-creation.

Figure 7. value co-creation

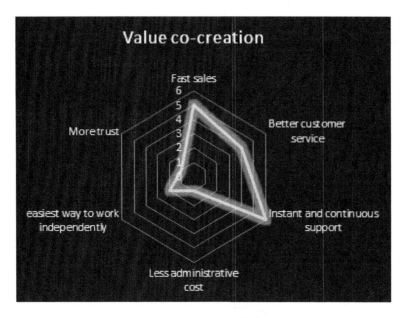

Target People

According to the respondents in this study, the largest number of target customers are social media users. There are certainly other media users along with social media but in this study, the author focused particularly on social media users and found that they are the highest target customers for social media marketing. In addition, there are some people who like to buy goods only for the sake of a discount. They are well known as discount lovers. They are the second largest target customers. Conversely, group buyers and corporate buyers are fewer targets for this kind of marketing. However, loyal and frequent buyers can be a good target market for social media marketing.

Figure 8. Target people

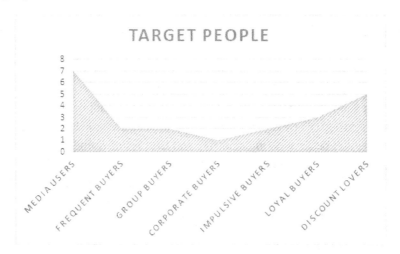

Handling Difficulty

According to the survey conducted in this study, the respondents answered positively about handling difficulty. Especially, usage of Facebook and WeChat as a platform to conduct social media marketing considered as the easiest tool as per the respondents. Here, one matter to draw attention is that the user of a particular platform may find it easier than another platform. For example, Facebook is not allowed to use in China, as a result, most users use WeChat as a platform or QQ. They are not familiar with Facebook. On the other hand in some other Asian countries like India, Pakistan, and Bangladesh, Facebook is considered as the major platform for social media communication.

Figure 9. handling difficulty

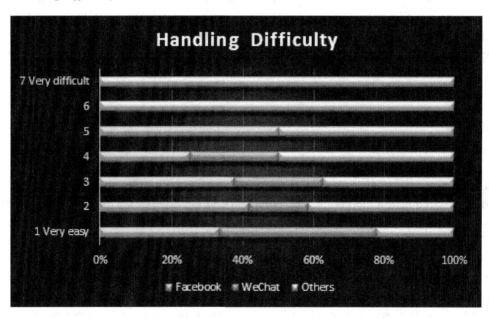

DISCUSSION

Social value co-creation (Devereux & Gallarza, 2019) has been investigated recently with an attempt to satisfy various stakeholders and to increase their benefits. Social media marketing can generate more social value co-creation with more and more business activities performed with the help of social media with less expense and more affordable price for the consumers. Value co-creation mostly refer to creating more value for the business and the customers' perspective, however, social value co-creation refers the same with an additional focus of societal and economic development perspective. Mobile phones may play the most vital role in creating social value co-creation by conducting business activities including information sharing, advertising, selling, collecting feedback from the users and sometimes ensuring warranty for the buyers. Social value co-creation is more crucial in this aspect due to social media marketing. If social media goes against a particular seller, it's hardly possible for the seller to stay in the market. According to Khajeheian and Arbatani (2011), the social media platform has changed the business circumstance in a different way where low barriers exits to enter (M = 1.40, SD = 0.5), exit market is considered as a major drawback in terms of developing country (M = 1.89, SD = 0.7), competition is observed as a medium level (M= 3.47), profitability rate is medium as well (M= 2.80). The result indicates that the social media market is not a noticeably enhanced market in the developing countries, however, due to social value-co creation, this may form a unique business opportunity in the future. Even small investors and entrepreneurs are interested to invest on advertising using social media more and more recently.

This is the ultimate outcome of this study. Value-co creation through more use of mobile devices along with the benefit of social media marketing. It has been represented in two different categories. The first one is the primary outcome and the second one is a secondary outcome. The primary outcome includes user intention and motivation. When people decide to start a new business, they look for a suitable platform. With various antecedents, moderators and mediators, the final decision depends. The opportunity for value co-creation primarily depends on user intention and motivation at this stage. So the primary stage is just to make a decision but not the actual start-up. However, the secondary outcome of this framework is to start-up the actual business with the help of social media and mobile devices and maintain proper customer relationship. In this kind of business, value co-creation can be affected positively and adversely due to a simple mistake or misunderstanding. As a result, maintaining a proper customer relationship may result in a successful start-up and more value co-creation.

CONCLUSION

As per the findings in this paper, mobile phones, in particular, smartphones play a vital role in value co-creation via social media marketing. The emergence of smartphones with multidimensional facilities helps users to enjoy shopping. Mobile phones in the present era not only improved communication system but also changed the way of social media marketing and created more value by a recent increase in online shopping via mobile apps. The countries who are not yet successful with social media marketing may think about adopting more strategies via mobile phones and adopt flexible apps for shopping. In addition, a secure and flexible mobile payment may enhance the probability of increased purchase by potential customers. The proposed framework in this study is an exemplary way to generate more value in social media marketing using mobile devices. With the antecedents, moderators, and mediators, the framework motivates social media entrepreneurs to go ahead and conduct more and more social media marketing activities.

This study is an attempt to enhance social media marketing activities with the usage of mobile phones which may create more value for the concerned parties associated in this activity. It can be a cornerstone for social media entrepreneurs, stakeholders and managers and also it contributes the theory by adding the new framework.

FUTURE RESEARCH DIRECTION

This study could be a base study for further experimental research which may exploit tremendous opportunities in social media marketing with the help of mobile devices. Due to limited number of data and individual case study, this research may not generate same result for any regions in the world. So, future research may try to discover the same on European or American perspective or even compare the differences among different regions.

REFERENCES

Almunawar, M. N., Anshari, M., Susanto, H., & Chen, C. K. (2018). How people choose and use their Smartphones. In *Management Strategies and Technology Fluidity in the Asian Business Sector* (pp. 235–252). IGI Global. doi:10.4018/978-1-5225-4056-4.ch014

Devereux, M. T., & Gallarza, M. G. G. (2019). Social value co-creation: Insights from consumers, employees, and managers. In Corporate Social Responsibility: Concepts, Methodologies, Tools, and Applications (pp. 55-79). IGI Global.

Dreamgrow. (2018). *21 Social Media Marketing Statistics You Need to Know in 2018*. Retrieved from https://www.dreamgrow.com/21-social-media-marketing-statistics/

Hossain, S. F., Nurunnabi, M., Hussain, K., Saha, S. K., & Wang, S. (2019). Effects of variety-seeking intention by mobile phone usage on university students' academic performance. *Cogent Education*, *6*(1). Advance online publication. doi:10.1080/2331186X.2019.1574692

Hossain, S. F. A. (2019). Social Networking and Its Role in Media Entrepreneurship: Evaluating the Use of Mobile Phones in the Context of Online Shopping–A Review. *Journal of Media Management and Entrepreneurship*, *1*(1), 73–86. doi:10.4018/JMME.2019010105

Hossain, S. F. A., Ying, Y., & Saha, S. K. (2019). Systematic Mobile Device Usage Behavior and Successful Implementation of TPACK Based on University Students Need. In *Science and Information Conference* (pp. 729-746). Springer.

Keswani, S. (2019). Emotional Finance Plays an Important Role in Investment Decisions. In *Behavioral Finance and Decision-Making Models* (pp. 89–103). IGI Global. doi:10.4018/978-1-5225-7399-9.ch005

Khajeheian, D. (2013). New Venture Creation in Social Media Platform; Towards a Framework for Media Entrepreneurship. In *Handbook of Social Media Management: Value Chain and Business Models in Changing Media Markets* (pp. 125–142). Springer Science & Business Media. doi:10.1007/978-3-642-28897-5_8

Khajeheian, D., & Roshandel Arbatani, T. (2011). *Remediation of media markets toward mediaentrepreneurship, how recession reconstructed media industry*. Paper presented at the meeting of European Media Management Education Association Conference, Moscow.

Leung, L., & Liang, J. (2019). Psychological Traits, Addiction Symptoms, and Feature Usage as Predictors of Problematic Smartphone Use Among University Students in China. *Substance Abuse and Addiction*, 321-341. doi:10.4018/978-1-5225-7666-2.ch017

Liu, H., Wu, L., & Li, X. (2019). Social media envy: How experience sharing on social networking sites drives millennials' aspirational tourism consumption. *Journal of Travel Research*, *58*(3), 355–369. doi:10.1177/0047287518761615

Pacauskas, D., Rajala, R., Westerlund, M., & Mäntymäki, M. (2018). Harnessing user innovation for social media marketing: Case study of a crowdsourced hamburger. *International Journal of Information Management, 43*, 319–327. doi:10.1016/j.ijinfomgt.2018.08.012

Prasad, P., & Saigal, P. (2019). Social Media Marketing: Tools and Techniques. In Application of Gaming in New Media Marketing (pp. 202-214). IGI Global.

Sahni, K., & Appiah, K. (2019). The dynamics of social media and value co-creation. In *Leveraging Computer-Mediated Marketing Environments* (pp. 22–42). IGI Global. doi:10.4018/978-1-5225-7344-9.ch002

Schaupp, L. C., & Bélanger, F. (2019). Social commerce benefits for small businesses: An organizational level study. In Social Entrepreneurship: Concepts, Methodologies, Tools, and Applications (pp. 1237-1255). IGI Global.

Seoexpert. (2018). *85+ Social Media Stats & Facts That Matter to Marketers in 2019*. Retrieved from https://seoexpertbrad.com/social-media-marketing-statistics/

Shareef, M. A., Mukerji, B., Dwivedi, Y. K., Rana, N. P., & Islam, R. (2019). Social media marketing: Comparative effect of advertisement sources. *Journal of Retailing and Consumer Services, 46*, 58–69. doi:10.1016/j.jretconser.2017.11.001

Solomon, M., Russell-Bennett, R., & Previte, J. (2012). *Consumer behaviour*. Pearson Higher Education AU.

Statista. (2019). *Future use of social media among marketers worldwide by platform 2018*. Retrieved from https://www.statista.com/statistics/258974/future-use-of-social-media-among-marketers-worldwide-by-platform/

Statista. (2019). *Social Media Statistics*. Retrieved from https://www.statista.com/topics/1164/social-networks/

Van Huy, L., Thinh, N. H., Pham, L., & Strickler, C. (2019). Customer Trust and Purchase Intention. *International Journal of E-Services and Mobile Applications, 11*(1), 1–23. doi:10.4018/IJESMA.2019010101

Yang, K. C., Kang, Y., & Wang, R. P. (2019). Integrating Social and Mobile Media in Environmental Marketing Communications in China: Opportunities and Challenges. In Environmental Awareness and the Role of Social Media (pp. 43-71). IGI Global.

ADDITIONAL READING

Achtenhagen, L. (2012). Entrepreneurs in Media. Encyclopedia of New Venture Management, 154-157. doi:10.4135/9781452218571.n60

Chen, Y. R. (2017). Perceived values of branded mobile media, consumer engagement, business-consumer relationship quality and purchase intention: A study of WeChat in China. *Public Relations Review, 43*(5), 945–954. doi:10.1016/j.pubrev.2017.07.005

Delacroix, E., Parguel, B., & Benoit-Moreau, F. (2018). Digital subsistence entrepreneurs on Facebook. *Technological Forecasting and Social Change*. Advance online publication. doi:10.1016/j.techfore.2018.06.018

Faulds, D. J., Mangold, W. G., Raju, P., & Valsalan, S. (2018). The mobile shopping revolution: Redefining the consumer decision process. *Business Horizons*, *61*(2), 323–338. doi:10.1016/j.bushor.2017.11.012

Fuentes, C., & Svingstedt, A. (2017). Mobile phones and the practice of shopping: A study of how young adults use smartphones to shop. *Journal of Retailing and Consumer Services*, *38*, 137–146. doi:10.1016/j.jretconser.2017.06.002

KEY TERMS AND DEFINITIONS

Media Entrepreneurs: Entrepreneurs who primarily and mostly depend on various media including social media to sell their products.

Smartphones: The recent updated creation of mobile telephones which has multidisciplinary usage within a single device apart from making phone calls and sending text messages.

Social Media: The most powerful and popular media which has been recently attracted by the marketers and entrepreneurs.

Social Media Marketing: It is a proven tool which indicate the strong focus of companies toward social media advertising in order to reach the customer in a more effective way.

Value Co-Creation: Combination of generating value through different stakeholders involved in business activity.

This research was previously published in the Encyclopedia of Organizational Knowledge, Administration, and Technology; pages 2166-2180, copyright year 2021 by Business Science Reference (an imprint of IGI Global).

Chapter 35
The Impact of Social Media Platforms "Instagram" and "Snapchat" on the Purchasing Decision – Structural Equation Modelling Approach:
Social Media Platforms

Eman Ali Alghamdi
DAMAC Properties, Riyadh, Saudi Arabia

Naima Bogari
King Abdulaziz University, Jeddah, Saudi Arabia

ABSTRACT

Social media (SM) tools have an immense potential in e-marketing and online shopping. However, there is a lack of researches on the use of social media platform as effective marketing tools. This study has aimed to investigate the revolution of social media in Saudi Arabia through understanding the impact of two popular SM platforms (Instagram and Snapchat) on the purchasing decision of Saudi customers through advertisements and blogger recommendations. Structural equation modeling (SEM) was used to develop a model, which was tested using Confirmatory factor analysis (CFA). The results indicated a positive impact of social media platforms on the purchasing decision of young female users. Moreover, the effectiveness of these platforms in generating electronic-word of mouth (eWOM) among consumers was highlighted. However, further research is needed to promote marketeers and consumers' awareness in the digital marketplace.

DOI: 10.4018/978-1-6684-6287-4.ch035

INTRODUCTION

Several paradigms' shifts have been observed since the last few decades; however, no shift is more revolutionary than the advent of internet (Cummins et al., 2014). Various aspects of different individuals and societies are significantly affected as a result of recent boom in social media (SM) (Ting et al., 2016). Furthermore, social media (SM) offers a myriad of applications in product promotion and marketing, since it relies on variables linked to customer responses and usage of advanced communication tools. SM enables companies to interact with customers using innovative technology and acquire a deeper understanding of their emotions and the motivating factors behind their consumption of products (Straker & Wrigley, 2016). The use of social media platforms including Instagram and Snapchat has significantly increased among Saudi users due to extensive smartphone usage and the passion of users.

This is the reason companies utilize SM tools to a great extent for generating higher revenues (Sakkthivel & Sriram, 2015), and the consumers to carry out research about the product using the WOM feature on SM before purchasing non-durable goods or services (Woo et al., 2015). Companies should utilize customer feedback to improve the quality of products and services, develop more user-friendly devices, and ensure that their staff conduct the business in a polite and sincere manner (Boon-Long & Wongsurawat, 2015). Consumer interaction with such ads is called pre-purchase search motivation, where their attitudes are influenced by the social networking advertisements (Mir, 2014). It is important for advertisers and marketers to consider the consumer behavior throughout the stages of purchasing that is likely to include; recognition of the consumers' needs; search for information; evaluation of alternative products; making the purchase, and post-purchase evaluation or the outcomes (Cao et al., 2014). The use of WOM provides the consumers with specific information at each of these stages.

The recent boom in SM has resulted in companies to recognize the effectiveness of utilizing such platforms for marketing and advertising. Over 3 billion people have internet access globally and are willing to search for new products and interact with online communities to seek and share product reviews (Boon-Long & Wongsurawat, 2015). Therefore, companies need to understand the influence of consumer reactions towards SM-based advertisements and manage the brand in the online environment (Schneider et al., 2016). The use of WOM is an effective way to promote sales for those products to generate information searches for products (López & Sicilia, 2013). There is a significant impact of using SM on the decisions made by consumers regarding online purchasing in the form of increased e-commerce awareness (Makki & Chang, 2015). Similarly, the consumer passion for mobile devices allows companies to develop their websites through making them more mobile-friendly (John, 2015).

The growing popularity and usage of SM platforms have forced marketers to examine their marketing strategies to remain prevalent amongst the youth (Yavisha and Krishna, 2013). Therefore, the present study aims to investigate the revolution of social media in Saudi Arabia by understanding the impact of two popular SM platforms (Instagram and Snapchat) on the purchasing decision of Saudi customers through advertisements and blogger recommendations.

THEORETICAL FRAMEWORK AND HYPOTHESIS DEVELOPMENT

There is a significant lack of research surrounding the use of Instagram and Snapchat as effective e-marketing tools. It is known that these marketing strategies are more effective, as compared to the physical advertising in the intention of buying products. Therefore, the present study aims to highlight the influence of these platforms through two main factors on the consumer's purchasing decision (Figure 1). These factors were in the form of advertisements on Instagram and Snapchat platforms, and blogger and celebrity-based recommendations on SM. These two factors serve as the independent variables of interest for this study; whereas, purchasing decision in the primary dependent variable. Consumer's age has been added as control variable to examine the impact on bloggers and celebrities' followers that motivate them to purchase the advertised product. The study findings would enable better recommendations to be made for the new entries to the Saudi Market, based on appropriate segmentation through the relevant SM platform.

Figure 1. The study framework

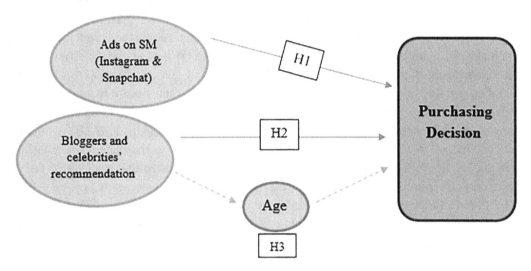

Social Media Revolution

Previous studies have shown poor integration of SM with the marketing strategy, despite of the tendency of most of the companies to use SM as a marketing tool (Nadeem, 2015; Makki and Chang, 2015; van Asperen et al., 2018). For instance; Nadeem (2015) examined how customer loyalty (CL) has come under an undeniable influence of SM. The attitudes of consumers towards online shopping in Saudi Arabia are extremely significant and worthy of examination due to factors such as the lack of autonomy faced by Saudi women to drive. Further research within the Saudi context by Makki and Chang (2015) highlighted that Saudi customers; regardless of gender, relied more on smartphone or tablet use to access the internet, as compared to personal computer usage. Therefore, the use of SM in the form of Instagram may be an effective way to increase product awareness and promote e-marketing in Saudi Arabia. As evidenced by Facebook's food retailer experiment, SM plays an influential role in influencing purchasing decisions. Further studies highlighted the positive relation between SM and undergraduate students' intention to purchase products (Song & Yoo, 2016). According to Carlson and Christopher (2015), the effectiveness of communication through SM can be observed through the followership. A recent study conducted by van Asperen et al. (2018) showed positive association between social media engagement and customer loyalty; however, only consuming social media is directly related to affective loyalty. This also paved the way of measuring the level of engagement of customers with the social media of the company in relation to their degree of loyalty.

The Impact of Advertising Through SM on the Purchasing Decision

The use of SM is a cost-effective way to communicate with customers, promote brands, and ultimately generate revenue (Min and Youjeong, 2016). Socio-demographic variables and product categorizations play a significant role in influencing the decision of consumers to buy a specific product (Woo et al., 2015). The aforementioned study further suggested that companies should consider such factors in the marketing plans, when segments are being targeted. Boon-Long and Wongsurawat (2015) found that Thailand fans commenting on the official Facebook page of Samsung Mobile primarily focused on the experience issues, business practice issues, information requests and comments about products developments and lunches. A recent study conducted by Siddique (2017) highlighted the effect of digital media on customer purchasing behavior. The results depicted that in recent times, the individuals allude to online advanced correspondence sources and discover them as dependable and valuable. These platforms have formed an important link between entertainment and mobile shopping that pushes companies to develop mobile sales and focus on the influence of 'Word of Mouth' (WOM) generated by the mobile shoppers (Teng et al., 2017).

H1: The advertisements on social media platform has positive impact on consumer intention to make purchasing decision.

Bloggers and Celebrities role in eWOM

According to a study by Hui-Ye Chiu et al. (2014), blogs enable a high level of interaction between blog visitors and the bloggers, by allowing visitors to leave comments on a posted article or recommend other blogs. According to Fu and Chen (2012), companies can use blogs to communicate with customers, shape customers' attitudes and create high levels of interaction and loyalty through eWOM and readers' comments. Kowalczyk and Pounders (2016) found that consumers will spread positive WOM for celebrities, who they follow on SM and particularly those whom they deem to be authentic. Furthermore, Young (2017) analyzed that age and gender are important factors for celebrities to use either Snapchat or Instagram, as opposed to factors such as income level and area of profession. The transition from celebrity-focused television programs and magazines to celebrity websites and SM profiles enables consumers to engage more deeply with them (Raithel, 2018). A recent study showed the impact of celebrity endorsement on consumers' word-of-mouth and decision behavior (Loureiro et al., 2018). In the similar context, the present study has focused on the popularity of these SM applications among young users. The second hypothesis developed for this study has been outlined below.

H2: As influencers, the recommendations of celebrities and bloggers has positive impact on consumer intention to purchase any product.

The Relationship Between Social Networks and eWOM

Interaction across multiple online channels between customers and firms is extremely essential for creating a holistic online shopping experience (Kandampully et al., 2015). This type of social communication requires an intensified search into consumer behavior to create a unified customer experience within e-commerce context. San-Martín et al. (2016) revealed that satisfaction, perceived control, perceived entertainment and subjective norm greatly affect WOM in the context of mobile phone commerce. Moreover, regulatory focus generates a longer-lasting effect on consumers' post-consumption behaviors. Younger populations are more prone to utilize SM for communicative purposes (Boulianne, 2015; Van Deursen et al., 2015). Gvili and Shalom (2018) were successful in proposing conceptual framework to explain consumer engagement with electronic WOM through social media. The results depicted that social capital and credibility significantly affect consumer attitude toward eWOM through social media.

The social eWOM is characterized differently from the anonymous eWOM due to the presence of unique characteristics. These characteristics include; information trustworthiness, interpersonal relationships, intended audience, and source evaluations (Pihlaja et al., 2017). A similar study conducted by Tien et al. (2018) focused on the impact of customer to customer eWOM by utilizing information persuasion in reference to purchase decision making. The results depicted that the likelihood of the adoption of a eWOM message increases as a result of perceived usefulness and credibility together. Therefore, viral marketing campaigns are needed for encouraging marketers to improve purchase intentions by spreading useful and credible customer to customer eWOM (Tien et al., 2018). In this regard, the third hypothesis was developed as outlined below:

H3: The effect of consumer's age on his/her intention to purchase the product is positively related based on SM celebrities' recommendation and make purchasing decisions.

Recently, it has been evidenced that people represent their companies through branded content on their personal accounts of Snapchat, Instagram etc. This clearly depicts the fact that consumers follow other consumers to get assistance in purchasing decisions (Glucksman, 2017). The social media brand influencers have achieved significant rise as it has successfully captured the attention of brand consumers and promote relevant and relatable content to clients (Glucksman, 2017). In the similar context, a study has ascertained that social media influencers are represented as an independent entity, who are responsible for shaping the attitude of audience through blogs (Garrido-Moreno et al., 2018). In this regard, the fourth hypothesis has been outlined.

H4: The type of SM (Instagram or Snapchat) used for advertisements and bloggers' recommendation and the purchasing decision are positively associated.

METHODOLOGY

Design

This study has used an analytical and descriptive approach to study the framed hypotheses. Both primary and secondary sources were used. Given the objectives of the study, a quantitative survey design was adopted, which used a positively-worded statement related to the relationships. Only qualifying questions were included to ensure the selective participation of only Instagram and Snapchat users. The data collection period was initiated on March 19, 2017 and continued until April 9, 2017.

The questionnaire incorporated a group of questions that covered the expected consumer's behavior and their feelings toward online shopping, in addition to measuring their willingness to use SM for seeking information pertaining to the relevant product. Direct questions that addressed the level of consumer acceptance for certain SM characteristics related to the advertised product were incorporated. The aim of the questions was to explore the consumer's interaction with these platforms, since the current study focused on two relatively new SM platforms.

Participants

The target sample was in the form of male and female SM users who specifically used Instagram or Snapchat. The total number of initial respondents were 746. Following a screening process and data cleaning to eliminate missing values and duplicated responses, the final number of respondents came down to 524 (i.e. N = 524). A non-probability method was used that relied on convenience samples from two main cities in Saudi Arabia, which included Jeddah and Khobar (Saunders, 2011). These cities were selected due to their culturally diverse natures and familiarity with current market trends. Additionally, these cities are significant economic hubs. Care was taken to ensure equality in the number of participants from both the cities for increasing accuracy in the data analysis.

The survey consisted of three dimensions, which were inclusive of advertisements on the two SM platforms; blogger recommendations on SM and purchasing decision. In addition to the control demographic variables, the survey had two major categories, which individually measured the participants' sensitivity to advertisements and bloggers' recommendations about products. In this regard, participants were asked to respond according to a 5-point Likert-type scale, where 1 indicated 'strongly agree' and 5 indicated 'strongly disagree'. The questionnaire was checked for internal consistency and reliability before commencing with the study.

Testing Procedures

Study dimensions were tested through structural equation modeling analysis, using Stata v. 14. The test was applied on the questionnaire items in a sample of 524 participants across the three dimensions. The reliability and dimensionality of all items was assessed through confirmatory factor analysis, using maximum likelihood estimation (ML). After modifying the model of each dimension, all the dimensions were consolidated into one model to be analyzed and assessed (Gefen et al., 2000). All the models were identified by setting any latent factor means to 0 and latent factor variances to 1. Following this, all item intercepts, item factor loadings and item residual variances were estimated.

Measures

First Dimension: Ads on SM (1st Main Independent Variable)

Prior to analysis, four items utilized the five-point Likert scale, where higher values indicated greater levels of purchasing for all items. The items' statements were as follows: "The ads on social media attracts my attention to products I haven't used before" (symbolized by E); "Social media is one of my choices when I seek information about certain brands" (symbolized by G); "The comments under posts help me to assess the advertised products before I buy it" (symbolized by I), and; "The comments under product ads help me to identify the competing products from other brands and compare between them" (symbolized by J).

Model fit statistics reported in table-1 include the obtained model χ^2, its scaling factor (in which values different than 1.000 indicate deviations from normality), its degrees of freedom, its p-value (in which non-significance is desirable for good fit), Comparative Fit Index (CFI) (in which values higher than .95 are desirable for good fit), and the RMSEA, or Root Mean Square Error of Approximation. Additionally, a point estimate and 90% confidence interval (in which values lower than .06 are desirable for good fit) were included. Sources of local misfit were identified using the normalized residual covariance matrix, which were available via the RESIDUAL output option in Stata, in which individual values were calculated as:

(observed covariance – expected covariance) / SD (observed covariance)

Relatively large positive residual covariances were observed among items I and J, indicating that the residuals of these items were highly related to each other. Modification indices, available via the MODINDICES output option in Stata, corroborated this pattern. After correlating the residuals for I with J, the new factor model global fit better than the initial factor model, as reported in table-1. Thus, the four items and the residuals between I and J appeared to measure the latent variable. This latent variable was in the form of advertisements.

Table 1. Advertisements measurement

Model (Ads)	# Items	Chi Square Value	Chi Square DF	Chi Square p-value	CFI	RMSEA Estimate	RMSEA Lower CI	RMSEA Higher CI	RMSEA p-value	SRMR
One Factor	4	26.130	2	<.0001	.954	.152	.103	.206	<.001	.057
One Factor (After Mofcation)	4	0	1.000	0.83	1	0.0001	0.000	0.069	0.911	0.001

Further examination of local fit via normalized residual covariances and modification indices yielded no interpretable remaining relationships. Thus, this factor model was retained as shown in figure 2.

Figure 2. Standardized loadings, means and errors for advertisements

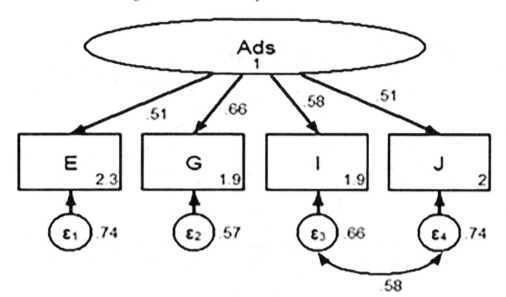

Second Dimension: Bloggers on SM (2ⁿᵈ Main Independent variable)

Prior to analysis, three items utilized the five-point Likert scale, where higher values indicated greater levels of purchasing for all items. The three items' statements were as follows: "Reviewing posts by bloggers and celebrities is one of my daily interests" (symbolized by S); "I like products posted by the blogger on his account on Instagram or Snapchat because I like his/her taste" (symbolized by T), and; "I like products posted by the blogger on his account on Instagram or Snapchat because I like his/her lifestyle" (symbolized by U). Model fit statistics reported in table-2 were the same as earlier.

Although a one-factor model was initially posited to account for the pattern of covariance across these 3 items, it resulted in a perfect fit, as shown in figure 3. Although each item had a significant factor loading, a single latent factor did not adequately describe the pattern of relationship across these nine items as initially hypothesized. Thus, the three items appeared to measure the latent variable in the form of bloggers, as shown in figure 3.

Table 2. Bloggers measurement

Model (Bloggers)	# Items	Chi Square Value	Chi Square DF	Chi Square p-value	CFI	RMSEA Estimate	RMSEA Lower CI	RMSEA Higher CI	RMSEA p-value	SRMR
One Factor	3	0.0000	0	0	1.000	.000	.000	.000	1.000	.000

Figure 3. Standardized loadings, means and errors for bloggers

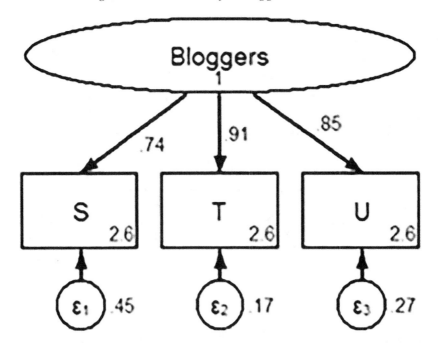

Third Dimension: Purchasing (Dependent Variable)

Prior to analysis, twelve items utilized the five-point Likert scale, where higher values indicated greater levels of purchasing for all items. The statements for these items were as follows: "I rely on readers' comments and opinions about the advertised product before I make purchase decision" (symbolized by K); "Watching video advertisements of a product that I want to purchase on Instagram or Snapchat has a direct impact on my decision to buy it" (symbolized by M); "I often buy a product that has been advertised on social media" (symbolized by O); "The blogger's appearance leads me to ask for additional information about the brand he/she uses" (symbolized by V); "I may buy a product that appears in the blogger's post just because he/she advertised it on his/her account" (symbolized by W); "I may buy a product that appears in the blogger's post just to get the discount he offered" (symbolized by X); "I may buy a product that appears in the blogger's post just because it has a gift promotion with it" (symbolized by Y); "Bloggers' experiments are my first choice when I seek for information about product to find out what I want" (symbolized by AA); "Bloggers' own experiences with the product that I'm interested in is (inspired me) to make a purchase decision" (symbolized by AB); "Bloggers' own experiences with the product that I'm interested in help me make the purchase decision faster" (symbolized by AC); "I consider bloggers' own experiences with the product that I'm interested in as an initial assessment for its (quality) before purchase it" (symbolized by AD), and; "I consider bloggers' own experiences with the product I'm interested in as an initial assessment for its efficiency before purchase it" (symbolized by AE). Model fit statistics reported in table-3 were the same as earlier.

Although a one-factor model was initially posited to account for the pattern of covariance across these 12 items, it resulted in a poor fit, as shown in table-3. Although each item had a significant factor loading, a single latent factor did not adequately describe the pattern of relationship across these 12 items as initially hypothesized. Sources of local misfit were identified using the normalized residual covariance matrix, available via the RESIDUAL output option in Stata, in which individual values were calculated as:

(observed covariance – expected covariance) / SD (observed covariance)

Consequently, the items were removed one by one in several models. The final model showed the significance of three factors. These were: FCP or followers' comments purchase (KMO); BAP or Bloggers' Appearance Purchase (VWXY, with a correlation between the residuals X and Y), and; BEP or Bloggers' Experience Purchase (AA AB AC AD AE, with a correlation between the residuals AD and AE). The modification indices which were available via the MODINDICES output option in Stata, corroborated this pattern. After three different factors, the new model showed a better global fit than the initial factor model, as reported in table-3.

Table 3. Purchasing measurement

Model (Purchasing)	# Items	Chi Square Value	Chi Square DF	Chi Square p-value	CFI	RMSEA Estimate	RMSEA Lower CI	RMSEA Higher CI	RMSEA p-value	SRMR
One Factor	12	1015.067	54	<.0001	.764	.184	.174	.194	<.001	0.93
One Factor (After Mofcation)	12	128	49.000	<.0001	1	0.055	.044	.067	.212	.030

Thus, only the 12 items appeared to measure the three-latent variables (FCP, BAP and BEP) as shown in figure 4.

Further examination of local fit via normalized residual covariance and modification indices yielded no interpretable remaining relationships and thus this factor model was retained. Additionally, the correlation between 0.58 and 0.76, indicated the lack of multicollinearity (<.9) issues among the three factors.

All Dimensions

The reliability and dimensionality of five dimensions was assessed. In this regard, the first dimension had 4 items, where each of them assessed the advertisements. The second dimension had 3 items, with each assessing bloggers and the third dimension contained 12 items, that assessed three factors for purchasing [FCP (3 items) BAP (4 items) and BEP (5 items)].

Figure 4. Standardized loadings, means and errors for purchasing

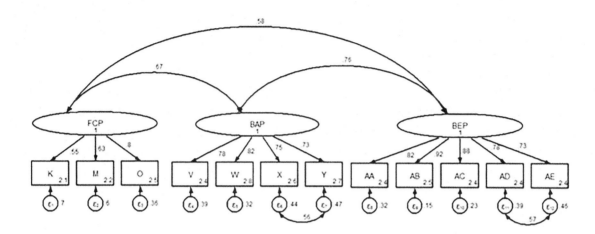

All the models were identified by setting any latent factor means to 0 and latent factor variances to 1. Following this, all item intercepts, item factor loadings, and item residual variances were estimated. Prior to analysis, the 19 items utilized a five-point Likert scale, where higher values indicated greater levels of advertisements, bloggers and purchasing with regard to the three factors, for all items. Model fit statistics reported in table-4 were the same as earlier.

Table 4. All five factors

Model (All five factors)	# Items	Chi Square Value	Chi Square DF	Chi Square p-value	CFI	RMSEA Estimate	RMSEA Lower CI	RMSEA Higher CI	RMSEA p-value	SRMR
One Factor	19	462.160	138	<.0001	.950	.060	.060	.074	<.001	.049

Each item had a significant factor loading to its dimension in the form of advertisements, bloggers, FCP, BAP and BEP. These five latent factors adequately described the pattern of relationship across these nineteen items as initially hypothesized. Sources of local misfit were identified using the normalized residual covariance matrix, available via the RESIDUAL output option in Stata, in which individual values were calculated as:

(observed covariance – expected covariance) / SD (observed covariance)

Further examination of the local fit via normalized residual covariances and modification indices yielded no interpretable remaining relationships. Thus, the five-factor model was retained as shown in Figure 5.

Figure 5. Standardized loadings, means and errors for all five factors

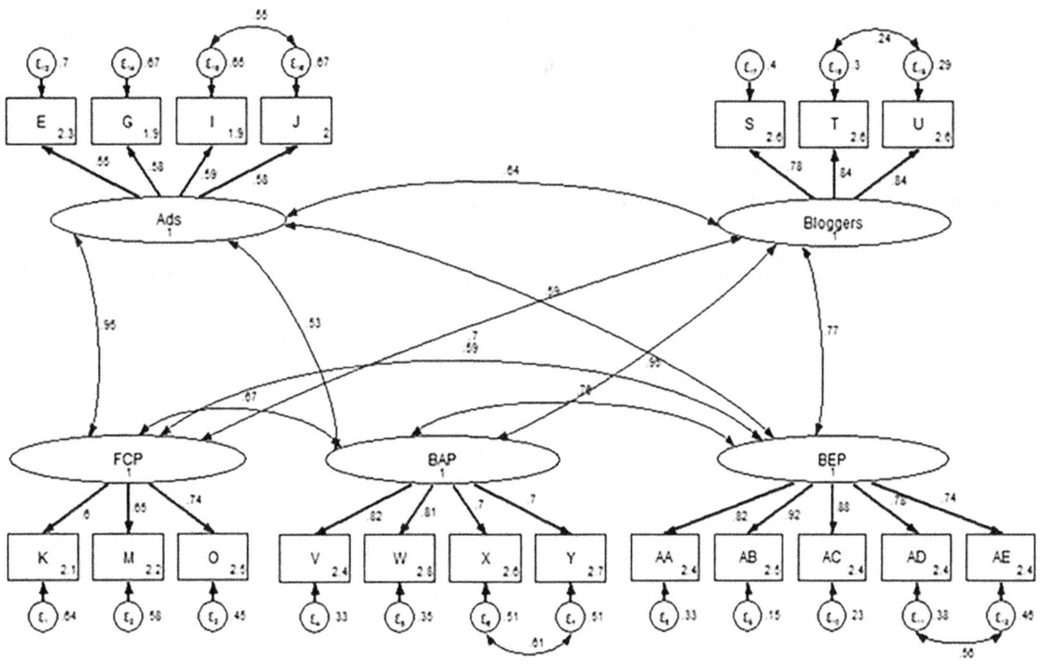

RESULTS

Profile of Respondents

Table 5 has shown that 68% of participants used both platforms, while the residual percentage is approximately equal for each platform separately. Through this, insights may be gained regarding the strong relationship between Instagram and Snapchat. It is notable that these results negate the fourth hypothesis, which stated that there was a positive relationship between choosing either Instagram or Snapchat and the purchasing decision.

The demographic data of the participants has been tabulated in table-5. Based on gender, it was seen that there were a greater number of female respondents as compared to male ones, which indicated the greater willingness of females to utilize SM platforms for e-shopping as compared to males. Based on age, it was seen that the greatest number of users fell within the 18-24 years age bracket (32.2%). This was followed closely by users within the 25-30 years age bracket (29.6%) and those users who were aged between 31- 39 years (26.9%). Lastly, the least number of users were found to fall within the age bracket of 40 years or above (11.3%). These results have been tabulated in table-5.

Based on educational and occupational grounds, it was seen that the most dominant cohort was in the form of bachelor degree holders (61.6%), followed by postgraduate degree holders (19.7%). This was followed by high-school students (12.4%) and diploma holders (6.3%). It was seen that most of the respondents were students, standing at 45.2% of the sample population. As evidenced by the results, most of the respondents earned a monthly income of 5000 SR or less (45.8%). This indicates that most of the respondents therefore belonged to a students' cohort. The results further indicated that 25% of the respondents earned between 5000 to 9999 SR and that 21.8% earned between 10000 to 19999 SR. Lastly, only 7.4% of the respondents earned 20000 SR or more. Further investigation is necessary regarding the impact of the relationship between the monthly income and online shopping through social media, on the purchasing decision.

Table 5. Demographic profile of the respondents

Control Variables		Frequency	Percentage
Gender	Male	226	43.1
	Female	298	56.9
Age	18-24	169	32.2
	25-30	155	29.6
	31-39	141	26.9
	40 and above	59	11.3
Education Level	High School	65	12.4
	Diploma	33	6.3

continues on following page

Table 5. Continued

	Bachelor	323	61.6
	Post-graduate	103	19.7
	Occupation		
	Student	237	45.2
	Government-sector employee	131	25
	Private sector-employee	134	25.6
	Employer/business owner	22	4.2
Monthly income in SR	5,000 and less	240	45.8
	5,000 - 9,999	131	25
	10,000 - 19,999	114	21.8
	20,000 and more	39	7.4
Use of Social Media	Instagram	79	15%
	Snapchat	89	17%
	Both	356	68%

RESULTS OF STATISTICAL TESTING

Multiple – Sample SEMPart (Confirmatory Analysis and Path Analysis)

The following questions were formulated in order to test H1 and H2, which stated the presence of a positive relationship between the intention to make the purchasing decision and the advertisements on SM platforms in addition to celebrity or blogger recommendations about products through SM.

Q1: Are ads and bloggers related to FCP, BAP and BEP?

The results from the path analyses predicted the three purchasing dependent variables (FCP, BAP and BEP) from the main independent variables (advertisements and bloggers) before accounting for any control variables. These have been presented in table-6.

Table 6. Coefficient and standard errors for the first path

	FCP		BAP		BEP	
	β	SE	β	SE	β	SE
Ads	.96***	.14	.027	.07	.35***	.09
Bloggers	.34***	.039	1.02***	.06	.75***	.05

N=524 (For all three dependent variables)

*p<.05; weighted; two-tailed tests

**p<.01; weighted; two-tailed tests

***p<.001; weighted; two-tailed tests

A path model was tested using Stata Version 14. The model demonstrated that bloggers were significantly and positively associated with all dependent variables. When bloggers increase by one point, the dependent variables were predicted to be increased by 0.34 (FCP), 1.02 (BAP) and 0.75 (BEP). Additionally, the advertisements were significantly and positively associated with FCP and BEP. For every point increase in the advertisement variable, the dependent variables were predicted to be increased by 0.96 (FCP) and 0.35 (BEP). However, advertisements were seen to not be significantly associated with BAP. The first path model fit was acceptable as shown in figure 6 (CFI = .932, RMSEA = .077, 95% CI = 0.071, 0.084, p = .001, p < .001). The question formulated below was used to test H3, which suggested that there was a positive relationship between the effects of consumer's age on purchase decision. It is based on SM celebrities' recommendation that influences purchasing decision, after being controlled by demographic variables (control variables).

Figure 6. Standardized loadings, means and errors for first path model

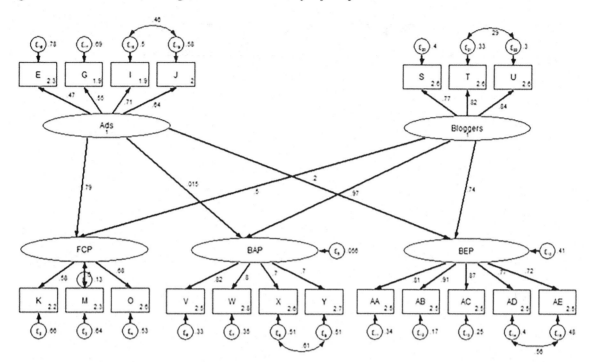

Q2: Are ads and bloggers related to FCP, BAP and BEP after controlling for number of SM platforms, hours spending in SM, number of bloggers you follow, age, gender, education, occupation, income, and city?

Other characteristics that may be associated with FCP, BAP, BEP, advertisements and bloggers are control variables in the second path, as shown in table-7.

Even when controlling variables, advertisements and bloggers are still significantly associated with FCP, ($\beta = .99$ and .33, respectively). It was seen that one-point increases in advertisements and bloggers were associated with values of 0.99 (FCP) and 0.33 (FCP) respectively. The study found that only one of the control variables was associated with FCP. Additionally, it was found that age showed a statistically significant association with FCP ($\beta = -.09$), whereby, FCP is predicted to decrease by -0.09 for increases in the categories of every year. Additionally, the association between advertisements, bloggers and BAP remained as the first path analysis. It was seen that only bloggers showed a statistically significant association with BAP, ($\beta = 1$), whereby one-point increases in bloggers were associated with one-point increases in BAP). Out of the control variables, gender and city were seen to be associated with BAP. It was also found that females showed a statistically more significant association with BAP than males, as represented by 0.16 ($\beta = .16$). Furthermore, Jeddah was found to score higher than Khobar, by 0.12 ($\beta = -.12$) on FCB and BAP. The second path model fit was acceptable as shown in figure 7, (CFI = .91, RMSEA = .06, 95% CI = 0.058, 0.068, p = .001, p < .001).

Table 7. Coefficient and standard errors for the second path

	FCP		BAP		BEP	
	β	SE	β	SE	β	SE
Ads	.99***	(.14)	.05	(.067)	.35***	(.09)
Bloggers	.33***	(.04)	1***	(.06)	.74***	(.05)
Hours	-.06	(.04)	-.06	(.04)	.004	(.05)
NBloggers	.045	(.041)	-.03	(.04)	-.08	(.05)
Age	-.09*	(.04)	.022	(.04)	.05	(.04)
Gender	.10	(.06)	.16*	(.06)	.03	(.07)
Education	-.03	(.033)	-.05	(.04)	-.06	(.04)
Occupation	-.003	(.034)	-.016	(.04)	.002	(.04)
Income	.016	(.035)	-.023	(.037)	.01	(.04)
NSocial	-.0002	(.036)	-.05	(.04)	.04	(.04)
City	-.12*	(.05)	-.12*	(.06)	.001	(.06)

N=524 (For all three dependent variables)

*p<.05; weighted; two-tailed tests

**p<.01; weighted; two-tailed tests

***p<.001; weighted; two-tailed tests

Q3: Does age mediate the relationship between bloggers and FCP, BAP and BEP after controlling for advertisements, number of SM platforms, hours spending in SM, number of bloggers you follow, age, gender, education, occupation, income, and city?

As seen from table-8, the results indicated that age did not mediate the relationship between bloggers and FCP, BAP and BEP (β =.004, -.001 and -.002, respectively). Additionally, the results in figure 8 showed that the other variables were similar to those seen in the previous path model, meaning that there was no significant change. The third path model fit was seen to be acceptable (CFI = .87, RMSEA = .077, 95% CI = 0.072, 0.081, p = .001, p < .001).

Figure 7. Standardized loadings, means and errors for second path model

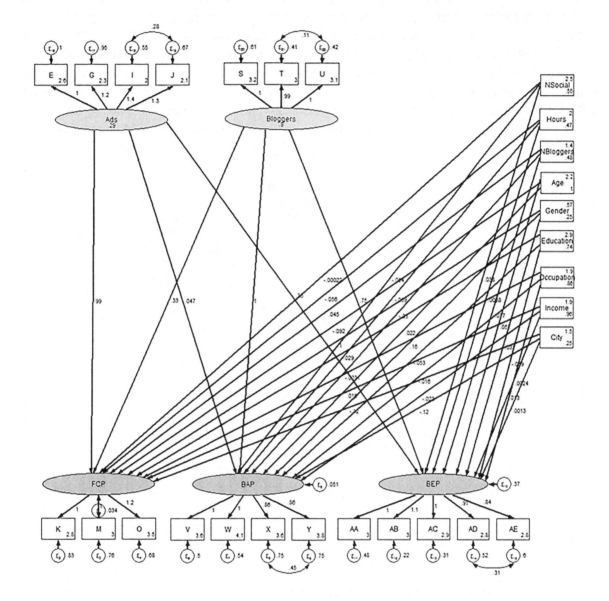

DISCUSSION

The findings suggested that Instagram and Snapchat are important SM platforms that motivate consumers to undertake the purchasing decision. Primary analysis was started where the first dimension, or SM advertisements, were considered as a one-factor model, thereby resulting in a poor fit. Following this, a little modification was run on the model by estimating structural equation modelling and the resulted model showed a good fit and thereby supported H1. This result was found to be consistent with the results obtained by Ahmed and Leo (2014), where it was seen that 61% of respondents considered advertising about Asia Airlines on SM platforms to be persuasive in terms of influencing them to buy tickets and

55% considered the overall impact of advertising, pricing and online accessibility to be influential in this regard. It was further seen that the second dimension, or 'bloggers and celebrities' recommendations on SM' was considered as a one-factor model, which resulted in a perfect fit and supported H2. These results were in line with a recent study by Djafarova and Rushworth (2017) which highlighted the positive role of Instagram celebrities on the purchasing decision of young female users. Additionally, advertisements which were significantly associated with followers' comments and online reviews by bloggers positively influenced a consumer's purchasing decision. These results are similar to those obtained by Bolton et al. (2013), which highlighted how the Y generation was more easily influenced by SM content.

Table 8. Coefficient and standard errors for the third path

	FCP		BAP		BEP	
	β	SE	β	SE	β	SE
Ads	.99***	(.13)	.05	(.07)	.35***	(.09)
Bloggers	.33***	(.04)	1	(.06)	.75***	(.05)
Hours	-.06	(.04)	-.06	(.04)	.003	(.05)
NBloggers	.04	(.04)	-.03	(.04)	-.08	(.05)
Age	-.09	(.04)	.03	(.04)	.06	(.04)
Gender	.1	(.06)	.15*	(.06)	.03	(.07)
Education	-.03	(.03)	-.05	(.04)	-.06	(.04)
Occupation	-.003	(.03)	-.02	(.04)	.002	(.04)
Income	.02	(.04)	-.02	(.04)	.01	(.04)
NSocial	-.0002	(.04)	-.05	(.04)	.04	(.05)
City	-.12	(.05)	-.12*	(.06)	.001	(.07)
Age Mediated Bloggers	.004	(.005)	-.001	(.002)	-.002	(.003)

N=524 (For all three dependent variables)

*p<.05; weighted; two-tailed tests

**p<.01; weighted; two-tailed tests

***p<.001; weighted; two-tailed tests

Figure 8. Standardized loadings, means and errors for third path model

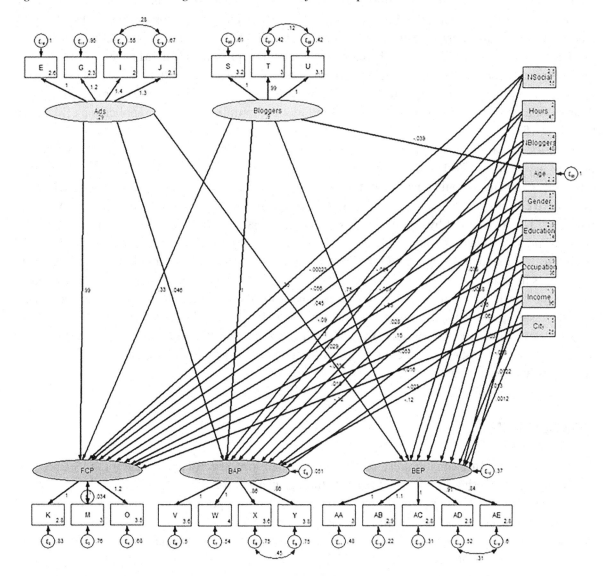

It was additionally seen that participants from Jeddah were more easily influenced by bloggers' appearance on SM platforms and chose to purchase products that had featured on their posts or been used by them. This may be justified by the greater openness of the residents towards market updates, a finding that supports the theory of consumers' authentication (Young, 2017). This is in line with a study by Makki and Chang (2015), which found that Saudi females greatly prefer SM channels such as Instagram. These findings supported H3. The involvement with social media enables active engagement between organizations and their customers via online two-way communication. A similar study conducted by Garrido-Moreno et al. (2018) analyzed the impact of social media platforms on level of engagement of the consumers with the prosthetic manufacturers. The results were somewhat similar to the present study as it depicted the significance of social media users and organizations across industries that are actively connected on SM.

Through these results, it was seen that satisfaction with mobile purchasing is an essential part of influencing consumer purchasing decision. This satisfaction significantly impacts the WOM shopping recommendations made by experienced shoppers, as highlighted by in a previous study (San-Martín, Prodanova & Lopez Catalan, 2016). Therefore, smartphones applications and SM pages should be made mobile-friendly and cater to user expectations to increase user satisfaction with mobile purchasing (Anil, Jay & Tingting, 2015). Therefore, it is essential for businesses in Saudi Arabia to completely revamp their mobile purchasing facilities through creating mobile-optimized sites and applications (Makki & Chang, 2015).

Additionally, a study highlighted that psychological or social benefits needed to be incorporated in order to have a more effective long-term strategy for relationship marketing (Song & Yoo, 2016). Additionally, companies should be aware of the power that dissatisfied customers can exert through social networks if customer engagement is not managed properly (Boon-Long & Wongsurawat, 2015). Although Instagram is not preferred by companies, it could be a valuable tool in "talking" about sustainability issues using appropriate and interesting pictures (Dovleac, 2015). Furthermore, Snapchat could be used as an effective marketing tool in eWOM, albeit at a lesser level than that afforded by Instagram, due to differences in photo-saving features. In the similar context, Lisichkova and Othman (2017) investigated the impact of influencers on the online purchase intentions of the consumers. These results are consistent with the results proposed in the present study. Claesson and Tägt Ljungberg (2018) applied the perspectives of social influence and influencer marketing to gain an understanding of how young consumers are engaged on the Instagram. Therefore, it can be stated that social influence is perceived to engage customers in an online context.

CONCLUSION

This study has aimed to evaluate the effectiveness of SM platforms, specifically Instagram and Snapchat, in impacting the purchasing decisions of SM users, through using a structural equation modelling approach. A positive influence of SM platforms was seen on impacting the purchasing decisions of young Saudi users. Instagram and Snapchat were found to be particularly effective in drawing attention from marketers and consumers for revolutionizing digital marketing in this era. Additionally, the study highlighted the significance of WOM generation in pushing consumers to evaluate products for providing provide feedback to companies. Whether ads were directly posted on Instagram and Snapchat by companies, or products were recommended by celebrities and bloggers, WOM generated under these posts was found to be extremely attractive in motivating purchasing decisions. Since visual marketing greatly influences the Y generation's purchasing decision, social marketing should be focused on developing applications that utilize this tool. However, this study had few limitations, as it did not clarify the impact of consumer's usage for the two platforms on their purchase decisions. Furthermore, the sample size was restricted due to data unavailability and complications in procuring samples from other regions within Saudi Arabia. Moreover, the model presented in the study has not referred to a specific consumer behavior; therefore, future studies need to incorporate larger sample sizes from Saudi Arabia and /or other regions of the world to evaluate the cross-cultural effect and variation in consumer behaviors.

CONFLICT OF INTEREST

The research has no conflict of interest and is not funded through any source.

ACKNOWLEDGMENT

The authors are very thankful to all the associated personnel in any reference that contributed in/for the purpose of this research.

REFERENCES

Bolton, R. N., Parasuraman, A., Hoefnagels, A., Migchels, N., Kabadayi, S., Gruber, T., ... Solnet, D. (2013). Understanding Generation Y and their use of social media: A review and research agenda. *Journal of Service Management*, *24*(3), 245–267. doi:10.1108/09564231311326987

Boon-Long, S., & Wongsurawat, W. (2015). Social media marketing evaluation using social network comments as an indicator for identifying consumer purchasing decision effectiveness. *Journal of Direct, Data and Digital Marketing Practice*, *17*(2), 130–149. doi:10.1057/dddmp.2015.51

Boulianne, S. (2015). Social media use and participation: A meta-analysis of current research. *Information Communication and Society*, *18*(5), 524–538. doi:10.1080/1369118X.2015.1008542

Cao, P., Meister, S., & Klante, O. (2014). How social media influence apparel purchasing behavior. *Marketing Review St. Gallen*, *31*(6), 77–86. doi:10.136511621-014-0427-y

Claesson, A., & Tägt Ljungberg, N. (2018). Consumer Engagement on Instagram: Viewed through the perspectives of social influence and influencer marketing. Lund University.

Cummins, S. W., Peltier, J. A., Schibrowsky, J., & Nill, A. (2014). Consumer behavior in the online context. *Journal of Research in Interactive Marketing*, *8*(3), 169–202. doi:10.1108/JRIM-04-2013-0019

Djafarova, E., & Rushworth, C. (2017). Exploring the credibility of online celebrities' Instagram profiles in influencing the purchase decisions of young female users. *Computers in Human Behavior*, *68*, 1–7. doi:10.1016/j.chb.2016.11.009

Dovleac, L. (2015). The role of new communication technologies in companies' sustainability. *Bulletin of the Transilvania University of Brasov Economic Sciences Series V*, *8*(1), 33.

Fu, J. R., & Chen, J. H. (2012). An investigation of factors that influence blog advertising effectiveness. *International Journal of Electronic Business Management*, *10*(3), 194.

Garrido-Moreno, A., Lockett, N., & García-Morales, V. (2018). Social media use and customer engagement. In Encyclopedia of Information Science and Technology (4th ed., pp. 5775–5785). Hershey, PA: IGI Global. doi:10.4018/978-1-5225-2255-3.ch502

Gefen, D., Straub, D., & Boudreau, M. C. (2000). Structural equation modeling and regression: Guidelines for research practice. *Communications of the Association for Information Systems*, *4*(1), 7.

Glucksman, M. (2017). The rise of social media influencer marketing on lifestyle branding: A case study of Lucie Fink. *Elon Journal of Undergraduate Research in Communications*, 8(2), 77–87.

Gvili, Y., & Levy, S. (2018). Consumer engagement with eWOM on social media: The role of social capital. *Online Information Review*, 42(4), 482–505. doi:10.1108/OIR-05-2017-0158

Hui-Ye Chiu, T., Chen, C. C., Joung, Y. J., & Chen, S. (2014). A study of blog networks to determine online social network properties from the tie strength perspective. *Online Information Review*, 38(3), 381–398. doi:10.1108/OIR-01-2013-0022

Kandampully, J., Zhang, T., & Bilgihan, A. (2015). Customer loyalty: A review and future directions with a special focus on the hospitality industry. *International Journal of Contemporary Hospitality Management*, 27(3), 379–414. doi:10.1108/IJCHM-03-2014-0151

Kowalczyk, C. M., & Pounders, K. R. (2016). Transforming celebrities through social media: The role of authenticity and emotional attachment. *Journal of Product and Brand Management*, 25(4), 345–356. doi:10.1108/JPBM-09-2015-0969

Lim, Y. J. (2017). Decision to use either Snapchat or Instagram for Most Powerful Celebrities. *Research Journal of the Institute for Public Relations*, 3(2), 1–16.

Lisichkova, N., & Othman, Z. (2017). The impact of influencers on online purchase intent. Digitala Vetenskapliga Arkivet.

López, M., & Sicilia, M. (2013). How WOM marketing contributes to new product adoption: Testing competitive communication strategies. *European Journal of Marketing*, 47(7), 1089–1114. doi:10.1108/03090561311324228

Loureiro, S. M. C., & Sarmento, E. M. (2018). *The role of word-of-mouth and celebrity endorsement in online consumer-brand relationship: the context of Instagram*. Academic Press.

Makki, E., & Chang, L. C. (2015). Understanding the effects of social media and mobile usage on e-commerce: An exploratory study in Saudi Arabia. *International Management Review*, 11(2), 98.

Mir, A.A., (2014). Effects of pre-purchase search motivation on user attitudes toward online social network advertising: A case of university students. *Journal of Competitiveness*, 6(2).

Pihlaja, J., Saarijärvi, H., Spence, M. T., & Yrjölä, M. (2017). From Electronic WOM to Social eWOM: Bridging the Trust Deficit. *Journal of Marketing Theory and Practice*, 25(4), 340–356. doi:10.1080/10696679.2017.1345593

Raithel, P. (2018). *The impact of consumers 'actual behaviour on social media on their purchase behaviour* [Doctoral dissertation]. Dublin Business School.

Sakkthivel, A. M., & Sriram, B. (2015). Influence of Social Network Websites over Women Consumers from Islamic Religion: A Structural Equation Modelling Approach. *Journal of Internet Banking and Commerce*, 20(2).

San-Martín, S., Prodanova, J., & Lopez Catalan, B. (2016). What makes services customers say "buy it with a mobile phone"? *Journal of Services Marketing*, 30(6), 601–614. doi:10.1108/JSM-02-2015-0081

Saunders, M. N. (2011). *Research methods for business students (5th ed.)*. Pearson Education India.

Schneider Hahn, I., Scherer, F. L., Basso, K., & Brachak dos Santos, M. (2016). Consumer trust in and emotional response to advertisements on social media and their influence on brand evaluation. *BBR-Brazilian Business Review, 13*, 4.

Shin, D., Song, J. H., & Biswas, A. (2014). Electronic word-of-mouth (eWOM) generation in new media platforms: The role of regulatory focus and collective dissonance. *Marketing Letters, 25*(2), 153–165. doi:10.100711002-013-9248-z

Siddique, R. (2017). Effect of digital media on consumer purchasing decision. *Science Business, 11*(4), 803-829.

Song, S., & Yoo, M. (2016). The role of social media during the pre-purchasing stage. *Journal of Hospitality and Tourism Technology, 7*(1), 84–99. doi:10.1108/JHTT-11-2014-0067

Straker, K., & Wrigley, C. (2016). Emotionally engaging customers in the digital age: The case study of "Burberry love". *Journal of Fashion Marketing and Management, 20*(3), 276–299. doi:10.1108/JFMM-10-2015-0077

Teng, S., Khong, K. W., Chong, A. Y. L., & Lin, B. (2017). Persuasive electronic word-of-mouth messages in social media. *Journal of Computer Information Systems, 57*(1), 76–88. doi:10.1080/08874417.2016.1181501

Tien, D. H., Rivas, A. A. A., & Liao, Y. K. (2018). *Examining the influence of customer-to-customer electronic word-of-mouth on purchase intention in social networking sites. Asia Pacific Management Review*.

Ting, H., de Run, E. C., & Liew, S. L. (2016). Intention to use Instagram by generation cohorts: The perspective of developing markets. *Global Business and Management Research, 8*(1), 43.

van Asperen, M., de Rooij, P., & Dijkmans, C. (2018). Engagement-based loyalty: The effects of social media engagement on customer loyalty in the travel industry. *International Journal of Hospitality & Tourism Administration, 19*(1), 78–94. doi:10.1080/15256480.2017.1305313

Van Deursen, A. J., Bolle, C. L., Hegner, S. M., & Kommers, P. A. (2015). Modeling habitual and addictive smartphone behavior: The role of smartphone usage types, emotional intelligence, social stress, self-regulation, age, and gender. *Computers in Human Behavior, 45*, 411–420. doi:10.1016/j.chb.2014.12.039

Woo, J., Ahn, J., Lee, J., & Koo, Y. (2015). Media channels and consumer purchasing decisions. *Industrial Management & Data Systems, 115*(8), 1510–1528. doi:10.1108/IMDS-02-2015-0036

Yasin, A. S., & David, L. G. (2014). An Impact of Advertising and Pricing on Consumers Online Ticket Purchasing. *International Journal of Innovation, Management and Technology, 5*(5), 383.

This research was previously published in the International Journal of Online Marketing (IJOM), 10(1); pages 72-94, copyright year 2020 by IGI Publishing (an imprint of IGI Global).

Chapter 36

Facebook Advertising as a Marketing Tool:
Examining the Influence on Female Cosmetic Purchasing Behaviour

Barween Hikmat Al Kurdi
iD https://orcid.org/0000-0002-7336-381X
The Hashemite University, Jordan

Muhammad Turki Alshurideh
iD https://orcid.org/0000-0002-7336-381X
The University of Jordan, Jordan & University of Sharjah, UAE

ABSTRACT

Social media platforms are widely used these days for the advertising and marketing of products. Facebook is considered one of the main social media platforms used by users these days. Currently, there are limited studies investigating the use of Facebook as an advertising communication platform, especially for the purchase of cosmetic products. This study targeted female consumers to ascertain to what extent Facebook advertising influenced their cosmetic buying behaviour through using a set of factors that were selected, namely, advertisement quality, advertisement design, message strength, advertisement repetitiveness, and message content. Smart PLS was used to assess the study model and to test the study's hypotheses. The study found that the main factors affecting consumer behaviour were advertisement quality and advertisement repetitiveness. The paper discusses the study's findings by presenting a set of implications and making recommendations.

DOI: 10.4018/978-1-6684-6287-4.ch036

1. INTRODUCTION

Advertising is known to be one of the major marketing tools because of its significant impact on consumer mindset and behaviour (Al-Dmour & Al-Shraideh, 2008; Alshurideh et al., 2020). Nowadays, the majority of business organizations are using digital marketing sites and social marketing platforms to advertise their products and services (Al Dmour et al., 2014; Alshurideh et al., 2019; Kumar & Singh, 2020). Facebook as a social media site is considered one of the more popular social media platforms used actively by consumers, especially the younger generation (Simoncic et al., 2014; Tufekci, 2012). A study by Niazi et al. (2012) found that consumer behaviour analysis is helpful for advertisers to understand the purchasing trends of consumers in response to different advertising situations.

Scholars such as Ayanwale et al. (2005) and Adelaar et al. (2003) have highlighted that the major aim of any advertiser is to reach potential customers and create an impact on their buying behaviour. To influence consumer behaviour requires focusing on what message is delivered to customers' minds and how that message is delivered. However, as a result of vastly growing markets, Niazi et al. (2012) identify that it is becoming increasingly difficult for companies to differentiate their products or services based on functional attributes such as benefits and performances. Even if a company manages to differentiate, this never lasts long as competitors are able to copy their opposition's products so reducing the differentiation margins. However, the use of Facebook as a communication tool means that cosmetics brands can access consumers on social media, which adds a competitive advantage for these organisations. However, although Facebook is a well-known social media platform, it is currently not used actively to promote fashion brands (Navarro-Beltrá et al., 2020).

As a result, targeting customers through social media platforms has become a trend these days to increase online and mobile shopping. Eventually, online shopping will also become the main source of buying, especially during times of natural crisis, for example, pandemics or flooding. These events often force customers to change their buying behaviour to purchase online rather than visiting stores. Online or eshopping, according to The Portal of Statistics (2018) in the USA, generated about 17.3 billion US dollars using mail order to household sales in 2013. Also, Clement (2020) declared that USA online physical goods sales amounted to more than \$365 billion and was expected to exceed \$600 billion in 2024.

In addition, cosmetic sales are expected to continue to grow in both the USA and in other global markets. The USA market is considered the most valuable personal care and beauty market globally with cosmetic sales revenue estimated to reach approximately 84 billion US dollars in revenue in 2016 (The Statistics Portal, 2018). A large number of consumers, especially the younger generation, are starting to rely on social media sites as a marketing platform to search, evaluate and buy a large variety of products including cosmetic products. For example, it was estimated that social media users spend on average about 257 minutes a month interacting with social media content (Aguilar, 2015). Accordingly, the market value of these social windows have increased greatly, for example, Aguilar (2015) claimed that Instagram is worth more about \$37 billion.

With social media attracting a generation of users actively using this platform to enhance how they feel about themselves and to achieve social and economic goals (Chave, 2017), their consumer responses needs to be investigated. This study sheds more light on a set of Facebook advertisement dimensions that influence cosmetics buying. These dimensions are advertisement quality, advertisement design, advertisement message strength, advertisement repetitiveness and whether the advertisement meets consumer needs.

2. RESEARCH PROBLEM AND IMPORTANCE

This study aims to reveal the effect of Facebook cosmetic advertisements on consumer behaviour and to determine what factors shape their responces to buy the advertised products. These factors are the general quality of the advertisement, advertisement design, strength of the message posted by the advertisement, and advertisement repetitiveness. The goal and objectives of this study are to determine whether these factors arouse customer attention and influence their buying behaviour. Therefore, this research investigated the online behaviour of customers buying cosmetic products as a result of social media advertising. In particular, the study attempted to identify what influenced the cosmetic purchasing behaviour of consumers on social media platforms. The study also attempted to determine the extent to which consumer behaviour contributed to product awareness through social media advertising.

This study target female users as other studies did such as Apriliana (2019) and Agneta (2018). That is because marketers now start preparing special Facebook ads for female users to increase their engagement with well-known females-oriented products such as cosmetics, clothing and gifts (Zhang, Sung, & Lee, 2010).

There have been many previous studies conducted on the effectiveness of determiners that improve and affect the purchasing behaviour of customers using social media (Khorsheed et al., 2020). However, not many studies shed more light on Facebook advertising determinants that influence consumers buying cosmetics. Therefore, this study can contribute tofuture cosmetic advertising research to achieve a more coherent and comprehensive understanding of consumer responses to cosmetic advertising using Facebook. Therefore, it is important to identify a set of determinants or factors to analyze consumer behaviour or responses to cosmetic advertisements. This is important to not only improve and encourage further research on the advertising sector, but also for social media advertising research.

Lack of literature regarding the advertisement characteristics is witnessed especially those increase Facebook ads feasibility and reaction. Quality of advertising is essential to be discussed as confirmed by Horrell et al. (2019) especially the quality of message information, advertisements design and content. It is important to give more research attention to Facebook advertisement design to create and increase the interest in the ads topic as clarified also by Carter-Harris (2016). Additionally, message strength posted through Facebook adverting needs more investigation as declared by Jung, Choo, & Lee (2013), Li & Suh (2015) and Ji, Chen, Tao, & Li (2019) who mentioned that as much as the ads message strength increase supported be message repetition as much as the influence will bring more credibility, emotion, intention ties, and reaction. The Facebook audience is not like other traditional internet audiences. Meeting the target market needs usually starts by giving more attention theoretically to social media ads designing in general and how to meet Facebook audiences' needs in particular. This will lead to motivate the target audience to exert more attention, attitude and behaviours towards both internet advertising and Facebook advertising especially the youth population as declared by Celebi (2015). Bsed on the previous discussion regarding the ad characteristics practically, this study adds to the knowledge an important piece of research, which can be considered as a milestone in social media platform advertisement designing especially those designed and delivered using the Facebook platform (Ramo & Prochaska, 2012).

3. LITERATURE REVIEW

This section discusses the main constructs of the study, namely, advertisement quality, advertisement message strength, consumer needs met by the advertisement, advertisement repetitiveness and advertisement design. Each of these variables are discussed and the extent to which they support each of the study's hypotheses.

Essentially, there is a need to discuss the development and evolution of advertisements using social media as a medium. With the research done by Pelling and White (2009), it was found that social media has become the most popular communication channel for younger Internet users. With this information, there is no doubt that marketers are now using social media as their main platform for advertising, to capture a larger target market and their younger audience. Not only is social media the most effective communication platform, but it is also the most effective for advertising currently (Alshurideh et al., 2019; Al Kurdi et al., 2020). The IAB (2009) notes that social media advertising is unique, as it allows consumers to scan advertisements selectively, and share them with their connections online. Because the younger generation accesses social media for all events and as their main source of information, new opportunities arise to build customer relationships with these virtual advertising platforms (Chu, 2011; Alshurideh et al., 2017).

Many companies use social media in advertising because of the advantages it has over traditional platforms, in which companies suffer because of a myriad of issues like cost, lack of time, difficulties in finding their appropriate target audience as well aslimited markets and customer information available. With social media, however, companies can advertise using the Internet, smartphones and social networking websites. These communication channels allow companies to reach their appropriate target market efficiently and in a more precise manner as well as customize their products to fit their customer needs in their advertising messages. This information helps to reduce advertising and promotion costs as well as provide a quick response to changes in the market place because of the easy and quick processing and accessing of customer information and needs. Companies collect the data from the cookies to run marketing campaigns aimed at a very specific market segment including the product group, geolocation, search term and their demographics.

As a result, during the twentieth century, social media has become more than just a platform for posting pictures and catching up with friends, consumers are also able to actively engage with brands as a part of their purchasing decision-making and experience (Elmerraji, 2015). Owing to the competitiveness of this new platform and format, there is a significant focus on the quality of the advertisement. There have also been many studies examining consumer behaviour based on this issue, as consumers are more likely to rely on the website's content quality as a source of information when they have favorable attitudes toward the site (Poh & Adam, 2002; Alshurideh et al., 2019).

The most effective social media tool are social networking sites likeFacebook, which allow companies to enhance and facilitate information exchange in the market place and trigger high expectations from brands bought and held by consumers (Awata, 2010; Alshurideh et al., 2019). Facebook, for example, has been used to promote brand loyalty among six beauty brands, namely, Estee Lauder, MAC Cosmetics, Clinique, L'Oreal, Maybelline and CoverGirl. The six brands were chosen because of their performance on both the annual loyalty leaders list of 2011 and the beauty digital index in 2011 (Shen & Bissell, 2013; Klimisch, 2013). There were also many studies examining consumer behaviour in accordance with such social media's development, as consumers relied on the website's content, system design and interactivity as well as information availability as sources of information quality when they used social sites to purchase products (Poh & Adam 2002; Alshurideh et al., 2019; Salloum et al., 2020; Al Kurdi et al., 2020).

3.1 Social Media Advertising Quality

As the number of social media users is growing rapidly, organisations have realized that they should use and utilize social media to reach customers professionally, especially when such a medium is used by millions daily (Parsons, 2013). The quality of the advertisements is an important factor that influences consumer behaviour, especially women and the cosmetics field. This is because it is globally known that women pay more attention to detail than men do and tend to respond more favorably to the advertised object than males would (Darley & Smith, 1995). For the study, advertisement quality is considered as a variable, however, for Hsieh and Chen (2011), it seems important that an advertisement is simplistic for it to be noticed by customers. Although a simplistic advertisement will stick in consumer minds, advertisements must also be attention-grabbing, and unique or creative (Leavens & Racine, 2009). Accordingly, the advertisement should include a clear message for the audience not only to capture their attention or to appeal to them, but there is also a need to know what the product is and why they should buy it. This will to motivate them to buy and repeat buying (Haugtvedt et al., 1992; Balasubramanian, 1994; Schünemann et al., 2003; Alshurideh, 2019). Another characteristic for the quality of the advertisement is targeting audiences' emotions (Olney et al., 1991). As advertisements have the power to make people happy or comforted, the ultimate goal for the advertiser is to create a sense of happiness, which the customer can sense, feel and enact (Schmitt, 2000).

Considering that cosmetics are considered a quality product, most women expect, especially for a high-end brand, that the advertisement not only fits the brand's image (Bruhn et al., 2012) but contributes to their personalities (Lin, 2010). Although quality is highly-appreciated by most consumers, women have a keen eye for quality, and will not be convinced of purchasing an item if its quality does not hold their attention (Jones, 1997; Al-Dmour et al., 2014 a, b). Based on the quality aspect, the effect of advertisement quality can be deduced as:

H1: There is a significant effect of advertisement quality on consumer purchasing behaviour through using Facebook as a social media site.

3.2 Strength of the Advertisement Message

Although advertising is considered to be one of the competitive advantages that a company might possess, it is also an integrated marketing tool that helps a company achieve success in selling products/ services as well as motivating and educating consumers (Greene et al., 1994; Al-Dmour & Al-Shraideh, 2008). As a consequence, a company should use a strong, persuasive and creative message to deliver its image to targeted customers (Alshurideh et al., 2017). In addition, for the message to have an impact on consumers, the company will need to determine the message's objectives using product knowledge, benefits and emotions as the strongest drawpoints to attract customers (Derks et al., 2008; Alshurideh, 2010; 2016; 2017; 2019). These objectives also enhance a brand's image, aid in its recognition and recall, and help create brand differentiation in consumer minds (Kohli et al., 2007; Al Kurdi et al., 2020).

When the message portrays the consumer's thoughts and acknowledges them individually, they are immediately drawn to it. In the case of cosmetics, it is highly-regarded and appreciated when the advertisement portrays an image that women see as suitable (MacKay & Covell, 1997). In this way, the image allows them to feel that although they do not particularly need this product, it gives them many benefits, so they are not only willing but also almost obligated to buy the product (Alshurideh, 2019). Hence, the message in the advertisement should be very personal to women and effectively portray the brand's personality. Based on these needs, the effect of message strength in the advertisement can be deduced as:

H2: There is a significant effect of the advertisment's message strength on consumer purchasing behaviour through using Facebook as a social media site.

3.3 Advertisement Meets Customers' Needs (Customized Advertising)

One of the main objectives a company sets is satisfying customer needs and wants (Alshurideh et al., 2012; Alshurideh, 2014; Al-dweeri et al., 2017). When creating advertisements, it is consumer needs and wants that the company must think about, as these needs will lead to better and more positive reactions from the customers. For example, social media enables companies to reach a larger sector of their target markets using better interaction means to understand customers better and influence their needs (Mangold & Faulds, 2009). Innovation in technology has created more opportunities for consumers to gather large amounts of information through the Internet while consuming a plethora of digital entertainment choices (Bright & Daugherty, 2012). In this sense, when an organisation uses customization in advertisements, it becomes more effective in a way that it makes customers feel important, even if they do not currently have this need. This 'control revolution' that allows consumers to complete their interaction with the companies, represents a vast population of new consumers, showcases their ability to process information in media environments, which is 'fundamentally different from their predecessors' (Prensky, 2001, p. 1). Based on these aspects, the effect of consumer needs being met by the advertisement can be deduced as:

H3: There is a significant effect of advertisements meeting consumer needs based on their purchasing behaviour through using Facebook as a social media site.

3.4 Repetitiveness of the Advertisement

Repetition in advertisements is most certainly one of the strongest communication tools companies can use to help keep their brands in their current and potential customers' minds when purchasing (Kent & Allen, 1994; Ghodeswar, 2008). Increasing message exposures through repeated advertising and message processing time were expected to alter the content of message in the recipients' thoughts (Anand & Sternthal, 1990; Alshurideh, 2019). More specifically, in response to initial message exposures, people would attempt to learn the content of the message and most of their thoughts would be consistent with the communication advocacy (Anand & Sternthal, 1990). The more consumers are exposed to a message, the most likely they will remember it. This usually happens when communication and advertising data are made easily visible and are already accessible with less effort to be received by viewers (Boyd, 2008). However, if the advertisement is repeated too often without being different in some aspects, customers will become accustomed to it and begin to tune out of the advertisement. Therefore, the company must use repetition in more creative ways, repeating the same message with different imagery or develop creative repetition through various types of media with which the customer is familiar, so that they can distinguish the differences, perceive quality and no longer feel bored (Campbell & Keller, 2003; Moorthy & Hawkins, 2005; Ghodeswar, 2008). Based on these aspects, the effect of advertisement repetitiveness can be deduced as:

H4: There is a significant effect of advertisement repetitiveness on consumer purchasing behaviour through using Facebook as a social media site.

3.5 Design of the Advertisement

One of the most influential factors that affect the attention of customers is the advertisement design (Lee & Benbasat, 2003). This is due to the idea that it provides the first impression of the product in customers' minds; whether it makes the customer look twice or skip the advertisement altogether. In the design, companies try to make the advertisement imaginative, using colors and stunning imagery to capture the audience's attention (Scarles, 2004). Of course, for a more successful advertisement, the company must use an innovative design in which the advertisement contains a memorable slogan that customers retain in their minds about the product during the purchase (Robinson et al., 2007). The main element of the advertisement should be providing the most important information about the product. The company should also use the space wisely, use contrasting colours and different font sizes (Klimisch, 2014). The advertisement design, however, should be simple and eye-catching, if there are too many colours and pictures, the message is usually lost owing to the excessive contrast (Rosen & Purinton, 2004). In addition, the advertisements' designs should be considered from the viewers' perspectives as their opinions are critical (Al-Dmour et al., 2014). Based on these aspects, the effect of advertisement design can be deduced as:

H5: There is a significant effect of the advertisement design on consumer purchasing behaviour through using Facebook as a social media site.

4. STUDY MODEL

The research model has been built based on studying a set of variables that affect consumer purchasing behaviour through social media site interaction. These variables were advertisement quality, advertisement design, message strength, message repetitiveness and whether it met consumer needs. The study's model, as seen in Figure 1, illustrates the relationship between the study's variables.

5. STUDY HYPOTHESES

Based on the study's model illustrated in Figure 1, the study's hypotheses can be summarized as:

H1: There is a significant effect of advertisement quality on consumer purchasing behaviour through using Facebook as a social media site.
H2: There is a significant effect of advertisement message strength on consumer purchasing behaviour through using Facebook as a social media site.

H3: There is a significant effect of advertisements meeting consumer needs based on their purchasing behaviour through using Facebook as a social media site.

H4: There is a significant effect of advertisement repetitiveness on consumer purchasing behaviour through using Facebook as a social media site.

H5: There is a significant effect of advertisement design on consumer purchasing behaviour through using Facebook as a social media site.

Figure 1. Study model

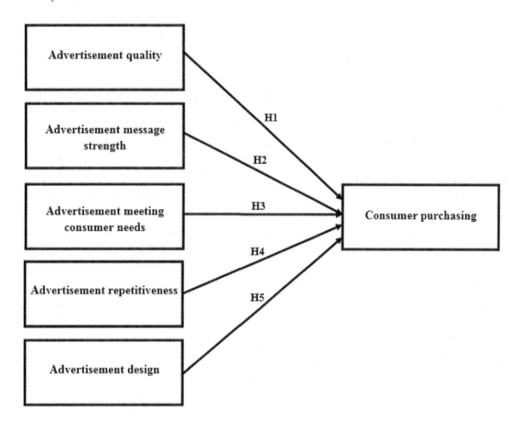

6. METHODOLOGY AND DATA COLLECTION TOOLS

The study's data was collected based on two types of sources, namely, primary and secondary data. The primary data was collected by designing a special survey, which consisted of 31 questions. The secondary data was sourced by previewing a large number of previous studies that were relevant to online and social media advertising. These studies were used to develop the study's model and prepare the survey items. The study's population were customers who bought cosmetic products via the Facebook platform in Jordan. A random sample of 515 consumers was targeted to complete the study's survey. The study's response rate was 75% as 387 surveys were completed by the study's sample. Seventeen questionnaires were invalid and 360 valid surveys were used for the data analysis.

The study constructs were bulit based on previous litreture. Table 1 below shows were the mian construct came from.

Table 1. Vareibles - refernces table

No.	Study constructs	References
1.	Advertisement quality	(Schwarz & Abrams, 2009)
2.	Advertisement message strength	(Loda & Coleman, 2005)
3.	Advertisement meets consumer needs (Customized advertising)	(Dehghani, 2013)
4.	Advertisement repetitiveness	(Kievik, Giebels, & Gutteling, 2020)
5.	Advertisement design	(Visser, Gattol, & Helm, 2015)

A pilot study was conducted for measuring the reliability of the questionnaire items. There was random selection of 40 customers out of the determined population for this pilot study. Taking into consideration 10% of the analysis' total sample size, 400 customers was set as the sample size and for this, there was great emphasis on the research guidelines. For evaluating the pilot study outcomes, there was utilization of Cronbach's alpha test for internal reliability via IBM SPSS Statistics ver. 23, which helped in yielding acceptable conclusions for the measurement items. By considering the stated trend of researches on social science, 0.70 reliability coefficient is considered as acceptable (Nunnally & Bernstein, 1978). Table 2 presents the Cronbach's alpha values in terms of the subsequent 7 measurement scales.

Table 2. Cronbach's Alpha values for the pilot study (Cronbach's Alpha ≥ 0.70)

No.	Study constructs	Cronbach's Alpha
6.	Advertisement quality	0.793
7.	Advertisement message strength	0.834
8.	Advertisement meets consumer needs (Customized advertising)	0.864
9.	Advertisement repetitiveness	0.853
10.	Advertisement design	0.799
11.	Consumer purchasing	0.816

Table 3. Study construct's reliability and numbers of items used

No.	Study constructs	Number of items	Cronbach's Alpha
12.	Advertisement quality	5	0.832
13.	Advertisement message strength	5	0.722
14.	Advertisement meets consumer needs (Customized advertising)	5	0.788
15.	Advertisement repetitiveness	5	0.770
16.	Advertisement design	6	0.891
17.	Consumer purchasing	5	0.727

To add more, to ascertain to what degree the study participants agreed or disagreed with the survey items, a Likert scale was used. Table 3 illustrates the number of items used and provides an overview of each study construct's reliability.

7. DATA DESCRIPTIVE ANALYSES

This section provides an overview of the study sample's demographic distribution, comments on the respondents buying behaviour and their use of cosmetics products. Regarding the age variable, the highest percentage of participants using Facebook were females in the age category of 20 to 40 years, which represented about 73% of the total sample size. Regarding the occupation variable, the highest percentage was for students (28%), then private sector jobs (25.5%) followed by governmental jobs (24.8%). However, the lowest occupation variable was for freelancer jobs (5.7%). Regarding the educational level, the highest percentage was for Bachelor degree holders (45.2%), then Diploma holders with 23.6%. In addition, the marital status for the study sample was single females with 56.7% and married females with 40.8%. Also, it was found that the distribution of the study's participants for the makeup variable was highest for the "yes" category, who used these products frequently (76.4%), while the lowest percentage was for the "no" category (3.8%), who used the products infrequently. Twenty percent of the study's sample reported that they used makeup for specific situations and for important events such as weddings and birthday parties Concerning the factors that urged customers to buy cosmetics products, it was found that there were a set of reasons such as liking the product (32.5%), the product's price and products from well-known brands (10%), how cosmetic products were advertised (9%), package appeal and friend's recommendations (3%). However, customers who cared about the majority of reasons and considered all reasons when buying cosmetic products was about 34% of the total study sample. Regarding the place where the study sample purchased cosmetic products, the study found that about 52% bought these products from cosmetics shops, 25% from mall shops, 14% from pharmacies and only about 8% used online shopping platforms.

8. ANALYSIS AND HYPOTHESES TESTING

8.1 Partial Least Square Analysis Methodology

8.1.1 Assessment of the Measurement Model (Outer Model)

The software named Smart PLS was used by Ringle, Wende and Will (2005), seems to be very operative for the Partial Least Squares-Structural Equation Modeling (PLS-SEM)(Alshurideh, Salloum, Al Kurdi, & Al-Emran, 2019)). This study evaluates PLS-SEM by testing it on some measurement and structural models (Alshurideh, Al Kurdi, & Salloum, 2019). The relation of indicators and latent constructs to themselves refers to the measurement model (outer model) and structural model, respectively. SEM-PLS was adopted to measure the proposed model (Anderson & Gerbing, 1988) along with the highest probability method. Several measurements were taken including Factor Loadings, Average Variance Extracted and Composite Reliability to get results about reliability and convergent validity. Factors loadings are used to assess the parameters like weight and correlation value of each questionnaire variable as a perceived indicator. However, if higher load value is found, it can benefit the depiction of the factor's dimensionality. The Composite Reliability (CR) is considered to be eligible for measuring reliability. The CR gives value as output by engaging factor loadings in the assembled formula. Average Variance Extracted (AVE) is the average of the variation of values of a certain variable, which also portrays latent construct. Convergence of each factor can be observed using AVE but for this discriminate validity has to be greater than one. Table 4 in the following section gives an overview of the reliability and validity concerns for the study's variables and interrelated items used in the study survey to collect the primary data. The conditions imposed for effective measurement of reliability and convergent validity were met adequately in the results of this study as explained in section 8.1.2 and as shown in Table 4.

8.1.2 Convergent Validity

Factor loadings, variance extracted and reliability (consisting of Cronbach's Alpha and composite reliability) were used as indicators to get an approximate value of convergent validity. If the reliability coefficient and composite reliability (CR) for the constructs collectively surpass the boundary of 0.7, it signifies internal consistency between several measurements of a construct (Hair et al., 1998). Table 4 represents scores of Cronbach Alpha outstripping the adequate value of 0.7 and composite reliabilities lying in the window of 0.715-0.818. Also, the range 0.511-0.715 of average variance extracted (AVE), fulfilled the condition of explaining at least 50% of variance extracted for a given data set underlying the latent construct (Falk & Miller, 1992). Accordingly, the study constructs achieved convergent validity.

Table 4. Convergent validity results assure acceptable values (Factor loading, Cronbach's Alpha, composite reliability >= 0.70 & AVE > 0.5)

Constructs	Items	Factor Loading	Cronbach's Alpha	CR	AVE
Advertisement quality	QOA_1	0.891	0.832	0.715	0.611
	QOA_2	0.763			
	QOA_3	0.709			
	QOA_4	0.852			
	QOA_5	0.757			
Advertisement message strength	SMA_1	0.735	0.722	0.743	0.539
	SMA_2	0.779			
	SMA_3	0.861			
	SMA_4	0.703			
	SMA_5	0.892			
Advertisement meeting consumer needs	AMC_1	0.835	0.788	0.717	0.652
	AMC_2	0.791			
	AMC_3	0.827			
	AMC_4	0.833			
	AMC_5	0.731			

continues on following page

Table 4. Continued

Constructs	Items	Factor Loading	Cronbach's Alpha	CR	AVE
Advertisement repetitiveness	ROA_1	0.743	0.770	0.818	0.715
	ROA_2	0.773			
	ROA_3	0.703			
	ROA_4	0.821			
	ROA_5	0.816			
Advertisement design	DOA_1	0.738	0.891	0.767	0.533
	DOA_2	0.842			
	DOA_3	0.775			
	DOA_4	0.865			
	DOA_5	0.721			
	DOA_6	0.739			
Consumer purchasing	CP_1	0.861	0.727	0.773	0.511
	CP_2	0.792			
	CP_3	0.781			
	CP_4	0.723			
	CP_5	0.851			

8.1.3 Discriminant Validity

Table 4 demonstrates the AVE values as being higher when compared to the squared correlation among the constructs in the measurement model, so the necessary conditions for discriminant validity were fulfilled (Fornell & Larcker, 1981; Hair et al., 1998). If the AVE value exceeded 0.5, it was likely the construct had ended up with a 50% of measurement variance. Discriminate value was used to be calculated by Partial Least Squares (Smart Pls Ver. 3.2.6). Table 4 depicts the results of AVE analysis with data in bold diagonals representing the square root of AVE scores, whereas the data in off-load diagonal demonstrated correlations among the constructs. Table 4 clearly shows that the AVE values were between 0.729-0.859, which was higher than 0.5. This higher value indicated a higher variance of all constructs with the measures of themselves instead of other constructs in the model, which caused the discriminate validity to go up.

Table 5. Fornell-Larcker Scale

	QOA	SMA	AMCN	ROA	DOA	CP
QOA	**0.729**					
SMA	0.309	**0.822**				
AMCN	0.454	0.322	**0.811**			
ROA	0.391	0.577	0.545	**0.815**		
DOA	0.389	0.329	0.273	0.452	**0.859**	
CP	0.476	0.328	0.345	0.477	0.542	**0.779**

The observations of loadings and cross-loadings as shown in Table 5 and 6, denoted that rather than loading measurement items on other conducts, their latent constructs were used. All values are seen satisfactory.

Table 6. Cross-loading results

	QOA	SMA	AMCN	ROA	DOA	CP
QOA_1	**0.891**	0.235	0.216	0.333	0.326	0.437
QOA_2	**0.763**	0.432	0.342	0.521	0.466	0.377
QOA_3	**0.709**	0.444	0.287	0.271	0.455	0.535
QOA_4	**0.852**	0.355	0.376	0.265	0.462	0.434
QOA_5	**0.757**	0.551	0.498	0.374	0.222	0.340
SMA_1	0.287	**0.735**	0.367	0.393	0.364	0.564
SMA_2	0.372	**0.779**	0.259	0.378	0.268	0.277
SMA_3	0.311	**0.861**	0.260	0.288	0.195	0.222
SMA_4	0.235	**0.703**	0.338	0.250	0.274	0.241
SMA_5	0.371	**0.892**	0.509	0.470	0.403	0.331
AMC_1	0.463	0.301	**0.835**	0.388	0.444	0.345
AMC_2	0.372	0.414	**0.791**	0.222	0.377	0.242
AMC_3	0.228	0.519	**0.827**	0.544	0.351	0.239
AMC_4	0.531	0.328	**0.833**	0.416	0.566	0.423
AMC_5	0.382	0.296	**0.731**	0.301	0.488	0.494
ROA_1	0.396	0.294	0.284	**0.743**	0.322	0.322
ROA_2	0.375	0.562	0.223	**0.773**	0.288	0.252
ROA_3	0.247	0.189	0.304	**0.703**	0.192	0.209
ROA_4	0.230	0.436	0.205	**0.821**	0.444	0.334
ROA_5	0.226	0.371	0.241	**0.816**	0.433	0.322
DOA_1	0.345	0.239	0.435	0.239	**0.738**	0.189
DOA_2	0.153	0.165	0.322	0.200	**0.842**	0.122
DOA_3	0.121	0.145	0.244	0.344	**0.775**	0.270
DOA_4	0.154	0.330	0.242	0.253	**0.865**	0.415
DOA_5	0.173	0.339	0.144	0.341	**0.721**	0.266
DOA_6	0.348	0.311	0.372	0.321	**0.739**	0.392
CP_1	0.436	0.222	0.522	0.418	0.220	**0.861**
CP_2	0.355	0.201	0.221	0.210	0.423	**0.792**
CP_3	0.235	0.233	0.442	0.301	0.259	**0.781**
CP_4	0.404	0.265	0.134	0.220	0.342	**0.723**
CP_5	0.311	0.145	0.191	0.226	0.352	**0.851**

8.2. Assessment of Structural Model (Inner Model)

8.2.1 Coefficient of etermination - R^2

The coefficient of determination (R^2 value) measure is commonly used to assess the structural model (Dreheeb, Basir & Fabil, 2016). The model's predictive accuracy is calculated using this coefficient and further calculations lead to squared correlation among a certain endogenous construct's actual and predicted values (Hair et al., 2016). The coefficient can also predict the joined effect of an exogenous latent variable on an endogenous latent variable. The coefficient can be defined as the squared correlation between actual and predicted values of the variables, so this coefficient can also help for determining the endogenous constructs secured by exogenous constructs. Chin (1998) states that the if the value exceeds 0.67, it is considered high, the values between 0.33 to 0.67 are considered direct, and if the value ranges between 0.19 and 0.33, it is considered weak. Also, there is a demonstration of moderate predictive power as the supporting power is 63.6%. According to Table 7, the R^2 values for the consumer purchasing was found to be more than 0.67; and hence, the predictive power of these constructs was considered as high.

Table 7. R^2 of the endogenous latent variables

Constructs	R^2	Results
Consumer purchasing	0.688	High

8.2.2 Test of the Hypotheses - Path Coefficient

A structural equation model using SEM-PLS with a high probability approximation was used to assess the proposed hypothesis and the association among the structural model's theoretical constructs (Alshurideh, Gasaymeh, Ahmed, Alzoubi, & Kurd, 2020; Kurdi, Alshurideh, Salloum, Obeidat, & Al-dweeri, 2020). Table 8 and Figure 2 represent these results, and it is visible that data supported all hypotheses. All exogenous variables were verified in the model (QOA, SMA, AMCN, ROA, DOA and CP). Based on the data analysis, hypotheses H1, H2, H3, H4 and H5 were supported by the empirical data. The results showed that consumer purchasing was significantly influenced by the advertisement quality ($\beta= 0.383$, P<0.001), advertisement message strength ($\beta= 0.034$, P<0.001), advertisement meeting consumer needs ($\beta= -0.117$, P<0.05), advertisement repetitiveness ($\beta= 0.372$, P<0.001), and advertisement design ($\beta= 0.022$, P<0.05), namely, hypothesis H1, H2, H3, H4 and H5, respectively. A summary of the hypotheses testing results is shown in Table 8.

9. RESULTS AND DISCUSSION

This study is important because it determined practically the main factors that affected consumer buying behaviour in the cosmetics field using social media platforms as a way of communicating and advertising. It was found that the most important advertising factor which affected cosmetic buying consumer behaviour using social media tools was the quality of the advertisement, followed by advertisement repetition. The variables related to advertisement design and advertisement message strength had less influence on consumers buying cosmetic products advertised using social media platforms.

Figure 2. Path Coefficient Result (Significant at p** < = 0.01, p* < 0.05)

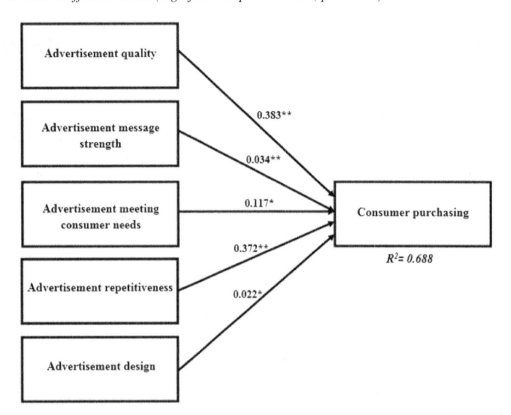

Table 8. Results of structural model (significant at p** < = 0.01, p* < 0.05)

Hyp.	Relationship	Path	*t*-value	*p*-value	Direction	Decision
H1	Advertisement quality -> Consumer purchasing	0.383	27.746	0.000	Positive	Supported**
H2	Advertisment message strength -> Consumer purchasing	0.034	10.356	0.001	Positive	Supported**
H3	Advertisement meeting consumer needs -> Consumer purchasing	0.117	3.326	0.021	Positive	Supported*
H4	Advertisment repetitiveness -> Consumer purchasing	0.372	2.158	0.000	Positive	Supported**
H5	Design of the advertisement -> Consumer purchasing	0.022	1.992	0.036	Positive	Supported*

In general, the study findings came up in the same stream of other studies in the same context. Agneta (2018) studied the effect of Facebook advertising on cosmetics buying and sales by Kenyan women and if such advertising method affects their attitude and belief. The study revealed that Facebook advertising do influence females' customers' attitude, perception, behaviour which in turn affect cosmetics buying and sales. In addition, Kane, Chiru, & Ciuchete (2012) explored how social media (e.g. Facebook) can be used to influence users' perception and buying behaviour of ecological products. The scholars studied five product categories and one of them was eco-beauty and cosmetics products. The study findings denoted that Facebook could be considered as an effective mean to build green attitudes towards consumers' minds and hearts. Additionally, Apriliana (2019) studied the influence of Instagram cosmetics advertising on girls' attitudes and consumptive behaviours in Yogyakarta. The study findings confirmed that using the Instagram platform to advertise cosmetics products do influence females' users' attitudes and purchasing behaviours.

Increasing the buying behaviour towards a specific cosmetic item usually increased because of advertisement type and quality (Al-Dmour & Al-Shraideh, 2008; Alshurideh et al., 2017). This issue has been confirmed by Ampofo (2014), who found that advertising affected cosmetic buying and increased customers purchasing these products. Ampofo (2014), Alshurideh et al. (2014) and Al-Dmour et al. (2014) confirmed that consumers also need to be informed properly about products otherwise the products will not be known and bought by consumers.

The results of the study on the factors that affected social media advertising and how it affected consumer purchasing behaviour toward specific cosmetic items emphasized the importance of advertisement quality and repetition of such advertisements. Customers become more familiar and aware of cosmetic products as they become more familiar with advertisements that were constantly repeated (Alshurideh, 2019; Alshurideh, 2016). This result is confirmed by Khraim (2011) who studied how demographics affected the cosmetic buying behaviour of young female consumers in the UAE. The study found that female consumers tended to compare cosmetic product brands, prices and where they were produced. The study noted that the cosmetic products' country of origin influenced the buying of these cosmetic products and the way they advertised positively (Al-Duhaish et al., 2014; Alshurideh et al., 2018; Alshurideh et al., 2017).

Moreover, the study found that the strength of the message in the advertisement affected consumer purchasing, as it emphasized the importance of analyzing the advertisement's strengths. For example, this may require analysing the advertisement's persuasive message or the hedonistic factors that the recipient is exposed to during the advertisement. Manipulating what the consumers have in their minds or what they will think about impacts on how consumer behaviour is used to strengthen the message. This happens with how and when the consumer is exposed to a message under specific conditions (Petty & Cacioppo, 1986). These conditions build up the message by further elaboration, tweaking the quality that the consumer seeks to portray in the product or service, and this has a significant impact on consumer thinking when purchasing the product.

In addition, the advertisement design also influenced consumers buying using social media platforms. This result was confirmed by De Keyzer et al. (2015) who found that perceived personalization affected and improved consumer responses towards Facebook and social network site advertising. A major task of advertisers, as identified by Tellis (2003), is to develop creative means for grabbing or holding consumers' attention, using a clear, precise messages, and persuading consumers of that message. This not only covers the uniqueness of the advertisement but also how attention-grabbing the design of the advertisement is and how it influences consumers' behaviour. Advertisements are also more effective and influential when they target educated people, as many consumers believe that subliminal messages in advertising are useless, as there has to be a cognitive side to advertising for people to have a more understanding (Tellis, 2003).

10. THEORETICAL AND MANAGERIAL IMPLICATIONS

Studying customers' responses is coming within the priority of any organization especially for social media advertising in general and for the Facebook platform posting in special. This study aims to investigate if a set of Facebook advertising characteristics may influence users' behaviour. These characteristics are advertisement quality, advertisement design, advertisement message strength, advertisement repetitiveness, and whether the advertisement meets consumers' needs to influence consumer purchasing. The study confirms such relationships and suggests a set of theoretical and managerial implications. Firstly, additional research is needed to give more light on studying how Facebook advertisements' design and quality influence users' reactions. Such issues are important and highlighted by many scholars such as Lohse & Rosen (2001) and Sumner, Khoo, Recker, & Marlino (2003) who talked about the importance of investigating the use of design, architecture, photographic-quality graphics, content, and the presence of advertisements on users' behaviours. Secondly, a need arises to investigate the advertisement's repetitiveness effects, especially when using personalized advertising to different groups of customers who targeted via the Facebook platform (Al-Dmour, Alshurideh, & Salehih, 2014; Hölli, 2019). Thirdly, advertisement message strength does not take much interest from scholars. It is essential to study such phenomenon especially how emotional strength of a message posted via Facebook can influence message reaction and message sharing (Ji, Chen, Tao, & Li, 2019).

The study findings provide a set of valuable managerial implications for designers, executors, and social media advertisers in different aspects. First, it is important when designing any social media ads especially those ill be posted using the Facebook site to focus more on the ads interrelated quality and design dimensions (i. g, information, content communicated by the company) which enable increasing the users' reactions as part of viral advertising strategy especially when such ads target different Facebook groups and how to create advertising pass-on among the group members (Chu, 2011).

Facebook ads repetition is an important advertising process that needs to be considered. Accordingly, it is important for advertisers when repeat posting to care about posting time and day, caring about the level of interaction and engagement during the posting by studying the numbers and types of comments and likes as confirmed by (Goldfarb & Tucker, 2011). Additionally, this study found that Facebook ads designed to meet users' needs affecting their purchase. Thus, studying such needs is important to be known first then determine the characteristics of the main ads that suit the target market needs while the ad characteristics differ from users group to another. If social media ads meet users' need that will help decision-makers in evaluating the Facebook advertising effectiveness as declared by (Belanche, Cenjor, & Pérez-Rueda, 2019) and which of these characteristics is noticed or skipped (Van den Broeck, Poels, & Walrave, 2020).

11. RECOMMENDATIONS

From the study's findings, a set of recommendations are suggested. Initially, companies should concentrate more on the quality of the advertisement presented through social media sites, in general, and specifically on the Facebook platform because it has the greatest influence on the users' awareness and attention when buying cosmetics. Accordingly, scholars and practitioners have shed more light on studying the effect of advertisement design and how it can attract more social media users and followers. It is also good for both scholars and practitioners to study and test the effect of a free sample marketing approach to attract customers (Alshurideh et al., 2018), especially within the cosmetic product buying context. This is because many studies have identified the importance of vouchers and free samples in the cosmetics field to increase consumer numbers and rate of beauty product purchasing. In addition, just over four in ten (42%) consumers will interact with a brand online for discounts or information on sales or money-saving tips, and this is as motivating for Twitter followers (52%) as it is for Facebook fans (50%) (Page, 2012).

In addition, companies should repeat advertisements often using social media to have a greater impact on the target market. This is because social media advertisement repetition increases the chance of holding consumer attention and intention to buy. Based on this, companies should improve the design of advertisements on social media, which may increase purchaser awareness and attention, especially targeting specific segments, ages, incomes and occupations. In addition, cosmetic companies should strengthen and design promotional messages effectively as well as increase the repetition of such messages to the appropriate audiences. Companies should also focus on presenting cosmetic advertisements through Facebook because it is the most popular social media tool that the youth target and access currently. Thus, more studies are needed to research Facebook advertising especially for cosmetic brand campaigns focusing on the advertisements' quality, design, message strength and repetition effect.

REFERENCES

Adelaar, T., Chang, S., Lancendorfer, K. M., Lee, B., & Morimoto, M. (2003). Effects of media formats on emotions and impulse buying intent. *Journal of Information Technology*, *18*(4), 247–266. doi:10.1080/0268396032000150799

Agneta, A. A. (2018). *Effects of facebook advertising on cosmetics sales and purchase by women in kenya* (Master Thesis). University of Nairobi.

Aguilar, C. (2015). *Cosmetic Firms Reinvent Their Marketing Using Instagram*. Available online at: https://www.entrepreneur.com/article/241377

Al-Dmour, H., Alshurideh, M., & Salehih, S. (2014). A Study of Jordanians' Television Viewers Habits. *Life Science Journal*, *11*(6), 161–171.

Al-Dmour, H., & Al-Shraideh, M. T. (2008). The influence of the promotional mix elements on Jordanian consumer's decisions in cell phone service usage: An analytical study. *Jordan Journal of Business Administration*, *4*(4), 375–392.

Al Dmour, H., Alshurideh, M., & Shishan, F. (2014). The influence of mobile application quality and attributes on the continuance intention of mobile shopping. *Life Science Journal*, *11*(10), 172–181.

Al-Dmour, H. H., Alshurideh, M., & Salehih, S. (2014). A study of Jordanians' television viewers habits. *Life Science Journal*, *11*(6), 161–171.

Al-Duhaish, A., Alshurideh, M., & Al-Zu'bi, Z. (2014). The impact of the basic reference group usage on the purchasing decision of clothes (A field study of Saudi youth in Riyadh city). *Dirasat: Administrative*, *41*(2), 205–221.

Al-dweeri, R. M., Obeidat, Z. M., Al-dwiry, M. A., Alshurideh, M. T., & Alhorani, A. M. (2017). The impact of e-service quality and e-loyalty on online shopping: Moderating effect of e-satisfaction and e-trust. *International Journal of Marketing Studies*, *9*(2), 92–103. doi:10.5539/ijms.v9n2p92

Al Kurdi, B., Alshurideh, M., Salloum, S. A., Obeidat, Z. M., & Al-dweeri, R. M. (2020). An Empirical Investigation into Examination of Factors Influencing University Students' Behavior towards Elearning Acceptance Using SEM Approach. *International Journal of Interactive Mobile Technologies*, *14*(02), 19–41. doi:10.3991/ijim.v14i02.11115

Alshurideh, D. M. (2019). Do electronic loyalty programs still drive customer choice and repeat purchase behaviour? *International Journal of Electronic Customer Relationship Management*, *12*(1), 40–57. doi:10.1504/IJECRM.2019.098980

Alshurideh, M. (2010). *Customer service retention–A behavioural perspective of the UK mobile market* (Doctoral dissertation). Durham University.

Alshurideh, M. (2014). The Factors Predicting Students' Satisfaction with Universities' Healthcare Clinics' Services: A Case-Study from the Jordanian Higher Education Sector. *Dirasat: Administrative Sciences*, *161*(1524), 1–36. doi:10.12816/0007482

Alshurideh, M., Al Kurdi, B., Abu Hussien, A., & Alshaar, H. (2017). Determining the main factors affecting consumers' acceptance of ethical advertising: A review of the Jordanian market. *Journal of Marketing Communications*, *23*(5), 513–532. doi:10.1080/13527266.2017.1322126

Alshurideh, M., Al Kurdi, B., Abumari, A., & Salloum, S. (2018). Pharmaceutical Promotion Tools Effect on Physician's Adoption of Medicine Prescribing: Evidence from Jordan. *Modern Applied Science*, *12*(11), 210. doi:10.5539/mas.v12n11p210

Alshurideh, M., Al Kurdi, B., & Salloum, S. A. (2019). Examining the main mobile learning system drivers' effects: A mix empirical examination of both the Expectation-Confirmation Model (ECM) and the Technology Acceptance Model (TAM). In *International Conference on Advanced Intelligent Systems and Informatics* (pp. 406-417). Springer.

Alshurideh, M., Gasaymeh, A., Ahmed, G., Alzoubi, H., & Kurd, B. (2020). Loyalty program effectiveness: Theoretical reviews and practical proofs. *Uncertain Supply Chain Management*, *8*(3), 599–612. doi:10.5267/j.uscm.2020.2.003

Alshurideh, M., Masa'deh, R., & Alkurdi, B. (2012). The effect of customer satisfaction upon customer retention in the Jordanian mobile market: An empirical investigation. European Journal of Economics. *Finance and Administrative Sciences*, *47*(12), 69–78.

Alshurideh, M., Salloum, S. A., Al Kurdi, B., & Al-Emran, M. (2019, February). Factors affecting the social networks acceptance: an empirical study using PLS-SEM approach. *Proceedings of the 2019 8th International Conference on Software and Computer Applications*, 414-418. 10.1145/3316615.3316720

Alshurideh, M. T. (2016). Exploring the main factors affecting consumer choice of mobile phone service provider contracts. *International Journal of Communications, Network and Systems Sciences*, *9*(12), 563–581. doi:10.4236/ijcns.2016.912044

Alshurideh, M. T. (2016). Is customer retention beneficial for customers: A conceptual background. *Journal of Research in Marketing, 5*(3), 382–389. doi:10.17722/jorm.v5i3.126

Alshurideh, M. T. (2017). A theoretical perspective of contract and contractual customer-supplier relationship in the mobile phone service sector. *International Journal of Business and Management, 12*(7), 201–210. doi:10.5539/ijbm.v12n7p201

Alshurideh, M. T., Salloum, S. A., Al Kurdi, B., Monem, A. A., & Shaalan, K. (2019). Understanding the quality determinants that influence the intention to use the mobile learning platforms: A practical study. *International Journal of Interactive Mobile Technologies, 13*(11), 157–183. doi:10.3991/ijim.v13i11.10300

Alshurideh, M. T., Shaltoni, A. M., & Hijawi, D. (2014). Marketing communications role in shaping consumer awareness of cause-related marketing campaigns. *International Journal of Marketing Studies, 6*(2), 163–168. doi:10.5539/ijms.v6n2p163

Ammari, G., Alkurdi, B., Alshurideh, A., & Alrowwad, A. (2017). Investigating the impact of communication satisfaction on organizational commitment: A practical approach to increase employees' loyalty. *International Journal of Marketing Studies, 9*(2), 113–133. doi:10.5539/ijms.v9n2p113

Ampofo, A. (2014). Effects of Advertising on Consumer Buying Behaviour: with reference to deamnd for cosmetic products in Banglore: India. *New Media and Mass Communication, 27*(7), 48–67.

Anand, P., & Sternthal, B. (1990). Ease of message processing as a moderator of repetition effects in advertising. *JMR, Journal of Marketing Research, 27*(3), 345–353. doi:10.1177/002224379002700308

Anderson, J. C., & Gerbing, D. W. (1988). Structural equation modeling in practice: A review and recommended two-step approach. *Psychological Bulletin, 103*(3), 411–423. doi:10.1037/0033-2909.103.3.411

Apriliana, N. S. (2019). The Influence Of Cosmetics Advertisement On Instagram Towards Teenage Girls' Attitude And Consumtive Behavior In Yogyakarta. *Proceeding of International Conference on Communication, Culture and Media Studies (CCCMS), 3*(1), 253-259.

Awata, K. (2010). *An exploration of the impact of social media on branding strategies.* Academic Press.

Ayanwale, A. B., Alimi, T., & Ayanbimipe, M. A. (2005). The influence of advertising on consumer brand preference. *Journal of social sciences, 10*(1), 9–16. doi:10.1080/09718923.2005.11892453

Balasubramanian, S. K. (1994). Beyond advertising and publicity: Hybrid messages and public policy issues. *Journal of Advertising, 23*(4), 29–46. doi:10.1080/00913367.1943.10673457

Belanche, D., Cenjor, I., & Pérez-Rueda, A. (2019). Instagram Stories versus Facebook Wall: An advertising effectiveness analysis. *Spanish Journal of Marketing-ESIC., 23*(1), 69–94. doi:10.1108/SJME-09-2018-0042

Boyd, D. (2008). Facebook's privacy trainwreck: Exposure, invasion, and social convergence. *Convergence, 14*(1), 13–20. doi:10.1177/1354856507084416

Bright, L. F., & Daugherty, T. (2012). Does customization impact advertising effectiveness? An exploratory study of consumer perceptions of advertising in customized online environments. *Journal of Marketing Communications*, *18*(1), 19–37. doi:10.1080/13527266.2011.620767

Bruhn, M., Schoenmueller, V., & Schäfer, D. B. (2012). Are social media replacing traditional media in terms of brand equity creation? *Management Research Review*, *35*(9), 770–790. doi:10.1108/01409171211255948

Campbell, M. C., & Keller, K. L. (2003). Brand familiarity and advertising repetition effects. *The Journal of Consumer Research*, *30*(2), 292–304. doi:10.1086/376800

Carter-Harris, L. (2016). Facebook targeted advertisement for research recruitment: A primer for nurse researchers. *Applied Nursing Research*, *32*, 144–147. doi:10.1016/j.apnr.2016.07.006 PMID:27969019

Celebi, S. I. (2015). How do motives affect attitudes and behaviors toward internet advertising and Facebook advertising? *Computers in Human Behavior*, *51*, 312–324. doi:10.1016/j.chb.2015.05.011

Chave, J. (2017). *Consumer Insight 2017: Cosmetics Europe: The Personal Care Association*. Available online at: https://www.cosmeticseurope.eu/files/6114/9738/2777/CE_Consumer_Insights_2017.pdf

Chin, W. W. (1998). The partial least squares approach to structural equation modeling. *Modern Methods for Business Research*, *295*(2), 295-336.

Chu, S. C. (2011). Viral advertising in social media: Participation in Facebook groups and responses among college-aged users. *Journal of Interactive Advertising*, *12*(1), 30–43. doi:10.1080/15252019.2011.10722189

Clement, J. (2020). *United States: retail e-commerce sales 2017-2024*. Statista. Available online at: https://www.statista.com/statistics/272391/us-retail-e-commerce-sales-forecast/

Cline, T. W., & Kellaris, J. J. (2007). The influence of humor strength and humor—message relatedness on ad memorability: A dual process model. *Journal of Advertising*, *36*(1), 55–67. doi:10.2753/JOA0091-3367360104

Darley, W. K., & Smith, R. E. (1995). Gender differences in information processing strategies: An empirical test of the selectivity model in advertising response. *Journal of Advertising*, *24*(1), 41–56. doi:10.1080/00913367.1995.10673467

Dehghani, M. (2013). *The Role of Social Media on Advertising: A Research on Effectiveness of Facebook Advertising on Enhancing Brand Image* (Master Thesis). Eastern Mediterranean University (EMU)-Doğu Akdeniz Üniversitesi (DAÜ).

Derks, D., Bos, A. E., & Von Grumbkow, J. (2008). Emoticons and online message interpretation. *Social Science Computer Review*, *26*(3), 379–388. doi:10.1177/0894439307311611

Dreheeb, A. E., Basir, N., & Fabil, N. (2016). Impact of System Quality on Users' Satisfaction in Continuation of the Use of e-Learning System. *International Journal of E-Education, e*-Business, *e*- Management Learning, *6*(1), 13–20.

Elmerraji, K. (2015). *Social Media Marketing: Instagram could be a shopper's paradise*. Available online at: https://tcapushnpull.com/tag/social-media-marketing/

Falk, R. F., & Miller, N. B. (1992). *A primer for soft modeling.* University of Akron Press.

Fornell, C., & Larcker, D. F. (1981). Evaluating structural equation models with unobservable variables and measurement error. *JMR, Journal of Marketing Research, 18*(1), 39–50. doi:10.1177/002224378101800104

Ghodeswar, B. M. (2008). Building brand identity in competitive markets: A conceptual model. *Journal of Product and Brand Management, 17*(1), 4–12. doi:10.1108/10610420810856468

Goldfarb, A., & Tucker, C. (2011). Online display advertising: Targeting and obtrusiveness. *Marketing Science, 30*(3), 389–404. doi:10.1287/mksc.1100.0583

Greene, W. E., Walls, G. D., & Schrest, L. J. (1994). Internal marketing: The key to external marketing success. *Journal of Services Marketing, 8*(4), 5–13. doi:10.1108/08876049410070682

Hair, J. F., Black, W. C., Babin, B. J., Anderson, R. E., & Tatham, R. L. (1998). Multivariate data analysis (Vol. 5). Prentice Hall.

Hair, J. F. Jr, Hult, G. T. M., Ringle, C., & Sarstedt, M. (2016). *A primer on partial least squares structural equation modeling (PLS-SEM).* Sage Publications.

Haugtvedt, C. P., Petty, R. E., & Cacioppo, J. T. (1992). Need for cognition and advertising: Understanding the role of personality variables in consumer behavior. *Journal of Consumer Psychology, 1*(3), 239–260. doi:10.1016/S1057-7408(08)80038-1

Hölli, M. (2019). *How Social Media Advertising and Repetitive Marketing Messages Affect the Online Purhasing Behavior?* (Master Thesis). Aalto University School of Business.

Horrell, L. N., Lazard, A. J., Bhowmick, A., Hayes, S., Mees, S., & Valle, C. G. (2019). Attracting Users to Online Health Communities: Analysis of LungCancer. net's Facebook Advertisement Campaign Data. *Journal of Medical Internet Research, 21*(11), 1–7. doi:10.2196/14421 PMID:31682589

Hsieh, Y. C., & Chen, K. H. (2011). How different information types affect viewer's attention on internet advertising. *Computers in Human Behavior, 27*(2), 935–945. doi:10.1016/j.chb.2010.11.019

Ji, Y. G., Chen, Z. F., Tao, W., & Li, Z. C. (2019). Functional and emotional traits of corporate social media message strategies: Behavioral insights from S&P 500 Facebook data. *Public Relations Review, 45*(1), 88–103. doi:10.1016/j.pubrev.2018.12.001

Jones, J. P. (1997). Is advertising still salesmanship? *Journal of Advertising Research, 37*(3), 9–16.

Jung, J., Choo, H. J., & Lee, H. K. (2013). The effects of fashion mobile word-of mouth-Focus on Facebook. *Journal of the Korean Society of Clothing and Textiles, 37*(2), 186–201. doi:10.5850/JKSCT.2013.37.2.186

Kane, K., Chiru, C., & Ciuchete, S. G. (2012). Exploring the eco-attitudes and buying behaviour of Facebook users. *Amfiteatru Economic,* (31), 157–171.

Kent, R. J., & Allen, C. T. (1994). Competitive interference effects in consumer memory for advertising: The role of brand familiarity. *Journal of Marketing, 58*(3), 97–105. doi:10.1177/002224299405800307

Khorsheed, R. K., Othman, B., & Sadq, Z. M. (2020). The Impacts of Using Social Media Websites for Efficient *Marketing. Journal of Xi'an University of Architecture & Technology, 12*(3), 2221–2235.

Khraim, H. S. (2011). The influence of brand loyalty on cosmetics buying behavior of UAE female consumers. *International Journal of Marketing Studies, 3*(2), 123–133. doi:10.5539/ijms.v3n2p123

Kievik, M., Giebels, E., & Gutteling, J. M. (2020). The key to risk communication success. The longitudinal effect of risk message repetition on actual self-protective behavior of primary school children. *Journal of Risk Research, 23*(12), 1–16. doi:10.1080/13669877.2020.1738527

Klimisch, J. (2013). *How to Create an Effective Small Business Advertisement*. VerticalRespose. https://www.verticalresponse.com/blog/how-to-create-effective-small-business-advertising/

Kohli, C., Leuthesser, L., & Suri, R. (2007). Got slogan? Guidelines for creating effective slogans. *Business Horizons, 50*(5), 415–422. doi:10.1016/j.bushor.2007.05.002

Kumar, P., & Singh, G. (2020). Using Social Media and Digital Marketing Tools and Techniques for Developing Brand Equity With Connected Consumers. In *Handbook of Research on Innovations in Technology and Marketing for the Connected Consumer* (pp. 336–355). IGI Global. doi:10.4018/978-1-7998-0131-3.ch016

Leavens, D., & Racine, T. P. (2009). Joint attention in apes and humans: Are humans unique? *Journal of Consciousness Studies, 16*(6-7), 240–267.

Lee, W., & Benbasat, I. (2003). Designing an electronic commerce interface: Attention and product memory as elicited by web design. *Electronic Commerce Research and Applications, 2*(3), 240–253. doi:10.1016/S1567-4223(03)00026-7

Li, R., & Suh, A. (2015). Factors influencing information credibility on social media platforms: Evidence from Facebook pages. *Procedia Computer Science, 72*, 314–328. doi:10.1016/j.procs.2015.12.146

Lin, L. Y. (2010). The relationship of consumer personality trait, brand personality and brand loyalty: An empirical study of toys and video games buyers. *Journal of Product and Brand Management, 19*(1), 4–17. doi:10.1108/10610421011018347

Loda, M. D., & Coleman, B. C. (2005). Sequence matters: A more effective way to use advertising and publicity. *Journal of Advertising Research, 45*(4), 362–372. doi:10.1017/S0021849905050464

Lohse, G. L., & Rosen, D. L. (2001). Signaling quality and credibility in yellow pages advertising: The influence of color and graphics on choice. *Journal of Advertising, 30*(2), 73–83. doi:10.1080/00913367.2001.10673639

MacKay, N. J., & Covell, K. (1997). The impact of women in advertisements on attitudes toward women. *Sex Roles, 36*(9), 573–583. doi:10.1023/A:1025613923786

Mangold, W. G., & Faulds, D. J. (2009). Social media: The new hybrid element of the promotion mix. *Business Horizons, 52*(4), 357–365. doi:10.1016/j.bushor.2009.03.002

Moorthy, S., & Hawkins, S. A. (2005). Advertising repetition and quality perception. *Journal of Business Research, 58*(3), 354–360. doi:10.1016/S0148-2963(03)00108-5

Navarro-Beltrá, M., Medina, I. G., & Correia, P. A. (2020). The Dialogical Potential of Facebook: The Case of Fashion Brands. *International Journal of Interactive Mobile Technologies, 44*(2), 278–299.

Niazi, G. S. K., Siddiqui, J., Alishah, B., & Hunjra, A. I. (2012). Effective advertising and its influence on consumer buying behavior. *Information Management and Business Review, 4*(3), 114–119. doi:10.22610/imbr.v4i3.971

Nunnally, J. C., & Bernstein, I. H. (1978). *Psychometric Theory.* McGraw-Hill.

Olney, T. J., Holbrook, M. B., & Batra, R. (1991). Consumer responses to advertising: The effects of ad content, emotions, and attitude toward the ad on viewing time. *The Journal of Consumer Research, 17*(4), 440–453. doi:10.1086/208569

Page, M. (2012). *How Beauty Brands Use Social Media.* SmartInsights. https://www.smartinsights.com/social-media-marketing/social-media-platforms/using-social-media-for-beauty-brands/

Parsons, A. (2013). Using social media to reach consumers: A content analysis of official Facebook pages. *Academy of Marketing Studies Journal, 17*(2), 27–36.

Pelling, E. L., & White, K. M. (2009). The theory of planned behavior applied to young people's use of social networking web sites. *Cyberpsychology & Behavior, 12*(6), 755–759. doi:10.1089/cpb.2009.0109 PMID:19788377

Petty, R. E., & Cacioppo, J. T. (1986). The elaboration likelihood model of persuasion. In *Communication and persuasion* (pp. 1–24). Springer.

Poh, D. M. H., & Adam, S. (2002) An exploratory investigation of attitude toward the website and the advertising hierarchy of effects. In *AusWeb02, the Web enabled global village: proceedings of AusWeb02, the eighth Australian World Wide Web Conference* (pp. 620-631). Southern Cross University.

Prensky, M. (2001). Digital natives, digital immigrants part 1. *On the Horizon, 9*(5), 1–6. doi:10.1108/10748120110424816

Ramo, D. E., & Prochaska, J. J. (2012). Broad reach and targeted recruitment using Facebook for an online survey of young adult substance use. *Journal of Medical Internet Research, 14*(1), e28. doi:10.2196/jmir.1878 PMID:22360969

Ringle, C. M., Wende, S., & Will, A. (2005) *SmartPLS 2.0 (Beta) Hamburg.* Available in http://www.smartpls.de

Robinson, H., Wysocka, A., & Hand, C. (2007). Internet advertising effectiveness: The effect of design on click-through rates for banner ads. *International Journal of Advertising, 26*(4), 527–541. doi:10.1080/02650487.2007.11073031

Rosen, D. E., & Purinton, E. (2004). Website design: Viewing the web as a cognitive landscape. *Journal of Business Research, 57*(7), 787–794. doi:10.1016/S0148-2963(02)00353-3

Salloum, S. A., Alshurideh, M., Elnagar, A., & Shaalan, K. (2020). Mining in Educational Data: Review and Future Directions. In *Joint European-US Workshop on Applications of Invariance in Computer Vision* (pp. 92-102). Springer. 10.1007/978-3-030-44289-7_9

Scarles, C. (2004). Mediating landscapes: The processes and practices of image construction in tourist brochures of Scotland. *Tourist Studies*, *4*(1), 43–67. doi:10.1177/1468797604053078

Schmitt, B. H. (2000). *Experiential marketing: How to get customers to sense, feel, think, act, relate.* Simon and Schuster.

Schünemann, H. J., Best, D., Vist, G., & Oxman, A. D.GRADE Working Group. (2003). Letters, numbers, symbols and words: How to communicate grades of evidence and recommendations. *Canadian Medical Association Journal*, *169*(7), 677–680. PMID:14517128

Schwarz, M., & Abrams, Z. (2009, October 8). *Method and system for managing advertisement quality of sponsored advertisements*. Google Patents. Available online at: https://patentimages.storage.googleapis.com/ac/f1/73/53814f76f66863/US20090254414A1.pdf

Shen, B., & Bissell, K. (2013). Social media, social me: A content analysis of beauty companies' use of Facebook in marketing and branding. *Journal of Promotion Management*, *19*(5), 629–651. doi:10.1080/10496491.2013.829160

Simoncic, T. E., Kuhlman, K. R., Vargas, I., Houchins, S., & Lopez-Duran, N. L. (2014). Facebook use and depressive symptomatology: Investigating the role of neuroticism and extraversion in youth. *Computers in Human Behavior*, *40*, 1–5. doi:10.1016/j.chb.2014.07.039 PMID:25861155

Sumner, T., Khoo, M., Recker, M., & Marlino, M. (2003). Understanding educator perceptions of" quality" in digital libraries. *2003 Joint Conference on Digital Libraries, 2003. Proceedings*, 269–279.

Tellis, G. J. (2003). *Effective Advertising: Understanding When, How, and Why Advertising Works.* Sage Publishing.

The Statistics Portal. (2018). Available online at: https://www.statista.com/topics/1008/cosmetics-industry/

Tufekci, Z. (2012, May). Facebook, youth and privacy in networked publics. *Sixth International AAAI Conference on Weblogs and Social Media*, 338-345.

Van Den Broeck, E., Poels, K., & Walrave, M. (2020). How do users evaluate personalized Facebook advertising? An analysis of consumer-and advertiser controlled factors. *Qualitative Market Research*, *23*(2), 309–327. doi:10.1108/QMR-10-2018-0125

Visser, M., Gattol, V., & Van der Helm, R. (2015). Communicating sustainable shoes to mainstream consumers: The impact of advertisement design on buying intention. *Sustainability*, *7*(7), 8420–8436. doi:10.3390u7078420

Zhang, J., Sung, Y., & Lee, W. (2010). To play or not to play: An exploratory content analysis of branded entertainment in Facebook. *American Journal of Business*, *25*(1), 53–64. doi:10.1108/19355181201000005

This research was previously published in the International Journal of Online Marketing (IJOM), 11(2); pages 52-74, copyright year 2021 by IGI Publishing (an imprint of IGI Global).

Chapter 37
Consumer Socialization Process for the Highly Connected Customers:
The Use of Instagram to Gain Product Knowledge

Ree C. Ho
Taylor's University, Malaysia

Teck Choon Teo
RVi Institute, Myanmar

ABSTRACT

Over the past two decades, social media has developed exponentially and significantly changed the customers' shopping behavior. Social media apps enable customers to interact with retailers and other customers closely, and influences their purchase decision. Hence, it is small wonder that businesses are investing time and resources to promote their products and brand image on social media applications. Instagram is best known for its enriched visual features in both image and footage and suitable for developing strong brand engagement. It is a viable platform for businesses to promote their products to customers. This chapter proposes a framework of product learning process with the use of Instagram. It contributes in effective management of social media marketing and provides marketers with the guidelines in using Instagram creatively to roll out customer engagement strategies.

INTRODUCTION

The emergence of the internet, particularly Web 2.0 has provided access to the views and opinions of a wide range of individuals opening up opportunities for new forms of communication and knowledge formation. Previous ways of navigating and filtering available information are likely to prove ineffec-

DOI: 10.4018/978-1-6684-6287-4.ch037

tive in today's context. Social media provides the connectivity needed for virtual environments (Kaplan & Haenlein, 2010). It has become a significant part of daily personal communication. In 2015 90% of young adults in the age group 18-29 often use of social media (Perrin, 2015). Additionally, social media enables users to share their product experiences through consumer reviews (Y. Chen, Fay, & Wang, 2011). Thus, it promotes communication among consumers (Abzari, Ghassemi, & Vosta, 2014). Social media referred as Social Networking Sites (SNS). Social networking sites is cyber-environment where individuals can create a personal profile, share photos, images and text with each other.

Arguably, Instagram may not be the most popular social media sites. However, known for its visual features in both image and footage with limited words. Does the lack of text by Instagram affect perceptions of popularity? This chapter explores the viability of Instagram in developing product attitude via consumer socialization process. Contents from Instagram are validated as antecedents in molding consumer socialization process. The two components of the consumer socialization process, namely peer communication and product involvement elucidates consumers learning about product knowledge.

Aims and Motivations

Social media generally refers to a collective of online communication channels built on community-based input, interaction, and collaboration. Typically, it is comprised of social networking sites, video sharing platforms, blogs and micro-blogging platforms, forums and messaging platforms. Social media channels are two-way communication platforms that enable people to respond and react to information. Primarily it is a medium for people to connect with each other; social media provides a unique opportunity for brands to leverage the power of peer-to-peer recommendation and word of mouth. The increasing marketing communication in the social media space has catapulted Instagram, translating into augmented popularity.

Instagram reaches the younger generation, and appeals to diverse societies more prevailingly than other social networking services (Abbott, Donaghey, Hare, & Hopkins, 2013; Salomon, 2013). As the reach and impact of social channels has grown and advertising models become established across key platforms, social media has evolved from being fan and community building platforms into highly powerful paid media channels capable of driving real business results at every stage of the customer touchpoints. As a result, social interaction gained in social media can assist consumer in making purchase decision. To tap into these opportunities, it is important to understand customer's purchase intent and delineate the moments in people's lives where social can play a role. For example, hospitality/tourism segment used social media for pre-trip planning as well as post-trip to share experiences with family and friends.

Understanding this initial start-point enable brands to define clearly their business objectives and strategies. Instagram is delivering clear business value beyond traditional likes, shares and comments in the form of images and videos. As such, the sharing of images rather than words alone has made communication with friends and broader groups of users who share similar interests more ideal, convenient and fascinating via the trend of aesthetic content in image and footage where consumers comment, post, and share consumer experience (Virtanen, Björk, & Sjöström, 2017). This chapter aims to uncover the consumer socialization process in the use of Instagram content, and the understanding of the product knowledge by consumers in facilitating the purchase decision. The elements such as the label and designs, color can sway the perception of consumers into actual purchase. Indeed, the consumer socialization process within Instagram can go beyond social purpose.

BACKGROUND

Growth of Social Commerce

Social commerce hawks merchandises directly through social media networks. It is unlike social media marketing i.e. you are not redirecting users to an online store, instead enabling them to checkout directly within the network they are using at that moment. It provides people the convenience to complete the transaction. One outstanding example is the Facebook Social Commerce; it is undoubtedly the biggest and most popular player. Facebook's major development such as Facebook Marketplace is hugely popular with people, giving Amazon and Google Shopping a "run" for their money. Another excellent example is the Instagram Social Commerce is the most promising platforms when it comes to creating a social selling strategy. Shoppable Posts, Instagram's latest development now allow brands the ability to tag items in organic posts which, when tapped, brings up a new page which leads to a checkout. It is small wonder that social commerce is making a huge impact on the world of e-commerce and marketing. Consequently, this led to the phenomenal growth of social commerce.

From marketing standpoint, social commerce has become part of our daily lives, particularly with the young people. Young people are ubiquitously known, have used social networking services, activities checking of their friends' updates, to catch up on the latest updates in their hobby, or simply to stalk the Instagram of their ex-girl/boyfriend. Consumers are exposed to brand and product via social network. Young people are more in tune with social media. They are also more prone to impulse purchases. Effectively, it capitalizes on young people's impulse urges by giving them a direct checkout within the updates they find most captivating.

Accordingly, social commerce giants are cashing in, changing their promotional tactics to align with customers' expectations vis-a-vis implementing highly engaging, eye-catching social promotions, etc. High level of interactions among consumers to learn about product and to share shopping experience with the use of consumer generated contents (Wang, Yu, & Wei, 2012). Consumers also use and distribute consumer related contents, such as product review, feedback and 'like' posts (Daugherty, Eastin, & Bright, 2008; Sparks & Bradley, 2017; Teixeira, Pereira, & Dionísio, 2018). The social media contents obtained via social media application is useful in the final purchase decision (Duverger, 2013; Fong & Burton, 2006).

Progressively, as more people are turning to social media in more areas of their lives, they are spending more time on their phone; expecting quick fix to every problem, and sharing everything they do on social media. It triggers companies and consumers alike to exploit full use of social media app, subsuming Instagram, for business purposes (Ashley & Tuten, 2015). The only logical action then is for marketers to take advantage of these behaviors and start selling through the channels that people engaged with the ease of checkout expectancy.

About Instagram

According to Salomon (2013), Instagram is the most popular image-based social media apps in both IOS and Android smart mobile device platform. In the initial years of the inception, it started as a photo sharing social network platform. However, gradually it evolved to include video, stories geo-tagged, livestream video and linking to more social network accounts. The main feature is the distribution of short and interesting message mainly in the form of image and video footage that attracts many young people to use Instagram (H. Chen, 2018). Additionally, it has simple and straightforward short messages, which is easy to understand. As Ilich and Hardey (2018) puts it aptly, a picture tells thousand words. Instagram can reach followers instantaneously and the response is correspondingly efficient and effective. Resulting in businesses adopting Instagram's business account where it can specifically target their customers.

Instagram has excelled as an effective communication and marketing tool to display products with visual descriptions. Hence, it becomes a useful social networking platform instantly to individuals and companies. Interestingly, the acquisition of Instagram by Facebook has potentially made Instagram even more attractive and appealing to millions of users.

Use of Instagram in Business

Without a doubt, social media platforms today play a significant part in the growth of several businesses. Many marketers are quick to consider engaging various social media platforms to attract and reach their target customers. Aside from the hugely popular Facebook and Twitter, Instagram is the next best choice to market business on social media platforms. In social media marketing, it is essential to review the number of audiences that you can reach. It is astonishing that Instagram has that eminence, boasting of over one billion monthly active users.

Turning to visuals, it has always been an important element in marketing. For example, if a message released to the public but no one remembers it, then it has failed! Communicating does no good if it does not retained by the audience. Today, it is easy for information to be ignored if it is not in a digestible format. Thus, integrating visual content can enhance how much the audience absorbs and remembers.

In addition to helping marketers communicate a message that intrinsically remembered, Instagram proffer effective visuals content that is highly desirable when it comes to increasing customer engagement. Hautz, Füller, Hutter, and Thürridl (2014) posited that images and footage as determinant in influencing consumer to buy. By combining visual and text, Instagram is then able to maximize the marketing value. Given its usefulness and convenience, in the customer's memory recall process, other writers also cited that product information can be diffused faster with Instagram (De Veirman, Cauberghe, & Hudders, 2017). It increases higher publicity effectiveness with Instagram's image (Colliander & Marder, 2018) and the credibility of celebrities' Instagram profile in influencing female to purchase fashion (Djafarova & Rushworth, 2017).

CONCEPTUAL FRAMEWORK DEVELOPMENT

Instagram consists of two words, "instant' and "telegram". It captures and shares moments with a steady stream of images and footage. The principal application is connecting people and companies visually with its followers. Creators and publishers can tag business partners in branded content through feed and stories in Instagram. With countless followers tagging along, it translates into both social and business values. It is small wonder that the number of monthly active Instagram users increased exponentially. Due to the apps' visual nature and appeal, it enjoys a massive user engagement rate. In addition, Instagram is also a valuable marketing tool for fashion brands having an Instagram profile.

In present times, Instagram is more than attracting attention and admiration, arguably it is a moneymaking machine. Many companies acknowledged the tremendous influence of Instagrammers and companies are happy offering free products, hoping that Instagrammers will post pictures with their products and recommend them. Astutely some companies even willing to compensate Instagrammers to promote their products, without telling their followers that they are paid for doing so. It can be a product placement on social media, a combination of paid electronic Word-of-Mouth (eWOM) and paid user generated content (UGC). The product placement on social media is the contemporary form of celebrity endorsement and gravitate towards Influencer Marketing. Virtual word of mouth essentially focus was on specific individuals rather than a target market as a whole. According to Liu, Chou, and Liao (2015), product placement on social media was one of the most valuable marketing strategies.

Instagram Marketing

Social media are nowadays a central part of the personal social life. Besides communicating with friends, social media also allows users to connect to strangers all over the world with whom they share the same interest. Besides the continuous sales increment indicated that e-commerce has enormous market potential. The spectacular success of e-commerce conglomerates e.g. Alibaba, Amazon and Groupon, have set as an example for firms to change the brick-and-mortar model of their business to brick-and-click.

In the same vein, Instagram continues to grow and evolve as a marketing platform. Hence, it is imperative for businesses to build effective Instagram marketing strategies compared to having a thorough understanding of the Instagram marketing landscape and measurable outcomes. In light of this, Instagram created an algorithm that re-organized people's feeds so they would theoretically see more content that is relevant to them. This improves user-experience and the priorities of certain types of content. It can optimize one's posts to get the maximum engagement and reach possible. The principle of Instagram business viability is about its distribution of small chunk of contents, small size, short and fast enough for users to obtain and absorb it. It is efficient especially in the content creation as in the use of other social media case in making word of mouth spread faster and achieves its marketing value.

Studies shows that Instagram can increase the brand awareness leading to purchase decision (Colliander & Marder, 2018; Djafarova & Rushworth, 2017). High level of interactivity also facilitates good communication and collaboration within users in learning product information and experience (Tsekouropoulos et al., 2012). Invariably advertising on social media has become of big importance in the past years. Hence, what about the outcome of consumer socialization in product learning?

Consumer Socialization

Consumer socialization refers to collective processes by which young people acquire skills, knowledge, and attitudes relevant to their functioning as consumers in the marketplace (Basu & Sondhi, 2014). Quintal et al., 2016). It postulates that one obtains related skills in a social context that will subsequently affect the cognitive, effectiveness, and attitude while making decisions. Furthermore, socialization agents identified as the sources of influence that transfer norms, attitudes, motivations, and behaviors to children (Quintal, Phau, Sims, & Cheah, 2016). Children constitute a significant marketing segment. Today, they not only make purchases for themselves but also influence family purchase decisions. The purchase behavior determines the way they socialized with others to act as consumers.

According to Niu (2013), the purchasing power of teenagers has greatly increased and attributed to family communication patterns. In addition, the adolescent life cycle and family communication patterns, family socio-economic status and parental marital status also affect adolescent cyber purchasing behavior. Hence, the adolescent consumers do not gain these skills, knowledge and attitudes in solitary but through socialization. Other researchers such as Peters, Chen, Kaplan, Ognibeni, and Pauwels (2013) and Wang et al. (2012) shared the same view.

The impact of consumer socialization not just on the young people, but the entire population (De Gregorio & Sung, 2010; Taylor, Lewin, & Strutton, 2011). A significant relationship existed between social structural factors and socialization processes. Peers appear to be the most important agents of consumer socialization, contributing to a variety of desirable as well as undesirable consumer decision outcomes. Apart from this, the information can also be helpful in allowing marketers to be more effective in targeting various markets by formulating marketing strategies according to demographic factors, socialization process and decision-making styles. Hence, these consumer socialization dimensions are mediating the relationship between the contents obtained from Instagram and the intention to adopt purchase, as shown in Figure 1.

Figure 1. The conceptual framework

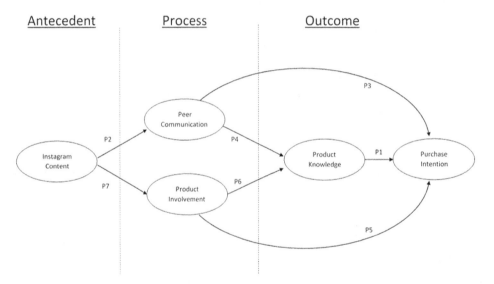

Product Knowledge

Product knowledge has gained attention in consumer behavior research. Product knowledge is an essential component in sales and marketing. Understanding products' features allows companies to present their benefits accurately and persuasively. Customers respond to enthusiastic sales staffs who are passionate about their products and eager to share the benefits with customers. By engaging customers, it is then possible to turn product features into benefits. Using one's knowledge to lead customer through the sales process, and make customer's experience an enjoyable one that they will want to revisit.

Customers have the tendency to know more of the product before purchase. The more customer know about the product, the more likely they will purchase the products and more competent in using it for full potential. Product learning is therefore important for all kinds of products and services. Wood and Lynch Jr (2002) accentuated that if customers are familiar with the product knowledge, they will invariably enjoy the product experience. Conversely, unfamiliarity may become disadvantageous for the customers.

Turning to self-service technologies with regard to technological interfaces, this allow customers to produce services independent of involvement of direct service employee. Increasingly Self-Service technologies are replacing many face-to-face service interactions with the intention to make service transactions more accurate, convenient and faster. With the widespread of contents by social media, people are becoming more comfortable and experience with technology, they are more willing to perform transactions over the Internet.

In other social media apps, the power of e-WoM (Electronic Word of Mouth) has been examined extensively (Hennig-Thurau, Gwinner, Walsh, & Gremler, 2004). People precisely like sharing information, social media, review websites and forums have become so successful. Therefore, e-WoM served as service chain, if one share information and then his/her friends shared the information with other friends and so on. This is the reason why e-WoM could become viral. Knowledge obtained from social media engagement is useful in helping consumer to make purchase decision. With refining image and video contents enriched with interactivity features, it is expecting that knowledge could be gained by following the Instagram posts. This then attributed to the high adoption and distribution speed of Instagram compared to other older social media apps. Therefore, we postulated the following proposition.

Proposition 1:

Product knowledge gained from consumer socialization can exert influence on purchase intention.

Instagram Content

Followers usually search for customized content from company that they are interested. In order to illustrate the application of the product, marketers must create engaging content on Instagram and show users how to use the products in their daily life. Consumers like to get ideas and see what products fit them personally. Hence, the trick is to keep content as actionable as possible.

In creating a thought-provoking story with the product, this can engage consumers and creates a compelling reason for them to click on the site and start shopping. This strategy can work for much of any product category. For example, agriculture revolution: agriculture technology uses storytelling to describe the communities benefiting from its sustainable food security initiatives around the world. The Instagram post can show a community that now has sustainable food security because of the nonprofit's project. Being open and telling brand story is a good way to build an online community.

With the high adoption of visual contents in social media, consumer socialization starts with the distribution of contents in the form of posts, image and footage. According to De Vries, Gensler, and Leeflang (2012), the most sought-after content has to be informative and entertaining. Interestingly, entertaining posts are the content normally do not directly relate to brand. The post published by the retailers should be customer-centric and this normally attracts the customers. If the content is relatable and can tell stories, then users will connect with the brand and will have a positive experience before they ever see the company's website. Consumer interaction with branded content becomes a matter of interest (Sabate, Berbegal-Mirabent, Cañabate, & Lebherz, 2014). Businesses should then recognize the benefits of getting closer to core customers in implementing customer centric strategies (Stefanou, Sarmaniotis, & Stafyla, 2003; Tian Xie & Johnston, 2004). Hashtags have become a uniform way to categorize content on many social media platforms. Hashtags allow Instagrammers to discover content and accounts to follow. It contributes to the increases of favorable posts, including the higher number of 'likes'. It also highlights the significance of high level of interactivity within social media users during the socialization process.

Peer Communication

By using social media marketing, companies virtually promote their brand image and MVC (Mission Vision and Culture) for minimum cost. This is an important advantage of word of mouth communication. Conversely, any errors or complaints on its services and/or products can adversely affect the companies' brand equity resulting in significant revenue loss. These errors affect the companies' images because young people communicate with their peers about everything at any time. Peer communication plays an important role in the socialization process fundamentally. As potential users develop greater independence from their parents and family, influence from peers and groups will have serious impact largely because of the large amount of time they spend together and the substantial behavioral and attitudinal similarities between them (Armağan & Çetin, 2013). These peers and groups become influential, important and valuable source of information on different brands and products.

Undoubtedly, Internet has the ability to link a piece of content to another. More specifically social media has transmuted how consumers and marketers communicate. Different social media platform (such as blogs, online discussion forums, and online communities) has an effect on marketing performance and especially social media has changed how consumers and marketers. For example, Instagram grabs attention of the younger generation, and is attractive to diverse societies, more appealing than other social networking services. Youngsters today spend more time on Instagram than Facebook (Salomon, 2013). This is because young mobile users who are extremely motivated to take photos or pictures using their mobile phones, and share them with others instantly. As such, the sharing of images rather than words alone has made communication with friends and broader groups of users who share similar interests conveniently. Social media provides firms with a more personal touch and communication channel with the consumers (Saji, Chauhan, & Pillai, 2013). It can enrich the two-way conversation in a shorter time possible as compared with traditional marketing communication channel. It is often wider coverage as it is much easier to find other users with similar interests together. From the business' perspective, friends with common interests invite and join the related retailer's social media, triggering the growth of social network groups. Hence, we developed the proposition as follow:

Proposition 2:

The contents gained from Instagram can exert influence on the peer communication during the consumer socialization.

Consumers often seek relevant information from various sources in their environment and attempt to make informed decisions. Hence, marketing through social media communication is new additional promotion mix strategy. In social networking, effective mode of communication between people and companies are crucial. Unlike traditional communication media, social networking site exploits its interactive images enabling the content to be more informative and representational. Users find social networking particularly useful because it can shared information and connected with their friends (Ho & Rezaei, 2018). From the decision-making stance, such online activities are crucial to companies as substantial amounts of users can make decision through social networking communication. It certainly has become an indispensable platform to get more customers and generate favorable attitude and intention in the marketplace in order to yield desired outcome (Brodie, Ilic, Juric, & Hollebeek, 2013; Mangold & Smith, 2012). Moreover, for the young online users, they tend to treat peer comments as important (Madell & Muncer, 2007). This led us to posit the proposition below:

Proposition 3:

Peer communication during consumer socialization can exert influence on purchase intention.

The elicitation of normative beliefs about Instagram provides knowledge about users' motivation to comply with relevant persons when it comes to using new application. Ting, Ming, de Run, and Choo (2015) accentuate that young people have no influence from their parents or the elderly. This indicates strong influence of people who are of similar age, such as their siblings, close friends and friends in the context of developing markets. Based on the consumer socialization process, peer communication at both individual and group levels are the antecedents for the product learning stage. Hence, it is critical for marketers to understand the social networking behavior as it is a contemporary phenomenon. Conversely, social networking is also a media for learning new things. The positive influence from siblings and friends, including Facebook friends, is important especially when it comes to new and innovative products.

With a variety of types of contents, Instagram can then be a platform for retailers to promote their products. Such understanding will assist companies in developing comprehensive strategies to not only target the users directly but also use referents to generate interest among potential users. During the consumer socialization process, followers and peers create information and shares experiences. The consumer learns more from peers rather than from retailer (Zhang & Daugherty, 2009). For instance, images posted in social media by local food and beverage industry can assist foreign travelers in understanding the local cuisines and impress them to patron the local restaurant.

Hence, consumers can expect to learn about efficacy of brand and product knowledge during their interactions with other users in Instagram. Indeed, social media is undergoing the socialization process which enables sharing and learning among the users by enjoying the outcomes of consumer socialization (Luczak & Younkin, 2012). Based on the discussion above, we developed the following proposition:

Proposition 4:

Peer communication during consumer socialization can exert influence on product knowledge.

Product Involvement

Product involvement is the degree of participation and actions conducted by consumers during the product consumption process. It is often associated with consumer's perceived enjoyment while consuming the product based on his own intrinsic values, needs and interests (Thong, Hong, & Tam, 2006). The user's predisposition to ponder over the outcome of a purchase and consumption experience will be contingent on their level of involvement and knowledge of the product itself. The possibility that any causal search occurs, users who are more knowledgeable were able to determine the correct underlying causes. This suggests that marketers need to be in a position to support less knowledgeable users in arriving at an accurate causal determination. Lee, Park, and Han (2008) further supports the notion that the level of involvement of Korean consumers tend to depend on the quality of information provided by the reviewers.

Instagram offers the hashtag (#) function in identifying relevant photos and videos. This way, users can browse specific hashtag to locate pictures/videos of their interest, such as "#travels" for travel destination or "#asianfood" for Asian food inspiration. Using suitable and relevant hashtags, the consumers can find the advertisement on their own. Thus, by identifying the key Instagrammers, the target audience faster and easily reached (Latiff & Safiee, 2015). Both through the Instagrammers' followers and hashtag posted by like-minded people.

Product Involvement During Consumer Socialization

Given the consumer socialization process, Lee et al. (2008) highlighted that the purchase intention is higher when there is higher level of customer's involvement in the negotiation stage with the retailer. Dellarocas (2003) reiterated that online word-of-mouth has imperative implications for managers in terms of brand building, product development, and quality assurance. Kim, Haley, and Koo (2009) provided further support to cues that the more effort and time spent by consumers in product evaluation, the higher possibility in product purchase.

Product involvement affects consumers in the decision-making process to purchase the products. The complexity of product search information, period in adopting, the level of the attitude and preferences about the product may lead to the customer perception on the various alternative in the same product category and brand loyalty (Bauer, Falk, & Hammerschmidt, 2006). Therefore, if a firm is seeking to win over consumer's loyalty of rival brand or enter into an established market may be better off targeting in its introductory efforts when consumers are already highly involved. The product involvement could be categorized into two major aspects with regard to enduring involvement and situational involvement (Bloch & Richins, 1983). In enduring involvement, it occurs when the consumer is actively involved in the process, and has more emotional attached during the purchase. While in situational involvement, it occurs when the consumer's perception on the product's importance is temporary as he/she is expecting to gain specific enjoyments or benefits from the product. The importance of product involvement in online shopping could understated during the consumer socialization process. Hence, we developed the following proposition:

Proposition 5:

Product involvement during consumer socialization can exert influence on purchase intention.

One significant factor that exerts influence on purchase intention is the influence of reference group. Reference group is people who act as a reference point for a consumer and with whom the consumer shares similar values, plays a major role in influencing the final purchase decision of the consumer. Rajput and Khanna (2014) concluded that reference groups are the external influencers such as favorite stars, celebrities, peers and relatives who considerably influence one's purchase decisions and behavior.

Product involvement in social commerce refers to as a situation where a particular consumer expresses constant interest with a particular product category (Peng, Zhang, Wang, & Liang, 2019). Herrington and Capella (1995) suggested that shoppers spend less time making a purchase when under time pressure. Significant factors are the influence of reference group and peer influence on purchase decisions (Akar & Nasir, 2015; Niu, 2013). According to Ting et al. (2015), communication is the foundation of social interaction, the essential means through which people initiate and maintain social relationships.

However, peers have increasing influence on their attitudes, beliefs, and behaviors. As young adults develop greater autonomy from their family, intrinsically peer influence becomes more important. They are particularly vulnerable to influence from their friends because of the considerable attitudinal and behavioral similarity between them and their friends (Armağan & Çetin, 2013). The main sources of information used by young adult concerning all kinds of products come mainly from peers. Consumers tend to interact with peers about consumption matters, which greatly influence their attitudes toward products and services (Wang et al., 2012). More importantly, they place greater level of trust in interpersonal information sources. Especially in their parents who are perceived as the most credible information source with respect to their learning about new products (Fan & Li, 2010). Hence, we posit the following proposition.

Proposition 6:

Product involvement during consumer socialization can exert influence on product knowledge.

An increasingly connected world has fast-forwarded the rate of information transfer across the globe. Social media has provided the platform for consumers to communicate simultaneously not only with their friends and acquaintances but also with relative strangers with unprecedented ease. Researchers who study consumer behavior attribute a great deal of importance to the product involvement variable (Charters & Pettigrew, 2006; Lin & Chen, 2006).

Product involvement can influence the decision-making process regarding a product. The extent to which consumers will search for information about the product, the timing in adoption of the product, the manner in which the consumer's attitudes and preferences regarding the product are influenced by the consumer's perceptions of alternatives in the same product category and brand loyalty (Hong, 2015). It has facilitated the ability of people to share more about themselves, their families, and their friends through a variety of media. Thus, developing and sustaining social and business relationships. However, Fischer and Reuber (2011) observed that two factors that can moderate the social interaction, i.e. community orientation and community adherence. Conversely, findings of Lu, Zhao, and Wang (2010) revealed that the absence of physical contact between buyer and seller could reduce the likelihood for successful transaction.

It is common for Instagram to have a large number of 'likes' and 'follows" after more followers viewed images and watched the clip related to the product. With the increased adoption of visual contents, the customers' are more likely to distribute and co-create the contents. Hence, with these differences in research, it is imperative to ascertain the role of product involvement in Instagram with the following proposition.

Proposition 7:

The contents gained from Instagram can exert influence on the product involvement during the consumer socialization

CONCLUSION

Social networking has become an important communication tool enabling individuals and organizations to connect effectively. More specifically, Instagram utilizes its interactive images to make the content more representative and informative. This chapter focuses on consumer socialization process and the use of Instagram in providing practical implications for both consumers and marketers. Firstly, the peer communication and product involvement are important dimensions for better understanding the behavior of networked consumers. In addition, the effect of visual contents distributed by Instagram can stimulate the consumer shopping activities. It can expedite the marketing message diffusion with the simple liking or sharing the visual contents (Chang, Yu, & Lu, 2015).

Interestingly, the use of Instagram is less expensive and more effective as compared to conventional marketing tools. From the marketer's perspective, one of the biggest and the most obvious limitations of digital marketing is that there is no interaction between the customers and the medium used for marketing. Traditional marketing is a one-way street where a business is able to broadcast or provide information to their target audience about its product or service. This brand building exercise hopes to attract the attention of the right people and converting them into customers.

On the other hand, Instagram marketing conducted via the Internet or any electronic devices. Realistically any business, regardless of its size can leverage digital marketing to reach out to their target market, connect with prospects and convert more of them into customers/clients. By following the posts, image and video footage, prospect can learn about the new products and brand messaging. In addition to its role in brand awareness, there is also better engagement between customers and the retailers (Choudhury & Harrigan, 2014). Inversely, retailers can also learn, observe and gain new ideas from the followers. However, business need to ensure quality of its product and service is what they claimed to be.

In conclusion, social networks are mature and generated much business values. However, the most popular social media site contrasts greatly by level of usage in different online platforms. Understanding these differences in different types of social media is central when targeting specific audiences. Additionally, the popularity of one social media application in a specific context may not necessary be so in another context. The main finding of this chapter is to explore the consumer socialization process needed for online purchase via Instagram. Furthermore, this chapter confirmed that consumers' product knowledge acquired would ultimately lead to swift purchasing behavior. Instagram can be useful in providing a platform for customers to learn about product knowledge others. Therefore, consumer socialization process further enhanced with contents from Instagram that served as the antecedent. Hence, we learned that consumer socialization process could provide the necessary avenue to make Instagram the ideal shopping mode.

LIMITATIONS AND FUTURE RESEARCH DIRECTIONS

While this chapter emphasizes on the relationship of the contents distributed by Instagram and purchase intention, it is worthwhile to take note that consumer socialization process is ever changing in today's highly connected networked world. The importance of peer group factor and social media in building the knowledge, skills and attitudes required to function in the market place. It has an overwhelming impact on their brand choice and consumption behavior. Throughout the consumer socialization, consumers develop the knowledge, skills and values they will use in making and influencing purchases now and in future. Therefore, they not only are consumers, but also have a considerable influence in the purchase decisions depending on their purchase experience in different products. Invariably the amount of influence exerted by consumers differs from product group and during the decision-making process. As in some products, some consumers are merely purchasers while in other products they are influencers in their social networks for other consumers. Hence, the purchase behavior developed by the way they have been socialized to act as consumers. Hence, future researches could investigate the consumer socialization of Instagram based on the role of the consumer during product purchase process.

Instagram has a strongly visual-oriented focus as the photographs and short videos are the most common content (Murthy, Gross, & McGarry, 2016). Instagram users are mainly driven by social interaction (Blight, Ruppel, & Schoenbauer, 2017) which explains the higher level of engagement and brand community commitment found among its users (Phua, Jin, & Kim, 2017). High levels of interaction are important, because they can encourage a word-of-mouth effect and fan community building which are strong contributors to the success of social media campaigns (See-To & Ho, 2014). This raise an important question. Will the consumers engage in impulsive buying after they learned about the product knowledge from others? Further studies should investigate the relationship between Instagram contents and the likelihood of impulsive purchase behavior to examine how these two constructs correlate with each other.

REFERENCES

Abbott, W., Donaghey, J., Hare, J., & Hopkins, P. (2013). An Instagram is worth a thousand words: An industry panel and audience Q&A. *Library Hi Tech News*, *30*(7), 1–6. doi:10.1108/LHTN-08-2013-0047

Abzari, M., Ghassemi, R. A., & Vosta, L. N. (2014). Analysing the effect of social media on brand attitude and purchase intention: The case of Iran Khodro Company. *Procedia: Social and Behavioral Sciences*, *143*, 822–826. doi:10.1016/j.sbspro.2014.07.483

Akar, E., & Nasir, V. A. (2015). A review of literature on consumers' online purchase intentions. *Journal of Customer Behaviour*, *14*(3), 215–233. doi:10.1362/147539215X14441363630837

Armağan, E., & Çetin, A. (2013). Peer communication and impacts on purchasing decisions: An application on teenagers. *International Journal of Social Sciences and Humanity Studies*, *5*(2), 60–72.

Ashley, C., & Tuten, T. (2015). Creative strategies in social media marketing: An exploratory study of branded social content and consumer engagement. *Psychology and Marketing*, *32*(1), 15–27. doi:10.1002/mar.20761

Basu, R., & Sondhi, N. (2014). Child socialization practices: Implications for retailers in emerging markets. *Journal of Retailing and Consumer Services*, *21*(5), 797–803. doi:10.1016/j.jretconser.2014.06.008

Bauer, H. H., Falk, T., & Hammerschmidt, M. (2006). eTransQual: A transaction process-based approach for capturing service quality in online shopping. *Journal of Business Research*, *59*(7), 866–875. doi:10.1016/j.jbusres.2006.01.021

Blight, M. G., Ruppel, E. K., & Schoenbauer, K. V. (2017). Sense of community on Twitter and Instagram: Exploring the roles of motives and parasocial relationships. *Cyberpsychology, Behavior, and Social Networking*, *20*(5), 314–319. doi:10.1089/cyber.2016.0505

Bloch, P. H., & Richins, M. L. (1983). A theoretical model for the study of product importance perceptions. *Journal of Marketing*, *47*(3), 69–81. doi:10.1177/002224298304700308

Brodie, R. J., Ilic, A., Juric, B., & Hollebeek, L. (2013). Consumer engagement in a virtual brand community: An exploratory analysis. *Journal of Business Research*, *66*(1), 105–114. doi:10.1016/j.jbusres.2011.07.029

Chang, Y.-T., Yu, H., & Lu, H.-P. (2015). Persuasive messages, popularity cohesion, and message diffusion in social media marketing. *Journal of Business Research*, *68*(4), 777–782. doi:10.1016/j.jbusres.2014.11.027

Charters, S., & Pettigrew, S. (2006). Product involvement and the evaluation of wine quality. *Qualitative Market Research*, *9*(2), 181–193. doi:10.1108/13522750610658810

Chen, H. (2018). College-aged young consumers' perceptions of social media marketing: The story of Instagram. *Journal of Current Issues and Research in Advertising*, *39*(1), 22–36. doi:10.1080/10641734.2017.1372321

Chen, Y., Fay, S., & Wang, Q. (2011). The role of marketing in social media: How online consumer reviews evolve. *Journal of Interactive Marketing*, *25*(2), 85–94. doi:10.1016/j.intmar.2011.01.003

Choudhury, M. M., & Harrigan, P. (2014). CRM to social CRM: The integration of new technologies into customer relationship management. *Journal of Strategic Marketing*, *22*(2), 149–176. doi:10.1080/0965254X.2013.876069

Colliander, J., & Marder, B. (2018). 'Snap happy' brands: Increasing publicity effectiveness through a snapshot aesthetic when marketing a brand on Instagram. *Computers in Human Behavior*, *78*, 34–43. doi:10.1016/j.chb.2017.09.015

Daugherty, T., Eastin, M. S., & Bright, L. (2008). Exploring consumer motivations for creating user-generated content. *Journal of Interactive Advertising*, *8*(2), 16–25. doi:10.1080/15252019.2008.10722139

De Gregorio, F., & Sung, Y. (2010). Understanding attitudes toward and behaviors in response to product placement. *Journal of Advertising*, *39*(1), 83–96. doi:10.2753/JOA0091-3367390106

De Veirman, M., Cauberghe, V., & Hudders, L. (2017). Marketing through Instagram influencers: The impact of number of followers and product divergence on brand attitude. *International Journal of Advertising*, *36*(5), 798–828. doi:10.1080/02650487.2017.1348035

De Vries, L., Gensler, S., & Leeflang, P. S. H. (2012). Popularity of brand posts on brand fan pages: An investigation of the effects of social media marketing. *Journal of Interactive Marketing*, *26*(2), 83–91. doi:10.1016/j.intmar.2012.01.003

Dellarocas, C. (2003). The digitization of word of mouth: Promise and challenges of online feedback mechanisms. *Management Science*, *49*(10), 1407–1424. doi:10.1287/mnsc.49.10.1407.17308

Djafarova, E., & Rushworth, C. (2017). Exploring the credibility of online celebrities' Instagram profiles in influencing the purchase decisions of young female users. *Computers in Human Behavior, 68*, 1–7. doi:10.1016/j.chb.2016.11.009

Duverger, P. (2013). Curvilinear effects of user-generated content on hotels' market share: A dynamic panel-data analysis. *Journal of Travel Research, 52*(4), 465–478. doi:10.1177/0047287513478498

Fan, Y., & Li, Y. (2010). Children's buying behaviour in China: A study of their information sources. *Marketing Intelligence & Planning, 28*(2), 170–187. doi:10.1108/02634501011029673

Fischer, E., & Reuber, A. R. (2011). Social interaction via new social media:(How) can interactions on Twitter affect effectual thinking and behavior? *Journal of Business Venturing, 26*(1), 1–18. doi:10.1016/j.jbusvent.2010.09.002

Fong, J., & Burton, S. (2006). Electronic Word-of-Mouth: A Comparison of Stated and Revealed Behavior on Electronic Discussion Boards. *Journal of Interactive Advertising, 6*(2), 7–62. doi:10.1080/15252019.2006.10722119

Hautz, J., Füller, J., Hutter, K., & Thürridl, C. (2014). Let users generate your video ads? The impact of video source and quality on consumers' perceptions and intended behaviors. *Journal of Interactive Marketing, 28*(1), 1–15. doi:10.1016/j.intmar.2013.06.003

Hennig-Thurau, T., Gwinner, K. P., Walsh, G., & Gremler, D. D. (2004). Electronic word-of-mouth via consumer-opinion platforms: What motivates consumers to articulate themselves on the internet? *Journal of Interactive Marketing, 18*(1), 38–52. doi:10.1002/dir.10073

Herrington, D. J., & Capella, L. M. (1995). Shopper reactions to perceived time pressure. *International Journal of Retail & Distribution Management, 23*(12), 13–20. doi:10.1108/09590559510103963

Ho, R. C., & Rezaei, S. (2018). Social Media Communication and Consumers Decisions: Analysis of the Antecedents for Intended Apps Purchase. *Journal of Relationship Marketing, 17*(3), 204–228. doi:10.1080/15332667.2018.1492322

Hong, I. B. (2015). Understanding the consumer's online merchant selection process: The roles of product involvement, perceived risk, and trust expectation. *International Journal of Information Management, 35*(3), 322–336. doi:10.1016/j.ijinfomgt.2015.01.003

Ilich, K. L., & Hardey, M. (2018). 'It's all about the packaging': Investigation of the motivations, intentions, and marketing implications of sharing photographs of secondary packaging on Instagram. *Information Communication and Society*. doi:10.1080/1369118X.2018.1478983

Kaplan, A. M., & Haenlein, M. (2010). Users of the world, unite! The challenges and opportunities of Social Media. *Business Horizons, 53*(1), 59–68. doi:10.1016/j.bushor.2009.09.003

Kim, S., Haley, E., & Koo, G.-Y. (2009). Comparison of the paths from consumer involvement types to ad responses between corporate advertising and product advertising. *Journal of Advertising, 38*(3), 67–80. doi:10.2753/JOA0091-3367380305

Latiff, Z. A., & Safiee, N. A. S. (2015). New business set up for branding strategies on social media–Instagram. *Procedia Computer Science, 72*, 13–23. doi:10.1016/j.procs.2015.12.100

Lee, J., Park, D.-H., & Han, I. (2008). The effect of negative online consumer reviews on product attitude: An information processing view. *Electronic Commerce Research and Applications*, 7(3), 341–352. doi:10.1016/j.elerap.2007.05.004

Lin, L.-Y., & Chen, C.-S. (2006). The influence of the country-of-origin image, product knowledge and product involvement on consumer purchase decisions: An empirical study of insurance and catering services in Taiwan. *Journal of Consumer Marketing*, 23(5), 248–265. doi:10.1108/07363760610681655

Liu, S.-H., Chou, C.-H., & Liao, H.-L. (2015). An exploratory study of product placement in social media. *Internet Research*, 25(2), 300–316. doi:10.1108/IntR-12-2013-0267

Lu, Y., Zhao, L., & Wang, B. (2010). From virtual community members to C2C e-commerce buyers: Trust in virtual communities and its effect on consumers' purchase intention. *Electronic Commerce Research and Applications*, 9(4), 346–360. doi:10.1016/j.elerap.2009.07.003

Luczak, C., & Younkin, N. (2012). Net generation: A conceptual framework of the consumer socialization process. *Academy of Marketing Studies Journal*, 16(2), 47.

Madell, D. E., & Muncer, S. J. (2007). Control over social interactions: An important reason for young people's use of the internet and mobile phones for communication? *Cyberpsychology & Behavior*, 10(1), 137–140. doi:10.1089/cpb.2006.9980

Mangold, W., & Smith, K. T. (2012). Selling to Millennials with online reviews. *Business Horizons*, 55(2), 141–153. doi:10.1016/j.bushor.2011.11.001

Murthy, D., Gross, A., & McGarry, M. (2016). Visual Social Media and Big Data. Interpreting Instagram Images Posted on Twitter. *Digital Culture & Society*, 2(2), 113–134. doi:10.14361/dcs-2016-0208

Niu, H.-J. (2013). Cyber peers' influence for adolescent consumer in decision-making styles and online purchasing behavior. *Journal of Applied Social Psychology*, 43(6), 1228–1237. doi:10.1111/jasp.12085

Peng, L., Zhang, W., Wang, X., & Liang, S. (2019). Moderating effects of time pressure on the relationship between perceived value and purchase intention in social E-commerce sales promotion: Considering the impact of product involvement. *Information & Management*, 56(2), 317–328. doi:10.1016/j.im.2018.11.007

Perrin, Andrew. (2015). Social media usage. *Pew Research Center*.

Peters, K., Chen, Y., Kaplan, A. M., Ognibeni, B., & Pauwels, K. (2013). Social media metrics—A framework and guidelines for managing social media. *Journal of Interactive Marketing*, 27(4), 281–298. doi:10.1016/j.intmar.2013.09.007

Phua, J., Jin, S. V., & Kim, J. J. (2017). Gratifications of using Facebook, Twitter, Instagram, or Snapchat to follow brands: The moderating effect of social comparison, trust, tie strength, and network homophily on brand identification, brand engagement, brand commitment, and membership intention. *Telematics and Informatics*, 34(1), 412–424. doi:10.1016/j.tele.2016.06.004

Quintal, V., Phau, I., Sims, D., & Cheah, I. (2016). Factors influencing generation Y's purchase intentions of prototypical versus me-too brands. *Journal of Retailing and Consumer Services*, 30, 175–183. doi:10.1016/j.jretconser.2016.01.019

Rajput, N., & Khanna, A. (2014). Dynamics of young indian consumers' buying behvior towards branded apparels: Gender perspective. *Archives of Business Research*, 2(5), 84–106. doi:10.14738/abr.25.596

Sabate, F., Berbegal-Mirabent, J., Cañabate, A., & Lebherz, P. R. (2014). Factors influencing popularity of branded content in Facebook fan pages. *European Management Journal*, *32*(6), 1001–1011. doi:10.1016/j.emj.2014.05.001

Saji, K. B. (2013). Role of content strategy in social media brand communities: A case of higher education institutes in India. *Journal of Product and Brand Management*, *22*(1), 40–51. doi:10.1108/10610421311298687

Salomon, D. (2013). Moving on from Facebook: Using Instagram to connect with undergraduates and engage in teaching and learning. *College & Research Libraries News*, *74*(8), 408–412. doi:10.5860/crln.74.8.8991

See-To, E. W. K., & Ho, K. K. W. (2014). Value co-creation and purchase intention in social network sites: The role of electronic Word-of-Mouth and trust–A theoretical analysis. *Computers in Human Behavior*, *31*, 182–189. doi:10.1016/j.chb.2013.10.013

Sparks, B. A., & Bradley, G. L. (2017). A "Triple A" typology of responding to negative consumer-generated online reviews. *Journal of Hospitality & Tourism Research (Washington, D.C.)*, *41*(6), 719–745. doi:10.1177/1096348014538052

Stefanou, C. J., Sarmaniotis, C., & Stafyla, A. (2003). CRM and customer-centric knowledge management: An empirical research. *Business Process Management Journal*, *9*(5), 617–634. doi:10.1108/14637150310496721

Taylor, D. G., Lewin, J. E., & Strutton, D. (2011). Friends, fans, and followers: Do ads work on social networks? *Journal of Advertising Research*, *51*(1), 258–275. doi:10.2501/JAR-51-1-258-275

Teixeira, N., Pereira, H. G., & Dionísio, P. (2018). Online consumer generated content it's for real! the rise of social influence marketing. *The Business & Management Review*, *9*(3), 358–366.

Thong, J.YL, Hong, S.-J., & Tam, K.Y. (2006). The effects of post-adoption beliefs on the expectation-confirmation model for information technology continuance. *International Journal of Human-Computer Studies, 64*(9), 799-810.

Ting, H., Ming, W. W. P., de Run, E. C., & Choo, S. L. Y. (2015). Beliefs about the use of Instagram: An exploratory study. *International Journal of business and innovation, 2*(2), 15-31.

Tsekouropoulos, G., Andreopoulou, Z., Koliouska, C., Koutroumanidis, T., Batzios, C., & Lefakis, P. (2012). Marketing policies through the internet: The case of skiing centers in Greece. *Scientific Bulletin-Economic Sciences*, *11*(1), 66–78.

Virtanen, H., Björk, P., & Sjöström, E. (2017). Follow for follow: Marketing of a start-up company on Instagram. *Journal of Small Business and Enterprise Development*, *24*(3), 468–484. doi:10.1108/JSBED-12-2016-0202

Wang, X., Yu, C., & Wei, Y. (2012). Social media peer communication and impacts on purchase intentions: A consumer socialization framework. *Journal of Interactive Marketing*, *26*(4), 198–208. doi:10.1016/j.intmar.2011.11.004

Wood, S. L., & Jr, L. (2002). Prior knowledge and complacency in new product learning. *The Journal of Consumer Research*, *29*(3), 416–426. doi:10.1086/344425

Xie, T. (2004). Strategic alliances: Incorporating the impact of e-business technological innovations. *Journal of Business and Industrial Marketing*, *19*(3), 208–222. doi:10.1108/08858620410531342

Zhang, J., & Daugherty, T. (2009). Third-person effect and social networking: Implications for online marketing and word-of-mouth communication. *American Journal of Business*, *24*(2), 53–64. doi:10.1108/19355181200900011

KEY TERMS AND DEFINITIONS

Consumer Socialization: The process undergone by social media users in which they develop the skills, attitude and knowledge as consumers.

Instagram Marketing: The use of Instagram with the goal of developing a positive brand identity and building relationship with online customers.

Peer Communication: The exchange of information, product reviews and comments by peers in one's social virtual community.

Product Involvement: Defined as the perceived relevance of a product class based on the consumer's inherent needs, interest, and value during the purchase process.

Product Knowledge: The amount of accurate information about the products including the alternatives and product features that consumers believe they know.

Product Learning: It refers to learning about product consumption through interactions among the consumers, resellers and socialization agents in Instagram.

Purchase Attitude: Consumer's positive or negative feelings related to accomplishing product purchase in the Internet.

Purchase Intention: The possibility that the consumer would purchase the related products after the consumer socialization process.

This research was previously published in Strategies and Tools for Managing Connected Consumers; pages 1-19, copyright year 2020 by Business Science Reference (an imprint of IGI Global).

Chapter 38
Travel Instagramability:
A Way of Choosing a Destination?

Cecília Avelino Barbosa
Université Lyon 2, France

Marina Magalhães
ICNOVA, NOVA University of Lisbon, Portugal

Maria Rita Nunes
iD https://orcid.org/0000-0001-5435-6529
Polytechnic Institute of Tomar, Portugal

ABSTRACT

Digital technologies enabled the emergence of ever-broader networks of connection, communication, and sharing between users across the globe, forging new cultural, social, political, and economic scenarios. This chapter aims to investigate this transformation in the perspective of tourism communication, through a reflection on the impacts of new media on the relationship between consumers and the choice of their tourism destinations. For this, it proposes a literature review on the reconfiguration of tourism communication in the culture of participation. It develops an empirical analysis of the content among the most followed digital influencers' profiles and those with greater engagement in Portugal.

INTRODUCTION

The digital expansion rapidly transformed the processes of production, circulation and consumption of information. It redefined the unidirectional communication model (from one to all) until now dominated by the large media conglomerates, to a network-based communication model (from all to all) (Di Felice, 2010). This change gained a fast pace from the web 2.0 and digital social networks, such as Facebook, YouTube, Twitter and, more recently, Instagram. Creating personal pages and profiles has enabled each user to become a content producer and potential media (Alves, 2017).

DOI: 10.4018/978-1-6684-6287-4.ch038

This new paradigm of networked communication and the rapid growth of collective speaking by users have not challenged traditional media only. Political campaigns, educational teaching-learning strategies and market relations between company-consumers have also redefined themselves, giving special appreciation to the opinions of ordinary users in their media channels (blogs and profiles on social networks). Companies, public organisations, management institutions or the State agencies, from the most diverse segments, in which tourism is included, started to pay attention to this consumption practices and concerned to the management of this digital presence. To establish a direct relationship with their customers, answer criticisms and follow suggestions launched by users in the informational flood of networks.

Marketing, in general, has also been adapting to the digital culture, adapting products and services to the needs of each individual. That is possible due to the large volume of information, from the most diverse media, confronting with a demand for customisation and information (Magalhães, 2018b). In the era when marketing and advertising ideals are closer to human aspirations and values (Kotler et al., 2010), seeking to generate experiences and sensations obligate strategies also to change. Instead of the old tripod: press office - public relations - advertising, as the focus of organisational communication, the strategy started to integrate several media, mainly digital, besides the "voices" of ordinary users (Terra, 2011).

The rupture between public and private space (Kaufman, 2015). The connected culture forges the feeling that people are closer, through expressions of solidarity, help, knowledge share and decision-making recommendations - whether these "experts" are valid or not (Raine & Wellman, 2012). Those who achieve greater social engagement (calculated by the number of followers or friends and their reactions), who share opinions on different topics and experiences with a service or product are known as digital influencers, who have recognised performance in platforms like Instagram.

Previously, only celebrities were considered capable of reaching a large audience. Nonetheless, the emergence of digital social networks arises new "specialists". Hitherto ordinary users can also attract thousands of followers who share the same interests or admire their choices and lifestyle (Raine & Wellman, 2012). The proximity between the digital influencer and the follower or fan, provided by the inherent interactivity of digital networks, is also an advantage that attracts investment from brands and companies from different segments. In the tourism area, these influencers are also known as travel Instagrammers, one of the types of Instagrammers used to promote hotels and destinations (Fonseca, 2019), among other tourism products and services.

Aware of the need to investigate the impacts of new media on tourism, this work intends to approach the topic from the perspective of the relationship between influence marketing and tourism in the landscape of digital social networks. In this sense, with a focus on the active role of consumers. This chapter has a theoretical-analytical nature, which starts with a literature review on the transformations in communicative processes in digital culture and then reflects on the relationship between marketing influence and tourism in our contemporaneity infused by the digital world.

The analytical part of this work focuses on investigating the phenomenon, empirically, through content analysis (Bardin, 2006) and a netnographic study (Amaral et al., 2008) from the profiles of digital influencers on the social network Instagram, in Portugal, in the "Travel" segment of Primetag (2019) study. Semi-structured interviews with the Instagrammers were also done. The corpus comprises the posts published during the European summer of 2019 by profiles with the biggest number of followers and the highest engagement level. The study's main goal is to identify the strategies used by digital influencers in the promotion of tourist destinations. Also, to classify resources, products and services prevalent in the posts. By identifying the strategies used, the researchers can analyse how the power of Instagrammers is used to influence their audience to visit places (Morais, 2018), whether it be instagrammable or not.

Here, instagrammable can be understood as Martins (2019) says: "everything that is shareable on the social network". Capable of arousing people's desire to know or consume. This neologism, arising from the growth of Instagram, a social network of the most frequent users. It was formulated to name a market trend that covers several segments. Destinations of the everyday that have been reinvented "since now the consumer is much more concerned with the experience he will have and, mainly, if will be able to share" (Morais, 2018).

BACKGROUND

To think about the impacts of the new media on tourism, especially regarding the relationship between consumers and the choice of their travel destinations, it is necessary to reflect on a broader transformation, which involves the very operating structures of a network society.

The acceleration of the informatisation process begun in the 1970s and has initiated a series of changes in the forms of organisation in the most diverse spheres of society. According to Castells (2016), these changes occurred through the centralisation of the role of information, the flexibility of production, the global network logic, the diffusion and convergence of digital Information and Communication Technologies - ICT. These resources enabled the emergence of increasingly broad networks of connection, communication and sharing among users from all over the world, forging new cultural, social, political and economic scenarios.

In the economic sphere, social networks constituted a material basis to restructure capitalist modes of production, steering industrial development towards informational. Then, the generation, processing and transmission of information became the fundamental sources of productivity and power due to new technological conditions (Castells, 2016). This transformed the contemporary economic and technological system into informational, global and networked capitalism, which permeates all spheres of daily life, from professional to personal, from the public to private.

The communication was one of the most affected areas by this change. the expansion of generation and circulation of knowledge, the connected communicative architectures enabled the experimentation of new forms of protagonism by groups, movements and individuals. With the internet, firstly from blogs, which occupied a place never seen before in the democratic model of production and circulation of information, and recently, with the popularisation of smartphones (which is possible to photograph, write, film, edit and post in real-time). Because of the multiplication of private communication channels on the web (such as the creation of personal pages or profiles on social networks) (Porto & Flores, 2013) the content production is simpler and more accessible, contributing to the multiplication of these voices.

Di Felice (2010) states that the collective taking of the word on social networks is the expression of a transition of communicative paradigms. Before the internet, a one-to-all communication model prevailed, that is, a few broadcasters, holders or actors in the mass media spoke to an entire receiving audience. It had limited possibility of feedback or interaction. Such a model was also considered a vertical or pyramidal model. The top of the pyramid being historically dominated by states and large media conglomerates and the receiving public, was located at its base or periphery. This does not mean that the audience was necessarily passive, but the public only had stricter or alternative channels of social response.

However, the advent of the internet caused the transition from this unidirectional and pyramidal model, characteristic of mass media, to a reticular or rhizomatic communication model (Di Felice, 2010). Everyone can potentially speak to everyone, as long as they are digitally connected. In this social network, the formulas of the mass society, based on the separation of identity between sender and receiver, company and consumer, institutions and citizens, informant and politician, are no longer sufficient to translate the complexity of the dynamics of contemporary interactions (Di Felice, 2010).

Therefore, the former receiving public (reader, listener, viewer), previously technologically unable to intervene in the communicative process, finds in the network communication model and digital technologies the opportunity to participate in the process of message construction and circulation. In other words, contemporary society would have gone from the media of mass to a mass of infinity media, through the empowerment of users with attributes previously restricted to the mainstream media and used in favour of the interests that move them. Thus, each person is a potential media, able to achieve things that previously only the organised media could achieve (Alves, 2017).

This change in the communicative paradigm is both a vector and a product of convergence culture (Jenkins, 2009). According to Jenkins (2009), this is related to three phenomena: the convergence of the media, the participatory culture and collective intelligence. In this culture of convergence that was born with the web, the products of old media (traditional mass media) and new media (digital natives) become hybrid, challenging the entire communication market - personal, social, educational, political, business, tourist, etc. - to constantly reinvent itself. With the arrival of social networks, this market needed to understand audiences' migratory behaviour that now goes anywhere on the network in search of the experiences they want (Jenkins, 2009). This happens because convergence is a process that adapts itself according to each technological novelty, affecting the most different spheres of daily life.

In the business area, this transformation is also quite evident, especially in the relationship between the company, brand, product or service with the customer. If in the mass communication paradigm consumers had limited space for giving feedback on their consumption experiences, in general, restricted to customer service, they can now share their assessments with the world - the companies and other consumers - in the era of convergence.

In the field of tourism, the tourist is also a producer of information. According to Toffler & Toffler (2006), when we create something for our consumption, we are prosumer = producer + consumer. Also, according to these same authors, with the development of technology and, above all, with the advent of the internet, the concept of prosumer deepens and ends up also encompassing people who create values (information) and share them with strangers, in the most varied forms. This can happen through countless digital channels, from their blogs and profiles on social networks to the pages, websites and platforms of the companies themselves, such as Uber, Airbnb and other companies from Silicon Valley that were born under the sign of the culture of collaboration or participation (Morozov, 2019).

This change reveals how collaborative networks are no longer restricted to family groups, the neighbourhood or friends to include a varied and extensive system of members in the participatory media, which connect individuals over common interests, no matter whether this interest is professional, a passion for jazz, or housing around etc. (Rainie & Wellman, 2012). Therefore, new technologies would have contributed to these networks being more diversified and of greater reach, also reconfiguring how people use them to learn, solve problems, support and advise each other.

To Rainie and Wellman (2012), the lines between information, communication and action are increasingly blurred, insofar as connected individuals use the internet, mobile phones and social networks to obtain information at their fingertips and act from them, delegating their claims to specialists, regardless of whether they are well known or not. Thus, the web can be seen as a vast store of information, which can help connected individuals to search for content, discover and contact other individuals who have similar experiences, comparing opinions in the face of decision making (Magalhães, 2018a).

This transformation challenged marketing in general, which realised the importance of customisation for information about products and services on social media (Magalhães, 2018b). Its strategy increasingly seeks to get closer to human values and aspirations, valuing experiences and sensations (Kotler et al., 2010), since social networks have brought a loss of control by companies over the content of what is said, when and where it is spoken about their brands and products (Kaufman, 2015, p. 141).

The profusion of the opinions from ordinary users and the reach that such opinions can achieve on social networks reveal the importance of quality management of the digital presence by companies in different segments. From the perspective of tourism, investigating the impacts of new media on the parallel between consumers and the choice of their destinations. It would be a starting point for those who are engaged in tourist communication in networked society. Therefore, based on this question, the participation of digital influencers and influencer marketing in the contemporary scenario will be analysed, adopting the social network Instagram as an empirical observation.

MAIN FOCUS OF THE CHAPTER

Communication and Tourism

In a consumer society (Baudrillard, 2017), communication, and its diverse media, are tools for persuasion to achieve this consumption (Fonseca, 2019), which in tourism happens with the consumption of places (Varley, Schilar & Rickly, 2020).

Communication is the basis of the relationship between the destination and its client, the tourist. Within this relationship, there is a need for an ever-closer approximation between the tour operators to attain the traveller's needs and desires. Travellers are usually quite informed and demanding (Marujo, 2008). In this way, there is a need for specific communication, tourist communication.

According to Wichels (2014), tourist communication is not restricted to the promotion of a destination, but it is rather a means capable of promoting ideas and ideals, cultural exchanges, notions of environmental and patrimonial protection of a locality. Besides, communication in tourism is also present in the stories that travellers tell from their perspective, with reports of how the travel was experienced when they are back to their home. Through communication, a destination, an attraction, a product, becomes socially existing (Baldisserra, 2010).

For Rodriguez (2009), tourist communication consists of actions that gather knowledge about the travels of people who travel more than 24 hours and who stay overnight in a different place from their region of origin. Besides, this author points out that tourist advertising carried out in newspapers and specialised magazines would be characterised as communication with no informative value, but rather commercial.

However, the need for communication between tourist destinations, their promoters, agents and tourists has undergone several changes. Roughly speaking, from the most recent registration of tourism practice to the arrival of the internet, group trips needed intermediation, that is, the presence of an agent that connects the (mass) tourist to its destination, providing ticket flights, accommodation reservations, itineraries and everything else necessary for the trip to proceed, and to effective communication between tourist and destination. With the internet, there was less noise in this communication. The tourist now has direct access to destinations, hotels and routes through the websites of companies and tourist destinations, in direct communication between customers and tourists, a moment called disintermediation (Cacho & Azevedo, 2010), which fundamentally changed the way how travellers do tourism (Hays, Page & Buhalis, 2013). Therefore, communication from all to all (Di Felice, 2010) also took place in tourist communication. The new tourists classified by Poon (1993), are people who are interested in expanding their horizons from the displacement of their place of residence, but who also influence other travellers to move or not. Thus, they assume a place of the provider of local tourist information.

This way, tourist communication became more complex, involving not only brochures, pamphlets and travel fairs. Due to the economic importance of the activity, the Destination Management Organisations (DMOs) have to rethink how they were communicating with their tourist or potential tourists (Iglesias-Sánchez, Correia, Jambrino-Maldonado & Heras-Pedrosa, 2020). A whole new world of resources was suddenly available: an enormous amount of information on possible travel destinations and use direct links to buy airline tickets, book tours and accommodation, all just at a click, or even better tap, away. This reveals the entry of other actors in the tourism market who disrupted established practices and fuelled further cycles of destination production, acquisitions, mergers, and consolidations of market power (Gibson, 2019). "Far from a standalone sector merely concerned with 'leisure' (as opposed to parts of the economy deemed more 'productive'), tourism is utterly imbricated in the Spatio-temporal dynamics of contemporary capitalism" (p.5). Airbnb, Trip Advisor, Instagram and also Google Translate are examples of this now dominant player bridging e-commerce, property, social media, and big data services.

It is noted that, as the whole society has undergone profound changes with the advent of the internet, the shift to web 2.0 has also led to paradigmatic changes in communication between tourists and destinations (Panas, Vasiliadou & Halkiopoulos, 2020). The client or the tourist who previously used the websites of the companies themselves or the destinations also seeks information and opinions from other tourists who registered, through a tourist communication, their experiences and travel reports (Wichels, 2014). Thus, there was a complexification of the definitions of communication in tourism. Tourists are, now, capable of organising their tourism, influenced by information that the internet offers through the tourists themselves. Baldissera (2010) reinforces the concept that tourist communication is not just about formal communication generated by public and private audiences. For this author, tourist communication encompasses both formal and informal communication, the latter consisting of the communication generated by different subjects in the touristic chain.

The relationship between communication and tourism conducted over the internet has also divided the power to influence these same tourists. The impact of User Generated Content (USG) in destination management is challenging (Iglesias-Sánchez *et al.*, 2020). The power of information is shared between tour operators (government, entrepreneurs, workers), the media and users/tourists. The latter are both recipients of information from the media, as well as providers of information and influence on the travel and tourist destinations of other travellers.

Social Media and Tourism Communication

Social media are the activity, the practices and behaviours of people who communicate online to share information, knowledge and opinion using, according to Brake and Safko (2009) conversational media (Hays, Page, & Buhalis, 2013). On conversational media, Brake and Safko (2009, p.6) say that "conversational media are Web-based applications that make it possible to create and easily transmit content in the form of words, pictures, videos, and audios."

From their own experience, travellers connected through information-sharing platforms such as TripAdvisor, Facebook or Instagram, can share moments they had or are having at that exact moment, with the most genuine details, impressions and experiences possible. Fans, followers or just friends, get to know the reality of a certain destination in an instant, what went well or not and how interested they are to also carry out that type of experience.

In tourism, social media is forcing traditional travellers' intermediaries, such as travel agencies, flight operators, to work throughout the social media platforms, adapting themselves to this new way to communicate in the tourism sector.

The new technology information through social media expanded the word-of-mouth influence. Now, with feedback, comments, ratings (1 to 5 stars), the tourist influences a large number of other tourists. The power of information in tourism is also shared. Amid the profusion of suggestions, recommendations and complaints about experiences shared on the networks, some gain more importance than others. This is the case of digital influencers, users who reach a large number of followers who are interested in their content, whose opinions have the power to influence other users through the trust achieved (Magalhães, 2018b). The place of worship previously restricted to celebrities and famous people came to be occupied by ordinary users, close to their followers, who managed to create real communities around their beliefs, lifestyle and interests (Wellman & Rainie, 2012).

Thus, the concept of digital influencers or social media influencers includes "all individuals who have recognition and respect in their chosen niche and consequently have a big following on their social media accounts" (Fonseca, 2019, p. 53). They are recognised as able to influence their followers into potentially making decisions and "can range from popular speakers to niche industry experts and even to current customers, employees and members of the media" (Fonseca, 2019, p. 54).

Faced with this scenario, the communication strategy of entities and organisations started to value the "voices" of the common user on social networks (Terra, 2011). Such a strategy constitutes what is called influence marketing, which corresponds to the planning, control of social networks by opinion leaders and social media multipliers, through their recommendations (Barreiro, Dinis & Breza, 2019).

According to Magalhães (2018b), "specialists" like bloggers, YouTubers or instagrammers are already considered professionals, as many digital influencers are hired by brands and associations to advertise their products and services. These users sometimes become a *creative worker in social media* (Duffy & Wissinger, 2017) and can be paid to advertise a variety of products and services.

Namely, on Instagram, this social network originated the phenomenon of so-called *instafame, in* which the presence of an attentive audience can be the most potent status symbol. Marwick (2015) defines *instafamous* as a new type of microcelebrity based on "a collection of self-presentation practices endemic in social media, in which users strategically formulate a profile, reach out to followers, and reveal personal information to increase attention and thus improve their online status (Senft 2013)" (p. 138).

In the contemporary informational flood, after the marketing realised the potential of these microcelebrities to attract "eyes", consumer brands have been investing in individual users to help them to increase their online popularity. Second to Fernandes (2018), furthermore, investing in instafamous also can be an advantageous idea when trying to reach a large number of people for less than a campaign run in traditional media. This is the case of Brazilian instagrammer Maju Trindade (@bymajuvuew), "a 19-year-old girl who reaches almost five million people every day using only her image and low-cost technologies" (p. 58) and the British travel influencer, Jack Morris (@doyoutravel), which has over 2.2

million followers on Instagram, and together with his girlfriend Lauren Buller (@gypsea_lust) influence millions of people through their content (Terttunen, 2017).

From the perspective of tourism, digital influencers must know "the target and the trends" and have a role in motivating and influencing "the process of seeking information and decision-making in relation to a specific tourist destination disclosed by them" (Barreiro, Dinis, Breza, 2019, p. 8).

Femenia-Serra and Gretzel (2020), reveal the inner dynamics of influencer marketing for tourism destinations through the example of the Spanish city of Benidorm. The destination started to work with many influencers to promote Benidorm in the French market and attract a higher number of tourists. The main focus was on young people aiming to change the destination image. They did a campaign called 'The Other Benidorm' with french influencer Léa Camilleri, who has over 365 thousand followers on Instagram. Léa was invited to do this campaign with videos and photos because she is a young influencer who has her image related to sustainable places, another objective of Benidorm marketing. According to Femenia-Serra and Gretzel (2020) data from an internal report demonstrate that the campaign 'The Other Benidorm' had a fruitful impact.

Therefore, to think about this relation between digital influencers and tourism promotion on Instagram in Portugal, this article will examine the phenomenon from the perspective of tourist destinations. This network was established due to its wide growth in the preference of Portuguese users, has quadrupled the number of users since 2013, according to data from the survey The Portuguese and Social Networks, 2019. The same study also revealed that currently, 68% of Portuguese have a profile on this network (Marktest, 2019), which demonstrates the need to analyse how the global trends of influential marketing at Instagram are reflected in this country.

TRAVEL AND DIGITAL INFLUENCERS ON INSTAGRAM: A CASE OF STUDY

This second part was turned to an empirical investigation about the active role of consumers, driven by the following question: what are the strategies used by digital influencers in the promotion of tourist destinations?

Methods

This is quantitative research, in the first place, because it works with an expressive volume of data from the published information in the selected profiles. Also, it identifies the dimension of the analysed contents, and how many of them mentioned the promotion of tourist destinations on Instagram. Moreover, this study is qualitative because it investigated what strategies were adopted by digital influencers in the production of this type of content.

From a pre-observation of the corpus of the study, a table of references with the most recurring categories was created, interested in identifying the resources, products and services that appear more frequently in the posts. The idea is not to confine publications in specific categories that refuse the others, as if the strategies were adopted purely or isolated by the Instagrammers. On the contrary, a preliminary observation intended to establish such categories as starting points to analyse how a post can even fit into more than one classification category, considering the combination of possible strategies in the network studied.

Content analysis and netnography methods were applied in both quantitative and qualitative analyses. It was complemented together with semi-structured interviews. Netnography, in a similar way to ethnography, allows the researcher to understand symbols, meanings as well as the practices of social groups, but in a specific context, in the web (Kozinets, 2010). For Hine (2000) in virtual ethnography, the field's construction is done by reflexivity and subjectivity. Like virtual ethnography, netnography is a specific type of online ethnography: 'Netnography is participant-observational research based on online hanging out, download, reflection, and connection' (Kozinets, 2015, p.67). Regarding participant observation, Hine (2000, p. 47) says:

The ethnographer is not a simple voyeur or disengaged observer but is also to some extent a participant sharing some of the concerns, emotions and commitments of the research subjects. This extended form of experience depends also on interaction, on a constant questioning of what it is to have an ethnographic understanding of a phenomenon ()

The nethnographic field was thus constructed considering the digital interaction of the Instagrammers not only with their followers but also with the authors, through interviews made by direct message from the platform. As the researchers are familiarised with the social network since 2012 and the authors started to follow the Portuguese Instagrammers studied since this research was started in June 2019. Regarding their digital interaction, the data was collected from June 21, 2019, to September 23, 2019. Throughout these three months, it was observed publications, comments, photo editions, publicity and hashtags. At the end of the first phase of analysis, the study intended to interview all profile owners, but only half of the population researched replied to the interview intent.

Research Corpus

A study developed by Primetag (2019), entitled Social Influence Report, analysed 1,682 Instagram accounts in Portugal, adopting as a criterion the minimum of 10,000 followers and 52 publications made throughout 2018. The profiles were divided by the study into several segments, such as Fashion and Beauty, Sports and Fitness, Travel, Gastronomy, Music, Cinema and TV. In the Travel segment, the Instagram accounts with the most followers in the country are those of Ana Sampaio (331 thousand), João Cajuda (305 thousand), Honeymooners - Joana and André (216 thousand), Teresa Freitas (216 thousand) and 55 Secrets (164 thousand) (updated on 07.22.2020).

From the five accounts with the most followers set out to study initially, Ana Sampaio, the profile with the most followers, had made one publication alone during the period determined for the study, from June 21 to September 23, 2019. Making a more extensive analysis of Ana Sampaio's profile and @55secrets, it was found that these accounts do not have a high frequency of publications. Ana Sampaio, for instance, during the whole year of 2019, has published nine times in total, without regularity in time. Therefore, because it was only one post made during the summer of 2019 to observe, which also applies to @55secrets, the authors suggested the exclusion of these two profiles for thematic analysis and possible comparison with the other profiles.

Besides, the authors decided to include in the research the three profiles with "higher engagement", according to the same Primetag study. Gonçalo Saraiva's account (@goncalo_sairava27) has the highest engagement rate, 14%, followed by Inês Brandling's account (@inesbrandling) with 13.7% engagement and finally Vitor Almeida (@vitoralmeida) with 12%. This way, three out of the five profiles with the largest number of followers in Portugal and the three profiles with the highest engagement index of Portugal were analysed.

The Primetag study used the following formulas to calculate the engagement (E) of content and accounts:

E publications = (L + C) / F

E account = (E1 + E2 + E3…) / number of publications

(L) is the total number of likes, (C) the total number of comments and (F) the total number of followers at the date of data collection. Since the variables are volatile, engagement is a relative and not an absolute indicator (Primetag, 2019, p. 48).

Profile Analysis

In the quantitative analysis, a study of the number of publications made in the proposed period was done, as well as an update on the number of followers, as Table 1 shows. The Primetag study measured the engagement index, and they did not extend to the group of Instagrammers with the largest number of followers.

Table 1. Quantitative analysis of the accounts with a greater number of followers and with more engagement

Instagrammer	Number of followers in a thousand	Number of publications*	Engagement index
WITH GREATER NUMBER OF FOLLOWERS			
Ana Sampaio – @anasbarros	331	1	*not applicable*
Joao Cajuda – @joaocajuda	305	45	*not applicable*
Honeymooners – @honeymooners	216	18	*not applicable*
Teresa Freitas – @teresacfreitas	216	21	*not applicable*
55 secrets – @55secrets	164	1	*not applicable*
WITH HIGHER ENGAGEMENT			
Gonçalo Saraiva – @goncalo_saraiva27	21,6	50	14%
Inês Brandling – @inesbrandling	82,3	19	13,7%
Vitor Almeida – @vitoralmeida	18	50	12%

*between June 21, 2019, and September 23, 2019

After this first phase of quantitative analyses and the choice of a representative and heterogeneous group of six profiles of Portuguese Instagrammers, it was made in deep content analysis and netnography in each profile. It was completed with a semi-structured interview with three of them. The six profiles were contacted by direct message on Instagram on July 22 2020. Gonçalo Saraiva, Vitor Almeida and Teresa Freitas answered. On the other hand, João Cajuda, Inês Brandling and the Honeymooners have never answered the questions even after several requests made through comments in the publications.

João Cajuda and the couple Honeymooners kept publishing and recording stories and were contacted again on the 25th and 29th July and the 3rd and 11th August 2020. Inês Brandling, meantime, did her last publication at the beginning of the Coronavirus quarantine on March 13 2020, saying the hashtag in Portuguese: *#euficoemcasa* (I stay at home) and as it was observed she has no more used her profile and consequently did not answer.

Among the six analysed profiles, João Cajuda and Inês Brandling stand out for being the only ones with publications with the hashtag "pub", which indicates paid advertising for the brand in question. Both make publicity for major brands with subsidiaries in Portugal, for example, Nespresso coffee (@ nespresso.pt) and EasyJet (@easyjet_pt), and mainly for Portuguese beverages' brands like Mateus Rose wine (@mateusrosewine) and Bohemia beer (@cerveja_bohemia). Among the paid publications directly linked to tourism, it highlights the two airline companies with which João Cajuda has partnered, the aforementioned EasyJet and Lufthansa (@lufthansa). The only tourist destination to partner with an instagrammer was the Swedish city of Malmo (@malmotown), in partnership with Inês Brandling. When it comes to professionalisation and profitability directly linked to the career of an Instagrammer, João Cajuda and Inês Brandling stand out.

They are what Duffy and Wissinger (2017) call as "creative worker in social media", a nod toward wider culture's fetishisation of entrepreneurship. According to the authors, this kind of influencers seem to have attained a career dream: They get paid to do what they love. Duffy and Wissinger (2017) also warn that, in some cases, this career "conceal less auspicious realities, including the demands for emotional labour, self-branding labour, and an always-on mode of entrepreneurial labour" (p. 4653).

It cannot be affirmed that the same happens with João Cajuda and Inês Brandling because none of them answered the messages and interviews the authors have sent to them. But as a result of the analysis, amongst all of the six explored profiles, the only one that seems to have a direct relation with tourism is that of João Cajuda. In addition to the 13 publications of brand advertising, João also made seven publications disseminating directly from the account @leva.me.tours "Leva-me" (Take me), that he owns, is described in his profile as an *"Unforgettable Travel Agency" with "tours by João Cajuda and Mariana Vaz"*. Through some of the profile texts, it was realised that in the summer of 2019 he accompanied a group to the Sahara Desert in Morocco.

João Cajuda is also the profile that on June 21 and September 23, 2019, posted photos and videos in more different destinations, sometimes he indicates the country and sometimes the city, but there are 19 locations. It does not mean that the Instagrammer has travelled to so many different destinations in a relatively short period. Analysing the texts of the publications and comments, as well as a correlation of dates, scenarios and even costumes used in the photos, it was perceived that in the summer of 2019 he travelled to Sardinia (Italy), Bordeaux (France) and Marrakesh (Morocco).

However, he merged the photos of the ongoing trips, with travel publications to the United States due to Lufthansa's partnership, to promote that *"@lufthansa now flies the iconic A380 to New York via Frankfurt or Munich"*. The same is repeated in the publication whose location is Miami, to promote the new flight of the airline also departing from Frankfurt or Munich. João continues to intercalate his travels in the summer of 2019 with publications of the type #TBT (throwback Thursday) with photos in destinations such as the Philippines, Seychelles, Costa Rica and Thailand to directly or indirectly promote Leva-me Tours travel itineraries. Finally, the publications are also interspersed with posts made in Portugal, whether to promote Mateus Wine and Nespresso Coffee or simply to demonstrate his love for his country.

It is important to consider that all six Instagrammers analysed in this paper posted at least one photo of the country on their network in the proposed period. Teresa Freitas was the one who posted the least. She made only one publication at *Casa de Serralves*, a foundation and museum in Porto. *Casa de Serralves* is a pink building built in the 1930s in the Art Deco style. It emphasised the property's colour as this is the differential of Teresa Freitas' profile: all her photos are in pastel tones. She also treats all photos so that the trees and green grass are in shades of pink and lilac bringing to all her publications the same thematic colour. Teresa can not be considered a travel Instagrammer, because she uses Instagram only to publicise her work as a designer and conceptual photographer. She creates digital content for major brands such as Netflix, Pandora, Dior, Fujifilm, Huawei, etc. In the interview, she answered that she "does not work from Instagram directly, I work for the brands and after I post the results on my Instagram". Which means she uses it more as her portfolio than any other strategy.

Along the same lines is Vitor Almeida, who also published a photo of *Casa de Serralves*. Vitor is an architect, and most of the photos published are of monuments, buildings and bridges around the world, the other part is photos of himself. Even so, his photos are also taken, mostly in iconic places, stairs, museums, and so on. Unlike Teresa Freitas, who did not post a single photo of her, Vitor Almeida, who calls himself an "Instagram Lover" in his profile description, also uses the network for his self-branding. He is an architect, but there are no photos of his projects. Vitor is keen for the application itself. In three summer, months, he made 50 publications. With this high number of publications, Vitor Almeida generated a total of 12% engagement.

Despite not knowing about Primetag's study and being among the three profiles with the highest engagement rate, in an interview Vitor justifies such engagement due to his strategy of getting to know his audience. And he said: "I know when they will react a lot - when the photo has a lot of impacts - and when the photo is cooler and has less interaction. It is important to give what people like, but it is also important to make the feed something with my identity". When asked if he considers this to be his career, he replies: "It is just a hobby! Although partnerships may arise, namely travel, but always to photograph ".

Moving to the first in the ranking of accounts with the most engagement in the Primetag study, Gonçalo Saraiva also made a total of 50 publications in the 90 days of summer 2019. Gonçalo's differential is that he was the only one who made absolutely all 50 publications in the same destination: Porto. He is a Social Communication student at the University of Coimbra, and his account is dedicated to Portugal. Most of the photos are taken in Coimbra. He highlights local culture through pictures of students and their traditional clothing, pictures of the daily life of a Portuguese and pictures of landscapes and architecture. In an interview, Gonçalo stated that like Teresa Freitas, he uses Instagram as "a kind of portfolio" for his photographs. His objective is "To show what Portugal has to offer through my photographic vision". Gonçalo knew about the study by Primetag, but he already used the study results for self-promotion in a highlight of the stories, even so, he says he has no engagement strategy and no commercial partnerships.

In the same city, the couple André and Joana, who after publishing dozens of posts around the world dressed in wedding suits, in the summer of 2019, started to publish only photos whose location indicated the Oncological Institute of Portugal, which is in Porto. This is because Joana was undergoing cancer treatment. Instead of having the white dress, makeup and hairstyle and be taken in many places around the world, the photos started to be on the sofa at home or in the hospital corridors. Even with this change of scenery and costumes, the account has not changed its initial theme proposal. With an account entitled "@honeymooners", whose goal is to help *"enjoy the most incredible 'trip' for two"* according to the account description. With the word trip in quotes, the couple probably wants to convey the idea that a trip can be a travel to the other side of the world and a joint battle against cancer.

Inês Brandling, who can gather a large number of followers (82.3 thousand) and a high engagement rate (13.7%) while optimising in 19 publications, nine advertisements. Inês makes gastronomic reviews of several Portuguese restaurants, which opens up the possibility of advertising drinks and desserts while making small travel diaries, and this earned her the partnership with the Swedish city of Malmo. Inês probably gets this engagement for the pictures of beautiful dishes and the tips and information she gives about destinations and restaurants. She is the only one who is dedicated to providing these services to her followers.

Of the six accounts studied here, three of them have only photos of gastronomy, landscapes and anonymous people and others, in addition to photos of landscapes also post many photos of themselves as tourists. João Cajuda, Joana and André, the couple Honeymooners, and Vitor Almeida position themselves as travellers and post photos enjoying the destinations they travelled to. Inês Brandling, despite writing in the first person, does not appear in any of the photographs and Gonçalo Saraiva and Teresa Freitas only comment on what is being represented in the photos, be it light, colour or action, all usually in no more than two lines of text.

Finally, it cannot be affirmed that there was unanimity in the destinations promoted or that the photos were taken only in "instagrammable" destinations. .Marwick (2015) explains that the "Internet is a visual medium, and more and more individuals are using images rather than written self-descriptions to express themselves". Due to the photographic nature of the medium, "on Instagram, textual description and replies to followers are de-emphasised in favour of images, particularly selfies" (p. 138). All photos call for good editing, angle and light, even in photos taken in a hospital, as was the case of Joana and André. Among all the accounts, João Cajuda is the one who posts the most photos in "instagrammable" places. He benefits from the places, unusual experiences and resources like underwater cameras and drones. João Cajuda, who works alone with tourism and social networks, edits videos of places he visits. In summer 2019, out of the 45 publications, seven were videos.

Portugal is present in every account. A second recurrent destination is the United States of America and San Francisco and San Diego, which are present in Teresa Freitas' accounts. Miami and New York are present in the accounts of Vitor Almeida and João Cajuda. Inês Brandling posted photos at Universal Studios in Hollywood (Table 2). Each profile was examined in the intention to answer the research question on the strategies used by digital influencers in promoting tourist destinations in three groups: (i) Those that promote themselves through a touristic destination; (ii) Those who promote a tourist destination to promote themselves, and (iii) those who promote a tourist destination due to some partnership.

In group 1 are João Cajuda and Vitor Almeida, both use appealing destinations, and take pictures of themselves, matching their clothes with the scenario, in desirable experiences. As Marwick (2015) summarises, "In the broadcast era, celebrity was something a person was; in the Internet era, micro-celebrity is something people do" (p. 140) or in this case, to where this micro-celebrity is travelling to. Besides, they use photography resources, high-quality cameras and hashtags to give more impact to the posts. In group 2 are Gonçalo Saraiva and Teresa Freitas, who use the cities' architectural beauties to promote their work as photographers and designers, whether looking for a specific angle and light or in the post position. In group 3 are João Cajuda and Inês Brandling. The two influencers were either hired by brands or even by the tourist destination and used storytelling resources, videos, and practical tips for destinations. The couple André and Joana did not fit into any of the categories.

Among the six explored profiles, João Cajuda is the only "creative work in social media" (Duffy and Wissinger, 2017) which relates Instagram as entrepreneurial and self-branding labour. Cajuda works on and with Instagram whether to promote brands, destinations or the travel agency Leva-me Tours.

Unlike João Cajuda, Inês Brandling, who also did some publicity posts, does not relate her image to her profile. A good performance of the influencer image requires considerable self-branding labour (Duffy and Wissinger, 2017) which is crucial for maintaining and gaining followers and fans.

Except for Gonçalo Saraiva, the Portuguese accounts here analysed demonstrated that their own country was not the main focus of their work. On the contrary, the Instagrammers benefit from many other landscapes to promote their work, whether as a tourist agent, photographer or designer.

The six influencers studied used the quality of the photographs and the thematic consistency of their profiles, as a way to keep their followers engaged and to promote tourism destinations were they live or visit.

Table 2. Qualitative analysis of the six accounts studied

Instagrammer	Thematic	Number of different locations	Photos in which they appear	Number of #pub	Brands	Strategy for the promotion of tourist destinations
WITH GREATER NUMBER OF FOLLOWERS						
João Cajuda – @joaocajuda	Travel and lifestyle	19 countries and cities (Bordeaux, Thailand, Philippines, etc.)	23 out of 45 posts	13	Nespresso Easyjet, Lufthansa, Mateus Rosé	Lifestyle, drones and underwater camera
Honeymooners – @honeymooners	Romance	2 places (Portugal and Portuguese Institute of Oncology)	18 out of 18 posts	-	-	Romantic trips
Teresa Freitas – @teresacfreitas	Fashion and landscape	7 cities (Venice, Saint Petersburg, San Francisco, etc.)	0 out of 21 posts	-	-	Photo editing
WITH MORE ENGAGEMENT						
Gonçalo Saraiva – @goncalo_saraiva27	Portugal (landscape and culture)	1 (Porto)	0 out of 50 posts	-	-	Hashtag
Inês Brandling – @inesbrandling	Gastronomy and literature	3 Cities (Lisbon, Copenhagen and Malmo)	0 out of 19 posts	9	Malmo Town, Grom Gelato, Bohemia Beer	Practical tips (prices, travel time, etc.)
Vítor Almeida – @vitoralmeida	Architecture and Design	3 Cities (Miami, NY and Porto)	6 out of 50 posts	-	-	hashtag

FUTURE RESEARCH DIRECTIONS

In this chapter, the question of the power of Instagrammers in promoting tourist destinations was analysed from the perspective of the strategies adopted by the content producers. It is also important to investigate, in future studies, how these strategies to influence followers from the perception of the audience.

To verify how this marketing influence is reflected in the Portuguese scenario, or even in different contexts, it is possible to adopt it as a method to analyse data referring to the engagement between

Instagrammers and their followers. From that, the in-depth interview method can be conducted with the followers who reveal greater interaction with the observed profiles to measure the influence of Instagrammers on their consumption habits in the travel or any other segment.

Besides, it is also important to update the data collected to continue monitoring the issue of promoting tourist destinations on Instagram. Primetag Study analysed Instagram accounts in 2018, and this article set out to study the same accounts in 2019. Even with just a few months separating one study from the other, there were major differences between the accounts' publications. One account that was more active in 2018 started to post less in 2019 and another that made publications around the world in 2018, started to post only one place in 2019. Everything is changeable, especially regarding people's accounts (not companies, brands, etc.).

Therefore, this research must be constantly updated and developed in different circumstances. For example, through a quick search in the accounts of the same Instagrammers surveyed, there is a big difference from the content posted during the summer of 2020 and what was published in 2019. This year, in post confinement and pandemic context, some stopped publishing, and some started to travel only in Portugal.

This shows the importance of taking data from summer 2020 and so on, for future analysis on the strategies to promote tourist destinations. A future comparative study on what happened in online tourism promotion until 2019 and what will happen in the post-Covid-19 era seems crucial.

For now, this study reveals that Portugal is not being publicised in the most followed accounts of the country, the opposite of other destinations. However, with Covid-19, these influential Instagrammers can be a great tool to encourage national travellers to stay safe in their own country and visit other places in Portugal. Also, it could help the sector, the one most affected.

CONCLUSION

Analysing the impact of the new media on tourism communication, this study proposed to focus on the use of Instagram in the promotion of destinations. After a literature review about the transformation of communication in the networked society, emphasising the multiplication of voices in the culture of convergence, it was reflected on how tourist communication has been reconfigured after the advent of social networks.

The proliferation of new actors in the production of content on digital platforms, where diverse consumption experiences are shared, including tourist ones, there is a latent need for further research, especially in the most far-reaching publication of digital influencers, such as in followers as engagement.

From this research, it is possible to affirm that Instagram is a large influential media platform. Consequently, many of the so-called influencers in the travel segment of Primetag study do have a constant and professional account promoting some destinations and/or themselves and their production/business. It is also noted that none of the publications of the Instagrammers has any relation with the official promotion of the tourism bureau of Portugal. It demonstrated the lack of engagement of the tourism sector in such an innovative and important area of marketing. It also showed a lack of connection between the tourism governmental organisation and the Instagrammers' influence to promote certain destinations or even the country. Therefore, the study revealed that new media is a powerful tool to promote destinations. The influence in tourism consumption behaviour is a field to be explored by DMOs, companies, and other stakeholders in the tourism sector.

REFERENCES

Alves, R. C. (2017). Performance em ciberjornalismo: tecnologia, inovação e eficiência. In G. L. Martins, L. S. A. Reino, & T. Bueno (Eds.), *Performance em ciberjornalismo: tecnologia, inovação e eficiência* (pp. 33–49). Editora UFMS.

Amaral, A., Natal, G., & Viana, L. (2008). Netnografia como aporte metodológico da pesquisa em comunicação digital. *Sessões do Imaginário: cinema, cultura, tecnologia da Imagem, 13*(20), 34-40.

Baldissera, R. (2010). Comunicação Turística. *Rosa Dos Ventos. REvista Do Programa de Pós-Graduação Em Turismo, 1*(1), 6–15.

Bardin, L. (2006). *Content analysis* (L. de A. Rego & A. Pinheiro, Trans.). Edicoes 70.

Barreiro, T., Dinis, G., & Breda, Z. (2019). Marketing de influência e influenciadores digitais: Aplicação do conceito pelas DMO em Portugal. *Marketing & Tourism Review, 4*(1), 1–19.

Baudrillard, J. (2017). *A sociedade do consumo*. Edições 70.

Cacho, A., & Azevedo, F. (2010). O turismo no contexto da sociedade informacional. *Revista Brasileira de Pesquisa em Turismo, 4*(2), 31–48. doi:10.7784/rbtur.v4i2.266

Castells, M. (2016). A sociedade em rede. A era da informação: economia, sociedade e cultura (17th ed.). Paz e Terra.

Di Felice, M. (2010). Mídias nativas: as manipulações tecnológicas do mundo e o fim dos pontos de vista centrais. In. C. Alvares & M. J. Damásio (Eds.), *Teorias e práticas dos Média: Transformando o Local no Global* (pp. 87-106). Lisboa: Edições Universitárias Lusófonas.

Duffy, B., & Wissinger, E. (2017). Mythologies of Creative Work in the Social Media Age: Fun, Free, and "Just Being Me". *International Journal of Communication, 11*, 4652–4671.

Femenia-Serra, F., & Gretzel, U. (2020). Influencer Marketing for Tourism Destinations: Lessons from a Mature Destination. In J. Neidhardt & W. Wörndl (Eds.), *Information and Communication Technologies in Tourism 2020* (pp. 65–78). Springer International Publishing. doi:10.1007/978-3-030-36737-4_6

Fernandes, L. C. (2018). *Publicidade online: A influência dos instafamous nos hábitos de consumo dos jovens* (Unpublished bachelor's thesis). Federal University of Rio de Janeiro (UFRJ), Rio de Janeiro, BR.

Fonseca, P. D. R. (2019). *Impact of Instagrammers on consumers travel behaviour in the hospitality sector* (Unpublished master's thesis). Estoril Higher Institute for Tourism and Hotel Studies (ESHTE), Estoril, PT.

Gibson, C. (2019). Critical tourism studies: New directions for volatile times. *Tourism Geographies, 22*(4-5), 1–19. doi:10.1080/14616688.2019.1647453

Hays, S., Page, S. J., & Buhalis, D. (2013). Social media as a destination marketing tool: Its use by national tourism organisations. *Current Issues in Tourism, 16*(3), 211–239. doi:10.1080/13683500.2012.662215

Hine, C. (2000). *Virtual Ethnography*. Sage. doi:10.4135/9780857020277

Iglesias-Sánchez, P. P., Correia, M. B., Jambrino-Maldonado, C., & de las Heras-Pedrosa, C. (2020). Instagram as a co-creation space for tourist destination image-building: Algarve and costa del sol case studies. *Sustainability (Switzerland)*, *12*(7), 1–26.

Jenkins, H. (2009). *Cultura da Convergência*. Aleph.

Kaufman, D. (2015). *O Despertar de Gulliver: Os desafios das empresas nas redes digitais* (Unpublished doctoral dissertation). University of São Paulo, São Paulo, SP.

Kotler, P., Hermanwan, K., & Setiawan, I. (Eds.). (2010). *Marketing 3.0: as forças que estão definindo o novo marketing centrado no ser humano*. Elsevier. doi:10.1002/9781118257883

Kozinets, R. V. (2010). *Netnography: Doing Ethnographic Research Online*. Sage.

Kozinets, R. V. (2015). *Netnography: Redefined* (2nd ed.). Sage.

Magalhães, M. (2018a). *Net-ativismo: protestos e subversões nas redes sociais digitais*. Colecção ICNOVA.

Magalhães, S. C. B. C. (2018b). *Gestão da Imagem de uma Empresa no Facebook: Estudo de Caso New Look* (Unpublished master's thesis). Lusofona University of Porto, Porto, PT.

Marketest. (2019). *Os Portugueses e as Redes Sociais 2019*. Retrieved from https://www.marktest.com/wap/a/grp/p~96.aspx

Martins, K. (2018). *Experiência Instagramável em São Paulo*. Retrieved from http://www.sonhosdelola.com.br/experiencia-instagramavel-em-sao-paulo/

Marujo, M. (2008). A Internet como novo meio de comunicação para os destinos turísticos: O caso da Ilha da Madeira. *Revista Turismo Em Análise*, *19*(1), 1–25. doi:10.11606/issn.1984-4867.v19i1p25-42

Marwick, A. E. (2015). Instafame: Luxury Selfies in the Attention Economy. *Public Culture*, *27*(1 (75)), 137–160. doi:10.1215/08992363-2798379

Morais, F. (2018). *Ambientes instagramáveis*. Retrieved from https://www.mundodomarketing.com.br/artigos/felipe-morais/37971/ambientes-instagramaveis.html

Morozov, E. (2019). *Big Tech: a ascensão dos dados e a morte da política*. Ubu Editora.

Panas, G., Vasiliadou, S., & Halkiopoulos, C. (2020). Data Analysis Evaluation of Web Technologies Enhancing Communication in Tourism Industry: Case Study in Kefalonia Island. In V. Katsoni & T. Spyriadis (Eds.), *Cultural and Tourism Innovation in the Digital Era* (pp. 171–187). doi:10.1007/978-3-030-36342-0_14

Poon, A. (1993). *Tourism, technology and competitive strategies* (Vol. 2). CAB International.

Porto, D., & Flores, J. (2013). *Periodismo Transmedia: Reflexiones y técnicas para el ciberperiodista desde los laboratórios de médios interactivos*. Editora Fragua.

Primetag. (2019). *Social Influence Report by Primetag*. Retrieved from https://primetag.com/social_influence_report/

Rainie, L., & Wellman, B. (2012). *Networked: the new social operating system*. MIT Press. doi:10.7551/mitpress/8358.001.0001

Ruibal, A. R. (2009). *Periodismo turístico: análisis del turismo a través de las portadas*. S. L. Editorial UOC.

Safko, L., & Brake, D. K. (2009). *The social media bible*. John Wiley and Sons, Inc.

Terra, C. F. (2011). O que as organizações precisam fazer para serem bem vistas nas mídias sociais sob a ótica da comunicação organizacional e das relações públicas. In *Proceedings of V Congresso Abrapcorp 2011: Redes Sociais, Comunicação, Organizações* (vol. 1, pp. 1-15). São Paulo, SP: ABRAPCORP.

Terttunen, A. (2017). *The influence of Instagram on consumers' travel planning and destination choice. Master Thesis in Hospitality, tourism and experience management*. University of Applied Sciences.

Toffler, A., & Toffler, H. (2006). *Revolutionary Wealth*. Knopf Doubleday.

Varley, P., Schilar, H., & Rickly, J. M. (2020). Tourism non-places: Bending airports and wild escapes. *Annals of Tourism Research, 80*, 102791. doi:10.1016/j.annals.2019.102791

Wichels, S. (2014). *Comunicação Turística: desafios e tendências na contemporaneidade. Estudo de caso: Tenerife* (Unpublished master's thesis). University of Coimbra, Coimbra, PT.

This research was previously published in Impact of New Media in Tourism; pages 173-190, copyright year 2021 by Business Science Reference (an imprint of IGI Global).

Chapter 39
Social Media as a Tool for Gastronomy:
An Analysis Through Instagram on Turkish Cuisine

Gonca Güzel Şahin
Atilim University, Turkey

ABSTRACT

Many countries that have unique local gastronomy cultures develop and promote their regions for the purpose of economic effects for regional development instruments and to protect and sustain local culture and meet the demands of today's tourists. For the purpose of security and providing the sustainability of local culture diversities in the world, national and international organizations register and put under protection the local gastronomy assets. This occurs in various proportions. In order to compete with regional tourism, a variety of tourist attractions should be developed. Turkish cuisine one of three top cuisines in the world. The aim of this chapter is to emphasize the importance of marketing strategy on social media for the traditional Turkish cuisine and Turkish cultural cuisine.

INTRODUCTION

Unlike traditional media, digital marketing is all marketing activities using mobile devices, interactive media and internet to support all marketing activities of a product. The preference in marketing activities affected by low-cost internet due to its ability to reach large masses has led to the change of general marketing strategies. With these changing strategies, campaigns organized in digital environment within the digital marketing applications, low costs that have arisen, easy access to the target audience and rapid implementation of these applications are of great advantages provided. Businesses who want to excel in the competitive environment and want to bring new goods or services to the market have to keep up with the technological era in today's conditions. The Internet is one of the most important digital revo-

DOI: 10.4018/978-1-6684-6287-4.ch039

lutions today. In particular, the Internet has become a pioneer of many innovations and changes since the beginning of the 21st century.

This concept, which is called digital marketing and carries marketing to virtual environment, creates significant advantages for organizations with its unique characteristics and provides great convenience in reaching the target audience. Businesses that benefit from the opportunities of the digital age can reach larger masses at a lower cost with the advantages created by the internet environment and can effectively carry out their activities by promoting the goods and / or services they market. With the developing technology and changing consumer habits, mobile device usage rate is increasing day by day and accordingly, shopping opportunities over mobile devices are developing rapidly. Because of these developments, organizations now allocate significant budgets for digital marketing activities (Koçak Alan et.al., 2018). Thus, it enables enterprises to act according to the results obtained (Özdaş, 2017). Digital marketing is the most important communication tool in reaching consumers today. This concept is also referred to as e-marketing, online marketing, online marketing or interactive marketing. It is known that digital marketing has many advantages over traditional marketing. Due to these advantages, digital marketing is preferred by the companies for low cost and quick and easy access to the target audience. The necessity of adapting to the developing technology triggers the continuous standing of the enterprises. Compared to the promotional activities through traditional mass media, advertisements on the internet are both cost-effective and updateable and measurable. In the product promotion and campaigns carried out over the internet, some statistical data and important information such as the number of people interested in the product are obtained.

As a result of this, the efficiency of the marketing activities is very important in shaping the marketing strategies of the enterprises. With the new regulations that have emerged with the technology and the internet, which has become a part of people's lives, it has started to reach the consumers who are wanted by the commercial enterprises and institutions in this way. The internet, which is also referred to as the digital revolution, not only benefits the people, but also the commercial enterprises. Digital marketing provides benefits in many areas such as advertising at a lower cost, determining consumer wishes and expectations by applying strategies and understanding consumer reactions instantly. In this way, it is possible to provide to identify marketing strategies that are appropriate to consumer wishes and expectations, to implement and control these strategies, and to integrate traditional marketing approach with changing and developing technology and to expand the use of smart phones that almost every individual has (Bulunmaz, 2016).

Thanks to smart phones and tablets, mobile applications and social media usage rates have increased, and consumers can take advantage of unlimited informations regarding their orders. In addition to internet marketing, digital marketing also conveys information about the product to consumers in areas that do not require internet use (sms, landline phones, etc.). Different from being a traditional brand, becoming a digital brand and creating brand awareness has become important. Enterprises that adopt digital marketing reach more consumers through the channels used, provide information about their products, create orders and control customer satisfaction after service. However, increasing the value of digital marketing and relations with potential consumers surfing the internet is one of the reasons why it is preferred. This is due to some of the characteristics typically described in electronic and digital marketing. Among these features, supplier companies provide many more advantages such as establishing stronger relationships with consumers, faster information sharing, loss of distances between organizations and enterprises and global accessibility (Heikkinen, 2012). Thanks to digital marketing methods, it has become easier for consumers to reach producers, ask questions about goods or services and express their wishes and complaints. Similarly, producers can easily reach consumers at any time. In the process of purchasing through digital marketing, consumers can examine multiple products at the same time, make comparisons with other alternative products and these made life easier for consumers in their complex and strenuous living conditions (Yöndar Karabeyoğlu, 2018). However, the competition in the markets is escalating and advancing towards globalization. Information is becoming the most important element for markets (Şengün, 2015). Another advantage of the information is that it can be tested and developed according to consumer expectations in the development and implementation of digital marketing strategies.

Many reasons such as the increasing competition environment, the change in marketing understanding, and the constant change in the demands and expectations of consumers show the importance and necessity of digital marketing for both producers and consumers. In today's information, communication and technology era, enterprises that stay away from technological and digital marketing along with traditional marketing understanding are seen to be very difficult to gain a place in the market in an increasingly competitive environment. Digital marketing is an environment where innovations and changes are rapidly consumed, enabling businesses to interact quickly and at lower costs when meeting consumers. Therefore, it is necessary to analyze the profile of the target group that we will provide goods and services with, and to create innovative strategies in this direction and to create a program by using all the opportunities provided by the media.

Before the formation of social media, it is necessary to talk about the development of internet use. The emergence of the discovery of the "World Wide Web", which is considered a revolution in this system, was developed by Tim Berners-Lee and the term "Web 1.0" refers to websites. In Web 1.0, websites were created for information purposes only. This means that when users visit their website, they only get information. The information age on the Internet, developed by O'Reilly Media in 2004, the term Web 2.0 has now developed a network system that transforms mutual communication by sharing information with users. At the same time, with Web 2.0, users have moved to a system where they can interact and share and create their own site content. Thus, the foundations of social media that can share information, photos and videos were established (Yücel Güngör et.al., 2016: 130).

In recent years, with the effect of technological developments, these sources of influence tend to develop and the diversity of social media tools in electronic media has increased and the individual content created by users has been integrated into the applications (Tham et.al., 2013). With technological advancement, the adoption and use of social media is increasing as it provides more contribution and interaction of users (Zhai, et.al., 2015). Today, those who share in social media are not only the shares of individuals, but also sites that they accept members on their own platform, share photos and videos about the goods and services they produce and share their opinions and suggestions easily. Therefore, social media is a marketing tool for businesses (Şengün, 2015). Social media can be defined as websites and applications that allow users to create and share content or join social networks. Social networking sites are special websites and applications that allow users to interact with people around the world (Parsons, 2017).

As of January 2019, the number of internet, mobile and social media users worldwide is given. Accordingly, it is seen that the world population is 7 billion 676 million and 5.112 billion people use mobile telephones, the ratio of this to the total population is around 67%. However, it is understood that 4.388 billion people use the internet and 3.484 billion people in total internet users are active social media users and it is around 79% when we compare to the total number of internet users. In addition, the number of social media users via mobile devices is 3,256 billion. The ratio of the number of social media mobile users to the total number of internet users is around 74%. According to the data of the month January

2019 the number of internet users in Turkey and they are given the general rate of mobile use. Number of Internet users in Turkey, where 72% of the total population, and the number of active Internet users shows that 59.36 million people. While the number of active social media users is 52 million and 63% of the country's population, the number of mobile social media users is 44 million and the ratio of the country's population is 53%. According to data from the month of January 2019 on the basis of monthly active usage in Turkey, here are some social media user numbers. Accordingly, the number of Facebook users is 43 million, followed by 38 million Instagram users. While 9 million people use Twitter and Snapchat is 6.35 million people, the number of members registered to LinkedIn is 7.3 million (2019 Turkey Using the Internet and Social Media Statistics. Accessed: 29/03/2019, https://dijilopedi. com/2019-turkiye-internet-kullanim-ve-sosyal-medytothey-statistics/).

Social networks are used in place of traditional communication tools like other technological communication tools. Social networking sites affect our lives both personally and socially. Accordingly, the opportunities provided by these sites include photo-video sharing, messaging etc. and become a part of our lives as applications that create communication and interaction. Social media, which is described as the biggest revolution after the Internet, does not matter where and how you are. While acquiring information on social media, the person becomes a source of information. Every item shared on social media can spread rapidly around the world and affect people. The rapid dissemination of information sharing on social media has become a preferred tool by both individuals and businesses. People can get information on social media, and their activities such as sharing and messaging information resulted in the emergence of new types of media: Instagram, twitter, youtube, facebook etc. These are the platforms that enable the sharing of information through social networking sites, supporting them, forming groups, creating new technological areas and making mutual communication and interaction (Boys & Ellison, 2008). The most important feature of social media channels that use different methods and technologies is quality service. It is the virtual environment where users choose the channels that are suitable for them according to their personal characteristics and they are selective in this regard.

Social media is primarily based on text, sound, photography and video, and it is a more convenient way of sharing information than traditional media. For this reason, more and more businesses are using social media as a marketing tool. With the increasing demand for social media and the increasing number of users, marketing activities are integrated into social media channels. Thus, visibility and image of enterprises can be improved more easily thanks to social media (Heikkinen, 2012).

Social media marketing is a process that enables people to promote internet sites, goods and services through social networks in electronic and virtual environments, and to create interaction by reaching out to the masses that cannot be reached by conventional advertising and marketing methods. For many reasons such as changes in consumer demands and expectations, changes in living conditions, increase in social media usage areas, increasing competition environment, businesses have started to carry out their marketing activities through social media.

Social media marketing requires a very different perspective than traditional marketing. Therefore, businesses have to be more careful because they communicate directly with their customers through social media (Needles &Thompson, 2013). The social media platform has become a platform where not only products are researched, purchased and evaluated, but also products are defended by customers. With the Internet becoming the most effective communication tool in recent years, it motivates the changes in the purchasing decision process of consumers quite well. Social networks are particularly effective in acquiring information (Bendahou & Berbou, 2015).

Social media marketing is mostly within the scope of promotion efforts. The realization of activities such as product promotion, promotions and public relations by the enterprises via social media is very effective in reaching and segmenting the target market.

In this way, businesses should determine their marketing activities and strategies through invaluable information such as how people think about social media, how they behave and their positive and negative comments. In particular, it is possible to increase product sales by developing special offers for users who meet in common with each other on social media. Businesses that increase the number of active members will increase their relations with their customers and shape the marketing mix with the information they obtain in feedback (Özdaş, 2017).

Social media marketing has improved with consumers getting information about the products exhibited by companies and consulting with other consumers who use the product, however rumor marketing and viral marketing methods have started to be preferred in social media. With the exception of the mass media on the subjects that attract consumers' attention, rumor is a special area where viral marketing is made and among them consumers can make their personal preferences. Word of mouth marketing is one of the important factors affecting the development of social media. Viral marketing is another advertising and promotion method that is spreading spontaneously in social media. Unlimited feature of social media is among the reasons why consumers prefer social networks. Rumor and viral marketing are not only preferred by consumers but also by producers.

The fact that rumor and viral marketing is effective in social media marketing brought about the necessity of using different applications related to activities such as production, promotion, customer potential to be served by the enterprises. One of these applications is SOLOMO. The word "social", "local" and "mobile" is composed of the first two letters of the word "SoLoMo" are the programs and applications used in social, local and mobile platforms in order to easily find sales and service areas of enterprises. With SoLoMo, businesses can communicate or access their customers at the most convenient time and place. With the help of smart phones, which are the most widely used communication tools in recent years, companies create their own applications in order to promote the goods and services they produce more and aim to enable customers to use these applications.

Social Media Marketing in Tourism

The fact that consumers cannot see and experience the touristic products before, the benefits of the products to the consumers are subjective, their opinions about the touristic product do not gain clarity create disadvantages for the touristic consumers. In recent years, with the development of technology and the increase in usage areas, it has become easier for tourist consumers to learn more about touristic products. In addition, comments and sharing on touristic businesses, destinations and touristic products have provided insight to potential tourists, making it easier for them to choose destinations. Two factors that are constantly changing and developing in the tourism industry, which are generally based on manpower; technology and people. With the development of technology, the use of internet has become widespread in the enterprises in tourism sector and changes in consumer demands and demands have occurred. The internet, which is used as a marketing tool in the tourism sector, has started to be used more. It has demonstrated its impact in many areas including tourism marketing mix (Sü & Doğdubay, 2012). With the developments in the digital age, the traditional process in social media is transformed with creative ideas and people share their travel experiences in digital environment with the services provided in this transformation (Munar & Jacobsen, 2013).

Touristic goods and services are not objective and have the characteristics of products that people evaluate as perceived. Based on the subjective nature of touristic products, the experience and recommendations that consumers share on the internet are more reliable than those demanding goods and services. Instead of sites, booklets, brochures where only positive promotions of the enterprises in the tourism sector are made, the comments and evaluations of the consumers who share their real experiences are more effective in the decision-making processes of potential consumers. In other words, sharing of information and opinions of different social network users with a common interest in social media is more realistic by the consumers and it is among the reasons for preferring social media together with comments, and the opportunity to share their experiences on social media after travel. The fact that touristic goods and services are abstract, production and consumption are synchronous and the inability to be tried before have made it necessary for the promotion activities of the enterprises to be more effective. In recent years, with the development of technology, businesses have established more productive websites and thus, activities such as promotion, customer relations, direct marketing, and distribution are effectively carried out in less time. Social media, which serves numerous purposes with its contents, is a mixture of consumer-based emotions, thoughts, impressions, experiences and communication and its place in the tourism sector is mostly social (Xiang & Gretzel, 2010, p.180). It is revealed by the researches that tourists gather information on social media to decide and make purchases or reservations for the travels they plan, this shows how important the social networks are for the tourism enterprises. In this context, visually sharing the activities carried out by consumers on social media with an expectation of appreciation and interpreting the quality of goods and services on social networks affect the preferability of tourism enterprises (İbiş & Engin, 2017). The fact that businesses operate on social media platforms in order to maintain their continuity in the competitive environment will be among the purchasing desires and preferences of consumers not only within national borders but also internationally.

Hospitality and airline companies and other stakeholders in the tourism industry are increasingly using social media and are increasingly using sites such as Facebook and Twitter to increase their brand awareness. Social media can be used at any point in a trip, and a traveler can plan everything from booking to the restaurant to eat (Sü & Doğdubay:2012: 71). One of the reasons why businesses attach importance to social media is to deliver the right messages to the right people at the right time and to be preferred by consumers. The intensive use of social media by consumers has been recognized by businesses and they have started to develop new strategies on this issue. Another benefit provided by social media for both businesses and consumers is the easy access to the masses that are difficult to reach, mutual producer and consumer accessibility, and direct communication with the interlocutors in a shorter period of time, at lower costs. The creation of new and different communication opportunities by social media has led to an increase in the benefit of both producers and consumers. With social media, it has made it possible to reach a large number of different sources of information about the destinations that tourist consumers want to experience.

Today's tourist consumers actively use websites, mobile applications and social media in travel planning and information services. Tourists conduct research on their travels online and share their holiday experiences and discuss them on common platforms, as a result the majority of tourism businesses now creating their own profile pages on social media platforms. Using social media tools and being active in social media can be an economical and effective way for tourism enterprises that do not have an extensive marketing budget. However, if the information in this social media tool is constantly updated, social media will be a successful method for businesses. People openly share their travel experiences that they previously only shared with acquaintances within their communities trough social media. They write on blogs, share photos on Instagram or Facebook, upload videos to Youtube, and announce their location on Foursquare.

Social Media Marketing in Gastronomy and Gastronomy Tourism

Derived from the Greek word gastros, the gastronomy is known as a science that deals with the culinary culture and roots of classical civilizations (Kivela & Crotts, 2006). With a more detailed definition, gastronomy is a branch of science that includes the artistic and scientific elements and it contains the studies of understanding and applying all the features starting from the historical development process of food and beverages in a detailed way, and developing and adapting it to today's conditions (Hatipoğlu, 2010). With the emergence of the concept of social media, there are significant differences in the communication tools and communication strategies provided by the communication between businesses and customers. Content created by the consumers on social platforms has become accessible to the business through social media (Mangold & Faulds, 2009). Gastronomy tourism, a concept related to individuals who want to discover new flavors and the cultures to which these flavors belong; it can be defined as a visit to food / beverage producers, food festivals, restaurants, local or rural areas in order to taste a special food / beverage (Long, 2004). Gastronomy, food or culinary tourism, which is the result of individuals' desire to try food / drinks belonging to different cultures, is considered within the scope of cultural tourism. It is known that the diversity of regional dishes is related to the cultural richness of the countries. Turkey, due to the geopolitical situation throughout the history have hosted many civilizations and rich farmland geography is one of the world's richest cuisine with sophisticated culinary culture.

According to a study by Groupon and the National Restaurant Association, social media has become the most used marketing strategy by restaurants. However, in a global study conducted by Hospitality Technology, especially in the USA, the social media sites that restaurants use most in digital marketing have been identified as Facebook and Twitter (Garcia, 2013). Groups of people who have such an active and active role in social networks provide businesses with a wide market opportunity to reach a large number of consumers at the same time. Therefore, the communication of these groups of people on the internet between brands and products becomes important because such online communities are natural communication environments. The development of social media is an indicator that social media-based life and mass communication will become widespread in the coming years. From digital menus to targeted social media campaigns with online orders, technology has evolved the marketing strategies of food and beverage businesses. When people are looking for a place to eat, planning a meal with friends, or looking for a suitable place to eat while traveling, they use social media tools including location-oriented sites, commenting sites, and booking services to evaluate online suggestions shared by other users. Customers use the Internet and social networks when planning, announcing, and documenting their outdoor activities. Experienced restaurant owners follow how their customers use their social media tools to share their dining experiences with friends and followers. On the other hand, the fact that accommodation and tourism businesses offer abstract and experiential products and rely on the online and offline information offered by other users when determining and evaluating product alternatives that visitors will purchase reveals the importance of social media for businesses offering tourism products (Sigala et.al., 2012). Because of the abstract nature of food and beverage products, which can be considered as touristic products, the positive or negative experiences of those who have experienced these products before are important sources of information for potential consumers. For this reason, businesses that use social media channels in the most effective way to reach consumers today have a great advantage in competition (Eryılmaz, 2014). Some studies have shown that the use of social media for business purposes is aimed at increasing the customer buying tendency. Especially small and medium-sized enterprises use social media to advertise low-budget advertising in order to increase their sales. However, it is stated that the main purpose of the social media usage of restaurants should be to increase the value of the company. With effective and efficient social media management, company value is enhanced. At the same time, businesses manage customer feedback through social media and suffer a significant loss of income when they manage it badly (Kim et.al., 2015).

Social networking sites such as Facebook, MySpace, Twitter, LinkedIn can be used for staff recruitment, advertising and feedback from customers in the restaurant industry. For example, McDonald's has established a global online community for quality information sharing (Dipietro et.al., 2012). In addition to Facebook, other social media channels such as Twitter, Foursquare and blogs are seen as beneficial for the operators. Twitter is a popular tool that is used successfully in the restaurant industry to promote promotions. Foursquare is a useful tool in the restaurant industry as a location-oriented application. Social media marketing is vital for large-scale restaurants. In order to fill the empty tables of high-capacity restaurants, it uses more effective advertisements. Social media offers low-budget advertising. Restaurants that target families with children, such as themed restaurants, should use social media more effectively (Needles & Thompson, 2013).

Traditional eating and drinking habits as cultural heritage are the identity of a society and are among the most effective tools to define societies. Cultural values of a society, livelihoods, and the effects of the globalizing world affect the lifestyles of societies. As one of the oldest and greatest tastes of humanity, eating and drinking activity developed in time parallel to urbanization and industrialization and has become an important part of today's life. Gastronomy is a branch of science and art that examines the relationship between culture and food and mentioned in the French literature as "the art of eating good". As part of cultural heritage, "gastronomy" is an important identity element of a society. The field-to-table production process of foods, the human factor contributing to the emergence of a local dish, the materials used and the preparation techniques during service and presentation represent the gastronomic heritage of that region. Turkish Cuisine enriched its development due to agricultural and animal husbandry coming from ancient Turks with the diversity of Anatolian geography. Islam, in the influence of Seljuk and Ottoman palace cuisine made Turkish Cuisine one of the most special cuisines in the world.

In many regions, gastronomy states importance as a marketing factor. For example, some travel agencies present the advantage of gourmet holiday to Italy and France regularly. These regions become like foremost vine destination in the world (Kivela & Crotts, 2008:356). The vines which marketing by a true integrated way, constitute a chance for destination and restaurants sector (Cambourne et.al., 2003:268). In these days, gastronomy is important because it is accepted that gastronomy is a target for travelling to a destination. Gastronomy becomes the most important reason for tourists to travel because of tourists' requests about new and special experience and alternative types of tourism (Rand & Heat, 2006:210). Local foods and local vines are strong and effective means for tourism destinations in a region. The foods which have original geographic sources provide to make region's image and agricultural tourism strong and be a label. This situation has a big importance for the curious of food, vine and tourism. The existence the potential of food and vine culture can provide to have working possibilities which assist to regional and agricultural progresses, and begin to operate the encamping companies. Gastronomic tourism presents some alternative chances for agricultural societies to associate with tourism and their own food and drinks. This process assists not only agricultural improvement and marketing the regions, but also protect the cultural inheritance and improve them (Alonso & Yi Liu, 2011; Green & Dougherty, 2008;

Hall et.al., 2003). It is seen that gastronomic tourism provides the progress of agricultural and pastoral places and produce local food with the experience which tourists get from food (Quan & Wang, 2003). Also, gastronomic tourism provides the advantage of competition and being label for region or country. Gastronomic identity ensures an important measurement of difference, improvements and advancement processes for a region. Consequently, cultural cuisine is on important state with respect to improvements of destination and economic progress (Henderson, 2009).

According to Quan and Wang (2003), food tourism holds several implications such as: adding value to agricultural products; providing a theme to build up attractions; utilising culture of foods as a food related event; incorporating food into mega events; and enhancing the local identity for destination marketing and development, therefore local and regional foods should not be regarded as trivial and ignored in tourism marketing. Food as a tourism product and experience can contribute to the competitiveness of the destination if appropriately developed and executed.

Recently, different methods have been used to marketing gastronomy tourism. These methods include the use of social media. With social media, more alternatives are available on food and beverages destinations. In order to evaluate and market their gastronomic alternatives well, destinations should form their strategies and social media elements meticulously. While developing these strategies, it is necessary to know social media users, how often they use them and their characteristics. Especially when it is intended to eat out, people use social media during the planning and consumption stages. Many food and beverage businesses also share the experiences of their customers with their followers in social media and follow the activities of customers in social media.

The rising star of gastronomy has influenced mass media, as well as influencing consumers, food and beverage businesses, employees and destinations. Mass media that meet the needs of the masses such as information, education, culture and entertainment have not been indifferent to the demand for gastronomy. In fact the kitchen is one of the most important elements of the culture and the people's interest in eating and drinking has increased the demand for publications on gastronomy. As a result, the number of publications on gastronomy for mass media has increased rapidly. Radio, television, newspapers and magazines as well as the Internet is the most effective communication tool of our age. The internet is the most impressive mass communication tool for gastronomy with its ability to present all written, visual and auditory sensory dynamics together. Blogs, web sites and social media posts where information on gastronomy are shared are the most used and most remarkable communication tools. Since technological developments have a big impact on marketing activities in virtual environment, it is sufficient for consumers to use only their fingers to access information. Accordingly, food and beverage businesses seek to gain customers through social media, and successful ones create competitive advantage (Perumal et.al., 2017).

Eating is both a social and a biological phenomenon and can also express the lifestyle of individuals. In the digital world, this sociality has brought "food moments" on social media and applications and these posts include cooking for many people, shared meals and even consuming them together. This new trend has focused the world on food sharing leading to a new online sharing. In this sense, social media uses the social and sharing characteristics of people with food to create new ways for people to access delicious food. One of the most widely used applications in social media is to share the photos of the edible meals in the profiles. As one of the most basic needs of human being, eating is becoming a symbol out of necessity as the habit of eating out in today's modern society starts to develop. The choices of what people eat, who they eat with, and where they eat are becoming more and more connected with this (http://www.ortakkullanimhareketi.com/2015/01/dusunulecek-sey-turkiyede-yemek-paylasm.html, accessed:15.12.2019)

The taste experiences in social media, criticisms, positive and negative comments are examined by the users and they are effective in choosing food businesses. The best result of this situation; food and beverage companies can analyze customer profiles and provide more efficient services according to their expectations and needs through social networks (İbiş & Engin, 2017: 325). Accordingly, the visuals of the food and beverages exhibited by businesses on social media make it a driving force for people to experience these flavors. Therefore, the products shared by the enterprises in the digital environment motivate people to tend to purchase (Hanan & Karim, 2015).

In the world, the known oldest cuisine culture appeared in Mesopotamia. In course of time, this cuisine created China and Anatolian cuisines. Anatolian cuisine constitues base of Ancieny Egypt, Ancient Greek and Ancient Rome cuisine. The known European cuisine derived from Ancient Rome cuisine as well. The root of East Asia cuisine depends on China cuisine.When it is looked the developing process of Turkish cuisine, it is seen that after Turk settled in Anatolia, they began to adopt Anatolian cuisine and combined and enriched with Middle Asia cuisine carried with them. In the later periods, in the parallel expanding of geography of Ottoman Emprise, gastronomical richness which are belong to other regions was joined Turkish Cuisine. Therefore, during this process Turkish cuisine gained the feature of fusion cuisine. For this reason, Turkish cuisine is one of the living oldest and best cuisines in the world (Akgöl, 2012; Bilgin & Samancı; 2008, Hatipoğlu, 2008).

The concept of cuisine culture includes food, different kind of food and beverages, preparing, cooking, servicing, storing, consuming types of foods. As eating habit is a part of culture, it can show difference among every society. As a society's eating behaviour and culture is related with life style, changig life will cause to change eating behaviour and culture. Every nation has cuisine culture in respect of cultural stucture. Turkish cuisine is one of the most gorgeous and colorful cuisines in the world. The variety of Turkish cuisine is related to many factors. The geographical location of Turkey and historical processes has been through contribute highly to forming the Turkish cuisine culture and creating diversity of cuisine.(Durlu-Ozkaya, 2009). Turkish cuisine is famous for using a variety of products for producing a variety of foods (Sürücüoğlu & Özçelik, 2005:10). It is known that geographical region differeces such as nomadic and agricultural economics structure made Turkish cuisine to be diversity and different. In addition, the oil, yoghurt and cheese, which has an important place in the humanbeing and nourishment are produced and expended by Turks (Aktaş & Ozdemir, 2007:24).

It is obvious that when culinary culture is mentioned not only food and beverages, which are, belong to a country but also preparation of food and service methods and equipments and kitchenware which are used in preparation and service, position and architecture of kitchen, food types and food ceremony and similar activities are tried to described. Turkish cuisine, France cuisine, China cuisine, Indian cuisine, Italian cuisine, and Mexico cuisine can be good examples for universal cuisines. Local cuisine, represent ethnical society in which food are produced and consumed (Chuang, 2009:87). Maviş (2003:58), described the concept of cuisine as "food, different kind of food and beverages, preparing, cooking, servicing, storing, process of consuming foods; accordingly enviroment and equipment, eating behaviour and belief which occurs in this concept, all applications in overall and unique cultural structure.

The Turkish cuisine which is inheritor of Ottoman cuisine, affected to Balkan and the Middle East and it affect this cuisines. Arabian cuisine also affected to Turkish cuisine. Especially, in southeast region cuisine, Arabian eating habit has a great affect. As palace cuisine affected by western countries and it affects their countries. Certainly, Turkish people's religions of Islam affects the improvements of their cuisine culture. In the Holy Koran, pig is the only animal to forbid to eat. However, eating donkey, horse, mule, lizard, slug and reptile is advised that people should not eat them. Today, in Turkish cuisine, these kinds of animals are not used in food. In Islam, alcohol is forbidden to drink, and people do not use it to drink.

In Turkish communities, eating habit changes according to socio-economic status. When income increases, the amount and quality of food, which are, consumed increases. The difference between Ottoman palace cuisine and local folk cuisine occurs because of the socio-economic status. The cuisine culture which was brought Turks from Middle Asia was enriched and diversified as result of affecting other communities (Baysal, 1993:20). In geographical places where Turkish people lived affected the cuisine culture's variety as well. The nourishment type which is consist of meat and fermented milk comes from the Middle Asia, developed agricultural system comes from Mesopotamia, fruit and vegetables come from Mediterranean and Aegean cultures, and they determine the Turkish cuisine has one of the best known cuisines with seven different regions and different local foods. When these regions are researched, southeast and east Anatolia have kebabs and spicy foods, the Mediterranean and Aegean have salads with olive oil, black sea has delicious foods with anchovy, interior of Anatolia has pastries, and Marmara has all kinds of Anatolian foods. Red pepper from Gaziantep, tart green olives from Bodrum, dried apricots from Cappadocia, anchovy pilaff from Trabzon, spicy kebabs from Adana, hallucinogetic honey from kars, creamy milk puddings and syrupy pastries-these are the tastes of the Turkish kitchen.

Based on these, this study proposes to reveal the content of instagram posts concerning Turkish cusine. Specifically the *research questions* is: what are the contents (Brand Content, Branding Elements, Culturel Figures, Information Content, Product Image, Local Foods, Local Desserts, Local Drinks, Information of Destination, Service Details, Athmosphere, Special Price & Promotions, Health Claims, Links, Followers who liked post, Followers who Commented, Service Equipment, Cooking Details) instagram posts concerning Turkish cusine?

METHODOLOGY

A Content Analysis Through Instagram on Turkish Cuisine

Content analysis is a qualitative/quantitative research technique. According to Hsieh and Shannon (2005) interpretation of what is contained in a message is called content analysis. Through systematic classification process of coding and identifying themes or patterns, content analysis is a "research method for the subjective interpretation of the content of text data . It is a "method of analysing written, verbal or visual communication messages." Cole (1988) also noted that content analysis is the study of recorded human communications such as dairy entries, books, newspaper, videos, text messages, tweets, Facebook updates etc. and content analysis is actually the study of contexts, meanings, subtexts, intentions contained in the messages. Table 1 indicates the content that is analysed for this study.

In this study, a total of 100 photos and videos shared on Instagram with the tag turkishcuisine" have been reviewed. 80 of these shares are composed of photographs and 20 of them are videos. Content analysis has been conducted on these photos and videos shared on Instagram.

Table 1. Criteria for analysis of contents of posts

Turkish Cuisine	Photos	Videos
Information Content	Recognizable information about the product. It includes phsical designing, looks/tastes, ingredients, or place of purchase	Recognizable information about the product. It includes phsical designing, looks/tastes, ingredients, or place of purchase
Brand Content	A brand is a name, term, sign, symbol, design, or a combination of these elements that is ideftify the goods or services.	A brand is a name, term, sign, symbol, design, or a combination of these elements that is ideftify the goods or services.
Branding Elements	Logos, colors, fonts, trademarks, or slogans	Logos, colors, fonts, trademarks, or slogans
Product Image	Pictures of the products sold or their ingredients, with no labels or branding elements	Pictures of the products sold or their ingredients, with no labels or branding elements
Local Foods	Traditional Turkish foods	Traditional Turkish foods
Local Desserts	Traditional Turkish desserts	Traditional Turkish desserts
Local Drinks	Traditional Turkish alkohol and non alkohol drinks	Traditional Turkish alkohol and non alkohol drinks
Cultural Figures	The culinary culture of Turkey. It includes food culture, cooking characterized by distinctive ingredients, techniques and dishes, regional food preparation traditions, customs and ingredients	The culinary culture of Turkey. It includes food culture, cooking characterized by distinctive ingredients, techniques and dishes, regional food preparation traditions, customs and ingredients
Information of Destination	Information about destinations which they need to be positioned and promoted.	**Information about destinations which they need to be positioned and promoted.**
Service Details	**Food and Beverage Services** can be defined as the process of preparing, presenting and serving of **food and beverages** to the customers.	**Food and Beverage Services** can be defined as the process of preparing, presenting and serving of **food and beverages** to the customers.
Athmosphere	The physical environment of product such as music, colour and furnishings.	The physical environment of product such as music, colour and furnishings.
Special Price & Promotions	Pricing products, pricing strategy, promotional pricing	Pricing products, pricing strategy, promotional pricing
Health Claims	Product development through healthy based production.	Product development through healthy based production.
Links	Link to an external page or additional content	Link to an external page or additional content
Followers who liked post	Numbers of followers who liked post	Numbers of followers who liked post
Followers who Commented	Numbers of followers who Commented	Numbers of ollowers who Commented
Service Equipment	Food and beverage service equipment such as cutlery, tableware, glassware, chandeliers	Food and beverage service equipment such as cutlery, tableware, glassware, chandeliers
Cooking Details	Details of cooking *techniques and recipes*	Details of cooking *techniques and recipes*

According to Figure 1, while 37% of the photos shared on instagram with "turkishcuisine" hashtag have brand content (Image is generated by the brand, or third party sponsored by brand, as opposed to consumer), 7% have branding elements (Logos, colors, fonts, trademarks, or slogans) . While 16% of the videos shared on instagram with "turkishcuisine" hashtag have brand content (Image is generated by the brand, or third party sponsored by brand, as opposed to consumer), 2% have branding elements (Logos, colors, fonts, trademarks, or slogans).

Figure 1. Brand content & branding elements of Turkish cuisine

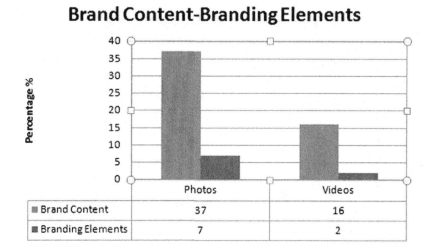

Figure 2. Local foods & local desserts & local drinks

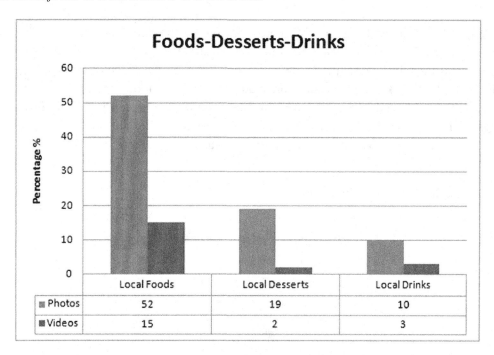

According to Figure 2, while 52% of the photos and 15% of the videos shared on instagram with "turkishcuisine" hashtag have local foods (Traditional Turkish foods), 19% of the photos and 2% of the videos have local desserts. 10% of the photos and 3% of the videos contain local drinks. (Traditional Turkish alcohol and non-alcoholic drinks)

Figure 3. Service & price & athmosphere

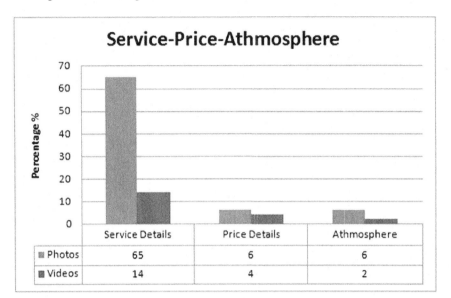

According to Figure 3, while 65% of the photos shared on instagram with "turkishcuisine" hashtag have service details (**Food and Beverage Services** can be defined as the process of preparing, presenting and serving of **food and beverages** to the customers), 6% have price details (the amount of money expected, required & low **price** or recent **price** reduction) and 6% have atmosphere details (refers to incorporation of tangible and intangible environmental features such as music, colour, brightness and furnishings). While 14% of the videos shared on instagram with "turkishcuisine" hashtag have service details, %4 have price details and 2% have atmosphere details.

Figure 4: Infirmation Content & Product Image

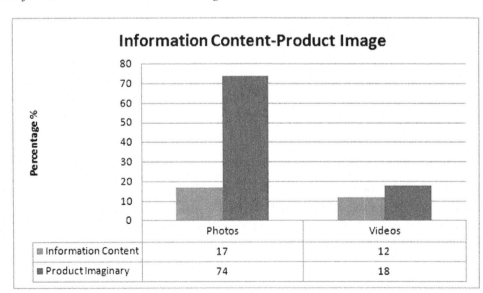

According to Figure 5 While 17% of the photos shared on instagram with "turkishcuisine" hashtag have information content (Recognizable information about what the product looks/tastes like, ingredients, or place of purchase), 74% have product images (Pictures of the products sold or their ingredients, with no labels or branding elements). While 12% of the videos shared on instagram with "turkishcuisine" hashtag have information content, 18% have product images.

Figure 5. Cultural figures & destination information & health information

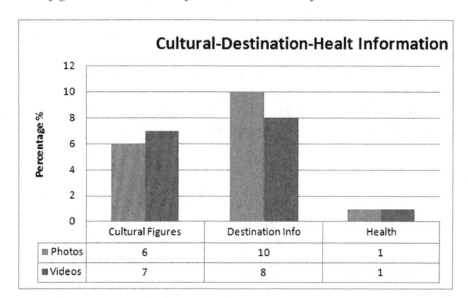

According to Figure 5, while 6%of the photos shared on instagram with "turkishcuisine" hashtag have cultural figures (Turkish food culture. A ***cuisine*** is a style of cooking characterized by distinctive ingredients, techniques and dishes, and usually associated with a specific ***culture*** or geographic region. Regional food preparation traditions, customs and ingredients often combine to create dishes unique to a particular region), 10% have destination information (a place to **which** one is journeying) and 1% have health information (Specific reference that the product shown is a healthy choice or may improve physical health). While 7% of the videos shared on instagram with "turkishcuisine" hashtag have cultural figures, 8% have destination information and 1% have health information.

While 51% of the photos shared on instagram with "turkishcuisine" hashtag have service equipment (used for **food** preparation and interior decoration such as chandeliers or ovens to the smallest piece of cutlery, furniture, or linen participate in creating overall ambience of the outlet), 9% have cooking details (***Details of Cooking*** Techniques, recipes). While 6% of the videos shared on instagram with "turkishcuisine" hashtag have service equipment, 12% have cooking details.

When the content of the most liked shares has been analyzed, it has been observed that the videos are liked mostly and these videos have the characteristics of Information Content, Brand Content, Product Images, Local Foods, Cultural Figures, Information of Destination, Service Details, Cooking Details.

FUTURE RESEARCH DIRECTION

The purpose of this paper is to formulate and discuss social media as a tool for marketing of gastronomy. The approach taken in the paper is to review the relevant literature and focus on the social media most important for future research on gastronomy marketing. The paper finds that there are a number of research avenues for gastronomy marketing researchers and marketing practitioners to conduct investigations on but the most important areas are branding, digital -marketing and social media marketing for Turkish cuisine. The paper is relevant to food and beverages firms and destination management organizations in the development of marketing activities/capabilities to increase their customer base. In addition, as this paper takes a global perspective it is also helpful to compare different international research directions. Changing demographics and the aging of the global population mean different marketing approaches will be needed to market gastronomy services to different consumers and also consumers from developing countries such as Italy and Spain. This paper is a key resource for gastronomy marketing practitioners wanting to focus on future growth areas and also marketing academics interested in gastronomy marketing that want to stay at the forefront of their research area of expertise.

CONCLUSION

Turkey is an important tourism destination in terms of natural scenery and internationally known as one of the most favourite countries for its natural beauties. On the other hand, Turkey is in need of increasing the varieties of its tourism marketing possibilities by giving more importance to "cultural" and "heritage" tourism like many other successful destinations such as France, Italy, Spain, China are doing for years. In this sense, the concept of culinary tourism product has been accepted as a new aspect. This new dimension will contriubute on tourism marketing of Turkey in many different ways.

According to academic studies, the tourists who come to travel to Turkey, want to know and try to the Turkish cuisine culture. The success of a destination affected to the power of competition. It is easier that the marketing activities, which makes with strength and original attractiveness, are more successful because these original components provide to have the power of competition to destinations. When the improvements about tourism are researched, it is seen that gastronomy has an important role for marketing the touristic destinations. The marketing activities which used gastronomic factors that relate to destinations, the income which are from gastronomic tourism activities and requiring new products prove with serious numeric data. Gastronomy carries a potential to increase the worth of many destinations. The ottoman and Turkish cuisines which are in the world's best cuisines, assist big additions to be label for destinations with a right location and attractive image.

Gastronomy tourism is one of the most important elements of tourism marketing and this new concept will contribute at a great level on the tourism marketing of Turkey. To achieve this aim, cooperation between local inhabitants and private sector should be realized. Gastronomy Tourism will positively push local economic growth and these results will be efficient and satisfactory for both sides. Gastronomy tourism has potential to get worth to many destinations for Turkish cuisine, which is one of richest cuisine in the world, with correct positioning and with attractive image, which will be created will highly, contributes to branding destination. In Turkey, the type of being branding has moved into public policy arguments for Turkey to be in today's global world. The argument turns around how to create and sustain the image of country that is attractive for tourists while making benefit. Turkey is represented with a number of natural beauties such as sun, sea, sand and the ruggedness of the Mediterranean coastline.

The lack of enough public relations and advertisement activities of turkish cuisine is the most important problem we face in tourism marketing of Turkey. In summary, turkish cuisine has a great potential and by taking the necessary actions this potential will be realized and achive the successful level of main european destinations such as France, Italy and Spain. Today's culinary traditions have been impressed by a long history of transmigration, together with regional product availability. Chefs have associated cultural traditions and local products, producing new forms and styles of cooking. Scaffoldings from different geographical regions across the country will emphasize the rich variety susceptible in Turkish culinary tourism influenced, not only by global but also by regional pressures, which can be branded under the umbrella of the cuisine in Turkey.

With the rapid development of technology, social media, which has emerged as one of the most important trends of the recent years, has become one of the most used platforms for the communication of consumers and businesses. As well as the websites of the enterprises, the shares of those who consume their products and services in the virtual environment is also evaluated by the potential consumers. Brands should be establish a new organizational structure to be constantly available on their social media accounts and increase their online sensibility to connect with the consumer, from the selection process of the product or service to post-purchase feedback. In this new model of organization, the importance of "social media experts" will increase day by day. Considering that social media usage will continue to increase, it is inevitable that destinations and marketing strategies of food and beverage businesses will undergo a major transformation from digital menus to online orders with technology-shaped social media campaigns. To reach consumers with more informative and compelling content on social media with local food cultures of the destinations and businesses in Turkey that has a rich culinary culture are becoming extremely important. Food-oriented social media management should be handled with a professional approach as one of the most effective promotion tools of our age in the marketing process of Turkish culinary culture, destinations and businesses.

REFERENCES

Akgöl, Y. (2012). *Gastronomi Turizmi ve Türkiye'yi Ziyaret Eden Yabancı Turistlerin Gastronomi Deneyimlerinin Değerlendirilmesi. In Yayımlanmamış Yüksek Lisans Tezi*. Mersin Üniversitesi Sosyal Bilimler Enstitüsü.

Alonso, A., & Liu, Y. (2011). The potential for marrying local gastronomy and wine: The case of the Fortunate Islands. *International Journal of Hospitality Management, 30*(4), 974–981. doi:10.1016/j.ijhm.2011.02.005

Baysal, A. (1993). Türk Yemek Kültüründe Değişmeler ve Beslenme Sağlık Yönünden Değerlendirme Türk Mutfak Kültürü Üzerine Araştırmalar. Ankara: Türk Halk Kültürünü Araştırma ve Tanıtma Vakfı Yayınları. No:3.

Bendahou, C., & Berbou, H. (2015). The impact of culture on the use of social media in travel destination search. *The Journal of MacroTrends in Social Science, 1*(1), 59–73.

Bilgin, A., & Samancı, Ö. (2008). *Türk Mutfağı*. T.C Kültür ve Turizm Bakanlığı.

Boyd, D. M., & Ellison, N. B. (2008). Social Network Sites: Definition, History and Scholarship. *Journal of Computer-Mediated Communication, 13*(1), 210–230. doi:10.1111/j.1083-6101.2007.00393.x

Bulunmaz, B. (2016). Gelişen Teknolojiyle Birlikte Değişen Pazarlama Yöntemleri ve Dijital Pazarlama. *TRT Akademi, 1*(2), 348–365.

Cambourne, B., Macionis, N., Hall, C. M., Sharples, E., & Mitchell, R. (2003). *Food Tourism Around the World: Development, Management and Markets.* Butterworth-Heinemann.

Chuang, H.-T. (2009). *The Rise of Culinary Tourism and Its Transformation of Food Cultures: The National Cuisine of Taiwan. The Copenhagen Journal of Asian Studies, 27*(2), 84–108.

Cole, F. L. (1988). Content analysis: Process and application. *Clinical Nurse Specialist CNS, 2*(1), 53–57. doi:10.1097/00002800-198800210-00025 PMID:3349413

Dipietro, R. B., Crews, T. B., Gustafson, C., & Strick, S. (2012). The Use of Social Networking Sites in the Restaurant Industry: Best Pactices. *Journal of Foodservice Business Research, 15*(3), 265–284. doi:10.1080/15378020.2012.706193

Durlu-Özkaya, F. (2009). *Turk Mutfağında Zeytinyağı.* Ankara: Eflatun Yayınevi.

Eröz Sü, S., & Doğdubay, M. (2012). Turistik Ürün Tercihinde Sosyal Medyanın Rolü ve Etik İlişkisi. *Dokuz Eylül Üniversitesi İktisadi ve İdari Bilimler Fakültesi Dergisi, 27*(1), 133–157.

Eryılmaz, B. (2014). *Sosyal Medya Kullanımının Müşteri Tercihleri ÜZerine Etkileri: Konaklama İşletmetlerinde Bir İnceleme.* Sakarya Üniversitesi.

Garcia, K. (2013). *Social Media Damage Control: Learning form the Restaurant Industry.* http://www.gannetwisconsinmedia.com/images/uploads/attachments/eMarketer_Social_Media_Damage_Control_Learning_from_the_Restaurant_ındustry.pdf

Green, G.P. & Dougherty, M.L. (2008). Localising linkages for food and tourism: culinary tourism as a community development strategy. *Community Development, 39*(3), 148-158.

Hall, M. C., Sharples, L., Mitchell, R., Macionis, N., & Cambourne, B. (2003). *Food tourism around the world: development, management and markets.* Butterworth-Heinemann: Elsevier.

Hanan, H., & Karim, M. S. A. (2015). Influence of Social Media in Food Festival Destination Image. *International Conference on Tourism and Ethnicity in ASEAN and Beyond 2015.*

Hatipoğlu, A. (2008). *Türk mutfağının dünya mutfağındaki yeri.* www.foodinlife.com.tr

Heikkinen, H. (2012). *Social Media and Internet Marketing's Influence on Decision Making Process of German Nature Tourists* (Bachelor's Thesis). Oulu University ofApplied Sciences.

Hsieh, H. F., & Shannon, S. E. (2005). Three approaches to qualitative content analysis. *Qualitative Health Research, 15*(9), 1277–1288. doi:10.1177/1049732305276687 PMID:16204405

İbiş, S., & Engin, Y. (2017). Öğrencilerin Yiyecek Ve İçecek İşletmesi Seçiminde Sosyal Medyanın Rolünün Belirlenmesi. *Mehmet Akif Ersoy Üniversitesi Sosyal Blimler Enstitüsü Dergissi, 8*(17), 322–336. doi:10.20875b.68247

Kim, S., Koh, Y., Cha, J., & Lee, S. (2015). Effects of Social Media on Firm Value for U.S. Restaurant Companies. *International Journal of Hospitality Management, 49*, 40–46. doi:10.1016/j.ijhm.2015.05.006

Kivela, J. & Crotts, J. (2006) Tourism and Gastronomy: Gastronomy's Influence on How Tourists Experience a Destination, *Journal of Hospitality & Tourism Research, 30*(3), 354-377.

Koçak Alan, A., Tümer Kabadayı, E., & Erişke, T. (2018). İletişimin Yeni Yüzü: Dijital Pazarlama Ve Sosyal Medya Pazarlaması. *Elektronik Sosyal Bilimler Dergisi, 17*(66), 123–134. doi:10.17755/esosder.334699

Mangold, W. G., & Fauld, D. J. (2009). Social Media: The New Hybrid Element of the Promotion Mixed. *Business Horizons, 52*(4), 357–365. doi:10.1016/j.bushor.2009.03.002

Maviş, F. (2003). *Endüstriyel Yiyecek Üretimi*. Detay Yayıncılık.

Munar, A. M., & Jacobsen, J. K. S. (2013). Trust and Involvement in Tourism Social Media and Web-Based Travel Information Sources. *Scandinavian Journal of Hospitality and Tourism, 13*(1), 1–19. doi:10.1080/15022250.2013.764511

Needles, A., & Thompson, G. (2013). Social Media Use in the Restaurant Industry: A Work in Progress. *Center for Hospitality Research Publications, 13*(7), 6–16.

Özdaş, N. (2017). *Dijital Pazarlamada Marka Yönetiminin Önemi Ve Hızlı Tüketim Sektörüne Yönelik Bir Uygulama*. Yüksek Lisans Tezi. Üsküdar Üniversitesi. SBE.

Parsons, H. L. (2017). *Does Social Media Influence an Individual's Decision to Visit Tourist Destinations? Using a Case Study of Instagram*. Cardiff Metropolitan University.

Perumal, I., Devi, U. K., & Halim, N. S. B. A. (2017). Social Media in Food and Beverages Industry: Case of Klang Valley, Malaysia. *International Journal of Business and Management, 12*(6), 121. doi:10.5539/ijbm.v12n6p121

Quan, S., & Wang, N. (2003). Towards a structural model of the tourist experience: An illustration from food experiences in tourism. *Tourism Management, 25*(3), 297–305. doi:10.1016/S0261-5177(03)00130-4

Rand, G., & Heath, E. (2006). Towards a framework for food tourism as an element of destination marketing. *Current Issues in Tourism, 9*(3), 206–234. doi:10.2167/cit/226.0

Şengün, G. (2015). *Turizm Pazarlamasında Sosyal Medyanın Rolü: Üniversite Öğrencileri Üzerine Bir Araştırma*. Yüksek Lisans Tezi. Atılım Üniversitesi Sosyal Bilimler Enstitüsü.

Sigala, M., Christou, E., & Gretzel, U. (2012). *Social Media in Travel, Tourism and Hospitality: Theory, Practice and Cases*. Ashgate Publishing Limited.

Sü, E. & Doğdubay, M. (2012). Turistik Ürün Tercihinde Sosyal Medyanın Rolü ve Etik İlişkisi. *Dokuz Eylül Üniversitesi İktisadi ve İdari Bilimler Fakültesi Dergisi, 27*(1), 133-157.

Sürücüoğlu, M. S. & Özçelik, A. O. (2005). *Eski Turk Besinleri ve Yemekleri*. Turk Mutfak Kulturu Uzerine Arastırmalar. Turk Halk Kulturunu Arastırma ve Tanıtma Vakfı Yayın. Ankara: Birlik Matbaacılık.

Tham, A., Croy, G., & Mair, J. (2013). Social Media in Destination Choice: Distinctive Electronic Word-of-Mouth Dimensions. *Journal of Travel & Tourism Marketing*, *30*(1–2), 144–155. doi:10.1080 /10548408.2013.751272

Xiang, Z., & Gretzel, U. (2010). Role of social media in online travel information search. *Tourism Management*, *31*(2), 179–188. doi:10.1016/j.tourman.2009.02.016

Yöndar Karabeyoğlu, D. (2018). *Türkiye'de Dijital Pazarlamada Marka ve Tüketici İlişkisinin İncelenmesi.* İstanbul Üniversitesi.

Yücel Güngör, M., Doğan, S., & Güngör, O. (2016). Yiyecek İçecek Endüstrisi ve Sosyal Medya. In O. N. Özdoğan (Ed.), *Yiyecek İçecek Endüstrisinde Trendler II (Kavramlar, Yaklaşımlar, Başarı Hikayeleri)* (pp. 129–156). Detay Yayıncılık.

Zhai, S., Xu, X., Yang, L., Zhou, M., Zhang, L., & Qiu, B. (2015). Mapping the popularity of urban restaurants using social media data. *Applied Geography (Sevenoaks, England)*, *63*, 113–120. doi:10.1016/j. apgeog.2015.06.006

KEY TERMS AND DEFINITIONS

Gastronomy: Gastronomy is known as a science that deals with the culinary culture and cooking techniques.

Gastronomy Tourism: Gastronomy tourism is a type of tourism that is related to visiting food producers, food festivals, restaurants, special places, or to prepare a food cooked by a famous chef.

Social Media Marketing: Social media marketing is a form of digital marketing that utilizes social networking websites as a marketing tool.

Turkish Cuisine: Turkish cuisine consists of Anatolian traditions and the heritage of sophisticated Ottoman cuisine which can be described as a fusion and refinement of Central Asian, Middle Eastern, Eastern European and Balkan cuisines.

This research was previously published in the Handbook of Research on New Media Applications in Public Relations and Advertising; pages 313-332, copyright year 2021 by Information Science Reference (an imprint of IGI Global).

Chapter 40
The Video–on–Demand Market in Germany:
Dynamics, Market Structure and the (Special) Role of YouTube

Nadine Lindstädt-Dreusicke
Pforzheim University, Pforzheim, Germany

Oliver Budzinski
Ilmenau University of Technology, Ilmenau, Germany

ABSTRACT

The markets for audiovisual content are subject to dynamic change. Where once "traditional" television was dominating, i.e. linear audiovisual media services, markets display nowadays the strong growth of different types of video-on-demand (VoD), i.e. nonlinear audiovisual media services including paid-for VoD such as Netflix and advertised-financed VoD like YouTube. This article aims at providing insights into the VoD market in general and the competitive environment in particular. For doing so, the authors first present recent developments in the German VoD market. In the second part of this article, the authors focus on the (perhaps special) role of YouTube in the market for audiovisual (online) services. Thereby arguments for and against YouTube exerting competitive pressure on i) other non-linear audiovisual media services (e.g. Netflix) as well as ii) on other linear audiovisual media service providers (TV stations) are discussed. The article concludes that there are numerous pros and cons speaking for a relevant role of YouTube for both markets.

INTRODUCTION

Watching video on the internet is still on the rise not least due to broadband connections as well as technologies favoring video usage on mobile devices (Crawford, 2015; Kupferschmitt, 2015). According to the ARD/ZDF Onlinestudie 2017, 72 per cent of the German speaking population from 14+ years watches moving images[1] on the internet at least rarely, whereas 53 per cent do so at least once per week (Koch

DOI: 10.4018/978-1-6684-6287-4.ch040

& Frees, 2017, p. 443; Kupferschmitt, 2017, p. 448). The latter figures are highest in the young(er) age groups (14-29 years: 88 per cent; 30-49 years: 70 per cent), whereas consumption decreases in the older age groups (50-69 years: 34 per cent; 70+ years: 17 per cent) (Koch & Frees, 2017, p. 443). Altogether, consumption of video streaming services (e.g. Netflix, Amazon Prime Instant Video, Maxdome, etc.) has increased within one year by 11 percentage points (from 12 per cent at least once per week in 2016 to 23 per cent in 2017; Koch & Frees, 2017, p. 443). Lower frequency consumption even increased by 20 percentage points to 38 per cent in 2017 (Kupferschmitt 2017, pp. 448-449).

In line with consumption growth, the overall market for audiovisual online content in general and video-on-demand (VoD) in particular displays high dynamics. Among the various players are online media libraries of traditional TV stations (both commercial TV providers and public service broadcasters), video portals such as YouTube as well as video streaming providers such as Netflix and Maxdome – just to mention a few. Particularly, the market for video streaming services is currently highly competitive. At the beginning of October 2015 Amazon, for instance, announced to remove devices of Apple (i.e. Apple TV) and Google (i.e. Google Chromecast) from their website, informing the market place providers that from October, 29th, 2015 on those devices cannot be sold anymore on Amazon (Horizont Online, 2015).[2] Watchever, the German VoD player of the French media company Vivendi, by contrast, launched a new content concept in order to set itself apart from its competitors in October 2015 – however, at the end of 2016 Vivendi shut down Watchever (Schobelt, 2015; Meedia, 2016). In addition to this, new and well established players from abroad have entered the market, such as Amazon Prime Instant Video in February 2014 or Netflix in September 2014. Both have taken leading positions in the German VoD market throughout the past years. In 2018, the traditional broadcasters such as ProSiebenSat.1 as well as RTL announced their plans to further expand their video-on-demand activities in order to compete with the leading players Netflix and Amazon (Meedia, 2018a, 2018b; Winterbauer 2018). Also, Deutsche Telekom aims to play a role in the market and announced plans to start investing in own content production as well as to open up their streaming-service Entertain TV for non-Telekom customers, the latter effective from October 2018 on (Meedia, 2018c).

This paper aims at providing insights into the dynamic VoD market and elaborating on the competitive environment. The authors therefore start with presenting recent developments in the German VoD market including business models, market structures and dynamics (section 2). Following in section 3, the authors focus on the (perhaps special) role of YouTube in the market for audiovisual (online) services. Thereby, arguments for and against YouTube exerting competitive pressure on other-non-linear audiovisual media services (i.e. VoD players such as Netflix and Amazon) as well as on other linear audiovisual media service providers (i.e. TV channels such as ProSieben and RTL) are discussed.

In order to specify the term video-on-demand, the authors follow the 2010 Audiovisual Media Services Directive from the European Union (2010, p. L95/12). According to it, linear audiovisual media services are services delivered by a media service provider "for simultaneous viewing of programmes on the basis of a programme schedule". Television broadcasting is, thus, falling under this definition. Non-linear audiovisual media services (also referred to as on-demand audiovisual media services) by contrast are services delivered by a media service provider "for the viewing of programmes at the moment chosen by the user and at his individual request on the basis of a catalogue of programmes selected by the media services provider". The latter corresponds to the International Telecommunication Union (ITU) definition of VoD[3]: "A service in which the end-user can, on demand, select and view a video content and where the end-user can control the temporal order in which the video content is viewed (e.g. the ability to start the viewing, pause, fast forward, rewind, etc.)" (ITU, 2009, p. 6). A report by the European Commission (2014, pp. 7-9) classifies on-demand services as displayed in Table 1. While the authors follow the understanding of the terms linear and non-linear audiovisual media services/video-on-demand in this paper, they do not want to preclude economic market delineation by these definitions, in particular as the dynamics of the markets imply ongoing endogenous changes of market definitions in this industry.

Table 1. Classification of on-demand audiovisual services[4]

Classification	Subcategories
On demand audiovisual media services (according to the AVMS Directive)	Catch-Up TV (also referred to as Replay TV), e.g. media libraries of private or public service broadcasters
	Preview TV, i.e. users pay for a TV program to watch it prior to their broadcast release
	VoD, i.e. providing on demand access to a catalogue of audiovisual services, not being dependent on their broadcast on television. E.g. Netflix, Amazon Prime Video
	Branded services on sharing platforms
Other on demand audiovisual services (outside the definition of the AVMS Directive)	Video-sharing platforms, e.g. YouTube
	Social networks permitting users to upload videos, e.g. Facebook
	Video pages of newspapers websites, e.g. website with video content on Spiegel Online
	Promotional websites containing video content

Source: modified and extended from European Commission (2014, p. 9)

THE VIDEO-ON-DEMAND MARKET IN GERMANY

Business Models on the VoD Market

VoD providers use fairly diverse and different types of business models. Industry studies usually distinguish two main categories depending on the financing of the services – namely *user financed VoD models* from *advertising financed VoD models*.

- Advertising Financed VoD Models (AVoD)

To start with the latter, video-on-demand providers can (partly) finance their services through advertising revenues, also referred to as AVoD (advertising financed or ad-supported video-on-demand) (inter alia, Bitkom, 2017b; Goldmedia, 2018). In this model, the VoD provider offers the streaming of videos to the user "for free", more precisely without monetary payment from the user, or at a reduced monetary price. In return, the user "pays" with her "attention" while watching the videos by being exposed to particularly different in-stream-video ad formats such as pre-, mid-, postroll-advertising.[5] Advertising financed VoD Models show the characteristics of a platform market[6] as do advertising-financed media markets in general (inter alia, Dewenter, 2003; Anderson & Gabszewicz, 2006; Gabszewicz et al., 2006; Kaiser & Wright, 2006; Crampes et al., 2009; Lindstädt, 2010; Seamans & Zhu, 2010; Reisinger, 2012; Anderson & Jullien, 2015; Crawford, 2015; Gabszewicz et al., 2015; Gimpel, 2015; Peitz & Reisinger, 2015; Tichem & Tuinstra, 2018; Budzinski & Kuchinke, 2019). Video-on-demand providers as platforms serve two distinct customer groups – namely users and advertisers – through internalizing the indirect network externalities that occur between those two customer groups. An increasing presence of users on an AVoD-platform increases the utility for each advertiser placing advertising on this platform because of the increased reach and the subsequently increased probability to turn advertising into turnover. This represents a positive indirect network externality. The other way around, however, is more ambiguous: an increasing amount of advertising need not necessarily increase utility of each user; for some user it will actually represent a disutility. Altogether, the indirect network externality in this direction may be positive or negative but it certainly will be lower than the one from users to advertisers. Consequently, the platform experiences incentives to subsidize the user side (monetary price of zero) and shift the financing of the service on the advertising side (efficient asymmetric price structure). Managing the indirect network externalities like this can be an important growth factor for a VoD-platform and promote profitability. Since the platform character of a VoD-service is not natural (i.e. alternative, non-platform business models exist as well, see below), AVoD is an artificial platform, i.e. a strategically chosen business model (profit maximization).

AVoD can be viewed as a special variant of data-based services (Budzinski, 2016; Budzinski & Kuchinke, 2019; Budzinski & Stöhr, 2019). Personalized user data has become an important factor particularly when it comes to modern digital online services: the user "pays" with the provision of her personal data. The platform element of the AVoD-business model actually runs on so-called targeted advertising where the platform employs personalized user data in order to provide each user individually with tailor-made advertising according to her stated (e.g. comments on goods at Amazon, Facebook-likes, etc.) or revealed (e.g. cookie-tracked or account-based data on her individual search, movement and consumption history on the internet) preferences. In combination with the indirect network externality, targeted advertising further increases the effectiveness of advertisements and, thus, further increases the willingness-to-pay of advertisers. A second way of utilizing personalized user data is individualized services like algorithm-based individualized recommendation and search services on the platform. Based upon the individual history of videos watched and positive comments, each user receives her own individual recommendations which other videos she might like. And when she searches within the platform, search results are listed according to her preferences as the algorithm has concluded them from the available personalized data. Both individualized services benefit the user and, c.p., increase her video consumption on the platform, thus, at the end of the day, increasing turnover and profits of the platform. Thus, the volume and the quality of personalized data influence competitiveness.[7]

Providers using this type of AVoD business model are, for instance, YouTube, MSN Movies as well as Hulu (a provider in the United States).

- User Financed VoD Models (PVoD)

User financed VoD models, by contrast, refer to the situation where the user directly pays with money for consuming VoD content. Currently, this is the most common financing model among leading commercial VoD providers (e.g. Bitkom, 2017a, 2017b) – with the notable exception of video portals à la YouTube. The authors distinguish two different subcategories (modified from Berthelmann, 2018, p. 16). Both can be applied to streaming and downloading.

- **Pay-Per-View:** This type is also referred to as transactional video-on-demand (TVoD). It refers to a time-limited access to the video content wherefore the user has to make a one-time payment.

The content is available only for a limited time period (e.g. 24 hours). An example is, for instance, the iTunes store where videos can be rented;

- **Flatrate-Pricing:** This service is also known as subscription-based video-on-demand (SVoD). By paying a flatrate subscription fee (e.g. monthly) the user has unlimited access to the video content offered by the provider. Examples are, for instance Netflix or Amazon Prime Video.

In the following, the authors summarize both the TVoD and the SVoD model under the term paid-for video-on-demand (PVoD). Examples include Maxdome, Netflix, Amazon Prime Video, Google Play, Apple iTunes, and Sky Online (Bitkom, 2017a).

Germany's VoD Market – Structure, Dynamics, and Relevant Players

The digital distribution of video content has become increasingly important within the German video rental market. In a study by the BMWI (2017) on the economic role of the movie industry in Germany the developments of the revenues and the digital share in the video rental market in Germany from 2008 until 2015 are pointed out. According to this study already 66 per cent of the revenues have been generated through digital video in 2015, coming from only 2 per cent in 2008 (BMWI, 2017, p. 112).

The media market for audiovisual online content in Germany is highly dynamic – not least due to the recipients' increasing interest of video usage on the internet throughout the past years. Kupferschmitt (2017, p. 448) shows the developments of video usage from 2007 until 2017 built upon the results of the ARD/ZDF-Onlinestudie. According to this, video consumption at least on a rarely base increased from 28 per cent of all users in 2007 up to 72 per cent in 2017. Weekly video consumption rocketed from 16 per cent in 2008 up to 56 per cent in 2016, however, then for the first time dropped 3 percentage points from 2016 to 2017 resulting in 53 per cent of the German speaking population 14+ years using video content on the internet on a weekly base (Kupferschmitt, 2017, p. 448).

According to a Bitkom (2017a) survey, 77 per cent of the German internet users (14+ years) stream TV shows, movies, or other types of video over the internet. The younger the target group, the more attractive video streaming gets (14-29-years old: 88 per cent; 30-49-years old: 90 per cent) (see also Koch & Frees, 2017, p. 443). According to the 2017 Digitization Report of the Medienanstalten, 42.2 per cent (plus 9 percentage points compared to the previous year) of the population in Germany (14+ years) use OTT[8] content at least once a month (Kunow, 2017, pp. 32-33). Heavy consumption (i.e. at least once a week and several times a week) experienced even greater increases. The most popular platforms are AVoD platforms such as YouTube[9] that have been the key drivers of the market throughout the past years (Koch & Frees, 2017, p. 443). The BVDW (2017) survey shows that AVoD portals so far are used more often than PVoD services. However, whereas the latter increased from 2016 to 2017 the usage frequencies of AVoD decreased during this time frame.

The importance of mobile video consumption has increased owing to faster mobile internet connections making it attractive and affordable to stream videos on smartphones and tablets (Bitkom, 2017a)[10], wherefore mobile is now the key driver in the market for moving images (von Rauchhaupt, 2017) due to allowing video consumption independent of time and location (Berkemeyer, 2017). This strengthens users' incentives for using non-linear over linear services.

According to von Rauchhaupt (2017), the German VoD market is revenue-wise the third largest within Europe after Great Britain and France. A study by Bitkom (2017a, 2017b) illustrates the development of AVoD and PVoD revenues in Germany from 2010-2016 with a forecast for 2017. According to this,

PVoD revenues (432 million in 2016) exceed AVoD revenues with the SVoD model forecasted to head TVoD for the first time in 2017.[11] The strong increase of SVoD revenues since 2014 coincides with the market entry by the two major PVoD players Amazon Prime Instant Video and Netflix, both offering a SVoD model (Goldmedia, 2016). The growth of VoD is predicted to continue. According to Goldmedia's market forecast 2018-2023 an increase of gross revenues up to € 2.5 billion in 2023 (coming from € 1.1 billion Euros in 2017) is expected (Absatzwirtschaft, 2018; Hein, 2018; Herrmann, 2018b).

In 2016, 38 PVoD providers were competing for users and market shares in the German VoD market (BMWI, 2017, p. 187; Goldmedia, 2016). This market segment is characterized by relevant market entries (Herrmann, 2018b)[12] but also exits like the shutdown of the VoD service Watchever at the end of 2016 (Meedia, 2016). Recent entries most prominently include Netflix[13] and Amazon Prime Instant Video[14], accompanied by increased and expanded activities of Sky and Maxdome[15] (BMWI, 2017, p. 187).

Up to now, Amazon and Netflix take the leading role in the German PVoD market (Absatzwirtschaft, 2018). According to Goldmedia[16] (2016), the most consumed PVoD service in Germany is Amazon. A figure by Goldmedia (2016) shows that in April 2016 32 per cent of the VoD consumers used an Amazon pay video offer (this corresponds to 22 per cent of all internet users in Germany[17]), followed by Netflix (17 per cent of the VoD users, corresponding to 11 per cent of all internet users in Germany). Limited to consumers between 14 and 75 years old[18], a study by Deloitte displays—based on usage figures—Amazon with 37 per cent and Netflix with 25 per cent market share as PVoD market leaders in Germany in 2017 (Statista, 2017, p. 28). Notably, as the Goldmedia (2016) study also shows, the German TV station providers (linear audiovisual media services) considerably lack behind in the PVoD market, according to usage figures: while pay-TV provider Sky follows the leading duo with a 12 per cent market share, the free-TV companies are only present with ProSiebenSat.1 (Maxdome, 11 per cent). The other big commercial TV-provider, RTL, as well as the public service providers (ARD, ZDF) stick with VoD market shares below 2 per cent each. ProSiebenSat.1, RTL, ARD and ZDF are the companies whose attempts to establish VoD platforms raised antitrust concerns by the Federal Cartel Office of Germany (FCO) some eight years ago (see Budzinski & Lindstädt-Dreusicke, 2019). As of now, only one of them enjoys a relevant market position, however, with considerable distance to the top players.

Amazon's leading position may partly be due to a bundling strategy, including its video streaming service into the Amazon Prime subscription fee, i.e. bundling video streaming with premium delivery services for other goods bought from Amazon. So far, this strategy was not challenged by the FCO. The position of the two market leaders, Amazon and Netflix, may be further strengthened if forecasts based on GfK data analysis claiming that further market growth is likely to concentrate on these two players prove to be adequate (von Rauchhaupt, 2017). Among the reasons may be their investments into own content productions and exclusive content rights.[19] Netflix, for instance, is intensively generating original content and aiming to hold exclusive rights to movies and television shows (Aguiar & Waldfogel, 2018). Just recently, Netflix announced that it is planning to offer its users over 1,000 own productions (i.e., films, series, documentaries) in their archives by the end of 2018 (Jacobsen, 2018). Amazon also invests in its own content productions (W&V, 2018), markedly in the German market (Herrmann, 2018a). On the other hand, the big incumbent international market player from the U.S. are currently within a horizontal and vertical merger wave, which includes the target of combating the Amazons and Netflixs on their digital battle ground (Stöhr et al, 2019).

IS YOUTUBE A RELEVANT MARKET PLAYER ON THE VOD MARKET IN GERMANY?

As already mentioned in the introduction, different studies use strongly varying market delineations for VoD markets. Some studies focus on PVoD only (e.g. Goldmedia, 2018), other studies and reports (e.g. Kunow & Ünal, 2017) include AVoD portals (e.g. YouTube), media libraries (e.g. ARD Mediathek), social networking sites distributing video content (e.g. Facebook), TV platform providers (e.g. Sky) or gaming video platforms (e.g. Twitch). In this paper, the authors cannot provide a well-derived market delineation. Lack of data is one reason, but it is also controversial how helpful market delineation actually is when it comes to heterogeneous and dynamic markets (Farrell & Shapiro, 2010; Kaplow, 2011, 2015). For our purposes it suffices to single out YouTube (originally a video sharing platform), the largest AVoD platform in Germany (SevenOneMedia, 2017, pp. 28-29), and to discuss the pros and cons of YouTube exerting competitive pressure on (other) non-linear audiovisual media service providers like Amazon and Netflix and linear audiovisual media service providers like TV stations.

According to a survey conducted by the BVDW (2017) on Digital Trends with focus on VoD 51 per cent of the respondents (n=1,049) stated that they use AVoD portals such as YouTube, MyVideo, Clipfish at least once a week. PVoD services such as Netflix, Maxdome or Amazon Prime Video are used by 30 per cent of the respondents at least once a week. Even though the ARD-ZDF Onlinestudie 2017 shows different numbers (video usage – at least once a week – in percent for 2017: 31 per cent for video portals and 23 per cent for video streaming services) the quintessence is the same (Koch & Frees, 2017, p. 443). AVoD is currently used more often than PVoD and, thus, plays a decisive role in overall video consumption. Also Kunow (2017, pp. 33-34) reveals that concerning VoD content, AVoD portals, and particularly YouTube (29.5 per cent), are the most used ones by the population in Germany for consuming professional VoD content at least once a month – compared to media libraries of TV channels with 28.4 per cent and online video libraries (e.g. Netflix) with 23 per cent. It gets even more interesting when looking at age specific usage patterns. Both, the ARD-ZDF Onlinestudie 2017 as well as the BVDW survey reveal that the younger the consumers are the more they use AVoD portals (Kupferschmitt 2017, p. 450; BVDW 2017, p. 7).[20] Also, they use AVoD more often than PVoD.

With respect to YouTube, the Social Media Atlas 2017/2018 revealed that 100 per cent of the 14-19-years old and 96 per cent of the 20-29-years old internet users consume video contents from YouTube (Statista, 2018a).[21] Consequently, this video platform is obviously highly relevant, especially for the younger generation. However, and as this study shows, YouTube even seems to be a fairly relevant media tool for the older age groups. When it comes to entertainment consumption, the attention of the user is viewed to be the relevant scarce resource (attention economics; inter alia, Falkinger, 2008). Since users have only limited (media) time during the day to spend on video consumption one can argue that they can spend time either on AVoD portals (e.g. YouTube) or on PVoD services (e.g. Netflix). This limitation may differ considerably between different age groups (and life circumstances) as adults often have stronger limits to the time they can spend for entertainment (job, family, etc.) than teenagers. Still, every minute spent on watching audiovisual content can be either devoted to a PVoD offering or to an AVoD offering. In line with this reasoning, YouTube might serve as a substitute for PVoD services and, thus, should exert competitive pressure on PVoD providers such as Amazon or Netflix.

An argument that would speak against considering YouTube as a relevant competitor to PVoD services is that a lot of YouTube content was non-commercial, i.e. content like a private cat video, a funny observation, your own dancing performance, etc. uploaded by users without commercial intent.[22] This non-commercial content might not be comparable to the professional programs provided by PVoD providers like Amazon or Netflix. However, while a lot of YouTube content may still be non-commercial, there is also a lot of commercial content on YouTube. Actually, the platform has become increasingly professionalized and commercial during the last decade or more (Döring, 2014; Ross & Weghake, 2015) and its most popular contents is rather commercial, purpose-created and business-strategically uploaded. Next to advertising-purpose YouTube channels of business companies, this includes commercial YouTube channels from traditional entertainment industries (using it as an additional distribution channel for music, movies, broadcastings, comedy, sports, etc. – and thus in direct competition with other online and offline distribution channels) as well as more YouTube-specific entertainment contents like fitness videos, styling and lifestyle videos, or gaming and e-sports video content. This latter area of social media stars is a highly commercial multimillion-dollar business generating big money from advertising revenues as well as from product placements (so-called influencer) and merchandising (Budzinski & Gaenssle, 2018). As such, the largest part of the most popular YouTube contents is directly comparable in terms of commercialization and professionalism to the contents of other non-linear and linear audiovisual media services like PVoD à la Netflix, Amazon, Sky – or traditional TV stations.

In addition to this, viewing habits – concerning consumption time and content types might differ. One would assume that the consumption time of YouTube videos is usually shorter (even though people might watch several videos in a row). The PVoD content, by contrast, might usually be watched for a longer time period. The assumed differences could go along with the different types of videos aired on AVoD portals à la YouTube and PVoD platforms. Whereas YouTube contains a lot of short(er) videos, music videos, etc. the users on PVoD platforms can watch whole movies, episodes of series[23] or documentaries. On the other hand, consumers may also watch considerable long chains of videos on YouTube, fuelled by the website's individualized algorithmic recommendation service.

Looking at actual figures, however, the following can be observed: according to the ViewTime Report 2017, YouTube is watched on average 8 minutes/day by the 14-69-year old users in Q2/2017 (SevonOne-Media, 2017, pp. 28-29).[24] PVoD is – according to that report – used on average for 9 minutes/day by the 14-69-years old and on average 14 minutes/day by the 14-49-years old in Q2 2017 (SevenOneMedia, 2017, p. 9). Thus, the differences in viewing time are marginal and hardly conclusive.[25] In particular, for the young generation, however, YouTube (as well as other AVoD portals) may be a close substitute for other ways of watching audiovisual content, be they linear or non-linear.

Furthermore, there are differences in the content types of consumed videos. The most favored content types on YouTube have been in Q2/2017 for the 14-69-years old: music videos (32 per cent), social media stars (27 per cent), news/documentaries/sports (14 per cent), series/movies/TV shows (7 per cent), and private videos (6 per cent) (SevenOneMedia, 2017, p. 29). On the one hand, viewing habits depart from (other) linear and non-linear audiovisual media services where series, movies and TV shows dominate. On the other hand, there is some overlap hinting to direct competitive pressure at least for some niches. Moreover, the degree of substitution is determined by the subjective utility of the individual user, i.e. what she thinks are close alternatives for dedicating her media time. Watching a gamer playing a popular video game or an e-sports event (all falling into the category social media stars) may be a close substitute to watching a tennis game or a traditional sports event as well as watching YouTube lifestyle stars to watching a TV show. It appears to be plausible that the degree of substitution between YouTube (AVoD) and PVoD-contents as well as TV will be wildly varying across consumers but in general it may be higher for young consumers than for old consumers. While this all hints to YouTube not being a perfect competitor to PVoD and TV, it also appears to be very plausible that it does exert imperfect competitive pressure – and that this will increase with the changing generations.

While this paper approached the relevance of YouTube and its competitive pressure on other audiovisual media providers from a theory-based media economics perspective, further research is necessary to empirically test these arguments (Budzinski et al., 2019). The dynamics concerning YouTube and its increasing impact on VoD providers are obviously at hand. Very recently, on June, 18th, 2018, YouTube has started its new subscription-based service YouTube Premium[26] in Germany (Pimpl, 2018). With this service the user gets the opportunity to watch advertising-free on-demand videos for € 11.99 per month. The videos can be streamed or downloaded for 30 days for being watched offline (YouTube Premium, 2018). This service is bundled with YouTube Music – a paid-for, advertising-free music streaming service.[27] This new YouTube service directly competes with PVoD services such as Netflix. YouTube Premium offers YouTube originals (films and series) and thereby also competes in the field of own productions with Netflix and Amazon Prime Video (YouTube Premium, 2018).

The preceding discussion focused on the question if YouTube is a relevant market player for the VoD market in Germany with respect to the audience side. Surely, it is also interesting to assess YouTube's direct market relevance on the advertising side. A recent study by the British market researcher WARC, for instance, has shown that large parts of advertising spending worldwide are invested in social media channels such as YouTube and Facebook (Nötting, 2018). In this context, it will furthermore be interesting to observe how Facebook's video platform Facebook Watch that has started in the United States last year and worldwide at the end of August 2018 (Perez, 2018) will perform. For both platforms – YouTube and Facebook – advertising presents the major revenue source wherefore they most probably put competitive pressure on other advertising financed audiovisual markets (linear and non-linear). The relevance of the video advertising sector is also clearly at hand as current and forecasted advertising figures show. Statista (2018b), for instance, shows the increasing relevance of video advertising: gross revenues in video advertising (both mobile and desktop) were at 321 million Euros in 2017 and are expected to increase up to 417 million Euros in 2019 and even up to 688 million Euros in 2023. Consequently, further research should also be conducted with a stronger focus on the advertising side.

CONCLUSION

The markets for audiovisual content are subject to dynamic change. Where once "traditional" television was dominating, i.e. linear audiovisual media services, markets display nowadays strong growth of different types of video-on-demand, i.e. nonlinear audiovisual media services, including both PVoD like Amazon Prime and Netflix and AVoD like YouTube. This paper has given insights into the recent developments of the German VoD market by presenting relevant business models, market structures and dynamics. In addition to this, the authors have put a focus on the perhaps special role of YouTube in the market for audiovisual (online) services. Thereby arguments for and against YouTube exerting competitive pressure on i) other non-linear audiovisual media services (such as Netflix and Amazon Prime) as well as on ii) other linear audiovisual media service providers (such as TV stations) have been discussed. The authors conclude that there are numerous pros and cons speaking for a relevant role of YouTube for both markets: YouTube for instance plays a decisive role for online video consumption and is used more frequently than PVoD portals, particularly among the younger age groups. At the same time, studies show decreasing usage figures of linear television, again specifically among the younger ones. Due to the consumers' limited available media time this platform should consequently exert competitive pressure on other audiovisual media providers – both online (e.g. watching YouTube videos instead of Netflix) and offline (e.g. watching YouTube videos instead of traditional television, such as ProSieben). However, content types of YouTube might be different to those of PVoD and traditional channels. Oftentimes existing literature emphasizes the lack of professional and commercial content shown on YouTube whereas other studies display the development of YouTube towards an increasingly professionalized and commercialized platform. On the other hand, the purposes for viewing might differ between traditional and PVoD (e.g. longer consumption) compared to YouTube (e.g. brief "in between" consumption). Whereas our reasoning in this paper is based on a media economics theory perspective, further research is necessary to empirically test these arguments (see Budzinski et al., 2019).

ACKNOWLEDGMENT

An earlier version of this paper was presented under the title "The New Media Economics of Video-on-Demand Markets: Lessons for Competition Policy" at the conference on "Institutional Change through Digitization" (Hamburg, September 2018) and the 51st Hohenheimer Oberseminar (Düsseldorf, October 2018). Following the conference feedback, the original manuscript has been separated into two papers: this and a second paper called "Antitrust Policy in Video-on-Demand Markets: The case of Germany". We thank the participants of both conferences as well as Michael Berlemann, Sophia Gaenssle, Gordon Klein and Annika Stöhr for helpful comments on earlier versions of this paper. Furthermore, we are grateful to Milena Wehner for valuable editorial assistance.

REFERENCES

Absatzwirtschaft. (2018). *Top-Studie: Video-on-Demand wird zum Massenmarkt – Umsätze wachsen so schnell wie nie*. Retrieved from http://www.absatzwirtschaft.de/top-studie-video-on-demand-wird-zum-massenmarkt-umsaetze-wachsen-so-schnell-wie-nie-134313/

Aguiar, L., & Waldfogel, J. (2018). Netflix: Global Hegemon or Facilitator of Frictionless Digital Trade? *Journal of Cultural Economics*, *42*(3), 419–445. doi:10.100710824-017-9315-z

Anderson, S. P., & Gabszewicz, J. J. (2006). The media and advertising: a tale of two-sided markets. In V. A. Ginsburgh & D. Throsby (Eds.), *Handbook of the Economics of Art and Culture* (Vol. 1, pp. 567–614). Amsterdam: North Holland. doi:10.1016/S1574-0676(06)01018-0

Anderson, S. P., & Jullien, B. (2015). The Advertising-Financed Business Model in Two-Sided Media Markets. In S. P. Anderson, J. Waldfogel, & D. Strömberg (Eds.), *Handbook of Media Economics* (Vol. 1, pp. 41–90). Amsterdam: North Holland.

Armstrong, M. (2006). Competition in Two-sided Markets. *The Rand Journal of Economics*, *37*(3), 668–691. doi:10.1111/j.1756-2171.2006.tb00037.x

Berkemeyer, K. (2017). *Der leise Tod des Fernsehens: Die nächste Zielgruppe springt ab*. Chip Online. Retrieved from http://www.chip.de/news/Netflix-und-Co.-Naechste-Bevoelkerungsgruppe-entdeckt-VoD-fuer-sich_118040541.html

Berthelmann, T. (2018). Digital Media Report 2018 – Video-on-Demand. Statista Digital Market Outlook – Segment Report.

Bitkom. (2017a). *Umsatz mit Video-Streaming knapp an der Milliardengrenze*. Retrieved from https://www.bitkom.org/Presse/Presseinformation/Umsatz-mit-Video-Streaming-knapp-an-der-Milliardengrenze.html

Bitkom. (2017b). *Video-on-Demand Markt boomt*. Retrieved from https://www.bitkom.org/Presse/Pressegrafik/2017/170113-Video-on-Demand-print.jpg

BMWI. (2017). *Wirtschaftliche Bedeutung der Filmindustrie in Deutschland. In Studie im Auftrag des Bundesministeriums für Wirtschaft und Energie (BMWI). Durchgeführt von Goldmedia GmbH Strategy Consulting*. Berlin: HMS Hamburg Media School GmbH und DIW Econ GmbH.

Budzinski, O. (2017). Wettbewerbsregeln für das Digitale Zeitalter – Die Ökonomik personalisierter Daten, Verbraucherschutz und die 9. GWB-Novelle. *List Forum für Wirtschafts- und Finanzpolitik, 43*(3), 221-249.

Budzinski, O., & Gaenssle, S. (2018). The Economics of Social Media Stars: An Empirical Investigation of Stardom, Popularity, and Success on YouTube. *Ilmenau Economics Discussion Papers, 24*(112). Retrieved from https://ssrn.com/abstract=3108976

Budzinski, O., & Kuchinke, B. A. (2019forthcoming). Industrial Organization of Media Markets and Competition Policy. In B. von Rimscha (Ed.), *Handbook Economics and Management of Media and Communication*. Berlin: DeGruyter.

Budzinski, O., & Lindstädt-Dreusicke, N. (2019). *Antitrust Policy in Video-on-Demand Markets: The Case of Germany*.

Budzinski, O., Lindstädt-Dreusicke, N., & Gaenssle, S. (2019). YouTube vs. Netflix – An Empirical Analysis of Consumer Behavior and Competition in Audiovisual Online Markets. *Paper presented at the EMMA (European Media Management Association) conference 2019*, Limassol, Cyprus. Academic Press.

Budzinski, O., & Stöhr, A. (2019). Competition Policy Reform in Europe and Germany - Institutional Change in the Light of Digitization. *European Competition Journal, 15*(1), 15–54. doi:10.1080/17441 056.2018.1555942

Budzinski, O. (2016). Wettbewerbsordnung online: Aktuelle Herausforderungen durch Marktplätze im Internet. *ORDO, 67*, 385-409.

Bundeskartellamt. (2018). Online advertising. In *Competition and Consumer Protection in the Digital Economy*. Retrieved from https://www.bundeskartellamt.de/SharedDocs/Publikation/EN/Schriftenreihe_Digitales_III.pdf?__blob=publicationFile&v=5

BVDW – Bundesverband Digitale Wirtschaft. (2017). *Digitale Trends. Umfrage zum Thema "Video on Demand"*. Bundesverband Digitale Wirtschaft (BVDW). Retrieved from https://www.bvdw.org/fileadmin/bvdw/upload/studien/Digital_Trends_VOD.pdf

Caillaud, B., & Jullien, B. (2003). Chicken & egg: Competition among intermediation service providers. *The Rand Journal of Economics*, *34*(2), 309–328. doi:10.2307/1593720

Conseil, N. P. A. (2007). *Video on Demand in Europe*, Study carried out by the NPA Conseil for the Direction du développement des medias and the European Audiovisual Observatory. Retrieved from http://www.obs.coe.int/documents/205595/264625/VOD+2007+EN.pdf/4d2bd6f9-98ca-40b3-ae36-00fa009ffc41

Crampes, C., Haritchabalet, C., & Jullien, B. (2009). Advertising, Competition and Entry in Media Industries. *The Journal of Industrial Economics*, *57*(1), 7–31. doi:10.1111/j.1467-6451.2009.00368.x

Crawford, G. S. (2015). The Economics of Television and Online Video Markets. In S. P. Anderson, J. Waldfogel, & D. Strömberg (Eds.), *Handbook of Media Economics* (Vol. 1, pp. 267–339). Amsterdam: North Holland.

Dewenter, R. (2003). *The Economics of Media Markets*. Helmut Schmidt Universität. Retrieved from http://opus.unibw-hamburg.de/opus/volltexte/2003/138/pdf/10.pdf

Döring, N. (2014). Professionalisierung und Kommerzialisierung auf YouTube. *merz medien + erziehung, 58*(4), 24-31.

European Audiovisual Observatory & DDM. (2009). *Video on demand and catch-up tv in Europe*. Retrieved from http://www.obs.coe.int/documents/205595/264625/VOD+2009+EN.pdf/78bbecb7-7c8f-4b67-8771-1189872a9637

European Commission. (2014). *On-Demand Audiovisual Markets in the European Union*. Luxembourg: Content & Technology by the European Audiovisual Observatory and the Council of Europe.

European Union (2010). Directives. Directive 2010/13/EU of the European Parliament and of the Council of 10 March 2010 on the coordination of certain provisions laid down by law, regulation or administrative action in Member States concerning the provision of audiovisual media services (Audiovisual Media Services Directive). *The Official Journal of the European Union.*

Evans, D. S. (2002). The Antitrust Economics of Two-sided Markets. *AEI-Brookings Joint Center for Regulatory Studies*, 1-73.

Evans, D. S. (2003). Some Empirical Aspects of Multi-sided Platform Industries. *Review of Network Economics*, *2*(3), 191–209. doi:10.2202/1446-9022.1026

Evans, D. S. (2004). The Antitrust Economics of Multi-Sided Platform Markets. *LECG Global Competition Policy: Economic Issues & Impacts*, 237-294. (Previously published in 2003 in. *Yale Journal on Regulation, 20*(2), 325–382.

Evans, D. S., & Schmalensee, R. (2005). The Economics of Interchange Fees and their Regulation: An Overview. *Proceedings – Payments System Research Conferences* (pp. 73-120). Federal Reserve Bank of Kansas City.

Evans, D. S., & Schmalensee, R. (2007). The Industrial Organization of Markets with Two-Sided Platforms. *Competition Policy International*, *3*(1), 151–179.

Falkinger, J. (2008). Limited Attention as a Scarce Resource in Information-Rich Economies. *Economic Journal (London)*, *118*(532), 1596–1620. doi:10.1111/j.1468-0297.2008.02182.x

Farrell, J., & Shapiro, C. (2010). Antitrust Evaluation of Horizontal Mergers: An Economic Alternative to Market Definition. *The B.E. Journal of Theoretical Economics*, *10*(1), 1–40. doi:10.2202/1935-1704.1563

Gabszewicz, J. J., Laussel, D., & Sonnac, N. (2006). Competition in the Media and Advertising Markets. *Manchester School*, *74*(1), 1–22. doi:10.1111/j.1467-9957.2006.00479.x

Gabszewicz, J. J., Resende, J., & Sonnac, N. (2015). Media as multi-sided platforms. In R. G. Picard & S. S. Wildman (Eds.), *Handbook on the Economics of the Media* (pp. 3–35). Cheltenham: Edward Elgar Publishing.

Gaenssle, S. & Budzinski, O. (2019). Stars in Social Media: New Light Through Old Windows. *Ilmenau Economics Discussion Papers*, *25*(123). doi:10.2139/ssrn.3370966

Gimpel, G. (2015). The Future of Video Platforms: Key Questions Shaping the TV and Video Industry. *The International Journal on Media Management*, *17*(1), 25–46. doi:10.1080/14241277.2015.1014039

Goldmedia. (2016). *Pay-VoD in Deutschland auf dem Weg zum Milliardenmarkt.* Pressemeldung. Retrieved from https://www.goldmedia.com/fileadmin/goldmedia/2015/Studien/2016/VoD/160705_Pressemeldung_VoD_Forecast_Deutschland_2021.pdf

Goldmedia. (2018). *Pay-VoD in Germany – Forecast 2018-2023.* Retrieved from https://www.goldmedia.com/fileadmin/goldmedia/2015/Studien/2018/VoD_Forecast/180604_Goldmedia_Video-on-demand_Forecast_Germany_2018_sample.pdf

Haucap, J., & Stühmeier, T. (2016). Competition and Antitrust in Internet Markets. In J. Bauer & M. Latzer (Eds.), *Handbook on the Economics of the Internet* (pp. 183–210). Cheltenham: Edward Elgar.

Hein, D. (2018). *Video-on-Demand-Markt wächst bis 2023 auf 2,5 Milliarden Euro.* Horizont. Retrieved from https://www.horizont.net/medien/nachrichten/Goldmedia-Studie-Video-on-Demand-Markt-waechst-bis-2023-auf-25-Milliarden-Euro-167580

Herrmann, S. (2018a). *Amazon packt nächstes Deutschland-Original an.* W&V. Retrieved from https://www.wuv.de/medien/amazon_packt_naechstes_deutschland_original_an

Herrmann, S. (2018b). *Streaming geht ab wie eine Rakete.* W&V. Retrieved from https://www.wuv.de/medien/streaming_geht_ab_wie_eine_rakete

Horizont Online. (2015). *Amazon verbannt Videogeräte von Apple und Google aus dem Angebot.* Retrieved from http://www.horizont.net/marketing/nachrichten/Videostreaming-Amazon-verbannt-Videogeraete-von-Apple-und-Google-aus-dem-Angebot-136685

Horizont Online. (2017). *Disney kündigt eigenen VoD-Service an - und kappt Zusammenarbeit mit Netflix.* Retrieved from https://www.horizont.net/medien/nachrichten/Streaming-Offensive-Disney-kuendigt-eigenen-VoD-Service-an---und-kappt-Zusammenarbeit-mit-Netflix-160163

ITU – International Telecommunication Union. (2009). Series Y: Global Information Infrastructure, Internet Protocol Aspects and Next-Generation Networks. Internet protocol aspects – IPTV over NGN. Requirements for the support of IPTV services.

Jacobsen, N. (2018). *Netflix forciert Wachstum: 1000 Eigenproduktionen bis Jahresende*. Meedia. Retrieved from https://meedia.de/2018/05/15/netflix-forciert-wachstum-1000-eigenproduktionen-bis-jahresende/

Jurran, N. (2014). *Amazon startet Prime Instant Video in Deutschland*. Heise. Retrieved from https://www.heise.de/newsticker/meldung/Amazon-startet-Prime-Instant-Video-in-Deutschland-2122284.html

Kaiser, U., & Wright, J. (2006). Price Structure in Two-sided Markets: Evidence from the Magazine Industry. *International Journal of Industrial Organization, 24*(1), 1–28. doi:10.1016/j.ijindorg.2005.06.002

Kaplow, L. (2011). Market Definition and the Merger Guidelines. *Review of Industrial Organization, 39*(1-2), 107–125. doi:10.100711151-011-9305-9

Kaplow, L. (2015). Market Definition, Market Power. *International Journal of Industrial Organization, 43*, 148–161. doi:10.1016/j.ijindorg.2015.05.001

Koch, W., & Frees, B. (2017). ARD/ZDF-Onlinestudie 2017: Neun von zehn Deutschen online. *Media Perspektiven, 9*, 434–446.

Kunow, K. (2017). Current status of the digitisation of television infrastructures and television and video consumption in Germany. In K. Kunow & A. Ünal (Eds.), Digitisation. Imposed enrichment: Is there a need for privileging plurality? (pp. 18-38). Berlin: die medienanstalten – ALM GbR.

Kunow, K., & Ünal, A. (Eds.). (2017). Digitisation. Imposed enrichment: Is there a need for privileging plurality? Berlin: die medienanstalten – ALM GbR.

Kuper, E.-S. (2009). *Internet Protocol Television – IPTV. In Rechtlicher Rahmen und Besonderheiten im Rundfunk- und Medienrecht, Telekommunikationsrecht, Urheberrecht und im Wettbewerbs- und Kartellrecht*. Hamburg: Kovac.

Kupferschmitt, T. (2015). Bewegtbildnutzung nimmt weiter zu – Habitualisierung bei 14- bis 29-Jährigen, Ergebnisse der ARD/ZDF-Onlinestudie 2015. *Media Perspektiven, (9)*, 383–391.

Kupferschmitt, T. (2017). Onlinevideo: Gesamtreichweite stagniert, aber Streamingdienste punkten mit Fiction bei Jüngeren, Ergebnisse der ARD/ZDF-Onlinestudie 2017. *Media Perspektiven, (9)*, 447–462.

Lindstädt, N. (2010). Multisided Media Markets: Applying the Theory of Multisided Markets to Media Markets. *Zeitschrift für Wettbewerbsrecht, 8*(1), 53–80.

Martens, D., & Herfert, J. (2013a). Der Markt für Video-on-Demand in Deutschland. *Media Perspektiven, (2)*, 101–114.

Martens, D. & Herfert, J. (2013b). *Der VoD-Markt Deutschland. Fakten und Einschätzungen zur Entwicklung von Video-on-Demand*. House of Research.

Meedia. (2016). *Jetzt ist es amtlich: Netflix-Konkurrent Watchever streamt nur noch bis Ende des Jahres*. Retrieved from http://meedia.de/2016/11/15/jetzt-ist-es-amtlich-netflix-konkurrent-watchever-streamt-nur-noch-bis-ende-des-jahres/

Meedia. (2018a). *Kartellamt gibt grünes Licht für Streaming-Plattform von ProSiebenSat.1 und Discovery*. Retrieved from https://meedia.de/2018/07/23/kartellamt-gibt-gruenes-licht-fuer-streaming-plattform-von-prosiebensat-1-und-discovery/

Meedia. (2018b). *RTL rüstet gegen Netflix & Co. auf: Sender-Gruppe will kräftig in Video-on-demand investieren*. Retrieved from https://meedia.de/2018/06/25/rtl-ruestet-gegen-netflix-co-auf-sender-gruppe-will-kraeftig-in-video-on-demand-investieren/

Meedia. (2018c). *Und wieder ein Netflix-Konkurrent: Die Deutsche Telekom will ihren Streamingdienst öffnen und ausbauen*. Retrieved from https://meedia.de/2018/08/27/und-wieder-ein-netflix-konkurrent-die-deutsche-telekom-will-ihren-streamingdienst-oeffnen-und-ausbauen/

Nielsen. (2016). *Wie die Deutschen Video-on-Demand und Klassisches Fernsehen nutzen*. Retrieved from http://www.nielsen.com/de/de/insights/reports/2016/global-video-on-demand.html

Nötting, T. (2018). *Werbeboom bei Online-Video*. W&V. Retrieved from https://www.wuv.de/digital/werbeboom_bei_online_video?

Pakalski, I. (2017). *Verkaufsbann für Apple TV bleibt bestehen*. Golem. Retrieved from https://www.golem.de/news/amazon-verkaufsbann-fuer-apple-tv-bleibt-bestehen-1712-131546.html

Peitz, M., & Reisinger, M. (2015). The Economics of Internet Media. In S. P. Anderson, J. Waldfogel, & D. Strömberg (Eds.), *Handbook of Media Economics* (Vol. 1). Amsterdam: North Holland.

Perez, S. (2018). *Facebook Watch is launching worldwide*. Techcrunch. Retrieved from https://techcrunch.com/2018/08/29/facebook-watch-is-launching-worldwide/?guccounter=1

Pimpl, R. (2018). *Youtube startet Bezahldienste für Filme und Musik auch in Europa*. Horizont. Retrieved from https://www.horizont.net/medien/nachrichten/Google-Angriff-auf-Netflix-Spotify-und-Co-Youtube-startet-Bezahldienste-fuer-Filme-und-Musik-auch-in-Europa-167779

PwC. (2015). *Video-on-Demand*. Retrieved from https://www.pwc.de/de/technologie-medien-und-telekommunikation/whitepaper_video_on_demand.html

Reisinger, M. (2012). Platform Competition for Advertisers and Users in Media Markets. *International Journal of Industrial Organization*, *30*(2), 243–252. doi:10.1016/j.ijindorg.2011.10.002

Rochet, J. C., & Tirole, J. (2003). Platform Competition in Two-Sided Markets. *Journal of the European Economic Association*, *1*(4), 990–1029. doi:10.1162/154247603322493212

Rochet, J. C., & Tirole, J. (2006). Two-sided Markets: A Progress Report. *The Rand Journal of Economics*, *37*(3), 645–667. doi:10.1111/j.1756-2171.2006.tb00036.x

Roson, R. (2005). Two-Sided Markets: A Tentative Survey. *Review of Network Economics*, *4*(2), 142–160. doi:10.2202/1446-9022.1070

Ross, W., & Weghake, J. (2015). 10 Jahre YouTube: Von dem Aufstieg einer Plattform und der Entwicklung neuer Märkte zum Kollateralschaden einer Google-Regulierung? *ORDO*, *66*(1), 195–220. doi:10.1515/ordo-2015-0111

Schobelt, F. (2015). *Kampf dem Déjà-Vu: So will Watchever neue Zuschauer gewinnen*. W&V. Retrieved from https://www.wuv.de/marketing/kampf_dem_deja_vu_so_will_watchever_neue_zuschauer_gewinnen

Seamans, R., & Zhu, F. (2010). *Technology Shocks in Multi-Sided Markets: The Impact of Craigslist on Local Newspapers*. NET Institute. Retrieved from http://www.netinst.org/Seamans_Zhu_10-11.pdf

SevenOneMedia. (2017). *Viewtime Report 2017. Focus on video usage.* Retrieved from http://viewer.zmags.com/publication/385b0226#/385b0226/1

Statista. (2017). Video-on-Demand in Deutschland, Dossier.

Statista (2018a). Anteil der befragten Internetnutzer, die YouTube nutzen, nach Altersgruppen in Deutschland im Jahr 2017, based on Faktenkontor. IMWF. Retrieved from https://de.statista.com/statistik/daten/studie/691565/umfrage/anteil-der-nutzer-von-youtube-nach-alter-in-deutschland/

Statista. (2018b). Videowerbung in Deutschland, Statista Digital Market Outlook. Retrieved from https://de.statista.com/outlook/218/137/videowerbung/deutschland#market-marketDriver

Stöhr, A., Noskova, V., Kunz-Kaltenhäuser, P., Gaenssle, S., & Budzinski, O. (2019). Happily Ever After? – Vertical and Horizontal Mergers in the U.S. Media Industry. *Ilmenau Economics Discussion Papers, 24*(115).

Tichem, J., & Tuinstra, A. (2018). Market Power of Online Streaming Video Platforms: Recent Insights. *Journal of European Competition Law & Practice*, *9*(1), 50–54. doi:10.1093/jeclap/lpx085

Ünal, A. (2015). Gefährliches Raubtier oder zahmes Pflänzchen. Netflix im Dschungel des deutschen Video-on-Demand-Markets. In K. Kunow & A. Ünal (Eds.), Digitalisierungsbericht. Digitale Welten analoge Inseln – die Vermessung der Medienwelt (pp. 15-25). Berlin: die medienanstalten – ALM GbR.

Von Rauchhaupt, J. (2017). *Wie VoD den Medien- und Mediamarkt durcheinanderwirbelt*. Adzine. Retrieved from https://www.adzine.de/2017/07/wie-vod-den-medien-und-mediamarkt-durcheinanderwirbelt/

Winterbauer, S. (2018). *Attacke auf Netflix & Co: ProSiebenSat.1 und Discovery wollen neues Streamingportal mit zehn Millionen Nutzern aufbauen*. Meedia. Retrieved from https://meedia.de/2018/06/25/attacke-auf-netflix-co-prosiebensat-1-und-discovery-wollen-neues-streamingportal-mit-zehn-millionen-nutzern-aufbauen/

Wippersberg, J., & Scolik, R. (2009). Einleitung: WebTV – Fernsehen auf neuen Wegen. In R. Scolik & J. Wippersberg (Ed.), WebTV – Fernsehen auf neuen Wegen. Beiträge zu Bewegtbildern im Internet (pp. 7-30). Wien: Lit.

Woldt, R. (2013). Fernsehen „auf Abruf" – von der Nische in den Mainstream? *Media Perspektiven*, *(2)*, 115–125.

W&V – Werben & Verkaufen. (2018). *Wie Amazon mit Eigenproduktionen Prime-Kunden akquiriert*. Retrieved from https://www.wuv.de/digital/wie_amazon_mit_eigenproduktionen_prime_kunden_akquiriert

YouTube Premium. (2018). *YouTube Premium*. Retrieved from https://www.youtube.com/premium

ENDNOTES

[1] The term moving images or video usage includes – according to the ARD/ZDF-Onlinestudie 2017 – the following: video portals such as YouTube, moving images on Facebook, video streaming services (e.g. Netflix); TV shows on the internet live or non-linear, Live TV on the internet, watching TV shows non-linear, video podcasts, shows in the online media libraries of the TV stations (Koch & Frees, 2017).

[2] This sales ban is still on so that no Apple TV or Google Chromecasts can be purchased on Amazon. This still holds for Apple although Apple TV has started to include the Amazon Video app on Apple TV – once the reason behind Amazon's decision (Pakalski, 2017).

[3] For differing VoD definitions see, for instance, Conseil, N.P.A (2007); European Audiovisual Observatory & DDM (2009); Kuper (2009); Wippersberg & Scolik (2009); Martens & Herfert (2013a, 2013b); Woldt (2014).

[4] See European Commission (2014, pp. 9-11) for further details on the classification and subcategories.

[5] These in-stream video ads have to be distinguished from in-page video ads that are video ads embedded in banners (Bundeskartellamt, 2018, p. 1).

[6] Platform economics or the theory of two-sided markets has its origin in economic analyses of the credit card industry in the context of antitrust lawsuits filed against MasterCard and Visa. See for platform economics in general Evans (2002, 2003, 2004); Caillaud & Jullien (2003); Rochet & Tirole (2003, 2006); Evans & Schmalensee (2005, 2007); Roson (2005); Armstrong (2006); Haucap & Stühmeier (2016).

[7] Other data-based business models include data-based price discrimination, data trading and data technologies, which currently do not appear to be relevant in the prevailing AVoD business models. See generally Budzinski (2017), Budzinski & Kuchinke (2019), and Budzinski & Stöhr (2019).

[8] OTT (over-the-top) services include: television content via live streaming or via media libraries; video-on-demand offers accessible via video portals, social media platforms or online video libraries (Kunow, 2017, p. 29).

[9] According to Kunow (2017, p. 33), YouTube is the most used platform among video portals for VoD content consumption.

[10] According to Nielsen (2016), already 41 per cent of the Germans stream VoD on the tablet.

[11] In 2015 a PWC study showed that TVoD was still favored by the respondents (age 18+; n= 1,023). With specific view to age groups the TVoD model was favored by the 31-45-years old and the age group 46+. The 18-30-years old, however, already favored the SVoD model in 2015 (Statista, 2017, p. 20; PwC, 2015).

[12] For 2019, for instance, Disney plans on launching a VoD service for their films and series in the United States (Horizont Online, 2017). The question is how long it will take until Disney expands its activities to other geographical markets as well. In addition to this, CBS revealed plans on expanding their streaming services internationally.

[13] In the United States, Netflix – a provider that originally started in 1997 as an online video rental store sending DVDs and Blue Rays by postal service to its customers – has been operating in the VoD market since 2007 (Ünal, 2015, pp. 15, 23). Netflix entered the VoD market in Germany in September 2014.

[14] Amazon Prime Instant Video started in Germany in February 2014, giving subscribers of Amazon Prime the opportunity of an unlimited streaming-access of more than 12,000 movies and TV shows (Jurran, 2014).

[15] Maxdome is the VoD offer of the ProSiebenSat.1 group.

[16] Goldmedia focuses on PVoD only and does not include AVoD such as YouTube.

[17] The ARD/ZDF-Onlinestudie 2017 showed similar figures – 22 per cent using video content on Amazon at least on a rarely base (Kupferschmitt, 2017, p. 451).

[18] Base: over 2,000 consumers, only VoD users (Statista, 2017, p. 28, based on Deloitte).

[19] The issue of the vertical integration of content production and content provision marks an upcoming trend in the industry with content producers starting to seek powerful positions in the video market (Gimpel, 2015).

[20] In the ARD-ZDF Onlinestudie 2017: usage of AVoD portals in total: 57 per cent; for the 14-29-years old: 91 per cent; for the 30-49-years old: 79 per cent (Kupferschmitt, 2017, p. 450). In the BVDW survey: usage of AVoD portals in total: 51 per cent; for the 16-24-years old: 74 per cent; for the 25-34-years old: 66 per cent (BVDW, 2017, pp. 3, 7).

[21] 4th quarter 2017, base: 3,500 internet users, 14+ years (Statista, 2018a, based on Faktenkontor; IMWF).

[22] The term user generated content has become popular for this type of non-commercial videos. However, on the ambiguities and widespread problematic (mis-)use of this term see Gaenssle & Budzinski (2019).

[23] Particularly with PVoD platforms (especially with SVoD providers) a typical viewing pattern especially of the younger viewers is binge watching – i.e. watching several episodes or even a whole series in a row (SevenOneMedia, 2017, pp. 42-45).

[24] The average usage time for free online videos in total is 15 minutes/day in Q2 2017 (SevenOneMedia 2017, p. 9).

[25] It has to be noted, however, that within 30 months, the PVoD usage has increased from on average 3-9 minutes/day among the 14-69-years old and, thus, shows remarkable growth (SevenOneMedia, 2017, p. 10).

[26] The VoD service originally started in the US and has been formerly known as YouTube Red (Pimpl, 2018).

[27] The music streaming service is also available separately to YouTube Premium as YouTube Music Premium for € 9.99 per months (Pimpl, 2018).

This research was previously published in the Journal of Media Management and Entrepreneurship (JMME), 2(1); pages 108-123, copyright year 2020 by IGI Publishing (an imprint of IGI Global).

Chapter 41
Consumers' Stickiness to Mobile Payment Applications:
An Empirical Study of WeChat Wallet

Elizabeth D. Matemba
Harbin Institute of Technology, Harbin, China

Guoxin Li
Harbin Institute of Technology, Harbin, China

Baraka J. Maiseli
University of Dar es Salaam, Dar es Salaam, Tanzania

ABSTRACT

WeChat wallet incorporates compelling features facilitating users to conduct financial transactions more conveniently. The authors' survey discovered that most users appreciate WeChat wallet services. Previous studies, however, inadequately address critical factors that motivate consumers' stickiness to this promising technology. Scholars concentrate only on the technological features and considers societal traditional practices. This work establishes a psychometric theoretical model that integrates novel constructs, which balances technological features and traditional values, predicting WeChat wallet customers' stickiness. To this end, a questionnaire, with Likert scale items, was administered to 450 Chinese and foreigners in China. The authors measured their model's reliability and validity using composite reliability, convergent validity, and discriminant validity. The study applied the common latent factor approach to test the common method bias. Structural equation modeling and SPSS were used for data analysis. The study reveals that perceived availability of merchant support, convenience, social influence, and red envelope (traditional Chinese culture for sharing monetary values during festivals and special events) preference promote consumers' stickiness behaviors to WeChat wallet. In addition, perceived security insignificantly moderates the relationships between convenience/social influence and consumers' stickiness. This study gives scholars an important research avenue to explore further the relationships between traditions and diffusion of technology.

DOI: 10.4018/978-1-6684-6287-4.ch041

INTRODUCTION

Consumers' stickiness refers to a condition that reinforces customers to remain connected with products or services over extended periods. For example, a customer surfing an e-commerce website may stay longer on the website if s/he receives desirable products offered from a reputable Company. In addition, a person may reuse a convenient and a more secure mobile payment application for financial transactions. In business settings, studying stickiness of consumers on products/services marks an essential component that elevates reputation, popularity, and earnings of a Company. Guided by the advantages, this study has investigated potential factors that make people remain sticky to the WeChat wallet—a mobile payment application, widely used in China, which has captured a considerable attention of scholars (Lien & Cao, 2014; W. Liu, He, & Zhang, 2015; Wang, Hahn, & Sutrave, 2016; Zhou, 2013).

Most related studies focus on continuance intention to use mobile payment technologies, the goal being to reveal psychological intentional factors for a person to continue using the technology. Zhou found that trust, flow, and satisfaction promote customers' continuance intention on mobile payments (Zhou, 2013). In (Yuan, Liu, Yao, & Liu, 2016), the authors introduced four continuance intention predictors of mobile banking in China: satisfaction, perceived usefulness, perceived task-technology fit, and perceived risk. Gao et al. found that system quality, privacy, and security concerns determine continuance intention toward mobile purchase (Gao, Waechter, & Bai, 2015). Ahmed established an integrated model suggesting that trust, subjective norms, satisfaction, and perceived usefulness significantly influence intentions of people to continue using mobile transfer technologies. These factors highlight useful guidelines that may help developers design technologies, hence developing customers' usage intentions for their products. Our study moves a step ahead to identify, analyze, and discuss factors—unexplored from previous studies—that binds customers with WeChat wallet.

In China and some East/Southeast Asian countries, people consider WeChat wallet as their common ways of lives: they can securely add their credit/debit cards into the (digital) wallet and execute financial transactions through merchant stores that accept payments through the application. Additionally, WeChat wallet embeds a feature called red envelope that emulates a traditional value of Chinese to share (virtual) monetary gifts in important occasions. Our decision to select WeChat wallet among several other payment methods revolves in three pillars: popularity, reputation, and ongoing plans of extending the application to countries outside China.

Using our experiences from the WeChat wallet application, we conducted a preliminary study to understand stickiness levels of users to the application. Our quick observations from a few people discovered four behavioral factors for consumers' stickiness: red envelopes preference, perceived availability of merchant support, convenience, and social influence. Surprisingly, literature lacks discussions on the first two factors, despite their obvious societal impacts. In addition, we discovered that security, as a moderating variable, plays a central part in determining consumers' stickiness levels.

The current research attempts to answer six questions, all tailored to the WeChat wallet application:

1. Does convenience directly affect consumers' stickiness?
2. Does preference of people on red envelope directly affect social influence?
3. Does perceived availability of merchant support directly affect social influence?
4. Does social influence directly affect consumers' stickiness?
5. Can perceived security moderates the relationship between consumers' stickiness and convenience/ social influence?

Results from our study may assist developers to design products or to offer services that connect well with people. Also, other mobile payment methods, such as Alipay (Tang & Yu, 2010), may be revised along the guidelines recommended in this study. Developers that intend to introduce mobile payment systems should carefully consider the proposed factors to grab customers' attentions. More specifically, the study emphasizes on building products/services that touch the actual lives of people. For instance, we have demonstrated that integrating rewarding features (red envelope) into mobile payment systems increases customers' stickiness to the technology. In addition, the study has surfaced perceived availability of merchant support as an important determinant for customers' stickiness. Despite their values, previous studies have never reported these two factors. Given the trends of information system (IS) literature, we believe that results from the current study introduce breakthroughs worth discussing at this time in which developers struggle to obtain reliable means of retaining their customers.

THEORETICAL BACKGROUND

The proposed conceptual model builds on concepts related to consumers' continuance usage of technologies. Consumers' stickiness, a central construct in our model, establishes a relatively stronger attachment between consumers and technologies, and the associated motivational factors for using technologies may hold consumers over a longer period. Consumer's stickiness refers to the ability to retain a customer within a specific product or service. Consider, for instance, a customer surfing products in the electronic commerce website: how long the customer stays in the website determines his/her stickiness level. To provide a comprehensive understanding and contextualization of the current study, we highlight the technology continuance model.

Pioneered by Bhattacherjee (Bhattacherjee, 2001), the IS continuance model theorizes that satisfaction and perceived usefulness directly influence people in their behavioral intentions to continue using technologies (Figure 1). Furthermore, the model assumes that an individual should confirm the original expectations before being satisfied with or before discovering usefulness of the technology. The author's model, adapted from expectation-confirmation theory in consumer behavior literature, could explain 33% and 41% of the variances in satisfaction and in IS continuance intention.

As noted from the author, the IS continuance model establishes a preliminary explanation on the acceptance-discontinuation anomaly. Results highlight reasons for users to discontinue technologies despite their earlier acceptances.

Figure 1. Continuance model of information system

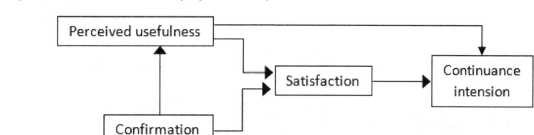

The IS continuance model has continuously been receiving attention of scholars. Developers, also, have developed interests in the model because it provides a commercial value: understanding the continuance behavior of customers for a given product predicts sustainability of the developer in the market. High demands of the IS continuance model have given rise to several variants, all aiming at predicting determinants for customers continuance intention to use technologies. In (Zhou & Li, 2014), the authors noted that social influence plays a fundamental role in mobile SNS (social network service) continuance intention in China. Hu and Zhang added perceived ease of use, which translates to convenience in some studies, as a behavioral determinant into the IS continuance model (J. Hu & Zhang, 2016). In (Kefi, Mlaiki, & Kalika, 2010), it was found that convenience (perceived ease use) indirectly impacts customers to continue using Facebook.

Moving beyond acceptance-discontinuation observation, the current study proposes cognitive factors for customers' stickiness, taking WeChat wallet as our target product for hypotheses testing. Our intuition is that, in a socially high influential environment (for example schools and universities) and for a given well-established technology, early adopters of the technology may not or may partially confirm their initial expectations, and they may rely on information they receive from their colleagues or friends. In addition, a cultural society with limited options to select a technology may ignore certain constructs, such as satisfaction and perceived usefulness found in the classical IS continuance model, which determine their stickiness levels to the technology. In this respect, and in view of our initial survey of this study in China, we have strategically eliminated some constructs in the original IS continuance model.

CONCEPTUAL MODEL AND HYPOTHESES DEVELOPMENT

Conceptually, our model predicts customers' stickiness through four cognitive factors: convenience, red envelopes preference, perceived availability of merchant support, and social influence. We, also, postulate that perceived security determines strengths of the relationships between convenience/social influence and customers' stickiness (Figure 2). The conceptual paths contain the proposed six hypotheses.

Figure 2. Proposed conceptual model

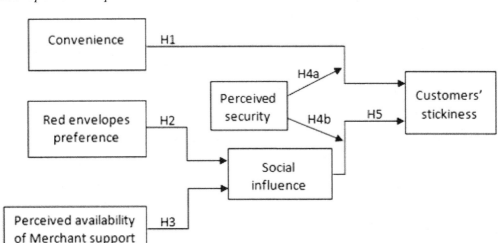

Convenience

Convenience, a construct in which a person applies little effort to complete a task (Baptista & Oliveira, 2015; Clarke III, 2001; Luna, Montoro-Ríos, Liébana-Cabanillas, & Luna, 2017; Riquelme & Román, 2014), can explain customers' stickiness. In the today's challenging world, people prefer executing tasks within a shorter time to attain satisfactory results. Given two mobile payment applications, say "A" and "B": if "A" incorporates fewer and easy-to-follow steps to transfer money compared with "B", for instance, assuming other factors remain constant, most people would naturally feel comfortable using "A". In a multitasking environment, convenience helps a person to complete one task quickly and switch on to another task, hence maximizing performance in achieving results. In addition, given a technology with features convenient to use, people with memory losses or relatively poor learning abilities may adequately fulfill their demands and continue using such a technology.

Sharma et al. observed that late adopters of technology consider convenience as a central construct that determines usefulness of the technology (Sharma et al., 2017), and hence these people may have higher levels of stickiness with a convenient technology. Additionally, the authors found that, in the context of the Canadian personal cellular telephone and Internet use, service convenience provided a significant prediction for the overall satisfaction, an observation that predicts customers' stickiness with the technology. The findings from Aagja et al. suggest that perceived level of service convenience increases with customer satisfaction (Aagja, Mammen, & Saraswat, 2011), which in turn allows people to continue using the service.

Therefore, we hypothesize that:

H1: Convenience of using WeChat wallet application increases with customers' stickiness on the application.

Red Envelope Preference

For most people, giving/receiving gifts have been their common life styles. In special occasions (weddings, graduations, or birthdays of babies), and in expressing appreciation or happiness, a person may send gifts, of any form, to the people s/he loves. Upon receiving the prize, a person may feel valued and respected. In job settings, scholars have associated monetary reward and job performance: rewarding employees may change their previous work attitudes and behaviours, an aspect that may motivate them to improve productions (Clarke III, 2001; Luna et al., 2017; Oghuma, Libaque-Saenz, Wong, & Chang, 2016; Riquelme & Román, 2014). In their seminal work on gift-exchange behavior between males and females, Areni et al. observed that countries embrace different cultures of giving gifts (Areni, Kiecker, & Palan, 1998). The authors isolated forms of memorable gifts (sacrifice as value, family tradition, and surprise as value) among groups of people, and discovered that females could more effectively describe gifts that their parents gave them. According to Areni et al., these experiences signal memorability because daughters could remember the gifts imbued with family values.

One form of monetary gift, red envelope or red packet, prevails in Chinese and some other East/ Southeast Asian societies. As a tradition, people in these societies perceive "red" as a good luck, a symbol to protect them against "evil spirits". In light of this tradition, WeChat wallet integrates red envelope as a feature to enable people send/receive gifts. From our investigation, original perceptions of people on giving/receiving gifts change when they unexpectedly receive red packets that can address their needs.

We can imagine, for example, a 60-year old parent receiving a red packet of 5000 Yuan from her grandson during a Chinese New Year. Perhaps the parent may feel cared, an advantage that may engage the parent in using WeChat wallet. For the relationship that involves youngsters, the gift-receiving partner may develop a behavior to use the feature and, as a courtesy, probably to send a red packet to the other communicating end.

On 18 February 2015, Tencent collaborated with CCTV Spring Festival Gala—probably to gain a larger market share—and introduced a feature called *WeChat wallet shake*. This feature allows users to shake their handsets to acquire unoccupied red envelopes. Statistics show that, approximately after one week since partnership of the two Companies, WeChat users shared over 3.27 billion red envelopes, and customers opened 1.65 million red envelopes every 60 seconds. In addition, during the gala promotion, the number of shakes reached 11 billion, a peak of 810 million per minute. In the New Year, people even shook multiple smartphones to elevate their chances of grabbing the red envelopes[1]. This increased interest of people to use *WeChat wallet shake* probably amplified social influence because people could reflect how the application gained a wide attention.

Hence, because of the contributions of rewards through red packets towards social influence, we hypothesize that:

H2: Preference of people to use red envelope positively affects social influence.

Perceived Availability of Merchant Support

Customers can use WeChat wallet to purchase goods from merchant stores, such as supermarkets. The purchase includes the following procedures (Figure 3): (1) a customer collects desirable goods from the store and proceeds to the point-of-sale for payments; (2) a seller computes the cost of items and informs the customer; and (3) if the merchant supports WeChat wallet, the customer will scan the quick-response (or QR for short) code and pay for the goods. In these steps, merchant support for WeChat wallet marks an essential step. After the process, customers may notice characteristics of the payment method, including convenience and speed. Given the (already accepted fact of) convenience of paying the merchants through WeChat wallet, a natural conception may be that customers will probably persuade other people to use the application for undertaking payments.

Surprisingly, despite the significance of merchant support on mobile payments, we located no works that show how customers respond to this factor. Our preliminary informal survey, in which we asked colleagues questions regarding their feelings on the factor, discovered that customers intensively consider availability merchant stores supporting WeChat wallet before asserting their decisions on usage. In essence, customers with higher perceptions on the availability of merchants that support WeChat wallet are likely to influence their friends to use the application.

Backed by these evidences, we hypothesize that:

H3: Perceived availability of merchant support on WeChat wallet increases with social influence.

Figure 3. Steps for executing payments through WeChat wallet

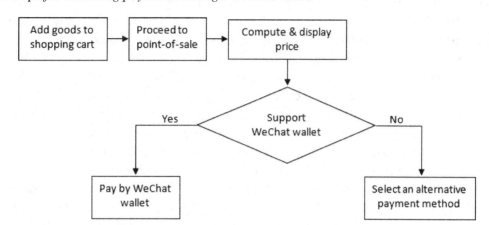

Perceived Security

Security forms an integral component for all mobile payment systems. Security relieves people from threats and danger. In the context of IS, security refers to protection of information systems against modification of or unauthorized access to information: storage, processing, and transmission[2]. Lack of security creates fears among IS users, and hence hesitance to apply the technology. Customers would like to conduct their financial transactions anonymously without inclusion of third parties. Having WeChat wallet convenient to use, for instance, cannot justify higher levels of customers' stickiness to the application. If a customer recognizes that an unintended person intercepted and received one of his transactions, he may immediately discontinue using the application to avoid financial losses in later transactions. This decision ignores the application's convenience. Furthermore, although social influence dictates directly customers' stickiness, customers may become sluggish towards the technology under conditions of poor security. Studies have confirmed how sensitive customers become on the security of their finances. Matemba and Li, and Shah et al. confirmed that successful adoption of Internet services in South Africa and Malaysia depends on the security levels of the systems and infrastructures that facilitate users' transactions (Matemba & Li, 2018; Shah Alam, Ali, & Mohd. Jani, 2011). Susanto et al. found that perceived security significantly influences trust (Susanto, Chang, & Ha, 2016), an observation that determines stickiness level of a customer to the technology. Supported by these findings, we hypothesize that:

H4a: High level of security in the WeChat wallet application strengthens the relationship between convenience and customers' stickiness to the application.
H4b: Perceived security moderates the relationship between social influence and customers' stickiness to the application.

Social Influence

Relationships and interactions among people mark an essential life component that may change minds of people in the society—a phenomenon called social influence, which occurs when other people affect one's beliefs, opinions, behaviors, or emotions[3]. Kelman revealed three forms of social influence: compliance, identification, and internalization (Kelman, 1958). The first form allows people to keep their opinions private while expressing agreements with others. Under compliance, people change their behavior—probably because of social pressures—but unnecessarily change their attitude. According to Kelman, people unwillingly comply to expect reward or to avoid punishment from the society. The next form of social influence, identification, occurs when a respected or liked person, such as a famous celebrity, influences behaviors or attitudes of people. As a motivating example, most Companies promote their products through advertisements containing admirable people to influence perceptions of customers, the intention being to increase sales and to widen visibility of the products. Internalization, on the other hand, causes people to accept external beliefs or behaviors and agree with them publicly and privately. In this case, people accept changes because they anticipate rewards that would positively impart their lives.

Social influence, regardless of its forms, affects psychological processes in people. More specifically, most social behaviours and attitudes directly determine customers' stickiness to a technology. For instance, an individual may persuade a colleague to execute a behavior, which s/he may become sticky to it. For example, under natural settings, we possibly all have been inclined to attitudes and behaviors from great people, in particular those with notable successes. We can imagine successful people, such as Jack Ma[4]—co-founder of the Alibaba Group—that have inspired millions of entrepreneurs in the world. In another example, consider online social interactions in e-commerce websites: consumers undertaking shopping of goods may develop steep inclinations to ratings and reviews from other shoppers (Amoroso & Ackaradejruangsri, 2017). In view of our study, users of the WeChat wallet application may impart their positive/negative perceptions to their friends, non-users of the application. Depending on the perceptions and nature of the impact, the influenced people may acknowledge the impacts and start using the application or they may develop opposite reactions and reject the application.

To further support our intuition, Agnihotri et al. demonstrated that salesperson's use of social media accelerates interactions between the communication parties (Agnihotri, Dingus, Hu, & Krush, 2016), and hence customers may elevate their trust on the salesperson and his/her products—an indicator for customers' stickiness. The authors noted a central role played by social media in relaying information to and steering the stickiness levels of customers. Liu et al. found that microbloggers influence customers' stickiness through content and technology gratification (I. L. Liu, Cheung, & Lee, 2016).

Therefore, from the mentioned evidences on how social influence affects behaviors and attitudes of people, we hypothesize that:

H5: Social influence positively affects customers' stickiness on the WeChat wallet.

Customers' Stickiness

We define stickiness as a condition in which a technology remains in use with a customer over a longer period. According to our conceptual model, convenience and social influence directly affect customers' stickiness, a target behavioral construct of the model. In industrial settings, most developers would prefer sticky customers (who constantly use their technologies) that would increase Company's reputation, sales, and profits. These practical benefits make the current study useful.

METHODOLOGY

Instrument Design and Data Collection

We designed an instrument that contains questionnaire items adapted from previous studies on mobile payment technologies (Table 8 in the Appendix). Selection of studies for adaptation featured the ones with well-designed and valid scales, the purpose being to avoid errors due to responses biases. From the conceptual model (Figure 2), the items for convenience originated from two studies: Luna et al., who investigated factors that necessitate people in Brazil to accept NFC (near field communication) technologies for mobile payments (Luna et al., 2017), and Kim et al., who empirically examined factors influencing the intention of customers to use mobile payments (C. Kim, Mirusmonov, & Lee, 2010). Riquelme et al. inspired us to design the items for perceived security (Riquelme & Román, 2014). The seminal work by Riquelme et al. explored types of customers and predicted impacts of privacy and security on consumers' online trust. The works in (Koenig-Lewis, Marquet, Palmer, & Zhao, 2015; Oliveira, Thomas, Baptista, & Campos, 2016; Sharma et al., 2017; Sun, Liu, Peng, Dong, & Barnes, 2014) assisted design of the items under social influence. The proposed constructs (red envelope preference, perceived availability of merchant support, and customers' stickiness) contain items designed from scratch. However, experts in the field reviewed rigorously the associated questions to ensure readability and correctness of inter-construct reliabilities.

To facilitate the analyses and to optimize chances for valid responses, the current study applied open-ended types of questions—carefully designed to ensure exhaustiveness and mutual exclusiveness. Using the five-point Likert scale, we measured the items through different levels with anchors spanning from strongly disagree to strongly agree. This type of scale—widely used in social and medical sciences (Hartley, 2014; Joshi, Kale, Chandel, & Pal, 2015) —offers a general approach for data collection and, therefore, can more easily be understood[5].

Data collection and analysis follow a quantitative approach. Our target respondents included foreigners and natives in China. Therefore, before collecting data, we prepared the English questionnaire and then sent it to people with excellent spoken and written English for proofreading. All errors captured at this stage (for instance, errors revolving in grammar and concision) were corrected, and the revised questionnaire received an intensive technical check from a colleague with similar research interests. We then translated the questionnaire into Chinese to allow natives understand the questions. To enhance quality of the translation, we distributed different questions of the English questionnaire to four intellectual Chinese people and requested them to translate. Next, we collapsed the translations into a single document and then sent it to another Chinese person for proofreading. This stage served a purpose of removing issues due to grammar, sentence constructions, and flow, thus improving quality of the Chinese questionnaire. We moved further into distributing the questionnaires to at most ten randomly selected respondents, and the remarks we received were that both groups (foreigners and Chinese) unambiguously understood the questions. This questionnaire-refinement stage helped us to minimize common bias problems of the instrument.

After being satisfied with the previous stage, we conducted a pre-test (pilot study) on 30 respondents from randomly selected respondents originated from different Universities in China. This pre-test stage, conducted before administering the instrument into a practical environment, facilitated instrument validation. Results collected from this stage demonstrated higher levels of validity and reliability (above cut-off values), suggesting that the instrument could capture meaningful data when deployed to a larger population.

Using the online survey tools, we collected data in November 2017 through separate links of foreigners[6] and Chinese[7]. Four hundred and sixty-two respondents received the links, and were requested to complete and submit their responses over the Internet. Analyzing the received data, we identified 12 incomplete cases, which were eliminated to retain 450 complete responses (222 males and 228 females). Despite the availability of several methods for data collection, we opted the Internet-based approach because of the nature of the target respondents: millennial group, which includes candidates more inquisitive to understand cutting-edge technologies, and which largely possesses Internet-enabled mobile handsets that they could use to submit their responses to us. Besides, this middle-age group prefers convenient data collection methods, not the traditional ones (paper-based questionnaire) that demand manual operations and that consume time.

Statistical Data Analysis

The current study applied structural equation model (SEM) approaches for data analysis (Barbara, 2001). Given the hypothesized model, SEM—a powerful tool for multivariate data analysis—helps to establish systematically and logically mathematical relationships among constructs of the model. SEM approaches (1) can simultaneously analyze multiple independent variables, which the proposed conceptual model contains; (2) support correlation of multiple variables (multicollinearity conditions); (3) facilitate data analysis through measurement errors; and (4) flexibly allow analysis of non-experimental data that represent complex theoretical propositions. These benefits elevated our confidence to apply SEM methods in statistically analyzing paths of the conceptual model. The confidence to use SEM approaches in the current study emanates from the distribution characteristics of our data. Using SPSS, we measured kurtosis of the proposed constructs and found that the kurtosis values for most of them lie within the acceptable ranges (H.-Y. Kim, 2013), hence signaling favorable normality conditions required by SEM-based methods.

The study applied AMOS23 (analysis of moment structures) software, configured under maximum likelihood estimation, to measure validities and reliabilities of the proposed constructs. In addition, the software assisted in evaluating model fitness and in analyzing fit indices. The model measurement stage included the following fit indices (Bentler, 1990; Bentler & Bonett, 1980; Browne & Cudeck, 1993): normed Chi-Square to degree-of-freedom (CMIN/DF), goodness-of-fit index (GFI), adjusted GFI (AGFI), normed-fit-index (NFI), root mean squared error of approximation (RMSEA), comparative fit index (CFI), and root mean squared residual (RMR).

CMIN/DF refers to the minimum discrepancy divided by the degree of freedom, and, for correct models, this value should approach unity. GFI measures fitness between the hypothesized model and the covariance matrix, while AGFI corrects GFI, which gives values depending upon weights attached to each latent factor (Baumgartner & Homburg, 1996). NFI analyzes the discrepancy between chi-squared values of the hypothesized and null models (Bentler & Bonett, 1980), but Bentler stated that this fit index tends to be negatively biased (Bentler, 1990). RMSEA addresses issues related to sample size by analyzing discrepancy between the population covariance matrix and the optimum hypothesized model (Brown, 2014; L. t. Hu & Bentler, 1999). CFI gives information on the discrepancy between the hypothesized model and the data. This index can address issues on sample size inherent in CMIN/DF and NFI. RMR refers to the square root of the discrepancy between the model covariance matrix and the sample covariance matrix.

Selection of these indices builds from the authors in (Hair, Black, Babin, Anderson, & Tatham, 1998), who found that fitness of the model can more effectively be established if the associated indices originate from different classes: absolute fit, incremental/comparative fit, and absolute fit with penalty clauses. The former class incorporates fit indices (Chi-Squared test, GFI, AGFI, NFI, RMSEA, CFI, and RMR) that explain the degree of fitness of the priori model on the data. In other words, absolute fit indices explain how data may be reproduced by the priori model (McDonald & Ho, 2002). Table 1 (first and second columns) summarizes cut-off values of GFIs adopted in our study. However, there has been controversial discussions within a scholarly community regarding the more appropriate thresholds for the cut-off values (Lance, Butts, & Michels, 2006). The current study used conversional evaluation rules on the indices to analyze the measurement model and test our hypotheses (Hair et al., 1998).

Model Measurement Analysis and Adjustments

Running AMOS23 on the initial hypothesized model with the collected data, we observed a relatively poor model fit in view of the recommended thresholds (Table 1, second and third columns). But reconfigurations and purifications of data may be employed to further improve the model (Anderson & Gerbing, 1988; Bagozzi & Yi, 1988). Therefore, refining the model's fitness, recommendations in (Byrne, 2016) were followed: (1) inspecting values of the fit indices in the "model fit summary" of the AMOS output files and analyzing their impacts on the model; (2) adjusting the values to ensure that they fall within the recommended thresholds; and (3) re-executing the modified model to confirm fitness. Following these steps, we decided to omit one item from customers' stickiness: "If I could, I would like to discontinue using WeChat wallet." This item—coded in reverse mode—appeared to introduce conditions that encouraged model's misfit, probably because the respondents misunderstood the item. After this adjustment, we repeated the measurements (CFA or confirmatory factor analysis) and obtained the required values of the fit indices (Table 1, third column).

Reliability and Validity Measurements

In high-quality surveys, scholars recommend reliable instruments that generate consistent and accurate results. These instruments ensure that they reliably measure the target elements. Validity of an instrument, unlike reliability that concentrates on the measurement process, deals with research methods and designs. A valid instrument embeds characteristics that ensure accurate measurements of the items hypothesized by the research. Both reliability and validity concerns may threaten results, and therefore scholars should treat well these aspects. We desire an instrument with both reliability and validity characteristics.

We measured reliability and validity using three quantitative indicators: convergent validity, discriminant validity, and composite reliability (CR). The former indicator confirms the degree of relationship between two measures of theoretically related construct, and can be measured through the average variance extracted (AVE) that measures the amount of variance captured by a construct relative to the one attributed to the measurement error. Discriminant validity, which confirms degree of validity between theoretically unrelated constructs, can be revealed using maximum shared variance (MSV, square of the highest correlation coefficient between latent constructs), average shared variance (ASV, average of the squared correlation coefficients between latent constructs), and $\sqrt{AVE}$. CR refers to the sum of all true score variances and covariances in the relevant composite of indicator variables divided by the total variance in the composite. The authors in (Hair, Black, & Babin, 2010) discussed conditions for an instrument to qualify reliability and validity tests (Table 2).

Table 1. Model measurements

Fit Index	Threshold	Initial Measurement Model	Modified Measurement Model
CMIN/DF	≤ 3.000	2.51	2.44
GFI (%)	≥ 90.0	89.2	90.1
AGFI (%)	≥ 80.0	86.3	87.2
NFI (%)	≥ 90.0	91.0	92.0
CFI (%)	≥ 90.0	94.3	95.1
RMR	≤ 0.05	0.11	0.097
RMSEA	≤ 0.08	0.58	0.06

Table 2. Threshold values of reliability and validity of constructs

Reliability	Convergent Validity	Discriminant Validity
CR > 0.70	AVE . 0.50	MSV < AVE
		ASV < AVE
		$\sqrt{AVE}$ > Inter-construct correlations

Additionally, we applied Cronbach's alpha to evaluate data adequacy in our survey. The metric was administered for all conditions of the instrument, including the one achieved by removing undesirable items from the questionnaire—to confine the Cronbach's alpha within the acceptable ranges. The Cronbach's alpha measures internal data consistency: how items in a group for a given construct relate with each other. A higher value of this metric implies acceptable threshold of internal consistency of items, and vice versa (Table 3).

Table 3. Interpretation of Cronbach's alpha cut off values

Cronbach's Alpha	Internal Consistency
$\alpha \geq 0.9$	Excellent
$0.8 \leq \alpha < 0.9$	Good
$0.7 \leq \alpha < 0.8$	Acceptance
$0.6 \leq \alpha < 0.7$	Questionable
$0.5 \leq \alpha < 0.6$	Poor
$\alpha < 0.5$	Unacceptable

Common Method Bias (CMB) Test

In survey-based studies, CMB refers to errors caused by an instrument used to capture responses from people. The authors in (MacKenzie & Podsakoff, 2012) discussed dangers, causes, and remedies of CMB, and their seminal work introduced useful techniques to find more appropriate approaches to improve the instrument. According to the authors, most causes of CMB revolve in the following factors: complex or abstract questions, ambiguous items, double-barreled items, and application of a common method (for instance, multi-item scale approach used in our study).

Noting the influence of CMB that would likely impact our results, we applied techniques suggested by MacKenzie and Podsakoff (MacKenzie & Podsakoff, 2012) to ensure that the instrument becomes unbiased. For instance, as highlighted in earlier sections, we carefully designed the questions and revised them accordingly in light of comments and recommendations from experts in the field. After the attempts to minimize CMB, the common latent factor approach (CLF) (Doty & Glick, 1998; Malhotra, Kim, & Patil, 2006; Podsakoff, MacKenzie, Lee, & Podsakoff, 2003) was applied to quantitatively discover possible instrument bias problems. As suggested by the authors, we computed standardized regression weights with and without the common latent factor, and then took the corresponding differences. Next, we located all difference values greater than 20% to identify construct relationships that suffer from CMB problems. Unlike CMB test using the Harman's, which has been criticized by scholars that it gives inaccurate and unreliable results (Chang, Van Witteloostuijn, & Eden, 2010), most classical studies have reported that CLF can more accurately measure CMB.

FINDINGS

Descriptive statistics highlights essential details on the participants (Table 9 in the Appendix): over 80% of the respondents aged 20-40 years (youth group) approximately; and equal numbers of males and females participated in our survey. Furthermore, the Appendix highlights the following results: respondents with bachelor's and master's degrees dominated the study, with only 19.8% of them being those with doctor's degrees; and salary of over 89% of the respondents ranged between 0-4000 RMB (note that most respondents were students receiving standard monthly incomes from their sponsors). Lastly, 76.7% of the respondents had, on average, an experience of between 1-4 years in using WeChat wallet; and the number of Chinese respondents slightly exceeded that of the foreigners. Table 4 summarizes means and standard deviations for various constructs, with most users having the "Agree" response to the items under convenience (mean ± standard deviation: 6.16±0.90).

Table 1 shows conformance of the final proposed model with the acceptable thresholds of the fitness indices. Furthermore, in view of the recommended thresholds (Table 2), our instrument demonstrates promising reliability and validity characteristics (Table 4). Measuring internal data consistency, we found acceptable values of the Cronbach's alpha for different constructs (Table 5). Regarding the CMB issues, results suggest lack of biasedness in our instrument.

Table 6 summarizes standardized factor loadings, SFL, and reliabilities, R^2, of the individual items. As recommended by Black et al., SFL > 0.7 and R^2 > 0.5 (Hair et al., 2010). From the results, the item CST3 (third item in customers' stickiness) yielded values much lower than those recommended in (Hair et al., 2010). Other few items that land relatively outside the recommendations by Back et al. include Conv1 (first item of convenience) and CST4 (fourth item of customers' stickiness).

Table 7 gives standardized regression coefficients and *p*-values of the conceptualized paths. Note from the Table that, because of the moderating effects of security, we replaced the original constructs by their standardized means. Results highlight that, of all the hypotheses, only two—moderation of security on convenience (H4a) and on social influence (H4b)—were unsupported. Hence, the study supports the remaining constructs' inter-relationships: social influence, red envelope preference, convenience, and perceived availability of merchant support. Of the supported hypotheses, red envelope preference and perceived availability of merchant support demonstrated higher impact (Table 7), meaning that these constructs influences, to a greater extent, customers' degree of stickiness to the WeChat wallet.

Table 4. Cronbach's alpha of different constructs

Construct	No. of Items	Alpha	Mean	Standard Deviation
Convenience	4	0.838	6.16	0.90
Red envelope	4	0.872	5.12	1.42
Perceived Merchant support	4	0.841	5.72	1.02
Perceived security	4	0.888	5.28	1.14
Social Influence	4	0.878	4.87	1.29
Stickiness	3	0.782	5.58	1.05

*Table 5. Master validity (*** means $p < 0.001$)*

	CR	AVE	MSV	1:Conv1	2:RedEnv	3:Merch	4:PS	5:SInf	6:CST
1	0.854	0.598	0.340	**0.773**					
2	0.874	0.634	0.317	0.349***	**0.797**				
3	0.849	0.587	0.378	0.583***	0.563***	**0.766**			
4	0.892	0.674	0.313	0.469***	0.359***	0.460***	**0.821**		
5	0.888	0.668	0.410	0.261***	0.515***	0.508***	0.517***	**0.817**	
6	0.816	0.605	0.410	0.483***	0.510***	0.615***	0.559***	0.641***	**0.778**

DISCUSSION

Results from this study highlights roles played by males and females in technologies. With nearly equal proportions of participations in the survey, we can conclude that these groups of people receive equal exposure to and interaction with the WeChat wallet application. Future studies may further analyze on how each group responds to questions in the questionnaire. Perhaps this analysis may reveal other interesting behavioral aspects of men and women regarding acceptance, usage, and continuance usage of technologies. Recalling the descriptive statistics results, approximately 84% of the respondents were youths, aged between 25—35 years, and a small percentage were elders. These statistics may be attributed to the environment under which the target population was extracted, but also provides an idea that youths are more inclined to recent technologies. Furthermore, approximately 79% of the respondents showed that they receive salary between 0-4000 RMB, and this range matches average salary payments of University students in China, a country selected to undertake the study. Because of the nature of communications in the country, most respondents use WeChat for chatting and other social services, including WeChat wallet, hence accounting for 76.6% of the respondents with experience in using the application.

Table 6. Standardized factor loadings and individual items reliabilities

Definition	Items	Factor Loadings	R^2
Convenience	Conv1	0.60	0.36
	Conv2	0.79	0.62
	Conv3	0.84	0.71
	Conv4	0.84	0.71
Red envelope	RedEnv1	0.70	0.49
	RedEnv2	0.80	0.64
	RedEnv3	0.84	0.71
	RedEnv4	0.84	0.71
Merchant support	Merch1	0.72	0.52
	Merch2	0.83	0.69
	Merch3	0.64	0.41
	Merch4	0.84	0.71
Perceived security	PS1	0.85	0.72
	PS2	0.91	0.83
	PS3	0.73	0.52
	PS4	0.77	0.59
Social influence	SInf1	0.80	0.64
	SInf2	0.88	0.77
	SInf3	0.90	0.81
	SInf4	0.67	0.45
Customer's stickiness	CST1	0.88	0.77
	CST2	0.86	0.74
	CST3	0.22	0.05
	CST4	0.55	0.30

We found that most hypotheses were supported (Table 7), suggesting that the conceptualized model may find useful applications in practical settings. The supported hypotheses reveal the following ideas.

First, consumers increase their stickiness levels for a convenient technology, such as the WeChat wallet. With an exploding trend of modern technologies, people would probably prefer technological features that can quickly capture their necessary needs without difficulties. Several WeChat wallet users, contacted informally through supplementary questions, expressed their sticky behavior on the application because of its GUI (graphical user interface) friendliness—easy-to-follow and shorter payment steps, appealing and readable features, and all-in-one integration capability (inclusion of essential services, such as chatting and calling, into the same application). This result calls upon a need for developers to focus on designs that comfort users. For instance, developers should avoid integrating complex features into their products to ensure that users achieve their goals conveniently and effortlessly. Given the today's world, flooded with sophisticated technologies, users can easily develop habits of discontinuing using technologies that fail to meet their expectations.

Second, users' preferences to use red envelopes can change behaviours of people. Of all the investigated path relationships, the one between red envelopes preference and social influence depicts the highest standardized estimate. This observation shows an important contribution that the interaction between these constructs can increase the number of WeChat wallet users. Non-users of the application may start using red envelopes if users persuade them on the benefits of the feature. Consequently, the increase in the number of users brings a commercial value to the developers. Therefore, to improve their sales, developers should creatively incorporate features—similar to red envelopes—that entertain users.

Third, merchant support plays a vital role in determining the social aspects of people. From the results, perception of people on the availability of merchant services in the area attracts non-users of WeChat wallet for subscriptions. The observation implies that authorities (and developers) should connect more merchants to the WeChat wallet service, and this advancement may change customers' perceptions.

Fourth, social influence determines customers' stickiness to the WeChat wallet. This result means that users' attachment levels depend upon the information they have received from their colleagues and friends. Decision-making evolves constantly in human lives, and the aspect can be achieved through persuasion (for instance, through word-of-mouth). People can, therefore, decide to remain sticky with WeChat wallet when they acquire positive convincing characteristics of the application.

Table 7. Remarks on hypotheses test using standardized estimates and p-values

H#	Conceptualized Path	Standardized Estimate	*p*-Value	Remarks
H1	CST ← Conv	0.197	< 0.001	Supported
H2	Slnf ← RedEnv	0.312	< 0.001	supported
H3	Slnf ← Merch	0.300	< 0.001	Supported
H4a	CST ← Conv_X_PS	-0.090	0.05	Unsupported
H4b	CST ← Slnf_X_PS	-0.080	0.05	Unsupported
H5	CST ← Slnf	0.307	< 0.001	Supported

For the unsupported hypotheses, one can still gather some useful critical ideas. Considering H4a—which gives a moderation effect of perceived security on the convenience/customers' stickiness relationship—our original conception was that the relationship would be weakened under conditions of poor security, and vice versa. Nevertheless, the results ascertain otherwise: users find that security plays an insignificant role in determining strength of the relationship. Similar arguments hold true for the moderation effect of security on social influence/customers' stickiness relationship. Conversely, most previous studies believe that security concerns impose limitations for people to execute financial transactions, say through WeChat wallet (Miyazaki & Fernandez, 2001; Salisbury, Pearson, Pearson, & Miller, 2001). Factors attributing this deviation of our results from those in the literature may be as follows: nature of respondents, instrumental design, study location, and type of the selected mobile payment application. For example, since its conception in China, WeChat wallet has been popularized in the country for more than four years. We speculate that the time may be sufficient for users to develop trust on the application, hence ignoring security concerns.

CONCLUSION

Summary

The current study has introduced a psychometric model to measure customers' stickiness on the WeChat wallet. We have revealed behavioral factors necessitating continuance usage of the application. Using SEM approaches, the study tested and validated four hypotheses (H1, H2, H3, and H5) that measure relationships between constructs: convenience, red envelopes preference, perceived availability of merchant support, social influence, and customers' stickiness. However, the study found that security insignificantly moderates relationships between convenience/social influence and customers' stickiness.

To achieve satisfactory results, we followed systematic procedures to validate our instrument. For instance, to ensure clarity, concision, and readability, professionals in the field revised questions from the English questionnaire. In addition, well-versed and intellectual Chinese individuals did proper translation of the English questionnaire into the Chinese language. Furthermore, we undertook a pilot study of the selected number of participants. These procedures helped us to reduce common method bias of the instrument. Other important steps to strengthen our study were to analyze model fitness by investigating threshold values of the corresponding indices.

Theoretical Contributions, Implications, and Recommendations

In the original IS continuance model, Bhattacherjee postulated that perceived usefulness, confirmation, and satisfaction significantly determine IS continuance intention (Bhattacherjee, 2001). An intuitive loose explanation of the model is that perceived usefulness and confirmation can jointly cause satisfaction, which can consequently determine IS continuance intention. These findings have been confirmed by some previous studies that the determinants capture customers' intentions to continue using technologies (Bhattacherjee, Perols, & Sanford, 2008). Nevertheless, our conception revolves in the intuitive assumption that customers that have applied a technology over a longer period tend to ignore motivational factors proposed by Bhattacherjee. We think that a technology that has remained robust for a reasonably longer period may make most customers either royal or sticky to it irrespective of their satisfactions. In other words, the factors proposed by Bhattacherjee et al. become meaningful only during the initial stages of IS usage. After users have been satisfied with the technology, they probably may start to concentrate on other technological aspects that they disregarded initially.

Satisfaction, a central factor in the Bhattacherjee's model, makes sense in situations where users have several options of similar technologies that they can switch to during early stages of IS usage. During this time, customers experiment with the technologies to recognize their usefulness. Over a certain time, customers may gain adequate experience that they can use to determine their continuance intentions. The present study shows that scholars may investigate continuance intention determinants for well-established products considering satisfaction. Using an example of WeChat wallet, we have demonstrated that experienced users focus on convenience and social influence to express their continued usage behavior.

Most previous studies on technology continuance focus on behavioural factors revolving in the characteristics of the technology. These studies ignore traditional practices of people in the society, including various forms of traditional rewarding mechanisms among people. The present study reveals that embedding popular traditional practices into mobile payment applications may increase customers' stickiness. Probably this observation gives a reason why WeChat wallet has been successful in the market. Societies possess different cultural and traditional values, and scholars may modify slightly the proposed model to suit such environments. The pivotal idea should be to convert the existing natural forms of payments and encapsulate them digitally into the mobile payment system, as with the case of red envelopes uncovered in our study.

The current study has established critical new factors, namely red envelopes preference and perceived availability of merchant support, for customers' stickiness. In the first factor, we can recognize the value of incorporating cultural aspects into mobile payment applications. Transforming the Chinese culture of sharing gifts into digital (red envelopes) motivates WeChat wallet users to send monetary gifts to their beloved ones. Even more importantly, users conveniently share the gifts without physical visitations encountered in traditional settings. Therefore, we recommend other methods of mobile payments to revise their implementations and include cultural features that users admire. Before designing and deploying the product, scholars should undertake intensive studies to understand cultural demands of the target society. As a motivating hypothetical example, we may have a society with people that prefer sharing traditional objects (for instance, cows, goats, and chicken) during special events. Developers can digitally code and embed this physical sharing aspect into the mobile payment application, and users may probably enjoy the transformation and remain intact with the technology.

The second proposed factor insists on having multiple merchant stores supporting WeChat wallet. Users cannot execute transactions without merchant support, thus making the factor critical. Going further to the practical world, the current study recommends developers to expand their services because users seem to care the perceived number of merchants. Users can easily abandon a mobile payment technology that has a limited support by merchants.

In China, two major instant messaging applications exist: WeChat (which integrates WeChat wallet) and QQ (developed by the Chinese Company called Shenzhen Tencent Computer System Limited). Recently, QQ customers have been migrating towards the WeChat application. We interviewed some candidates in Harbin (the city in China) and observed that QQ has lost popularity, especially within the Chinese community. The strong reason given for this paradigm shift was that WeChat is convenient to use, a fact that strengthens our argument that convenience steers continuance intention of customers to use WeChat wallet. Consumers added that the login mechanism of WeChat is simple, and that they can easily synchronize messages between the application and their Computers. In addition, WeChat offers effective password recovery options, and integrates electronic wallet with relatively easier steps to follow when transferring digital money to friends. Our results validate this argument through the supported hypothesis H1, giving an implication that convenience can raise customers' stickiness to a technology. Other developers may harness the value of this finding and improve ways through which customers interact with features of their technologies.

The results for social influence, another critical construct proposed in our study, shows that interaction of people in the society can influence their inclination capabilities with the technologies. When users describe appealing features of the application, such as WeChat wallet, to their colleagues, usually some psychological behaviors are built to such colleagues and they may start using the application. Therefore, our results give developers insights on how they can promote and strengthen social networks linked to their products (technologies). In doing so, network of customers sticky to the promoted technologies will grow. Recalling lives in China, for example, most foreigners depend on information from natives to understand superior messaging and mobile money transfer technologies. Of the foreigners we informally interviewed, a larger percentage said that they have remained sticky to WeChat wallet because of the influence they received from their (Chinese) colleagues. Hence, technology developers may effect our results to the development process by ensuring that the society is properly connected to the technology.

Limitations

Despite the promising findings, the current study endures some limitations. First, online survey tools dominated the data collection process. Although this approach suited our study, there could be a possibility that a few users were uncomfortable filling out online surveys—a natural habit of some individuals—hence introducing biased responses. Nevertheless, our assumption was that the selected sample included intellectuals actively involved in completing online surveys. We were unable to identify actual respondents' habits towards this mode of data collection.

Second, a sample size of 450 people may be insufficient to represent the whole population in China. Therefore, scholars should carefully use our results by considering this limitation. Future studies should increase the sample size and include samples from different distributions. Our results show that youngsters, students with bachelor's and master's degrees, dominated the study. Investigating other types of WeChat wallet users would add value to the current findings.

Third, combining Chinese and foreigners into a single survey may have introduced biased responses. Given the origin of the WeChat wallet, Chinese respondents could have subjective perceptions towards the application. Similarly, foreigners from countries with similar mobile payment applications could have introduced technological competitive issues, which probably lead to inappropriate attempt of the survey. Scholars should further measure severity of this limitation and find effective means to deal with this distribution differences.

Lastly, our study predicts behavioral factors that encourage people to continue using the technology over a longer period. However, predicting human behavior may be a relatively non-trivial task, and the current results cannot explain the complexity. To strengthen the current results, we recommend an experimental study to monitor WeChat wallet usage habits over regular intervals of time.

ACKNOWLEDGMENT

The National Natural Science Foundation of China (Grant No. 71272173, 71771063) supported this research. The authors of this work are grateful for Mr. Nelson Muchonji, Mrs. Zainab Katima, and Ms. Lauren Brown for their support in data collection.

REFERENCES

Aagja, J. P., Mammen, T., & Saraswat, A. (2011). Validating service convenience scale and profiling customers: A study in the Indian retail context. *Vikalpa, 36*(4), 25–50.

Agnihotri, R., Dingus, R., Hu, M. Y., & Krush, M. T. (2016). Social media: Influencing customer satisfaction in B2B sales. *Industrial Marketing Management, 53*, 172–180. doi:10.1016/j.indmarman.2015.09.003

Amoroso, D., & Ackaradejruangsri, P. (2017). How Consumer Attitudes Improve Repurchase Intention. *International Journal of E-Services and Mobile Applications, 9*(3), 38–61. doi:10.4018/IJESMA.2017070103

Anderson, J. C., & Gerbing, D. W. (1988). Structural equation modeling in practice: A review and recommended two-step approach. *Psychological Bulletin, 103*(3), 411–423. doi:10.1037/0033-2909.103.3.411

Areni, C. S., Kiecker, P., & Palan, K. M. (1998). Is it better to give than to receive? Exploring gender differences in the meaning of memorable gifts. *Psychology and Marketing, 15*(1), 81–109. doi:10.1002/(SICI)1520-6793(199801)15:1<81::AID-MAR6>3.0.CO;2-J

Bagozzi, R. P., & Yi, Y. (1988). On the evaluation of structural equation models. *Journal of the Academy of Marketing Science, 16*(1), 74–94. doi:10.1007/BF02723327

Baptista, G., & Oliveira, T. (2015). Understanding mobile banking: The unified theory of acceptance and use of technology combined with cultural moderators. *Computers in Human Behavior, 50*, 418–430. doi:10.1016/j.chb.2015.04.024

Barbara, M. B. (2001). *Structural equation modeling with AMOS: Basic concepts, applications, and programming.* New York, NY: Taylor & Francis Group.

Baumgartner, H., & Homburg, C. (1996). Applications of structural equation modeling in marketing and consumer research: A review. *International Journal of Research in Marketing, 13*(2), 139–161. doi:10.1016/0167-8116(95)00038-0

Bentler, P. M. (1990). Comparative fit indexes in structural models. *Psychological Bulletin, 107*(2), 238–246. doi:10.1037/0033-2909.107.2.238 PMID:2320703

Bentler, P. M., & Bonett, D. G. (1980). Significance tests and goodness of fit in the analysis of covariance structures. *Psychological Bulletin, 88*(3), 588–606. doi:10.1037/0033-2909.88.3.588

Bhattacherjee, A. (2001). Understanding information systems continuance: An expectation-confirmation model. *Management Information Systems Quarterly, 25*(3), 351–370. doi:10.2307/3250921

Bhattacherjee, A., Perols, J., & Sanford, C. (2008). Information technology continuance: A theoretic extension and empirical test. *Journal of Computer Information Systems, 49*(1), 17–26. doi:10.1080/08874417.2008.11645302

Brown, T. A. (2014). *Confirmatory factor analysis for applied research.* Guilford Publications.

Browne, M. W., & Cudeck, R. (1993). Alternative ways of assessing model fit. *Sage focus editions, 154*, 136-136.

Byrne, B. M. (2016). Testing instrument equivalence across cultural groups: Basic concepts, testing strategies, and common complexities.

Chang, S.-J., Van Witteloostuijn, A., & Eden, L. (2010). From the editors: Common method variance in international business research. Journal of International Business Studies, 41(2), 178-184.

Clarke, I. III. (2001). Emerging value propositions for m-commerce. *The Journal of Business Strategy*, *18*(2), 133.

Doty, D. H., & Glick, W. H. (1998). Common methods bias: Does common methods variance really bias results? *Organizational Research Methods*, *1*(4), 374–406. doi:10.1177/109442819814002

Gao, L., Waechter, K. A., & Bai, X. (2015). Understanding consumers' continuance intention towards mobile purchase: A theoretical framework and empirical study–A case of China. *Computers in Human Behavior*, *53*, 249–262. doi:10.1016/j.chb.2015.07.014

Hair, J. F., Black, W. C., & Babin, B. J. (2010). *RE Anderson Multivariate data analysis: A global perspective*. New Jersey: Pearson Prentice Hall.

Hair, J. F., Black, W. C., Babin, B. J., Anderson, R. E., & Tatham, R. L. (1998). Multivariate data analysis (Vol. 5). Upper Saddle River, NJ: Prentice Hall.

Hartley, J. (2014). Some thoughts on Likert-type scales. *International Journal of Clinical and Health Psychology*, *14*(1), 83–86. doi:10.1016/S1697-2600(14)70040-7

Hu, J., & Zhang, Y. (2016). Understanding Chinese undergraduates' continuance intention to use mobile book-reading apps: An integrated model and empirical study. *Libri*, *66*(2), 85–99. doi:10.1515/libri-2015-0090

Hu, L., & Bentler, P. M. (1999). Cutoff criteria for fit indexes in covariance structure analysis: Conventional criteria versus new alternatives. *Structural Equation Modeling*, *6*(1), 1–55. doi:10.1080/10705519909540118

Joshi, A., Kale, S., Chandel, S., & Pal, D. (2015). Likert scale: Explored and explained. *British Journal of Applied Science and Technology*, *7*(4), 396–403. doi:10.9734/BJAST/2015/14975

Kefi, H., Mlaiki, A., & Kalika, M. (2010). Shy people and Facebook continuance of usage: Does gender matter? *Paper presented at the AMCIS*.

Kelman, H. C. (1958). Compliance, identification, and internalization three processes of attitude change. *The Journal of Conflict Resolution*, *2*(1), 51–60. doi:10.1177/002200275800200106

Kim, C., Mirusmonov, M., & Lee, I. (2010). An empirical examination of factors influencing the intention to use mobile payment. *Computers in Human Behavior*, *26*(3), 310–322. doi:10.1016/j.chb.2009.10.013

Kim, H.-Y. (2013). Statistical notes for clinical researchers: Assessing normal distribution (2) using skewness and kurtosis. *Restorative Dentistry & Endodontics*, *38*(1), 52–54. doi:10.5395/rde.2013.38.1.52 PMID:23495371

Koenig-Lewis, N., Marquet, M., Palmer, A., & Zhao, A. L. (2015). Enjoyment and social influence: Predicting mobile payment adoption. *Service Industries Journal, 35*(10), 537–554. doi:10.1080/02642 069.2015.1043278

Lance, C. E., Butts, M. M., & Michels, L. C. (2006). The sources of four commonly reported cutoff criteria: What did they really say? *Organizational Research Methods, 9*(2), 202–220. doi:10.1177/1094428105284919

Lien, C. H., & Cao, Y. (2014). Examining WeChat users' motivations, trust, attitudes, and positive word-of-mouth: Evidence from China. *Computers in Human Behavior, 41*, 104–111. doi:10.1016/j. chb.2014.08.013

Lin, H.-F. (2008). Determinants of successful virtual communities: Contributions from system characteristics and social factors. *Information & Management, 45*(8), 522–527. doi:10.1016/j.im.2008.08.002

Liu, I. L., Cheung, C. M., & Lee, M. K. (2016). User satisfaction with microblogging: Information dissemination versus social networking. *Journal of the Association for Information Science and Technology, 67*(1), 56–70. doi:10.1002/asi.23371

Liu, W., He, X., & Zhang, P. (2015). Application of red envelopes–new weapon of wechat payment. *Paper presented at the 2015 International Conference on Education, Management, Information and Medicine*. Atlantis Press. 10.2991/emim-15.2015.139

Luna, I. R., Montoro-Ríos, F., Liébana-Cabanillas, F., & Luna, J. G. (2017). NFC technology acceptance for mobile payments: A Brazilian Perspective. *Revista Brasileira de Gestão de Negócios, 19*(63), 82–103. doi:10.7819/rbgn.v0i0.2315

MacKenzie, S. B., & Podsakoff, P. M. (2012). Common method bias in marketing: Causes, mechanisms, and procedural remedies. *Journal of Retailing, 88*(4), 542–555. doi:10.1016/j.jretai.2012.08.001

Malhotra, N. K., Kim, S. S., & Patil, A. (2006). Common method variance in IS research: A comparison of alternative approaches and a reanalysis of past research. *Management Science, 52*(12), 1865–1883. doi:10.1287/mnsc.1060.0597

Matemba, E. D., & Li, G. (2018). Consumers' willingness to adopt and use WeChat wallet: An empirical study in South Africa. *Technology in Society, 53*, 55–68. doi:10.1016/j.techsoc.2017.12.001

McDonald, R. P., & Ho, M.-H. R. (2002). Principles and practice in reporting structural equation analyses. *Psychological Methods, 7*(1), 64–82. doi:10.1037/1082-989X.7.1.64 PMID:11928891

Miyazaki, A. D., & Fernandez, A. (2001). Consumer perceptions of privacy and security risks for online shopping. *The Journal of Consumer Affairs, 35*(1), 27–44. doi:10.1111/j.1745-6606.2001.tb00101.x

Oghuma, A. P., Libaque-Saenz, C. F., Wong, S. F., & Chang, Y. (2016). An expectation-confirmation model of continuance intention to use mobile instant messaging. *Telematics and Informatics, 33*(1), 34–47. doi:10.1016/j.tele.2015.05.006

Oliveira, T., Thomas, M., Baptista, G., & Campos, F. (2016). Mobile payment: Understanding the determinants of customer adoption and intention to recommend the technology. *Computers in Human Behavior, 61*, 404–414. doi:10.1016/j.chb.2016.03.030

Podsakoff, P. M., MacKenzie, S. B., Lee, J.-Y., & Podsakoff, N. P. (2003). Common method biases in behavioral research: A critical review of the literature and recommended remedies. *The Journal of Applied Psychology*, *88*(5), 879–903. doi:10.1037/0021-9010.88.5.879 PMID:14516251

Riquelme, I. P., & Román, S. (2014). Is the influence of privacy and security on online trust the same for all type of consumers? *Electronic Markets*, *24*(2), 135–149. doi:10.100712525-013-0145-3

Salisbury, W. D., Pearson, R. A., Pearson, A. W., & Miller, D. W. (2001). Perceived security and World Wide Web purchase intention. *Industrial Management & Data Systems*, *101*(4), 165–177. doi:10.1108/02635570110390071

Shah Alam, S., Ali, M. Y., & Mohd. Jani, M. F. (2011). An empirical study of factors affecting electronic commerce adoption among SMEs in Malaysia. *Journal of business economics and management*, *12*(2), 375–399. doi:10.3846/16111699.2011.576749

Sharma, S. K., Sharma, S. K., Govindaluri, S. M., Govindaluri, S. M., Al-Muharrami, S., Al-Muharrami, S., ... Tarhini, A. (2017). A multi-analytical model for mobile banking adoption: A developing country perspective. *Review of International Business and Strategy*, *27*(1), 133–148. doi:10.1108/RIBS-11-2016-0074

Sun, Y., Liu, L., Peng, X., Dong, Y., & Barnes, S. J. (2014). Understanding Chinese users' continuance intention toward online social networks: An integrative theoretical model. *Electronic Markets*, *24*(1), 57–66. doi:10.100712525-013-0131-9

Susanto, A., Chang, Y., & Ha, Y. (2016). Determinants of continuance intention to use the smartphone banking services: An extension to the expectation-confirmation model. *Industrial Management & Data Systems*, *116*(3), 508–525. doi:10.1108/IMDS-05-2015-0195

Tang, J., & Yu, S. (2010). Online payment system of vending machine based on alipay. *Journal of Mechanical & Electrical Engineering, 5*, 035.

Wang, Y., Hahn, C., & Sutrave, K. (2016). Mobile payment security, threats, and challenges. *Paper presented at the 2016 Second International Conference on Mobile and Secure Services (MobiSecServ)*. 10.1109/MOBISECSERV.2016.7440226

Yuan, S., Liu, Y., Yao, R., & Liu, J. (2016). An investigation of users' continuance intention towards mobile banking in China. *Information Development*, *32*(1), 20–34. doi:10.1177/0266666914522140

Zhou, T. (2013). An empirical examination of continuance intention of mobile payment services. *Decision Support Systems*, *54*(2), 1085–1091. doi:10.1016/j.dss.2012.10.034

Zhou, T., & Li, H. (2014). Understanding mobile SNS continuance usage in China from the perspectives of social influence and privacy concern. *Computers in Human Behavior*, *37*, 283–289. doi:10.1016/j.chb.2014.05.008

ENDNOTES

[1] https://www.fastcompany.com/3065255/china-wechat-tencent-red-envelopes-and-social-money

[2] https://oit.unlv.edu/network-and-security/definition-information-security

[3] https://web.archive.org/web/20120322041448/http://qualities-of-a-leader.com/personal-mbti-type-analysis

[4] https://en.wikipedia.org/wiki/Jack_Ma

[5] https://psyc450.wordpress.com/2011/12/05/the-likert-scale-advantages-and-disadvantages/

[6] https://www.wjx.cn/jq/18085635.aspx

[7] https://www.wjx.cn/jq/18134982.aspx

This research was previously published in the Journal of Database Management (JDM), 29(3); pages 43-66, copyright year 2018 by IGI Publishing (an imprint of IGI Global).

APPENDIX

Table 8. Construct items

Items	Constructs Measurements	Reference
Social Influence		
SI1	People who influence my behavior think that I should use WeChat wallet.	(Koenig-Lewis et al., 2015; Oliveira et al., 2016; Sharma et al., 2017; Sun et al., 2014)
SI2	People who are important to me think that I should use WeChat wallet.	
SI3	People whose opinions I value prefer that I use WeChat wallet.	
SI4	The use of WeChat wallet improves my status in the society.	
Convenience		
CN1	WeChat wallet includes fewer number of easy-to-follow steps to send/receive money.	(Kim et al., 2010) (Luna et al., 2017)
CN2	Interaction with WeChat wallet is clear and understandable.	
CN3	WeChat wallet offers a more convenient way to send/receive money.	
CN4	WeChat wallet saves my time to send/receive money.	
Red envelopes		
RE1	I use red envelope to send money to my friends.	
RE2	Red envelope motivates me to use WeChat wallet.	New variable
RE3	Red envelope increases the interaction between my friends and I.	
RE4	Overall, red envelope is my favorite feature in WeChat wallet.	
Merchant support		
MS1	I feel pleased when I locate merchants that accept WeChat wallet.	New variable
MS2	I use WeChat wallet because many merchants accept it.	
MS3	I will continue using WeChat wallet as long as many merchants support it.	
MS4	I considered availability of merchants' support before using WeChat wallet.	
Satisfaction		(Lin, 2008; Oghuma et al., 2016)
SF1	My Decision to use WeChat wallet was a wise one.	
SF2	I am pleased with my experience of using WeChat wallet.	
SF3	Overall, I am satisfied with WeChat wallet.	
SF4	My feelings on the services of WeChat wallet are better than I expected.	
Consumers' stickiness		(Baptista & Oliveira, 2015)
CS1	I intend to continue using WeChat wallet in the future rather than discontinue its use.	
CS2	I will always try to continue using WeChat wallet in my daily life.	

continues on following page

Table 8. Continued

Items	Constructs Measurements	Reference
CS3	If I could, I would like to discontinue using WeChat wallet.	
CS4	My intentions are to continue using WeChat wallet than to use alternative means.	
Perceived security		(Riquelme & Román, 2014)
PS1	WeChat wallet appears to be a more secure payment method.	
PS2	I feel secured using WeChat wallet.	
PS3	I feel totally safe proving sensitive personal information to the WeChat wallet.	
PS4	WeChat wallet includes adequate security features.	

Table 9. Descriptive statistics (frequency and percentage) of consumers' stickiness

Measure	Value	Frequency	%
Gender	Male	222	49.3
	Female	228	50.7
Age	Less than 20 years	17	3.8
	20 to 25 years	145	32.2
	26 to 30 years	141	31.3
	31 to 35 years	91	20.2
	36 to 40 years	35	7.8
	Above 40 years	21	4.7
Education	Bachelor's degree	226	50.2
	Master's degree	135	30.0
	Doctor of Philosophy (PhD	89	19.8
Income	Less than 2000 RMB	287	63.8
	2000 to 4000 RMB	114	25.3
	4000 to 6000 RMB	21	4.7
	6000 to 8000 RMB	13	2.9
	8000 to 10000 RMB	5	1.1
	Above 10000 RMB	10	2.2
WeChat wallet experience	Less than 1 year	48	10.7
	1 to 2 year(s)	185	41.1
	2 to 4 years	160	35.6
	Above 4 years	57	12.7
Nationality	Chinese	241	53.9
	Foreigners	209	46.4

Chapter 42
Twitting for Talent by Linking Social Media to Employer Branding in Talent Management

Deepika Pandita
Symbiosis International University, India

ABSTRACT

This paper reconnoiters and gives importance to how social networking has been tactically applied as a current means by many companies for branding their companies and inventive talent acquisition approaches in India. This research backs to the arenas of the domain talent management and has crucial suggestions for industry practitioners concerning the practicality of social network websites (SNWs) to organizational branding, talent management. Interviews were taken, which was a qualitative way of getting responses from 78 focussed group discussion with HR professionals working in information technology companies (IT). Later the data was analysed to their talent acquisition techniques that endorse the increasing consumption of (SNWs) social networking websites as part of their talent strategy.

INTRODUCTION

Research conducted in the area Human Resources Management utilizing SNWs can be mostly seen in these main categories: talent acquisition and selection techniques(Warning & Buchanan, 2010), employee policies (Brown & Vaughn, 2011), networking on the job (Simon, & Engle, 2017), and evaluating jobs (Bohnert & Ross, 2010); relations of the employer and the employee; (Sanchez Abril et al 2012) study on employee privacy; Väyrynen et al (2013) study on consequences on workstation of digital exposure; Mainierio and Jones's (2013) study on harassment of the employee in the workplace; A rising trend among many Indians is the extensive use of internet and presents a seamless environment for discovering diverse opportunities for employment and Talent Management policies. (Carpentier, M.et al 2019) There has been some research on the use of digital media on Human Resources (Sharma, 2019). Therefore, it is vital to examine the impact of SNWs on the processes of Talent Management that have an

DOI: 10.4018/978-1-6684-6287-4.ch042

impact on the organization. The literature has acknowledged that the commercialization of SNWs has given rise to the development of the social network theory. (Lewis et al, 2008). Researchers like Boyd Ellison (2007) predicted the prospective of skills of communication like SNWs in the research of social networks. Therefore, the primary purpose of this study is to develop the prospect of SNWs as a means of social networking in the background of the structural approach and discovering its practice in Talent Management in the Indian scenario. To be more precise, the objectives of the research are dual: (1) to emphasize the amount to which SNWs are being implemented and are demonstrating to be a valuable mechanism for Talent Management and branding the employer; and (2) to measure and analyze the hands-on practices for the companies using SNWs for decisions pertaining to Employer Branding, Talent Acquisition, Employee Engagement and the role of HR Manager. The outcome of this research shall be useful for HR researchers and industry practitioners, as it highpoints the effectiveness of SNWs in Human resources practices like the acquisition of talent and processes relating to the selection, ensuring engagement of the employees, and branding the employer.

REVIEW OF LITERATURE

Social Websites

The SNWs are web-based facilities that permit the employees to build private or public summary for themselves, communicate with number of internet workers with whom they are a part of the common association, and interpret and pass through the list of networks and the ones made in the organization (Ellison & Boyd 2007). The theory is being determined from the viewpoints of equally with social network theories and social capital. The method of social network emphases associations in the midst of the individuals (i.e., organizations, work units or individuals) and thus differentiates the situation from any old-fashioned structural perspectives of research that scrutinize each individual in remoteness (Brass, Galaskiewicz et al, 2004). The supporting evidence underlying the theory of social network is that the individuals are entrenched in the systems of interrelated relations which deliver prospects for and restraints on individual behavior (Burt, 2010). The theory of social capital has been recognized as a conception having importance to the learning of "processes of the social network" (Adler et al, 2002). Burt (2000) was among the first investigators who connected the network theory to the notion of the theory of social capital. Agreeing to Burt (2000), to help in the creation of social capital there are two networks. In order to create social capital, a closure argument related to network is required for a system of intensely interrelated elements. (Rothkrantz 2015).

The current study on the social capital theory has presented the benefits people be able to acquire from their social networks; robust links deliver them with expressive sustenance (capital bonding), and fragile links deliver them with no redundant facts and diverse viewpoints (capital bridging) (Putnam, 2000). Backing up the significance of social networks, exploration of this study has established social capital to be related with novelty, enactment and existence of organizations and groups in the system, and with the outcomes of the individual, like attitudes at work, performance on the job, and search for employment (Vlaisavjevic, et al2016). A country like India is extremely varied with different cultures, religions, geographical locations, and administrative disparities through its zone (Budhwar & Varma, 2013). Separately from the mixed environment, aspects resembling exclusion in the caste system, cost of living and numerous such motives act as a hindrance in emerging group associations (Intra and inter) among the individuals (Barker, 2010). Developments in technology have aided in pledge such encounters (Singh et al 2012). Presently, social media is observed as a method to overcome these boundaries in constructing and instituting associations in India (Pillai & Chauhan, 2013). The structure of the networking permits diverse people to attach within bigger and more mixed systems and to connect to various individuals in various and different means, disregarding their own formal social systems and social structures.

Social Capital is described as: "features of social organization such as networks, norms and social trust that facilitate coordination and cooperation for mutual benefit" (Putnam, 1995). Some authors, such as (Ahern & Hendryx 2003) and (Baker 2000), have opted for vaguer descriptions of the concept, stating, for example, what they understand it to 'refer to' rather than committing themselves to a rigid definition. Fukuyama offers a more specific but significantly different definition of social capital as: "an instantiated informal norm that promotes cooperation between two or more individuals" (Fukuyama, 1999, p.1) rather than the resources which this norm provides access to. (Yilmaz & O'Connor 2012).

Figure 1. Proposed Model of Research

Talent Management

In the recent years is the reputation of make the most of the talent as a competitive advantage is a major topic that has emerged. (Scullion, Collings, & Caligiuri, 2010). "Talent management is including all the processes relating to human resources in the organization. It generally mentions the following activities like talent sourcing, screening of the candidate, talent selection, induction, employee retention, and employee development, deployment of manpower and renewal of the workforce with analysis. Some researchers have distinctly classified talent management as creating talent pools in the organization. Theories in Talent Management have concentrated on the hypothesis that capitalizing on employee talent is a foundation of continued competitive advantage (e.g., Al Ariss et al 2014). Therefore, practices of

Talent Management are broadly associated with Human Resources practices in organizations antedating the increasing performance of the business (Katou & Budhwar, 2012). Talent Attraction is the whole purpose of an organization's communication before and during the process of recruitment is to attract potential job applicants to the organization (Breaugh & Starke, 2000). Concepts like employee engagement and employer branding are emphasized inside the space of the approaches of Talent Management. (Christensen Hughes & Rog, 2008). Talent Acquisition is the competence to attract, recruit, develop, and retain high caliber talent is the single-most-important determinant of organizational effectiveness and a source of competitive advantage (Borstorff, Marker, & Bennett, 2007). Discovering the right candidate is a perplexing job for human resource professionals, which is obligatory to frequently look at innovative and varied ways of acquiring talent in the organization. As the struggle for acquiring manpower gets extreme, newer strategies pertaining to talent acquisition are essential to be articulated to empower companies to look for the right talent for the right positions (Scholz 2012).

In the organization, human resources policies and practices can generate an atmosphere where social media related communications between the employees and the employers are more probable to develop (Parker & Cross, 2004), which could be advantageous for the Talent Management processes of the company. The present study relates to the same judgement and recommends that social network structures of relationships enable a smooth function of Talent Management practices in the organization. (Shujaat, et al 2019). Furthermore, for years, although readings on social networks have been steered in arenas like anthropology and sociology, modern progress in the Internet techniques and Web Sites deliver a rich and unparalleled prospect to re-visit some conventions and discoveries relating to the behavior and structure of social networks particularly in various settings of the organization. The research problem in this research wishes to report that the use of SNWs influences the Talent Management policies and practices of the organization.

RESEARCH METHODOLOGY

Considering the objectives of the research, the study is clearly investigative and consequently working in inductive and qualitative means (Glaser & Strauss, 1967). A theory named Grounded theory (Corbin & Strauss, 1990) has stood utilized, which permits the author to improve a model that is thoroughly interrelated to the background of the occurrences that are being premeditated (Cresswell, 1998). To investigate a phenomenon, the grounded theory approach is used which is a set of processes that have been used. The grounded theory approach is anticipated to permit this to be inspected in greater wisdom, providing comprehensions on the practices of Human Resources of contemporary organizations (Kerr & Robinson, 2015). In this research, specialists in Human Resources, Human Resources managers, Sr. Human Resources managers, and specific consultants in the area of HR were tenaciously nominated as the frame of samples due to their vital role in providing solutions in the domain of HR and services in their groups. Furthermore, these managers in HR and HR consultants broadly use the Internet and the web at their workroom for their corresponding job characteristics and responsibilities. Henceforth, it is a motive to accept that they can deliver worthwhile evidence about the practice of SNWs in companies (look at Table 1 for particulars of the collected sample).

The data was collected from managers of IT/ITES companies and organizations that completely deliver staffing support to IT/ITES companies were carefully chosen for this research. The samples who were interviewed were mid-managers Human Resource specialists in their respective organizations. Though, the precise roles of respondents speckled depending on how their organization was implementing Talent Management. For instance, in companies where SNW was being utilized more generally, the author had a chat with the Head of HR accountable for acquiring manpower, talent acquisition director, or a senior Human Resource Manager. In the event of organizations pertaining to staffing, the founding member of the Director were interviewed for the company.

Table 1. Design of Research Sample

N = 78	Types	No. of Companies	No. of Companies in Percentage
Company size	<100	14	18
(employees)	100–500	31	40
	501–1000	18	22.8
	>1000	15	19.2
Type of Org	IT Companies	25	32.4
	ITES Companies	36	43.2
	Staffing Companies	17	23.2
Talent acquisition team	Yes	55	71
	No	23	29
Age	25–35	18	23.1
	35–45	25	32
	45–55	22	28.2
Gender	Male	57	75
	Female	21	25
Qualification	Graduate	31	39.7
	Post Graduate	28	35.9
	Above Master's	19	24.4
Seniority In current position	More than 15 years	33	42.8
	10 to 14 years	27	32.1
	5 to 9 years	15	19
	Less then year	54	5.1

Given the nature of this study, which is exploratory, mostly semi-structured interviews were selected for collection of the data. The author then resorted to questions that were open-ended like "what is the effectiveness of SNWs in organizations" and "how does the HR Manager use SNWs in the function of HR", which presented the samples a chance to enlighten their views and explanations for the use of SNWs in their organizations. Senior HR managers accountable for acquiring talent or managers of talent acquisition (N = 78) were selected and they got interviewed. In this research, the author has treated an individual interview with an HR manager as one data point.

The average time of the interview was for around 30-45 minutes. All these interviews with the HR Professionals were recorded on tape and transcribed. The transcripts delivered the substance for the investigation. Various categories and subcategories (Table 3) were emerged out of the interviews taken.

The coding process for this data was of two steps. Firstly, from the various expressions, there were themes that were derived and then based on commonality some sub-themes were also derived which were related to the main themes. The sub-themes under talent management practices comprised talent attraction and talent selection, under employer branding it consisted of the attractiveness of the employer and employer of choice, and Employee Value Proposition. Under the theme of Employee engagement, it consisted of blogs, intranet and web pages of the company. Lastly, the role played by HR Manager also was a sub-theme in this study.

FINDINGS

This research data analysis was predominantly concentrated on categorizing SNWs content significant to the HR managers' viewpoints about the practice of SNWs in the organization for processes relating to Talent Management practices specifically focussed on employer branding, talent acquisition and employee engagement. The role of HR Manager also plays a key role as per the findings from this research. From the interview which was taken a total of 173 expressions were pulled out. Each of the final categories emerged from the analysis of the interview comprised of subcategories, replicating parallel elements impelling the key subjects. For instance, in the space of expressions stating to leveraging SNWs in building the brand of the organization, approximately some expressions denoted to the wide-ranging reach of SNWs that help in crafting a good image of the company in a gigantic way, although others mentioned as the practice of "social media" by their companies.

The research results specify that the most commonly arising expressions associated with the usage of SNWs in the companies were firstly through the talent procurement and the process of selection of the organization (78% of respondents). Secondly, in prominence is the usage of SNWs in employer branding and developing approaches for the same (61% of respondents). Thirdly, the next most repeatedly happening comments related to the use of SNWs as a tool to manage the engagement of the employees (53% of respondents). Lastly, the HR manager`s role in the change in the Talent Management practices had the least number of comments (46% of respondents).

Table 2. Analysis of Interview (Categories)

1. Usage of SNWs in sourcing human capital and acquisition of the potential candidates
1a. Creating Talent Pool by attracting passive applicants
1b. Background Verification and offer process
1c. Talent Acquisition Sources: looking for cost effective ways
2. Employer Branding through SNWs
2a. Creating Employee Value Proposition for attracting talent by making a best place to work
2b. Making it as an employer of Choice by creating strategies for employee retention and engagement.
3. Use of SNWs for creating employee engagement measures for existing employees.
4. Starring role of the Human Resource Manager for inculcating the use of SNWs to the employees.
4a. The Characteristics of HR Manager
4b. The Characteristics of top leadership in the organization.

Table 3. Categories and Sub Categories

Respondent Category and Subcategory	Respondents (*N* = 78)	Percentage	Overall Percentage
Use of SNWs in talent management process			
Talent attraction	67	86%	
Talent selection	60	76%	38.9% plunge in this category
Cost associated with TM (sourcing)	63	80%	
Employer branding with SNWs			
Attractiveness of the employer	62	78%	
Employer of choice	21	28%	Overall 26.8% plunge in this category
EVP (Employer Value Proposition)	32	41%	
SNW and employee engagement			
Blogs, Intranet and Web Pages	38	47%	Overall 19.7% plunge in this category
SNW and the role of HR Manager			
HR manager and top leadership support	26	34% 19%	11.8% plunge in this category

RESULTS

SNWs, Acquisition and Selection of the Right Talent

Many companies are expending social websites to identify potential employees and improve their talent acquisition process. Information pertaining to potential candidates are provided using SNWs. It is a quick and most efficient tool to hire and select candidates. Some of the most cited messages for this theme of talent acquisition and selection are as follows:

Resumes and creation of talent pool are easy because of SNWs thus it's vital in filtering and screening in the sourcing of the candidates. (GM HR ITES Company)

Approaching the applicants differently is important as recruitment today happens in a variety of ways for various applicants. Creating an applicant`s pool is an easy affair nowadays as SNWs are a great mechanism for creating and connecting to various passive applicants. (Head-HR IT Company)

Linkedin as a tool is a great platform to connect to their professional & business networks. We use this not only to source but also to verify their background. (CEO of Staffing Organization)

The other sub-theme that became evident was to look at background checks for the candidates to be selected. The following quotes were reported and were echoed by 59 managers:

HR Recruiters use social networking tools to perform background checks that the right culturally fir candidate is got into the system. (Director HR ITES Company)

It is a common practice to check their background data and then select the right applicant. SNWs makes it very easy to get every information on the candidate. With the advancement in technology, the data can be pulled out in seconds.

However, 11% of the respondents said that they were neutral with the use of SNWs in the talent management process. Even though Human Resource managers were not tremendously tangible about social networks' success, they nevertheless acknowledged their significance.

SNWs and Employer Branding

The social media websites play an important role in building the brand image. This is a great effort in attracting the right talent to the organization. This study looked at three sub-themes that emerged as a part of collecting the data attractiveness of the employer, employee value proposition and employer of choice. The companies that had very good repute and stronger products and brands were able to invite the best talent. Nearly 78% of the HR Managers have reported that the role of social networks was able to increase the attractiveness for the potential candidates.

Some of the most cited messages areas for this theme of employer branding are as follows:

Our Social Networking Websites consisting of blogs, our HR practices get noticed by the potential applicants thus helps in building our brand especially our HR practices. (Senior Human Resource manager of an ITeS organization)

Our Culture of the company gets highlighted through social media networks. We highlight our vision, mission statements, and management style followed in our company. We also talk about the successes of some of our employees which helps in building the brand tremendously. (Senior Human Resource manager of an ITeS organization)

The following sub-theme was the aspect of the employer value proposition (EVP) wherein 41% of the managers agreed to work wonders for their company.

Some of the most cited messages are as below for this theme of Employer Value Proposition are given below:

We create our company page exhibiting our values, policies and the best practices for our employees. (Head Human Resources of an IT organization)

We project our company image as "employee-first as our employer brand". With the wide reach of SNWs one can easily do it on the web. The best advantage is that it reaches the active as well as the passive job seekers. (Manager Talent Acquisition, ITES organization)

The findings of this research are unswerving with the outcome of Rutledge (2008) that socializing technologies, such as LinkedIn, Facebook, Twitter and Myspace permit Human Resources and HR specialists the capability to associate with the accessible talent pool in the job market. Additionally, this research climaxes the usage of SNWs in getting applicants who are proactive as well as passive talents.

HR professionals widely use SNWs in the talent recruitment and selection method for examining the credentials of the candidates and examine the potential applicant before encompassing an offer of employment. There is no additional cost for such an opportunity. For instance, LinkedIn, an SNW has recommendations within the profiles that speak of representative behavior at work of the candidate. The investigation of the interview publicized that Human Resource specialists are leveraging SNWs for making contacts that can fetch detailed statistics on the potential candidates before concluding the offer of employment. SNWs, for employers, is a low-priced and fast source of collecting any information relating to the background of the candidate. (Clark & Roberts, 2010).

In a country like India, one of the most important roles played in an individual`s life is through informal networks. Therefore, in innumerable instances, one of the biggest challenges faced by HR practitioners is receiving accurate facts of the potential candidates as hiring becomes an important function in the area of Talent Management. By the use of SNWs correct and accurate information is provided to the employer.

To sum it up, if policies and practices of Talent Management are to be leveraged it can only be utilized through the use of SNWs in any organization. SNWs can be developed in any organization for the improvement of many HR policies and social networks in the organization. SNWs can also be utilized for gaining access to free applicant profiles and curricula vitae (CVs), for accessing the "passive" applicants who are not open to market opportunities or applicants who are proactive and who are open to market opportunities, for dispersing accountabilities associated with talent acquisition which means an flexible sourcing of the applicants through social media networks and being less hooked on to acquisition of talent consultants and organizations.

PRACTICAL IMPLICATIONS

This research makes three important contributions to the prevailing social networking theories. Firstly, organizations get a lot of information about the candidates through SNWs before they hire a candidate. Secondly, how SNWs are a crucial way to build professional networks thus enhancing networking skills for the employees. Thirdly, the role of the HR Managers has changed from the time the SNWs act as an aid to them for building employer brand, selecting the right candidates and making their workplace a better place to work. It also aids the HR Managers who are a vital link in the organization to get the right talent so it helps them find SNWs are an excellent tool to acquire talent, select the best talent and engage employees. Secondly, there are always budgetary constraints for the HR Managers thus SNWs are the most cost-effective ways to enhance the employer brand. Thirdly, considering the reach SNWs have, it is an important tool to build talent pools in the organization for the HR Managers. Finally, in the process of talent acquisition, background verification has become easy and quick for the HR Managers as it's a one-click step thus enabling the credibility check of the candidate before a job offer is issued.

RECOMMENDATIONS

Companies can customize SNWs as a policy to capture imbedded and prohibited behaviours of the individuals in the organization, which is one of the crucial aspect for modern organizations. Therefore, it is acclaimed that organizations should make and form some unambiguous Talent Management processes and measures regarding the utilization of SNWs as selection policies (Davison et al., 2011) in the talent acquisition process. The same policies should be shared with new work force as soon as they join the organization typically during Induction and Orientation.

Training on social networking should be periodical and deployment agendas should be organised in the company, making maximum employees conscious of the information on the intranet and other usages of SNWs. Furthermore, companies should develop their social media practices to embed the use of SNWs to the employees within the organization to encourage sharing of the internal information. Therefore, in this paper there is valuable message for both the Human Resources and managers working in the IT sector who design to apply knowledge on technology and social media for shared purposes, and must communicate the significance of the same.

CONCLUSION AND FUTURE RESEARCH

There are limitations to this study. First, the collected samples were mainly collected through a qualitative process that is interviewed. It can be tested empirically in the future. The data depends profoundly on professionals from the HR fraternity and is also confined to a restricted sample of IT/ITeS companies. One can look at other sectors like manufacturing, media, automobile and so on to study the implications of social media in their sectors. Second, our research data were predominantly collected from Human Resources managers and practitioners. Data from other employees working in various departments like marketing, sales, commercial of the same organizations can be studied and their usage of SNWs may be deliberated for research in future.

REFERENCES

Adler, P. S., & Kwon, S. W. (2002). Social capital: Prospects for a new concept. *Academy of Management Review*, *27*(1), 17–40. doi:10.5465/amr.2002.5922314

Al Ariss, A., Cascio, W. F., & Paauwe, J. (2014). Talent management: Cur- rent theories and future research directions. *Journal of World Business*, *49*(2), 173–179. doi:10.1016/j.jwb.2013.11.001

Arevalo, J. A., & Aravind, D. (2011). Corporate social responsibility practices in India: Approach, drivers, and barriers. Corporate Governance. *The International Journal of Business in Society*, *11*, 399–414.

Barker, M. D. (2010). *The effect of reservations on caste persistence in India* (Unpublished MA thesis). Washington, DC: Georgetown University.

Barney, J. B. (1991). Firm resources and sustained competitive advantage. *Journal of Management*, *17*(1), 99–120. doi:10.1177/014920639101700108

Behera, K. (2019). Ranjan, Santanu K Rath, S Misra, R Damaševičius, and Rytis Maskeliūnas. "Distributed Centrality Analysis of Social Network Data Using MapReduce. *Algorithms*, *12*(8), 161. doi:10.3390/a12080161

Behera, R., Rath, S., Misra, S., Damaševičius, R., & Maskeliūnas, R. (2017). Large scale community detection using a small world model. *Applied Sciences (Basel, Switzerland)*, *7*(11), 1173. doi:10.3390/app7111173

Bhatnagar, J. (2009). Talent management. In P. Budhwar & J. Bhatnagar (Eds.), *A changing face of HRM in India* (pp. 180–206). Routledge.

Bohnert, D., & Ross, W. H. (2010). The influence of social networking web sites on the evaluation of job candidates. *Cyberpsychology, Behavior, and Social Networking, 13*(3), 341–347. doi:10.1089/cyber.2009.0193 PMID:20557256

Budhwar, P., & Varma, A. (Eds.). (2011). *Doing business in India. Divide England*. Routledge.

Burkholder, N. C., & Preston, E. Sr. (2004). *On staffing*. Wiley.

Burt, R. S. (2000). The network structure of social capital. *Research in Organizational Behavior, 22*, 345–423. doi:10.1016/S0191-3085(00)22009-1

Burt, R. S. (2010). *Neighbor networks: Competitive advantage local and personal*. Oxford University Press.

Carpentier, M., Van Hoye, G., & Weijters, B. (2019). Attracting applicants through the organization's social media page: Signaling employer brand personality. *Journal of Vocational Behavior, 115*, 103326. doi:10.1016/j.jvb.2019.103326

Cascio, W., & Boudreau, J. (2012). *Short introduction to strategic human resource management*. Cambridge University Press. doi:10.1017/CBO9781139227087

Clark, L. A., & Roberts, S. J. (2010). Employer's use of social networking sites: A socially irresponsible practice. *Journal of Business Ethics, 95*(4), 507–525. doi:10.100710551-010-0436-y

Coleman. (1990). *Foundations of Social Theory*. Cambridge, MA: Harvard University Press.

Cresswell, J. E. (1998). Stabilizing selection and the structural variability of owners within species. *Annals of Botany, 81*(4), 463–473. doi:10.1006/anbo.1998.0594

Cross, R., & Parker, A. (2004). *The hidden power of social networks*. Harvard Business School Press.

Davison, H. K., Maraist, C., & Bing, M. N. (2011). Friend or foe? The promise and pitfalls of using social networking sites for HR decisions. *Journal of Business and Psychology, 26*(2), 153–159. doi:10.100710869-011-9215-8

Eastman, M. J. (2011). *A survey of social media issues before the NLRB*. US Chamber of Commerce.

Farndale, E., Scullion, H., & Sparrow, P. (2010). The role of the corporate HR function in global talent management. *Journal of World Business, 45*(2), 161–168. doi:10.1016/j.jwb.2009.09.012

Fleming, H., & Asplund, J. (2007). *Human sigma: Managing the employee–customer encounter*. Simon and Schuster/ Gallup Press.

Granovetter, M. S. (1973). The strength of weak ties. *American Journal of Sociology, 78*(6), 1360–1380. doi:10.1086/225469

Hoffman, T. (2008). New ways to target top talent in '08. *Computerworld, 42*(5), 34–36.

Kaplan, A. M., & Haenlein, M. (2010). Users of the world, unite! The challenges and opportunities of social media. *Business Horizons*, *53*(1), 59–68. doi:10.1016/j.bushor.2009.09.003

Lewis, K., Kaufman, J., Gonzalez, M., Wimmer, A., & Christakis, N. (2008). Tastes, ties, and time: A new social network dataset using Face- book.com. *Social Networks*, *30*(4), 330–342. doi:10.1016/j.socnet.2008.07.002

Mainiero, L. A., & Jones, K. J. (2013). Sexual harassment versus work- place romance: Social media spillover and textual harassment in the workplace. *The Academy of Management Perspectives*, *27*(3), 187–203. doi:10.5465/amp.2012.0031

McDonald, P., & Thompson, P. (2016). Social media (tion) and the reshaping of public/private boundaries in employment relations. *International Journal of Management Reviews*, *18*(1), 69–84. doi:10.1111/ijmr.12061

Mitsuhashi, H., & Min, J. (2016). Embedded networks and suboptimal resource matching in alliance formations. *British Journal of Management*, *27*(2), 287–303. doi:10.1111/1467-8551.12134

Nyberg, A. J., Moliterno, T. P., Hale, D. Jr, & Lepak, D. P. (2014). Resource-based perspectives on unit-level human capital: A review and integration. *Journal of Management*, *40*(1), 316–346. doi:10.1177/0149206312458703

Parkes, C., & Borland, H. (2012). Strategic HRM: Transforming its responsibilities toward ecological sustainability—the greatest global challenge facing organizations. *Thunderbird International Business Review*, *54*(6), 811–824. doi:10.1002/tie.21505

Parry, E., & Tyson, S. (2008). An analysis of the use and success of online recruitment methods in the UK. *Human Resource Management Journal*, *18*(3), 257–274. doi:10.1111/j.1748-8583.2008.00070.x

Putnam, R. D. (2000). *Bowling alone: The collapse and revival of American community*. Simon & Schuster.

Robinson, S., & Kerr, R. (2015). Reflexive conversations: Constructing hermeneutic designs for qualitative management research. *British Journal of Management*, *26*(4), 777–790. doi:10.1111/1467-8551.12118

Rothkrantz, L. (2015). How social media facilitate learning communities and peer groups around MOOCS. *International Journal of Human Capital and Information Technology Professionals*, *6*(1), 1–13. doi:10.4018/ijhcitp.2015010101

Rutledge, P.-A. (2008). *Profiting from social networking*. Pearson Education.

Sampath, R. (2007). Generation Y to require new recruiting strategies, organization reshaping. *Natural Gas & Electricity*, *24*(21), 1–27.

Schweyer, A. (2010). *Talent management systems: Best practices in technology solutions for recruitment, retention and workforce planning*. Wiley.

Sharma, A. (2019). A Study to understand the relationship of Social Media with Employer Branding. *Research Journal of Social Sciences*, *10*(6), 284-292.

Shujaat, A., Rashid, A., & Muzaffar, A. (2019). Exploring the Effects of Social Media Use on Employee Performance: Role of Commitment and Satisfaction. *International Journal of Human Capital and Information Technology Professionals*, *10*(3), 1–19. doi:10.4018/IJHCITP.2019070101

Singh, N., Lehnert, K., & Bostick, K. (2012). Global social media usage: Insights into reaching consumers worldwide. *Thunderbird International Business Review*, *54*(5), 683–700. doi:10.1002/tie.21493

Strauss, A., & Corbin, J. M. (1990). *Basics of qualitative research, grounded theory, procedures and techniques*. Sage.

Varma, A., & Budhwar, P. S. (2013). *Managing human resources in Asia- Pacific*. Routledge. doi:10.4324/9780203157053

Warning, R. L., & Buchanan, F. R. (2010). Social networking web sites: The legal and ethical aspects of pre-employment screening and employee surveillance. *Journal of Human Resources Education*, *4*(2), 14–23.

Wright, P. M., Gardner, T. M., & Moynihan, L. M. (2003). The impact of HR practices on the performance of business units. *Human Resource Management Journal*, *13*(3), 21–36. doi:10.1111/j.1748-8583.2003.tb00096.x

Yilmaz, M., & O'Connor, R. (2012). Social capital as a determinant factor of software development productivity: An empirical study using structural equation modelling. *International Journal of Human Capital and Information Technology Professionals*, *3*(2), 40–62. doi:10.4018/jhcitp.2012040104

Zeidner, R. (2008). Employers give Facebook a poke. *HRMagazine*, *53*, 12–54.

This research was previously published in the International Journal of Human Capital and Information Technology Professionals (IJHCITP), 12(2); pages 1-12, copyright year 2021 by IGI Publishing (an imprint of IGI Global).

Chapter 43
Carnivalesque Theory and Social Networks:
A Qualitative Research on Twitter Accounts in Turkey

Sefer Kalaman
Yozgat Bozok University, Turkey

Mikail Batu
(iD) https://orcid.org/0000-0002-6791-0098
Ege University, Turkey

ABSTRACT

Carnivalesque theory has been used as a model and a structure in the works carried out in many fields such as communication, literature, and sociology. In fact, Carnivalesque appears in many environments/areas, particularly in the social networks, which are the manifestation of social life. This chapter examines social networks in the context of carnivalesque theory to reveal facts of carnivalesque in Twitter. Content analysis technique was used in the research. Research data came from 10 Twitter accounts which have a maximum number of followers in Turkey. These data were analyzed and examined in terms of grotesque, dialogism, carnival laughter, upside-down world, marketplace, and marketplace speech belonging to the carnivalesque theory. According to the findings, the structure of Twitter, which is one of the most popular social networks in Turkey, is largely similar to the structure of the carnival and features of carnivalesque theory.

DOI: 10.4018/978-1-6684-6287-4.ch043

INTRODUCTION

Human beings, who started living in the big communes, have the birth and development of many innovations in social, political, artistic and technological aspects since they have the common mind, the ability to work together and the ability to think and invent individually. These innovations have led to the transformation of the individual and society in many respects. The internet, which is the most recent example of these innovations, has led to the transformation of everyday life in more ways and numbers than ever before although it is included human life into more than half a century ago.

Figure 1.

The social networks within the Internet are the main actors of this transformation at the point of social relations. Social networks have influenced and changed the way people communicate, how they belong to a community, and how they display their selves. People are now socialized through this virtual network, belonging to the virtual communities in this network and express their ego with created virtual identities in these virtual networks.

These networks resemble a carnival because of their characteristics. People are doing that will never do in everyday life in this network. People say things they can never say and people act like they can never be this virtual network. This kind of virtual environment exists as their second life.

Social networks have a great deal of the characteristics of the carnivalesque theory of Michail Bakhtin. This digital network is a digital environment of carnival where makes people come together, form communities, act for a common purpose, oppose ins, derive a common language, produce a humor, laugh, change their bodies, reverse the existing order and authority just like the carnivalesque.

CARNIVALESQUE THEORY

Carnival

The settled life action that one of the most important turning points in the life of mankind trace to "Göbekli Tepe" that B.C. 10000 years in the Şanlıurfa province in Turkey. In time, the people coming together and forming large communities, and the formation of cities happened in B.C. 3900. The first samples of this city is now Turkey, Egypt, Iraq, are of such countries. At the time, these cities became the pioneers of civilization, production, education, art and many other fields of life. In Egypt, one of the most important of these civilizations, the whole habitat is designed with a hierarchical order and is divided into different categories (slave, ruling class, workers, farmers, craftsmen) according to their status. The social activities of the people belonging to these classes take place in their class in the general and their relationship with other classes continues on the basis of superior-subordinate relationship. However, in some social celebrations, such as carnival or festivities, these classes coexist, and at the time of the carnival, these distinctions are relatively uncertail/transparent compared to other times.

This is the first festival of history recorded Feyyum in Egypt, one of the first cities of history interrupted routine of everyday life that determined by strict rules and restrictions, is at ease Pharaoh and minorities have power, contains the most difficult conditions for the rest of the people. These festivities outside the day-to-day operations and rules have a free time feature and on other days, these festivities eliminate the necessities that shape the life of the people. In the given banquets, it is replaced by the abundance, people can enter and see places where they are not allowed to enter in the normal time and they can be found in the same environment as the Pharaoh and the minority they serve in the whole year (Yurdakul, 2006: 20). This structure, which was the first example of the carnival, showed itself in the Middle Ages. Carnival culture was born as a new life space in the oppressive, rigid and restricted environment of the Middle Ages and has been strictly adopted by people. In other words, the carnival became a second life space in the Middle Ages, built by people on laughter. The carnival, which differs from culture to culture and from society to society, has come to life as a celebration, entertainment or festival that Christians gathered in communities before they entered the Great Lent.

Carnival is a festival life. The festival contains odd features of all the shows and funny rituals of the Middle Ages. All features and applications of real and ideal life at the carnival are suspended. Special type of communication that will never be possible in everyday life shows up during the carnival. In this type of communication, everything can be said clearly, all kinds of satire, mockery, place, humiliation (this may be a king or a noble), to ignore the rules of etiquette, and to perform the desired gesture and mimic forms (Bakhtin, 1984: 8- 10).

Bakhtin alleges these carnivals as an anarchic and emancipatory time period when it is razed the political, legal, and ideological authority of the church and the state. In this period of time, beliefs and rules are used as a mockery fact, and a clean and clear beginning is allowed to create new ideas (Kıpçak, 2016: 110). The suspension of the hierarchical structure and the fear, respect and sublime concepts that develop in relation to this hierarchical structure, the disappearance of the distance between individuals and the beginning of a more intimate relationship, the monotony of everyday life to replace the strange and unusual, sacrilege, obscenity, satirize holy, select the metaphorical king and queen and overthrow them, are some of the carnival's features (Brandist, 2011: 208-209).

From this point of view, there must be two lives of people living in the Middle Ages. The first is the real life that is formal, ordinary and be submit to ins and eupatrid. The second is the second life, the carnival life, where they live their true selves, behave freely from oppression and authority, transcend bodily and linguistic boundaries, and be turn distinction of ins-people, wielder-governed, noble- commons.

The person who transforms himself into a carnival wants to subvert all the moral and social rules imposed by the official life. The characteristics of the rebellious behavior; it provides an emotional discharge of absurdity, contrast, extravagance and illegality. H owever, if such behavior is separated from the daily life by the usual timetable, it also begins to adapt the social order. Carnival is an area of freedom under the surveillance of the power and within the limits of power. This liberating and at the same time adaptive order of the carnival has its own characteristics and determinative functions. When carnival participants turn into carnival itself, they fulfill these functions and violate the rules of daily and official times. While they all exist in each other, these functions, which form autonomous areas on their own, are carnival itself (Kıpçak, 2016: 116-117). During the carnival, the power of the king, kingdom, nobles and autocracy weakens. However, when the carnival is over and people return to their normal life, these power centers continue to manage more powerful than before.

Mikhail Bakhtin and Carnivalesque Theory

Born in 1895, Mikhail Bakhtin was a theorist in the human sciences, linguistics and literature. He makes mark in history with his work in the Soviet Union between 1920-1975. Bakhtin's work has been recognized by many scientific disciplines, scientists and researchers when he died more than the period he lived. However, Bakhtin's work has been used by different researchers as a concept, theory or inspiration in different disciplines. He included dialogue, dialogic and carnival concepts in own works. Another concept that Bakhtin discusses in depth is carnivalesque. Carnivalesque is a theory which based on carnival, characteristic structure of carnival and carnival features.

Bakhtin said that "In its history, carnivalesque is both a historical phenomenon and a literature trend". In this sense, carnivalesque has the characteristics that evaluate the multiplicity of life in the theoretical field and in this context can be applied to the language or culture area (Sözen, 2009: 66). It is necessary to explain some essential concepts in terms of the structure, characteristics and framework of the carnivalesque theory. These concepts, which form the basis of the carnivalesque theory, can be listed as grotesque, dialogism, carnival laughter, upside-down world, marketplace and marketplace speech.

In the carnival studies of Bakhtin, the grotesque form is mentioned quite a lot. Hegel said that grotesque has three feature in the context of the archaic Indian forms. According to this, it is possible to list the grotesque characteristics as the mergering of different natural areas, immeasurable and exaggerated dimensions and proliferation of different members and organs (hands, feet and eyes of Indian gods) of the human body. In particular, the destruction of the body, which is the basis of the grotesque form, is one of the indispensable elements of the carnival squares. In particular, the destruction of the body, which is the basis of the grotesque form, is one of the indispensable elements of the carnival squares. It is a common behavior to compare phenomenon individuals (king, religious leaders, nobles) to dead people or overthrow them (Uygun ve Akbulut, 2018: 78; Bakhtin, 1984: 44). However, people experience a metamorphosis by shedding their own assets and bodies in carnival with outfit, mask and exaggerated costumes. This situation, in the words of Bakhtin (1984: 48), means that both the man and the woman are freed from the idealized body structure imposed by the society and the body is free from its standard structure.

Another important concept of the carnivalesque theory, except for grotesque, is dialogism. Bakhtin includes highly of the concept of dialogism in his books and clarifies how dialogism has come to life in the carnival environment. Bakhtin expresses the common language used in carnival with the concepts of dialogue, dialogic and dialogism. Bakhtin also reveals how this language differs from the official language of prohibition in normal life. According to Bakhtin (1981: 426; 2001: 20), dialogism is a characteristic epistemological type of a world dominated by multilingualism. In this language world, the obligation of people to establish dialogue is a guarantee that communication will not be a monologue. Even the simplest daily conversation is basically dialogic. This multiplicity, which forms the basis of dialogism, forms the basis of a free and creative communication environment. In this context, the free expression of different ideas and the emergence of a discussion environment on these differences become one of the basic characteristics of dialogic communication (Kıpçak, 2016: 125).

An irreplaceable element of this communication is the laughing act. In other words; laughing does not just mean the loosening of the formal environment. The laughing act takes on a renewal mission at the carnival. As a form of carnival laughter, parodies destroy the subordinate and upper relations, and ensure to be reinterpreted the objects of everyday life. Laughter also allows for the creation of a creative environment. Hierarchical order transforms everyday life into a colorless, cold and diseased environment. In this context, laughing takes the role of a therapeutic role on the society by destroying the hierarchical structure and language (Gülüm, 2016: 131; Kıpçak, 2016: 119-120). Laughing refers to the fact that people are suspended the dominant culture and authority (Turan, 2008: 16). This smile is a revolt in its essence, this is to denigrate ins and it is a shout of freedom. This situation is to reverse the existing order, habits and life.

Life is turned upside-down during the carnival. Identities are turned upside-down. Tasks, occupations, moral norms, sexes are turned upside-down by reversing the established hierarchical order. This upside-down state is a description of a utopian world. When the carnival ends and life returns to its old order, it is replaced by a flat, oppressive and boring world. While the possible new world order is being abandoned, things are restored and the order continues (Kıpçak, 2016: 130).

The first concrete step in the upside-down world order, which is at the head of the Carnival environment, is undoubtedly depose rituals that the king to be declared a clown and the clown to be declared a king. This ritual is done in an order and accompanied by ceremonies. However, this is a behavior that is unique to the carnival time frame. Even if the carnival appears that authority have lost a little power, it will not dare demolish it. Because although the carnival environment depicts a free formation, it obtains permission from the authority to be realized and to be presented to the public (Uygun and Akbulut, 2018: 78).

Carnival is a non-discriminatory performance between the performers and the audience. At the Carnival, everyone is an active participant. In the carnival act everyone comes together and unite. The carnival is not watched, or even more strident, it is not even an execution; participants live in the carnival. Because carnival life is a life out of the usual way, it is a life that has been reversed. Carnival is the reversed face of the world (Derin, 2017: 328). In the same way, daily, formal and restricted language has turned into a structure called marketplace speech.

The well-known language of the marketplace has a structure in which there is blasphemy, slang and underbred communication. Another living area where this situation is experienced is carnivals. Carnival is an environment in which the oppression, slang, humiliation and ridicule occur as in the same marketplace where the repressive regime, formal and official language can be taken out. Here, everyday life can be turned upside-down, people can swear and mock with each other as well as the noble group, and their existence may be overthrown during the carnival period (Bakhtin, 1984: 17).

The place where this action takes place is the carnival square, in other words the marketplace. Carnival, which is one of the most prominent cultural and popular gathering events of early Modern Europe, also hosted the marketplace where trade developed. In the marketplace, merchants, sellers, touts exhibit their products. In the marketplace where a wide variety of products exist, the phenomenon of shopping in the atmosphere of the carnival like feasts also come to forefront. As a result, carnivals, which temporarily liberate their attendees, also is allow for a commercial exchange field that enable to settle the capitalist system. While people are temporarily moving away from the dogmatic seriousness of hierarchical structures at the carnival, they also find themselves in the midst of the capitalist logic and power mechanisms of the established system with the drunkenness of laughter. Crowds gathered together with the carnival transform this rich and fertile environment into an advertising environment. People who advertise their products or themselves are attracted to the public's attention by using all kinds of humorous language in the city square and the streets. In this context, it will not be wrong to say that the marketplace is the place where the announcements and advertising strategies are implemented in the carnivalesque sense (Kıpçak, 2016: 13-133).

The entertainment on the marketplace as well as the carnival has also become legal. This legalization took place by force. However, these entertainments have been partial and have led to conflicts and new prohibitions. During the whole Middle Ages, church and the state were forced to make more or less concessions and satisfy the marketplace. The small islets of the time, which are allowed to leave the official routine under the laughing sheath only and are strictly limited by the feast days, are spread all year. Obstacles have been removed provided there is nothing but laughing (Bakhtin, 2001: 110).

The elements such as marketplace, marketplace speech, grotesque, dialogism, upside-down world and carnival laughter are the main features that constitute the carnivalesque theory. Although carnivalesque theory is a theory used in literature, it is adaptable to many fields of science and art because of its characteristics. One of these areas is undoubtedly the field of communication. Because of its structure, the concepts of carnival and communication are two elements which are already very much related to each other. For this reason, the carnivalesque theory, which can be adapted to many communication environments, can also be adapted for social networks, one of the most important communication environments of the era.

SOCIAL NETWORKS AND CARNIVALESQUE THEORY, TWITTER AS A CARNIVALESQUE FIELD

The traditional media, which has been created through mass media such as radio, television and newspapers, have been replaced by digital media. A new media environment has been created with the internet technology that provides an interactive participation to the individual. In this platform, which is also called as social media, individuals have the opportunity to tell their thoughts and their attitudes towards any situation freely, to express, support or criticize even an event in another center of the world (Uygun ve Akbulut, 2018: 76-77). Considering the elements of number of users, generated content and popularity, this virtual environment, which is used for different purposes, is the most important environment for social networks. Social networks are a digital communication environment where incorporates different communication tools, users can enter anytime and anywhere they want, users can create accounts individually, communicate with other users and generate content.

Boyd and Ellison (2007) emphasize three features to define social networks that product of web 2 technology. First, social networks allow users to create an open or semi-open profile within a system with a limited number of boundaries. Second, social networks provide a list that users share links with others and access to this list. Third, social networks allow users registered in this network to have access to others' links.

In other words, social networks are a virtual communication/life area where people get together and share their feelings and thoughts, react to ins or people and institutions who have power, create communities for a specific purpose, generate humor, mock ins with this humor, distance from distress of everyday life, oppose the social hierarchical order and reverse the existing social structure, can freely exhibit their own self and create a space of freedom.

Social networks are similar to a carnival because of these features. Today, people's living space is now surrounded by computer networks. In the digital world that lives 24 hours a day, 7 days a week, social networks cover a large part of people's lives. The carnivalesque theory, which Bakhtin put forward years ago, has also been adapted to the social networks of today (Kıpçak, 2016: 107). Because the nature of the carnival is related to popular culture. There are carnival if there are locals. Although it is directed towards transformation into mass culture with capitalism, people are popular culture are people in basis of popular culture. Popular culture provides a free environment and endless pleasure like carnival. Popular culture is spreading more quickly thanks to mass media. New media tools that replace the traditional media order are effective tools in this formation. Considering all this, it is seen that the new media and social networks have become carnival (Uygun and Akbulut, 2018: 79).

In a study by Mclean and Wallace (2013: 1530) on the carnivalesque theory and blogs, which are one of the social networks, it was revealed that social networks have a large part of the features of the carnivalesque theory. The actions of people in this social networks such as laughter, parody, used masks and costumes, break off daily formal life and transform different life, used marketplace speech, mock about ins are very similar to the carnivalesque theory. In addition, in the study of Uygun and Akbulut (2018: 88), in the context of social media researches, the carnivalesque theory of Mihail Bahtin is frequently mentioned. Because of the features it contains and its unique style, social networks and carnivalesque are overlapping. From a general perspective, the upside-down world, tout, body destruction, grotesque images, features of humor and laughter are found in Instagram, one of the most popular social networks.

Carnivalesque theory and features of carnivalesque are in social networks such as blogs, Instagram and Facebook. At the same time, the structural features of the carnivalesque theory are largely similar

Twitter which is one of the most widely used environments of social networks. The accounts created on Twitter, the shares made on these accounts and the comments made on the shares correspond dimension of virtual environment such as marketplace, marketplace speech, grotesque, dialogism, upside-down world and carnival laughter which belong to carnivalesque theory.

Twitter is a social network established by Jack Dorsey and his colleagues in 2016 in San Francisco. The general purpose of Twitter provides to share opportunity to people in a web environment, like that feelings, thoughts, experiences, things in daily life. In other words, Twitter is a public sharing network that is open to everyone with internet access. The main feature that distinguishes Twitter from other social networks is that users can express themselves with a maximum of 140 characters, but there is no limit to the number or frequency of messages. Therefore, it shows a practical structure for writing and reading (Altunay, 2010: 36). As a result of its features, Twitter can be used by different people, states, institutions and organizations for different purposes.

For example, Twitter is a common place where protesters meet against Iranian elections, a public channel which gave the Zapatistas a right to speak and shared their thoughts with the whole world, the first mass media that Barack Obama has announced his presidential candidacy, a network of Haiti earthquake victims. In this context, it can be stated that new media and social networks carry their own democracy to the most powerful economies from the most repressive regimes (Altunay, 2010: 36).

According to Kıpçak (2016: 155), Twitter has parallels with the carnival environment with the above mentioned structural features and the usage patterns that arise from these structural features. The main determinants of the carnival can also be seen on Twitter and Twitter is becoming an online carnival. Throughout history, certain species may reappear when they meet the appropriate conditions. This is due to the fact that the species is updated according to time, but it has its core qualities. Carnivals can be repeated in a completely commercial way, far away from the traditional atmosphere. However, developing technologies and new media offerings; It creates a digital carnival that forms its presence on networks, independent of time and space. Twitter has a carnival qualities with humor, political satire, concealment of identities, advertising strategies and unique language.

METHODOLOGY

Method

The aim of the study is to examine social networks in the context of carnivalesque theory and to reveal the carnivalesque factors in Twitter, one of the most important social networks. In this study, a case study design which is one of the qualitative research methods is used. Case study that why and how to answer questions, is used for cases where the link between the content and the event is not clear and net (Sığrı, 2018: 161). In the case analysis, it is possible to examine in-depth details of a subject as well as to compare the details of many subjects. In this way, the issues that have not been previously considered on the subject can be transferred to the reader. Content analysis technique was used in the analysis of the data obtained with case study. Content analysis is a qualitative data analysis technique that aims to reach the concepts and relationships that can explain the collected data. In the first stage, the data summarized and interpreted in the descriptive analysis are subjected to a deeper process in content analysis (Sığrı, 2018: 280).

Population and Sampling

The population of the study is Twitter accounts which the most followed in Turkey. 10 Twitter accounts which have a maximum number of followers in Turkey, represent sample of study. This Twitter accounts (Cem Yılmaz, Recep Tayyip Erdoğan, Abdullah Gül, Galatasaray SK, NTV, Okan Bayülgen, Ata Demirer, Cüneyt Özdemir, T.C. Cumhurbaşkanlığı ve Fenerbahce SK) is the first 10 accounts with the most followers in Turkey (Socialbakers, 2019). In this study, the shares sent from these accounts are discussed. Data was analyzed and examined in terms of dialogism, upside-down world, carnival laughter, grotesque, marketplace and marketplace speech belonging to the carnivalesque theory.

SOLUTIONS AND RECOMMENDATIONS

Shares of 10 Twitter accounts which have a maximum number of followers in Turkey were analyzed and examined in terms of carnival laughter, dialogism, grotesque, upside-down world, marketplace and marketplace speech belonging to the carnivalesque theory.

Grotesque: With the development of new communication technologies, new applications are increasing and with these applications, it becomes easier to perform different operations on the existing images, change the image in any way and to remove new meanings from the image. In carnivalesque theory, grotesque imagery is deformed by different processes on the body, or new forms or images can be revealed which can be derived from new meanings. There is an entertainment-oriented production in which people in different borders accepted by the society in general terms can be displaced with a cynical content, the images of the powerful ones are destroyed and the irregularity, satire and irony are highlighted. In this respect, it is possible to share changed, converted images or directly modified/converted/produced characters/information on Twitter. Thus, a social criticism is the basis for social entertainment and the meanings are presented. Below are examples for the grotesque subtitle.

Figure 2. Examples of grotesque

In the first tweet, the character Hermione Jean Granger in Harry Potter has three different images. Sharing three different images of the same woman maters for grotesque content. In the second image in the first tweets, the bodily features of the person were changed and a completely different character was revealed. There are few similarities between the three photographs. In the second example, there is a text which can be explained with the sub-titles of satire and weird in grotesque title, and which hang in the match played by Galatasaray vs Konyaspor. In the article, the team name of Konyaspor was changed. The word "Konyaspor" was replaced by the word "konsantrasyon". The team of Galatasaray carried a banner photo containing this word on their Twitter account and shared it with all their followers in their social networks. In the two examples seen above, there are important contents for the grotesque title (out of existing reality) such as distortion, conversion in the messages shared on the Twitter account. Thanks to Twitter's opportunity of photo sharing, these photos were shared with all followers, and retweeters of the followers were also allowed to see people who were not followers.

Dialogism: There is dialogue in the essence of communication. Dialogue refers to the interaction and influence of two people in the communication process. Hence, there is mutual conversation in the dialogue, but the conversation does not have to be an agreement. In some cases, the end of the dialogue can turn into conflict. In the carnivalesque theory, people who have a dialogue can have different ideas. Dialogic communication is an interaction based on interaction and demonstrating the concrete outcome. This communication is based on reciprocity from the nature of explicity and dialogue. One of the social media, which is considered as the new media, Twitter also allows for dialogic communication, which allows for a carnival interaction. Below are two examples for dialogic communication.

Figure 3. Examples of dialogism

The first tweet above is an important example of dialogic communication within Twitter's opportunity. Due to Twitter's standard number of words, Twitter has short and concise dialogues. However, the established dialogue can also have a acrimonious content within the framework of the carnival speech. In the first example above, a follower of the famous comedian Cem Yılmaz wrote his opinion about the show tickets on the black market: "It's not hard to solve the black market problem. You can put the system to confirm that the person who bought the ticket was the same as the person who came to the show. Isn't that right, Cem Abi, Cem Bey?". However, Cem Yılmaz responded in a humorous way that this was not about him and therefore he was not the solution point: "Honey ... let me rewrite it; I don't sell tickets I'm going on stage. OK? Did you ever see a comedian who sold tickets in his/her pocket? Oh my Gosh!". In the second example, after a well-known journalist Cüneyt Özdemir shared "shortly after" that his statement in a previous tweet. Then a follower responded in a critical way: "You're saying soon, but it's coming in five hours". Then he explains the situation. In the two examples above, there was a direct interaction between the people who had a Twitter account and their followers. Twitter's application was used, and it was answered directly in a short time and the responses were retweeted by other users. Thus, they communicated directly with their followers within the framework of dialogic communication, tried to explain problems them, and by making this interaction clear to other followers, they have prevented new problems in the subjects mentioned.

Carnival Laughter: Humor and humor can be evaluated in laughter, is a form of expression that encountered in different areas of social life. The laughter, which is an individual and social behavior, can be found in almost every area of humor. Laughing action has an important and central point in the carnival period. Carnival participants put their thoughts into behavior how they can reflect the different codes of laughter in many cases. In social networks, laughter behavior can be implied with photographs, as well as with different emojis, word games or abbreviations. In this direction, the participant can perform the exaggerated laugh on Twitter like that the carnival, and create a deep content on the humorous subject. Participants can do these how using the words that will emphasize the same emojis, letters or laughter. Below are two examples of Twitter being a carnivalesque laughter environment.

Figure 4. Examples of carnival laughter

In the first tweeting photo, Galatasaray coach Fatih Terim poses with a spectacled boy wearing a Galatasaray shirt and a little girl with a downsendrome. However, the photograph can reflect the social sadness inside, but instead, it has been conveyed exaggerated laughter like carnival. Not only Fatih Terim, it is possible to see the same smile on children's faces. This photograph is a transfer of emotion that ignoring the existing situation and use the laughter.

In the second example, there is a photograph from the famous comedian Cem Yılmaz's show and a sentence he wrote himself. Cem Yılmaz wrote "The first 25 years are getting hard, but then you get used to" on a photograph taken from the program. The sentence is a carnival expression, mocked for years and deepening it with smile emojis.

In the examples shown above, there is a smile about the situation and laughing as if it is mocked in the framework of the carnivalesque theory. In this respect, samples were retweeted and appreciated by hundreds of followers. The extent to which the current situation can be ridiculed is clearly seen in Cem Yılmaz's message.

Upside-Down World: In the social life, there is a system accepted by the majority. This order takes place in a system in which the lives of people from different backgrounds are carried out in a certain framework. In carnivals, a new and critical world is established by going beyond the accepted and stereotyped order in social life. In this new world, words are changed, clothing is exaggerated and worn out of the standard. Through masks and colorful costumes, it is disguised and new identities are created. In this way, the hierarchy in real life is destroyed, everyone is equalized, and social anger, rage, joy and revolt are expressed. In this direction, the existing order is turned upside-down. Twitter enables this upside-down world to be applied in terms of its application features and it offers an environment of behavior that will turn the general life in the system to all people with certain technologies. Below are examples for the world that has been turned upside-down on Twitter.

Figure 5. Examples of upside-down world

In the first tweeting photo above, the famous comedian Ata Demirer shared a photo of herbs in her garden like an ordinary citizen. Ata Demirer's dress and the garden in the background in the photo are different from the known Ata Demirer image. The photograph is far from the person who is represented under bright lights in the media or scenes and represent the opposite of its existing image.

Okan Bayülgen who is the famous showman, shared a photo. Kabare Dada actors is in this photo. When looking at the actors, their clothes, their makeup and their postures are seen to be far beyond ordinary life on a carnivalesque basis. In the examples, via Twitter, was moved out of the world and was created upside-down world image by both disguise and going beyond the visible image.

Marketplace Speech: Public markets have a unique structure and language. The people can speak as they wish there, create their jokes by referring to the agenda and use a language that is natural, free from anyone, culture based and approach to culture humorously. Slang words, special sayings, abbreviations and implications can be found in this language. Through this intimate and direct language, the free environment is supported and a laugh-based festival is created. Thus, certain norms that are imposed on the people by some groups are avoided. Nowadays, marketplace speech can be reflected in social networks that users think are free. In Twitter, it is possible for users to communicate with political leaders and artists in everyday language without a problem. In some cases, Twitter users can express themselves by using local dialects and interesting dialogues can be experienced. The following tweets show examples of how marketplace speech is used in the context of carnivalesque theory.

Figure 6. Examples of marketplace speech

In the first tweets above, the message of the famous journalist Cüneyt Özdemir is communicating with his followers. In the language of the message, it is observed that the words used in the public and the exclamation words are chosen in daily life. This content directly reflects the marketplace speech of carnivalesque theory.

In the second share, there is a dialogue with a follower of the famous comedian Cem Yılmaz. When we look at the language of dialogue, it is seen that daily Turkish language is used, in addition, a cynical language is used, sarcasm is made and Nasreddin Hoca, which has an important place in Turkish culture, is the subject of speech. His follower said "Nasreddin Hoca is a Turkish hero who is sensitive to society and its problems, has a lot of skills and against evil people. His donkey is more talent than us, you handle it with yours.". Cem yılmaz in response to this tweet: "Gentleman, you have a internet! You have a gentleman internet! We understand that. Do not obey people you do not know, do not care about yourself. It is enough observation of the Nasreddin Hodja's donkey. Leave me the part of Nasreddin. Take care of your interests.". The whole of these statements directly reflects the subheading of the marketplace speech of the carnivalesque theory.

In the two above examples, there is a dialogic-based communication. Looking at the language used, a content is used in the street in daily life. Thanks to Twitter, the message was quickly responded and a dialogue took place. The words chosen in the speech will be used by people from every group in daily life and can be an example of the marketplace speech.

Marketplace: Today, as in the cities, there were marketplaces of villages and towns in the 20th century. Marketplaces were the places where there were many sought-after products, witnessed places of encounter, promotions were made, and there were places for today's advertising billboard. The marketplace is parallel to the carnival rituals with the language used, its purpose, color and design. Promotions or campaigns are brought to the front of the showcase, the official discourses are replaced by the expressions that the people are free and comfortable in this environment. Twitter is a square where people feel comfortable, away from the official and promotional campaigns and also meet people or institutions from different fields. Below are the shares on the marketplace in the context of the carnivalesque theory.

Figure 7. Examples of marketplace

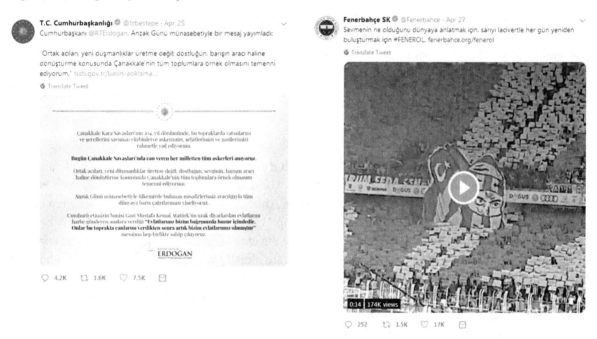

The first tweet in the photo above, Presidency Republic of Turkey published a document to mark Anzac Day in April 25. The message stated that it was remembered all soldiers who died from all nations in the Dardanelles War. This issue that great importance for the history of Turkey, has announced to everyone on Twitter with the signature of the President Recep Tayyip Erdoğan.

In the second example, a share was made on the Turkish football team Fenerbahçe's Twitter account. In the share, there are videos of "Fener OL" campaigns launched on April 4 by Ali Koç to remove Fenerbahçe from the economic crisis. Fenerbahçe Twitter account, which is shared by "Fener OL" campaign information, is presented to followers and more support is requested. In the two examples, thousands of people were reached via Twitter. Thus, large audiences were given the desired message through Twitter. In these messages, it was both expressed a national feeling for a painful event and requested support for a campaign by a team.

FUTURE RESEARCH DIRECTIONS

In this study, the similarity between the carnivalesque theory of Michail Bakhtin and the social networks was examined. To reveal this similarity, Twitter, which is one of the most important social networks, was analyzed by using qualitative content analysis technique. To obtain the data, 10 Twitter accounts which the most followers in Turkey were examined and similarities were found between these accounts and the carnivalesque theory.

In this study, although carnivalesque theory is discussed in social networks which is a branch of communication field, it is a theory which can be applied in almost all sub-dimensions of communication field (cinema, television, journalism etc.). Carnivalesque theory, however, is also a very appropriate theory for use in the fields such as literature, sociology, psychology, fine arts and political science. Especially first of all the communication field, the most appropriate research technique to be used in research in the fields as part of carnivalesque theory is qualitative content analysis. In addition, questionnaire and interview (semi-structured, unstructured) techniques are the methods that can be used to learn the emotions, thoughts and behaviors of target groups in these areas and to obtain data.

CONCLUSION

The carnivalesque theory of Michail Bakhtin is a literary theory which contains the basic features of carnival. Carnival laughter, dialogism, upside-down world, grotesque, marketplace and marketplace speech is the basic features of the carnivalesque theory. Although the theory of carnivalesque is a theory which is put forward in the field of literature, it is adaptable to many fields of science and art because of its characteristics. One of these areas is undoubtedly the area of communication. In fact, the concepts of carnival and communication are two elements that are already very much related to each other. For this reason, the carnivalesque theory, which can be adapted to many communication environments, can also be adapted for social networks, one of the most important communication environments. From this point of view, a study has been done to reveal the relationship and similarities between the carnivalesque theory and Twitter one of the social networks.

In this study, a case study design which is one of the qualitative research methods is used. In the study, with a maximum number of Turkey 10 Twitter follower examples of the account identified and analyzed. In the study, examples that obtained from 10 Twitter accounts with a maximum number of followers in Turkey, identified and analyzed. It is possible to see grotesque examples although not all of the pages examined have grotesque sharing. It was found that there was disguise and change words in the shares examined in the sub-title grotesque. It is thought that this situation is made due to the relevant shares and it has no special reason. It was found out that the shared messages that digress the fact and a distortion/changing was made. It was found that the followers did not react differently to the others. In terms of the dialogism in which mutual communication took place, it was seen that dialogue was established with followers in almost all accounts. This situation shows that there is interaction in the title of dialogism. n addition, it was determined that retweets were made under the shares and some headers were labeled with the hashtag sign. In this way, it was realized that the shares were seen on other people's pages and people from different sectors were able to reach the shares. In dialogism, it can be said that not only two people but also more people are affected by the existing dialogue.

The carnival laughter expresses a reaction with gestures and mimics in carnivalesque theory. This response does not have to be spoken or vocal. Similar cases were observed in the shares analyzed. There was a smile to mock the situation in the sharing. In almost every sub-title of the carnivalesque theory, it is possible to talk about the upside-down world. In the examined Twitter pages, examples of the upside-down world where the existing system was reversed, there is no difference in level between people and the routine order has been changed, was reached. In these examples, it has been seen that it is out of the general world, it was created new world by disguise, it was shared in opposite direction of image.

Marketplace speech is another topic in which oral expression becomes important for carnivalesque theory. In this title, the language of daily life is returned and the street mouth used by the people is preferred. Such samples were also found in the examined pages. These examples are expected to be seen. Because Twitter is a social network used by individuals belonging to different social groups. In this network, it is possible to come across every expression like carnival environment. On the examined pages, examples about the marketplace title were also seen. In these examples, it was determined that the account holders sent messages to thousands of people without any limits and interacted with these messages. Therefore, in the framework of carnivalesque theory, it was found equivalent marketplace expression.

As can be seen from the examples, carnivalesque shares subsist in Twitter which is one of the most popular social networks in Turkey. These shares represent carnivalistic details in real life in the context of carnivalesque theory. In this context, Twitter, which is one of the most important social networks, has a great similarity with the carnivalesque theory of Michail Bakhtin.

REFERENCES

Altunay, M. C. (2010). Gündelik Yaşam ve Sosyal Paylaşım Ağları: Twitter ya da "Pıt Pıt Net". *Galatasaray Üniversitesi İletişim Dergisi, 12*, 31–56.

Bakhtin, M. M. (1981). *The Dialogic Imagination*. Austin, TX: University of Texas Press.

Bakhtin, M. M. (1984). *Rabelais and His World*. Bloomington, IN: Indiana University Press.

Bakhtin, M. M. (1986). *Speech Genres and Other Late Essays*. Austin, TX: University of Texas Press.

Bakhtin, M. M. (2001). *Karnavaldan Romana*. İstanbul, Turkey: Ayrıntı Yayınları.

Boyd, D. M., & Ellison, N. B. (2007). Social Network Sites: Definition, History, and Scholarship. *Journal of Computer-Mediated Communication, 13*(1), 210–230. doi:10.1111/j.1083-6101.2007.00393.x

Brandist, C. (2011). *Bahtin ve Çevresi, Felsefe, Kültür ve Politika*. Ankara, Turkey: Doğu Batı Yayınları.

Derin, Ö. (2017). İtici Bir Güç Olarak Oluşsal Şiddet. *Felsefe ve Sosyal Bilimler Dergisi, 24*, 317–335.

Gülüm, E. (2016). Karnavalesk Bir İmgelemin Taşıyıcısı Olarak Bektaşi Mizahı. *Milli Folklor, 28*(112), 130–141.

Kıpçak, N. S. (2016). *Yeni Karnaval Olarak Yeni Medya: Karnavalesk Nitelikleri ile Twitter*. İstanbul, Turkey: Marmara Üniversitesi Sosyal Bilimler Enstitüsü Radyo TV Sinema Anabilim Dalı, Doktora Tezi.

Mclean, P. B., & Wallace, D. (2013). Blogging the Unspeakable: Racial Politics, Bakhtin, and the Carnivalesque. *International Journal of Communication, 7*, 1518–1537.

Sığrı, Ü. (2018). *Nitel Araştırma Yöntemleri*. İstanbul, Turkey: Beta Yayınları.

Socialbakers (2019). *Twitter statistics for Turkey*. Retrieved from https://www.socialbakers.com/statistics/twitter/profiles/turkey/

Sözen, M. F. (2009). Bakhtin'in Romanda "Karnavalesk" Kavramı ve Sinema. *Akdeniz Sanat Hakemli Dergi*, 2(4), 65–86.

Turan, M. (2008). Kaos Teorisi: Bauman ve Bakhtin. *Ankara Üniversitesi Dil ve Tarih-Coğrafya Fakültesi Felsefe Bölümü Dergisi*, 19(1), 45–66.

Uygun, E., & Akbulut, D. (2018). Karnavalesk Kuramı ve Instagram Ortamına Yansımaları. *Yeni Medya Elektronik Dergi*, 2(2), 73–89. doi:10.17932/IAU.EJNM.25480200.2018.2/2.73-89

Yıldız, T. (2014). Diyaloji Diyalektiğe Karşı. *Psikoloji Çalışmaları Dergisi*, 34(1), 79–85.

Yurdakul, S. (2006). *Bir Ürün ve Toplumsal Bütünleşme Aracı Olarak Modern Kent Karnavalları ve Türkiye'deki Örneklerde Görülen Uygulama Farklılıkları*. İstanbul, Turkey: Marmara Üniversitesi Sosyal Bilimler Enstitüsü, İletişim Bilimleri Anabilim Dalı, Yüksek Lisans Tezi.

ADDITIONAL READING

Bakhtin, M. M. (2004). *Dostoyevski Poetikasının Sorunları*. İstanbul: Metis Yayınları.

Castells, M. (2010). *The Rise of the Network Society*. Malden, MA: Wiley-Blackwell.

Cross, M. (2011). *Bloggerati, Twitterati: How Blogs and Twitter Are Transforming Popular Culture*. Santa Barbara, Denver, Oxford: Praeger.

Karimova, G. (2010). Interpretive Methodology From Literary Critcism: Carnivalesque Analysis of Popular Culture: Jackass, Southpark and Everyday Culture. *Studies in Popular Culture*, 33(1), 37–51.

Lindahl, C. (1996). Bakhtin's Carnival Laughter and the Cajun Country Mardi Gras. *Folklore*, 107(1-2), 57–70. doi:10.1080/0015587X.1996.9715915

Rheingold, H. (1994). *The Virtual Community: Homesteading on the Electronic Frontier*. New York: Harper Perennial.

St John, G. (2008). Protestival: Global Days of Action and Carnivalized Politics in the Present. *Social Movement Studies*, 7(2), 167–190. doi:10.1080/14742830802283550

Theall, D. F. (1999). The Carnivalesque, the Internet and Control of Content: Satirizing Knowledge, Power and Control. *Continuum (Perth)*, 13(2), 153–164. doi:10.1080/10304319909365789

Tufekci, Z. (2008). Can You See Me Now? Audience and Disclosure Regulation in Online Social Network Sites. *Bulletin of Science, Technology & Society, Vol*, 28(: 1), 20–36. doi:10.1177/0270467607311484

Vaneigem, R. (2012). *The Revolution of Everyday Life*. Oakland: PM Press.

KEY TERMS AND DEFINITIONS

Mikhail Bakhtin: Was a Russian philosopher, literary critic, semiotician[4] and scholar who worked on literary theory, ethics, and the philosophy of language. His writings, on a variety of subjects, inspired scholars working in a number of different traditions (Marxism, semiotics, structuralism, religious criticism) and in disciplines as diverse as literary criticism, history, philosophy, sociology, anthropology and psychology. Although Bakhtin was active in the debates on aesthetics and literature that took place in the Soviet Union.

Carnival: The carnival, whose origin is based on the Middle Ages and which varies from culture to culture, from society to society, is a celebration, entertainment or festival that Christians gathered in communities before Great Lent.

Carnivalesque: The carnivalesque, which Mikhail Bakhtin formulated from the concept of carnival, is a theory based on the basic characteristics (grotesque, dialogism, carnival laughter, upside-down world, marketplace and marketplace speech) of the Middle Age carnivals and argues that people communicate with a second identity in a community by getting rid of their everyday identities.

Content Analysis: Content analysis is a technique that provides an objective and systematic description and analysis of text content such as news, advertising texts, interview, television programs.

Qualitative Research: is primarily exploratory research. It is used to gain an understanding of underlying reasons, opinions, and motivations. It provides insights into the problem or helps to develop ideas or hypotheses for potential quantitative research.

Social Networks: Social networking is a virtual communication environment where people come together with different purposes such as information, entertainment and socialization, communicate independently of time and space, create and display their own profile and access other users' profiles.

Twitter: İs an American online news and social networking service on which users post and interact with messages known as "tweets".

This research was previously published in New Media and Visual Communication in Social Networks; pages 270-288, copyright year 2020 by Information Science Reference (an imprint of IGI Global).

Chapter 44
Paradigms of Public Relations in an Age of Digitalization:
Social Media Analytics in the UAE

Badreya Al-Jenaibi
The United Arab Emirates University, UAE

ABSTRACT

This study explores the uses of social media in public relations (PR) departments in the United Arab Emirates (UAE). It seeks to lay the basis for understanding the place of social media in the UAE and to contribute to the analysis of the issue of social change in the PR offices. The chapter assesses the state of PR in the UAE in relation to global media and highlights needs in this area for both public and private enterprises. Presenting interview data taken from a cross section of 40 organizations throughout the UAE, it addresses perceptions of benefits, challenges, public acceptance, and future strategies of social media in relation to global SM as whole. It finds that barriers to the use and acceptance of SM in PR have mostly been lifted.

INTRODUCTION

In the contemporary world, public relations have been shown to be an essential tool for business market-ing. When large investments in marketing strategies have not yielded desired results in a timely fashion (Kaplan, 2012), corporations have been compelled to seek professional help (Harris, 2008) from the public relations expert. Traditionally, Public Relations intervention has taken the form of placing adver-tisements in newspapers (Motti, 2011). These efforts however are rapidly being replaced given the onset of Social Media Public Relations, or SMPR (Dave, 2008). Yet to date little research has been performed to date on the use of SMPR techniques in the UAE. This research critically analyzes the operations of SMPR departments in organizations in the United Arab Emirates. It adopts a multidimensional approach to offer a socio-scientific perspective on this subject matter. Both qualitative and quantitative methods were chosen in combination to produce optimal results (Meyette, 2003).

DOI: 10.4018/978-1-6684-6287-4.ch044

Social Media has been defined as the democratization of substance and / or content and the comprehension of the responsibility (Powell, et al., 2011) played by various people across the globe during the reading and propagation of information (Kietzmann, Hermkens, McCarthy & Silvestre, 2011). It is identified in part with websites like Facebook, Friendster, and MySpace which permit their clients to allocate content (Kaplan, 2012), Media along with many others (Caverlee, Webb, 2008), and with websites intended for photo and video sharing, like Flickr, YouTube, and Photo bucket (Jarboe, 2009). The Social Media category also includes news collection and online reference websites (Elavsky & Elavsky, 2011), like Digg and Wikipedia, and micro-blogging sites like Twitter (Garfield, 2010).

Overall, the online experience is becoming an ever more important means through which organisations relate to their customers and clients. Today, Facebook and Twitter marketing are considered vital constituents in a contemporary Social Media marketing strategy (Gillin, 2008). Given its potential to establish and relay certain attitudes, social media also can play an important role in public relations. Various researchers like Kaplan, Andreas, Michael and Haenlein (2010) have documented the dual role of Social Media pathways arising out of its interactive model. Social media is recognized as having the potential to both grant corporations an influential business presence (Kietzmann, Hermkens, McCarthy & Silvestre, 2011) and to act as centres for clients to locate and interact with a corporation's services (Reisner, 2009) and products. Among its contributions to business presence is the ability of Social Media Pathways to assist corporations in creating and maintaining (Hill, 2005) a constructive social status. For example, entrepreneurs can craft and sustain their business profiles on social networking sites. Research shows that social media pathways can help a business entrepreneur to craft more cohorts (Gregory, 2004) and/or followers by leveraging its ability to collate information (Botan &Taylor, 2006) and send out updates on a regular basis (Dave, 2008). Such exposure helps to gain new customers while also avoid losing already established consumers.

To take full advantage of social media, PR must recognize and successfully incorporate the features that distinguish social media. As a means of communication, on-line interaction differs from traditional forms of exposure (Grosseck & Holotescu, 2008). In contrast to static and repetitive advertising and sound-bites, social media often entails instant and interactive correspondence (Grossman, 2009), including dialogue in place of monologue. It is comprised of a complex network of inter-related signs and symbols (Hobsbawm, 2009) with which browsers and users can instantly respond without recrimination. In such an environment, a company or organisation must respond to continual questioning (Ihator, 2001), appraisal, and/or criticism. Thus social media is distinct from traditional media in part due to the self-regulating nature (Weinberg & Pehlivan, 2011) in which social media often operates. Although many companies have set up websites on the internet to gain recognition in the virtual domain, many *do not realise the potential* of on-line interaction (Chafkin, 2007), and in some instances are not generating any business at all.

The making of the public relations profession in UAE has been affected tremendously by the socio-economic, educational and cultural development of the country (Ayish & Badran, 1997). Ministries and government administrations established their in-house public relations departments and sections to respond to growing demands from their various publics. But is the UAE, with its impressive PR media systems investment in place, earnestly incorporating social media?

This general question leads to several research questions addressed in this paper: Is the UAE doing enough to incorporate social media as an aspect of PR? What are the impacts of social media to the already established PR institutions in the UAE? What are the common challenges in public relations in the UAE, particularly with respect to gender?

While touching upon SM in general, this study will focus on the impact, negative and positive, of SM actually used in PR in the UAE. The study will assess the manner in which PR experts are making use of SM to achieve factual results. This study also seeks to demonstrate the extent to which organizations across the UAE use SM as a tool of interactive communication with the public. Previous studies have concentrated on the use of internet by UAE organizations as a tool for PR outside of SM. Studies have tended to focus only on a few organizations, but this study surveyed 40 organizations across the UAE and 40 PR practitioners' interviews. This study is of practical importance as it will assist in establishing the impact of SMPR techniques in UAE PR departments in organizations.

LITERATURE REVIEW

In general the PR output may be defined as "one-way official communication" (Ayish & Badran, 1997, p. 382). Extensive literature has been dedicated to detailing the myriad advantages and challenges that are associated with the use of SM as a PR tool within organizations across the world. It documents how PR experts were indeed one of the first to harness the power (Boyd, 2008) of the novel technology. The internet has had an immense impact on the manner in which PR experts have run their day-to-today (Cassidy, 2006) affairs over the last ten years (Ayish, 2005).

According to a study conducted by the department of Mass Communication of the United Arab Emirate University, none of the private firms in UAE used the term "Public Relations" to define relations with the public (Department of Mass Communication, 1994). But public sector organizations in the UAE generally do have small-to-medium sized PR departments. These departments execute a more restricted version of their complementary PR roles within the private sector. Arthur (1993) found that the number of private firms practicing PR in United Arab Emirates witnessed remarkable growth in terms of customers. He further established that in these firms, PR serves two main functions. These include marketing and advertising of products and services.

A 2004 study investigated twenty websites belonging to UAE public and private organizations and found that they highly valued the internet as a PR tool for its ability to leverage IT to improve performance and contribute significantly to the growth of a firm's output (Ayish, 2005). The study established that private institutions were amalgamating PR into a more inclusive package of effective communication aimed at a range of audiences. Most private institution websites incorporated three main features, namely: advertising, public relations, and marketing. The study also revealed that the PR staff is not directly involved in the design and modification of their institution's websites, and leave the IT department with the task of amassing and classifying the information. According to this study, this state of affairs has the negative effect of suggesting a low standing for the role of PR personnel in virtual communication, as compared with their traditional responsibility in direct personal interaction. PR employees thus do not appear have an impact in managing the manner in which information flows to the public in such organizations (Ayish, 2005).

In the UAE, PR has become a thriving industry with an impressive future – a remarkable state of affairs given the gloomy outlook for it held just a few years ago. Its current growth is reflected in the conclusions of research conducted by Kirat (2006) suggesting that:

Journalism and Mass Communication departments launched PR programs to meet the growing needs of the job market with qualified practitioners. International public relations agencies chose Dubai as a base for their activities in the UAE and the region (Kirat, 2006, p. 255).

But in a prior study (2005), Kirat explained that the Arab world had long faced a growing number of problems in successfully implementing PR in an emerging age of globalisation and global media. These were highlighted as "misconceptions, confusion in tasks and prerogatives, lack of professional man-power and the absence of a culture of democracy, transparency and public opinion"(Kirat, 2005, p. 256). Conceding that planning and research were badly missing in Arab public sector organisations, Kirat further suggested that, despite its drawbacks, PR was nevertheless the profession of the future for the nations of the Arab World: "Arab countries need public relations to meet the challenges of democracy, public opinion, civil society and globalization" (Kirat, 2005, 257). An extensive follow-up study the next year found that the UAE had already developed PR programmes in a large section of its global media. Yet both studies make apparent that PR is still approached in relation to traditional forms of media rather than social media. While the UAE integrated PR systems sophisticated enough to effectively incorporate desired ideological and systemic faculties, the integration and acknowledgement of the role of social media in PR is less clear.

The significance of social media in itself is relatively clearly recognized. For example, in a recent study conducted by Evans et al. (2011) it was found that:

Public relations practitioners consider micro blogging to be a valuable asset to a campaign's social media strategy. They believe that Twitter offers a form of communication not offered by other social media applications, and they believe micro blogging will continue to be an essential part of an integrated communications campaign. (P. 19)

However, despite this rhetoric, little practical evidence exists suggesting social media is actually being implemented and employed significantly in the UAE. Although the Middle East has vast potential as a hotspot for online growth (Skinner, 2011), possessing one of the world's fastest growing regional economies and enormous investments in telecommunication infrastructure (Ryan, 2011), surprisingly, according to research and media opinion, the Middle East, and in particular the UAE, appears much less active in the social media scene than most international spectators might normally expect (Evans, 2011).

In an analysis of a number of Emirates-based organisations, Kirat (2007) found that all twenty four organisations had a homepage, while only two thirds of them were actively posting their publications over the internet, and only one third were using electronic newspapers to monitor their coverage in the media and to gather news, data and information of importance for the various tasks they perform. Only three of the twenty four organisations had an online newsroom, while only two had a virtual tour detailing the organisation and its operations (Kirat, 2007). Other findings included the fact that none of the surveyed organisations' Web sites had film or video of any kind. It was concluded that "Organizations in the United Arab Emirates still have a lot to do to take advantage fully and rationally of what interactive communication, Internet and online publications are offering for a better performance and more effective public relations" (Kirat, 2007, p. 259). Kirat also concluded that, while the proper use of online applications is able to provide unprecedented access, public relations practitioners in the UAE are not utilising the Internet in such a way that would allow target publics to connect directly with their organization

(Kirat, 2007). Overall, Kirat (2005) and Ayish (2005) suggested that the integration of internet tools into contemporary public relations practices was necessary for success to be achieved.

Prior research conducted by Ayish (2005) analysed the use of the Internet as a public relations tool by twenty government and private organisations in the UAE. Ayish (2005)found that UAE public relations staff members continued to play their traditional role, i.e., acting in person in real world situations. When it came to online communications, they did not seem to have a large say in controlling the flow of information to the public. Ayish (2005) questioned how representative the online face of these firms is, noting that what "appears online about a certain organisation must be in tune with what is carried out in real world communications" (Ayish, 2005, 381). While it is true that the skill and expertise in UAE PR practices in traditional media may be applied to new social media (Howard, 2011), continual reliance on traditional media is still a concern. In research conducted by Parkesh and Sharma (2010), the effectiveness of online methods by a management consultancy was addressed in relation to the launching of a world music festival event in Abu Dhabi in 2009. The choice of a well-planned integrated marketing communication (IMC) strategy incorporating an online strategy was found to be crucial for the successful launch of the event, and it helped to register a visitor ratio of 89%, or five times their target, and a staggering rate of 99% for the visitors planning to visit the festival again in 2010 (Prakash & Sharma, 2010). The conclusion they drew stated that:

Traditional communication media may not be sufficient to succeed in the current media clutter and over-communicated market place. In this context, social networking media are emerging as a new media type and are an important addition to the current media. Understanding the target audience and preparing a customised media mix involving traditional and modern media may have a synergistic effect on end results (p. 371)

The problems regarding the successful implementation and integration of social media as crucial aspect of PR in the UAE is perhaps best addressed at an institutional level. For example, recent active research has been conducted regarding the implementation process of social media and the lack of response from the institution of education. In one such study conducted by Prakash, Dayal and Eastaugh (2011), it was found that among a number of problems related to the implementation of social media as a phenomena in the UAE, were difficulties in integrating the dynamics of social media into university research programs. For instance, a study conducted by Al-Jenaibi (2011) discussed how the lack of university-based education had:

Underlined the gender issues associated with PR in the UAE, which have led to the study of inequality in the field, such as how male and female workers differed significantly in their views about gender fairness in work locations, roles, status, ranks and tasks, responsibilities, and work-life balance (p. 19)

Universities and other educational institutions in the UAE should be encouraged to incorporate into their research programs issues relating to social media. The relation between socio-economic status and social media in UAE PR, for example, requires much further research.

THEORY AND METHODOLOGY

The methodology employed by this study relied on assessing the state of SMPR in the UAE from patterns found primarily in statements by 40 individuals located in organizations spread across the UAE. The interview questionnaire handed to Public Relation Officers contained of 13 questions. The researcher chooses big, known local PR institutions, organizations and banks in the UAE which used the social media. Big institutions have branches in all emirates that present the UAE organizations and institutions in general. Interview questions were judged by three media professors, during the interview interviewees answered the questions freely without recording them. Interviews take 30 to 40 munities in the interviewees' offices. The researcher scripts the interviews and divided them in different themes in the analysis part.

This method draws from a brand of Uses and Gratification Theory (UGT) that was developed to understand mass media in 1974 by theorists Blumler, Katz, and Gurevitch. (Uses & Gratification theory, 1973-1974). Applied then to understanding mass media, it suggests that receivers are responsible in selecting media that satisfies their needs, for example, for knowledge social communication (Katz, 1987). It maintains that mass media is actively incorporated into their lives by audiences. The theory states how the receivers use the media in order to satisfy their specific gratification (Katz & Gurevitch, 1974). In this case interview data was interpreted to determine a) whether PRSM was satisfying the professional needs of PR professionals to deliver their services, and b) the understanding of PR professionals of the effectiveness of PRSM in satisfying the expectations of their audiences.

Gratification theory is an audience-centred approach that transfers the focus of research from the purpose of the communicator to the needs of the audience. (Katz & Gurevitch, 1973). When an audience looks for media, it is looking to satisfy a specific need, be it entertainment, business, or new information (McQuail, 1994). The high use of Twitter, Faceboook or many other social networking sites reflects the satisfaction of audience needs through chatting, updating statuses, tweeting and re-tweeting, etc.

A key component of the theory is the dependence of gratification upon expectations (Severin & Tankard, 1997). Individuals search for media that satisfies or fulfils their expectations. People approach sites with expectations, and if not met, gratification is not satisfied, and further use is discouraged (Rubin & Windahl, 1982). A gratification-based need for media is motivated not only by psychological reasons (Grant, 1998), but also by social circumstances. For instance, people new in a region would likely have a need to find a good place for dinner or need information for places to visit. To get this information, they might look to find a source of social media they can trust.

The research methodologies leveraged the advantages of combining quantitative and qualitative techniques for better results (Meyette, 2003). The study was conducted using a longitudinal sample of Public Relations practitioners and institutions across the seven Emirates of the UAE (including Abu Dhabi, Dubai, Umm Al Qaiwain, Sharjah, Ajman, Ras Al Khaimah and Fujarah). The diversity of organizations spread across the Emirates was recognized as benefiting the accuracy of the study (Stenbecka, 2001). The interview questionnaire handed out to PR Officers contained of 13 questions. They were distributed to different organizations, namely the UAE Municipalities, Emirates Identity Authority, Abu Dhabi Food Control Authority, Police headquarters, Al Ain Hospital, Tawam hospital, AlNoor Hospital, Daman insurance offices, Abu Dhabi National Oil Company (ADNOC), Abu Dhabi Education Council - ADEC, Abu-Dhabi national bank, Dubai Islamic bank, Zayed centre for heritage and history, Abu Dhabi Islamic Bank, Bank of Sharjah, RAK bank, First Gulf Bank, Commercial bank of Dubai, Commercial bank of Abu-Dhabi, Dubai Internet City, Sama Dubai TV station, Abu-Dhabi TV station, Sharjah TV station,

Dubai Electricity and water authority, Road and transport authority, Awqaf and Minors affairs Foundations, UAE Courts, UAE airports in (Al Ain, Fujairah and Sharjah), Hilton Hotels, Social support centres, General Directorate of Residence and Foreigners Affairs (GDRFA), Al Ain distribution company, Abu Dhabi Transmission & Despatch Company (TRANSCO) and Dubai Women establishment.

The primary aim of the research was gain an initial understanding of a set of basic questions about SMPR as a basis for future research. This aim includes: a) to obtain a general gauge of the kinds of social media sites preferred by the PR practitioners, b) find the reasons why users decided to use these sites, c) learn more about various difficulties they came across while using various social networking sites, and d) solicit opinions about how obstacles could be overcome. The research also was designed to understand how the public in the UAE reacts to social media, and to that end a query was included about public interactions with these sites. The questionnaire also included some queries which helped provide an accurate picture of how social media is actually being used, under what conditions, and essential information about future plans to develop social media, get customer feedback, track customers.

DISCUSSION OF FINDINGS

Types of Social Media Used for Public Relations

- With respect to the types of social media tools used by PR officers to conduct their work in the United Arab Emirates:

In the UAE, the most commonly used social mediaSM tools include familiar names, such as Facebook, YouTube, Twitter, MySpace, LinkedIn, Flickr, Yahoo, Hotmail, and Google, Esky, notlog.net, government website. Four of these – Facebook, YouTube, Twitter and MySpace – were used most frequently. A few lesser known social media and related tools were mentioned, including EskyCity, Netlog, and black berry messenger. Nevertheless Blackberry Messenger was mentioned as mainly used for tracking information. Generally, the majority of the interviewees networked with the public through the internet. Curiously, some interviewees mentioned that they did use a variety of sites and were not specify particular about the type of social media used. Facebook, YouTube, Twitter and MySpace are used as a primary source. Most of the interviewees use the website of the Emirates identity card as a source of tracking or giving any information. Twitter, Facebook and Google are all seen as particular effective as means of communication by some interviewees while BlackBerry Messenger is mainly used for tracking information. Generally, the majority of the interviewees networked with customers through the internet.

- Frequency of use of social media in organizations in the United Arab Emirates: In the United Arab Emirates, Typical uses of social media in organizations in the UAE:

According to interview responses, in the UAE social media is widely used on a daily basis— for a wide variety of purposes. These include during important events and activities of an organization. Used, for query purposes and, in making announcements about new services, social media tools are also used in organizations to access the and search for information and data work; and, for searching information---, including searching information about other companies' services and prices, for example. There are additional uses of social media in organizations in UAE. They are. In addition, it is used for marketing or promotion services, and to inform the public about new services or products. Used to show some Interviewees noted its usefulness for presenting ideas and proposals, social media tools are also used in participating in some competitions in the a relevant area of work. Finally, they are used to keep, and keeping in touch with the public on a regular basis. Despite few interviewees saying their organizations use social media rarely, it can be concluded that social media is extensively used in organizations in the UAE.

The Purposes of Using Social Media

Most of the interviewees said that their purpose in using the social media is to connect with the largest number of members in the community. Also, it helps them to get closer from people and knowing every new. While other PR practitioners said that their aim "is to know about the opinions of publics and their complaints and it helps develop the organization as it is quick and can track the errors soon (identity card) and to deliver the largest number of information aimed at the institution for dissemination to the public and it helps them to connect with internal and external public". Many of them believe that it helps to build a good reputation and image of the company and it helps them to earn new information process anticipates their future evolution of life. Interviewee # 12 said that "they use social media in order to increase the public awareness and encourage them".

In summary, most of the PR offices in the UAE states that they get to learn new skills of work and facilitate communication and it saves the time, money and energy. In conclusion, different companies use the social media for various different purposes. Interviewee # 39 said the website is increasing now days so we need good management in social networking and there should be committees to solve issues of social media.

Although more than 16 interviewees say that they actively track customer feedback, 5 interviewees mentioned that the tracking of the customer feedback is done by customer services, not the PR office, because they have separate offices. One interviewee said that they "keep track of customer feedback especially in events section." (Interviewee # 17, 2012). Another added that "in order to know about customer feedback, an evaluation and survey is done about the quality of service in the institution." (Interviewee # 21, 2012). Two interviewees said that they keep track customers by using a database system and tracking the feedback through surveys (Interviewee # 23 & 25, 2012). Another two interviewees agreed that customers are vital for the success of the company, so it is important to keep a track of their feedback, which they actively do (Interviewee # 13 & 14, 2012). One of these added " P.R must take into consideration the opinions and suggestions of their customers."(Interviewee # 13, 2012). Overall, most of the companies have some kind of technique through which they track the feedbacks of their customers.

Perceived Purposes of Using Social Media

Most of the interviewees said that their main purpose in using social media is to connect with the largest number of members in the community. Getting closer to people was also mentioned as important. One response reflecting the host of functions the PR could perform: "to know about the opinions of publics and their complaints and it helps develop the organization as it is quick and can track the errors soon (via the identity card) and to deliver the largest number of information aimed at the institution for dissemination to the public and it helps them to connect with internal and external public." (Interviewee # 40, 2012). Many of respondents believe that it helps to build a good reputation and image of the company.

Role of Social Media in Eliminating the PR Responsibilities

The majority of the interviewees stated that social media is simply another tool of public relations—it is still required that did not eliminate the need for direct interpersonal explanation of certain issues or giving answers to questions raised by a customer, because of this reason, it communication and exchanges. Thus, it was felt that SMPR does not eliminate the actual traditional interpersonal public relations roles, despite the fact that they it can play a crucial role in getting access to many people within a short period of time at less cost;, and in meeting the target targets set within an organization. Even though majority of the some interviewees said that social media will not eliminate the public relations roles, some did not state whether it will or not; traditional PR would be replaced, but just said that social media facilitates the work of the administration of public relations and strengthens these relations. For those few interviewees who believed that social media eliminates the roles of public relations, they said that it eliminates did suggest elimination, their views were limited to face-to-face communication, and felt that it SMPR reduces, but does not eliminate replace, public relations as a whole.

Benefits of Using Social Media When Distributing New Plans

The interviewees stated several benefits. Helping public awareness efforts in a bid Interviewees felt social media tools have a positive impact in reaching a large number of people at a fast rate, and that it is cheaper as compared to traditional media forms, such as the television and the radio. They noted that SMPR supported P.R practitioners efforts to develop their workplaces services, for example, it serves as a good source of transferring knowledge amongst the people and/or customers, social media tools, are helpful in conveying message of helps both convey an organization and in obtaining organization's message and obtain new information regarding a certain from customers on a given topic. In addition, social media tools also, has a positive impact of reaching a large number of people at a fast rate and that it is cheaper as compared to traditional media forms, such as the television and the radio; and, it helps to spread the rights and duties of people in the community. Through social media tools, an organization is capable of receiving opinions and/or comments about its services or products from customers and to get new ideas. Saving time and boosting communication, social media tools further helps public relations PR officers to consult about certain issues with the their clients of an organization. Finally, social networking tools help to identify the new characters from different countries and to on certain issues, as well as follow-up of on strategic plans and creative ideas.

Social Media Is SMPR as a Time Saver

The majority of the interviewees agreed that it SMPR saves time and that it is a quick form of communication to advertise in the websites and to track the views of the world—the social networking sites can send typical PR functions, like advertising, tracking public opinion, and sending information to users worldwide in few seconds. Some interviewees, however, stated that it saves time but only rarely. On a negative note,, and one said that it does not save time at all; it is because some experiments are done on social networking sites, which could lead to novel experimentation with it often leads to a loss of time.

Challenges PR Officers Comes Across on the Use When Using of Social Media

Although many interviewees failed to give a clear response on the thought, still, there are some general ideas of what kind of regarding challenges PR faces when using the social media. The majority rejected the fact that public relation officers come across in using social media; there are some general patterns discernable. A majority rejected the very idea that PR officers face challenges while using various social media tools at the workplace. To some of them, there are no challenges experienced while using social media tools since for some, this stems from the fact that their use of social networking tools is quite low. One said there are always problems linked with use of social media tools which are slowly solved despite to begin with. One interviewee noted the using social media tools presented problems that are time-consuming to solve (Interviewee # 36, 2012). Although many of them not experiencing did not experience any difficulties, problems, several problems were pointed out by those interviewees who said they experienced problems. They mentioned include inadequate publicity of by the site they use, d, a lack of instant Facebook function, bad signals, and a host of infrastructural problems related to poor internet connection, and 'hanging.' Further problems associated with the use of social media tools amongst PR officers in the UAE includes, including things like 'hanging', "poor signals," (Interviewee # 38, 2012) low speeds in loading pages and that people have . Some mentioned the challenge presented, not to SMPR implementation, rather, to traditional PR by SMPR. In other words, they mention a tendency of ignoring to ignore PR officers or having public relations officers as consider them a secondary option when it comes to obtaining information which that could be accessed through the social networking sites. Mainly, within an organization, challenges related to use of social networking sites are dealt with by a specific team.

Acceptance of Services Through Social Media in the United Arab Emirates

Views of Public Acceptance of Social Media PR Services in the UAE

Many interviewees believe that there is a general acceptance of services through social media in the United Arab Emirates. To a large extent, this is because they have witnessed a significant interaction through the social networking sites and that social media is popular acceptance has come from witnessing its popularity in the country. Stating that people find it easier using social media in the country and have acclimatized to it nowadays, the interviewees said that social media is accepted particular with new services provided by companies on social sites. Interviewees indicated that people now are more acclimated to using social media in the country as it has gotten easier to use, and they are particularly open to any new public services. Two interviewees gave two different statistics high statistical estimates regarding the use of social sites: 60% and 70% respectively (Interviewee # 12 & 29, 2012). One Another said that, according to a UNESCO study, the United Arab Emirates is amongst the countries highly engaged in social networking via social media tools (Interviewee # 11, 2012). Despite many interviewees agreeing To the contrary, one said that many people across the country accept services via social media; one on the contrary said that many people are not even aware of the services provided by social media—it is thus not greatly accepted by the audience in the United Arab Emirates.

Future Strategies of Using Social Media

A variety of future strategies for using SMPR were pointed out by respondents. They include planning to increase the plans geared toward increasing public interaction of the public with services offered by an organization through social media, making an online census online, and increasing use of websites to reach potential customers. Planning to focus on the development of more services that can be provided through the social media and to start using electronic communication (in other government departments), some interviewees said that they plan planned to use more varied types of social media (like including Twitter) and to diversify their use of social sites. Organizations in the United Arab Emirates also intended to use social media more in the future for advertisement purposes and dissemination of information. Someone mentioned a desire to formulate a plan in which all employees will would start using social media in a bid to facilitate communication, update their sites more frequently, subscribe to their social networking sites, and harmonize with social blogs so that they do the two would not overlap—all blogs will would be officially registered. Clearly, even though few interviewees stated they does not intent to employ any appropriate strategy in the future, most of them intend to employ various strategies with the objective of reaping maximum benefits out of the social media?

- *Tracking the customers' feedback:* More than 16 interviewees say that they actively track the customer feedback, and 5 interviewees mentioned that the track of the customers' feedback is done by the customer services not the PR office because they have separate offices. Interviewee # 9 said that they "keep a track of the customer feedback especially in events section". Interviewee # 17 added that "in order to know about the customer's feedback an evaluation and survey is done about the quality of service in the institution". Interviewee #28 and #33 said that they keep track customers by database system and track the feedback through surveys. Thus, interviewee # 33 and 30 say that customers are very vital for the success of the company so it is important to keep a track of their feedback which they actively do. Interviewee # 38 added " P.R take into consideration the opinions and suggestions of their customers". In addition many interviewees agreed that tracking customer's feedback, evaluation and survey is done about the quality of service in the institution. So basically most of the companies have some kind of technique through which they track the feedbacks of their customers.

With or Against Social Media

People who are with/ support the social media, mentioned some reasons like they believe it helps in immediate access to information, it is a new, fast and modern technology, it helps communicate with public and delivery of the message, to follow-up the opinion of publics and to communicate with them always and always bring awareness among them, to get the benefits from the experience and the experts' people, it enables to track more about the culture and values of people, it helps to facilitate the process and work, it reaches a large amount of publics and it gives more experience in dealing with public in better way. Interviewees #35 and # 31 were in support of social media because they believed that" it helps solving problems in the PR offices". But other few interviewees had a different opinion. They believe that social media is a waste of time, it makes the communication uncomplicated. Most of interviewees did not give any recommendations or suggestion regarding the use of social media or anything related to the same. Some interviewees recommended that they will look forward to create courses to get more experience and skills that help the employees to deal with the publics. Interviewee # 18 said that "improvement of the social media should be the main focus and the social media should be supervised to create awareness programs on how to use these social sites"

CONCLUSION

According to respondents, public relations organizations in the UAE use the same major social media tools that are popular worldwide, especially Facebook, YouTube, Twitter and MySpace. They used these services frequently for queries, placing announcements, marketing and promotion, participating in competitions, and actively tracking customer feedback. In general, they were drawn to social media given the perception that it provided the fastest, easiest, and most effective means to connect with the largest number of customers. Where in the past infrastructural and technical barriers presented a significant challenge to accept use of SM for PR, a majority of respondents felt such barriers have been overcome, though some elements remain. Most did not see the medium as a threat that might replace direct inter-personal PR, though some recognized its limitations. Among benefits cited were its aforementioned fast, relatively inexpensive ability to link organization with customer, and its ability to enhance PR services and communication across the board. The removal of barriers has led to a feeling among respondents that the general public now largely accepts SM interaction, with only a small number claiming a general lack of awareness on the part of the public. The generally positive view of the status and prospects of SMPR has led to active plans to more fully incorporate it into core organizational functions in the future, especially advertising, as part an integrated internal PR plan.

The use of social media has become so global that its use has become standard, and so organizations, whether public or private, are seen as untrustworthy if they cannot or do not communicate their dealings and ambitions with transparency to their clients through this medium. This is therefore of prime importance to the industry of public relations, and public relations education, to deal with global media.

In terms of recommendations, the author recommends that the socio-economic effects of social media, for which substantial literature exists, be incorporated by the educational institutions in the UAE and by private businesses with a vested interest. Although it is clear that journalism and mass communication departments have launched PR programs to meet the growing needs of the job market with qualified practitioners, and that many international public relations agencies have chosen Dubai as a base for their activities in the UAE, it is clear that more integration of social media research is required. The future of public relations in the UAE is very promising, though more has to be done to integrate social media in PR instead of relying on traditional media. Although it is facing a number of problems, PRSM appears to be a job of the future. However, the issues pertaining to socio-economic factors such as gender equality are yet to be addressed by anyone other than researchers, and in truth, the research in this area has not been forthcoming. If it is to continue to develop itself as a driving force in the global media industry, then UAE and its institutions must integrate the rising tide of social media and research associated with it. In its current state, the UAE seems to be overlooking a great deal, while having the means to facilitate whatever is deemed necessary. As a whole, it would seem clear that the UAE is a significant driving force in PR and that its success in relation to the global media is a problem for universities and businesses that need to address the dynamics and research on social media.

REFERENCES

Al-Jenaibi, B. (2011). Gender Issues in the Diversity and Practice of Public Relations in the UAE Case Study of P.R. Male Managers and Female P.R. Practitioners. *The Journal of Politics*, *2*(3), 1–22.

Arthur, R. (1993). *Advertising and the media in the Gulf*. Galadari Publishers.

Ayish, M., & Badran, B. (1997, March 5–7). *Public relations technician and manager roles in the United Arab Emirates*. Paper presented at the International Conference on Strategic Planning in Public Relations, UAE University, Al Ain.

Ayish, M. I. (2005). Virtual public relations in the United Arab Emirates: A case study of 20 UAE organizations' use of the Internet. *Public Relations Review*, *31*(3), 381–388. doi:10.1016/j.pubrev.2005.05.013

Bagersh, S. (2011). Changing Roles in the UAE Media World: Instructor, Journalist, Marketer. *Middle East Media Educator*, *1*(1), 37–40.

Botan, C., & Taylor, M. (2006). Public relations: State of the field. *Journal of Communication*, *54*(4), 645–661. doi:10.1111/j.1460-2466.2004.tb02649.x

Boyd, d. (2008). Why youth (heart) social network sites: The role of networked publics in teenage social life. In D. Buckingham (Ed.), *Youth, Identity, and Digital Media* (pp. 119142).Cambridge, MA: MIT Press.

Cassidy, J. (2006, May 15). Me media: How hanging out on the Internet became big business. *The New Yorker*, *82*(13), 50.

Caverlee, J., & Webb, S. (2008). A Large-Scale Study of MySpace: Observations and Implications for Online Social Networks. *Association for the Advancement of Artificial*. Retrieved September 17, 2012 from http://faculty.cs.tamu.edu/caverlee/pubs/caverlee08alarge.pdf

Chafkin, M. (2007). How to kill a great idea! *Inc. Magazine*. Retrieved on August 22, 2012 from https://www.inc.com/magazine/20070601/features-how-to-kill-a-great-idea.html

Department of Mass Communication (DMC). (1994). *Identification of public relations needs in government and private institutions in the United Arab Emirates. Department of Mass Communication*. Faculty of Humanities and Social Sciences, United Arab Emirates University.

Elavsky, C. M., Mislan, C., & Elavsky, S. (2011). When talking less is more: Exploring outcomes of Twitter usage in the large-lecture hall. *Learning, Media and Technology*, *36*(3), 3. doi:10.1080/17439 884.2010.549828

Evans, A., Twomey, J., & Talan, S. (2011). Twitter as a Public Relations Tool. *The Public Relations Journal*, *5*(1).

Gillmor, D. (2004). *We the media: Grassroots journalism by the people, for the people*. O'Reilly Media. doi:10.1145/1012807.1012808

Grant, A. E. (1998). *Dependency and control.* Paper presented to the Annual Convention of the Association of Educators in Journalism and Mass Communications, Baltimore, MD.

Gregory, A. (2004). Scope and structure of public relations: A technology driven view. *Public Relations Review, 30*(3), 245–254. doi:10.1016/j.pubrev.2004.05.001

Grosseck, G., & Holotescu, C. (2008). Can we use Twitter for educational activities? *Proceedings of the 4th international scientific conference eLearning and software for education.* Retrieved on May 12, 2012 from http://adl.unap.ro/else/papers/015.-697.1.Grosseck%20GabrielaCan%20we%20use.pdf

Grossman, L. (2009). *Iran protests: Twitter, the medium of the movement.* Retrieved on May 10, 2012 from https://www.time.com/time/world/article/0,8599,1905125,00.html

Harris, K. (2008). Using Social Networking Sites as Student Engagement Tools. *Diverse Issues in Higher Education, 25*(18).

Hiebert, R. E. (2004). Commentary: New technologies, public relations and democracy. *Public Relations Review, 31*(1), 1–9. doi:10.1016/j.pubrev.2004.11.001

Hill, J. (2005). *The voice of the blog: The attitudes and experiences of small business bloggers using blogs as a marketing and communications tool* (Unpublished dissertation). University of Liverpool. Retrieved on June 15, 2012 from https://jeffreyhill.typepad.com/voiceblog/files/MBADissertation.pdf

Hobsbawm, A. (2009). Social media beachcombing: Survival of the twittest? *BusinessWeek.* Retrieved on May 14, 2012 from http://businessweek.com/print/managing/content/may2009/ca2009058_879008.htm

Howard, P. N. (2011, February 23). The Arab Spring's cascading effects. *Miller-McCune.* Retrieved on May 14, 2012 from http://www.miller-mccune.com/politics/the-cascading-effects-of-the-arabspring-28575/spring-28575/

Ihator, A. S. (2001). Communication style in the information age. *Corporate Communications, 6*(4), 199–204. doi:10.1108/13563280110409836

Kadragic, A. (2010). Commentary: Media in the UAE: The Abu Dhabi powerhouse. *Asia Pacific Media Educator, 20,* 247–252.

Kaplan, A. M. (2012). If you love something, let it go mobile: Mobile marketing and mobile social media 4x4. *Business Horizons, 55*(2), 129–139. doi:10.1016/j.bushor.2011.10.009

Kaplan, A. M., & Haenlein, M. (2010). Users of the world, unite! The challenges and opportunities of Social Media. *Business Horizons, 53*(1), 59–68. doi:10.1016/j.bushor.2009.09.003

Katz, E. (1987). Communication research since Lazarsfeld. *Public Opinion Quarterly, 51*(4 PART 2), 525–545. doi:10.1093/poq/51.4_PART_2.S25

Katz, E., Blumler, J. G., & Gurevitch, M. (1974). 05/uses-and-gratifications-research-by.html" Uses and gratifications Research. *Public Opinion Quarterly, 37*(4), 509–523. doi:10.1086/268109

Katz, E., Blumler, J. G., & Gurevitch, M. (1974). Ulilization of mass communication by the individual. In J. G. Blumler & E. Katz (Eds.), *The uses of mass communications: Current perspectives on gratifications research* (pp. 19–32). Sage.

Katz, E., Haas, H., & Gurevitch, M. (1973). On the use of the mass media for important things. *American Sociological Review*, *38*(2), 164–181. doi:10.2307/2094393

Kietzmann, J. H., Hermkens, K., McCarthy, I. P., & Silvestre, B. S. (2011). "Social media? Get serious! Understanding the functional building blocks of social media" (PDF). *Business Horizons*, *54*(3), 241–251. doi:10.1016/j.bushor.2011.01.005

Kietzmann, J. H., Hermkens, K., McCarthy, I. P., & Silvestre, B. S. (2011). Social Media? Get Serious! Understanding the Functional Building Blocks of Social Media. *Business Horizons*, *54*(3), 241–251. doi:10.1016/j.bushor.2011.01.005

Kirat, M. (2005). Public relations practice in the Arab World: A critical assessment. *Public Relations Review*, *32*(3), 323–332. doi:10.1016/j.pubrev.2005.05.016

Kirat, M. (2006). Public relations in the United Arab Emirates: The emergence of a profession. *Public Relations Review*, *32*(3), 254–260. doi:10.1016/j.pubrev.2006.05.006

Kirat, M. (2007). Promoting online media relations: Public relations departments' use of Internet in the UAE. *Public Relations Review*, *33*(2), 166–174. doi:10.1016/j.pubrev.2007.02.003

McQuail, D. (1994). *Mass Communication: An Introduction* (3rd ed.). Sage Publications.

Motti, N. (2011). *Oren Meyers and Eyal Zandberg. On Media Memory: Collective Memory in a New Media Age*. Palgrave MacMillan.

Powell, G. R., Groves, S. W., & Dimos, J. (2011). *ROI of Social Media: How to improve the return on your social marketing investment*. John Wiley & Sons.

Prakash, K, Dayal, A, Eastaugh, D. (2011). *Retail physicality and identity change as innovation strategies: the case of Better Life*. Academic Press.

Prakash Vel, K., & Sharma, R. (2010). Megamarketing an event using integrated marketing communications: The success story of TMH. *Business Strategy Series*, *11*(6), 371–382. doi:10.1108/17515631011093070

Reisner, R. (2009). Jakob Nielsen critiques Twitter. *Business Week*. Retrieved August, 22, 2012, from https://www.businessweek.com/pring/managing/content/may2009/ca2009058_037210.htm

Rubin, A. M., & Windahl, S. (1982). *Mass media uses and dependency: A social systems approach to uses and gratifications*. Paper presented to the meeting of the International Communication Association, Boston, MA.

Ryan, P. (2011). Digital Tools of the Trade: The Social Media Forum. *Middle East Media Educator*, *1*(1), 48–53.

Severin, W. J., & Tankard, J. W. (1997). *Communication Theories: Origins, Methods, and Uses in the Mass Media* (4th ed.). Longman.

Skinner, J. (2011). Social Media and Revolution: The Arab Spring and the Occupy Movement as See through Three Information Studies Paradigms. *Sprouts: Working Papers on Information Systems, 11*(169).

Weinberg, B. D., & Pehlivan, E. (2011). Social Spending: Managing the Social Media Mix. *Business Horizons, 54*(3), 275–282. doi:10.1016/j.bushor.2011.01.008

This research was previously published in Recent Developments in Individual and Organizational Adoption of ICTs; pages 262-277, copyright year 2021 by Information Science Reference (an imprint of IGI Global).

APPENDIX: INTERVIEW Q's

RQ1: Does your organization use Social Media for public relations? How?

RQ2: When did you start using Social Media in the Public Relations department?

RQ3: What kinds of Social Media do you make use of within the Public Relations department and why?

RQ4: What are the reasons and benefits of using Social Media in the Public Relations department?

RQ5: How does the Public Relations department in organizations use Social Media to build its trust with the public?

RQ6: What are the guidelines for using Social Media within the Public Relations department?

RQ7: Who ought to manage Social Media in an organization?

RQ8: How has Social Media changed the face of public relations in Organizations in the United Arab Emirates?

RQ9: In what ways do the Social Media affect the organization's relations with the general public?

RQ10: How effective is the Social Media as a tool for marketing as well as an advertising tool?

RQ 11: What are the future plans for the Public Relations departments as regards to the usage and/or the implementation of Social Media?

RQ 12: Do you have some suggestions or recommendation?

Section 4
Utilization and Applications

Chapter 45
Maturity Profiles of Organizations for Social Media

Edyta Abramek
University of Economics in Katowice, Poland

ABSTRACT

The aim of the study is to analyze case studies of selected organizations in terms of their achievements in the use of social media. The profiling method applied in the study facilitated evaluating the model of the selected organization. It is an efficient technique for exploring data. Graphic objects show the individual characteristics of selected organizations. Graphical visualization makes it easy to gauge the trajectory, the direction of your company's social media strategy, and helps to make a decision to change it. Further analysis of the structure of these models may facilitate the discovery of relevant relationships between the analyzed variables.

INTRODUCTION

The paper focuses on how organizations perceive the potential of social media. Thanks to them people can: create (blogs, podcasts), collaborate and exchange knowledge (wiki sites), establish and maintain contact (social network sites), post posts (forums), organize content (tags, bookmarks), find and get information faster (RSS feeds, dashboards, widgets).

Thanks to them the recipient can become a prosumer. The prosumer by means of social media can demonstrate the activity of presenting his or her opinion, testing prototypes, participating in research or participating in competitions products and services. They allow the creation of products and services resulting from social participation.

Social media, unlike traditional media, transforms communications into interactive dialogue. Social media allows you to build closer, more lasting relationships between a company and a community. In the literature of the subject you can find various typologies of the maturity of an organization in the context of the use of social media. There are cases of organizations that are not in the social media at all. There are also organizations that are very active in social media. The least ripe in the social media are decentralized organizations, where the degree of coordination of activities in the use of social media

DOI: 10.4018/978-1-6684-6287-4.ch045

is low or there is no coordination at all. The most mature organizations are those that use social media to formulate business strategies.

The subject of the considerations presented in the article is:

- The maturity of organizations in the use of social media (Buyapowa, 2014;Jussila, Kärkkäinen, & Lyytikkä, 2011;Wilson, Guinan, Parise & Weinberg, 2011) in the company's activity on the example of selected organizations from Poland,
- And the ability to use this knowledge in formulating the vision and strategy of the company's development.

This study focuses on addressing the following research questions:

- **RQ1:** *What kind of social media strategy is actually used in the research organizations?*
- **RQ2:** *How do graphs of the maturity profiles looks like?*
  - **RQ2a:** *What strategy did the organization choose?*
  - **RQ2b:** *Did the organization choose one or does it realize actions specific to several strategies?*
  - **RQ2c:** *Do the strategies of selected organizations in the use of social media and the direction they take in this area are synchronized?*

The targets of the study are shown in Table 1.

Table 1. The targets of the study

The Main Subject	Realization of the Subject
Carrying out a comparative analysis of the maturity of selected organizations in terms of how social media is used.	Analysing of case studies of selected organizations in their use of social media.
Detail Goals	**Realization of the Goals**
Identifying the dominant direction of social media usage.	Working out of the maturity profiles of organizations in the context of the use of social media. Evaluating whether the organization has chosen the best strategy for its resources and objectives.
Determining whether the company does not lose the extra energy to carry out activities characteristic of other strategies which are not connected with its main strategy .	Assessing whether the organization's strategy and objectives are convergent.

BACKGROUND

Media is a tool for preserving and transmitting information. With the development of the Internet, social media was born. They have changed the role of the recipient, who became the creator or co-creator (Evans & McKee, 2010; Li & Bernoff, 2011). The recipient was "engaged". Social media has transformed communication with the recipient into an interactive dialogue. Table 2 shows the types and characteristics of the media. It is worth emphasizing the differences between the concepts: social media and social network. The concept of social network refers to communities centred on social networking sites.

Table 2. Types of social media

	Mass Media/Broadcast Media	**Social Media**	**Automated Media**
Characteristics	Content is created by the publisher. Content is controlled by the publisher - central control, restrictions imposed by law, licenses. Communication with the recipient is one-way. Content publishing is the final stage in the publishing process. The scope of the media is limited.	Content is created by the community. Content is subject to social control - control is individual, not limited. Communication with the recipient is interactive and multidirectional. Content publishing is just the beginning of the publishing process - content is spread through social interaction. The scope of the media is unlimited.	The content created (processing, selection, presented) is without human participation. The main role of the media is aggregation of content from different sources. The scope of the media is unlimited.
Types	TV, press, radio, books, journals, magazines, etc.	Social news sites, blogs, microblogs, forums, wikis, social networking sites (Facebook), social sharing sites, social event sites, social bookmarking sites, virtual social worlds (Second Life), collaborative projects (Wikipedia), content communities, virtual game worlds, etc. (Evans, 2010; Kaplan & Haenlein, 2010).	Personalized news reader such as Feedly, Google News/ Reader, Fark, Pulse, News 360, Netvibes.

Social media is the medium by which companies can reach their customers directly. Social media allows companies:

- To engage consumers in building a positive brand image and promoting it,
- To get feedback from consumers (due to communication in both directions),
- To engage consumers to improve products or services.

Consumers, through social media, can directly communicate with the company and have a real impact on building their image or co-creating products or services. Consumers who are referred to as prosumers for social media can be active in the company by: presenting their opinions, participating in research, participating in competitions, testing prototypes of products and services and co-creating them.

Most companies' social media strategies focus on promoting products and services and building brand awareness. Many companies are not able to capitalize on the potential that social media has to offer yet. Current reports and research in this area indicate that traditional companies are dominant in the Polish market (Surma, Krzycki, Prokurat, & Kubisiak, 2012) - companies treat social media as an additional marketing channel. And it is worth pointing out that the number of social media users is constantly growing. At the beginning of 2017 it was already 2.789 billion global social media users, of which 2.549 billion are using them by mobile devices. Compared to 2016 this is an increase of 21 percent. All social media users account for a total of 37 percent of the total population (Kemp, 2017; Sotrender, 2017a).

Formulating a company's growth strategy with the use of social media is still a challenge for businesses. Companies must first (Sotrender, 2017b):

- Recognize the demographics of their customers,
- Understand own customers' behaviours and expectations,
- Identify opinion leaders and brand ambassadors.

Developing a company's growth strategy using feedback from social media is possible through:

- Analysing various indicators (Reach, engagement),
- Analysing the needs of consumers and their expectations,
- Studying the subject matter of the statement and their context,
- Studying of speech leaders and discussion sites,
- Use of advanced data analytics.

The relevance and usefulness of the information itself and the current access to it are essential to formulating a company's development strategy.

SOCIAL MEDIA STRATEGY

Social media changes the way organizations and individuals communicate. They open a new dimension of organization's relations with their clients. Communication is possible in both directions. Thanks to them people can: create (blogs and micro-blogs, videos), maintain contact (virtual worlds, social portals), cooperate and exchange knowledge (web-pages of wiki-type), leave responses (discussion forums, comments), order the content (bookmarks/tags), find information faster (widgets, RSS feeds, dashboards for managers). Social media facilitate the development of online social networks by connecting a user's profile with those of other individuals.

Companies using social network sites like: Facebook, YouTube, QZONE, Instagram, Tumblr, Twitter and messengers like Facebook Messenger, WhatsApp, QQ, WeChat (Kemp, 2017) can quickly mobilize the community. Thanks to them people, communities and organizations can discuss, co-create, modify and share user-generated content faster and regardless of place or time. Literature studies allow us to assess how companies in Poland perceive and exploit the potential of social media. According to the report (Sotrender, 2017a), the most active in the social media are companies:

- Related to Internet and telecommunication media,
- FMCG (Fast Moving Consumer Goods) industry offering products that are regularly and bought almost daily by consumers such as groceries, cosmetics, personal cleaners and hygiene products, household chemicals,
- Related to traditional media.

But still, many organizations cannot identify the type of using social media strategy e.g. (Piskorski, 2011) or do not have them at all. The most important goal of formulating a strategy for using social media is primarily the relevance and usefulness of information for policy makers.

The goal of research was to characterize the types of social media strategy in organizations and identify on this basis, what type of social media strategy the tested organizations has on the current stage of development. The inspiration for the current research was the survey/study called "What is your current strategy of applying social media?" (Wilson et al., 2011). The study revealed the existence of four types of social media strategies:

- **Predictive Practitioner:** Involves the use of social media in a particular area, for example customer service, manufacturing, R&D, marketing.
- **Creative Experimenter:** Contains the use of social media for improvement of specific functional areas or practices of the organization.
- **Social Media Champion:** Represented by organizations, which have an inter-department team dealing with social media. This team coordinates and manages projects in the sphere of social media.
- **Social Media Transformer:** Includes organizations, in which there are many centralized teams dealing with social media. Teams can be scattered across different parts of the world, and yet they easily exchange knowledge thanks to modern technologies.

H. J. Wilson, P. J. Guinan, S. Parise and B. D. Weinberg (2011) have developed a questionnaire, on the basis of which, can be identify the type of organization's strategy for using social media.

The Research Process

The study covered three different organizations, located in Silesia (Poland). It was done using the research method used in the management sciences - case study analysis. The purpose of studying selected cases was to test the theory and its development on the basis of observed regularities. Case studies focused on the relationship between the strategy of using social media and the direction companies take in this regard. The test procedure is shown in Figure 1.

Figure 1. The research process

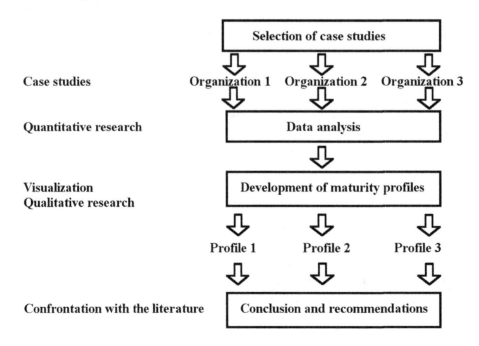

Studying the cases allowed us to recognize the phenomenon in real conditions. The sample selection process was random. The survey was based on survey data from three selected organizations. In the Table 3 was presented a summary of the selected participating organizations.

Table 3. Characteristics of the organizations and their area of actions

Organizations	Area of Action and the Nature of the Analysed Organizations	Problems	External Contacts	Target
Organization A	Education / University	Well known problems. Defined sequence of action.	Concentration on activities within the company. External contacts in the development phase, but still limited.	Efficiency Reliability
Organization B	Business / Business accelerator	Problems that require innovative ideas.	Contacts: external, dense and redundant, are basis of action.	Results
Organization C	Medicine / Dental Clinic	Known problems. Unknown sequence of solving of a problem.	External contacts as a source of information for the activities being undertaken.	Coordination of activities

ORGANIZATIONAL MATURITY PROFILES AND STRATEGIES FOR USING SOCIAL MEDIA: EXPERIMENTAL RESULTS

Thanks to the profiling method identified three maturity profiles of organizations in the use of social media (Figure 2). With regard to the fourth type of strategy, only the area of activity characteristic for this type of activity was indicated.

None of the analysed cases, was a social change initiator. Organizations of this type benefit from the social media on a wide scale, and they regularly use the data from these media and communicate through it. Organization B was the closest thing to this model.

The study revealed the following social media strategies:

- **Organization A - *Creative Experimenter*:** The object of research in this case is a university. Organizations that choose this strategy are looking for ways to improve the areas of their business or the practices that they use. Universities in Poland recognize the potential of social media. They communicate with students via e-mail, they also use Facebook, Instagram and Snapchat. They run programs for representatives (ambassadors) at home and abroad. University projects in Poland in relation to social media are still experimental. They are in the learning phase of projects in the sphere of social media. *In conclusion, we can notice moderate involvement and coordination of the work of university staff in the use of social media.*
- **Organization B - *Social Media Champion*:** The subject of research in this case is the business accelerator, a company that supports the development of startups. The operation of the company is based on the use of social media in daily activities. This company provides jobs (offices, halls), Internet, online tools, business networking. *In conclusion, we can see the great commitment and coordination of employees in the use of social media.*

- **Organization C - *Predictive Practitioner*:** The researcher in this case is a dental clinic. *In conclusion, there is a lack of involvement and coordination of staff practices in the use of social media. Employees are mainly engaged in performing their daily duties.*

Figure 2. Organizational maturity profiles
Source: Results of the questionnaire (Wilson et al., 2011).
* Lack of example

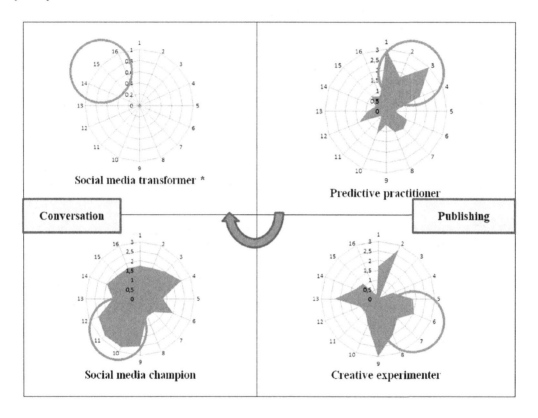

Corporate strategies for using social media can be analysed in the context of their innovation and business relevance. These are two main aspects that determine the success of the venture and are responsible for generating competitive advantage as well. Considerations are illustrated in Figure 3.

- *Predictive practitioners* organizations undertake typical projects in social media that are characterized by low innovation and low strategic importance. The risk of this projects to the organization is slight. Projects contribute to reducing operating costs in selected areas.
- *Creative experimenter* organizations are organizations that undertake activities of little or moderate importance to the organization. Actions, however, allow for the breaking of conventional practices, which can contribute to the acquisition of a new consumer segment.
- *Social media champion* organizations are important to the organization's strategy and operations. Changes are being made to well-established areas of business and are designed to increase competitive advantage.

- *Social media transformer* organizations - high innovation, high business value, high risk, failure can be a source of trouble for the organization.
- *Predictive practitioner* (Organization C) and *Social media champion* (Organization B) projects contribute to cost reduction and productivity growth, while *Social media transformer* (Lack of example) and *Creative experimenter* (Organization A) contribute to revenue growth and new value creation.

Figure 3. The value matrix of social media strategies
Source: Based on (Hartman, Sifonia & Kador, 1999; Wilson et al., 2011).
* Lack of example

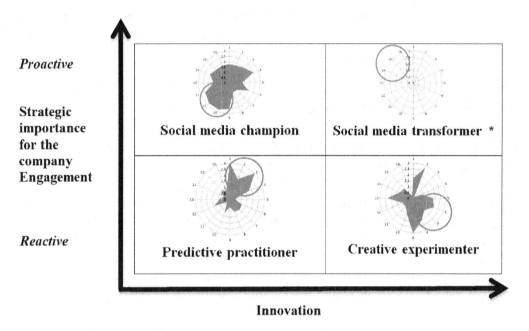

"Social maturity is not reserved only for massive brands that already have an established customer service machine. Smaller, lesser-known brands can, and should have mature customer service on social as well" (Conversocial, 2017). In addition, the level of maturity of organizations in the social media area was confronted with the Social Media Index. The results are shown in Figure 4.

Observers (Predictive practitioner, Organization C) - the businesses which have not integrated social channels into their customer service strategy. Conservative (Creative experimenter, Organization A) - high investment but low innovation; these tend to be larger brands without a solid strategy in social media. Contenders (Social media champion, Organization B) – the organization actively engaging with customers on a variety of social platforms, but without the budget or manpower. Social media transformer– the businesses with strong brand presences across social media.

Figure 4. Social Maturity Index
Source: Based on Conversocial (2017) and Wilson et al. (2011)

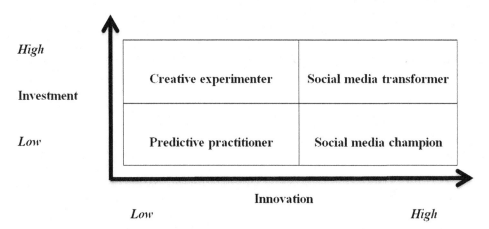

CONCLUSION AND FUTURE RESEARCH DIRECTIONS

The purpose of the research presented in the article was to analyse selected organizations and to assess the maturity of these organizations using the profiling method. The graphical presentation of the maturity profiles allowed to check if the organization did not waste energy on several strategies at the same time. This method has also allowed us to assess how much the strategies of selected organizations and their respective social media activities are synchronized. There are needed further in-depth research in this area, for example using multi criteria methods in order to assess which organization has the best fit for the chosen strategy.

Due to the growing interest of social media, today's companies need to be open to the usage of social media: dialogue, relationships with consumers building, interactivity.

The strategy in this area should be well known not only to the management but also to its employees. An organization's maturity survey on the use of social media with the profiling method allows for further recommendations for optimizing social media activities. This method is a kind of social media compass.

REFERENCES

Buyapowa. (2014). *The three stages of Social maturity.* Retrieved from http://www.welikecrm.it/wp-content/uploads/2014/06/Social-Maturity.pdf

Conversocial. (2017). *Social Maturity Index.* Retrieved from http://www.conversocial.com/hubfs/socialmaturity.pdf

Evans, D., & McKee, J. (2010). *Social Media Marketing: The Next Generation of Business Engagement.* Wiley Publishing, Inc.

Evans, L. (2010). *Social Media Marketing. Strategies for Engaging in Facebook, Twitter & Other Social Media.* Que Publishing.

Hartman, A., Sifonis, J., & Kador, J. (1999). *Net Ready. Strategies for success in the economy.* McGraw-Hill Companies.

Jussila, J. J., Kärkkäinen, H., & Lyytikkä, J. (2011). *Towards Maturity Modelling Approach for Social Media Adoption in Innovation.* In *Proceedings of the 4th ISPIM Innovation Symposium* (pp. 1-14). Wellington, New Zealand: ISPIM. Retrieved April from https://tutcris.tut.fi/portal/files/6640892/Jussila_2011_Towards_Maturity_Modeling_Approach_for_Social_Media_Adoption_in_Innovation.pdf

Kaplan, A. M., & Haenlein, M. (2010). Users of the World, Unite! The Challenges and Opportunities of Social Media. *Business Horizons, 53*(1), 59–68. doi:10.1016/j.bushor.2009.09.003

Kemp, S. (2017). *Digital in 2017, Global Overview.* Retrieved April, 2017, from https://wearesocial.com/blog/2017/01/digital-in-2017-global-overview

Li, Ch., & Bernoff, J. (2011). *Groundswell. Winning in a world transformed by social technologies.* Forrester Research.

Piskorski, M. J. (2011). Social Strategies That Work. *Harvard Business Review, 89*(11), 116–122. PMID:22111430

Sotrender. (2017a). *Facebook Trends Poland.* Retrieved April, from https://www.sotrender.com/trends/facebook/poland/201702/porownanie-branz, DC: Author.

Sotrender. (2017b). *Poznaj swoich odbiorców i zrozum ich zachowanie.* Retrieved from https://www.sotrender.com/pl/audience/, DC: Author.

Surma, K., Krzycki, M., Prokurat, S., & Kubisiak, P. (2012). *Raport z badania Polskie firmy w mediach społecznościowych.* Retrieved from https://www.hbrp.pl/b/raport-z-badania-polskie-firmy-w-mediach-spolecznosciowych/b9PFjezh

Wilson, H. J., Guinan, P. J., Parise, S., & Weinberg, B. D. (2011, July). *What's Your Social Media Strategy? Harvard Business Review.*

This research was previously published in Crowdsourcing and Knowledge Management in Contemporary Business Environments; pages 134-145, copyright year 2019 by Business Science Reference (an imprint of IGI Global).

Chapter 46
Speed of Use of Social Media as an Antecedent of Speed of Business Internationalization

Josep Rialp-Criado
https://orcid.org/0000-0002-0656-1592
Universitat Autònoma de Barcelona, Bellaterra, Spain

María-del-Carmen Alarcón-del-Amo
https://orcid.org/0000-0002-5195-3923
Universidad de Murcia, Murcia, Spain

Alex Rialp
Universitat Autònoma de Barcelona, Bellaterra, Spain & Norwegian University of Science and Technology, Trondheim, Norway

ABSTRACT

Despite various advances in international business and entrepreneurship literatures and increasing interest in speed of internationalization mainly among international entrepreneurship scholars, the relationship between the use of social media and the internationalization speed of the firm remains poorly investigated. This article presents the reflective construct "speed of use of social media" and proves its positive effect on the third order formative construct "speed of internationalization." Furthermore, using multi-group analysis, the article demonstrates that this effect is moderated by the industry where the company performs (business-to-customer vs. business-to-business) and its export intensity, but not by the size of the firm. The results obtained open an interesting area for further research in the role of Web 2.0 and social networking in future knowledge management systems of international new ventures companies.

DOI: 10.4018/978-1-6684-6287-4.ch046

INTRODUCTION

Globalization and emerging markets are offering amazing opportunities to new and old companies that move faster to foreign markets. For example, the world's best startup examples like Uber, AirBnB and BlaBlaCar are actually looking to be the first at customizing their business models to suit requirements of various APAC and MEA markets. Airbnb, for example, leveraged the advantages of being a first mover to the European and Asian Markets against its counterpart Wimdu. Late entrants such as Expedia and Amazon faced difficulty in instituting themselves in the region (and this came at a higher cost as well). But the speed of internationalization is not only relevant for startups, García-Carcía, García-Canal and Guillén (2017) found that firms from the 'old' Europe can also keep up with new trends in internationalization and profit from speeding their internationalization process, thus providing some hope to the managers of established multinationals from developed economies whose global leadership has been challenged by newcomers to the international scene.

In fact, different studies have focused on the speed of internationalization concept in the literature (Jones, Coviello and Tang 2011; Johanson and Vahlne 1977; Rialp, Rialp and Knight 2005; Zhang, Sarker, and Sarker 2013; Casillas and Acedo 2013; Casillas and Moreno-Menéndez 2014). In this sense, it is possible find studies relating speed of internationalization to investment in technology (Saarenketo, Puumalainen, Kylaheiko, and Kuivalainen, 2008); to technology-intensive sectors (Mohr and Batsakis 2014); and also, importantly, studies focused on the effect of speed of internationalization on performance (Hilmersson and Johanson 2016). However, as recognized by Mohr and Batsakis (2014 p. 601), "research on the speed with which firms expand their operations internationally is scarce at best, in particular, when compared to other questions related to international expansion such as, for example, entry mode choice".

In this sense, the possible antecedents of speed of internationalization, for example the relationship between information and communication technologies (ICTs) in general, and social media (SM) in particular, and internationalization speed remains poorly investigated (Morgan-Thomas and Jones 2009). Durkin, McGowan and McKeown (2013, p. 720) point out: "there is a deficit in the research with respect to a more strategic consideration of how SM can add value to the customer-SME relationships".

Therefore, this article attempts to delineate the role of SM usage in the internationalization process of firms and elaborate on how the speed of use of SM may accelerate the speed of internationalization. Internationalization has much of market relationships, as involve entering to new markets. Musteen, Francis and Datta (2010) indicate that firms sharing a common language with their international ties are able to internationalize faster than firms that do not share a common language. Therefore, the faster a company uses social networks sites, the faster the company can obtain a common language with their international ties that, at the same time, allow the company to develop a faster internationalization process. In this sense, according to Ibeh and Kasem (2011), social and business networks were found to be important in explaining the internationalization speed, but social ties seemed more influential at initial stages of the process.

Furthermore, brands can exploit the potential of social media by establishing an online brand community based on a structured set of social relations among admirers of a brand. Kananukul, Jung and Watchravesringkan (2015) prove that brand trustworthiness is formed through consumer's trust toward social network sites, brand trust induces a high degree of brand loyalty and those individuals with higher brand loyalty are likely to purchase the brand's products more frequently as well as in a higher volume.

Therefore, the firms' possession of intangible resources and assets (e.g. brand trustworthiness), acquired first for those firms that faster use social sites, explain the speed with which firms expand their international operation. Therefore, as previous authors have done (Mohr and Batsakis 2014), we draw on the resource- and knowledge based views (RBV/KBV) of the firm to identify another intangible resource that explains speed of internationalization.

It is not a surprise that any activity related to market relationship will be positively related to internationalization process. If this issue is accepted, higher speed of market relation activities should positively influence internationalization speed; in other words: if the company is faster using SM, it will increase the speed of internationalization (what does not mean that if the company does not use SM cannot be fast in its internationalization speed: the company would be faster in its internationalization process if its speed of use of SM was higher). The fact that SM are borderless, allows reinforce the idea that the speed of internationalization can be faster. Thus, this research proposes a model that introduces the direct effect of the speed of use of SM on the speed of internationalization and the moderating effect of industry, size and export intensity of the firm on the proposed relationship.

The remainder of this article is organized as follows: first it provides a brief overview of literature on speed of internationalization and SM. Subsequently, it develops the model and the hypothesis that explicates the relationships between the speed of use of SM and internationalization speed and shows how such relationship may be moderated by different characteristics of the firm. Then the basis of the empirical investigation is explained and finally, it concludes by discussing the theoretical and practical implications of the arguments and how they enhance the current understanding of international entrepreneurship.

BACKGROUND

Speed of Internationalization

Chetty, Johanson and Martín (2014) refer to physics to conceptualize the concept of speed of internationalization. As they mention, "speed" is defined and measured as "distance divided by time" in physics; therefore, they consider that speed has two components: time and distance and define speed of internationalization as "a relationship between the internationalization distance covered and the time passed to reach this" (p. 640). So, adopting this formula, it could be possible to assume, for example, that the number of foreign markets where a firm initiates its operations could be a proxy of the "distance" covered, while time could be the difference between the current year (2015) and its year of inception. This physic analogy could be generalized for conceptualizing other theoretical constructs related to speed. In fact, Chetty et al. (2014) refer to the internationalization process literature for conceptualizing internationalization distance, and found that the concept could be related to the firm's knowledge (mostly experiential) and to the firm's commitment to international markets.

We agree with Chetty et al. (2014) when they argue that "experience gained from international activities during a specific time period can be assumed to correspond to the firm's speed of international learning" (p.640), and experience is gained by conducting business in different markets: the diversity of markets' conditions allow firms to learn more in comparison with a situation where the conditions of the international markets were the same. Likewise, the potential for repetition is an intrinsic component of learning. Consequently, the more experiential knowledge gained during a specific period of time, the bigger the contribution to the speed of internationalization. On the other hand, international commitment supposes that firms invest resources in foreign markets instead of investing in the domestic one (Johanson and Vahlne 1977); therefore, international commitment reflects the firm's dependence on foreign markets. Although the commitment concept in the international business literature has been addressed from different approaches (da Rocha, Cotta del Mello, Pacheco and de Abreu Farias 2012), it is possible to identify a common point of view: the loose of value of committed resources when the firm moves to other markets.

Chetty et al. (2014) consider that "speed of committing internationally relates to international commitment and time" (p. 641), for instance, the more employees devoted to the international operations during a specific period of time or the more resources are committed to legal entities in international markets, the bigger the international commitment. Therefore, the larger the magnitude of resources committed internationally during a specific period of time the higher the speed of internationalization.

Speed of Implementation of Social Media

The term "Social Media" (SM) has been defined by the literature as "a group of Internet-based applications that build on the ideological and technological foundations of Web 2.0, and that allow for the creation and exchange of user-generated content" (Kaplan and Haenlein 2010, p. 61). SM comprise both the conduits and the content disseminated through interactions between individuals and organizations (Kietzman, Hermkens, McCarthy and Silvestre 2011). These technologies have the potential to provide greater access to customer information through customer-customer interactions or through company-customer interactions (Agnihotri, Kothandaraman, Kashyap and Singh 2012).

To measure "speed of use of SM" the research draws on the physics analogy employed previously by Chetty et al. (2014) for defining the concept of speed of internationalization. In this research, we define speed of use of SM as the relationship between the SM use distance and the time passed to reach this. Therefore, it is needed to identify the two components of the formula: distance covered and time, and then it can define speed of use of SM as a relationship between the SM use distance covered and the time passed to reach this distance.

Considering the previous literature on SM, the conceptualization of SM use distance could be related to the regular use of SM applications in the operations and transactions of the company. Regarding the time component, this research considers the number of years the firm has been operating since the existence of SM technologies. According to Michaelidou, Siamagka and Christodoulides (2011), a time-line based on Google trends shows a growing interest in SM since 2004. In addition, O'Reilly and Musser (2007) explain that in 2004 they realized that the Web was on the cusp of a new era, the Web 2.0. Therefore, 2004 can be considered the year when SM tools started being used by companies. So, the number of years a firm has been operating since 2004 could be considered the time dimension.

THEORETICAL MODEL AND HYPOTHESIS

The use of SM by international new ventures can potentially accelerate their internationalization due to (1) the pursuit of high, value-added IT applications to maintain a competitive edge; (2) the reduction in the costs of communicating with foreign customers/suppliers and of gathering information about foreign competitors; and (3) the support/enhancement of distinctive competencies and skills in other business functions (Zhang et al. 2013).

Pezderka et al. (2012, p. 9) assert that "those companies that develop superior capabilities in terms of communication with customers, relationship-building, reaching potential customers, bypassing costly physical presence in foreign markets, market research, being a front-runner in employing advanced export management technology, and cost reduction through Internet deployment, will experience enhanced export performance". Therefore, along with the emergence, further development and deployment of SM technologies, companies now have a greater ability than ever to take advantage of international market-growth opportunities (Mathews, Healy and Wickramasekera 2012) and therefore, the adoption and current use of SM may have unique implications for increasing the speed and benefits of internationalization (Okazaki and Taylor 2013).

Musteen et al. (2010) developed some hypotheses relating the structural, cognitive and relational aspects of the international network of SME CEOs to two internationalization outcomes - speed and performance drawing on social capital theory and the international entrepreneurship literature. Their findings indicate that firms sharing a common language with their international ties are able to internationalize faster than firms that do not share a common language. Therefore, the faster a company uses social networks sites, the faster will obtain a common language with their international ties that, at the same time, allow the company to develop a faster internationalization process. Ibeh and Kasem (2011) also remark the importance of the relational perspective in explaining the internationalization speed. According to these authors, both social and business networks were found to be important, but social ties seemed more influential at initial stages of the process.

Furthermore, social network sites (e.g. LinkedIn) enable users to connect and stay in touch with other people (Phan, Thomas and Heine 2011). Brands can exploit the potential of social media by establishing an online brand community, which is a specialized, non-geographically bound community, based on a structured set of social relations among admirers of a brand. Kananukul et al. (2015) prove that brand trustworthiness is formed through consumer's trust toward social network sites, brand trust induces a high degree of brand loyalty and those individuals with higher brand loyalty are likely to purchase the brand's products more frequently as well as in a higher volume. Accordingly, it can be expected that:

Hypothesis One: The higher the speed of use of social media, the higher the speed of internationalization of exporting firms.

The moderator variables used for this study are as follows: industry type, firm size and export intensity of the firm. Different papers that have analysed speed of internationalization have considered size as a control variable (Acedo and Jones 2007; Chetty et al. 2014; Hutzschenreuter, Kleindienst, Guenther and Hammes 2016; Luo, Zhao and Du 2005; Mohr and Batsakis 2017). In this sense, it is possible to find specialized literature where speed of internationalization is considered as an explanatory of firm performance (Hilmersson and Johanson 2016) where size and industry have also played the role of controls. Likewise, other papers that have been focused on explaining speed of internationalization and have considered, in line with the current research, possible determinants (for example, the learning acquired in the course of past internationalization activities (Casillas and Moreno-Menendez 2014); firms' possession of intangible resources, in particular, intangible assets (e.g. brand value) and different types of experiential knowledge of international operations (Mohr and Batsakis 2014); and/or individual-level and company-level antecedents, including propensity to act, risk tolerance, company-level organization of knowledge, ability to forge company-level consensus, and company-level responsiveness (Li, Qian and Qian 2015); have also considered size and industry as control variables.

Perrigot, Kacher, Basset and Clique (2012) analyzed the relationship between the presence of the company in SM and the industry where the company operated, finding a significant relationship. The industry type in which a business operates may influence the adoption of information system (IS) innovations, including Internet and e-business technologies (Levenburg et al. 2006); although other authors do not confirm this view (Teo 2007). In this sense, Swani, Brow and Milne (2014, p. 873) recognize that "social media research and stories of its effectiveness mainly focus on business-to-consumer (B2C) examples in which social media leads to increased brand awareness, loyalty, engagement, and sales (e.g., Kumar and Mirchandani 2012; Rapp, Beitelspacher, Grewal and Hughes 2013; Taylor, Lewin and Strutton 2011; Wiersema 2013)". From the point of view of these authors, B2B marketers seem hesitant to adopt social media marketing strategies. They refer to Giamanco and Gregoire (2012) to point out that only 5% of B2B marketers cite social media marketing as a well-optimized part of their marketing mix, 17% do not use social media at all, and 58% consider themselves in the initial stages of developing their social media strategies. Taking into account the consideration done for some authors that service businesses are more predisposed towards using the Internet for business activities than manufacturing enterprises (Goode and Stevens 2000), the relationship among speed of use of SM and speed of internationalization could be moderated differentiating between B2B and B2C companies. The need for B2C firms to connect with international customers, and every time more frequently, could suppose that these companies with a higher speed of use of SM could internationalize faster. Therefore, it can be hypothesized that:

Hypothesis Two: The higher the speed of use of social media, the higher the speed of internationalization of B2C than B2B.

Some authors verified that the size of the firm has a positive direct influence on export performance (Calof 1994; Majocchi et al. 2005; Williams 2011). For example, Bonaccorsi (1992) established that small firms export a lower share of their sales because of limited resources, lack of scale economies and high risk perception in international activity. Majocchi et al. (2005) find a highly significant relationship between firm size and export intensity, when size is measured by number of employees. Nazar and Saleem (2009) conclude that firm size has positive effect on export performance if measured in terms of total sales and has negative effects are found on export profits if measured by number of employees a firm have. However, the impact of size on exports is not free of controversy in the literature. Smaller firms are also seen by the academic literature as quicker and more flexible than the larger ones due to structural simplicity, and therefore efficient adaptation can provide them a competitive advantage in responding to the specific requirements of foreign buyers when export relation size increases (Verwaal and Donkers 2002). That is the reason why some authors, as Moen (1999) and Pla-Barber and Alegre (2007), did not find a significant relation between seize and export: Moen (1999) find that firm size and export intensity is not significantly related; while Pla-Barber and Alegre (2007) find that firm size is not a preponderant factor for the internationalization of biotech firms and mention that prior research had generally focused on manufacturing industries without taking into account the implications of dealing with heterogeneous technology profiles.

On the other hand, firm size has been found to positively predict the adoption of IS (Teo 2007; Huang et al. 2008); although some researchers (e.g. Goode and Stevens 2000) have failed to confirm this relationship. In this sense, Lorenzo-Romero et al. (2013) in their study of the use of SM as a marketing strategy by retailers, did not find many differences between large, medium, and small companies in the use of SM tools. Attending previous literature, we based on the assumption that for larger firms, less flexible than smaller ones, a higher speed of use of SM could benefit a faster internationalization. Therefore, we establish the following hypotehsis:

Hypothesis Three: The higher the speed of use of social media, the higher the speed of internationalization of larger firms than smaller firms.

Finally, it can be posited that the higher the export intensity of the firm, the higher the dependence of the firm of the international markets and its experiential knowledge obtained about them. The export intensity is characterized by a considerable amount of uncertainty, which stems from the lack of knowledge about foreign markets. That is the reason why managers need to develop their international contacts to achieve market entry to the leading markets. Just a passive following strategy will downsize the market opportunities and if the internationalization happens after all, it will take place in the economies with lower economic potential (Ojala 2009). On the other hand, and as it has been already mentioned, firms sharing a common language benefit from networking and internationalize faster than the ones that do not share common language (Musteen et al. 2010). Therefore, for those firms depending more on foreign markets, the higher speed of use of SM could facilitate a higher speed of internationalization. The knowledge needed to compete in foreign markets can be acquired through experience from practical operations abroad but nowadays it could also be obtained using SM. A firm using SM tools for connecting with its foreign customers could better know the differences in environmental conditions and is more likely to select the most attractive markets and adapt the marketing strategy to accommodate the specific needs of those markets abroad (Cavusgil and Zou 1994).

Hypothesis Four: The higher the speed of use of social media, the higher the speed of internationalization of high-export intensity firms than low-export intensity firms.

As it has been seen, the variables considered here as moderators are among the most frequently considered as possible firm-level determinants of export performance (Grandinetti and Mason 2012). For instance, the emergence of the size of the firm as a key determinant is not a surprise, as its relationship with export performance has been one of the most extensively studied in the export marketing literature (Moen 1999). However, no significant relationship was found between the size of the firm and export performance in some cases (Moen 1999; Contractor et al. 2005). Thus, the connection between firm size and performance is still a controversial issue (Brouthers and Nakos 2005). Studies on the relationship between firm size and internationalization highlight the fact that small size does not constitute *per se* a barrier to exporting and that, despite having fewer resources, SMEs can successfully enter foreign markets and achieve a high level of exports. This characteristic of "mixing empirical results" is also related to other determinants of export performance. In this sense, several empirical studies report a significant positive relationship between experience in foreign markets and performance (Lado et al. 2004), whereas other studies have suggested that international experience is negatively related to export performance (Brouthers and Nakos 2005).

Figure 1 shows the proposed model, in which the relationships that will be tested in the measurement and structural model, and the moderating effects, are included.

Figure 1. Proposed model

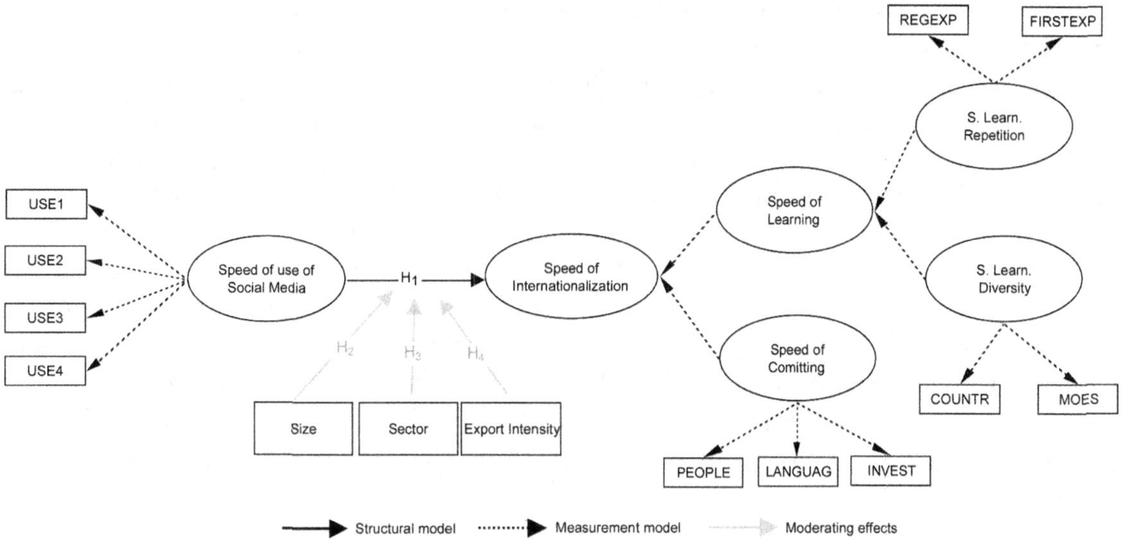

METHODOLOGY

Sample and Procedure

An online questionnaire to multi-industry sample of Spanish exporting firms was used as method of data collection in December 2014. A multiindustry sample enlarges the observed variance and emphasizes the generalization of the findings (Morgan, Kaleka, & Katsikeas, 2004; Navarro-García, Arenas-Gaitán, & Rondán-Cataluña, 2014).

Given that the study's unit of analysis was at the organization level, and the research focuses mainly on the internationalization process of the company and the use of SM, international and general manager/s in charge of the firm's foreign business activity were contacted. The final sample was obtained from the market research company GMI based on the ICEX (Spanish Institute for Foreign Trade) database of exporters. The non-probability method by quota sampling was used to ensure that the sample is representative of the Spanish exporting companies' population with regard to region of location. Maintaining sectorial proportionality, 1100 managers in charge of exports (i.e. export managers) received the questionnaire, and 337 fully valid ones were returned.

To analyse the possible non-response bias, we compared the number of times the Web page with the survey was requested with the number of completed research responses actually received, so we could make a reasonable estimation of active refusals: the web page was requested more than 970 times and the number of completed research responses was 337, which represents a 34% rate of non-refusal —overcoming the range of 15–20% mentioned by Menon, Bharadwaj and Howell (1996) —. Unfortunately, we could not compute differences in key variables among those answering the survey and those that did not because the directory where the contact information was found did not provide us with other types of information.

Likewise, to analyse the possible differences between earlier and late respondents (regarding those who answered first to the questionnaire and those who answered after the first and second re-call), we ran bivariate analysis and we did not find any significant differences in their responses.

The final sample consisted of 337 exporters. These companies are, in average, 52 years old, they have been regular exporters for almost 19 years —a similar percentage to the one obtained by Navarro-García et al. (2014)—, their average level of export intensity is 57%, and the number of exporting countries, in average, is 16 (being the maximum number of exporting countries by a firm 160). Most firms are small and medium-sized (67.1%), with the mean number of employees being 142.7. The big size companies (32.9%) have a mean number of employees of 9,035.1. The 58.8% of the sample are B2B and the 41.2% are B2C companies. We defined whether a given firm can be classified as SMEs or a large firm following OECD definition (OECD 2018); and we follow Horjmose, Brammer and Millingotn (2012) to establish if a firm was active in a business to business or a business to consumer sector (as these authors we based on the firm's primary activity as provided by CNAE, more precisely, we used the 4 digit CNAE code that characterized a firm's primary activity to allocate firms to the B2B or B2C sectors).

Table 1. Demographic information of the sample

Sample size	337	
Age	52 years old (average)	
Time being regular exporter	19 years (average)	
Export intensity	57% (average)	
Number of exporting countries	16 (average)	
Size	Small and Medium size (67.1%)	142.7 (average number of employees)
	Big size companies (32.9%)	9035 (average number of employees)
Industry	B2B	58.8%
	B2C	41.2%

Measures

Most of the measures used in the study were taken from previously validated sources, specifically those variables used to measure the third-order construct "Speed of Internationalization". In fact, following Chetty et al. (2014), "speed of internationalization" will be conceptualized as a formative higher-order construct created by two dimensions in this research: speed of international learning and speed of committing internationally. The construct "speed of international learning" is operationalized as a reflective first-order, formative second-order construct (i.e., a 'type II' construct according to the alternative second-order factor specifications provided by Jarvis et al. 2003), that is, formed by two constructs with reflective indicators: "Speed of learning from repetition of international activities' and 'speed of learning from diversity of international activities". The first one captures the speed of the time-based dimension of learning, i.e., learning by repetition and is reflected in indicators such as the speed of obtaining the first export order and achieving regular exports. The second one is reflected in indicators such as the speed of the geographic scope and of diversity of entry modes used in international operations. That is, the 'rate' at which the firm has entered foreign countries and used several different entry modes.

Regarding the measurement of "speed of committing internationally", this is expected to be reflected in indicators capturing the speed and degree of integration and specialization of the resources and the amount of resources (Johanson and Vahlne 1977). In other words, this research measures the speed at which the firm commits specific resources with indicators such as the "speed of committing staff in international activities" (e.g., number of full time employees currently active in international activities/ number of years operating) and the "speed of using a firm's foreign language skills", and the speed at which the firm invests significant resources internationally or "speed of entry modes commitment".

At the beginning of the questionnaire, we included a brief description about the objective of the research and definition of Social Media. In this research, we consider Social Media as interactive and user-generated content applications used by customers for communication and for the creation, editing, and dissemination of content. Social Media include blogs, social networks, customer forums, content aggregators, wikis, etc. (Constantinides and Fountain 2008).

As it has been mentioned in the section "Speed of implementation of Social Media", in this research we define speed of use of SM as the relationship between the SM use distance and the time passed to reach this. More precisely, SM relates the regular use of SM applications in the operations and transactions of the company to the number of years the firm has been operating since 2004 (2004 can be considered the year when SM tools started being used by companies (Michaelidou, Siamagka and Christodoulides 2011; O'Reilly and Musser 2007)). So, if a firm is using SM in one type of transactions while another firm is using SM for all its transactions, and both have been operating 12 years (the difference between 2015 and 2004) the speed of use of SM will be higher for the second one than for the first one. Likewise, a firm operating since 2008 could be faster in the use of SM than a firm operating since 2000 if the former is using SM tools in more transactions than the latter. Therefore, "speed of use of SM" reflects the intensification of the implementation of these media by the firm since the SM technology emergence in the world market.

The scale used to measure the "Speed of use of Social Media (SM)" was adapted from the scale used by Ifinedo (2011). More precisely, Speed of use of SM will be conceptualized in this research as a reflective construct formed by four observable variables relating operations and transactions where the firms use SM tools and the number of years the firm has been operating since the emergence of these media. To measure the general usage of SM this research used the four items proposed by Ifinedo (2011) that were anchored on a five-point Likert scale ranging from "strongly disagree" to "strongly agree" in which participants were asked to indicate an appropriate response. Then, to calculate the speed of use of SM, each item is divided by the number of years operating during the existence of these applications (since 2004).

We consider the construct "speed of use of SM" a reflective construct considering the decision rules for determining whether a construct is formative or reflective provided by Jarvis et al. (2003, table 1 p. 203): the direction of causality is from constructs to items, indicators are manifestations of the construct, changes in the indicators would not cause change in the construct but changes in the construct do cause change in the indicators. Furthermore, indicators are interchangeable, share a common theme and drop an indicator would not alter the conceptual domain of the construct. On the other hand, indicators covariance with each other and a change in one of the indicators is associated with changes in the other indicators. Finally, indicators have the same antecedents and consequences.

The operationalization of the constructs appears in Table 2.

Table 2. Constructs and measures

Construct	Indicators	Label	Measurement	Source
Speed of learning from repetition of international activities (REPETITION)	Speed of achieving regular exports	REGEXP	Number of years regularly exporting/number of years operating	Chetty et al. (2014)
	Speed of obtaining the first export order	FIRSTEXP	Number of years since the first export order/number of years operating	
Speed of learning from diversity of international activities (DIVERSITY)	Speed of geographic scope of a firm's international operations	COUNTR	Number of countries/number of years operating	Chetty et al. (2014)
	Speed of diversity of entry modes used in international operations	MOES	Number of entry modes/number of years operating	
Speed of international learning (LEARNING)	Speed of learning from repetition of international activities	REPETITION	Latent variable scores	Chetty et al. (2014)
	Speed of learning from diversity of international activities	DIVERSITY	Latent variable scores	
Speed of committing internationally (COMMIT)	Speed of committing staff in international activities	PEOPLE	Number of employees in international activities/number of years operating	Chetty et al. (2014)
	Speed of using a firm's foreign language skills	LANGUAGE	Number of languages used/number of years operating	
	Speed of entry modes commitment	INVEST	Entry mode with foreign investment (yes/no)/number of years operating	
Speed of internationalization (Speed Int.)	Speed of international learning	LEARNING	Latent variable scores	Chetty et al. (2014)
	Speed of committing internationally	COMMIT	Latent variable scores	
Speed of use of Social Media	Speed of using social media in regular activities	USE1	"Our company makes use of Social Media very often"/number of years operating during the existence of Social Media	Items adapted from Ifinedo (2011)
		USE2	"Our company uses Social Media, at all times, for its transactions"/number of years operating during the existence of Social Media	
		USE3	"Our company uses Social Media its critical operations"/ number of years operating during the existence of Social Media	
		USE4	"The number of business operations and activities in my company that requires Social Media"/number of years operating during the existence of Social Media	

The moderator variables were assessed as follows: firm size was measured by number of employees and divided into two groups, SMEs as those with less than 250 workers, and large companies as those with more than 205 workers. Sector was divided as B2C (retail and services) and B2B companies (manufacturing and construction). The export intensity was assessed as high export intensity and low export intensity. Export intensity, calculated as export sales as percentage of total sales, allows capture different levels of internationalization by exporting firms in this research and it is not considered as a proxy of level of international commitment, as done in other studies. Therefore, the scores were divided at the fiftieth percentile of the total group, and companies were assigned to the high export intensity group if they have a value above the fiftieth percentile, and to the low export intensity group if they have a value under the fiftieth percentile.

Data Analysis Technique

A structural equation modelling (SEM), specifically partial least squares (PLS), is proposed to assess the measurement and structural model. This technique is used because is more appropriate for this research in view of the research objectives and exploratory nature of the study (the conceptualization of speed of internationalization and speed of use of social media) (Lew and Sinkovics 2013), studies with small sample sizes (Fornell and Bookstein 1982), the non-normal distribution of most indicators (Chin et al. 2003) and, what is most important, the presence of second and third-order formative constructs in the measurement model (Hair et al. 2012).

We followed one of the PLS-based methods for estimating models with higher-order constructs, as Chetty et al. (2014) used to conceptualized speed of internationalization, the "two-stage" approach (e.g., Henseler, Wilson, Götz and Hautvast 2007; Wetzels, Oderkerken-Schröder and van Oppen 2009), and used latent variable scores in the estimation of the second and third-order constructs.

SmartPLS 2.0 software was used to analyse the data (Ringle et al. 2005). The stability of the estimates was tested via a bootstrap re-sampling procedure (500 sub-samples (Chin 1998)).

RESULTS

A PLS model is analysed in two stages: first, the assessment of the reliability and validity of the measurement model, and second, the assessment of the structural model.

Reliability and Validity Assessment

Firstly, following the approach of other studies (e.g. Ifinedo 2011; Alegre and Chiva 2013), procedural remedies for controlling common method biases were followed (Podsakoff et al. 2003): clear and concise questions were used in the questionnaire, respondents' anonymity was assured and the Harmon one-factor test was used to assess if such biases were a problem in the sample. Results show that common method bias was not a relevant concern in the data set: the factor analysis conducted in the overall sample resulted in two factors with eigenvalues greater than 1 (accounting for 67.3% of the total variance).

Secondly, an analysis of the validity and reliability of the scales employed in the model was performed. As one of the objectives is to analyse the moderator effect of size, sector and export intensity in the relationship proposed, this research also tested the reliability and validity for these subgroups, to asses that the measurement instrument is reliable. Therefore, we separated the companies into two groups for each moderator: SMEs –those with less than 250 employees- and large companies for size, B2C and B2B companies for sector, and companies with a high export intensity and companies with a low export intensity. Therefore, we will analyse the validity and reliability of the scales for the 7 models (Total, SMEs, big companies, B2C, B2B, high and low export intensity).

The scales' development was founded on the review of the most relevant literature, thus assuring the content validity of the measurements instruments (Cronbach,1971) (Table 2).

To analyse the reliability of the constructs, we first conducted an exploratory factor analysis (EFA) with SPSS software. The consideration of multiple items for each construct increases construct reliability (Terblanche and Boshoff 2008). Using EFA, and considering the different items for each construct, we found that only one dimension appeared for all constructs. Therefore, EFA confirmed the unidimensionality of the constructs considered in the model. The item-total correlation, which measures the correlation of each item with the sum of the remaining items that constitute the scale, is above the minimum of 0.3 recommended by Nurosis (1993) for all constructs in the sample used.

The results of the PLS for reflective indicators are reported in Table 3. Convergent validity is verified by analysing the factor loadings and their significance. We deleted one item (PEOPLE) of the "Speed of committing internationally" construct since the item loading estimates lower than 0.4 (Bagozzi and Yi 1988). The results of the final re-specified measurement model provide a good convergent validity. The individual item loadings in our models are higher than 0.6 (Bagozzi and Yi 1988), and the average of the item-to-factor loadings are higher than 0.7 (Hair et al. 2006). Also, we checked the significance of the loadings with a re-sampling procedure (500 sub-samples) for obtaining t-statistic values. They were all significant (p<.001). These findings provide evidence supporting the convergent validity of all the reflective constructs for the seven models. Composite reliability (CR) represents the shared variance among a set of observed variables measuring an underlying construct (Fornell and Larcker 1981). Generally, a CR of at least 0.60 is considered desirable (Bagozzi and Yi 1988). This requirement is fulfilled for every factor in the seven models. The average variance extracted (AVE) was also calculated for each construct; the resulting AVE values were greater than 0.50 (Fornell and Larcker 1981). Therefore, the four constructs for each model demonstrated acceptable levels of reliability.

Table 3. Internal consistency and convergent validity for constructs with reflective indicators

Variable	Indicator	Mean	SD	Loading	CR	AVE	
Total							
DIVERSITY	CONTRY	0.61	0.89	0.78	0.76	0.61	
	MOES	0.19	0.22	0.79			
REPETITION	FIRSTEXP	0.70	0.29	0.96	0.96	0.93	
	REGEXP	0.59	0.28	0.96			
COMMIT	LANGUAG	0.25	0.43	0.86	0.74	0.60	
	INVEST	0.03	0.04	0.67			
USE	USE1	0.44	0.29	0.95	0.98	0.93	
	USE2	0.39	0.24	0.95			
	USE3	0.40	0.25	0.97			
	USE4	0.41	0.26	0.98			

continues on following page

Table 3. Continued

		Group 1			Group 2		
Variable	**Indicator**	**Loading**	**CR**	**AVE**	**Loading**	**CR**	**AVE**
Size (Group 1= SME, Group 2=BIG)							
DIVERSITY	CONTRY	0.76	0.75	0.60	0.80	0.81	0.68
	MOES	0.78			0.85		
REPETITION	FIRSTEXP	0.96	0.96	0.92	0.97	0.96	0.93
	REGEXP	0.96			0.96		
COMMIT	LANGUAG	0.88	0.73	0.58	0.79	0.78	0.64
	INVEST	0.62			0.81		
USE	USE1	0.96	0.98	0.93	0.92	0.98	0.92
	USE2	0.95			0.96		
	USE3	0.97			0.97		
	USE4	0.98			0.97		
Sector (Group 1= B2C, Group 2=B2B)							
DIVERSITY	CONTRY	0.67	0.73	0.57	0.88	0.82	0.70
	MOES	0.83			0.79		
REPETITION	FIRSTEXP	0.97	0.97	0.94	0.96	0.56	0.91
	REGEXP	0.97			0.96		
COMMIT	LANGUAG	0.87	0.71	0.56	0.87	0.79	0.66
	INVEST	0.60			0.75		
USE	USE1	0.94	0.98	0.94	0.95	0.97	0.91
	USE2	0.98			0.92		
	USE3	0.98			0.96		
	USE4	0.98			0.98		
Export Intensity (Group 1= High, Group 2=Low)							
DIVERSITY	CONTRY	0.76	0.77	0.62	0.79	0.76	0.62
	MOES	0.81			0.78		
REPETITION	FIRSTEXP	0.97	0.97	0.93	0.96	0.96	0.92
	REGEXP	0.97			0.96		
COMMIT	LANGUAG	0.82	0.72	0.56	0.89	0.78	0.65
	INVEST	0.67			0.71		
USE	USE1	0.95	0.98	0.94	0.94	0.97	0.90
	USE2	0.98			0.90		
	USE3	0.98			0.97		
	USE4	0.98			0.98		

AVE: Average Variance Extracted; CR: Composite reliability.
*We have checked the significance of the loadings with a re-sampling procedure (500 sub-samples) for obtaining t-statistic values. They are all significant (p<0.01).

Table 4. Item weights and multicollinearity tests for constructs with formative indicators

Construct/ indicator	Group 1				Group 2			
	Weight	*t*-value (bootstrap)	Tolerance	VIF	Weight	*t*-value (bootstrap)	Tolerance	VIF
Total								
LEARNING								
REPETITION	0.603***	10.995	0.911	1.098				
DIVERSITY	0.638***	13.400	0.911	1.098				
Speed Int.								
LEARNING	0.285**	2.432	0.820	1.220				
COMMIT	0.845***	10.373	0.820	1.220				
Size (Group 1= SME, Group 2=BIG)								
LEARNING								
REPETITION	0.609***	9.960	0.908	1.101	0.550***	6.477	0.895	1.118
DIVERSITY	0.630***	11.197	0.908	1.101	0.676***	9.798	0.895	1.118
Speed Int.								
LEARNING	0.200**	2.544	0.784	1.276	0.507*	2.031	0.860	1.163
COMMIT	0.891***	18.261	0.784	1.276	0.693***	2.748	0.860	1.163
Sector (Group 1= B2C, Group 2=B2B)								
LEARNING								
REPETITION	0.574***	10.585	0.888	1.126	0.591***	9.805	0.89	1.125
DIVERSITY	0.649***	13.870	0.888	1.126	0.633***	10.400	0.89	1.125
Speed Int.								
LEARNING	0.226*	2.297	0.754	1.327	0.478*	2.351	0.855	1.169
COMMIT	0.868***	13.036	0.754	1.327	0.715***	4.050	0.855	1.169
Export Intensity (Group 1= High, Group 2=Low)								
LEARNING								
REPETITION	0.575***	7.967	0.921	1.085	0.653***	9.385	0.890	1.123
DIVERSITY	0.672***	11.104	0.921	1.085	0.572***	8.151	0.890	1.123
Speed Int.								
LEARNING	0.220*	2.366	0.788	1.269	0.427*	2.045	0.861	1.161
COMMIT	0.879***	14.838	0.788	1.269	0.759***	4.371	0.861	1.161
*p<0.05; **p<0.01; ***p<0.001.								

The weights for the two dimensions forming speed of internationalization are significant (see Table 4) for each model, with values higher for speed of committing internationally than for speed of international learning. This means that the former makes a higher contribution to speed of internationalization than the latter. In addition, the speed of learning from diversity of activities makes a more important and significant contribution to speed of international learning than learning from repetition of activities, as Chetty et al. (2004) included in their study. As a standard precaution when working with formative measures

(Mathieson, Peacock and Chin 2001), we tested for multicollinearity by calculating the variance inflation factor (VIF) and the tolerance values. A rule of thumb from econometrics states that VIFs greater than 10 reveal a critical level of multicollinearity. If the VIF is equal to 1 there is no multicollinearity among factors. In our case, the VIF is around 1, which indicates some correlation, but not enough to be overly concerned about (Henseler et al. 2009).

Finally, the comparison of bivariate correlations and square roots of the AVEs, presented in Table 5, show an adequate discriminant validity of all constructs for every model, since all diagonal values exceeded the inter-construct correlations. Discriminant validity indicates the extent to which a given construct is different from other latent variables.

Table 5. Discriminant validity: first order latent variables correlations and square root of the average variances extracted

Variable	Group 1				Group 2			
	DIVERSITY	REPETITION	COMMIT	USE	DIVERSITY	REPETITION	COMMIT	USE
Total								
DIVERSITY	0.78							
REPETITION	0.30	0.96						
COMMIT	0.57	0.27	0.77					
USE	0.56	0.22	0.57	0.96				
Size (Group 1= SME, Group 2=BIG)								
DIVERSITY	0.77				0.83			
REPETITION	0.30	0.96			0.32	0.97		
COMMIT	0.61	0.30	0.76		0.52	0.22	0.80	
USE	0.62	0.25	0.67	0.96	0.42	0.19	0.32	0.96
Sector (Group 1= B2C, Group 2=B2B)								
DIVERSITY	0.76				0.84			
REPETITION	0.33	0.97			0.33	0.96		
COMMIT	0.72	0.32	0.75		0.44	0.24	0.81	
USE	0.68	0.33	0.74	0.97	0.41	0.14	0.34	0.95
Export Intensity (Group 1= High, Group 2=Low)								
DIVERSITY	0.79				0.78			
REPETITION	0.28	0.97			0.33	0.96		
COMMIT	0.65	0.28	0.75		0.45	0.27	0.80	
USE	0.67	0.26	0.70	0.97	0.38	0.17	0.36	0.95

Diagonal values are the square root of the variance shared between the reflective constructs and their measures. In order to achieve discriminant
validity diagonal elements must be larger than off-diagonal.

On the basis of all criteria, we can accept this measure as a valuable instrument built from reliable and valid constructs for the seven models.

Structural Model

First, as in the validity assessment, the model was run separately for each subgroup to test the moderator effect and the relationship for each group (bootstrapping of 500 sub-samples was implemented). To assess the predictive ability of the structural model this research followed the approach proposed by Falk and Miller (1992) that the R2 value (variance accounted for) of each of the dependent constructs exceeds the 0.1 value. Table 6 shows that the R2 values in the dependent variables are higher than the critical level mentioned for each model.

Another test applied was the Stone-Geisser test of predictive relevance (Q2). This test can be used as an additional assessment of model fit in PLS analysis (Geisser 1975). The Blindfolding technique was used to calculate de Q2. Models with Q2 greater than zero are considered to have predictive relevance (Chin, 1988). In this case Q2 is positive for all predicted variables.

Table 6. Hypotheses and moderating effect testing

Path	Global		Multigroup analysis					
			Group 1		Group 2			
	Stand coefficients	t-value (bootstrap)	Stand coefficients	t-value (bootstrap)	Stand coefficients	t-value (bootstrap)	t[mgp]	*p*
Total Speed of use of SM→Speed Int.	0.977***	194.076						
R² (Speed Int.)	0.954							
Q² (Speed Int.)	0.936							
Size (Group 1= SME, Group 2=BIG)								
Speed of use of SM→Speed Int.			0.979***	252.749	0.979***	140.884	-0.174	0.8620[n.s.]
R² (Speed Int.)			0.958		0.959			
Q² (Speed Int.)			0.000		0.910			
Sector (Group 1= B2C, Group 2=B2B)								
Speed of use of SM→Speed Int.			0.982***	197.256	0.978***	117.074	2.881	0.004***
R² (Speed Int.)			0.965		0.956			
Q² (Speed Int.)			0.914		0.935			
Export Intensity (Group 1= High, Group 2=Low)								
Speed of use of SM→Speed Int.			0.981***	240.863	0.976***	122.387	3.822	0.000***
R² (Speed Int.)			0.963		0.953			
Q² (Speed Int.)			0.000		0.922			
***p<0.001; [n.s.]=not significant. T[mgp] = t-value for multi-group comparison test (see formula 1 in page 16).								

Second, the multigroup path coefficient differences were examined based on the procedure suggested by Keil et al. (2000) and Chin (2000). These authors suggest to apply an unpaired samples t-test to the group-specific model parameters using the standard deviations of the estimates resulting from bootstrapping. The parametric test uses the path coefficients and the standard errors of the structural paths calculated by PLS with the samples of the two groups, using the following expression of t-value for multigroup comparison test (1) (see Chin 2000) (m=group 1 sample size and n=group 2 sample size):

$$t = \frac{\beta_{group\,1} - \beta_{group\,2}}{\sqrt{\frac{m-1}{m+n-2} \times SE^2_{group\,1} + \frac{n-1}{m+n-2} \times SE^2_{group\,2}} \times \sqrt{\frac{1}{m} + \frac{1}{n}}} \qquad (1)$$

This statistic follows a t-distribution with m+n-2 degrees of freedom. The subsample-specific path coefficients are denoted as β, the sizes of the subsamples as m and n, and the patch coefficient standard errors as resulting from bootstrapping as SE.

Table 6 and Figure 2 show a synthesis of the results obtained for the causal and moderated hypothesis testing. Consistent with Chin (1988), bootstrapping (500 re-samples) was used to generate t-values. Support for each general hypothesis can be determined by examining the sign and statistical significance of the t-values. In the overall model, the results obtained allow state that the speed of use of social media influences in the speed of the internationalization[1].

Figure 2. Hypotheses testing

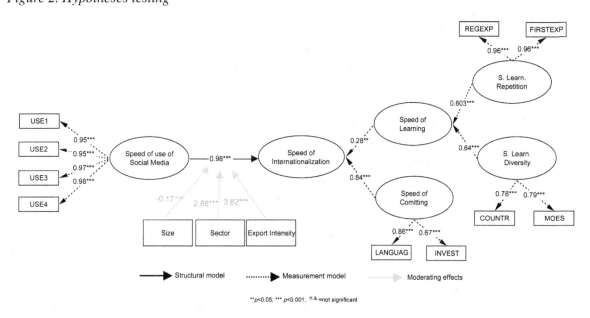

In addition, the impact of moderating variables on the proposed relationship was significant for the sector and for the export intensity, since t-value for multi-group comparison are significant at a level of 0.01. However, firm size does not have a moderator effect. In other words, whether the firms is B2C or

B2B or whether the firm have high export intensity or low export intensity have impact on the proposed hypothesis, being stronger this relationship in B2C companies and companies of higher export intensity.

CONCLUSION

The speed of use of SM by firms influences positively in the speed of their internationalization processes: *the more rapidly SM tools are integrated in the activities of the company, the higher the speed of internationalization.*

From an academic point of view, and drawing on the resource- and knowledge based views of the firm, with this result we contribute to the literature that identifies intangible resources to explain speed of internationalization. As we mention in the introduction, the faster a company uses social networks sites, the faster the company can obtain a common language with their international ties that, at the same time, allow the company to develop a faster internationalization process (Musteen et al. 2010). Furthermore, firms can establish online brand communities based on a structured set of social relations among admirers of a brand, these communities form brand trustworthiness that induces a high degree of brand loyalty and those individuals with higher brand loyalty are likely to purchase the brand's products more frequently as well as in a higher volume (Kananukul et al. 2015).

In addition, our results prove that sector and export intensity moderate the proposed relationship, while the firm size does not have a moderator effect. In other words, whether the firms are B2C or B2B or whether the firm has high export intensity or low export intensity have impact on the relationship between the speed of use of SM and the speed of internationalization: the effect is stronger in B2C companies and in higher export intensity companies.

In relation to the stronger effect in B2C companies, as Jussila, Kärkkäinen and Aramo-Immonen (2014) recognize, there are significant differences between the B2B and B2C companies in the markets, products and product development. For instance, products produced by B2C organizations are less complex and the development of new products takes significantly less time than products produced by B2B organizations, whose customers are less in number but are large organizations instead of single persons.

For B2B organizations the co-operation with customers is generally more direct and more intense than in the B2C organizations due to the number of buyers. This is precisely one of the aspects that the implementation and adoption of SM can change for B2C organizations: SM facilitates an intense and direct cooperation with customers, domestic and foreign, what accelerates and increases customer engagement, faithfulness, brand awareness, loyalty, and domestic and foreign sales (e.g., Kumar and Mirchandani 2012; Wiersema 2013).

This intense and direct cooperation with customers that SM permit is also behind the stronger effect of the speed of use of SM on the speed of internationalization in higher export intensity companies. For these companies, international markets constitute the main destiny of their products; and the possibility of contacting directly with their foreign consumers, obtain direct information as well as suggestions related to current and potential products through SM, accelerate the internationalization process.

Finally regarding possible moderators in the relationship between speed of use of SM and speed of internationalization, the results show that size does not have a moderator effect. In other words, the effect of the speed of use of SM on the speed of internationalization does not differ for smaller and medium size companies than for larger firms. Many scholars had thought that firm size is a good proxy of the stock of resources available to enhance the presence of the firm in foreign markets (Prasad et al.

2001), however the effect on the speed of internationalization of integrating SM in the regular activities of the company is not related to the stock of resources of the company. So, small and medium size companies are not in disadvantage regarding larger ones when the research focuses on the integration and exploitation of SM to accelerate the internationalization process. This contradicts to earlier studies of technology adoption suggesting that firm size correlates positively with the use of technology (e.g., Del Aguila-Obra and Padilla-Melendez 2006) and, as Jussila et al. (2014, p. 612) suggest: "possible explanations for this include the relatively limited financial resources needed for the adoption (see e.g., Michaelidou et al. 2011), and the ease of adoption and the cost effectiveness of at least some SM approaches, such as social networking sites or one-way communication related approaches used e.g., in marketing of smaller companies."

From our perspective, the effect of size on the internationalization process and results has obtained mixed evidences in the literature, for some authors smaller firms are in disadvantage (Nazar and Saleem 2009), while for others smaller firms are also seen quicker and more flexible than the larger ones due to structural simplicity, and therefore efficient adaptation can provide them a competitive advantage in responding to the specific requirements of foreign buyers (Verwaal and Donkers 2002). From our perspective, the result of the current research regarding the no moderation effect of size in the relationship between speed of use of SM and speed of internationalization reinforces previous works where size has not been found as a significant explanatory variable of exports (Moen 1999; Pla-Barber and Alegre 2007).

From a managerial point of view, our results reinforce Durkin, McGowan and McKeown (2013, p.720) statement that: "practitioners increasingly recognize that a business opportunity exists in effective SM adoption, to build and maintain issues of trust and commitment with key stakeholders in their network, such as customers, and to enhance and maintain quality in those networked relationships (Harris and Rae 2010)". In fact, our research allows us to transmit to practitioners that:

1. The speed of use of SM allows to firms to build and maintain trust and commitment with key stakeholders in their network, and to enhance and maintain quality in those networked relationships (Harris and Rae 2010).

2. Furthermore, and being focused in the international domain, as Mathews et al. (2012) point out, with a faster use of social media companies will have a greater ability to take advantage of international markets opportunities. Speed of internationalization is related to commitment and knowledge of international markets (Chetty et al. 2014) and the use of SM increase the commitment with customers and the knowledge acquisition of foreign markets. In fact, drawing on the literature on relationship marketing, the importance of commitment has been widely recognized in predicting continued use of organizational IT applications in general and web-based online services in particular (Kim and Son 2009). Likewise, the potential of SM to replicate dimensions of face-to-face interaction in a virtual environment and to accommodate high levels of self-disclosure, as suggested by Kaplan and Haenlein (2010), has the potential to significantly complement personal contact networking activity, a key marketing resource of owner/managers. So, in line with Gamboa and Gonçalves (2014, p. 711), "the more highly networked the organization, the more benefits that can be derived from using Web 2.0 tools".

3. A faster SM adoption allows the reduction in the costs of communicating with foreign customers/suppliers and of gathering information about foreign competitors. The support of distinctive competencies and skills in other business functions can be reasons explaining why the use of SM

by companies oriented towards international markets accelerate their internationalization speed (Pezderka et al. 2012; Zhang et al. 2013).

4. Furthermore, as some authors have identified (Durkin et al.2013; Gamboa and Gonçalves 2014; Calefato, Lanubile and Novielli 2015), the speed of use of social media allows companies to improve customer satisfaction and strengthen client (and other stakeholders) relations, both drivers of loyalty, via dynamic interaction with their fans on SM: "via SM, companies now have at their disposal tools that allow them to communicate with millions of customers simultaneously. This ability allows information to be delivered quickly through feedback and has lasting impact through the establishment of long-term relationships" (Gamboa and Gonçalves 2014, p. 711).

Therefore, our findings demonstrate the effect of quickly adopting SM in the internationalization process of the company: firms increasing the speed of use of SM in their activities will increase their speed of internationalization. Therefore, managers of companies, no matter size, with an interest in foreign markets should allocate more resources to SM integration and should try to take advantage of the SM sites that their target buyers tend to frequent. Considering the adoption literature, LinkedIn, Twitter, or Facebook are a natural choice because of their relative ease of trial and use, perceived advantages, and compatibility to current user needs and systems, which are major factors in organizational adoption of innovations (Jussila et al. 2014). This suggested adoption and integration is especially true for B2C companies and companies that highly rely in foreign markets to survive. Considering the importance of relationship building in foreign markets, SM offer a viable tool for internationalized companies to foster and speed customer–brand relationships up.

Although this study contributes to current literature by exploring and improving the understanding of the integration of SM in the activities of export-oriented companies, it is not free of some limitations that invite continued research. Firstly, the sample allows generalize the results to internationalized firms that have used exports to reach foreign markets. More detailed research should be performed considering other entry modes or ways of becoming an internationalized firm.

Another data limitation is related to its cross-section collection. Although the research has tried to collect information from a dynamic perspective, due to the fact it considers a longitudinal concept as "speed", future research should benefit of working with panel data.

This study also opens several areas for further research because it has identified a positive influence of the speed of implementation of SM in firms with an international orientation, increasing the speed of its internationalization process (because SM increase the direct and constant connection and interchange of information with foreign stakeholders of the company). Some studies have already discussed the potential and the role of Web 2.0 and social networking in future knowledge management systems of companies, for example Hustad and Teigland (2008) focused on multinational firms. The results of their study point out that when incorporated in an organization's routines, SM may enable companies to more fully leverage the knowledge sharing and creation potential of its employees across distributed locations than traditional knowledge management has done in the past. However, since few studies have focused on the role of SM in knowledge management, future research should pay attention to how internationalized companies proceed in their efforts of implementing these media (possible barriers companies could face to implement and use these tools in different operations) and how this may influence their existing knowledge management strategy, practices and organizational aspects.

ACKNOWLEDGMENT

This research was supported by the the Spanish Ministry of Economics and Competitiveness (ECO2013-44027-P).

REFERENCES

Acedo, F. J., & Jones, M. V. (2007). Speed of internationalization and entrepreneurial cognition: Insights and a comparison between international new ventures, exporters and domestic firms. *Journal of World Business*, *42*(3), 236–252. doi:10.1016/j.jwb.2007.04.012

Agnihotri, R., Kothandaraman, P., Kashyap, R., & Singh, R. (2012). Bringing" Social" into Sales: The Impact of Salespeople's Social Media Use on Service Behaviors and Value Creation. *Journal of Personal Selling & Sales Management*, *3*(3), 333–348. doi:10.2753/PSS0885-3134320304

Alegre, J., & Chiva, R. (2013). Linking Entrepreneurial Orientation and Firm Performance: The Role of Organizational Learning Capability and Innovation Performance. *Journal of Small Business Management*, *51*(4), 491–507. doi:10.1111/jsbm.12005

Bagozzi, R. P., & Yi, Y. (1988). On the evaluation of structural equations models. *Journal of the Academy of Marketing Science*, *16*(1), 74–94. doi:10.1007/BF02723327

Bonaccorsi, A. (1992). On the Relationship between Firm Size and Export Intensity. *Journal of International Business Studies*, *23*(4), 605–635. doi:10.1057/palgrave.jibs.8490280

Brouthers, L. E., & Nakos, G. (2005). The Role of Systematic International Market Selection on Small Firms' Export Performance. *Journal of Small Business Management*, *43*(4), 363–381. doi:10.1111/j.1540-627X.2005.00142.x

Calof, J. L. (1994). The Relationship Between Firm Size and Export Behaviour Revisited. *Journal of International Business Studies*, *25*(2), 367–387. doi:10.1057/palgrave.jibs.8490205

Casillas, J. C., & Moreno-Menéndez, A. M. (2014). Speed of the internationalization process: The role of diversity and depth in experiential learning. *Journal of International Business Studies*, *45*(1), 85–101. doi:10.1057/jibs.2013.29

Casillas, S., & Acedo, F. J. (2013). Speed in the Internationalization Process of the Firm. *International Journal of Management Reviews*, *15*(1), 15–29. doi:10.1111/j.1468-2370.2012.00331.x

Cavusgil, S. T., & Zou, S. (1994). Marketing strategy-performance relationship: An investigation of the empirical link in export market ventures. *Journal of Marketing*, *58*(1), 1–21. doi:10.1177/002224299405800101

Chetty, S., Johanson, M., & Martín, O. M. (2014). Speed of internationalization: Conceptualization, measurement and validation. *Journal of World Business*, *49*(4), 633–650. doi:10.1016/j.jwb.2013.12.014

Chin, W. W. (1988). The partial least squares approach to structural equation modeling. In G. A. Marcoulides (Ed.), *Modern Methods for Business Research*. Lawrence Erlbaum.

Chin, W. W. (2000). *Frequently Asked Questions—Partial Least Squares and PLS-Graph*. Available online at http://disc-nt.cba.uh.edu/chin/plsfaq/plsfaq.htm

Chin, W. W., Marcolin, B. L., & Newsted, P. R. (2003). A partial least squares latent variable modeling approach for measuring interaction effects: Results from a Monte Carlo simulation study and an electronic-mail emotion/adoption study. *Information Systems Research, 14*(2), 189–17. doi:10.1287/isre.14.2.189.16018

Constantinides, E., & Fountain, S. (2008). Web 2.0: Conceptual foundations and Marketing Issues. *Journal of Direct. Data and Digital Marketing Practice, 9*(3), 231–244. doi:10.1057/palgrave.dddmp.4350098

Contractor, F. J., Hsu, C. C., & Kundu, S. K. (2005). Explaining export performance: A comparative study of International New Ventures in Indian and Taiwanese Software Industry. *Management International Review, 45*(3), 83–110.

Cronbach, L. J. (1971). Test validation. In R. L. Thorndike (Ed.), *Educational Measurement*. Washington, DC: American Council of Education.

Da Rocha, A., Cotta del Mello, R., Pacheco, H., & de Abreu Farias, I. (2012). The international commitment of late-internationalizing Brazilian entrepreneurial firms. *International Marketing Review, 29*(3), 228–252. doi:10.1108/02651331211229741

Del Aguila-Obra, A. R., & Padilla-Melendez, A. (2006). Organizational factors affecting Internet technology adoption. *Internet Research, 16*(1), 9–110. doi:10.1108/10662240610642569

Durkin, M., McGowan, P., & McKeown, N. (2013). Exploring social media adoption in small to medium-sized enteprirses in Ireland. *Journal of Small Business and Enterprise Development, 20*(4), 716–734. doi:10.1108/JSBED-08-2012-0094

Falk, R. F., & Miller, N. B. (1992). *A Primer for Soft Modeling*. Akron, OH: University of Akron Press.

Fornell, C., & Bookstein, F. L. (1982). Two structural equation models: LISREL and PLS applied to customer exit-voice theory. *JMR, Journal of Marketing Research, 19*(4), 440–452. doi:10.1177/002224378201900406

Fornell, C., & Larcker, D. F. (1981). Evaluating structural equations models with unobservable variables and measurement error. *JMR, Journal of Marketing Research, 18*(1), 39–50. doi:10.1177/002224378101800104

Gamboa, A. M., & Gonçalves, H. M. (2014). Customer loyalty through social networks: Lessons from Zara on Facebook. *Business Horizons, 57*(6), 709–717. doi:10.1016/j.bushor.2014.07.003

García-García, R., García-Canal, E., & Guillén, M. F. (2017). Rapid internationalization and long-term performance: The knowledge link. *Journal of World Business, 52*(1), 97–110. doi:10.1016/j.jwb.2016.09.005

Geisser, S. (1975). The predictive sample reuse method with applications. *Journal of the American Statistical Association, 70*(350), 320–328. doi:10.1080/01621459.1975.10479865

Giamanco, B., & Gregoire, K. (2012). Tweet me, friend me, make me buy. *Harvard Business Review*, (July-August): 88–93.

Goode, S. & Stevens, K. (2000). An analysis of the business characteristics of adopters and non-adopters of World Wide Web Technology. *Information Technology and Management*, (1:1-2), 129–154.

Grandinetti, R., & Mason, M. C. (2012). Internationalization modes other than exporting. *European Business Review*, *24*(3), 236–254. doi:10.1108/09555341211222495

Hair, J. F., Black, W. C., Babin, B. J., Anderson, R. E., & Tatham, R. L. (2006). *Multivariate data analysis*. Upper Saddle River, NJ: Prentice-Hall.

Hair, J. F., Sarstedt, M., Pieper, T. M., & Ringle, C. M. (2012). The use of partial least squares structural equation modeling in strategic management research: A review of past practices and recommendations for future applications. *Long Range Planning*, *45*(5), 320–340. doi:10.1016/j.lrp.2012.09.008

Harris, L., & Rae, A. (2010). The online connection: Transforming marketing strategy for small businesses. *The Journal of Business Strategy*, *31*(2), 4–12. doi:10.1108/02756661011025017

Henseler, J., Ringle, C. M., & Sinkovics, R. R. (2009). The use of partial least squares path modeling in international marketing. In New Challenges to International Marketing. Emerald Group Publishing Limited.

Henseler, J., Wilson, B., Götz, O., & Hautvast, C. (2007). Investigating the moderating role of fit on sports sponsoring and brand equity: A structural model. *International Journal of Sports Marketing & Sponsorship*, *8*(4), 321–329. doi:10.1108/IJSMS-08-04-2007-B005

Hilmersson, M., & Johanson, M. (2016). Speed of SME internationalization and performance. *Management International Review*, *56*(1), 67–94. doi:10.100711575-015-0257-4

Hoejmose, S., Brammer, S., & Millington, A. (2012). Green supply chain management: The role of trust and top management in B2B and B2C markets. *Industrial Marketing Management*, *41*(4), 609–620. doi:10.1016/j.indmarman.2012.04.008

Hustad, E., & Teigland, R. (2008). Implementing social networking media and web 2.0 in multinationals: Implications for knowledge management. *Proceedings of the European Conference on Knowledge Management*, 323–332.

Hutzschenreuter, T., Kleindienst, I., Guenther, C., & Hammes, M. (2016). Speed of Internationalization of New Business Units: The Impact of Direct and Indirect Learning. *Management International Review*, *56*(6), 849–878. doi:10.100711575-016-0305-8

Ibeh, K. & Kasem, L. (2011). The network perspective and the internationalization of small and medium sized software firms from Syria. *Industrial Marketing Management*, *40*(3), 358-367.

Ifinedo, P. (2011). Internet/e-business technologies acceptance in Canada's SMEs: An exploratory investigation. *Internet Research*, *21*(3), 255–281. doi:10.1108/10662241111139309

Jarvis, C. B., MacKenzie, S. B., & Podsakoff, P. M. (2003). A Critical Review of Construct Indicators and Measurement Model Misspecification in Marketing and Consumer Research. *The Journal of Consumer Research*, *30*(2), 199–218. doi:10.1086/376806

Johanson, J., & Vahlne, J. E. (1977). The internationalization process of the firm: A model of knowledge development and increasing foreign market commitments. *Journal of International Business Studies*, *8*(1), 25–34. doi:10.1057/palgrave.jibs.8490676

Jones, M. V., Coviello, N., & Tang, K. T. (2011). International entrepreneurship research (1989–2009): A domain ontology and thematic analysis. *Journal of Business Venturing, 26*(6), 632–659. doi:10.1016/j. jbusvent.2011.04.001

Jussila, J. J., Kärkkainen, H., & Aramo-Immonen, H. (2014). Social media utilization in business-to-business relationships of technology industry firms. *Computers in Human Behavior, 30,* 606–613. doi:10.1016/j.chb.2013.07.047

Kananukul, C., Jung, S., & Watchravesringkan, K. (2015). Building customer equity through trust in social networking sites A perspective from Thai consumers. *Journal of Research in Interactive Marketing, 9*(2), 148–166. doi:10.1108/JRIM-03-2014-0019

Kaplan, A. M., & Haenlein, M. (2010). Users of the world, unite! The challenges and opportunities of social media. *Business Horizons, 53*(1), 59–68. doi:10.1016/j.bushor.2009.09.003

Keil, M., Tan, B. C., Wei, K. K., Saarinen, T., Tuunainen, V., & Wassenaar, A. (2000). A cross-cultural study on escalation of commitment behavior in software projects. *Management Information Systems Quarterly, 24*(2), 299–325. doi:10.2307/3250940

Kietzman, J. H., Hermkens, K., McCarthy, I. P., & Silvestre, B. S. (2011). Social media? Get serious! Understanding the functional building blocks of social media. *Business Horizons, 54*(3), 241–251. doi:10.1016/j.bushor.2011.01.005

Kim, S. S., & Son, J.-Y. (2009). Out of Dedication or Constraint? A Dual Model of Post-Adoption Phenomena and Its Empirical Test in the Context of Online Services. *Management Information Systems Quarterly, 33*(1), 49–70. doi:10.2307/20650278

Kumar, V., & Mirchandani, R. (2012). Increasing the ROI of Social Media Marketing. *MIT Sloan Management Review, 54*(1), 55–61.

Lado, N., Martínez-Ros, E., & Valenzuela, A. (2004). Identifying successful marketing strategies by export regional destination. *International Marketing Review, 21*(6), 573–597. doi:10.1108/02651330410568024

Levenburg, N., Magal, S. R., & Koslage, P. (2006). An exploratory investigation of organizational factors and e-Business motivations among SMFOEs in the US. *Electronic Markets, 16*(1), 70–84. doi:10.1080/10196780500491402

Lew, Y. K., & Sinkovics, R. R. (2013). Crossing borders and industry sectors: Behavioral governance in strategic alliances and product innovation for competitive advantage. *Long Range Planning, 46*(1–2), 13–38. doi:10.1016/j.lrp.2012.09.006

Li, L., Qian, G., & Qian, Z. (2015). Speed of internationalization: Mutual effects of individual- and company-level antecedents. *Global Strategy Journal, 5*(4), 303–320. doi:10.1002/gsj.1103

Lorenzo-Romero, C., Constantinides, E., & Alarcón-Del-Amo, M.-D.-C. (2013). Social media as marketing strategy: An explorative study on adoption and use by retailers. In C. Lorenzo-Romero, E. Constantinides, & M.-D.-C. Alarcón-Del-Amo (Eds.), Social media in strategic management. Advanced series in management (pp. 197–215). Emerald.

Luo, Y., Zhao, J. H., & Du, J. (2005). The internationalization speed of e- commerce companies: An empirical analysis. *International Marketing Review*, *22*(6), 693–709. doi:10.1108/02651330510630294

Majocchi, A., Bacchiocchi, E., & Mayrhofer, U. (2005). Firm size, business experience and export intensity in SMEs: A longitudinal approach to complex relationships. *International Business Review*, *14*(6), 719–738. doi:10.1016/j.ibusrev.2005.07.004

Mathews, S., Healy, M., & Wickramasekera, R. (2012). The Internetalisation of information, knowledge, and interaction components of the firm's internationalisation process. *Journal of Marketing Management*, *28*(5-6), 733–754. doi:10.1080/0267257X.2011.560887

Mathieson, K., Peacock, E., & Chin, W. W. (2001). Extending the technology acceptance model: The influence of perceived user resources. *The Data Base for Advances in Information Systems*, *32*(3), 86–112. doi:10.1145/506724.506730

Menon, A., Bharadwaj, S. G., & Howell, R. (1996). The quality and effectiveness of marketing strategy: Effects of functional and dysfunctional conflict in intraorganizational relationships. *Journal of the Academy of Marketing Science*, *24*(4), 299–313. doi:10.1177/0092070396244002

Michaelidou, N., Siamagka, N. T., & Christodoulides, G. (2011). Usage, barriers and measurement of social media marketing: An exploratory investigation of small and medium B2B brands. *Industrial Marketing Management*, *40*(7), 1153–1159. doi:10.1016/j.indmarman.2011.09.009

Moen, O. (1999). The relationship between firm size, competitive advantages and export performance revisited. *International Small Business Journal*, *18*(1), 53–72. doi:10.1177/0266242699181003

Mohr, A., & Batsakis, G. (2014). Intangible assets, international experience and the internationalisation speed of retailers. *International Marketing Review*, *31*(6), 601–620. doi:10.1108/IMR-09-2013-0186

Mohr, A., & Batsakis, G. (2014). Intangible assets, international experience and the internationalisation speed of retailers. *International Marketing Review*, *31*(6), 601–620. doi:10.1108/IMR-09-2013-0186

Mohr, A., & Batsakis, G. (2017). Internationalization Speed and Firm Performance: A Study of the Market-Seeking Expansion of Retail MNEs. *Management International Review*, *57*(2), 153–177. doi:10.100711575-016-0284-9

Morgan, N. A., Kaleka, A., & Katsikeas, C. S. (2004). Antecedents of Export Venture Performance: A Theoretical Model and Empirical Assessment. *Journal of Marketing*, *68*(1), 90–108. doi:10.1509/jmkg.68.1.90.24028

Morgan-Thomas, A., & Jones, M. V. (2009). Post-entry dynamics: Differences between SMEs in the development speed of their international sales. *International Small Business Journal*, *27*(1), 71–97. doi:10.1177/0266242608098347

Musteen, M., Francis, J., & Datta, D. K. (2010). The influence of international networks on internationalization speed and performance: A study of Czech SMEs. *Journal of World Business*, *45*(3), 197–205. doi:10.1016/j.jwb.2009.12.003

Navarro-García, A., Arenas-Gaitán, J., & Rondán-Cataluña, F. J. (2014). External environment and the moderating role of export market orientation. *Journal of Business Research, 67*(5), 740–745. doi:10.1016/j.jbusres.2013.11.037

Nazar, M. S., & Saleem, H. M. N. (2009). Firm-Level Determinants of Export Performance. *International Business & Economics Research Journal, 8*(2), 105–112.

Nurosis, M. J. (1993). *SPSS. Statistical data analysis.* SPSS Inc.

O'Reilly, T., & Musser, J. (2007). *Web 2.0 principles and best practices.* O'Reilly Media, Inc.

OECD. (2018). *Enterprises by business size (indicator).* OECD. doi:10.1787/31d5eeaf-en

Ojala, A. (2009). Internationalization of knowledge-intensive SMEs: The role of network relationships in the entry to a psychically distant market. *International Business Review, 18*(1), 50–59. doi:10.1016/j.ibusrev.2008.10.002

Okazaki, S., & Taylor, C. R. (2013). Social media and international advertising: Theoretical challenges and future directions. *International Marketing Review, 30*(1), 56–71. doi:10.1108/02651331311298573

Perrigot, R., Kacker, M., Basset, G., & Cliquet, G. (2012). Antecedents of Early Adoption and Use of Social Media Networks for Stakeholder Communications: Evidence from Franchising. *Journal of Small Business Management, 50*(4), 539–565. doi:10.1111/j.1540-627X.2012.00366.x

Pezderka, N., Sinkovics, R. R., & Jean, R. J. B. (2012). Do born global SMEs reap more benefits from ICT use than other internationalizing small firms? In M. Gabrielsson & V. H. Manek Kirpalani (Eds.), *Handbook of research on born globals* (pp. 185–213). Cheltenham, UK: Edward Elgar. doi:10.4337/9780857938046.00021

Phan, M., Thomas, R., & Heine, K. (2011). Social Media and Luxury Brand Management: The Case of Burberry. *Journal of Global Fashion Marketing, 2*(4), 213–222. doi:10.1080/20932685.2011.10593099

Pla-Barber, J., & Alegre, J. (2007). Analysing the link between export intensity, innovation and firm size in a science-based industry. *International Business Review, 16*(3), 275–293. doi:10.1016/j.ibusrev.2007.02.005

Podsakoff, P. M., MacKenzie, S. B., Lee, J. Y., & Podsakoff, N. P. (2003). Common Method Biases in Behavioural Research: A Critical Review of the Literature and Recommended Remedies. *The Journal of Applied Psychology, 88*(5), 879–903. doi:10.1037/0021-9010.88.5.879 PMID:14516251

Prasad, V. K., Ramamurthy, K., & Naidu, G. M. (2001). The influence of Internet-Marketing Integration on Marketing Competencies and Export Performance. *Journal of International Marketing, 9*(4), 82–110. doi:10.1509/jimk.9.4.82.19944

Rapp, A., Beitelspacher, L. S., Grewal, D., & Hughes, D. E. (2013). Understanding social media effects across seller, retailer, and consumer interactions. *Journal of the Academy of Marketing Science, 41*(5), 547–566. doi:10.100711747-013-0326-9

Rialp, A., Rialp, J., & Knight, G. A. (2005). The phenomenon of early internationalizing firms: What do we know after a decade (1993–2003) of scientific inquiry? *International Business Review*, *14*(2), 147–166. doi:10.1016/j.ibusrev.2004.04.006

Ringle, C. M., Wende, S., & Will, A. (2005). *SmartPLS (beta)*. Hamburg, Germany: University of Hamburg.

Saarenketo, S. K., Puumalainen, K., Kylaheiko, K., & Kuivalainen, O. (2008). Linking knowledge and internationalization in small and medium-sized enterprises in the ICT sector. *Technovation*, *28*(9), 591–601. doi:10.1016/j.technovation.2007.12.003

Swani, K., Brow, B. P., & Milne, G. R. (2014). Should tweets differ for B2B and B2C? An analysis of Fortune 500 companies' Twitter communications. *Industrial Marketing Management*, *43*(5), 873–881. doi:10.1016/j.indmarman.2014.04.012

Taylor, D. G., Lewin, J. E., & Strutton, D. (2011). Friends, fans, and followers: Do ads work on social networks? How gender and age shape receptivity. *Journal of Advertising Research*, *51*(1), 258–275. doi:10.2501/JAR-51-1-258-275

Teo, T. S. H. (2007). Organizational characteristics, modes of Internet adoption and their impact: A Singapore Perspective. *Journal of Global Information Management*, *15*(2), 91–117. doi:10.4018/jgim.2007040104

Terblanche, N. S., & Boshoff, C. (2008). Improved scale development in marketing: An empirical illustration. *International Journal of Market Research*, *50*(1), 105–119. doi:10.1177/147078530805000108

Verwaal, E., & Donkers, B. (2002). Firm Size and Export Intensity: Solving an Empirical Puzzle. *Journal of International Business Studies*, *33*(3), 603–613. doi:10.1057/palgrave.jibs.8491035

Wetzels, M., Oderkerken-Schröder, G., & van Oppen, C. (2009). Using PLS path modeling for assessing hierarchical construct models: Guidelines and empirical illustration. *Management Information Systems Quarterly*, *33*(1), 177–195. doi:10.2307/20650284

Wiersema, F. (2013). The B2B agenda: The current state of B2B marketing and a look ahead. *Industrial Marketing Management*, *42*(4), 470–488. doi:10.1016/j.indmarman.2013.02.015

Williams, D. A. (2011). Impact of firm size and age on the export behaviour of small locally owned firms: Fresh insights. *Journal of International Entrepreneurship*, *9*(2), 152–174. doi:10.100710843-011-0073-2

Zhang, M., Sarker, S., & Sarker, S. (2013). Drivers and export performance impacts of IT capability in 'born-global' firms: A cross-national study. *Information Systems Journal*, *23*(5), 419–443. doi:10.1111/j.1365-2575.2012.00404.x

ENDNOTE

[1]   Admitting that the studied relation could be reversed (the speed of internationalization could impact on the speed of use of social media), we replicated all the analysis changing the direction of the relationship among both constructs. The relationship was not significant (the coefficient was 0.023, with a significance level = 0.628 (t value = 0.485), what supports the direction of the relationship suggested in the current research.

This research was previously published in the Journal of Global Information Management (JGIM), 28(1); pages 142-166, copyright year 2020 by IGI Publishing (an imprint of IGI Global).

Chapter 47
Can Firm Performance and Corporate Reputation Be Improved by Communicating CSR in Social Media?
A Pilot Study Analysis

Julian Schröter
FOM University, Germany

Andreas Dutzi
https://orcid.org/0000-0003-3903-4470
University of Siegen, Germany

Eshari Withanage
University of Siegen, Germany

ABSTRACT

As stakeholders make their decisions based on corporate reputation, it is vital for the companies to ensure that their CSR activities are communicated effectively via social media (SM) channels. It can be argued that by leveraging CSR in SM channels, firms have the possibility in strengthening trust and loyalty of their stakeholders and thereby enhancing corporate reputation and firm performances. Hence, the study aims to examine how CSR communication has an impact on firm performances and reputation. Top 50 and bottom 50 companies that are ranked in the Social Media Sustainability Index (2016) are collected along with four reputation ranking indices and Twitter data for this study. Although there is no significant relationship between Twitter and corporate reputation, there is a significant relationship between Twitter and firm performances.

DOI: 10.4018/978-1-6684-6287-4.ch047

INTRODUCTION

Most firms use social media to advertise their products and services (Kietzman et al. 2011). One-way communication from firms towards consumers is fading (Trainor 2012). The power of firms has shifted from firms towards consumers (Bunting and Lipski 2000). The financial crisis has led firms adopting more cost-effective promotional channels like social media (Kirtis and Karahan 2011). However, there are firms which disregard the use of social media channels (Kietzman et al. 2011).

At the beginning of 2015, social media users have exceeded 2 billion (Kemp 2015). This increase is since firms and individuals are using social media either to discover new followers or to discover parties who accompaniment them (Cheliotis 2009). Between 2015 and 2018, the number of firms that use social media to interact with their consumers will be more than triple (The China Post 2012). Emergence of various social media channels have enabled to generate communication in a more cost effective and efficient way to both internal as well as external stakeholders (Jones et al. 2009). This dissemination of information leads to create impact on the image due to the active engagement of the users in the environment (Jones et al. 2009).

By maintaining a favourable status in the competitive market, firms can access critical resources (Podolny 1993). It can even be targeted for a joint venture (Dollinger et al. 1997). Corporate reputation is an intangible asset, which assess the overall firm's current assets, their position and expected future performances (Teece et al. 1997). Hence, corporate reputation is the driving force for firms to generate competitive edge over their competitors, as it will be difficult for another firm to just match the esteem that they have generated through reputation (Fombrun and Shanley 1990). Further studies have identified that corporate reputation is a strategic asset and a superior performer, which sustains in long term (Roberts and Dowling 1997).

Electronic word of mouth has the potential in developing threats towards corporate reputation (Aula 2010). In contrast, social media has a strong influence in creating firm's future equity value (Luo et al. 2013). Due to the rapid growth of social media, it has become vital for firms to understand not only how to effectively utilise these channels to endure corporate reputation but also how it can be derived to enhance better firm performance.

This study analyses the relationship between twitter communication concerning CSR, corporate responsibility, and firm performance. Top 50 firms and bottom 50 firms are selected from the Social Media Sustainability Index (2016) along with the reputation indices and twitter data (number of tweets, followers, and likes) are collected to find out if social media affects corporate reputation and firm performance.

LITERATURE REVIEW

Corporate Social Responsibility

In the early 1950s, firms considered CSR as an obligation towards the society (Balmer et al. 2007). With the introduction of the CSR pyramid by Carroll (1979), firms have a responsibility towards the society, which encompasses economic, legal, ethical, and philanthropic expectations of the society. It is a concept, where firms assimilate both environmental, as well as social concerns of the business processes and with their stakeholders (European Commission 2011). It engages in the societal philanthropy, environmental friendliness, being ethical, and business practices regarding concerns of sustainability, product safety, poverty, eliminating pollution, maintaining human rights, and growth of the economy (Rindova et al. 2005). CSR is an umbrella term, which classifies sustainability development, corporate citizenship, corporate philanthropy, and compliance (Verboven 2011). CSR integrates responsible business practices and policies into its business model to enhance the well-being of the society while maintaining profits (Hopkins 2007). Firms have social and environmental responsibility, influenced by business activities (Lantos 2011). Since firms are not legally bound to conduct social activities, they have the option of defining CSR and to include it in their business practices (Matten and Moon 2008).

Being ethical and conducting philanthropic practices are the main areas in which firms engage in CSR activities. Ethical responsibility can be achieved by minimising the harms that are made to the society by the business practices (Lantos 2001). Philanthropic CSR elaborates on the support for an activity that is provided by firms to enhance the society well-being (Carroll 1999). There are two motivations for firms to conduct philanthropic activities: intrinsic (altruistic) or extrinsic (strategic) motivations (Lantos 2001; Du et al. 2010). Altruistic institutional values and the environment are intrinsic motivations (Matten and Moon 2008). Strategic motives include generating profits (Lantos 2001). Irrespective of the motives of a company, CSR has become vital when measuring firm reputation and public image (Ellen et al. 2006).

When firms conduct CSR activities, they enhance stakeholder perception towards their image. Building image is vital for firms to create competitive advantage for their business (Barone et al. 2007). There is a trend in monitoring CSR due to the concern that the stakeholders have towards responsible business practices (Morsing and Schultz 2006). Stakeholders have high expectations for the values and the way how firms are operated (Carroll 1999). Firms can strive for public support which enhances their image and reputation by engaging in CSR activities (Barone et al. 2007). Stakeholder's demand is becoming an important aspect when dealing with social and environmental activities (Carroll 2007). It is a risk for the firms to link sustainability issues as it will tend to create criticisms (Fieseler et al. 2010). The firm must consider the importance of reporting and sharing honest information to ensure developing a good corporate reputation (Gill et al. 2008). The focus of a firm should be to generate revenue for their shareholders (Balmer et al. 2007). If firms fail to meet expectations regarding environmental responsibility, they can be criticised by the public, which in turn create negative publicity within the market. Hence, it is a challenging task for firms to balance between economic performance and ethics (Watson 1994).

Social capital can be built when firms communicate about CSR activities with their stakeholders (Etter and Fieseler 2010). Firms must build trust by being honest and transparent when communicating their CSR activities (Etter and Fieseler 2010). If firms compromise the quality of the goods that they produce to be socially sustainably or if it is perceived that the CSR activities will not lead to enhance corporate ability, then the stakeholder assessment of the CSR activities will not be positive (Bhattacharya and Sen 2004). The possibility in building resemblance between stakeholder's expectation and CSR agenda depends on communication with different stakeholders and obtaining their support (Dawkins 2004).

Corporate Reputation

Corporate reputation varies from one stakeholder to another. The perception of consumers will be varied to the perception of the suppliers (Honey 2009). In consumer perspective, corporate reputation is how consumers react to a firm's goods and services as well as to communication and interaction with firms (Walsh and Beatty 2007). Corporate reputation is formed by the beliefs and receptions of the consumers (Bunting and Lipski 2000). Although perceptions cannot always be compatible with reality, consumer perceptions are their own reality (Rayner 2003). The fields of marketing, economics, sociology, and management draws their attention towards the concept of corporate reputation (Brown et al. 2006). Corporate reputation can be seen in an economic perspective where it drives insider and outsider expectations for firm's attributions (Weigelt and Camerer 1998), or it can be a global impression which reflects perceptions of all stakeholders (Deephouse 2000; Fombrun and Shanley 1990). Considering the institutional view, corporate reputation can be depicted as the overall evaluation of the firm, considering whether it is good or bad (Weiss et al. 1999). It depends on the observer's perception as well as interpretation (Clark and Montgomery 1998). Studies have defined corporate reputation as a resource, which changes over time, contain relative stability, mirrors cumulative investments and remains distant to other organizational behavioural constructs (Ching et al. 1992; Fombrun and Shanley 1990).

Corporate reputation is an act of firm's past performances and not a function of market position (Shrum and Wuthnow 1988). According to Vergin and Qoronfleh (1998), Corporate reputation reflects daily behaviour of firms and each firm's decision affects their reputation. According to Yoon et al. (1993), the response of the purchaser is consistent with the attitude towards the reputation of the vendor. This reputational capital is the preliminary component of the social capital that sets the consistency, integrity, obligation, and honesty (Petrick et al. 1999). It is the accumulation of all stakeholder's perception of how firms meet demand and expectation of the stakeholder (Wartick 1992). Corporate reputation can enhance firm performance (Roberts and Dowling 2002; Eberl and Schwaiger 2005). Similarly, firms can generate several benefits through a favourable reputation, such as the ability to charge a premium price from consumers, be a threat to the rivalries, attract high investments, reduce employee turnover, and invest in R&D and new product developments (Carmeli and Tishler 2005; Fombrun and Shanley 1990). With this pricing strategy, financial analysts can rate firms higher which increases demand for the firm's shares, which in turn will boost their market value (Carmeli and Tishler 2005).

Corporate reputation has the potential of developing a competitive edge for firms. It is a firm's intangible and a most valued asset (Eberl and Schwaiger 2005). Once the reputation is damaged, it is not possible to redevelop (Firestein 2006). This has the potential to influence investment decisions (Walsh and Beatty 2007). Corporate reputation has a positive impact on employee commitments as well as job satisfaction (Alniacik et al. 2011). When firms have a good reputation, it allows them to hire the best employees and to retain the existing employees (Helm 2011). Corporate reputation can strengthen consumer loyalty and enhances consumer relationships (Andreassen and Lindestad 1998). This increases consumer purchases and retain consumers (Keh and Xie 2009). A good reputation is derived from good management and the decisions that are taking strategically for the success of the business operations (Honey 2009). However, favourable reputation does not guarantee the strength of the brand, although bad reputation can damage the brand (Page and Fearn 2005). Having a good reputation and doing mistakes creates contradictions (Rhee and Haunschile 2006).

Negative reputation decreases competitive edge in the market, damages brand value and the relationship between firms and their stakeholders (Rayner 2003). A loss of reputation might also affect the entire industry (Aula 2010). The firm's responses via social media and manipulation of information affect their reputation (Aula 2010). The commitment and active participation of everyone in the firm is vital to safeguard and maintain corporate reputation (Rayner 2003).

Social Media

Web 1.0 is more about commerce where Web 2.0 is more about people (Barsky and Purdon 2006). Social media is considered as Web 2.0 (Kaplan and Haenlein 2010) as it is the platform that allows development and conception of social media. Value creation and the power moved from firms towards consumers (Berthon et al. 2012). Social media is a method of linking and interrelating with users, being individuals or firms, via various online communication channels (Kirtis and Karahan 2011). Conventional media deviates with social media through two-way communication while building relationships among users (Drury 2008). Social media has numerous ways of communication channels, networking platforms (Kietzman et al. 2011).

Social media distributes information through social interactions and membership of the public (Abrahams et al. 2012). It intimates community engagement and social viral activity due to its accessibility and scalability (Li and Shiu 2012). The mechanisms of social media can be either online or word of mouth forums, like, discussion boards, blogs, chat rooms, email, social networking sites, such as Facebook, Twitter, Instagram, Printerest and YouTube (Mangold and Faulds 2009). Empirical studies proved multiple benefits that social media provides towards stakeholders, namely location-based recommendations (Zhao and Lu 2012), assessments of users, and internal information among managers to involve in shared clarifications (Hoehle et al. 2012), ability to advertise on new products and services, engage in branding, and boost consumer services (Park et al. 2010). Firms can also acquire information on individuals and their preferences, social interactions, and social influences (Li and Shiu 2012). Social media can circulate information in real time (Mangold and Faulds 2009). 92% of the marketers have specified that social media is vital for their business (Stelzner 2015).

Social media influence decisions as well as the attitudes of the consumers (Gruen et al. 2006). Conventional media channels allow individuals to communicate face to face, whereas social media allows individuals to communicate electronically (Abrantes et al. 2013). Social medial channels can affect firm's activities and influences customer's purchasing decisions (Gruen et al. 2006). Social media has become the operative and cost-efficient technique for firms to communicate with their consumers (Kaplan and Haenlein 2010). Hence, social media is a vital tool for management of the consumer relationship (Trainor 2012). These social-driven consumers are the centre of the commercial ecosystem (Greenberg 2010). The conventional customer relationship is not replaced with the use of social media. It is extending the relationship by using technological channels which enhance firms to be more consumer-centric (Trainor 2012).

Consumers want to communicate firm's activities rather than simply retrieving shared information (Trainor 2012). It has become a challenge for firms to control the information, which circulates within different social media channels (Kaplan and Haenlein 2010). Social media is more than a traditional marketing communication channel which is controlled by the consumers (Hoffman and Fodor 2010).

Marketing strategies should contain both traditional as well as social media to ensure successful marketing campaigns (Hanna et al. 2011). Social media should be considered as part of the promotional mix strategy (Mangold and Faulds 2009). Irrespective of the firm size, firms can engage in social media activities due to low investments (Kaplan and Haenlein 2010). Hence, social media enables even small businesses to compete with large firms and new entrants at low risk (Kaplan and Haenlein 2010). The social media channel should be chosen in which the firm can respond to consumer comments (Peters et al. 2013). If firms do not have much time to spend in social media channels, they should choose the channel which has the widest customer-spread. (Kaplan and Haenlein 2010).

Twitter has been considered for this study since it is the leading social medial channel that firms use to communicate their sustainability activities (Social Media Sustainability Index 2016). It allows the users to connect, view, and engage with various news, ideas, or the newest stories of firms, and personal characters of their interest (Twitter 2015). 58 million tweets are shared within a day among the 290 million active twitter registered users (Satistics Brain 2015). Twitter has become the top 10 most visited website (Satistics Brain 2015). CSR information can be spread to the interested user (follower), so twitter has become the most pervasive social media channel (Etter 2013). Two-way communication increases the usage of twitter between stakeholders (Burton and Soboleva 2011). Firms can provide response and feedback to the stakeholder's concerns. This commitment can generate favourable outcomes (Coyle et al. 2012).

CSR Communication In Social Media

Online communication affects the traditional concept of CSR and the relationship between firms and public (Rolland and Bazzoni 2009). To achieve a positive relationship with their stakeholders, firms need to communicate their CSR activities fruitfully in a two-way symmetric communication manner (Morsing and Schultz 2006). According to Morsing and Schultz (2006), there are three categories of stakeholder relations about how firms engage in communicating their CSR activities with their stakeholders. It is vital to develop communication between firms and stakeholders (Taylor et al. 2001). Since the corporate website is more static, it is not useful to interact with stakeholders (Fieseler et al. 2010). Social media channels enable stakeholders to engage with firms (Dellarocas 2003). Furthermore, social media enables access to stakeholders, who were unable to reach within the same intensity as before resulting in a more sophisticated and personalized dialogue (Etter and Fieseler 2010). A traditional corporate website has broader and sensitive users (Coupland 2005) instead.

Knowledgeable users scrutinize firm's comments on social media, especially with respect to CSR activities (Etter and Fieseler 2010). Stakeholders also expect firms to be active than being reactive when communicating via social media since reactive communication is 'greenwashing' (Etter and Fieseler 2010). Stakeholders are no longer passive users but engage in initiating and evaluating the contents of information (Dellarocas 2003). Hence, firms need to understand how to communicate their CSR activities to their stakeholders (Dawkins 2004). The stakeholder scepticism to go viral in online communication channels have made firms to use traditional mass media channels when presenting corporate information (Insch 2008). However, with the emergence of Web 2.0 it allowed firms to create a combination of both CSR agenda and shared social values (Kent and Taylor 1998). Social media improves conversation between firms and its stakeholders (Andriof and Waddock 2002). Stakeholder empowerment and new informational society have closely entailed the attractiveness of the relational approach (Castells 1997). This has directed towards the development of the public sphere. Collaborative communication affects others instead of creating a common view and firms are interested in selecting subjects that can be discussed and avoid evaluating any controversial issues (Coupland 2005; Schultz et al. 2011).

Online communication enables firms to develop a steady relationship with their stakeholders (Wright 1998). Two-way communication with limitless number of users is possible (Kent and Taylor 1998). Since social media has no rigid regulations or formal orders, it allows stakeholders to communicate with firms in a more open way (Fieseler et al. 2010). To address this risk, firms need to communicate to their stakeholders by well-trained and authorised spokes personnel. Facebook connects in a two-way relationship with parties who are already known to each other, Twitter on the other hand connects with both the known and unknown parties (Ravikant and Rifkin 2010). Twitter allows the users to address a message to a specific user or to reply to someone's tweets, which can be seen by everyone (Boyd et al. 2010).

Social Media and Corporate Reputation

Whenever the firm communicates about their CSR activities or products and services via various marketing channels, their reputation depends on the reactions of the stakeholders (Bunting and Lipski 2000). However, it is essential to get stakeholders engaging in communications (Jones et al. 2009). With the shift of power towards stakeholders, it has become difficult for firms to influence their reputation (Aula 2010). Some studies analyse the relationship between a firm's reputation and other various variables as consumer loyalty (Keh 2009), firm performance (Eber and Schwaiger 2005; Carmeli and Tishler 2005), and employee job satisfaction (Alniacik et al. 2011; Helm 2011). With the developed consumer frameworks, firms have the possibility in identifying the types of consumers who will interact with them via social media (Hoffman and Fodor 2010). Consumers prefer to integrate with the firm's activities which increases customer satisfaction (Trainor 2012). This consumer satisfaction increases corporate reputation (Carmeli and Tishler 2005). Consumers are no longer passive, so a new set of proficient consumers is created who actively participates in social media activities (Jones et al. 2009). Additionally, firms can influence social media as they develop a healthy reputation among users (Li et al. 2013). Firms can monitor how their products are being discussed among users and thereby companies can help developing trends and recognise potential problems (Li et al 2013). The firm's follower can intensify the messages and then retweet. Through social media communication, firms can change a negative to a positive impact (Li et al. 2013). Hence, any successful firm should make the full use of social media to enhance firm reputation (Li et al. 2013).

The public can now start a discussion about brands (Dijkmans et al. 2015). The firm can identify and address the consumer's attitude (Dijkmans et al. 2015). The content of the firm should be relevant, attractive, and useful. This will encourage the respective consumer to develop and engage in continuous communication (Dijkmans et al. 2015). Positive communication via social media can generates positive reputation (Meijer and Kleinnijenhuis 2006; Dijkmans et al. 2015). Firms need to boost their corporate reputation in the competitive business environment and thereby achieve the business objective (Fombrun and Shanley 1990). Hence, firms can enhance corporate reputation by actively communicating business activities to the users. A positive communication might increase a higher corporate reputation (Dijkmans et al. 2015).

Accordingly, the following hypotheses can be generated:

$H1_0$: There is no relationship between number of tweets, followers, likes and corporate reputation.
$H1_a$: There is a relationship between number of tweets, followers, likes and corporate reputation.

Social Media and Firm Performance

Stakeholders can obtain information, which is vital in making respective decisions and cannot be revealed via conventional media (Gao and Hitt 2012). There is no movement in prices without new information (Healy and Palepu 2001). Quality announcements for new products are used by inventors even prior to the emergence of social media (Chen et al 2011). Nowadays investors retrieve information via social media to evaluate firm's prospects (Gu et al. 2012). Investors, as well as consumers, are affected by comments on social media (Chen et al. 2011). Moreover, consumer's purchasing decision can be influenced via social media communications. This reaction will tend to increase the satisfaction of the stakeholders.

Stakeholder satisfaction can lead to enhance firm equity value (Luo et al. 2010), where firms can generate higher returns at a lower cost (Fornell et al. 2006).

Accordingly, these intangible assets (Matolcsy and Wyatt 2008) can influence firm's stock market valuation. Firms who heavily engage in social media should possess on IT intangible assets and solid prospects for future equity value of the firm in comparison to the firms who engage less in social media (Wyatt 2005). Social media can influence firm's future equity value (Luo et al. 2013). Due to the ability of real time communication, social media can create a negative image more rapidly than other communication channels (Luo et al. 2013). Although social media is an indicator for a firm's equity value, it is unable to treat the investments made for social media as a new cost. Hence, social media has a stronger predictive value than any other traditional online consumer behaviour metrics (Luo et al. 2013).

In comparison to traditional media channels, social media has the possibility in creating a stronger impact on the stock performances (Yu et al. 2013). The novelty and real-time characteristic of information, opposed to e.g., quarterly, or monthly reports, enables measuring a firm's performances by social media (Luo et al. 2013). Social media and financial performance are connected (Schniederjans et al. 2013). If firms are aware of the financial value, then they will consider in investing in social media (Luo et al. 2013). The value of the firm is also the influential effect that they create among other stakeholders using social media (Fisher 2009). Hence, social media communication can increase brand image, provide awareness about new products or sustainability activities (Hoffman and Fodor 2010).

The financial value of social media must be understood (Gilfoil and Jobs 2012). Irrespective of the expansion of social media, most firms still allocate only a negligible portion of their budgets on social media activities. One such reason for this can be due to the difficulty in measuring social media investments (Gilfoil and Jobs 2012). The value of consumers does not purely depend on the disbursements that they made but also on the opinions of other consumers influencing the firm's value (Fisher 2009).

Accordingly, the following hypotheses can be generated:

$H2_0$: There is no relationship between number of tweets, followers, likes and firm performance.
$H2_a$: There is a relationship between number of tweets, followers, likes and firm performance.

CSR Communication and Legitimacy Theory

Empirical studies can be found to justify the motives of the firms to engage in publishing social and environmental reports (Deegan 2002; Deegan and Rankin 1996). Due to the immense pressure that firms face with various environmental laws and stakeholders they have taken initiatives to prepare sustainability reports which depicts firm's environmental as well as social performances. While adhering to environmental laws and regulations firms needs to provide information to their stakeholders with respect to environmental impact on business operations. Wide varieties of motives can be found in studies to validate in providing information with respect to social and environmental aspects. Apart from the force made by the society to take mechanisms to control pollutions made when producing goods (Wiseman 1982) and services there are other factors which motivates firms to consider in taking responsibility activities (Gibson 1996). One such aim would be to create competitive edge by enhancing their image among public. These factors made firms to engage in providing information on their sustainability activities via annual reports.

Scholars have stated that irrespective of the vast availability of the theoretical perspectives to evaluate social and environmental perspectives, legitimacy theory can be considered as one of the most main perspective (Patten 1991; Deegan 2002; Adams et al. 1998). In order to illustrate disclosures with respect to social and environmental behaviours of firms, legitimate theory is the most used theory (Neu et al. 1998; Milne and Patten 2002). Legitimisation is considered as the resemblance between the actions of firms and social values, where the actions can lead to either to change the social value or to indicate value congruence. Hence, when there is an incongruence between the two value systems then it will lead to create a threat to the firm (Dowling and Pfeffer 1975). Firms have the possibility in mitigating such threats by effective communication where the society will then be able to obtain a clear understanding of firm's social legitimacy. Some of the legitimisation specimens can be, establishing committees with local councils, initiating environmental audits and complying with legislations (Bansal and Roth 2000).

With the rapid changes in the business world, it is vital for firms to ensure that they constantly meet the legitimacy and the relevance of the society's requirements and the beneficiaries of such conducts have been approved by the society itself. According to this social contract between firms and the society, firms are liable to comply with the terms of the contract. In cases where firms are unable to continue their operations, then the society can take actions to revoke the binding contract between them and the firm. Hence, it can be argued that the theory of legislation focuses on social contracts where the existence of the firm is depended on the frontier of firm's operations towards the society at large (Deegan 2002). Moreover, it is the duty of the managers to engage themselves in the process of legitimisation to prolong or maintain firm's legitimacy (Milne and Patten 2002). While continuing with the business operations firms are obliged to conduct socially desirable activities to gain rewards, be socially accepted by the society and to survive. With this perspective firms needs to disclose their social activities to be a good corporate citizen. By legitimising these social activities, firms have the possibility in ensuring their survival in the society.

Further arguments are raised indicating that legitimacy theory is related to firm's behaviour when responding societal demand and the act of their legitimation (Tilt 1994). The act of reporting creates an impact on the public towards firms (Neu et al. 1998). Firms can pursue legitimisation by either engaging in the activities that will not damage or cause harm towards the societal well-beings and to do the right thing. Nothing seems to be fixed in a vibrant society. The constant change makes every firm to be responsive. Failing to change accordingly to the change in the environment will tend to create a dissatisfaction among public. This in turn can also create pressure towards firms to meet the expectations of the society while using the legality to increase performances (Deegan and Rankin 1996). Hence, the concept of legitimacy is vital to analyse the link between firms and their environment.

One such strategy of legitimacy theory is communication (Tilt 1994). Societal legitimacy can be managed by engaging with the society thorough effective communication (Schuman 1995). Firms need to communicate sustainability activities, as in comparison to other communication channels used to communicate sustainability activities, namely, advertising, broachers or newsletters, annual reports have the legitimacy, which cannot be seen in other channels (Deegan 2002), use annual reports. It can be seen as a strategic document, which projects the sustainability activities that are conducted by the firm. Top management believes that this is the most effective method of informing and refining the community about firms view on environmental activities. Moreover, annual reports have the potential in influencing the perception of the community towards firms. In turn, it also has the possibility in image building while eliminating any unfavourable perceptions that the community has towards firms (Deegan 2002). Sustainability reports also have the likelihood in constructing relationships among them and outside society where it will lead to enhance firm performances as well (Gray et al. 1995). Henceforth, annual reports are the most common and acceptable way of communicating sustainability (Buhr 1998). However, with the emergence of various social media channels it has made things more complex for firms to reach legitimacy (Schultz et al. 2013).

Conceptual Framework

With respect to the above developed hypothesis, the following conceptual framework is developed to analyse the link between social media, corporate reputation, and firm performances, as illustrated in *Figure 1*.

Figure 1. Conceptual framework

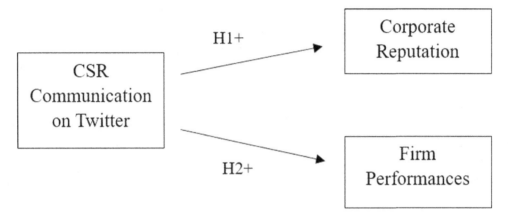

Methodology

To test the hypothesis H1 and H2, the top 50 and bottom 50 companies listed in the Social Media Sustainability Index in year 2016 are selected.

To measure firm's performance, data was collected from annual reports. The data include *profit before interest and taxes (PBIT)* and *net profit* for each firm for the year 2015. From each of the selected firms, the twitter data including *number of tweets, number of followers, number of likes,* and *account since* is collected on 28 April 2016 for both the top 50 and bottom 50 firms. These profit and twitter variables are listed in Table 1.

Table 1. Profit and twitter variables

Reputation Indices	Variable
PBIT	1
Net profit	2
Number of tweets	3
Number of followers	4
Number of likes	5
Account since	6

The four reputation indices listed in *Table 2* have measured corporate reputation by considering CSR as the key attribute. The index-position of the company used for measuring as ordinal scaled variables.

Table 2. Reputation rankings

Reputation Index	Institute	Publication	Variable
The reputation of the most visible companies	Harris Poll Reputation Quotient	Nielsen	7
Worlds most admired companies	Hay Group	Fortune	8
Global 100 most sustainable corporations in the world	Corporate Knights Magazine	Forbes	9
The companies with the best CSR reputations	Reputation Institute	Forbes	10

Spearman correlations were computed using all the 10 variables from Table 1 and Table2.

Results

The spearman correlation between the two firm performance variables (1-2) and the four twitter variables (3-6) and four corporate reputation variables (7-10) for the top 50 and bottom 50 firms are shown in Table 3 and Table 4. When evaluating the top 50 firms, there is a significant relationship between *number of tweets* and *PBIT* ($r=0.28$, $p=0.049$). Similarly, when assessing the bottom 50 firms, there is a significant relationship between *number of followers* and *PBIT* ($r=0.339$, $p=0.016$). However, there is no significant relationship between *number of tweets* with *corporate reputation*, *number of followers* and the four *corporate reputation indices*, and *number of likes* and the *corporate reputation indices* for both top 50 and bottom 50 firms ($p<0.05$ *level*).

Table 3. Relationship between firm performance, twitter, and corporate reputation indices– top 50 companies

	2	3	4	5	7	8	9	10
1. PBIT	,908**	**,280***	0,225	0,128	-0,203	0,064	-0,093	-0,006
2. Net profit	-	0,172	0,133	0,128	-0,174	0,077	-0,191	-0,09
3. Number of tweets		-	,584**	,402**	0,441	0,292	-0,125	0,357
4. Number of followers			-	,280*	0,447	0,086	-0,125	0,362
5. Number of likes				-	-0,212	-0,029	-0,257	0,072
6. Account since					-0,509*	-0,31	-0,108	-0,177
7. Reputation of most visible companies 2015					-	0,22	,81*	0,6
8. Worlds most admired companies 2015						-	-0,333	-0,086
9. Companies with best CSR reputation 2015							-	-0,006
10. Global 100 most sustainable corporations in world 2015								-
Note: **p≤0.01, *p≤0.05								

Table 4. Relationship between firm performance, twitter, and corporate reputation indices– bottom 50 companies

	2	3	4	5	7	8	9	10
1. PBIT	,988**	0,042	**-0,339***	-0,029	0,237	0,262	-0,102	-0,2
2. Net profit	-	0,047	,363**	-0,064	0,055	0,262	-0,069	-0,2
3. Number of tweets		-	,595**	,492**	0,091	0,310	0,308	0,314
4. Number of followers			-	,309*	-0,321	-0,381	-0,324	0,2
5. Number of likes				-	0,491	-0,31	-0,005	-0,029
6. Account since					-0,181	-0,262	0,102	-0,257
7. Reputation of most visible companies 2015					-	-0,6	0	0
8. Worlds most admired companies 2015						-	0,3	1
9. Companies with best CSR reputation 2015							-	-1
10. Global 100 most sustainable corporations in world 2015								-
Note: **p≤0.01, *p≤0.05								

DISCUSSION

There is no significant relationship between *number of tweets* and the *corporate reputation indices*, *number of followers* and the *corporate reputation indices*, and *number of likes* and the *corporate reputation indices* for both top 50 and bottom 50 companies considering H1. H1 was developed based on the following assumption: At present, consumers are motivated to interact with firms by communicating and sharing information and proving feedback wherever necessary. This interaction derives to enhance consumer satisfaction which in turn boost the reputation of the firm (Carmeli and Tishler, 2005; Trainor 2012). Hence, there can be an indirect influence on social media in generating corporate reputation. However, the results to test H2 shows a significant relationship between *number of tweets* and *PBIT* and *number of followers* and *PBIT*. Hence, the empirical findings, which stated that the increased stakeholder satisfaction could lead to enhance firm value (Luo et al. 2010), cannot be falsified. Moreover, firms with larger net revue seems to be more active in twitter.

Accordingly, the findings of the study provide a signal towards the firms that they should not believe that by being an active social media player in the market does not lead to enhance corporate reputation. However, there is an indirect effect towards firms, where, by communicating about their CSR activities via social media firms have the possibility in sharing their social activities in real time. This will aid firms to obtain the respective feedback from their stakeholders, where they can then make the necessary amendments to these activities if they receive any negative comments from their stakeholders. Prompt reactions towards negative feedback will enable firms to protect their reputation in the market place while positive feedback will enable firms to enhance stakeholder satisfaction, retain, and attract employees and consumers. Although communicating CSR activities via various social media channels does not have a direct impact on corporate reputation in short term, it can create an impact in long term.

Additionally, firms needs to have a better understanding on how they communicate effectively via twitter. Firms should not engage only in posting their brands and products but also in retweeting, sharing ideas, and forwarding of any vital information from other users. This will enable firms to actively involve with twitter. Social media enables firms to effectively communicate and maintain transparency of the firms CSR activities. This will also increase responsiveness of communicating CSR while using social media. Hence, if the firm wants to increase transparency and accountability, they are encouraged to get involved in various social media platforms. Social media will act as a signal towards policy makers. It is not only a marketing tool but also an element of distinctive policy of CSR communication.

However, firms might or might not engage in social media to communicate their CSR. The firms can still use traditional communication channels to fulfill the same need. The shift in power from firms to consumers has occurred due to the use of social media by firms as well as the stakeholders. The real time accessibility and the fact that information can be shared easily make companies less control their own reputation (Bunting and Lipski, 2000). Firms should ensure that only trained staff can share and communicate the respective information with their stakeholders (Hoffman and Fodor, 2010). With respect to the theoretical aspect, firms have the possibility in aiding CSR communication through social media and thereby enhance legitimacy. This will be possible due to collaborative alignment of CSR communication in various social media channels. Additionally, firms can attain corporate legitimacy by globally enhancing connectivity of corporate activities through CSR issues and finding the respective solutions.

Zero-correlation proves non-causality. Predicting real-world outcomes with social media has already been proven (Asur und Huberman 2010). According to the author, the rate of tweets is able to forecast revenues. Social media is part of the promotion mix of a company concerning advertising and customer involvement (Mangold und Faulds 2009). Social media content created by a company affects brand image (Coulter et al 2012). The link between firm performance and brand value improves shareholder value (Yeung und Ramasamy 2008). The causality assumption of this paper is the (indirect) link between the followers, meaning the interested and loyal users, and the revenue of a company. The more people follow a company, the more likely those people are buying products/services of the company, leading to revenue.

CONCLUSION

The analysis of the study has fulfilled the research gap by identifying that there is no statistical correlation between twitter and corporate reputation, there is significant relationship between twitter and firm performance. However, although corporate reputation does not have a direct impact on tweets short term, it has an indirect impact where it can strengthen corporate reputation. Similarly, unlike any other social media channel like Facebook, twitter allows the users to generate a dialogue with the users by retweeting. Hence, twitter, as a communication channel of CSR, will enable firms to focus more on generating a platform, in which the users are interested in generating a dialogue with the firm. It is vital for firms to allocate and invest in social media channels, which in turn has the potential in influencing and enhancing their reputation and firm performance, mostly in the long term. Hence, the study encourages firms to ensure that they continue in investing and involving in social media to communicate their CSR activities while the benefits can be generated in longer term.

Several limitations of this study can be identified according to the complexity of the research hypothesis, sampling framework, analysis methods and selection of firms. Hence, further studies can focus by incorporating several other social media communication channels like, Facebook, Pinterest or LinkedIn or developing a theoretical framework to identify other factors that can affect corporate reputation (trust, loyalty, technology, legal aspects etc.) and firm performance (assets, leverage, size, risk, corporate governance etc.). Another future research would be to increase the size of the data collection which will lead to enhance the validity and the reliability if the findings. Additionally, the study measures firm performance only with the use of PBIT and net profit. Hence further studies can be conducted with the computation of ratio analysis like, return on assets, return on equity, Tobin's q etc. A content analysis of the respective tweets can also be conducted as a future study and there by understand and examine how the users of social media reacts for any twitter message of the firm.

REFERENCES

Abrahams, A. S., Jiao, J., Wang, G. A., & Fan, W. (2012). Vehicle defect discovery from social media. *Decision Support Systems*, *54*(1), 87–97. doi:10.1016/j.dss.2012.04.005

Abrantes, J. L., Lages, C. R., & Jayawardhena, C. (2013). Drivers of in group and out group electronic word of mouth (eWOM). *European Journal of Marketing*, *47*(7), 1067–1088. doi:10.1108/03090561311324219

Adams, C. A., Hill, W. Y., & Roberts, C. B. (1998). Corporate social reporting practices in Western Europe: Legitimating corporate behaviour? *The British Accounting Review*, *30*(1), 1–21. doi:10.1006/bare.1997.0060

Alniacik, U., Cigerim, E., Akcin, K., & Bayram, O. (2011). Independent and joint effects of perceived CR, affective commitment and job satisfaction on turnover intensions. *Procedia: Social and Behavioral Sciences*, *24*, 1177–1189. doi:10.1016/j.sbspro.2011.09.139

Andreassen, T. W., & Lindestad, B. (1998). The effect of corporate image in the formation of customer loyalty. *Journal of Service Research*, *1*(1), 82–92. doi:10.1177/109467059800100107

Andriof, J., & Waddock, S. (2002). *Unfolding Stakeholder Thinking: Theory, Responsibility and Engagement*. Greenleaf Publishing.

Asur, S. and Huberman, B. A. (2010). *Predicting the Future with Social Media*. doi:10.1109/WI-IAT.2010.63

Aula, P. (2010). Social Media, Reputation Risk and Ambient Publicity Management. *Strategy and Leadership*, *38*(6), 43–49. doi:10.1108/10878571011088069

Balmer, J. M. T., Fukukawa, K., & Gray, E. R. (2007). The nature and management of ethical corporate identity: A commentary on corporate identity, corporate social responsibility and ethics. *Journal of Business Ethics*, *76*(1), 7–15. doi:10.100710551-006-9278-z

Bansal, P., & Roth, K. (2000). Why companies go green: A model of ecological responsiveness. *Academy of Management Journal*, *43*(4), 717–736.

Barone, M., Norman, A., & Miyazaki, A. (2007). Consumer response to retailer use of cause related marketing: Is more fit better? *Journal of Retailing*, *83*(4), 437–445. doi:10.1016/j.jretai.2007.03.006

Barsky, E., & Purdon, M. (2006). Introducing web 2.0: Social networking and social bookmarking for health librarians. *The Journal of the Canadian Health Libraries Association*, *27*(3), 65–67. doi:10.5596/c06-024

Berthon, R. P., Pitt, L. F., Plangger, K., & Shapiro, D. (2012). Marketing meets web 2.0, social media, and creative consumers: Implications for international marketing strategy. *Business Horizons, 55*(3), 261–271. doi:10.1016/j.bushor.2012.01.007

Bhattacharya, C. B., & Sen, S. (2004). Doing better by doing good: When, why, and how consumer respond to corporate social initiatives. *California Management Review, 47*(1), 9–24. doi:10.2307/41166284

Boyd, D., Golder, S., & Lotan, G. (2010). Tweet, tweet, retweet: conversational aspects of retweeting on Twitter. *Proceedings of the 43rd Hawaii International Conference on System Sciences (HICSS 43),* 1-10. 10.1109/HICSS.2010.412

Brown, T. J., Dacin, P. A., Pratt, M. G., & Whetten, D. A. (2006). Identity, intended image, construed image, and reputation: An interdisciplinary framework and suggested terminology. *Journal of the Academy of Marketing Science, 34*(2), 99–106. doi:10.1177/0092070305284969

Buhr, N. (1998). Environmental performance, legislation and annual report disclosure: The case of acid rain and Falconbridge. *Accounting, Auditing & Accountability Journal, 11*(2), 163–190. doi:10.1108/09513579810215455

Bunting, M., & Lipski, R. (2000). Drowned out? Rethinking corporate reputation management for the Internet. *Journal of Communication Management (London), 5*(2), 170–178. doi:10.1108/13632540110806758

Burton, S., & Soboleva, A. (2011). Interactive or reactive? Marketing with Twitter. *Journal of Consumer Marketing, 28*(7), 491–499. doi:10.1108/07363761111181473

Carmeli, A., & Tishler, A. (2005). Perceived organizational reputation and organizational performance: An empirical investigation of industrial enterprises. *Corporate Reputation Review, 8*(1), 13–30. doi:10.1057/palgrave.crr.1540236

Carroll, A. B. (1979). A three-dimensional conceptual model of corporate performance. *Academy of Management Review, 4*(4), 497–505. doi:10.5465/amr.1979.4498296

Carroll, A. B. (1999). Corporate Social Responsibility. *Business & Society, 38*(3), 268–295. doi:10.1177/000765039903800303

Carroll, A. B. (2007). A History of Corporate Social Responsibility, Concepts and Practices. In The Oxford Handbook of Corporate Social Responsibility. New York: Oxford University Press.

Castells, M. (1997). *The Power of Identity, the Information Age: Economy, Society and Culture* (Vol. 2). Blackwell.

Cheliotis, G. (2009). From open source to open content: Organization, licensing and decision processes in open cultural production. *Decision Support Systems, 47*(3), 229–244. doi:10.1016/j.dss.2009.02.006

Chen, Y., Liu, Y., & Zhang, J. (2011). When do third party product reviews affect firm value and what can firms do? The case of media critics and professional movie reviews. *Journal of Marketing, 75,* 116–134.

Ching, C., Holsapple, C. W., & Whinston, A. B. (1992). Reputation, learning and coordination in distributed decision-making contexts. *Organization Science, 3*(2), 275–297. doi:10.1287/orsc.3.2.275

Clark, B. H., & Montgomery, D. B. (1998). Deterrence, reputations and competitive cognition. *Management Science, 44*(1), 62–82. doi:10.1287/mnsc.44.1.62

Coulter, K. S., Bruhn, M., Schoenmueller, V., & Schäfer, D. B. (2012). Are Social Media replacing traditional media in terms of brand equity creation? *Management Research Review, 35*(9), 770–790. doi:10.1108/01409171211255948

Coupland, C. (2005). Corporate social responsibility as argument on the web. *Journal of Business Ethics, 62*(4), 355–366. doi:10.100710551-005-1953-y

Coyle, J. R., Smith, T., & Platt, G. (2012). I'm here to help. How companies' microblog responses to consumer problems influence brand perceptions. *Journal of Research in Interactive Marketing, 6*(1), 27–41. doi:10.1108/17505931211241350

Dawkins, J. (2004). Corporate responsibility: The communication challenge. *Journal of Communication Management (London), 9*(2), 108–119. doi:10.1108/13632540510621362

Deegan, C. (2002). The legitimising effect of social and environmental disclosures - a theoretical foundation. *Accounting, Auditing & Accountability Journal, 15*(3), 282–311. doi:10.1108/09513570210435852

Deegan, C., & Rankin, M. (1996). Do Australian companies report environmental news objectively? *Accounting, Auditing & Accountability Journal, 9*(2), 50–67. doi:10.1108/09513579610116358

Deephouse, D. L. (2000). Media reputation as a strategic resource: An integration of mass communication and resource-based theories. *Journal of Management, 26*(6), 1091–1112. doi:10.1177/014920630002600602

Dellarocas, C. (2003). The digitization of word of mouth: Promise and challenges of online feedback mechanisms. *Management Science, 49*(10), 1407–1424. doi:10.1287/mnsc.49.10.1407.17308

Dijkmans, C., Kerkhof, P., Buyukcan-Tetik, A., & Beukeboom, C. J. (2015). Online Conversation and Corporate Reputation: A Two-Wave Longitudinal Study on the Effects of Exposure to the Social Media Activities of a Highly Interactive Company. *Journal of Computer-Mediated Communication, 20*(6), 632–648. doi:10.1111/jcc4.12132

Dollinger, M., Golden, P., & Saxton, T. (1997). The effects of reputation on the decision to joint venture. *Strategic Management Journal, 18*(2), 127–140. doi:10.1002/(SICI)1097-0266(199702)18:2<127::AID-SMJ859>3.0.CO;2-H

Dowling, J. B., & Pfeffer, J. (1975). Organizational legitimacy: Social values and organizational behavior. *Pacific Sociological Review, 18*(1), 122–136. doi:10.2307/1388226

Drury, G. (2008). Opinion piece: social media: should marketers engage and how can it be done effectively? *Journal of Direct, Data and Digital Marketing Practice, 9*(3), 274–277. doi:10.1057/palgrave.dddmp.4350096

Du, S., Bhattacharya, C. B., & Sen, S. (2010). Maximizing Business Returns to Corporate Social Responsibility (CSR): The Role of CSR Communication. *International Journal of Management Reviews, 12*(1), 8–19. doi:10.1111/j.1468-2370.2009.00276.x

Eberl, S., & Schwaiger, M. (2005). Corporate Reputation: Disentangling the effects on financial performances. *European Journal of Marketing*, *39*(7/8), 838–854. doi:10.1108/03090560510601798

Ellen, P. S., Webb, D. J., & Mohr, L. A. (2006). Building Corporate Associations: Consumer Attributions for Corporate Socially Responsible Programs. *Journal of the Academy of Marketing Science*, *34*(2), 147–157. doi:10.1177/0092070305284976

Etter, M. (2013). Broadcasting, reacting, engaging – three strategies of CSR Communication. *Journal of Communication Management (London)*, *18*(4), 322–342. doi:10.1108/JCOM-01-2013-0007

Etter, M., & Fieseler, C. (2010). On Relational Capital in Social Media. *Studies in Communication Sciences*, *10*(2), 167–189.

European Commission. (2011). *Corporate social responsibility*. https://ec.europa.eu/growth/industry/corporate-social-responsibility/index_en.htm

Fieseler, C., Fleck, M., & Meckel, M. (2010). Corporate Social Responsibility in the Blogosphere. *Journal of Business Ethics*, *91*(4), 599–614. doi:10.100710551-009-0135-8

Firestein, J. P. (2006). Building and protecting corporate reputation. *Strategy and Leadership*, *34*(4), 25–31. doi:10.1108/10878570610676864

Fisher, T. (2009). ROI in social media: A look at the arguments. *Journal of Database Marketing and Customer Strategy Management*, *16*(3), 189–195. doi:10.1057/dbm.2009.16

Fombrun, C., & Shanley, M. (1990). What's in a name? Reputation building and corporate strategy. *Academy of Management Journal*, *33*(2), 233–258.

Fornell, C., Mithas, S., Morgeson, F. V. III, & Krishnan, M. S. (2006). Customer satisfaction and stock prices: High returns, low risk. *Journal of Marketing*, *70*(1), 3–14. doi:10.1509/jmkg.2006.70.1.3

Gao, G., & Hitt, L. M. (2012). Information technology and trademarks: Implications for product variety. *Management Science*, *58*(6), 1211–1226. doi:10.1287/mnsc.1110.1480

Gibson, K. (1996). The problem with reporting pollution allowances: Reporting is not the problem. *Critical Perspectives on Accounting*, *7*(6), 655–665. doi:10.1006/cpac.1996.0073

Gilfoil, D. M., & Jobs, C. (2012). Return on investment for social media: A proposed framework for understanding, implementing and measuring the return. *Journal of Economic and Business Research*, *10*(11), 637–650. doi:10.19030/jber.v10i11.7363

Gill, D. L., Dickinson, S. J., & Scharl, A. (2008). Communicating sustainability: A web content analysis of North American, Asian and European firms. *Journal of Communication Management (London)*, *12*(3), 243–262. doi:10.1108/13632540810899425

Gray, R., Kouhy, R., & Lavers, S. (1995). Corporate social and Environmental Reporting. *Accounting, Auditing & Accountability Journal*, *8*(2), 47–77. doi:10.1108/09513579510146996

Greenberg, P. (2010). The impact of CRM 2.0 on customer insight. *Journal of Business and Industrial Marketing*, *25*(6), 410–419. doi:10.1108/08858621011066008

Gruen, W. T., Osmonbekov, T., & Czaplewski, A. J. (2005). eWOM: The impact of customer to customer online know how exchange on customer value and loyalty. *Journal of Business Research*, *59*(4), 449–456. doi:10.1016/j.jbusres.2005.10.004

Gu, B., Park, J., & Konana, P. (2012). The impact of external word of mouth sources on retailers sales of high involvement products. *Information Systems Research*, *23*(1), 182–196. doi:10.1287/isre.1100.0343

Hanna, R., Rohm, A., & Crittenden, V. L. (2011). We're all connected. The power of social media ecosystem. *Business Horizons*, *54*(3), 265–273. doi:10.1016/j.bushor.2011.01.007

Healy, P. M., & Palepu, K. G. (2001). Information asymmetry, corporate disclosure and the capital markets: A review of the empirical disclosure. *Journal of Accounting and Economics*, *31*(1-3), 405–440. doi:10.1016/S0165-4101(01)00018-0

Helm, S. (2011). Employee's awareness of their impact on corporate reputation. *Journal of Business Research*, *64*(7), 657–663. doi:10.1016/j.jbusres.2010.09.001

Hoehle, H., Scornavacca, E., & Huff, S. (2012). Three decades of research on consumer adoption and utilization of electronic banking channels: A literature analysis. *Decision Support Systems*, *54*(1), 122–132. doi:10.1016/j.dss.2012.04.010

Hoffman, D. L., & Fodor, M. (2010). Can you measure the ROI of your social media marketing? *MIT Sloan Management Review*, *52*(1), 41–49.

Honey, G. (2009). *A short guide to reputation risk*. Gower.

Hopkins, M. (2007). *Corporate Social Responsibility and International Development: Is Business the Solution?* Earthscan.

Insch, A. (2008). Online communication of corporate environmental citizenship: A study of New Zealand's electricity and gas retailers. *Journal of Marketing Communications*, *14*(2), 139–153. doi:10.1080/13527260701858505

Jones, B., Temperley, J., & Lima, A. (2009). Corporate reputation in the era of web 2.0: The case of Primark. *Journal of Marketing Management*, *25*(9-10), 927–939. doi:10.1362/026725709X479309

Kaplan, A. M., & Haenlein, M. (2010). Users of the world, unite! The challenges and opportunities of social media. *Business Horizons*, *53*(1), 59–68. doi:10.1016/j.bushor.2009.09.003

Keh, T. H., & Xie, Y. (2009). Corporate reputation and customer behavior intentions: The roles of trust, identification and commitment. *Industrial Marketing Management*, *38*(7), 732–742. doi:10.1016/j.indmarman.2008.02.005

Kemp, S. (2015). *Digital, Social and Mobile Worldwide in 2015*. http://wearesocial.net/blog/2015/01/digital-social-mobile-worldwide-2015/

Kent, M. L., & Taylor, M. (1998). Building dialogic relationships through the World Wide Web. *Public Relations Review*, *24*(3), 321–334. doi:10.1016/S0363-8111(99)80143-X

Kietzmann, J. H., Hermkens, K., McCarthya, I. P., & Silvestre, B. S. (2011). Social media? Get serious! Understanding the functional building blocks of social media. *Business Horizons*, *54*(3), 241–251. doi:10.1016/j.bushor.2011.01.005

Kirtis, A. K., & Karahan, F. (2011). To be or not to be in Social Media arena as the most cost-efficient marketing strategy after the global recession. *Procedia: Social and Behavioral Sciences*, *24*, 260–268. doi:10.1016/j.sbspro.2011.09.083

Lantos, G. P. (2001). The boundaries of strategic corporate social responsibility. *Journal of Consumer Marketing*, *18*(7), 595–632. doi:10.1108/07363760110410281

Li, Y. M., & Shiu, Y. L. (2012). A diffusion mechanism for social advertising over micro-blogs. *Decision Support Systems*, *54*(1), 9–22. doi:10.1016/j.dss.2012.02.012

Luo, X., Homburg, C., & Wieseke, J. (2010). Customer satisfaction, analyst stock, recommendations and firm value. *JMR, Journal of Marketing Research*, *47*(6), 1041–1058. doi:10.1509/jmkr.47.6.1041

Luo, X., Zhang, J., & Duan, W. (2013). Social Media and Firm Equity Value. *Information Systems Research*, *24*(1), 146–163. doi:10.1287/isre.1120.0462

Mangold, G., & Faulds, D. (2009). Social media: The new hybrid element of the promotion mix. *Business Horizons*, *52*(4), 357–365. doi:10.1016/j.bushor.2009.03.002

Matolcsy, Z. P., & Wyatt, A. (2008). The association between technological conditions and the market value of equity. *The Accounting Review*, *83*(2), 479–518. doi:10.2308/accr.2008.83.2.479

Matten, D., & Moon, J. (2008). Implicit and Explicit CSR: A Conceptual Framework for a Comparative Understanding of Corporate Social Responsibility. *Academy of Management Review*, *33*(2), 404–424. doi:10.5465/amr.2008.31193458

Meijer, M. M., & Kleinnijenhuis, J. (2006). News and corporate reputation: Empirical findings from the Netherlands. *Public Relations Review*, *32*(4), 341–348. doi:10.1016/j.pubrev.2006.08.002

Milne, M. J., & Patten, D. M. (2002). Securing organizational legitimacy. *Accounting, Auditing & Accountability Journal*, *15*(3), 372–405. doi:10.1108/09513570210435889

Morsing, M., & Schultz, M. (2006). Corporate social responsibility communication: Stakeholder information, response and involvement strategies. *Business Ethics (Oxford, England)*, *15*(4), 323–338. doi:10.1111/j.1467-8608.2006.00460.x

Neu, D., Warsame, H., & Pedwell, K. (1998). Managing public impressions: Environmental disclosures in annual reports. *Accounting, Organizations and Society*, *23*(3), 265–282. doi:10.1016/S0361-3682(97)00008-1

Page, G., & Fearn, H. (2005). Corporate reputation: What do consumers really care about? *Journal of Advertising Research*, *45*(3), 305–313. doi:10.1017/S0021849905050361

Park, C. W., MacInnis, D. J., Priester, J., Eisingerich, A. B., & Iacobucci, D. (2010). Brand attachment and brand attitude strength: Conceptual and empirical differentiation of two critical brand equity drivers. *Journal of Marketing*, *74*(6), 1–17. doi:10.1509/jmkg.74.6.1

Patten, D. M. (1991). Exposure, legitimacy and social disclosure. *Journal of Accounting and Public Policy, 10*(4), 297–308. doi:10.1016/0278-4254(91)90003-3

Peters, D. H., Adam, T., Alonge, O., Agyepong, I. A., & Tran, N. (2013). Implementation research: What it is and how to do it. *British Medical Journal*, 1–7. PMID:24259324

Petrick, J. A., Scherer, R. F., Brodzinski, J. D., Quinn, J. F., & Ainina, M. F. (1999). Global leadership skills and reputational capital. Intangible resources for sustainable competitive advantage. *The Academy of Management Executive, 13*(1), 58–69. doi:10.5465/ame.1999.1567322

Podolny, J. M. (1993). A status-based model of market competition. *American Journal of Sociology, 98*(4), 829–871. doi:10.1086/230091

Ravikant, N., & Rifkin, A. (2010). *Why Twitter is massively undervalued compared to Facebook.* https://techcrunch.com/2010/10/16/why-twitter-is-massivelyundervalued-compared-to-facebook

Rayner, J. (2003). *Managing reputational risk. Curbing threats, leveraging opportunities.* John Wiley and Sons.

Rhee, M., & Haunschild, P. (2006). The liability of good reputation: A study of product recalls in the U. S. automobile industry. *Organization Science, 17*(1), 101–117. doi:10.1287/orsc.1050.0175

Rindova, V. P., Williamson, I. O., Petkova, A. P., & Sever, J. M. (2005). Being good or being known: An empirical examination of the dimensions, antecedents, and consequences of organizational reputation. *Academy of Management Journal, 48*(6), 1033–1049. doi:10.5465/amj.2005.19573108

Roberts, P. W., & Dowling, G. R. (1997). The value of a firm's corporate reputation: How reputation helps attain and sustain superior profitability. *Corporate Reputation Review, 1*(1), 72–76. doi:10.1057/palgrave.crr.1540020

Roberts, P. W., & Dowling, G. R. (2002). Corporate reputation and sustained superior financial performance. *Strategic Management Journal, 23*(12), 1077–1093. doi:10.1002mj.274

Rolland, D., & Bazzoni, J. O. (2009). Greening corporate identity: CSR online corporate identity. *Corporate Communications, 14*(3), 249–263. doi:10.1108/13563280910980041

Schniederjans, D., Cao, E. S., & Schniederjans, M. (2013). Enhancing financial performance with social media: An impression management perspective. *Decision Support Systems, 55*(4), 911–918. doi:10.1016/j.dss.2012.12.027

Schultz, F., Utz, S., & Göritz, A. (2011). Is the medium the message? Perceptions of and reactions to crisis communication via twitter, blogs and traditional media. *Public Relations Review, 37*(1), 20–27. doi:10.1016/j.pubrev.2010.12.001

Shrum, W., & Wuthnow, R. (1988). Reputational status of organizations in technical systems. *American Journal of Sociology, 93*(4), 882–912. doi:10.1086/228828

Social Media Sustainability Index. (2016). *The SMI-Wizness Social Media Sustainability Index.* http://sustainly.com/sites/default/files/The%206th%20Annual%20Social%20Media%20Sustainability%20Index.pdf

Statistic Brain. (2013). *Twitter Statistics.* https://www.statisticbrain.com/twitter-statistics/

Stelzner, M. (2012). *Social media marketing industry report.* https://www.socialmediaexaminer.com/report2015/

Taylor, M., Kent, M. L., & White, W. J. (2001). How activist organizations are using the Internet to build relationships. *Public Relations Review*, *27*(3), 263–284. doi:10.1016/S0363-8111(01)00086-8

Teece, D. J., Pisano, G., & Shuen, A. (1997). Dynamic capabilities and strategic management. *Strategic Management Journal*, *18*(7), 509–533. doi:10.1002/(SICI)1097-0266(199708)18:7<509::AID-SMJ882>3.0.CO;2-Z

The China Post. (2012). *Number of Companies Using Social Media to Triple in 3–5 years: study.* http://www.chinapost.com.tw/business/company-focus/2012/06/18/344660/Number-of.htm

The Companies with the Best CSR Reputations. (2015). https://www.reputationinstitute.com/CMSPages/GetAzureFile.aspx?path=~%5Cmedia%5Cmedia%5Cdocuments%5C2015-global-csr-reptrak- results.pdf&hash=f375854351576541ae88db1e043e7417e9f057f83955bb3768454dd8e0417353&ext=.pdf

The Global 100 Most Sustainable Corporations in the World. (2015). https://www.corporateknights.com/reports/2015-global-100/2015-global-100-results-14218559/

The Most Admired Companies. (2015). https://www.rankingthebrands.com/The-Brand-Rankings.aspx?rankingID=118&year=908

The Reputation of the Most Visible Companies. (2015). https://www.rankingthebrands.com/The-Brand-Rankings.aspx?rankingID=235&nav=category

Tilt, C. A. (1994). The influence of external pressure groups on corporate social disclosure. *Accounting, Auditing & Accountability Journal*, *7*(4), 47–72. doi:10.1108/09513579410069849

Trainor, K. J. (2012). Relating Social Media Technologies to Performance: A Capabilities-Based Perspective. *Journal of Personal Selling & Sales Management*, *32*(3), 317–331. doi:10.2753/PSS0885-3134320303

Twitter. (2015). *About.* https://twitter.com/about

Verboven, H. (2011). Communicating CSR and Business Identity in the Chemical Industry through Mission Slogans. *Business Communication Quarterly*, *74*(4), 415–431. doi:10.1177/1080569911424485

Vergin, R. C., & Qoronfleh, M. W. (1998). Corporate reputation and the stock market. *Business Horizons*, *41*(1), 19–26. doi:10.1016/S0007-6813(98)90060-X

Walsh, G., & Beatty, S. E. (2007). Customer based corporate reputation of a service firm: Scale development and validation. *Academy of Marketing Science*, *35*(1), 127–143. doi:10.100711747-007-0015-7

Wartick, S. L. (1992). The relationship between intense media exposure and change in corporate reputation. *Business & Society*, *31*(1), 33–49. doi:10.1177/000765039203100104

Watson, T. J. (1994). Management Flavours of the Month: Their Role in Managers Lives. *International Journal of Human Resource Management*, *5*(4), 889–905. doi:10.1080/09585199400000071

Weigelt, K., & Camerer, C. (1988). Reputation and corporate strategy: A review of recent theory and applications. *Strategic Management Journal, 9*(5), 443–454. doi:10.1002mj.4250090505

Weiss, A. M., Anderson, E., & MacInnis, D. J. (1999). Reputation management as a motivation for sales structure decisions. *Journal of Marketing, 63*(4), 74–89. doi:10.1177/002224299906300407

Wiseman, J. (1982). An evaluation of environmental disclosures made in corporate annual reports. *Accounting, Organizations and Society, 7*(1), 53–63. doi:10.1016/0361-3682(82)90025-3

Wright, D. K. (1998). *Corporate communications policy concerning the Internet: A survey of the nation's senior-level, corporate public relations officers.* The Institute for Public Relations.

Wyatt, A. (2005). Accounting recognition of intangible assets: Theory and evidence on economic determinants. *The Accounting Review, 80*(3), 967–1003. doi:10.2308/accr.2005.80.3.967

Yeung, M., & Ramasamy, B. (2008). Brand value and firm performance nexus: Further empirical evidence. *Journal of Brand Management, 15*(5), 322–335. doi:10.1057/palgrave.bm.2550092

Yoon, E., Guffey, H. J., & Kijewski, V. (1993). The effects of information and company reputation on intentions to buy a business service. *Journal of Business Research, 27*(3), 215–228. doi:10.1016/0148-2963(93)90027-M

Yu, Y., Duan, W., & Cao, Q. (2013). The impact of social and conventional media on firm equity value: A sentiment analysis approach. *Decision Support Systems, 55*(4), 919–926. doi:10.1016/j.dss.2012.12.028

Zhao, L., & Lu, Y. (2012). Enhancing perceived interactivity through network externalities: An empirical study on micro-blogging service satisfaction and continuance intention. *Decision Support Systems, 53*(4), 825–834. doi:10.1016/j.dss.2012.05.019

This research was previously published in the International Journal of Applied Management Sciences and Engineering (IJAMSE), 8(2); pages 1-20, copyright year 2021 by IGI Publishing (an imprint of IGI Global).

Chapter 48
Social Media and Social Entrepreneurship

Md Nazmul Islam
University of West of Scotland, UK

Vivek Chitran
University of Cumbria, UK

ABSTRACT

Information plays an important role in the individual lives of people, and social media as an aspect of online information phenomenon is an exciting topic to explore in terms of its impact on social entrepreneurship. Many theoretical fields have contributed to the development of social entrepreneurship, looking in particular at the financial, political, and psychological impacts. This chapter is unique since it focuses on social enterprises and the impact of evolving technologies on social entrepreneurship. This chapter contributes to the literature on social media usage in social enterprises and offers a better understanding of the issues in the specific context of developing countries.

BACKGROUND AND INTRODUCTION

Previous work has established a lengthy list of internal and external aspects that affect the acceptance of IT by SMEs (Ahmad et al., 2014; Brunswicker and Vanhaverbeke, 2013; Ongori and Migiro, 2010; Venkatraman and Fahd, 2016). Research also holds that internal factors are more influential than external factors in terms of the acceptance of IT in business (Fernández-Olmos and Ramírez-Alesón, 2017). The characteristics of leaders, entrepreneurs and administrative experts including creativeness, age and experience/knowledge of IT are particularly salient in terms of the impact that they have (Fernández-Olmos and Ramírez-Alesón, 2017; Fosso Wamba & Carter, 2014).

Other issues such as virtual benefits (Mehrtens, Cragg, & Mills, 2001; Pillania, 2007), ease of practice (Lane, Wafa and Hassan, 2014; Yang et al., 2014) the size of the business (Bogataj Habjan and Pucihar, 2017) and its structural readiness (Son and Han, 2011; Alshawi and Goulding, 2008) also have an impact on the adoption of IT in businesses. On the other hand, Government support, as well as rules

DOI: 10.4018/978-1-6684-6287-4.ch048

and procedures and the nature of the business and national setting (Gunasekaran and Ngai, 2009), are the key external factors that influence IT adoption.

Recently, the role of SM has captured the imagination of business researchers and academics. Organizations recognize the tactical value of social media and are making advances in terms of how it can be used strategically. On the other hand, they are taken as an influential means for concluding the worldwide digital gaps (Ali, 2011; Ozuem, Prasad and Lancaster, 2016). Social media can also exert a powerful influence over social conduct, social relations and socio-politics (Stepanova, 2011). Moreover, the dissemination of SM within organizations produces both prospects and challenges (Deng, Joshi, & Li, 2015).

THEORETICAL CONTEXT: SOCIAL MEDIA AND SOCIAL ENTREPRENEURSHIP

Social connection is considered a fundamental component in terms of the psychology of communities (Laroche et al., 2012). The evolution of technology from telegraph, radio and telephone to the computer and other modern devices has made it easier and faster for people to maintain interactions with each other. In an era of rapid technological development and ubiquitous digital technologies, the use of social media is possibly the most notable contribution in the field of networked society (Vodanovich et al., 2010; Harris, Rae & Misner, 2012). Recent studies demonstrate that around the globe there are now over one billion people that use social media for different purposes (Karikari et al., 2017; Anderson et al., 2016). This has revolutionised the process of obtaining information and this has in turn created increased online brand assurance amongst customers (Hammedi et al., 2015; Pagani and Malacarne, 2017; Brodie et al., 2013; Chang et al., 2015; Kim, 2016; Kumar et al., 2016).

Social media is comparatively a recent phenomenon facilitated by increasing global access to the internet. This has given rise to the concept of the so-called "Networked Society" (Castells 2003). The origins of social media interacting can be traced to the advent of Bulletin Board Systems (BBS) in 1978, where users could log in to share software and information as well as to send messages and post to public communication panels. At the same time, because of the increasing interest and availability of home computers, social media became increasingly familiar to users (Kaplan and Haenlein, 2010). More importantly, this BBS is considered as a predecessor of the World Wide Web.

In 1979, Tom Truscott and Jim Ellis, from Duke University came up with the idea of "Usenet", which was a worldwide conversation or communications system that allowed users to post public messages over the internet (Kaplan and Haenlein, 2010). This platform was mainly used for posting articles or news. The idea came into being in a major way in 1980. The difference between BBS and Usenet was the dependency of Usenet on a server to create a news feed and to forward messages and information to different servers. BBS was based on central administration or a server.

In 1991 the discovery of the World Wide Web (WWW) provided new energy to connect the nerd culture with an increasing counterculture. After successfully change the dot. Communism to dot. Commercialism, Web 1.0 had been changed into the new form of two-way communication with the launch of Amazon and eBay in the early 2000s. Consequently, web 2.0 has grown to facilitate a more democratic style of interaction among users (Kaplan and Haenlein, 2010). Indeed, Web 2.0 is predominantly an exchange process for gaining access to resources and co-creating value (Finch et al., 2012).

In 1997 Bruce and Susan Abelson initiated ''Open Diary,'' which was a premature social networking site that combined all online diary writers into one segment (Kaplan and Haenlein, 2010). At the same time Six Degree, which is considered the first distinguishable social media site was also formed in 1997 (Grizane and Jurgelane, 2017; Boyd and Ellison, 2007). This site added features which allowed users to create individual profiles and make friends with other users. SixDegrees.com permitted users to make personal profiles, invite Friends and browse the profiles of other users. Six Degrees endorsed itself as a means to allow individuals to send messages to others. Although this social networking site managed to attract millions of individuals, it closed in 2000 as a consequence of unsustainable business operations.Blogging sites were formulated in 1999 and added a new arm to the establishment of social media. Blogging remains popular among social media users. Blogging was first called "weblogging" in 1997 later transformed into "Blogging". The format because very popular (Kaplan and Haenlein, 2010).

In 2000 with the evolution of social networking sites like Myspace, LinkedIn and Facebook, and the increasing access to high-speed Internet services, social media usage grew ever more popular. The appearance of several sites changed how people in general, and entrepreneurs, in particular, shared common interests. For example, applications like Photobucket and Flickr delivered give photo sharing services to users. At this point social networking because a key consumer trend and sites such as Facebook and Twitter became, for some, an essential part of daily life. Around 2003 social media began to focus on conventional organisations and mass audiences. MySpace, which acquired around $580 million when it first appeared, is considered to be the first example of an SNS which managed to attract mainstream media attention.

Although several explanations exist regarding social media, there remains no objectively recognised definition, in terms of both functional and theoretical contexts (Treem & Leonardi, 2012; Omosigho and Abeysinghe, 2012; Kaplan & Haenlein, 2010; Xiang & Gretzel, 2010). Currently, existing definitions have either emphasized the specific structures of social media that have since become out-dated (Grizane and Jurgelane, 2017; Boyd & Ellison, 2007; Kaplan & Haenlein, 2010) or have focussed on the energetic aspects of social media usage (Scott & Orlikowski, 2014). As a consequence of the incessant and rapid advancement of Social media, it is difficult to define it using a single perspective (Kane et al., 2014).

This chapter focuses on both the substantial features of social media and the dynamic interpretations of social media. The concept of social media can be defined using different perspectives, and each explanation tends to have been instigated by the insight brought to bear from each corresponding study (Kaplan and Haenlein, 2010). In terms of behavioural observation, social media has been defined as a set of actions, performances, and behaviours of groups of people who gather to share information, knowledge, and views using familiar online media (Safko, 2012; Zafarani & Liu, 2014). In other words, social media is more about the thoughts that people produce and share rather than their perceptions (Lincoln, 2010). Three main characteristics of social media from a behavioural perspective are constructive, shared aptitude and conversation enabler (Lincoln, 2010; Ahlqvist et al. 2008). Constructive social media users add value to the sites or apps they use in social interactions. Social media diverts private individuals to become the pioneers of particular sources of information by sharing thoughts, perceptions and knowledge online. Social media platforms have continued to prosper and to shape society (Richey, 2016).

On the other hand, shared aptitude in the context of social media means working collectively and efficiently without any geographical restrictions. Social media is a collaborative tool which is easily adaptable and flexible in nature (Wang, Yu and Wei, 2012; Georgescu & Popescul, 2015; Ozuem, Prasad and Lancaster, 2016). Social media represents the evolution of a process of content distribution through social communications. The idea of enabling conversation is one of the key features of social media. The term 'enabler' refers to the use of social media practices and actions to achieve a course or function. Kadam, & Ayarekar (2014) suggested that the interactive nature of social media sites breaks down class and other barriers. Wikipedia, which has the ultimate aim to produce encyclopaedic content employs shared perceptions and contributions from a number of Web users. Wikipedia is an example of using social media as an enabler.

From a media viewpoint, Social media is an upgraded version of mass media and niche media. Social media has three explicit features. First, social media is collaborative. Thus, several authors have described social media as a mode of receiving and publishing messages to extensive audiences who can empower an exchange of dyadic and networked collaboration (Järvinen, Tollinen, Karjaluoto, & Jayawardhena, 2012; Lacka & Chong, 2016). Russo, Watkins, Kelly, and Chan (2008) defined social media as a collaborative platform that supports online communications and networking. Secondly, the content generated in social media is mainly produced by users rather than professionals. Finally, social media stresses the centrality of content and community rather than information.

From a conceptual perspective, social media is a platform on which people interact and it is constructed based on three key principles of content, communities and Web 2.0. This new way of communication enables users to generate, share, exchange and observe content in simulated groups and networks (Stockdale, Ahmed and Scheepers, 2012; Ahlqvist, Bäck, Halonen and Heinonen, 2008). Thus, social media is not viewed equally amongst business practitioners or academics and the concepts of Web 2.0 and User Generated Content are complex (Kaplan and Haenlein, 2010; Laroche et al., 2012). According to Boyd and Ellison, (2007) the socially interactive nature of social media encompasses content, communities and Web 2.0 technologies and delivers services through web-based and mobile applications.

Figure 1. Social media under a conceptual perspective

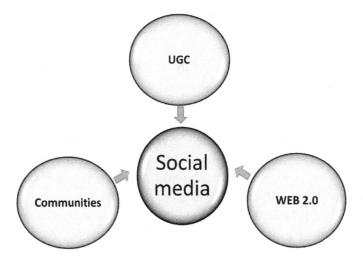

For hundreds of years, the construction and propagation of content have been evolving, and the possibilities for typical users to interconnect and influence mass audiences have only recently been realised with the arrival of Web 2.0 technologies. According to Kaplan and Haenlein, (2010) Web 2.0 was first evaluated in 2004 as a means of generating and publishing content and applications by software inventors and users in a collaborative manner. The author's introduced Web 2.0 as a platform for the revolution of social media, and a symbol of a new conceptual and technological foundation. From his point of view,

Web 2.0 signifies an ideological and scientific revolution with elementary functionalities in terms of where the World Wide Web (WWW) can be accessed by operators and end-users. Therefore Web 2.0 is considered as a key platform to produce and establish software and content in a collaborative manner instead of at the individual level (Kaplan and Haenlein, 2010).

Web 2.0 tends to refer to the broad phenomenon of social media. However, in this study, the term is used to review the technical aspects of social media. Web 2.0 incorporates a diverse range of applications including wikis, blogs, podcasts, social networking sites, debate forums, conference spaces, direct messaging, group journals and address records, cybernetic offices, joint whiteboards presentation systems and many more. Web 2.0 provides the possibility of an enhanced interactive setting that enables a high grade of interaction, support, alliance and assembly amongst users (Barnes et al., 2012). The features of Web 2.0 offer the opportunity to overcome the restrictions of distance for all businesses, whether large, medium or small (Barnes et al., 2012). In addition, Web 2.0 delivers the combined collaborative and participatory approaches to relationship building using tactics such as consumer relationship management. It depends on enterprise applications which are intricate and expensive (Barnes et al., 2012). Thus, industries all around the world are beginning to extensively embrace Web 2.0 in order to forge closer links with stakeholders in more effective ways (Barnes et al., 2012). However, Constantinides and Fountain (2008) suggest that the particular nature of Web 2.0 has not been fully understood and, more importantly, there is no universal definition of the term. Therefore, from a practical viewpoint, the term Web 2.0 is not universally understood (Barnes et al., 2012).

On the other hand, Ahlqvist et al. 2008 consider User Generated Content (UGC) to be something that users can engender and share on the web. However, Kaplan and Haenlein (2010) view UGC as the overall procedure through which individuals make use of social media. The term UGC is useful to distinguish between the various types of media content like audio, video, images, information, labels, assessments, playlists and so on that are publicly available.

User Generated Content (UGC) can be described as the collaborative outputs of all the opportunities that people take advantage of in social media settings (Ozuem, Almeida, and Azemi, 2016; Kaplan and Haenlein, 2010). UGC comprises several forms of media content which are openly accessible and formed by end-users; from text to video and audio resources (Kaplan and Haenlein, 2010). Tang, Fang, and Wang (2014) define UGC simply as media content used to exchange information and views with users. Others have also suggested that UGC is content that is made available on the web which is codified by users without having professional knowledge and practice. Such users, however, have a certain amount of creative ability (Shao, 2009; Christodoulides, Jevons, & Bonhomme, 2012; Organization for Economic Cooperation and Development, 2007).

UGC has the ability to appear in many forms and formats. Letters in newspapers can be regarded as the oldest examples of UGC whereby users had the ability to modify written content in newspapers (Fill, 2009). Currently, Most UGC takes the form of online media which ranges from podcasts, online forums, 'comments', pictures and videos, blogging and reviews (Simon, 2016).

Therefore, UGC is any form of content from digital images, videos, audio files, statements, tweets and blog discussions to forum posts, and everything in between which has been generated by amateur contributors or users. This form of content sharing is considered the consequence of users that endorse brands, rather than content created by the brand itself.

Social Media from a communication perspective refers to the revolution that occurred following the dawn of the information age which expanded human intellect and enhanced social practices and the sharing of intelligence. From this point of view, social media lets users create, discover, share, appraise, and collaboratively create information which is easily accessible online to mass audiences. This suggests that social media has changed the way we communicate from one-to-many (monologue) to many-to-many (dialogue).

Remarkably, even though experts have sought to define social media, limited attention has been given to exploring how organisations define and understand social media (Treem & Leonardi, 2012). The internet plays an integral role in the development of all types of businesses by giving them chances to diverse forms of social media tools like Facebook, Twitter and Instagram. These are used by millions of people on an hourly basis. On the other hand, through peer communications, social media exert a significant influence over consumer purchasing behaviours (Wang et al., 2012; Lueg et al. 2006; Okazaki 2009). At the same time, social media which can be used as powerful marketing tools can support enterprises to create new and dynamic business prospects (Jagongo and Kinyua, 2013). According to Hennig-Thurau et al., (2004) social media has changed the nature of communication between manufacturers and marketers and their targeted clients. Social media is now instrumental in the strategies of several industries (Laroche et al., 2012).

Conversely, social networking provides access to the resources businesses require that are normally very difficult for them to reach (Jagongo and Kinyua, 2013). Social media resources can increase contact between customers and suppliers. It can promote innovation and drive organisations to engage in strategic partnerships (Della Corte, Iavazzi and D'Andrea, 2015). In addition, social media is a platform for businesses to inspire and enhance the sense of intimacy and meaningful relationships they maintain with their customers (Felix et al., 2017; Mersey, Malthouse, & Calder, 2010; Swani, Brown, & Milne, 2014). It also creates more potential to link up with corporate allies internationally (Drummond, McGrath and O'Toole, 2017; Michaelidou, Siamagka, & Christodoulides, 2011). Kim and Ko (2012) and Ozuem, Howell and Lancaster, (2008) see social media as a two-way direct communications medium whereby marketers and consumers both contribute to a new way of trading, servicing and generating corporate models and standards. This would suggest that social interactions via social media are useful for communicating with likeminded individuals and for establishing networks with the public. Hogan & Quan-Haase, (2010) labelled social media as a "moving target" while Sorenson, (2013) contended that social media belongs to a period of rapid development that, at its peak, will overtake anyone's aptitude to make sense of it.

By reviewing different opinions about social media, it can be determined that social media is a platform which allows users to publish and observe a diverse form of information. It can thus be implemented as a strategy for marketing, which involves continuous updating. Enterprises continue to enjoy a variety of advantages from social media. Such a platform of communication has very wide reach. It is low cost to use and offers effective and efficient communications potential (Kaplan and Haenlein, 2010; Kim and Ko, 2012). Businesses can draw attention to different types of users in different parts of the world and they can link with current loyal, and potential customers (Wang et al., 2016; Schultz et al., 2012; Della Corte et al., 2015). This can be carried out effectively and in a more affordable way than with traditional media (Wang et al., 2012). Social media swap physical immediacy for a virtual interface (Barnes et al., 2012). Interaction is vibrant for business actors who can assemble resources quickly to build links (Finch et al., 2012).

Currently, corporate social networking platforms create the opportunity to involve the consumer to generate value in online experiences with offline outcomes. Moreover, whether carried out to fulfil needs or to enjoy interactions in social media platforms, individuals like the idea of contributing, creating and participating online (Laroche et al., 2012). Thus, consumer socialization means that this new and alternative way of communications has changed consumer behaviour permanently. (Lueg et al. 2006; Okazaki 2009).

The intense level of competency of social media compared to traditional ways of communicating through networks has encouraged established leaders to use online content such as Twitter, Facebook, Skype, LinkedIn and so on to build a more sustainable and dynamic environment for their businesses (Kaplan & Haenlein, 2010). The arrival of social media has created powerful options for relational and logistic communication (Lovejoy and Saxton, 2012). Therefore, it can be argued that social media provides an opportunity for all types of businesses to widen their scope and grow their operations to even greater levels of capacity.

Previous studies have claimed that non-profit making enterprises are unable to practice or adopt websites and that social media is underrealized as a tactical, collaborative stakeholder engagement tool (Kent, Taylor, &White, 2003; Saxton, Guo, & Brown, 2007; Chang et al., 2015; Kim, 2016). This perception was perhaps formulated due to a lack of opportunity to create more communications sites with comment options and argument panels. The arrival of social media sites like Facebook and Twitter make those observations invalid since they are free to use and have built-in interactive features (Lovejoy and Saxton, 2012). Therefore, any business, whether large or small, profit or non-profit can generate an online site and start to build a network and grow business activity.

Regardless of the prevalence and rising concentration on social media, an empirical enquiry is only in its embryonic stage. Research has demonstrated the importance and impact of social media usage for consumer marketing (Quinton & Wilson, 2016; Siamagka, Christodoulides, Michaelidou, & Valvi, 2015; Swani et al., 2014) as well as the implications and practices of social media in firms (Treem & Leonardi, 2012; Koch, Leidner and Gonzalez, 2013; Leonardi, 2014). Other research has focussed on branding in large organisations (Ali, Jiménez-Zarco, & Bicho, 2015; Hudson et al., 2015; Kilgour, Sasser, & Larke, 2015; Colleoni, 2013; Arora & Predmore, 2013; Dahnil, Marzuki, Langgat, & Fabeil, 2014). Yet very little has been written about the impact on or usage of social media in SMEs (Dahnil et al., 2014; Wang et al., 2016; Öztamur & Karakadilar, 2014) especially in social entrepreneurial firms.

Social Media as a Strategic Weapon

Although the literature exposes the various theoretical benefits of social media, most of these are operational in nature rather than strategic (Barnes et al., 2012). The adoption of ICTs has been considered a strategic weapon to reach an extensive market and compete with big enterprises for some time (Safari et al., 2015; Ongori and Migiro, 2010). Social media can be used as a tool to develop a dynamic strategy in business (Williams & Williams, 2008). Social networking sites have become central aspects of network resources for administrations. They add strategic value to business performance (Zhou, Wu, & Luo, 2007). Since they offer businesses the potential to interact with distant audiences, social media also create the opportunity to determine new prospects in business strategies. Social media, which offer a widespread source of information, have transformed the strategies of many companies (Mangold & Faulds, 2009). Once introduced as a part of business strategy, social media can play a significant role in managing customer relationships, enhancing communication and facilitating the sharing of knowledge amongst all stakeholders.

Social media help businesses to understand what the public think about their brands, and help them better understand competitors. This helps to inform future strategies. At the same time, social media can help firms to better engage with existing customers (Della Corte et al., 2015). They can influence customers to make repeat purchases. Social media offers an adaptive and sustainable business strategy to entrepreneurs by helping them to join forces and share a diverse range of knowledge with their networks (Drummond et al., 2017). However, Jagongo & Kinyua, (2013) suggest that policymakers in the world of social media should offer constructive online surfing tariffs and e-business strategies in order to inspire entrepreneurs to engage with technological advantages which could add a new dimension to any business format.

Social Entrepreneurship

Any discussion related to "social entrepreneurship" must begin with the term "entrepreneurship" (Martin and Osberg, 2007). Entrepreneurship is a leading component of economic growth and expansion (Anokhin et al. 2008; Rani 2013; Kedmenec et al. 2015). Alongside economic progression, entrepreneurship influences and transforms social conditions (Harding, 2007). Gurol & Atsan, (2006) claim that entrepreneurship is an engine to create new job opportunities, as well as social modifications. On the other hand, it is recognised as a potential breeding ground for technological advancements as well as product and market revolution (Mueller and Thomas, 2000). Entrepreneurship is the process of starting up a business and then contributing to the development of a strong economic position (Harding, 2007). Entrepreneurship is a process which seeks opportunities without concern for the currently controlled resources (Stevenson and Jarillo, 1990). Miller (1983), categorises entrepreneurial behaviour as "innovation, proactiveness and risk-taking". On the other hand, Shane (2003) states that revolution, evaluation and exploitation are all key aspects of entrepreneurship.

Dess et al. (1999) argue that there are two different ways of setting up corporate entrepreneurship. One is to develop an entirely new way to trade, and the other is to alter the present circumstances and curricula via strategic revitalization. Messeghem, (2003) agrees and suggests that launching a business is just a technique which is associated with nursing entrepreneurial behaviour. Such behaviour involves generating or adding to new activity as part of entrepreneurial actions (Stevenson and Jarillo, 1990; Messeghem, 2003). In this sense, the entrepreneur can come up with a new product or service in existing markets to dominate market share and to increase value for the enterprise (Certo and Miller, 2008).

Messeghem, (2003) also suggests that the dynamic detection of new opportunities is part of entrepreneurship and is a tactical dimension of the firm. According to Alvord et al. (2004), entrepreneurship is the process of forming a viable business organization. Thus, it can be said that entrepreneurship is the creation of value through innovation. However, entrepreneurial research has both academic and practical importance which invite further research (Abdulwahab and Al-Damen, 2015).

Social entrepreneurship is the arena in which entrepreneurs modify their actions to be directly knotted with the pivotal goal of bringing social value (Abu-Saifan, 2012). Last few decade, social entrepreneurship has become a progressively important global cultural phenomenon (Dacin et al. 2011; Thompson et al. 2000) because of the failure of government and other responsible authority to lessen toughest and most intractable social challenges such as poverty, social expulsion, and the diverse nature of environment (Harding, 2007).

According to Alvarez and Barney, (2007) the idea of developing new value is vital for the field of entrepreneurship and spreading this sense to the land of social entrepreneurship has directed to an evolving research stream of concentration to scholars (Mair & Martı, 2006; Austin et al., 2012; Certo and Miller, 2008; Trivedi and Stokols, 2011; Peredo and Chrisman, 2006; Dacin et al. 2011; Schendel and Hitt, 2007).

Social entrepreneurship is a multidimensional concept concerning the entrepreneurially virtuous activities to eradicate social problems or attain the social objectives (Mort et al., 2003; Thompson, 2002). Even though social entrepreneurship is comparatively new, the practice of this phenomenon is considerably older and has been undertaken with government support by private foundations for many years. Social entrepreneurship is a creative activity that can support needy and relegated groups and take an approach to explain social difficulties in inventive ways (Noruzi, Westover, & Rahimi, 2010; Unkwu, Jude and Obiajulu, Egbunike and Ozuem, 2016). Social entrepreneurship has been the subject of a great deal of academic attention in recent decades.

Awareness of social entrepreneurship within the academic world and amongst government only developed in the 1990s. This took place alongside the evolution of new media in the 2000s. In 2004, social co-operatives were launched in the UK to help social businesses to harness their returns and resources for social purposes. As the borders between government, not-for-profit, and commercial sectors have become increasingly blurred, and as further ground-breaking and profitable ways of addressing social problems have emerged, there has been a greater focus on how ideas like social entrepreneurship can address critical social problems (Dees & Anderson, 2003).

Even though the focus on social-oriented business has increased over the years (Dacin et al. 2011; Thompson et al. 2000), it is clear that the concept of social entrepreneurship remains indistinct (Haugh, 2005; Robinson and Lo, 2005; Certo and Miller, 2008; Dacin et al. 2011). Scholars like Smith, Bell and Watts, (2014) have suggested that more comprehensive research to look at how advanced social projects are determined is essential in order to comprehend the phenomena more clearly. In addition, since much research has emphasized the charitable nature of social enterprises, their commercial role has never fully come into focus (Dees, 1998).

In this study the process of resource mobilization in terms of developing market strategy considered as a leading research gap. During the growth phase, every organisation requires doing their marketing broadly which involve extensive resource acquisition. The selection of this gap was determined by many aspects. Regardless of the dominant theoretical evidence on the role of marketing in the development of commercial businesses, it is a surprising fact that there is a lack of academic research on marketing in the context of social enterprise (Agafonow, 2014; Shaw & Carter, 2007). On the other hand, to obtain the required funding, influence customers perception, spread business activity and distinguishable business model, social enterprises need to promote themselves (Agafonow, 2014).

Compared to developed countries, in developing countries like Bangladesh, Social enterprises operate in a condition of resource constrained. Regularly they are competing with several other organizations for resources together with the shortage of capital and expert employees. Lack of adequate funding is considered as a primary obstacle for the growth of social enterprises in developing countries especially in the Asian region (Kim and Lim, 2017).

Social media can deliver an excellent return for entrepreneurs and can help them to capitalise on social investments. Currently, almost all types of businesses are engaging in social networking communications (Bughin, 2008). The cooperative actions of entrepreneurial organisations and their partners through two-way communication on social media platforms has proven productive (Lacka & Chong, 2016; Singaraju et al., 2016). The co-creation of new products, facilities, concepts and systems has been accelerated with the evolution of social media (Drummond et al., 2017).

MANAGERIAL IMPLICATIONS

Social media has modified the way businesses deal with customers (Nadeem, 2012). Blogs, social networking sites, content communities, virtual worlds and collaborative projects collectively represent groups of individuals that generate and distribute content internally and outside of specialised practices. It is now one of the core elements of communicating with consumers (Ozuem, Patel, Howell, and Lancaster, G., 2017). Businesses are starting to form expressive and constant affairs that comprise regular connections with their clients. This new description of customer engagement permits firms to establish reliable relations that spread and exist a long time.

Research increasingly reveals numerous motives for the uptake of social media usage amongst companies (Scott & Orlikowski, 2014; Uyar and Boyar, 2015; Leonardi,2014). In several cases, researchers have focussed on the practice of internal social media stands (Scott & Orlikowski, 2014; Lee, 2016; Huang, Baptista & Galliers, 2013) by prominent companies communicating with international networks (Karjaluoto and Ulkuniemi, 2015). In this sense, social media offers many interactional benefits and outcomes that were previously difficult, and often impossible to attain. Social media facilitates an innovative way to share knowledge (Koch, Leidner and Gonzalez, 2013) and a new means to reach geographically isolated users (Scott & Orlikowski, 2014). Kaplan and Haenlin (2010) have underscored the significance of social media platforms and proposed some approaches to adopting social media in business. There is scope to explore social media more strictly in terms of its uses in social enterprise.

Indeed, most academic literature examines commercial enterprises rather than social enterprises when it comes to social media. A consequence of this is that researchers have perhaps overlooked an essential context (Lewis, 2015; Koch Gonzalez & Leidner, 2012; Vandenbosch and Eggermont, 2016; Kaplan and Haenlein, 2010) and have tended to depend on the inaccurate hypothesis that social entrepreneurs understand and thus unable to take full advantage from social media (Ho, 2016). Besides, such assumptions do overlook the fast-paced nature of technology and variation in the types of users and business settings that are implicated.

REFERENCES

Abdulwahab, M., & Al-Damen, D. (2015). The Impact of Entrepreneurs' Characteristics on Small Business Success at Medical Instruments Supplies Organizations in Jordan. *International Journal of Business and Social Science*, *6*(8), 164–175.

Abu-Saifan, S. (2012, February). Social Entrepreneurship: Definition and Boundaries. *Technology Innovation Management Review*, 22-27.

Agafonow, A. (2014). Value Creation, Value Capture, and Value Devolution. *Administration & Society*, *47*(8), 1038–1060. doi:10.1177/0095399714555756

Ahlqvist, T., Back, A., Halonen, M., & Heinonen, S. (2008). *Social media roadmaps: exploring the futures triggered by social media*. VTT. Retrieved from http://www.vtt.fi/inf/pdf/tiedotteet/2008/t2454.pdf

Ahmad, S., Abu Bakar, A., Faziharudean, T., & Mohamad Zaki, K. (2014). An Empirical Study of Factors Affecting E-Commerce Adoption among Small- and Medium-Sized Enterprises in a Developing Country: Evidence from Malaysia. *Information Technology for Development*, *21*(4), 555–572. doi:10.1080/02681102.2014.899961

Ainin, S., Parveen, F., Moghavvemi, S., Noor, I. J., & Nor Liyana, M. S. (2015). Factors influencing the use of social media by SMEs and its performance outcomes. *Industr Mngmnt & Data Systems*, *115*(3), 570–588. doi:10.1108/IMDS-07-2014-0205

Alalwan, A., Rana, N., Dwivedi, Y., & Algharabat, R. (2017). Social media in marketing: A review and analysis of the existing literature. *Telematics and Informatics*, *34*(7), 1177–1190. doi:10.1016/j.tele.2017.05.008

Ali, A. H. (2011). Power of Social Media in Developing Nations: New Tools for Closing the Global Digital Divide and Beyond, The. *Harv. Hum. Rts. J.*, *24*, 185.

Ali, I., Jiménez-Zarco, A. I., & Bicho, M. (2015). Using Social Media for CSR communication and engaging stakeholders. *Developments in Corporate Governance and Responsibility*, *7*, 165–185. doi:10.1108/S2043-052320150000007010

Alshawi, M., & Goulding, J. (2008). Organisational e-readiness: Embracing IT for sustainable competitive advantage. *Construction Innovation*, *8*(1), ci.2008.33308aaa.001. doi:10.1108/ci.2008.33308aaa.001

Alvarez, S., Barney, J., & Anderson, P. (2013). Forming and Exploiting Opportunities: The Implications of Discovery and Creation Processes for Entrepreneurial and Organizational Research. *Organization Science*, *24*(1), 301–317. doi:10.1287/orsc.1110.0727

Alvord, S. H., Brown, L. D., & Letts, C. W. (2004). Social entrepreneurship and societal transformation: An exploratory study. *The Journal of Applied Behavioral Science*, *40*(3), 260–282. doi:10.1177/0021886304266847

Anderson, S., Hamilton, K., & Tonner, A. (2016). Social labour: Exploring work in consumption. *Marketing Theory*, *16*(3), 383–400. doi:10.1177/1470593116640598

Anokhin, S., Grichnik, D., & Hisrich, R. D. (2008). The journey from novice to serial entrepreneurship in China and Germany: Are the drivers the same. *Managing Global Transitions*, *6*(2), 117–142.

Arora, P., & Predmore, C. E. (2013). Social media as a strategic tool: Going beyond the obvious. *Advanced Series in Management*, *11*, 115–127. doi:10.1108/S1877-6361(2013)0000011010

Austin, J., Stevenson, H., & Wei-Skillern, J. (2006). Social and commercial entrepreneurship: Same, different, or both? *Entrepreneurship Theory and Practice*, *30*(1), 1–22. doi:10.1111/j.1540-6520.2006.00107.x

Barnes, D., Clear, F., Dyerson, R., Harindranath, G., Harris, L., & Rae, A. (2012). Web 2.0 and micro-businesses: An exploratory investigation. *Journal of Small Business and Enterprise Development*, *19*(4), 687–711. doi:10.1108/14626001211277479

Bogataj Habjan, K., & Pucihar, A. (2017). Cloud Computing Adoption Business Model Factors: Does Enterprise Size Matter? *The Engineering Economist*, *28*(3).

boyd, d., & Ellison, N. (2007). Social Network Sites: Definition, History, and Scholarship. *Journal of Computer-Mediated Communication, 13*(1), 210-230.

Brodie, R. J., Ilic, A., Juric, B., & Hollebeek, L. (2013). Consumer engagement in a virtual brand community: An exploratory analysis. *Journal of Business Research, 66*(1), 105–114. doi:10.1016/j. jbusres.2011.07.029

Brunswicker, S., & Vanhaverbeke, W. (2013). *Open Innovation in Small and Medium-Sized Enterprises (SMEs): External Knowledge Sourcing Strategies and Internal Organizational Facilitators*. SSRN Electronic Journal.

Bughin, J. (2008). The rise of enterprise 2.0. *Journal of Direct Data and Digital Marketing Practice, 9*(3), 251–259. doi:10.1057/palgrave.dddmp.4350100

Castells, M. (2011). A network theory of power. *International Journal of Communication, 5*, 773–787.

Certo, S., & Miller, T. (2008). Social entrepreneurship: Key issues and concepts. *Business Horizons, 51*(4), 267–271. doi:10.1016/j.bushor.2008.02.009

Chang, C.-C., Hung, S.-W., Cheng, M.-J., & Wu, C.-Y. (2015). Exploring the intention to continue using social networking sites: The case of Facebook. *Technological Forecasting and Social Change, 95*, 48–56. doi:10.1016/j.techfore.2014.03.012

Christodoulides, G., Jevons, C., & Bonhomme, J. (2012). Memo to marketers: Quantitative evidence for change. How user-generated content really affects brands. *Journal of Advertising Research, 52*(1), 53–64. doi:10.2501/JAR-52-1-053-064

Colleoni, E. (2013). CSR communication strategies for organizational legitimacy in social media. *Corporate Communications, 18*(2), 228–248. doi:10.1108/13563281311319508

Constantinides, E., & Fountain, S. (2008). Web 2.0: Conceptual foundations and marketing issues. *Journal of Direct. Data and Digital Marketing Practice, 9*(3), 231–244. doi:10.1057/palgrave.dddmp.4350098

Dacin, M., Dacin, P., & Tracey, P. (2011). Social Entrepreneurship: A Critique and Future Directions. *Organization Science, 22*(5), 1203–1213. doi:10.1287/orsc.1100.0620

Dahnil, M. I., Marzuki, K. M., Langgat, J., & Fabeil, N. F. (2014). Factors Influencing SMEs Adoption of Social Media Marketing. *Procedia: Social and Behavioral Sciences, 148*, 119–126. doi:10.1016/j. sbspro.2014.07.025

Dees, J. G. (1998). *The meaning of social entrepreneurship*. Comments and suggestions contributed from the Social Entrepreneurship Funders Working Group.

Dees, J. G., & Anderson, B. B. (2003). For-Profit Social Ventures. *International Journal of Entrepreneurship Education, 2*, 1–26.

Della Corte, V., Iavazzi, A., & D'Andrea, C. (2015). Customer involvement through social media: The cases of some telecommunication firms. *Journal of Open Innovation: Technology, Market, and Complexity, 1*(1), 10. doi:10.118640852-015-0011-y

Deng, X., Joshi, K., & Li, Y. (2015). Introduction to the Social Media and Enterprise Minitrack: Job and Work Design Issues. In *System Sciences (HICSS), 2015 48th Hawaii International Conference on* (pp. 1818–1818). IEEE.

Dess, G. D., Lumpkin, G. T., & McGee, J. E. (1999). Linking Corporate Entrepreneurship to Strategy, Structure, and Process: Suggested Research Directions. *Entrepreneurship Theory and Practice, 23*(3), 85–102. doi:10.1177/104225879902300306

Drummond, C., McGrath, H., & O'Toole, T. (2017). The impact of social media on resource mobilisation in entrepreneurial firms. *Industrial Marketing Management.*

Drummond, C., McGrath, H., & O'Toole, T. (2017). The impact of social media on resource mobilisation in entrepreneurial firms. *Industrial Marketing Management.*

Durkin, M., McGowan, P., & McKeown, N. (2013). Exploring social media adoption in small to medium-sized enterprises in Ireland. *Journal of Small Business and Enterprise Development, 20*(4), 716–734. doi:10.1108/JSBED-08-2012-0094

Felix, R., Rauschnabel, P. A., & Hinsch, C. (2017). Elements of strategic social media marketing: A holistic framework. *Journal of Business Research, 70*, 118–126. doi:10.1016/j.jbusres.2016.05.001

Fernández-Olmos, M., & Ramírez-Alesón, M. (2017). How internal and external factors influence the dynamics of SME technology collaboration networks over time. *Technovation, 64-65*, 16–27. doi:10.1016/j.technovation.2017.06.002

Fill, C. (2009). *Marketing communications: Interactivity, communities and content* (5th ed.). Harlow, UK: Prentice Hall/Financial Times

Finch, J., Wagner, B., & Hynes, N. (2012). Resources prospectively: How actors mobilize resources in business settings. *Journal of Business Research, 65*(2), 164–174. doi:10.1016/j.jbusres.2011.05.017

Fosso Wamba, S., & Carter, L. (2014). Social Media Tools Adoption and Use by SMEs: An Empirical Study. *Journal of End User and Organizational Computing, 26*(1), 1–16. doi:10.4018/joeuc.2014040101

Georgescu, M., & Popescul, D. (2015). Social media–the new paradigm of collaboration and communication for business environment. *Procedia Economics and Finance, 20*, 277–282. doi:10.1016/S2212-5671(15)00075-1

Grizane, T., & Jurgelane, I. (2017). Social Media Impact on Business Evaluation. *Procedia Computer Science, 104*, 190–196. doi:10.1016/j.procs.2017.01.103

Gunasekaran, A., McGaughey, R., Ngai, E., & Rai, B. (2009). E-Procurement Adoption in the Southcoast SMEs. *International Journal of Production Economics, 122*(1), 161–175. doi:10.1016/j.ijpe.2009.05.013

Gurol, Y., & Atsan, N. (2006). Entrepreneurial characteristics amongst university students. *Education + Training, 48*(1), 25–38. doi:10.1108/00400910610645716

Hammedi, W., Kandampully, J., Zhang, T. T., & Bouquiaux, L. (2015). Online customer engagement: Creating social environments through brand community constellations. *Journal of Service Management, 26*(5), 777–806. doi:10.1108/JOSM-11-2014-0295

Harding, R. (2007). Understanding social entrepreneurship. *Industry and Higher Education, 21*(1), 73–86. doi:10.5367/000000007780222723

Harris, L., & Rae, A. (2009). Social networks: The future of marketing for small business. *The Journal of Business Strategy, 30*(5), 24–31. doi:10.1108/02756660910987581

Haugh, H. (2005). A research agenda for social entrepreneurship. *Social Enterprise Journal, 1*(1), 1–12. doi:10.1108/17508610580000703

Hennig-Thurau, T., Gwinner, K. P., Walsh, G., & Gremler, D. D. (2004). Electronic Word-of-Mouth Via Consumer Opinion Platforms: What Motivates Consumers to Articulate Themselves on the Internet? *Journal of Interactive Marketing, 18*(1), 38–52. doi:10.1002/dir.10073

Ho, T. (2016). Private Entrepreneurs in China: Social Entrepreneurs or Social Menaces? *Chinese Public Administration Review, 3*(1/2), 14. doi:10.22140/cpar.v3i1/2.52

Hogan, B., & Quan-Haase, A. (2010). Persistence and Change in Social Media. *Bulletin of Science, Technology & Society, 30*(5), 309–315. doi:10.1177/0270467610380012

Huang, J., Baptista, J., & Galliers, R. (2013). Reconceptualizing rhetorical practices in organizations: The impact of social media on internal communications. *Information & Management, 50*(2-3), 112–124. doi:10.1016/j.im.2012.11.003

Hudson, S., Roth, M. S., Madden, T. J., & Hudson, R. (2015). The effects of social media on emotions, brand relationship quality, and word of mouth: An empirical study of music festival attendees. *Tourism Management, 47*, 68–76. doi:10.1016/j.tourman.2014.09.001

Jagongo, A., & Kinyua, C. (2013). The Social Media and Entrepreneurship Growth (A New Business Communication Paradigm among SMEs in Nairobi). *International Journal of Humanities and Social Science, 3*(10), 213–227.

Järvinen, J., Tollinen, A., Karjaluoto, H., & Jayawardhena, C. (2012). Digital and social media marketing usage in B2B industrial section. *Marketing Management Journal, 22*(2).

Kadam, A., & Ayarekar, S. (2014). Impact of Social Media on Entrepreneurship and Entrepreneurial Performance: Special Reference to Small and Medium Scale Enterprises. *SIES Journal of Management, 10*(1).

Kane, G., Alavi, M., Labianca, G., & Borgatti, S. (2014). What's Different About Social Media Networks? A Framework and Research Agenda. *Management Information Systems Quarterly, 38*(1), 274–304. doi:10.25300/MISQ/2014/38.1.13

Kaplan, A. M., & Haenlein, M. (2010). Users of the world, unite! The challenges and opportunities of Social Media. *Business Horizons, 53*(1), 59–68. doi:10.1016/j.bushor.2009.09.003

Karikari, S., Osei-Frimpong, K., & Owusu-Frimpong, N. (2017). Evaluating individual level antecedents and consequences of social media use in Ghana. *Technological Forecasting and Social Change, 123*, 68–79. doi:10.1016/j.techfore.2017.06.023

Karjaluoto, H., & Ulkuniemi, P. (2015). Digital communications in industrial marketing. *Journal of Business and Industrial Marketing*, *30*(6). doi:10.1108/JBIM-04-2013-0092

Kedmenec, I., Rebernik, M., & Perić, J. (2015). The Impact of Individual Characteristics on Intentions to Pursue Social Entrepreneurship. *Ekonomski Pregled*, *66*(2), 119–137.

Kent, M. L., Taylor, M., & White, W. J. (2003). The relationship between Web site design and organizational responsiveness to stakeholders. *Public Relations Review*, *29*(1), 63–77. doi:10.1016/S0363-8111(02)00194-7

Kilgour, M., Sasser, S. L., & Larke, R. (2015). The social media transformation process: Curating content into strategy. *Corporate Communications*, *20*(3), 326–343. doi:10.1108/CCIJ-07-2014-0046

Kim, A., & Ko, E. (2012). Do social media marketing activities enhance customer equity? An empirical study of luxury fashion brand. *Journal of Business Research*, *65*(10), 1480–1486. doi:10.1016/j.jbusres.2011.10.014

Kim, D. (2016). Value ecosystem models for social media services. *Technological Forecasting and Social Change*, *107*, 13–27. doi:10.1016/j.techfore.2016.03.010

Kim, D., & Lim, U. (2017). Social Enterprise as a Catalyst for Sustainable Local and Regional Development. *Sustainability*, *9*(8), 1427. doi:10.3390u9081427

Kim, H. D., Lee, I., & Lee, C. K. (2013). Building Web 2.0 enterprises: A study of small and medium enterprises in the United States. *International Small Business Journal*, *31*(2), 156–174. doi:10.1177/0266242611409785

Koch, H., Leidner, D., & Gonzalez, E. (2013). Digitally enabling social networks: Resolving IT-culture conflict. *Information Systems Journal*, *23*(6), 501–523. doi:10.1111/isj.12020

Kumar, A., Bezawada, R., Rishika, R., Janakiraman, R., & Kannan, P. (2016). From social to sale: The effects of firm-generated content in social media on customer behavior. *Journal of Marketing*, *80*(1), 7–25. doi:10.1509/jm.14.0249

Lacka, E., & Chong, A. (2016). Usability perspective on social media sites' adoption in the B2B context. *Industrial Marketing Management*, *54*, 80–91. doi:10.1016/j.indmarman.2016.01.001

Lane, P., Wafa, S., & Hassan, R. (2014). Perceived Usefulness and Perceived Ease of Use of E-Commerce Adoption among Entrepreneurs in Sabah. *Kuwait Chapter of Arabian Journal of Business and Management Review*, *3*(9), 94–103. doi:10.12816/0018333

Laroche, M., Habibi, M. R., Richard, M. O., & Sankaranarayanan, R. (2012). The effects of social media based brand communities on brand community markers, value creation practices, brand trust and brand loyalty. *Computers in Human Behavior*, *28*(5), 1755–1767. doi:10.1016/j.chb.2012.04.016

Lee, J., & Hong, I. B. (2016). Predicting positive user responses to social media advertising: The roles of emotional appeal, informativeness, and creativity. *International Journal of Information Management*, *36*(3), 360–373. doi:10.1016/j.ijinfomgt.2016.01.001

Leonardi. (2014). Social media, knowledge sharing, and innovation. *Information Systems Research*, *25*(4), 796–816. doi:10.1287/isre.2014.0536

Lewis, S. (2015). Reciprocity as a Key Concept for Social Media and Society. *Social Media + Society*, *1*(1).

Lincoln, S. (2010). *Mastering Web 2.0*. London: Kogan Page.

Lovejoy, K., & Saxton, G. (2012). Information, Community, and Action: How Nonprofit Organizations Use Social Media*. *Journal of Computer-Mediated Communication*, *17*(3), 337–353. doi:10.1111/j.1083-6101.2012.01576.x

Lueg, J. E., Ponder, N., Beatty, S. E., & Capella, M. L. (2006). Teenagers' Use of Alternative Shopping Channels: A Consumer Socialization Perspective. *Journal of Retailing*, *82*(2), 137–153. doi:10.1016/j.jretai.2005.08.002

Mair, J., & Marti, I. (2006). Social entrepreneurship research: A source of explanation, prediction, and delight. *Journal of World Business*, *41*(1), 36–44. doi:10.1016/j.jwb.2005.09.002

Mangold, W. G., & Faulds, D. J. (2009). Social media: The new hybrid element of the promotion mix. *Business Horizons*, *52*(4), 357–365. doi:10.1016/j.bushor.2009.03.002

Martin, R. L., & Osberg, S. (2007). Social Entrepreneurship: The Case for Definition. Stanford Social Innovation Review, 29–39.

Mehrtens, J., Cragg, P. B., & Mills, A. M. (2001). A model of Internet Adoption by SMEs. *Information & Management*, *38*(3), 165–176. doi:10.1016/S0378-7206(01)00086-6

Mersey, R. D., Malthouse, E. C., & Calder, B. J. (2010). Engagement with Online Media. *Journal of Media Business Studies*, *7*(2), 39–56. doi:10.1080/16522354.2010.11073506

Messeghem, K. (2003). Strategic entrepreneurship and managerial activities in SMEs. *Estados Unidos*, *21*(2), 197–212.

Michaelidou, N., Siamagka, N. T., & Christodoulides, G. (2011). Usage, barriers and measurement of social media marketing: An exploratory investigation of small and medium B2B brands. *Industrial Marketing Management*, *40*(7), 1153–1159. doi:10.1016/j.indmarman.2011.09.009

Miller, D. (1983). The Correlates of Entrepreneurship in Three Types of Firms. *Management Science*, *29*(7), 770–791. doi:10.1287/mnsc.29.7.770

Mort, G. S., Weerawardena, J., & Carnegie, K. (2003). Social entrepreneurship: Towards conceptualisation. *International Journal of Nonprofit and Voluntary Sector Marketing*, *8*(1), 76–89. doi:10.1002/nvsm.202

Mueller, S. L., & Thomas, A. S. (2000). Culture and entrepreneurial potential: A nine-country study of locus of control and innovativeness. *Journal of Business Venturing*, *16*(1), 51–75. doi:10.1016/S0883-9026(99)00039-7

Nadeem, M. (2012). Returning Customer: Was That A Planned Purchase? *Skyline Business Journal*, *7*(1), 11–17.

Noruzi, M. R., Westover, J. H., & Rahimi, G. R. (2010). An Exploration of Social Entrepreneurship in the Entrepreneurship Era. *Asian Social Science, 6*(6), 3–10. doi:10.5539/ass.v6n6p3

Okazaki, S. (2009). The Tactical Use of Mobile Marketing: How Adolescents' Social Networking Can Best Shape Brand Extensions. *Journal of Advertising Research, 49*(1), 12–26. doi:10.2501/S0021849909090102

Omosigho, O., & Abeysinghe, G. (2012). Evaluating readiness of organizations to adopt social media for competitive advantage. *Information Society (i-Society), 2012 International Conference on,* 16-21.

Ongori, H., & Migiro, S. (2010). Information and communication technologies adoption in SMEs: Literature review. *Journal of Chinese Entrepreneurship, 2*(1), 93–104. doi:10.1108/17561391011019041

Organization for Economic Cooperation and Development. (2007, April 12). *Participative web: User-created content.* Retrieved from http://www.oecd.org/sti/38393115.pdf

Öztamur, D., & Karakadilar, I. S. (2014). Exploring the role of social media for SMEs: As a new marketing strategy tool for the firm performance perspective. *Procedia: Social and Behavioral Sciences, 150,* 511–520. doi:10.1016/j.sbspro.2014.09.067

Ozuem, W., Almeida Pinho, C., & Azemi, Y. (2016). User-Generated Content and Perceived Customer Value. In *Competitive Social Media Marketing Strategies. Mission* (pp. 50–63). Hershey, PA: IGI Global. doi:10.4018/978-1-4666-9776-8.ch003

Ozuem, W., Howell, K., & Lancaster, G. (2008). Communicating in the new interactive marketspace. *European Journal of Marketing, 42*(9/10), 1059–1083. doi:10.1108/03090560810891145

Ozuem, W., Patel, A., Howell, K., & Lancaster, G. (2017). An exploration of consumers' response to online service recovery initiatives. *International Journal of Market Research, 59*(1), 97–119.

Ozuem, W., Prasad, J., & Lancaster, G. (2016). Exploiting online social gambling for marketing communications. *Journal of Strategic Marketing, 26*(3), 258–282. doi:10.1080/0965254X.2016.1211728

Pagani, M., & Malacarne, G. (2017). Experiential engagement and active vs. passive behaviour in mobile location-based social networks: The moderating role of privacy. *Journal of Interactive Marketing, 37,* 133–148. doi:10.1016/j.intmar.2016.10.001

Peredo, A. M., & McLean, M. (2006). Social entrepreneurship: A critical review of the concept. *Journal of World Business, 41*(1), 56–65. doi:10.1016/j.jwb.2005.10.007

Pillania, R. (2007). Organisational issues for knowledge management in SMEs. *International Journal of Business and Systems Research, 1*(3), 367. doi:10.1504/IJBSR.2007.015835

Quinton, S., & Wilson, D. (2016). Tensions and ties in social media networks: Towards a model of understanding business relationship development and business performance enhancement through the use of LinkedIn. *Industrial Marketing Management, 54,* 15–24. doi:10.1016/j.indmarman.2015.12.001

Rani, S. H. (2013). Antecedents and Consequences of Entrepreneurial Quality among Graduate Entrepreneurs. *Asian Journal of Business and Management Sciences, 2*(9), 44–55.

Richey, M. (2016). *Exploring social media use in small firms: a cultural toolkit perspective* (PhD thesis). Loughborough University.

Robinson, J. A., & Lo, J. (2005). *Bibliography of Academic Papers on Social Entrepreneurship*. New York: New York University.

Russo, A., Watkins, J., Kelly, L., & Chan, S. (2008). Participatory communication with social media. *Curator (New York, N.Y.), 51*(1), 21–31. doi:10.1111/j.2151-6952.2008.tb00292.x

Safari, F., Safari, N., Hasanzadeh, A., & Ghatari, A. (2015). Factors affecting the adoption of cloud computing in small and medium enterprises. *International Journal of Business Information Systems, 20*(1), 116. doi:10.1504/IJBIS.2015.070894

Safko, L. (2012). *The social media bible* (3rd ed.). Hoboken, NJ: John Wiley & Sons.

Saxton, G. D., Guo, C., & Brown, W. (2007). New dimensions of nonprofit responsiveness: The application and promise of Internet-based technologies. *Public Performance & Management Review, 31*(2), 144–173. doi:10.2753/PMR1530-9576310201

Schendel, D., & Hitt, M. A. (2007). Introduction to volume 1. *Strategic Entrepreneurship Journal, 1*(1–2), 1–6. doi:10.1002ej.16

Schultz, R. J., Schwepker, C. H., & Good, D. J. (2012). An exploratory study of social media in business-to-business selling: Salesperson characteristics, activities and performance. *Marketing Management Journal, 22*(2), 76–89.

Scott, S., & Orlikowski, W. (2014). Entanglements in Practice: Performing Anonymity Through Social Media. *Management Information Systems Quarterly, 38*(3), 873–893. doi:10.25300/MISQ/2014/38.3.11

Shane, S. (2003). *A general theory of entrepreneurship: The individual-opportunity nexus*. Cheltenham, UK: Edward Elgar Publishing Limited.

Shao, G. (2009). Understanding the appeal of user-generated media: A uses and gratification perspective. *Internet Research, 19*(1), 7–25. doi:10.1108/10662240910927795

Shaw, E., & Carter, S. (2007). Social entrepreneurship: Theoretical antecedents and empirical analysis of entrepreneurial processes and outcomes. *Journal of Small Business and Enterprise Development, 14*(3), 418–434. doi:10.1108/14626000710773529

Siamagka, N. T., Christodoulides, G., Michaelidou, N., & Valvi, A. (2015). Determinants of social media adoption by B2B organizations. *Industrial Marketing Management, 51*, 89–99. doi:10.1016/j.indmarman.2015.05.005

Simon, J.P. (2016). User generated content – users, community of users and firms: Toward new sources of co-innovation? *Info, 18*(6), 4–25.

Singaraju, S. P., Nguyen, Q. A., Niininen, O., & Sullivan-Mort, G. (2016). Social media and value co-creation in multi-stakeholder systems: A resource integration approach. *Industrial Marketing Management, 54*, 44–55. doi:10.1016/j.indmarman.2015.12.009

Smith, R., Bell, R., & Watts, H. (2014). Personality trait differences between traditional and social entrepreneurs. *Social Enterprise Journal, 10*(3), 200–221. doi:10.1108/SEJ-08-2013-0033

Son, M., & Han, K. (2011). Beyond the technology adoption: Technology readiness effects on post-adoption behavior. *Journal of Business Research, 64*(11), 1178–1182. doi:10.1016/j.jbusres.2011.06.019

Sorenson, O. (2013). Status and reputation: Synonyms or separate concepts? *Strategic Organization, 12*(1), 62–69. doi:10.1177/1476127013513219

Stepanova, E. (2011). The role of information communication technologies in the "arab spring.". *Ponars Eurasia, 15*, 1–6.

Stevenson, H. H., & Jarillo, J. C. (1990). A Paradigm of Entrepreneurship: Entrepreneurial Management. *Strategic Management Journal, 11*, 17–27.

Stockdale, R., & Standing, C. (2004). Benefits and barriers of electronic marketplace participation: An SME perspective null. *Journal of Enterprise Information Management, 17*(4), 301–311. doi:10.1108/17410390410548715

Swani, K., Brown, B. P., & Milne, G. R. (2014). Should tweets differ for B2B and B2C? An analysis of fortune 500 companies' Twitter communications. *Industrial Marketing Management, 43*(5), 873–881. doi:10.1016/j.indmarman.2014.04.012

Tang, T., Fang, E., & Wang, F. (2014). Is neutral really neutral? The effects of neutral user generated content on product sales. *Journal of Marketing, 78*(4), 41–58. doi:10.1509/jm.13.0301

Thompson, J., Alvy, G., & Lees, A. (2000). Social entrepreneurship - A new look at the people and the potential. *Management Decision, 38*(5), 328–338. doi:10.1108/00251740010340517

Treem, J. W., & Leonardi, P. M. (2012). Social Media Use in Organizations: Exploring the Affordances of Visibility, Editability, Persistence, and Association. *Communication Yearbook, 3*(6), 143–189.

Trivedi, C., & Stokols, D. (2011). Social Enterprises and Corporate Enterprises: Fundamental Differences and Defining Features. *The Journal of Entrepreneurship, 20*(1), 1–32. doi:10.1177/097135571002000101

Unkwu, Obiajulu, & Ozuem. (2016) Understanding Social Entrepreneurship: An Exploration of Theory and Practice. *World Journal of Social Sciences, 6*(3), 86-99.

Uyar, A., & Boyar, E. (2015). An Investigation Into Social Media Usage of Publicly Traded Companies. *Journal of Corporate Accounting & Finance, 27*(1), 71–78. doi:10.1002/jcaf.22113

Vandenbosch, L., & Eggermont, S. (2016). The Interrelated Roles of Mass Media and Social Media in Adolescents' Development of an Objectified Self-Concept. *Communication Research, 43*(8), 1116–1140. doi:10.1177/0093650215600488

Venkatraman, S., & Fahd, K. (2016). Challenges and Success Factors of ERP Systems in Australian SMEs. *Systems, 4*(2), 20. doi:10.3390ystems4020020

Vodanovich, S., Sundaram, D., & Myers, M. (2010). Digital Natives and Ubiquitous Information Systems. *Information Systems Research, 21*(4), 711–723. doi:10.1287/isre.1100.0324

Wamba, S. F., & Carter, L. (2014). Social Media Tools Adoption and Use by SMES: An Empirical Study *Journal of Organizational and End User Computing, 26*(2), 1–17. doi:10.4018/joeuc.2014040101

Wang, X., Yu, Y., & Wei, Y. (2012). Social media peer communication and impacts on purchase intentions: A consumer socialization framework. *Journal of Interactive Marketing*, *26*(4), 198–208. doi:10.1016/j.intmar.2011.11.004

Williams, T., & Williams, R. (2008). Adopting social media: Are we leaders, managers or followers? *Communication World*, *25*(4), 34–37.

Xiang, Z., & Gretzel, U. (2010). Role of social media in online travel information search. *Tourism Management*, *31*(2), 179–188. doi:10.1016/j.tourman.2009.02.016

Yang, H., Lee, J., Park, C., & Lee, K. (2014). The Adoption of Mobile Self-Service Technologies: Effects of Availability in Alternative Media and Trust on the Relative Importance of Perceived Usefulness and Ease of Use. *International Journal of Smart Home*, *8*(4), 165–178. doi:10.14257/ijsh.2014.8.4.15

Zafarani, R., & Liu, H. (2014). Behavior Analysis in Social Media. *IEEE Intelligent Systems*, *29*(4), 1–4.

Zhou, L. X., Wu, W. P., & Luo, X. M. (2007). Internationalization and the performance of born-global SMEs: The mediating role of social networks. *Journal of International Business Studies*, *38*(4), 673–690. doi:10.1057/palgrave.jibs.8400282

KEY TERMS AND DEFINITIONS

Online Communities: A group of people who have shared interest and communicate through interactive platforms such as discussion boards, websites, e-mail, and chat.

Social Entrepreneurship: Social entrepreneurship mainly focuses on identifying various intractable social difficulties with the innovative concept to eliminate those problems as well as to elevate economic value and the condition of the society.

Social Marketing: Social marketing is the Combination of the concepts of commercial marketing and the social sciences. This is one of the cost-effective and most sustainable idea to influence an individual's behavior.

Social Media: Social media is a platform which allows to publish and observe the diverse form of information and thus it can be implemented as a strategy for marketing and communication, which involves continuous updating.

Social Networking Sites: Social networking sites give the opportunity to create and share a personal profile in the form of text, photo, video and audio in order to connect with other users.

User-Generated Content: User-generated content can be described by way of any form of content, it can refer to digital images, videos, audio files, statements, tweets, blog discussion form posts, and everything in between which has been generated and placed by amateur contributors or users.

Web 2.0: Web 2.0 consider as a platform to produce and established software and content in a collaborative manner instead of the individual company.

Chapter 49
Conspicuous Consumption via Social Media

Lee Kar Wai
Universiti Putra Malaysia, Malaysia

Syuhaily Osman
Universiti Putra Malaysia, Malaysia

ABSTRACT

Conspicuous consumption has been explored since 19th century, focusing on its conceptual or mathematical modelling. It has gained widespread attention in the Western culture as compared to East. However, the increased performance of luxury market and strong demand for luxury goods in developing countries urged investigation on the spread of this consumption pattern. This chapter examines conspicuous consumption in Malaysia via social media usage. A research was carried out involving 387 respondents in Klang Valley, Malaysia. The results suggest Malaysian are moderately materialistic and propend to conspicuous consumption. Through the exposure to social media, consumers are being situated in comparison with other social media users and inclined to learn and pick up the consumption styles that are being exposed to. Thus, high level of social media usage can lead to high inclination in consuming conspicuously.

INTRODUCTION

The worldwide luxury market has continued to shine in recent years. The Luxury Goods Worldwide Market Study, Fall–Winter 2018 conducted by Bain and Company found that the luxury market had shown positive performance across the industry and grew about 5%, an estimation of €1.2 trillion globally. As the emerging luxury market, 70% of consumers in China, Russia, and United Arab Emirates had reported an increase in their spending on luxury purchases (Deloitte, 2017). Consumers in developing countries such as Asian countries are now more exposed to prestige and luxury goods as well (Wan-Ismail, Zakaria, & Abdul-Talib, 2016). Indeed, Malaysians are increasingly brand conscious throughout the years (Bagheri, 2014). Luxury market has also shown increasing growth due to the important contribution

DOI: 10.4018/978-1-6684-6287-4.ch049

of the youth (Giovannini, Xu, & Thomas, 2015), particularly consumers from Generation Y has shown more interest in international brands (Tee, Gharleghi, & Chan, 2013).

There are analyses of globalism mentioned that consumer culture is spreading from the West to different parts of the world, where consumers from developing countries started to prefer luxury brands as similar to those Westerns (Ger & Belk, 1996). Social media can be a major contributor to this effect due its availability of variety data and information from the mass media, international tourism, and multinational marketing (Durvasula, Lysonski, & Watson, 2015; Zhou & Belk, 2004).

Moreover, according to statistic from Multimedia and Communications Ministry in 2017, Malaysia has a 117.3% of household broadband penetration and 98% out of the 24.5 million active internet are using social media. Assessing social media has become a daily routine for people where Malaysians spend up to three hours daily to access the internet on their mobile phones, and up to three and a half hours on social media. Through all the time spending on social media, users get to know and learn about new brands and luxury goods are not exceptional. According to The Star, 94% of Malaysians discover products and brands on Facebook and 62% of them make a purchase after the discovery (Lee, 2016). Supporting that, a study of Hajli (2014) had proved that social media can influence consumers purchase decisions; and high intensity of assessing to social media can also have direct influence on conspicuous consumption (Thoumrungjore, 2014).

Previous studies revealed the connection between consumers' attributes and conspicuous consumption, particularly social visibility, materialism, self-esteem, individualism, and desire for uniqueness (Chaudhuri et al., 2011). Among the values of luxury consumers, materialism is the crucial one (e.g., Fournier and Richins, 1991). According to Kasser (2003), it is characterized as the propensity to ascribe noteworthy significance to material belongings and eminence. Hence, individuals, who are highly materialistic, are bound to display high social status through the purchase of luxury goods (Fournier and Richins, 1991; Wang and Wallendorf, 2006). Specifically, materialism enhances interest in luxury brands (Gil, Kwon, Good, & Johnson, 2012) and a preference for luxury goods (Prendergast & Wong, 2003; Wong & Ahuvia, 1998). However, it was revealed that desires which driven by acquisition of money and possessions frequently prompt to problematic consequences as the association between endorsement of materialism and well-being very often were inverted (Dittmar, Bond, Hurst, & Kasser, 2014; Twenge et al., 2010).

Consumers in the Western countries seek brands that make them comfortable with; however, for consumers in Asian countries, the most elevated need in brands is with respect to status seeking. These attitude, value and practices encompassing conspicuous consumption are especially crucial to investigate because they are originally viewed as western ideals and have started to be a norm in East Asian due to the globalization (Podoshen, Li, & Zhang, 2011).

Conspicuous Consumption

Conspicuous consumption was originally coined by American economist Thorstein Veblen (1889) in his book, "The Theory of the Leisure Class", indicating wealthy people obtain products and services with the purpose to show monetary power as the motivations behind achieving or keeping up social status (Veblen, 1899). Likewise, Veblen goods are defined as luxury goods for which the quantity demanded increases as the price increases which against the law of demand. Initially, these concepts were heavily linked with the upper classes of society, whom are affordable to spend their disposable income on goods and services that are not based on the functionality; instead, on how luxury the product is in order to display wealth and gain higher social status.

The economics studies on conspicuous consumption remained consistent since the commence of Veblen's theory. Traditionally, this kind of demonstration-oriented consumption has connected with the display of status and wealth. Although the focus had been more on durables purchases, immaterial purchases are claimed to also demonstrate status (Chen, Yeh & Wang, 2008). For example, it can reveal different implications, including ethnicity, age, sexuality, hobbies, individual qualities, signalling of value, and other types of personality (Blumer, 1969; Davis, 1992).

Besides facilitating the understanding on the issue, these economic studies also recommended the policy makers to intervene conspicuous consumption with policy measures. For instance, the progressive consumption taxes, which penalize high levels of consumption, or the luxury taxes, which penalize specific status-conferring consumption such as purchases of high-end cars or boats (Becker, Murphy, and Werning 2005; Frank 1985b). Nonetheless, these measures have not been effective intervention due to three important points. Firstly, these measures were seek to increase equality in income and serve as part of the redistribution of wealth mechanism, yet there are limited evidence on the effectiveness of increasing equality in increase savings and reduce consumption (Ordabayeva & Chandon, 2010). Secondly, these measures neglected the conspicuous consumption among the lower classes, those who are most severely impact if they overspend (Trigg, 2001; Wan-Ismail, Zakaria, & Abdul-Talib, 2016). Thirdly, the economic studies tend to take a macro perspective and neglect individual consumers and their proclivity toward conspicuous consumptions.

In the context of Malaysia, the sector of luxurious goods in Malaysia has been developing alongside with countries around the world in the course of the years (Run, Butt & Nee, 2010), consumers are also more aware about the brands they are buying from, especially with the young generation. The young generation are more preferring luxury brands and products particularly undergraduates and young adults in the workforce (Kamaruddin & Mokhlis, 2003), limited attention has been devoted on the issue of conspicuous consumption. Mat et al. (2016) employed purposive sampling and mall-intercept survey at high-class shopping malls located in Kuala Lumpur, to investigate the luxury consumption of 400 luxury fashion consumers. The researchers define conspicuous consumption behaviour as luxury consumption behaviour; and reported that attitude, brand image, patron status, role model – celebrities, and quality found to be statistically significant in influencing conspicuous consumption behaviour. The findings showed that attitude is the most influential factor that predicts the assumption of luxury fashion products.

The phenomenon where a higher portion of expenditure was not spent on basic needs but on luxuries is seen in households with higher income levels. However, observations made in recent years over conspicuous consumption highlighted that in developing countries, lower class groups were also suggested in further studies to adapt with conspicuous consumption (Hamilton & Catterall, 2005; Trigg, 2001; Wan-Ismail et al., 2016). The overconsumption and preference towards luxury products had led to overspending and poorer financial management actions such as high level of personal debt and credit card debt, which describes a large group of Malaysian Consumers (Kapeller & Schütz, 2015; Sandhu & Paim, 2015). As indicated by the report from The Malaysian Reserved, thousands of Malaysians had been pulled into bankruptcy due to excessive personal loan and credit card usage (Hani, 2019). For many of those who are married, this situation is causing financial pressure to their families. As shown by the statistics from the Malaysian Department of Insolvency, the main reasons that lead to bankruptcy include personal loans (27.76%), hire purchase (24.73%), housing loans (14.09%), as well as credit cards debt (9.91%).

In the current age digital, social media has transform the ways users interacts and lives. It has become a platform where users share various elements of life including stories, experiences, activities and consumptions to friends and followers in social media (Yenicioglu & Christodoulides, 2014). While on the other hand, it also become a battlefield for corporations and brands to market products and engages consumers (Ashley & Tuten, 2015). These idealized personality and lifestyles advertised in social media can cause pressure on consumers to purchase conspicuous goods base on image and price instead of functionality (Escobar, 2016).The traditional conspicuous consumption theory has clearly changed along with the globalization and the advent of social media (Yenicioglu & Christodoulides, 2014). Nonetheless, there is a dearth of research on investigating social media usage in conjunction with conspicuous consumption. Further, Wilcox and Stephen (2012) had recommended future studies on the consumer to look into the effect of social media towards customers' choices to purchase luxuriously. These findings indubitably urge for further investigation on the issue.

Although past studies have attempted to examine the influence of social media to consumer behaviour such as decision making, purchase intention and buying behaviour (Goh, Heng, & Lin, 2013; Hajli, 2014; Wang, Yu, &Wei, 2012), a comprehensive model illustrates influence of social media usage to the conspicuous consumption is not prevalent. Due to the shifting of attitudes towards the display of wealth and the wide spreading of luxury products (and information about them) (Atsmon, Dixit, & Wu, 2011), this study adopted conspicuous consumption as the main discussion focus in order to gain more understanding upon linking social media usage and conspicuous consumption. Indeed, more research that delve into aspect of consumer behavior and psychology in the digital economy is deemed necessary (Ling Chang, Ling Tam, & Suki, 2016; Nathan, Fook Chiun, & Suki, 2016; Suki, 2016).

Materialism

Materialism is an aspect related to consumption that has gained widespread attention. In theory, the word "materialism" is alludes to the philosophical conceptualization that nothing exists aside from matter and its movement (Scott, 2009). According to Lange (1873-75), materialism is then noticed as a belief in "material, self-existent things." Today, in like manner use, materialism is related with an inclination to consider material belonging and physical solace as more essential than spiritual qualities. Materialism is a complex, multi-faceted marvel (Larsen, Sirgy, & Wright, 1999), broadly studied by researchers from different fields, for example advertising, anthropology, consumer behavior and marketing, economics, psychology, political science, and social sciences (Mannion & Caolan, 1995).

Two types of materialism that are most widely known are personality materialism and value materialism (Ahuvia & Wong, 2002; Srikant, 2013; Kasser et al., 2004). Belk (1984; 1985) has conceptualized materialism as a personality trait composed of possessiveness, non-generosity, envy, and preservation (Ger & Belk, 1996) which also known as personality materialism. These constructs are selected and defined as a general trait rather than an attitude towards only a particular target person and possession. In the Richins and Dawson's (1992) conception (value materialism), materialism refers to an instrumental or terminal value (Rokeach, 1973). Although both Richin and Dawson's measure (1992) and Belk's measure (1985) share some adapted items in common, Richins and Dawson's (1992) measure interprets materialism differently. According to them, materialism is an enduring belief in the desirability of acquiring and possessing things. Operationally, the Richins and Dawson's scale (1992) comprised three dimensions: acquisition centrality, the role of acquisition in happiness, and the role of possessions in defining success.

Materialism has been associated with various consumer behaviours including social consumption motivation (Fitzmaurice & Comegys, 2006), compulsive buying (Rindfleisch, Burroughs & Denton, 1997; Roberts, Manolis & Tanner, 2003), brand perception (Kamineni, 2005), attitude towards advertising

(Yoon, 1995), self-doubt and insecurity (Chang & Arkin, 2002), social influence conformity (Schroeder & Dugal, 1995), and self-esteem contingent on praise (Deci & Ryan, 1995). Although there are two different understanding of materialism as mentioned, they both implied a consistency in the popular belief that materialistic person likes to display luxury goods (Wong, 1997). Conspicuous consumption is one of the behaviour that is most frequently related to materialism, in which the satisfaction from using a product is not derived from the functionality of it; instead, the audience reaction. Richin (1994) stated that people who are materialistic prone to value things that can be shown in public more. In addition, they often feel more satisfaction in showing the products than actually using them. Based upon such indications, it is believed that individual high in materialism may incline to purchase conspicuously.

In addition, the influence of social media usage towards materialism was proven to be significant (Kamal, Chu, & Pedram, 2013). A more current study found that highly materialistic consumer tend to pay more attention to what is displayed as luxurious and branded (Audrin, Brosch, Sander & Chanal, 2018). In addition, it is worth to highlight that the more a materialistic consumer is exposed to luxuries and branded, the more it will lead to luxury purchases. Thus, being highly exposed to social media will not only provides consumers with more frequent exposure to luxuries, it will also affect the consumer intention to consumption conspicuously.

Social Media Usage

Social media is web-based service that allows users to interact, collaborate, and communicate through the creation, modification, and sharing of content (McCay-Peet & Quan-Haase, 2017). There are a variety of purpose for the usage of social media, such as entertainment, social interaction, personal identity, information, and empowerment (Muntinga, Moorman, & Smit 2011).

Prior study has proposed that consumers' traditional media consumption can affect their materialism level (Ger & Belk 1999; Goldberg & Gorn 1978) because the media caters consumers with values and norms which acted as factors towards consumption. Previously, researches that suggested the connection between media usage and materialism are generally domain in television consumption and print advertising (Churchill & Moschis 1979; Lens, Pandelaere, & Warlop 2010; Richins, 1987). Past studies revealed that television viewership can influence viewers' materialism in the East and in the West (Chu, Windels, & Kamal, 2016). The existence of this relationship is explained by Richins (1987) partly because of the advertisements found in TV. However, this relationship between TV consumption and materialism is significant only when the commercials are guesstimated as realistic and authentic by individuals. Due to the fact that materialistic person will compare more between their standards of living and others'; in which media consumption provides sources for that (Schiffman & Kanuk, 2004).

Although the consumption of television and printing media is decreasing throughout the years, materialism and conspicuous consumptions remain on the rise (Lim et al., 2014). This may due to the advancements in the usage of social media. Social media settings enable social interactions between consumers, as well as enable consumers to openly display their lifestyle. This platform appears to provide a setting that enhances social comparison behaviour (Vogel, Rose, Roberts, & Eckles, 2014) whereby social media support consumers by having an access data to friends.

In particular, Facebook is a setting that encourages social comparison behaviour with the accompanying reasons. First, when social media, one can freely see data about how others are doing. Rich data about others' livestyle can be a worthwhile resource for individuals who search out comparison targets for self-assessment. Second, given that most Facebook friends tend to have identical background, comparison targets sought on Facebook will probably have similar characteristics than those sought in different settings (Hargittai, 2007). Besides, social media makes it simpler for user to interface with both weak and strong ties (strength of users' relationship closeness to their friends on the network), data stream inside any given social network usually relies on the strength of those ties (Frenzen & Nakamoto 1993). Thus, on the off chance that one frequently utilizes Facebook, she or he will probably to encounter comparison targets and has chances to do comparison with those targets. At that point, it is normal that, as one's usage intensity is high, she or he will probably involve in social comparison activities (Jang, Park & Song, 2016), regardless of the culture (Chu, Windels, & Kamal, 2016). According to Ozimek and Förster (2017), people who score high in materialism are using social media especially Facebook to satisfy their need to do comparison with others. Rest on that finding, higher Facebook use is said to be triggered by materialistic comparison condition than the non-materialistic comparison condition.

Moreover, increasingly more luxury brands have turned towards marketing communication in social media (Kim & Ko, 2012) such as Facebook, Twitter, YouTube, and Instagram (Schwedt, Chevalier, & Gutsatz, 2012). Prior researches stated that social media marketing is a promising promotional strategy in marketing luxury brands as well (Kim & Ko, 2012; Phan, Thomas, & Heine, 2011; Schwedt et al., 2012). Besides influence from marketers, individuals now can be influenced not only by their close family and friends, they can be influenced by public figure such as bloggers, influencer in social media, and celebrities. All of these are due to the available of access to view and intimate idealized personality and lifestyles of others in social media (Escobar, 2016). Hence, it was reasonable to suggest that these exposures in social media, the idealized media pictures of riches in social media will strengthen and fuel the drive to get a greater amount of the wanted products and leads to increasing motivation of acquisition of luxurious products to show status which is conspicuous consumption.

The Study

Due to the scenario discussed above and based on the previous research findings as well, the following section of this chapter will discuss about the research undertook to examine such issues in Malaysian context. Particularly, this research is conducted to have a clearer view about to what extent that the conspicuous consumption can be related to social media. The research involved 387 respondents who were selected from shopping malls in Klang Valley, Malaysia through systematic sampling method. The research data was collected through the use of self-administrated questionnaire which contained the items questioning about the respondents social media usage and also the perception towards their conspicuous consumption.

Background of Respondents

In the demographic profile section, gender, age, ethnic, marital status, monthly income, and education level were examined. The summary of respondents' demographic data is presented in percentage form as shown in Figure 1.

The gender distribution of the respondents consisted of 41.9% male and 58.1% female. For age distribution, the respondents were consisted of 39.1% aged less than 25, followed by 37.4% aged more than 30, and 23.5% aged between 26 and 30. In term of the ethnic distribution, slightly more than half of the respondents (51.9%) were Chinese, followed by Malay (38.3%), Indian (9.3%), and lastly other ethnicity (0.5%). The reported ethnic ration found to be different from the actual ethnic ration in Malaysia. This might due to the tendency of luxury products to be more well-liked by Chinese than other ethnics (Mat et al., 2016). Data on marital status of the respondents showed that the highest number respondents are married (42.6%), and the rest are single (56.6%) and divorced (0.8%).

Figure 1. Demographic background of the respondents

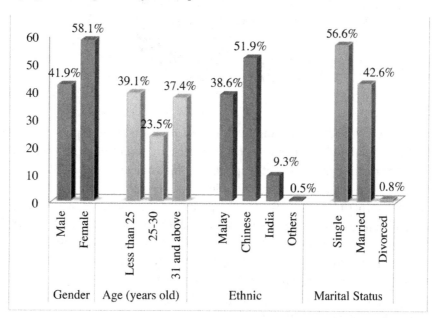

With respect to socio economic background (Figure 2 and 3), only two variables were asked from respondents, i.e., monthly income and highest education level. The data for monthly income shows that the largest income group comprised of income ranging from RM2001 to RM4000 (30.2%), followed by the group whom income less than RM2000 (28.2%). For those with income ranging from RM4001 to RM6000 and above RM6000 are accounted for 19.1% and 22.5% respectively.

Figure 2. Respondents' monthly income

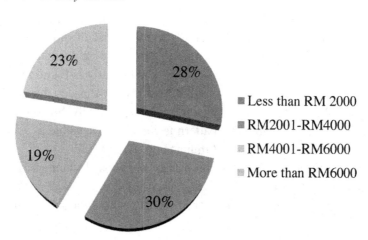

Figure 3. Respondents' highest education level

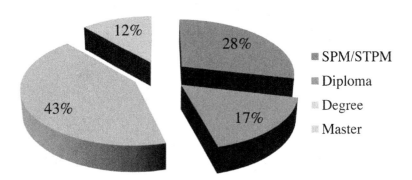

Meanwhile, in term of highest education level, largest proportion of respondent (41.3%) is degree holders, followed by SPM/STPM holders (27.6%). Others are diploma (16.8%) and master (11.4%) holders. PhD took the smallest proportion of respondent which occupied only 2.9% of total. This shows that most of the respondents had tertiary education level.

According to the Internet Users Survey 2017 done by Malaysian Communications and Multimedia Commission, more than half of the social media users in Malaysia are young adults aged below 35, who had at least secondary/post-secondary education or above with monthly above RM1000. Comparing to this statistics of the Internet user general demographic distribution in Malaysia, the social media users in this survey showed consistency where half of the social media users in current survey were consisted of young adults aged below 30 who most of them possess at least a tertiary certificate with monthly income ranged between RM2001 and RM4000.

Social Media Usage

The assessment of social media usage is consisted of two parts, usage pattern and absorption. Social media usage pattern includes self-reported assessments of social media behaviour, designed to measure the extent to which the respondents were actively engaged in social media activities, while absorption is referred to the extent of an individual's attention focuses in accessing social media.

Figure 4 shows that in terms of frequency, more than half of the respondents (59.4%) will access the social media as frequent as more than 5 times in a day. Only as little as 9.6% of the respondents access the social media less than 3 times a day. This shows that, social media site users are regular visitors where accessing the social media have become a daily routine. Aside from the daily usage frequency, in order to find out the exact amount of time consumers spent on social media, respondents were asked about how many hours they spent on using social media in a day. It was found that about 35.1% of the respondents spend less than 2 hours surfing on social media sites. Besides that, near to half of the respondents (47.0%) spend about 2 to 4 hours on using social media daily. Since half of the respondents are accessing the social media frequently, this pattern is considered sensible as according to Achariam (2015), Malaysians spend about 3 hours and 27 minutes on social media.

Furthermore, among the three social media sites listed (Facebook, Twitter, and Instagram), Facebook is the most used social media site, followed by Instagram. About 69.6% of the respondents primarily use Facebook the most, and only as little as 1.6% of the respondents do not own a Facebook account. According to the report of Malaysia Internet Users Survey 2017 done by Malaysian Communications and Multimedia Commission, the highest percentage of Internet users owned a Facebook account (97.3%), followed by Instagram (56.1%) in year 2016. The result for current study which showed Facebook as the most used social media site, followed by Instagram is seen to show similarity as reported in the Internet Survey 2017.

Figure 4. Social media usage pattern

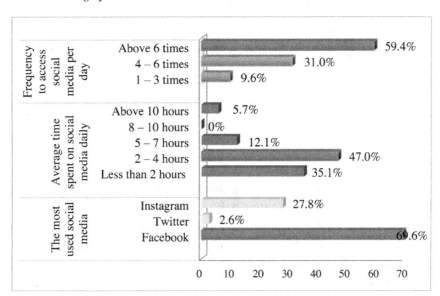

In addition, with the purpose to find out the audience consumers own in the social media environment, respondents were asked about the amount to friends and followers they have for each social media site (Figure 5). More friends and followers in social media means more audiences are able to view the content a user delivered through the form of news feed. The result showed that more than half of the respondents (59.5%) own less than 1000 Facebook friends, followed by 1001 to 2000 Facebook friends (32.3%), and 6.2% of the respondents own more than 2000 Facebook friends. This indicates that Facebook provided the most opportunities not only for the users to view but also deliver contents in the news feed.

As for the second most used social media site, Instagram is reported as the second most used social media site (27.8%). Result shows that 17.6% of the respondents not owning an Instagram account and more than half of the respondents (65.6%) have less than 500 Instagram followers. Although Twitter is listed as one of the most used social networking site for Malaysian and the ownership of Twitter has saw an increased as reported in Internet Users Survey 2017, Twitter is reported as the least used social media site (2.6%), and more than three quarter of the respondents (77.5%) do not own a Twitter account.

Overall, most of respondents own more than one social media user account. Social media is highly accessed by consumers with frequency up to 5 times a day. Lastly, the result enclosed that, the respondents owned biggest audience group in the platform of Facebook site, which it is seem acceptable since most of respondents were primarily using Facebook as the main social media site.

Figure 5. Number of friends/followers

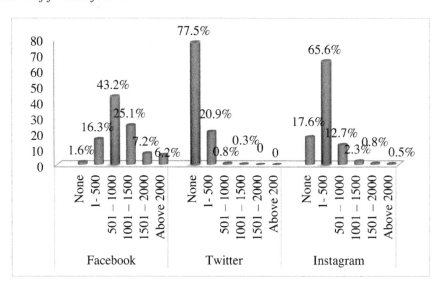

Based on the data shown in Table 1 about the absorption towards social media usage as perceived by the respondents, it was found that more than half of the social media users (67.5%) enjoy spending time on using social media. A total of 41.6% of them reported that social media can help to forget about daily problems. However, they will not get too involved in using social media until they forget about everything else outside the social media world (49.6%). Besides that, near to half of the users (49.4%) also remain neutral for the idea that they care a lot about using social media. Looking from these results, respondents were genuinely enjoying their time when using social media. However, as much as the respondents feel involved in using social media, they are not completely absorbed to the extent that they will forget everything else.

Table 1. Absorption towards social media usage

No.	Statement	Total Frequency/ (%)				
		1	2	3	4	5
1.	I genuinely enjoy the time spending on the social media.	4 (1.0)	10 (2.6)	112 (28.9)	188 (48.6)	73 (18.9)
2.	I feel that the social media helps me forget about daily problems.	25 (6.5)	57 (14.7)	144 (37.2)	119 (30.7)	42 (10.9)
3.	I feel totally absorbed while I am using the social media.	12 (3.1)	68 (17.6)	156 (40.3)	117 (30.2)	34 (8.8)
4.	I get so involved while using the social media that I forget everything else.	65 (16.8)	127 (32.8)	107 (27.6)	76 (19.6)	12 (3.1)
5.	I couldn't care less about using social media.	8 (2.1)	79 (20.4)	191 (49.4)	98 (25.3)	11 (2.8)

Materialism

In determining materialism of consumers, results showed more than half of the respondents (69.2%) tried to minimise possessions in order to keep their life simple. It was also enclosed that less than a quarter of respondents (22.7%) were likely to own many luxury possessions. This indicated that respondents are less prone to treat material possession as the central of living. However, only as low as 23.8% and 23.0% of respondents opposed the idea that they admired people with expensive belongings, and material possessions are important achievements in life respectively. Therefore, it is reasonable to say that there is still a considerable amount of respondents possessed neutral to positive opinion towards the idea that possession can show success.

Furthermore, the results also showed more that more than half of the respondents (65.2%) would be happier if they could own nicer things and afford to buy more things. In addition, only low amount of respondents (19.3%) felt okay for not being able to buy all the things that they like. This result also signified that respondents were treating possessions as the lead to happiness.

Table 2. Materialism

No.	Statement	Total Frequency/ (%)				
		1	2	3	4	5
	Acquisition of Centrality					
2.	I try to keep my life simple without having many material possessions.	3 (0.8)	27 (7.0)	89 (23.0)	199 (51.4)	69 (17.8)
5.	Buying things gives me a lot of pleasure.	20 (5.2)	75 (19.4)	145 (37.5)	122 (31.5)	25 (6.5)
6.	I like a lot of luxury in my life.	53 (13.7)	119 (30.7)	127 (32.8)	67 (17.3)	21 (5.4)
	Success					
8.	I admire people who own expensive cars, homes, and clothes.	29 (7.5)	63 (16.3)	124 (32.0)	128 (33.1)	43 (11.1)
9.	I think some of the more important achievements in life include buying material possessions.	24 (6.2)	65 (16.8)	149 (38.5)	127 (32.8)	22 (5.7)
11.	The things I own say a lot about how I am doing in life.	11 (2.8)	73 (18.9)	159 (41.1)	132 (34.1)	12 (3.1)
12.	I like to own things that impress people.	27 (7.0)	98 (25.3)	153 (39.5)	98 (25.3)	11 (2.8)
13.	I do not pay much attention to the material objects other people own.	11 (2.8)	57 (14.7)	162 (41.9)	130 (33.6)	27 (7.0)
	Happiness					
15.	My life could be better if I could buy certain things I do not currently own.	12 (3.1)	65 (16.8)	156 (40.3)	132 (34.1)	22 (5.7)
17.	I would be happier if I could afford to buy more things.	5 (1.3)	20 (5.2)	110 (28.4)	198 (51.2)	54 (14.0)
18.	It sometimes irritates me that I cannot afford to buy all the things I like.	11 (2.8)	64 (16.5)	162 (41.9)	130 (33.6)	20 (5.2)

Figure 6 showed the percentage of respondents falling in different category of materialism, namely low, moderate and high. The border score for each category is 11-25 (low), 26-40 (moderate), 41-55 (high). Majority of the respondents are moderately materialistic (85.0%). Only as little as 8.3% and 6.7% of the respondents are high and low in materialism respectively. This result indicates that consumers showed moderate level of materialism. Comparing this result to the result of past studies done (Kamal, Chu, & Pedram, 2013; Podoshen, Li, & Zhang, 2011), it is found that consumers in recent years are consistent compared to previous year which was also moderate for both Asian and American sample. These indicate that the respondents now are not highly inclined to show materialism as according to the frequency distribution, although respondents believed success is judged by the things people own and acquiring more possessions can lead to happiness, they did not treat material belongings as central of living.

Figure 6. Category of materialism

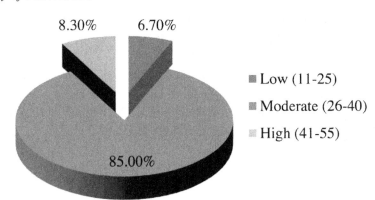

Perception Towards Conspicuous Consumption

In the section designed to determine the consumer perception towards conspicuous consumption, all of the items showed more negative responses as compared to positive. Based on data shown in Table 2, near to three quarter of the respondents (73.9%) opposed that their purchases are for the purpose to show their wealth. Besides that, respondents opposed frequent purchases of top-of-the-line products (67.7%).

In addition, slightly more than half of the responses dissented about wanting to be different by choosing product with exotic design (58.9%), wanting to show sophistication (54.5%), and wanting to know what others think about brands of their choices (53.7%). However, there were still about more than a quarter of respondents do consider products that can make good impression (32.3%), and make purchases which they feel can create style that others admire (30.8%). This might because of products' brand image can help to indicate quality and status (Mat et al., 2016). Conspicuous consumption as demonstration-oriented consumption can provide satisfaction not only from the consumption itself; it also provides satisfaction from the admiration received from others (Ekşi & Candan, 2018).

From the frequency distribution shown in Table 2, the three categories of consumer perception towards conspicuous consumption namely low, moderate, and high was determined. It can be seen in Figure 7 that the border score for reach category are 12-27 (Low), 28-43 (Moderate), and 44-60 (High). Data showed slightly more than half of the respondents (54.5%) are moderately propended in conspicuous consumption. Near to half of the respondents (41.3%) have low perception towards conspicuous consumption, and only as little as 4.1% of consumers are highly conspicuous. This result indicated that consumers in Malaysia are somehow low to moderately propend in conspicuous consumption. There is difference with the result from Western cultured sample that reported higher involvement in conspicuous consumption (Segal & Podoshen, 2013). Overall, it can be concluded that the results show moderate inclination of Malaysian in conspicuous consumption. Although Malaysian are less involved in conspicuous consumption as compared to Westerns, the affection for luxury is exceptionally pervasive in Asia Pacific area (Sandhu & Paim, 2015). Schaefer, Hermans, and Parker (2004) mentioned that East Asians might also have pressure to engage in this kind of consumption due to the need to maintain stature in the community.

Table 3. Conspicuous consumption

No.	Statement	Total Frequency/ (%)				
		1	**2**	**3**	**4**	**5**
1.	I buy some products because I want to show others that I am wealthy.	141 (36.4)	145 (37.5)	79 (20.4)	18 (4.7)	4 (1.0)
2.	It says something to people around me when I buy a high priced brand.	70 (18.1)	143 (37.0)	111 (28.7)	54 (14.0)	9 (2.3)
3.	I would be a member in a businessmen's posh club.	94 (24.3)	160 (41.3)	93 (24.0)	39 (10.1)	1 (0.3)
4.	I would buy an interesting and uncommon version of a product otherwise available with a plain design, to show others that I have an original taste.	61 (15.8)	124 (32.0)	128 (33.1)	70 (18.1)	4 (1.0)
5.	By choosing a product having an exotic look and design, I show my friends that I am different	83 (21.4)	145 (37.5)	102 (26.4)	54 (14.0)	3 (0.8)
6.	I choose products or brands to create my own style that everybody admires.	50 (12.9)	92 (23.8)	126 (32.6)	106 (27.4)	13 (3.4)
7.	I always buy top-of-the-line products.	115 (29.7)	147 (38.0)	89 (23.0)	32 (8.3)	4 (1.0)
8.	I show to others that I am sophisticated.	81 (20.9)	130 (33.6)	120 (31.0)	51 (13.2)	5 (1.3)
9.	Before purchasing a product, it is important to know what friends think of different brands or products I am considering.	86 (22.2)	122 (31.5)	99 (25.6)	68 (17.6)	12 (3.1)
10.	Before purchasing a product, it is important to know what kinds of people buy brands or products I am considering.	67 (17.3)	127 (32.8)	97 (25.1)	79 (20.4)	17 (4.4)
11.	Before purchasing a product, it is important to know what others think of people who use certain brands or products I am considering.	64 (16.5)	117 (30.2)	120 (31.0)	78 (20.2)	8 (2.1)
12.	Before purchasing a product, is important to know what brands or products to buy to make a good impression on others.	53 (13.7)	100 (25.8)	109 (28.2)	107 (27.6)	18 (4.7)

Figure 7. Category of perception towards conspicuous consumption

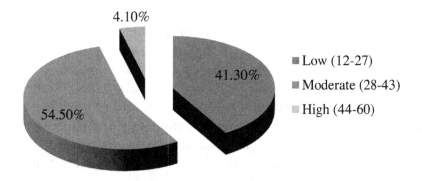

Effect of Social Media Usage on Materialism and Conspicuous Consumption

It was suggested that social media can influence materialism and conspicuous consumption. It is not hard to find that social media has become the key contribution to the success of luxury brands' marketing effort (Phan et al., 2011). More corporations and brands are turning to market products and engages consumers through social media (Ashley & Tuten, 2015). Aside from marketers, social media users will more likely to only present the best sides of themselves and their lives on social media platforms (Lin & Utz, 2015). These digital contents play some roles in brand expressions, triggering aspirations and provoking desires to be special and feel special, therefore influencing consumers on materialism as well as luxury consumption (Kamal, Chu, & Pedram, 2013; Escobar, 2016).

Although majority of respondents are moderately materialistic, only half of the respondents are moderately conspicuous in their consumption. Not to overlook, near to half of the respondents fell into the category of low involvement in conspicuous consumption. Despite these result, materialism was found to have direct influence on consumer perception towards conspicuous consumption (.Podoshen & Andrzejewski, 2012). Materialists believe that success and happiness can be visibly exhibited by the possession they own, which can be the reason for the demonstration-oriented consumption. This derivation is affirmed by empirical proof that discovered in contrasted with individual low in materialism, highly materialistic individuals are bound to value items that show monetary power (Richins, 1994a).

Looking at the effect of social media on link between materialism towards conspicuous consumption, it was discovered that under the influence of social media usage, there is a positive interaction effect of materialism on conspicuous consumption. It can be said deduced that social media usage showed positive moderation in the relationship of materialism and conspicuous consumption. When social media usage is high, high materialism becomes a strong predictor of conspicuous consumption. This result indicated that consumers who are highly materialistic are more inclined to do purchases conspicuously. By adding the influence of social media usage, idealized media pictures of riches in social media will strengthen and fuel the drive to consume getter amount of conspicuous products. According to Audrin et al. (2018), highly materialistic individuals tend to pay more visual attention on luxurious condition such as designer brands and products. In addition, the more highly materialistic individual exposed to visual images of luxurious products, the more they will select luxury products. This provides explanation on why intensive usage of social media can cause high materialism to be more intending to consume conspicuously.

CONLCUSION

Based on this study, Malaysia portrays a market where the use of social media and demand of luxury products has increased due to the growth of the nation's economy. Although the emphasize on overt display of consumption to demonstrate financial achievement had been rooted in Asian norm, this consumption pattern had not been widely spread as the results suggested only low to moderate consumer perception towards conspicuous consumption. However, with more common practice of luxury display in social media, there is possibility for more consumers to pick up such demonstration-orientated consumption pattern as social media usage was discovered to affect consumer purchasing behaviour. This effect of social media usage can be seen more critical on individuals who value material possessions. Materialists pay extra attention on material objects that are branded, expensive and visible. This information selection allows them to be only surrounded by luxuries and the comparison of luxuries, triggering them to involve more in conspicuous consumption.

This chapter provides more comprehensive understanding on the effect of social media usage towards materialism and conspicuous consumption. Besides that, the social media usage pattern and the extent of materialism and perception towards conspicuous consumption of consumer in Malaysia are disclosed. These results are relevant to two parties including market researchers and consumers. In exploring the effect of social media usage on materialism and conspicuous consumption, a new finding has given vital connotations to the theory, as well as to the practice. Current study implies to the literature by showing the effect of social media usage in the relationship between materialism and conspicuous consumption. Aside from the consistent result found between materialism and conspicuous consumption, this research reveals the effect of social media environment on the predictability of materialism towards conspicuous consumption. Intensive usage of social media can strengthen the drive to consume conspicuously, and it can be seen especially for those who are more materialistic.

The study identified the potential impacts of social media users' characteristics (materialism) able to exert an influence on conspicuous consumption. Consumers need to be aware that the dependence on the utilization of conspicuous goods to compensate for societal and situational underestimation or to adjust their status and self-esteem is inappropriate. The formal curriculum syllabus can advocate the young generations to abstained themselves from materialism and conspicuous consumptions; instead, focusing on developing social identity through knowledge, skills and abilities.

REFERENCES

Achariam, T. (2015). Malaysians use the internet an average of 12 hours a day. *The Sun Daily*. Retrieved from: https://www.thesundaily.my/news/1633825

Ahuvia, A. C., & Wong, N. Y. (2002). Personality and values based materialism: Their relationship and origins. *Journal of Consumer Psychology*, *12*(4), 389–402. doi:10.1207/S15327663JCP1204_10

Ashley, C., & Tuten, T. (2015). Creative strategies in social media marketing: An exploratory study of branded social content and consumer engagement. *Psychology and Marketing*, *32*(1), 15–27. doi:10.1002/mar.20761

Atsmon, Y., Dixit, V., & Wu, C. (2011). *Dimensions of brand personality.* Insights & Publications, McKinsey & Company. Retrieved from www.mckinsey.com/insights/marketing_sales/tapping_chinas_luxury-goods_market

Audrin, C., Brosch, T., Sander, D., & Chanal, J. (2018). More than meets the eye: The impact of materialism on information selection during luxury choices. *Frontiers in Behavioral Neuroscience*, *12*, 12. doi:10.3389/fnbeh.2018.00172 PMID:30197590

Bagheri, M. (2014). Luxury consumer behavior in Malaysia: Loud brands vs. quiet brands. *Procedia: Social and Behavioral Sciences*, *130*, 316–324. doi:10.1016/j.sbspro.2014.04.037

Bain & Company, Inc. (2019). *Luxury Goods Worldwide Market Study, Fall–Winter 2018*. Retrieved from https://www.bain.com/contentassets/8df501b9f8d6442eba00040246c6b4f9/bain_digest__luxury_goods_worldwide_market_study_fall_winter_2018.pdf

Becker, G. S., Murphy, K. M., & Werning, I. (2005). The equilibrium distribution of income and the market for status. *Journal of Political Economy, 113*(2), 282–310. doi:10.1086/427463

Belk, R. W. (1984). Three scales to measure constructs related to materialism: Reliability, validity, and relationships to measures of happiness. In T. Kinnear (Ed.), *Advances in Consumer Research* (Vol. 11, pp. 291–297). Provo, UT: Association for Consumer Research.

Belk, R. W. (1985). Materialism: Trait aspects of living in the material world. *The Journal of Consumer Research, 12*(3), 265–280. doi:10.1086/208515

Belk, R. W. (1996). Hyperreality and globalization: Culture in the age of Ronald McDonald. *Journal of International Consumer Marketing, 8*(3-4), 23–37. doi:10.1300/J046v08n03_03

Blumer, H. (1969). Fashion: From class differentiation to collective selection. *The Sociological Quarterly, 10*(3), 275–291. doi:10.1111/j.1533-8525.1969.tb01292.x

Boyd, D., & Ellison, N. (2008). Social network sites: Definition, history, and scholarship. *Journal of Computer-Mediated Communication, 13*(1), 210–230. doi:10.1111/j.1083-6101.2007.00393.x

Chang, L. D. M., Ling Tam, A. Y., & Suki, N. M. (2016). Moderating effect of races towards consumers' feeling of TCM usage. Handbook of Research on Leveraging Consumer Psychology for Effective Customer Engagement, 306-323.

Chang, L., & Arkin, R. M. (2002). Materialism as an attempt to cope with uncertainty. *Psychology and Marketing, 19*(5), 389–406. doi:10.1002/mar.10016

Chaudhuri, H. R., & Majumdar, S. (2006). Of diamonds and desires: Understanding conspicuous consumption from a contemporary marketing perspective. *Academy of Marketing Science Review, 2006*(11).

Chaudhuri, H. R., Mazumdar, S., & Ghoshal, A. (2011). Conspicuous consumption orientation: Conceptualisation, scale development and validation. *Journal of Consumer Behaviour, 10*(4), 216–224. doi:10.1002/cb.364

Chen, E. Y. I., Yeh, N.-C., & Wang, C. P. (2008). Conspicuous consumption: A preliminary report of scale development and validation. *Advances in Consumer Research. Association for Consumer Research (U. S.), 35*, 686–687.

Chu, S. C., Windels, K., & Kamal, S. (2016). The influence of self-construal and materialism on social media intensity: A study of China and the United States. *International Journal of Advertising, 35*(3), 569–588. doi:10.1080/02650487.2015.1068425

Churchill, G. A. Jr, & Moschis, G. P. (1979). Television and interpersonal influences on adolescent consumer learning. *The Journal of Consumer Research, 6*(1), 23–35. doi:10.1086/208745

Davis, M. (1992). Codes of ethics, professions, and conflict of interest: A case study of an emerging profession, clinical engineering. *Professional Ethics, A Multidisciplinary Journal, 1*(1/2), 179-195.

de Run, E. C., Butt, M., & Nee, C. Y. (2010). The influence of role models on young adults purchase. *Jurnal Kemanusiaan, 15*, 70–81.

Deci, E. L., & Ryan, R. M. (1995). Human autonomy: The basis for true self-esteem. In M. Kemis (Ed.), *Efficacy, agency, and self-esteem* (pp. 31–49). New York: Plenum.

Deloitte. (2017). *The new luxury consumers. Global Powers of Luxury Goods 2017*. Retrieved from: https://www2.deloitte.com/content/dam/Deloitte/global/Documents/consumer-industrial-products/gx-cip-global-powers-luxury-2017.pdf

Durvasula, S., Lysonski, S., & Watson, J. (Eds.). (2015). *Proceedings of the 1997 World Marketing Congress. A Cross-Cultural Examination of a Scale to Measure Trait Aspects of Vanity*. Springer.

Ekşi, O., & Candan, F. B. (2018). The effect of lifestyle on conspicuous consumption. *Current Debates in Business Studies*, (15), 109-125.

Escobar, A. (2016). The impact of the digital revolution in the development of market and communication strategies for the luxury sector (fashion luxury). *Central European Business Review*, *5*(2), 17–36. doi:10.18267/j.cebr.149

Fitzmaurice, J., & Comegys, C. (2006). Materialism and social consumption. *Journal of Marketing Theory and Practice*, *14*(4), 287–299. doi:10.2753/MTP1069-6679140403

Frank, R. H. (1985). *Choosing the right pond: Human behavior and the quest for status*. Oxford University Press.

Frenzen, J., & Nakamoto, K. (1993). Structure, cooperation, and the flow of market information. *The Journal of Consumer Research*, *20*(3), 360–375. doi:10.1086/209355

Ger, G., & Belk, R. W. (1996). Cross-cultural differences in materialism. *Journal of Economic Psychology*, *17*(1), 55–77. doi:10.1016/0167-4870(95)00035-6

Ger, G., & Belk, R. W. (1999). Accounting for materialism in four cultures. *Journal of Material Culture*, *4*(2), 183–204. doi:10.1177/135918359900400204

Giovannini, S., Xu, Y., & Thomas, J. (2015). Luxury fashion consumption and Generation Y consumers: Self, brand consciousness, and consumption motivations. *Journal of Fashion Marketing and Management*, *19*(1), 22–40. doi:10.1108/JFMM-08-2013-0096

Goh, K. Y., Heng, C. S., & Lin, Z. (2013). Social media brand community and consumer behavior: Quantifying the relative impact of user-and marketer-generated content. *Information Systems Research*, *24*(1), 88–107. doi:10.1287/isre.1120.0469

Goldberg, M. E., & Gorn, G. J. (1978). Some unintended consequences of TV advertising to children. *The Journal of Consumer Research*, *5*(1), 22–29. doi:10.1086/208710

Hajli, M. N. (2014). A study of the impact of social media on consumers. *International Journal of Market Research*, *56*(3), 387–404. doi:10.2501/IJMR-2014-025

Hamilton, K. L., & Catterall, M. (2005). Towards a better understanding of the low income consumer. *Advances in Consumer Research. Association for Consumer Research (U. S.)*, *32*(1), 627–632.

Hani, A. (2019, August 8). Credit cards, personal loans landing Malaysians in debt trap. *The Malaysian Reserve*. Retrieved from https://themalaysianreserve.com/2019/08/08/credit-cards-personal-loans-landing-malaysians-in-debt-trap/

Hargittai, E. (2007). Whose space? Differences among users and non-users of social network sites. *Journal of Computer-Mediated Communication, 13*(1), 276–297. doi:10.1111/j.1083-6101.2007.00396.x

Hudders, L., & Pandelaere, M. (2012). The silver lining of materialism: The impact of luxury consumption on subjective well-being. *Journal of Happiness Studies, 13*(3), 411–437. doi:10.100710902-011-9271-9

Jang, K., Park, N., & Song, H. (2016). Social comparison on Facebook: Its antecedents and psychological outcomes. *Computers in Human Behavior, 62*, 147–154. doi:10.1016/j.chb.2016.03.082

Kamal, S., Chu, S. C., & Pedram, M. (2013). Materialism, attitudes, and social media usage and their impact on purchase intention of luxury fashion goods among American and Arab young generations. *Journal of Interactive Advertising, 13*(1), 27–40. doi:10.1080/15252019.2013.768052

Kamaruddin, A. R., & Mokhlis, S. (2003). Consumer socialization, social structural factors and decision-making styles: A case study of adolescents in Malaysia. *International Journal of Consumer Studies, 27*(2), 145–156. doi:10.1046/j.1470-6431.2003.00297.x

Kamineni, R. (2005). Influence of materialism, gender and nationality on consumer brand perceptions. Journal of Targeting. *Measurement and Analysis for Marketing, 14*(1), 25–32. doi:10.1057/palgrave.jt.5740167

Kapeller, J., & Schütz, B. (2015). Conspicuous consumption, inequality and debt: The nature of consumption-driven profit-led regimes. *Metroeconomica, 66*(1), 51–70. doi:10.1111/meca.12061

Kasser, T., Ryan, R. M., Couchman, C. E., & Sheldon, K. M. (2004). Materialistic values: Their causes and consequences. *Psychology and Consumer Culture: The Struggle for a Good Life in a Materialistic World, 1*(2), 11–28.

Kim, A. J., & Ko, E. (2012). Do social media marketing activities enhance customer equity? An empirical study of luxury fashion brand. *Journal of Business Research, 65*(10), 1480–1486. doi:10.1016/j.jbusres.2011.10.014

Lange, F. A. (1873-75). *The History of Materialism* (B. Russell, Trans., 3rd ed.). New York: Arno Press.

Larsen, V., Sirgy, J. M., & Wright, N. D. (1999). Materialism: The construct, measures, antecedents, and consequences. *Academy of Marketing Studies Journal, 3*(2), 78–110.

Lens, I., Pandelaere, M., & Warlop, L. (2010). Effects of Advertising Exposure on Materialism and Self-Esteem: Advertised Luxuries As a Feel-Good Strategy? *ACR North American Advances., 37*(1), 1–5.

Lim, W. M., Ng, W. K., Chin, J. H., & Boo, A. W. X. (2014). Understanding young consumer perceptions on credit card usage: Implications for responsible consumption. *Contemporary Management Research, 10*(4), 287–302. doi:10.7903/cmr.11657

Mannion, C., & Brannick, T. (1995). Materialism and its measurement. *IBAR*, (16), 1-15.

Mat, A., Kori, N. L., Rahman, S. A., Munir, Z. A., & Bahry, N. S. (2016). Conspicuous consumption behaviour: A case study of luxury fashion consumers at selected malls in Kuala Lumpur, Malaysia. *Australian Journal of Basic and Applied Sciences*, *10*(11), 193–198.

McCay-Peet, L., & Quan-Haase, A. (2017). What is social media and what questions can social media research help us answer. The SAGE Handbook of Social Media Research Methods, 13-26.

Moav, O., & Neeman, Z. (2012). Saving rates and poverty: The role of conspicuous consumption and human capital. *Economic Journal (London)*, *122*(563), 933–956. doi:10.1111/j.1468-0297.2012.02516.x

Muntinga, D. G., Moorman, M., & Smit, E. G. (2011). Introducing COBRAs: Exploring motivations for brand-related social media use. *International Journal of Advertising*, *30*(1), 13–46. doi:10.2501/IJA-30-1-013-046

Nathan, R. J., Fook Chiun, D. C., & Suki, N. M. (2016). An online marketing strategies assessment for companies in airlines and entertainment industries in Malaysia. Handbook of Research on Leveraging Consumer Psychology for Effective Customer Engagement, 1-15.

Ordabayeva, N., & Chandon, P. (2010). Getting ahead of the Joneses: When equality increases conspicuous consumption among bottom-tier consumers. *The Journal of Consumer Research*, *38*(1), 27–41. doi:10.1086/658165

Ozimek, P., & Förster, J. (2017). The impact of self-regulatory states and traits on Facebook use: Priming materialism and social comparisons. *Computers in Human Behavior*, *71*, 418–427. doi:10.1016/j.chb.2017.01.056

Phan, M., Thomas, R., & Heine, K. (2011). Social media and luxury brand management: The case of Burberry. *Journal of Global Fashion Marketing*, *2*(4), 213–222. doi:10.1080/20932685.2011.10593099

Podoshen, J. S., & Andrzejewski, S. A. (2012). An examination of the relationships between materialism, conspicuous consumption, impulse buying, and brand loyalty. *Journal of Marketing Theory and Practice*, *20*(3), 319–334. doi:10.2753/MTP1069-6679200306

Podoshen, J. S., Li, L., & Zhang, J. (2011). Materialism and conspicuous consumption in China: A cross-cultural examination. *International Journal of Consumer Studies*, *35*(1), 17–25. doi:10.1111/j.1470-6431.2010.00930.x

Quoquab, F., Pahlevan, S., & Hussin, N. (2016). Counterfeit Product Purchase: What Counts—Materialism or Religiosity? *Advanced Science Letters*, *22*(5-6), 1303–1306. doi:10.1166/asl.2016.6739

Richins, M. L. (1987). Media, materialism, and human happiness. In W. Melanie & A. Paul (Eds.), *Advances in Consumer Research* (Vol. 14, pp. 352–356). Provo, UT: Association for Consumer Research.

Richins, M. L., & Dawson, S. (1992). A consumer values orientation for materialism and its measurement: Scale development and validation. *The Journal of Consumer Research*, *19*(3), 303–316. doi:10.1086/209304

Rindfleisch, A., Burroughs, J. E., & Denton, F. (1997). Family structure, materialism, and compulsive consumption. *The Journal of Consumer Research*, *23*(4), 312–325. doi:10.1086/209486

Roberts, J. A., Manolis, C., & Tanner, J. F. Jr. (2003). Family structure, materialism, and compulsive buying: A reinquiry and extension. *Journal of the Academy of Marketing Science, 31*(3), 300–311. doi:10.1177/0092070303031003007

Rokeach, M. (1973). *The nature of human values.* New York: Free press.

Sandhu, S. K., & Paim, L. (2016). Consuming for status among Malaysian working women. *Journal of Emerging Economies & Islamic Research, 4*(3).

Schiffman, L. G., & Kanuk, L. L. (2004). *Consumer behaviour* (8th ed.). Prentice-Hall Inc.

Schroeder, J. E., & Dugal, S. S. (1995). Psychological correlates of the materialism construct. *Journal of Social Behavior and Personality, 10*(1), 243.

Schwedt, G., Chevalier, M., & Gutsatz, M. (2012). *Luxury retail management: How the World's top brands provide quality product and service support.* Hoboken, NJ: Wiley.

Scott, K. (2009). *Terminal materialism vs. instrumental materialism: Can materialism be beneficial?* (Doctoral dissertation). Oklahoma State University.

Segal, B., & Podoshen, J. S. (2013). An examination of materialism, conspicuous consumption and gender differences. *International Journal of Consumer Studies, 37*(2), 189–198. doi:10.1111/j.1470-6431.2012.01099.x

Solomon, M. R. (1983). The role of products as social stimuli: A symbolic interactionism perspective. *The Journal of Consumer Research, 10*(3), 319–329. doi:10.1086/208971

Sommer, R. (2017). Michael Kors - A Fashionable Trend. *Seeking Alpha.* Retrieved from https://seekingalpha.com/article/4133212-michael-kors-fashionable-trend

Srikant, M. (2013). Materialism in consumer behavior and marketing: A review. *Management & Marketing, 8*(2), 329.

Suki, N. M. (2016). *Handbook of Research on Leveraging Consumer Psychology for Effective Customer Engagement.* https://www.igi-global.com/book/handbook-research-leveraging-consumer-psychology/149284

Sun, G., Wang, W., Cheng, Z., Li, J., & Chen, J. (2017). The intermediate linkage between materialism and luxury consumption: Evidence from the emerging market of China. *Social Indicators Research, 132*(1), 475–487. doi:10.100711205-016-1273-x

Tee, P. K., Gharleghi, B., & Chan, B. Y. F. (2013). Malaysian young consumer preferences in choosing international fashion brand. *Journal of Human and Social Science Research, 1*(1), 31–38.

Thoumrungroje, A. (2014). The influence of social media intensity and EWOM on conspicuous consumption. *Procedia: Social and Behavioral Sciences, 148*, 7–15. doi:10.1016/j.sbspro.2014.07.009

Trigg, A. B. (2001). Veblen, Bourdieu, and conspicuous consumption. *Journal of Economic Issues, 35*(1), 99–115. doi:10.1080/00213624.2001.11506342

Veblen, T. (1899). *The Theory of the Leisure Class: An Economic Study in the Evolution of Institutions*. Macmillan & Co.

Vogel, E. A., Rose, J. P., Roberts, L. R., & Eckles, K. (2014). Social comparison, social media, and self-esteem. *Psychology of Popular Media Culture, 3*(4), 206–222. doi:10.1037/ppm0000047

Wan-Ismail, W. N. A., Zakaria, N., & Abdul-Talib, A. N. (2016). Craving vs. Compulsion for Luxury Goods?: Trends and Patterns of Conspicuous Consumption Behavior in Asian Culture. In *Neuroeconomics and the Decision-Making Process* (pp. 287–297). IGI Global. doi:10.4018/978-1-4666-9989-2.ch015

Wang, X., Yu, C., & Wei, Y. (2012). Social media peer communication and impacts on purchase intentions: A consumer socialization framework. *Journal of Interactive Marketing, 26*(4), 198–208. doi:10.1016/j.intmar.2011.11.004

Wilcox, K., & Stephen, A. T. (2012). Are close friends the enemy? Online social networks, self-esteem, and self-control. *The Journal of Consumer Research, 40*(1), 90–103. doi:10.1086/668794

Wong, N. Y. (1997). Suppose you own the world and no one knows? In M. Brucks & D. MacInnis (Eds.), *Advances in consumer research* (Vol. 4, pp. 197–201). Provo, UT: Association for Consumer Research.

Yenicioglu, B., & Christodoulides, G. (2014). Branding in the age of digital connectivity. In *The Routledge companion to the future of marketing* (pp. 268–281). London: Sage.

Zhou, N., & Belk, R. W. (2004). Chinese consumer readings of global and local advertising appeals. *Journal of Advertising, 33*(3), 63–76. doi:10.1080/00913367.2004.10639169

Zhu, N. (2011). Household consumption and personal bankruptcy. *The Journal of Legal Studies, 40*(1), 1–37. doi:10.1086/649033

This research was previously published in Leveraging Consumer Behavior and Psychology in the Digital Economy; pages 60-80, copyright year 2020 by Business Science Reference (an imprint of IGI Global).

Chapter 50
How Social Media is Transforming Marketing?

İbrahim Kırcova
Yıldız Technical University, Turkey

Ebru Enginkaya
Yıldız Technical University, Turkey

ABSTRACT

Integrating companies to digital channels is a necessity to build and maintain a competitive advantage in today's market conditions. In the business environment, companies realize that sustainable competitive advantage can be gained only by understanding customers' needs and expectations, developing activities that meet their demands, ease their work, and engage them to the brand to create difference and value. Success in marketing will be driven by an effective communication and consumer experience. Marketing and brand managers are in the process of determining how social media tools impact them and what their digital transformation approach and communication strategy should be. This chapter examines the importance of social media for companies and benefits of social media on the performance of market-ing processes that enable better communication, planning, and execution from consumer engagement to consumer purchase.

INTRODUCTION

Marketing is in a state of change since digital technologies have become so pervasive in social media channels and consumer expectations. Companies are adopting changes through the adoption of social media channels and technology. Social media provide an individualized opportunity for marketing ex-ecutives to help them make better informed strategic decisions. Companies can catch the opportunity to carry their operations and make customer communication faster, focused, continuously and multichan-nel with the right data gained from social media platforms and in this way companies can present their segments differentiated and valuable experience.

DOI: 10.4018/978-1-6684-6287-4.ch050

Social media plays an important role in the shifting of marketing, along with different consumption patterns and various communication ways. Today, social media is an important interactive communication channel that allows for two-way, real-time interaction and feedback. Interaction and engagement with social media can help businesses to more effectively market to and communicate with its customers. Also, most of the consumers engage with brands through social media and brands use social media platforms as an information and a fundamental contact point with consumers (Clark, Black, & Judson, 2017).

Social media delivers measurable results in sales, leads, and branding. It also enables to reach a large number of people at a low cost. Relevant market and consumer data can be collected through different social media tools. The data gathered from social media channels can be designed to help marketing executives understand and capitalize on the evolving insights and trends that are impacting the company across all segments. With the data obtained from various social media channels, marketing managers identify and prioritize segments, develop comprehensive and relevant offerings, focus on and apply valuable social media marketing strategies to improve the omnichannel customer communication. By tracking and analyzing important trends and consumers on social media, companies can achieve higher levels of information while reducing costs. The objective of the chapter is to indicate the significance of social media channels in the marketing strategies of businesses with the rapid development of technology and innovations.

THE IMPORTANCE OF SOCIAL MEDIA PLATFORMS

In an increasingly competitive environment for each company main purpose is to offer faster, better quality and more affordable proposals than main competitors. For this purpose, companies utilize all kinds of technological innovation and possibilities. On the other hand, customer expectations are increasing and these high expectations are driving businesses. Focusing only on product or service quality is not enough, also it is important to meet customer expectations almost on a personal basis, to facilitate sales and after-sales processes and to provide the customer with a unique experience. However, for companies, it is not enough to communicate only with the customer, but also to interact with them. Being able to interact with customers is crucial in terms of knowing, understanding, meeting their expectations by interacting. Companies that are interacting with customers are more successful superior to competitors. Innovations in social media and continuous improvements are now key components of competitive and differentiation strategy that directly impact consumers.

The world of social media networks is dynamic and in constant change. Social media just keeps growing. According to statistical information by WeareSocial (2018); the number of internet users in 2018 is 4.021 billion, the number of social media users in 2018 is 3.196 billion, equaling 42% penetration. The average social media user spends 135 minutes a day online. Facebook's platform still dominates the global social landscape, with total users up 15 percent year-on-year to reach almost 2.17 billion at the beginning of 2018. There are now more than 50 million small businesses using Facebook Pages to connect with their customers. 4 million of those businesses pay for social media advertising on Facebook. 68% of marketers have published video content on Facebook. (Hainla, 2018). YouTube has 1.5 billion users and on average, people spend 40 minutes a day watching YouTube. Instagram has 1 billion monthly active users and Instagram Stories has 300 million users worldwide. Twitter has 300 million monthly active users. LinkedIn has 500 million, Pinterest has 200 million, Snapchat has 178 million users worldwide. The average internet user has 7 social media accounts and 88 percent of businesses are on social media (StrikeSocial, 2018).

Users who spend more and more time on social media platforms, starting with Facebook, Twitter, YouTube, and Instagram, are increasingly learning about other people's ideas about products and services they will buy and collecting information about brands. The purchases made are assessed and these evaluations are shared in a way that everyone can reach with various applications. These developments have led to the emergence of the concept of "social media marketing".

Social media is defined as "a group of internet-based applications that build on the ideological and technical foundations of Web 2.0, and that allow the creation and exchange of user generated content" (Kaplan & Haenlein, 2010). Carr and Hayes (2015) broadly defined social media as "internet-based channels that allow users to interact and selectively self-present, either in real-time or asynchronously, with both broad and narrow audiences who derive value from user-generated content and the perception of interaction with others".

The increase in the number of users on social media platforms has also led businesses and brands to focus on this concept. Individuals who are overwhelmed by the one-sided, repressive and compelling ways of traditional media tools prefer to spend time on social media platforms where control is largely in their hands. Today, individuals are talking, discussing and interacting with each other by sharing texts, graphics, audio files, video files, and photos on these platforms. Consumers share information about the products, services, brands, and experiences they choose to purchase. Whiting and Williams (2013) applied the uses and gratifications theory to social media to explain the many and varied reasons why consumers use and like social media. They provide a very rich and comprehensive understanding of why consumers utilize social media and what gratifications they receive from social media, which are: social interaction; information seeking; pass time; entertainment; relaxation; communicator utility; convenience utility; information sharing, and surveillance / knowledge about others.

Businesses and brands that are aware of the effect created by the people who have affected each other are taking part in these platforms and making their own communications. Brand communications made in traditional media with a massive budget can be made on social media platforms both modestly and in a more effective way. Social media platforms enable more and more people participate in this media day by day with applications that make the sharing environment interesting and attractive. Today, social media is an important tool for companies which offers diversity while simplifying interaction with the customer at very low costs by using internet technologies. Social media is an online tool that provides communication, collaboration, and sharing among people, communities, and companies through the internet and technological capabilities. Social media offers opportunities to interact, work, share, socialize, play, learn, buy and sell interactive and interconnected networks (Tuten & Solomon, 2015). Web 2.0, defined as platforms that allow users to generate and share information, documents, audio files, video files, photos and similar images with each other, can be used not only for websites where companies produce content, but also for users to create content, is the technical infrastructure that allows the labeling to be done and value creation pass through the consumer (Berthon, Pitt, Plangger, & Shapiro, 2012). Users who participate in platforms developed by others on the basis of membership express their opinions without being subject to any restrictions and their friends quickly learn their exchanges and interact.

Social media is the web-based technology and mobile media on which people and communities share, create, discuss and present their content through interactive platforms (Kietzman, Hermkens, McCarthy & Silvestre, 2011). The ability to promptly update, analyze and share information which is constantly being updated with the ease of use of social networking sites, such as Facebook, YouTube, LinkedIn,

Instagram, and other social networking sites such as sharing personal information, pictures, videos, content and profiles, has attracted great interest from users, the numbers have increased day by day and the spreads have been accelerated (Kaplan & Haenlein, 2010). With the new web technologies, it is extremely easy for consumers and businesses to create and publish their own web content (Zarrella, 2010).

CONTRIBTION OF SOCIAL MEDIA TO MARKETING STRATEGIES

Social media is a platform that all kinds of companies can benefit from. Due to the structural characteristics of social media platforms and their users' positions it has started to be considered as a new communication, marketing, and sales channel for companies. The power of social media is due to the multiplicity and the interaction of the participants. People have never come together in this way and have never interacted with each other before. No idea, ideology, activity or campaign has succeeded in bringing people together in this way. Even people from almost every region of the world who do not have anything in common with each other come together on the same platform. At the same time, these people easily share their common interests, common enjoyment, pleasures, thoughts, and the content they produce. It is very easy for people with common interests find each other, with the various software on the platforms.

The growing popularity and diversity of social networks have created significant opportunities for companies. Social networks are effective communication environments that enable companies to spread their marketing messages, deliver wider product offerings, manage the companies' reputation, build relationships to attract new customers, and make more purchases of existing customers. Nowadays, it is a necessity for brands and institutions exist in social media while companies, brands, institutions and all kinds of internet users interact with each other. With social platforms and other internet applications, there is a constant interaction between companies and consumers, and brands are finding a suitable channel for delivering all the values that make up their corporate identities to the target consumers. With integrated digital platforms, social media platforms provide benefits such as creating brand awareness in the target audience, promoting brand identity, attracting customers to products and services, and managing relationships with customers by the interoperability of digital platforms.

In addition to being present in social media by opening only the profile page for businesses, it develops various marketing tools to create various possibilities at low cost in basic fields such as marketing, sales, brand awareness, customer relationship management, complaint management. For example, to be a part of corporate identity, companies in the Facebook platform can reach to their target segments with customized advertisements, according to gender, age, occupation, education level, income level, geographic region and interests (Schmidt & Ralph, 2011). Social media platforms provide being selective in reaching the target market, directing to the goal and using resources properly.

Social Media as a New Marketing Channel

The important contribution of social media is the opportunity created from a marketing perspective that allows companies to communicate with their target market. Companies prefer to be a strong and well-known brand because competition in products and services does not provide lasting advantages. Companies realize that bringing products and services under the brand name is crucial to be in a competitive marketplace, for this reason, they are struggling to create brands by emphasizing their marketing communications or to put their existing brands in the forefront. To communicate the brand's existence to the target audience, to establish rational and emotional connections between the brand and the target market, and to provide strong reasons for the target consumers to prefer the brand, requires effective communication from multiple channels. It is not an easy process to differentiate between millions of products and services offered on the market and to provide the consumers to aware of the brand.

Social media emerges as a sophisticated and powerful new marketing channel. Social media tools provide marketers new opportunities for targeting campaigns using profile information, linking community members with social networks within friend groups, systematically developing word of mouth marketing from existing customer base, and as a result, marketing becomes attentive, personal and social. On social networks, advertising and branding objectives are based on personal characteristics such as gender, age, interests of consumers (Shih, 2011).

Today, it is not possible to carry out marketing communication by using just one channel. While using traditional media platforms, also using digital marketing, communication, and social media platforms together are a necessity for companies. This approach is defined as "integrated marketing communication" in the field of marketing. Although consumers are increasingly choosing social media platforms, traditional media tools are still preferred. Even if the influence diminishes over time, there is still more investment in television advertising. Print media advertisements such as newspapers and magazines are still at higher rates. The reason for this is that the transition from traditional media tools to social media tools takes place within a certain period of time. At the same time, some consumers prefer traditional media tools for reasons such as education, culture, and habits. For this reason, it is the right approach to conduct marketing communication, both in coordination with traditional media and social media.

Integrated marketing approach requires all marketing channels to be used in a coordinated way towards the same goal. It is possible that social media platforms and traditional media tools can be associated in many different ways. Such associations are becoming increasingly easier, especially due to the various possibilities of social media tools. For example, an image taken from outdoor advertising to a mobile phone is extremely easy to reach a website or a social media platform. Such multi-channel applications can also increase the power of communication. On the other hand, since small and medium-sized businesses do not have large advertising budgets, they do not have many chances to use traditional channels. It is possible for these businesses to increase brand awareness and customer loyalty by effectively engaging in marketing communications with limited budgets instead of large budget campaigns.

The sharing of the experience of the users who follow each other on the social media platforms, the reporting of the products and services and especially the recommendations of the popular ones and the influential people have led to the concept of "social marketing". For most people, the beliefs of people who trust and share product experiences can provide sympathy and interaction for brands and products. Many people who share content on the social media can quickly post their views and experiences about the products, services, and brands they buy on their own profiles or on the walls of related brands. Social media offer consumers the opportunity to interact with other people and brands without sacrificing any monetary or time cost. Consumers are now active members of brand communities by communicating with brands and expose their opinions and experiences. Today, in the social media communication environment, the control power of the companies is decreasing and the power passes from marketers to consumers (Miller & Lammas, 2011).

Social Media as Information Source

The number of members on social media platforms is expressed in billions. Most users are actively using more than one social media platform. Each of these platforms is used for different purposes and each one works with the different system. These platforms are a unique source of information because of the traces left by every event made in these media. Demographic, psychographic, and behavioral data provide significant easiness for creating marketing strategies and for market research. Qualitative and quantitative marketing research on social media platforms can be done much more easily with a small budget. It is a reality that marketing research based on extensive field research is carried out with a great budget. While it is easy to allocate budget for marketing research of large-scale brands, it is difficult for small and medium-sized enterprises to allocate resources and funds for such researches. This situation, which is in favor of large-scale, powerful brands in an increasingly competitive environment, is largely eliminated by market research in social media.

The tools presented for interacting directly with the target audience and the content displayed on social media are important data sources. Marketing research in social media can be done on a modest budget and is a much shorter period of time than traditional marketing research processes. The time spent to identify the population and select the sample of traditional marketing research can be quickly realized in the social media medium. Moreover, each company can conduct research covering all its followers on the social media platform. Businesses can learn simple, fast, and at very low cost through social media tools that can be obtained from market research at a very high cost. Companies are able to learn all the information through social media tools which are simple, fast and very low-cost way instead of traditional marketing researches. In addition, social media platforms have features such as optimizing research processes, adding valuable information and resolve possible mistakes.

Social media platforms accumulate all of their participants' information in a large database. By analyzing the information gathered on the social media platforms, it is possible to make suggestions to each company about the time, age group and the gender group about what content should be advertised. In this way, companies can communicate based on actual market knowledge rather than on insight or prediction. It is very clear that what products and services are offered to the market, which price ranges are attracted by consumers, and which keywords are used. Social media platforms are able to offer market intelligence, at a very low cost, with certainty that keeps businesses from making inaccurate decisions. A brand's position in social networks is one of the specific criteria for estimating sales and general status of a brand. Today, consumers increasingly convey their social relationships to the online world and make comments on brands without any hesitation. Especially young consumers play a big role in brand-product success or failure in comparison with other target segments. Social media channels are a new way of reaching young people (often early adopters, brand ambassadors, trend-setters) and conducting market research on them. With regard to campaigns, feedback is easily gained from social media metrics and it is easy to understand which campaigns are successful and which are not. Social media metrics ensure that the money spent on these platforms is spent most accurately by making precise measurements.

Social Media as a Communication Tool

Social media has become the crucial part of digital communications strategies. Social networks, which initially emerged as environments where individuals socialize, are now an important competitive tool for businesses. Businesses use these channels as a communication platform to reach a larger number of consumers and gain a competitive advantage. For many brands, social networks are the meeting medium with their target consumers. Social networks are now recognized as an important medium for businesses to strengthen their relationships with customers and to introduce their new products. Social networks provide information about the product and establish closer relationships with consumers. Businesses also have the opportunity to advertise their products, to receive feedback and ideas from customers through these tools. Businesses use social media not just for digital advertising, but for customer service, generating innovative ideas, and creating brand communities. The content that users generate about brands provides important data for companies and marketers (Smith, Fischer, & Yongjian, 2012).

The increasing number of social media platforms has led to a new marketing communication. More users on these networks and more time they spent on these networks have led to the emergence of new marketing communications. The impact of social media on branding products and services and establishing strong links with brands is indisputable, but recognizing products and services with our senses in the physical world will always preserve its existence and importance. For this reason, it is the best way for brands to use social media in an integrated way with traditional media tools and to increase their influence by providing transitions.

Almost every business has to make a difference in the intensely competitive environment in order to get a mind share, heart share, and market share. And with the awareness of the need to make this difference, companies has to express itself in a holistic approach to all communication channels. Large businesses can express themselves more easily and effectively using mass media tools. In small and medium-sized enterprises, it is difficult to reach the target market because it is not possible to use large, expensive tools like this. Moreover, it is even more difficult for a large number of companies to be chosen from among brands and products, to remain in mind, and to remain in a position that the target segment constantly prefers. For this reason, the work to be done must be accurate, effective, consistent and businesses have to make the right communication from the right channels. There are new opportunities in terms of businesses that use the rich possibilities of social media platforms in brand communication. Sharing audio and video files to the target consumers by generating the desired length and number is an important support for effective communication. Not only the social media pages, but also brands that strengthen their presence in blogs with audio and videos have the chance to say that they want to announce their target consumers in a variety of ways. Moreover, with the awareness that they can be reached as many digital platforms as possible, brands are going to diversify their content in social media. Especially high-tech products, technically complex products and services, business areas that require constant up-to-date information, contribute to enhancing brand awareness by providing content. The contents also have important functions in terms of feedback from the customers. Customers are turning to social media platforms to unleash their frustration or questions. 78% of people who complain to a brand via Twitter expect a response within an hour (Hainla, 2018). In terms of companies and brands, Twitter provides important contributions as a communication and interaction platform. It is possible to take advantage of Twitter in the areas of marketing communications such as branding, brand awareness, and brand extension due to instant messaging, updating, short comments on current topics and easy sharing interface that is easily accessible from all mobile devices (Ye, Fang, He, & Hsieh, 2012). Twitter also makes great contributions when launching of brands, announcements of changes in products and services, advertising campaigns, contests, slogans, logo selection, and gathering of consumer opinions.

Instagram has become a powerful platform for marketers and its potential cannot be overlooked any longer. Top brands on Instagram are seeing a per-follower engagement rate of 4.21%, which is 58 times higher than on Facebook and 120 times higher than on Twitter. 41% of marketers have used Instagram video and 44% plan to use Instagram video 90% of Instagram users are younger than 35. Instagram has become the social media network for targeting Millennials. 32% of teenagers consider Instagram to be the most important social network. Instagram Stories have helped to increase the amount of time people spend on this network, according to Instagram. Users under 25 years old spend more than 32 minutes a day on the platform, while those over 25 spend more than 24 minutes a day. People use Instagram as a way to follow their interests. This, leads to opportunities for everyone from global brands to local enterprises to reach and engage with their customers while they're diving deeper into their interests. Marketers are rapidly increasing their adoption of Instagram to promote everything from clothing to concerts. Instagram's latest internal figures show 25 million businesses have a business profile on the network, and over 200 million users visit at least one business profile every day (Mathison, 2018).

Interactive Communication Using Social Media

Social media is an important tool as a platform by which consumers can express their concerns on any issue, and can talk about their problems in any matter and also report the faults and deficiencies at the same time (Krishna, Dangayach, & Jain, 2011). The most fundamental feature of social media platforms, which are constantly growing, updating, evolving and open to all, is the continuous interaction between users because of the technologies and methods used. Social media is a platform where users can coexist, share, and act together, make suggestions, see, interpret, and create collective opinions and ideas. Social media tools have the power to create a common power of ideas and ideas among businesses, even among individuals with different knowledge (Jue, Marr, & Kassotakis, 2010).

Interaction on social media platforms is essential. Interaction is a structure that supports every kind of interaction between people, between people and institutions, between people and businesses. Interaction is the most important diversity of social media. The diverse sharing among consumers makes social media more common and more effective. Social media is sophisticated, allowing everyone to participate and spread it online. End-users form, create, shape and share content with this participatory nature of social media (Akar, 2011). As a new interactive channel, social media is a far more effective and useful medium than traditional media. For any business, the interactions that will take place in this media are the interactions directly related to the main subject. For example, it is very easy to learn from social media, which products will be produced, how the products will be designed, which colors will be preferred, and which products are not preferred.

As social media platforms use systems that support simultaneous communication, members and users can make simultaneous voice and video calls between themselves. This feature distinguishes social media platforms from traditional communication tools and provides significant advantages. A commercial message sent from social media platforms is instantly seen by the members participating on the platform, and when the members are interested in the message, with this interest interaction occurs. Interaction presents an important advantage for brand managers in their word of mouth communication. In this media, users who share the same interests, pleasures and feelings inform and advise each other about the messages coming from the brands. As a result of this, communication activities are more effective and successful. Social media platforms have changed consumers' behavior of searching, finding, reading, sharing and consuming information in a high incidence of information and contents which are positive or negative about products, services, brands and places and will continue to change depending on the development of social media platforms (Ye, Law, Gu & Chen, 2011).

There are various consequences of social media communication being rich in content, being continuous and effective. Users who come together on various platforms in social media are influencing each other and this is also reflected in their behavior. The information that a user posts, exhibit attitude about brand preferences, shopping habits, fashion, and trends. Interactions that take place in the social media can mobilize organizations, civil society institutions and create behavioral changes. As an interaction platform, all businesses need to establish their social media accounts and create awareness in this area. Businesses that do not need interaction with the customer should also take their place in these platforms in order to control the negative communications that may occur in these media and to communicate with the target consumers when required. Social media platforms are the most effective communication area in case of a crisis that may occur for any reason.

Content Creation and Content Sharing

Social media is based on content produced by users. Social media is also defined as the media created by the consumers. Social media; the recommendation or sharing of content, the criticism, and evaluation of products, services and brands, the discussion of popular topics of the day, the hobbies, the pursuit of interests, the sharing of expertise and experiences (Ryan & Jones, 2008).

Consumers who have a means of communication at all times of the day are constantly watching the developments in social media and have the chance to upload the content they produce in this domain. This opportunity has brought all users to the position of producing content for social media. The users who have posted their developments, news, interesting events, photos and videos to social media have moved from a simple consumer position to a different profile. Moreover, these posts are also seen by other consumers, create a significant content collection. The meaning of this content makes it possible to determine the interests of the users, their conversations, their pleasures, their likes. Businesses seeking to benefit from social media need to conceptualize and act accordingly. Sharing of text, audio, video, photographs and similar materials produced by users is essential. This content, which grows rapidly at almost every day, is being watched and reshared by different users. Comments, tags, and attachments made during sharing provide social media growth. The value of the platforms prepared for users to create and share content is increased by the number of members and content generated by the users. The platform's function is to provide quick and easy access by loading the loaded content with a specific algorithm. There are millions of different content on each social media platform. Structural and emotional links between users enrich the content of social media and the added value created by users is the power of social media. Users are able to access information in an easy and detailed way that they can not reach elsewhere with the content they create and share on social media platforms (Kushin & Yamamoto, 2010).

In social media, it is also important to create content that attracts the attention of the target consumers. Despite the advantages of social media platforms such as cost, speed, ease, and simplicity, a professional effort is necessary to create content and create interaction to draw interest of the target market. For this reason, businesses have to be careful to create an up-to-date, remarkable content policy on social media platforms.

It is imperative for brands to create powerful campaigns with creative content on social media to gain the trust of consumers and to drive sales. For example, beautiful food photos and recipes are at the core of Whole Foods. Users can browse seasonal recipes, Instagram food photos from other Whole Foods shoppers, and tips for healthy eating and smarter shopping. Whole Foods knows that by presenting users with useful, compelling content, they'll inspire visitors to shop – even if they don't explicitly tell them to do so. On Instagram (1.8 million followers), they'll post beautiful food photos from users, but rarely promote their own products or deals. Whole Foods is also a prolific video creator who updates its YouTube channel (53K followers) nearly every week. They have series on cooking how-tos, food trends, recipes, sourcing, and more. In addition to providing existing customers with inspiration, Whole Foods is creating content that will be surfaced in search when people look for recipes or cooking tips. This inspire existing customers to shop for ingredients – and introduce the brand to other potential customers (Eng, 2017).

Tracking Comments

Any kind of content shared on social media platforms is open to interpretation. Positive or negative comments increase interaction and turn into social media debates. Since the participants write their own ideas during interpretation, after a certain period of time comprehensive feedback accumulate under any content. Comments provide valuable information to companies or brands at least as much as obtained from comprehensive market research. Today, many brands use social media accounts and users' comments as an opportunity to improve their products, processes, and communication.

Social media platforms are places where brands do not have one-way communication and where customers have the opportunity to talk, comment and interact. In other words, brands have started to talk to their customers. The content of the conversation involves all kinds of customer information that brands need. Consumers review a wide variety of social media tools in their purchasing decisions. Consumers move away from traditional communication sources and perceive social media as a more reliable source of information. For this reason, the more the brands talk and engage with customers in social media, consumer interest in products and services much more (Mangold & Faulds, 2009).

Businesses take part with Facebook, which is one of the important tools of social media, with their corporate identities, make promotions of their products and brands, create pages and reach a large number of potential customers and manage their products more effectively by taking their opinions and comments. Twitter is an important business channel that allows companies to engage directly with their customers, partners and other stakeholders, both individually and globally. Through Twitter, businesses follow what consumers think about products, respond to customer requests, communicate with shareholders, and earn money with various creative, different advertisements. Celebrities and politicians are also in touch with their fans and voters in this new way (Tuncer, Özata, Akar & Öztürk, 2013). Twitter, which brings consumers together with brands and enables brands to express themselves in a more sincere way, enables them to follow and participate in creative tweets of brands, their dialogue with consumers and other brands. The important feature of Twitter is that it is very easy to create a brand-community in a very short time. If used correctly, the main advantage of Twitter among social media platforms is delivering messages directly to the large audience at low cost.

Building Brand Community

Social media is an efficient platform to build, grow and maintain a brand community. Brands use social media tools to maintain their relationships and engage consumers with their brands (Yan, 2011). Social media not only increases the communication power of the consumers, but also increases the communication power of the brands day by day. Social media platforms offer many opportunities to brands such as interacting with consumers, exchanging information, providing feedback about brand developments.

Social media is also an interactive, personal and sensitive environment for brands (Jothi, Neelamalar & Prasad, 2011). Brands need to be found on different social media platforms with corporate identities and use social media as part of their integrated marketing communications.

Businesses are trying to increase their brand awareness, gain new customers and profit by using social media applications like Facebook, Twitter, Instagram, YouTube (Kaplan & Haenlein, 2010). It is a fact that social media is a more difficult medium than the traditional media in terms of marketing communication in the intensely competitive environment created by millions of products and services offered by many substantial companies in the market. The messages that are received and spread in this media are not under the control of the brands. Users share their love, likes, and tales about the brands they are watching, sharing and spreading their opinions on various topics. Users easily talk, share, and spread their ideas about the brands they love, like, follow up on these platforms. One of the main problems for marketers is to establish emotional, cognitive and structural connections with the target consumers. Messages sent from traditional media channels are not enough to establish emotional bonds and connections with consumers. Traditional media is in the form of monologue because it is a one-way communication, interaction does not take place. Today's brands will fulfill expectations as much as they listen and monitor customers. In this sense, social media is a platform where brands listen to their customers. Businesses that listen and respond consumers gain a customer oriented organization identity by allowing their customers to direct themselves. In social media, online brand communities should be built and users should be actively involved in these communities. It is important to establish long-lasting relationships between brands and users, taking into account factors such as trust, continuity, interaction, and communication (Casalo, Flavian & Guinaliu, 2010).

Social media is the easiest and most cost-effective community creation platforms. At this point, businesses need to converge in listening than talking on social media platforms. It is possible to create a large participatory community with the interaction that will be created after learning what the target group is talking about, which topics to share, which trends to follow. The most important achievement on these platforms is constant interaction with a large mass of followers of the brand. Twitter offers a variety of facilitating solutions for small and medium-sized businesses that cannot achieve results through traditional marketing tools and processes in a highly competitive environment. Twitter can also be used to direct traffic to other social media platforms or web pages of a brand and create brand communities.

Collaboration through Social Media

Businesses are leveraging technology and social media to adapt to changes. Social media enables collaboration using a variety of applications. Social media, like all other digital platforms, is a platform where collaboration is intense. Co-operation and congruity represent the basic features of social media. It is possible to carry out large-scale events in a short period of time through collaborations that are created, shared and maintained in a short time among users. In addition to the activities performed by the users, there are many examples that can be reached to millions of users in cooperation with the content requested to share quickly. Especially in social awareness, political advocacy, social media events are important examples and opportunities for brands.

Any unexpected situation, brands and companies directly reach out to the consumers via social media tools and deliver the right information about the subject, thus preserving their corporate reputation. Today, many businesses are sharing a variety of information, innovation, and news with blogs. Many businesses around the world use blogs to interact with their target audience, listen to them and provide feedback. Blogs are an important means for the companies to communicate directly with their customers and to create collaboration. The companies ask consumers about their opinion about the products and services that are thought to be offered to the market. Blogs that users share about their own ideas and interests are also used by brands to advertise their target groups and to raise awareness. The software giant Microsoft is implementing new product developments based on feedback from corporate blogs. Besides, brands and companies can also use social media as an effective medium to remove the negative effects of negative communication that may occur in brands, products and etc.

Social Media as a Sales Channel

In addition to customer interaction, brand communication, information gathering, content creation and sharing, social media also used as a sales channel. Social media, which is the common point of millions of users, is a medium where sales of various products and services can easily be done. Most businesses have begun selling their products from sites they've established via social media accounts. Sales opportunities are frequently seen in different sectors such as the service sector, the fast-moving consumer goods sector, and the real estate sector.

It is also said that social media platforms are a function of supporting sales rather than generating direct sales. Customers who are directed to the landing page of the business from the social media platform are closer to purchasing with the effect created by the social media comments and interactions. Because of the effects that social media have on sales, directly and indirectly, brands are going to organize campaigns that will turn marketing communication into sales. Million dollar television commercials are no longer the primary factor affecting the intent to buy. The comments of consumers who use and experience products and services on social media now substitute for traditional communication media and channels (Qualman, 2013). Numerous companies in the fields of tourism, education, apparel, software and consumer electronics are actively participating in social media platforms and especially on Facebook and Instagram direct sales examples are frequently encountered.

Social Commerce

The increase in the number and type of social media platforms, the addition of more and more participants to these platforms is causing commercial activities on social media. The concept of "social commerce" has begun to evolve with the evaluation of e-commerce sites' interactions among users in social media platforms. As e-commerce sites began to use social media platforms effectively, e-commerce and social media platforms have emerged in the form of collaborative work. The concept of social trade refers to e-commerce transactions through social networks. This concept, which emerges due to the influence of social networking, decision-making mechanisms, has a different meaning due to the existence of a large number of different users who are influential in a user's purchasing process.

By using social networks effectively, e-commerce firms can easily reach the target consumers and find the opportunity to benefit from the interaction and to sell in this way. Businesses are using social media platforms increasingly for commercial purposes every day in favor of new methods developed by these platforms. The main goal of businesses is to convert the social media user into a customer. Social media platforms, which are not only focused on brand awareness and corporate reputation, but also function as a commercial platform, are partnering with e-commerce sites more and more each day. Through social media, it is possible to have privileges such as giving special discounts to consumers, individualize special campaigns, interacting with business and other consumers (Clark & Melancon, 2013).

Conversations, comments, shares, suggestions, complaints, and evaluations about products and services on social media platforms are actively engaging consumers. Consumers often make purchases by being influenced by the users they follow on their social media platforms or from the recommendations of their contacts and their purchasing decisions. Users who follow the brand accounts on social networking sites receive notifications from these channels and share them with other users. Facebook, Twitter, and Instagram provide important opportunities for users to keep each other informed. At the same time, these platforms offer diversified and effective ways of finding, discovering and examining new products that attract the attention of users. Users talk about their favorite products and brands, voluntarily advertise them, and often act as a purchasing consultant. Users who ask their friends in social media what they want to learn about a product or service take action by receiving suggestions from others.

Measurability of Social Media

One of the most important facets of social media is measurability. Measuring and monitoring consumers and trends are a priority for marketing strategies which could increase brand awareness, market share or revenues. Social media offers opportunities to acquire customer profile information, especially to identify potential customers. Through social media, information about users' preferences such as brand, product, service, political view, etc. can be collected easily and then it is possible to make personalized targeting to the customers in the frame of this information (Dam & Velden, 2015). The measurement is based on precise tracks of the members of the platform. For instance, measurements based on precise figures can be made on detailed topics such as how many members are on each platform, time of participation in the platform, the number of content produced, the content liked or disliked and followers. In addition, it is possible to determine exactly how far an advertisement message delivered from any social media platform has reached the target consumers, which members see this advertisement message, who responds to this message, who generates the content about this message, and which members share this message with others. Moreover, this measurement can be done by location, place and time dimension. It is also possible to learn and know at what time zone and in which geographical domain the target consumers respond.

Users' comments, feedbacks, interpretation they leave on websites, posts, Facebook likes, share numbers, Twitter messages, videos uploaded to YouTube provide important research interest for businesses. The social CRM system- that can be used to recognize both substantial and potential customers- needs to be restructured in order to be monitored, analyzed and find its direction (Karahasan, 2012). Increasing interaction with social media platforms has resulted in customer data that has accumulated on these platforms to reach a very large size. If this interaction is expected to increase further in the forthcoming years, businesses and brands that embrace more customer profiles with strategies customized to these platforms will face tremendous potential.

The monitoring and tracking people, institutions, products, competitors in the social media and analyzing the interactions in these platforms will ensure that significant information for companies and brands. The target group determination process can be performed easily with this valuable data. Because it is necessary to develop a different communication and interaction strategies for each platform by following diverse behaviors in different platforms, with the help of these analyzes it is possible to understand the expectations, wants and needs of the target consumers. An easily measurability feature of social media events allows businesses to reach their target groups effectively without the need for large advertising budgets.

Social Media as a Creative and Effective Advertising Tool

Social media platforms are considered as effective advertising media. Social media, which millions of users subscribe voluntarily, not being used as an advertising platform can be a significant loss for businesses. It is more difficult to advertise in social media than traditional channels, where control is entirely at the users. In today's competitive environment, any kind of business, especially small and medium-sized businesses, must take advantage of the opportunities available on social media platforms. When it is used in an integrated way with traditional media tools, social media platforms offer a wide range of opportunities as a new communication channel with different structures and different contents. Social media advertising has been growing in parallel with the emergence of these platforms in recent years and increasing day by day. Advertising on social media platforms requires a different process than traditional media tools. Unlike communication with mass advertising tools, the target consumers, segment, content, and interaction of the ads on social media platforms must be well planned and estimated in advance. Since social media platforms are enriched with diverse technologies almost every day, different advertising methods and techniques are applied and a new type of advertising is emerging swiftly. Essentially, advertising on social media platforms involves placing the ad on or around the content and being part of the content. Almost every social media platform has its own advertising format. In addition, when other digital channels are integrated as an advertising channel, the awareness of the brand on social media platforms increases.

On social media platforms, users are consistently talking about businesses, brands, people, events, and products. Conversations about any brand or product lead to intensive interaction with users and lead to intensive interaction. This phenomenon creates a new type of advertising. Advertising agencies specify which products are being spoken at what intensity and how intense are the conversations. In parallel with this, important and effective advertising tools can be determined. In this way, advertisers place banners on blogs or forums where users talk about the products and install banners in the areas next to their conversations. For example, a holiday resort operator may place banners on blogs or forums that have related user conversation spots on holiday plan or identify the blogs that most overlap with brand identity and target consumers. These services are very fast and detailed, varying according to processes and technology. Some agencies also specialize in finding the most effective users, not just the most relevant user conversations.

Video sharing on social media platforms is also very common. Increasingly more and more brands and users are sharing videos. These videos are watched with interest by other users, for this reason, videos are considered an effective advertising platform. Publishers and marketing communicators look for ways to place ads on video content created by users and find ways to use them. While pre-roll video advertising is prevalent before the video itself, YouTube and some similar sites still prefer to use overlay video ads. Ads make video watching difficult and annoy consumers. Due to these reasons, measures are taken such as keeping ads short, cutting the ad after cutting some part of the ads, or adding the option to skip. In addition, these platforms can also provide important metrics to find out which ads are liked, which ads are cut in half, and which ads are being watched several times by the same users.

Brands are creating different platforms for talking, entertaining, educating and creating brand loyalty by bringing users together using interesting content, games, surveys, puzzles and contests and similar activities to create their own social media communities. In this method, off-site advertising, users directed to specific communities where they can share valuable or interesting content they can join. Thus, users are given the opportunity to see themselves as a part of the brand and these platforms establish a deep relationship between the brand and identity/personality.

SOLUTIONS AND RECOMMENDATIONS

Today, a substantial portion of customers and leads are on social. Social media provide an opportunity for the consumers to access the company, reach new contents and click through to the website easily. Social media platforms offer highly targeted communication and content, which can be customized around customers' needs. Therefore, it can be said that companies should focus on the strategies to increase engagement and interaction with their target consumers. With the help of different kinds of social media platforms and tools, it will be possible to improve connection, communication and brand loyalty. Social media plays a bigger role in influencing brand perception. It is obvious that brands with active social media profiles have more loyal customers. Consequently, companies and brands should create appropriate social media strategies to generate the company or brand profile, improve public image, increase brand the sales.

FUTURE RESEARCH DIRECTIONS

In this study, it is broadly focused on the significance of social media platforms in marketing decisions and strategies. Technological and innovative changes and developments are evaluated in terms of social media marketing. Social media generates opportunities for strategic marketing and management actions. Main concepts between marketing decisions and social platforms are discussed in this book chapter. Different studies that will examine how social media will evolve and how it will be used in different markets and different sectors will also contribute to the literature.

CONCLUSION

The changes in the digital world raise interest in social media platforms and there is increasingly more engagement. Social media serves to a brand's and company's marketing plan as part of integrated marketing communications. Increasing brand recognition and corporate reputation and enhancing corporate image are the fundamental objectives of social media marketing and they serve for the purpose of increasing product and service sale. Companies can share their information related to themselves and their products with their target customers directly without public relations experts and communication agents. From this perspective, it can be said that companies' dependency on third parties with their marketing activities decreased.

All activities on social media platforms are done to increase the company's sales, market share, and profit. With this purpose, if the company serves through traditional distribution channels, communication on their social media platforms should have the purpose of leading target customers to companies' sales points. If the company has an online selling channel on the internet and the company is an e-commerce company, social media platforms should have the purpose of creating traffic to the company's e-commerce website. Social media is not only a brand communication, sales, and marketing platform, but also a platform for public relations and corporate reputation management. Therefore, every company should create social media accounts and start their presence on social media even to protect their corporate and brand name on social media. Social media activities can be seen and shared by target customers of the company and the other customers by nature. The voice of customers on social media should have listened.

Companies should set their objectives and plan their social media activities for the suitable target customers. Every company and brand should analyze their own target customers, calculate the risks on the related platform and build an engagement policy. In the future, it is expected that competition will be in these areas and therefore analyzing target customers is an important step to hinder negative propaganda that can be made by rivals who want to damage company and brand by using these platforms. It is important to know target customers' behavior, habits, the things they follow, the events and facts they criticize, their demographic and psychographic features in detail. Time spent on social media is very valuable and data gained from engagement leads strategies of companies and there is a need to be close to a user in brand management. Therefore, engagement, information flow, communication, and data should be well analyzed.

It is a fact that social media activities preferred more day by day. Interest in social media is increasing since these platforms are easy to use and effective campaigns can be created with low budgets. Social media has become essential for brands in order to create closer touch points with customers and to become proactive in the marketplace. Social media provides brands a new way to communicate with their consumers, offers a way of interaction that has previously not existed. Since the new competition is on digital platforms, every form of companies should build an effective social media strategy.

REFERENCES

Akar, E. (2011). *Sosyal Medya Pazarlaması*. Ankara: Efil Yayınevi.

Berthon, P. R., Pitt, L. F., Plangger, K., & Shapiro, D. (2012). Marketing meets Web 2.0, social media, and creative consumers: Implications for international marketing strategy. *Business Horizons*, *55*(3), 261–271. doi:10.1016/j.bushor.2012.01.007

Carr, C. T., & Hayes, R. A. (2015). Social Media: Defining, Developing, and Divining. *Atlantic Journal of Communication*, *23*(1), 46–65. doi:10.1080/15456870.2015.972282

Casalo, L. V., Flavian, C., & Guinaliu, M. (2008). Promoting Consumer's Participation in Virtual Brand Communities: A New Paradigm in Branding Strategy. *Journal of Marketing Communications*, *14*(1), 19–36. doi:10.1080/13527260701535236

Clark, M., Black, H. G., & Judson, K. (2017). Brand community integration and satisfaction with social media sites: A comparative study. *Journal of Research in Interactive Marketing*, *11*(1), 39–55. doi:10.1108/JRIM-07-2015-0047

Clark, M., & Melancon, J. (2013). The influence of social media investment of relational outcomes: A relationship marketing perspective. *International Journal of Marketing Studies*, *5*(4), 132–142. doi:10.5539/ijms.v5n4p132

Dam, J.-W., & Velden, M. (2015). Online profiling and clustering of Facebook users. *Decision Support Systems*, *70*, 60–72. doi:10.1016/j.dss.2014.12.001

Eng, H. (2017). *50 Best Content Marketing Brands of 2017*. Retrieved from https://insights.newscred.com/ best-content-marketing-brands-2017/

Fox, S. (2009). e-Riches 2.0: Next-Generation Marketing Strategies for Making Millions Online. New York: Amacom.

Hainla, L. (2018). *21 Social Media Marketing Statistics You Need to Know in 2018*. Retrieved from https://www.dreamgrow.com/21-social-media-marketing-statistics/

Jothi, P. S., Neelamalar, M., & Prasad, R. S. (2011). Analysis of social networking sites: A study on effective communication strategy in developing brand communication. *Journal of Media and Communication Studies*, *3*(7), 234–242.

Jue, A. L., Marr, J. A., & Kassotakis, M. E. (2010). *Social Media at Work: How Networking Tools Propel Organizational Performance*. Jossey-Bass.

Kaplan, A., & Haenlein, M. (2010). Users of the world, unite! The challenges and opportunities of Social Media. *Business Horizons*, *53*(1), 59–68. doi:10.1016/j.bushor.2009.09.003

Karahasan, F. (2014). *Taşlar Yerinden Oynarken Dijital Pazarlamanın Kuralları*. İstanbul: Doğan Kitap.

Kietzman, J. H., Hermkens, K., McCarthy, I. P., & Silvestre, B. S. (2011). Social media? Get serious! Understanding the functional building blocks of social media. *Business Horizons*, *54*(3), 241–251. doi:10.1016/j.bushor.2011.01.005

Krishna, A., Dangayach, G. S., & Jain, R. (2011). A Conceptual Framework for the Service Recovery Paradox. *The Marketing Review*, *11*(1), 41–56. doi:10.1362/146934711X565288

Kushin, M. J., & Yamamoto, M. (2010). Did Social Media Really Matter? College Students' Use of Online Media and Political Decision Making in the Election. *Mass Communication & Society*, *13*(5), 608–630. doi:10.1080/15205436.2010.516863

Mangold, W. G., & Faulds, D. J. (2009). Social media: The new hybrid element of the promotion mix. *Business Horizons*, *52*(4), 357–365. doi:10.1016/j.bushor.2009.03.002

Mathison, R. (2018). *22+ Useful Instagram Statistics for Social Media Marketers*. Retrieved from https://blog.hootsuite.com/instagram-statistics/

Miller, R., & Lammas, N. (2010). Social media and its implications for viral marketing. *Asia Pacific Public Relations Journal*, *11*(1), 1–9.

Qualman, E. (2013). *Socialnomics: How Social Media Transforms the Way We Live and Do Business*. John Wiley & Sons.

Ryan, D., & Jones, C. (2008). *Understanding Digital Marketing, Marketing Strategies for Engaging the Digital Generation*. London: Kogan Page.

Schmidt, S. M. P., & Ralph, D. L. (2011). Social Media: More Available Marketing Tools. *Business Review (Federal Reserve Bank of Philadelphia)*, *18*(2), 37–43.

Shih, C. (2011). *The Facebook Era: Tapping Online Social Networks to Market Sell and Innovate*. Boston: Pearson Education Inc.

Smith, A. N., Fischer, E., & Yongjian, C. (2012). How Does Brand-related User-generated Content Differ Across YouTube, Facebook, and Twitter? *Journal of Interactive Marketing*, *26*(2), 102–113. doi:10.1016/j.intmar.2012.01.002

StrikeSocial. (2018). *50 Powerful Social Media Statistics for Marketers in 2018.* Retrieved from https://strikesocial.com/blog/50-social-media-stats-every-marketer-should-know-in-2018/

Tuncer, S., Özata, Z., Akar, E., & Öztürk, M. C. (2013). *Sosyal Medya*. Eskişehir: Anadolu Üniversitesi Yayınları.

Tuten, T. L., & Solomon, M. R. (2015). *Social Media Marketing*. London: Sage Publication.

WeareSocial. (2018). *Digital in 2018*. Retrieved from https://wearesocial.com/blog/2018/01/global-digital-report-2018

Whiting, A., & Williams, D. (2013). Why people use social media: A uses and gratifications approach. *Qualitative Market Research*, *16*(4), 362–369. doi:10.1108/QMR-06-2013-0041

Yan, J. (2011). Social media in branding: Fulfilling a need. *Journal of Brand Management*, *18*(9), 688–696. doi:10.1057/bm.2011.19

Ye, Q., Fang, B., He, W., & Hsieh, J. J. P. A. (2012). Can Social Capital be Transferred Cross The Boundary of The Real and Virtual Worlds? An Empirical Investigation of Twitter. *Journal of Electronic Commerce Research*, *13*(2), 145–156.

Ye, Q., Law, R., Gu, B., & Chen, W. (2011). The Influence of User-Generated Content on Traveler Behavior: An Empirical Investigation on the Effects of E-word-of-mouth to Hotel Online Bookings. *Computers in Human Behavior*, *27*(2), 634–639. doi:10.1016/j.chb.2010.04.014

Zarrella, D. (2010). *The Social Media Marketing Book*. O'Reilly Media.

KEY TERMS AND DEFINITIONS

Brand Community: It refers to a community that formed on the basis of attachment to a product or brand and built upon shared values, common interest, and connections.

Content Marketing: It refers to creating content that builds a long-term relationship with the target market.

Conversion: It refers to any action on the websites or social media platforms.

Engagement: It is the metric that measures the reactions of users on social platforms and allows companies to see how consumers use, talk, and share content about brands.

Social Commerce: A form of e-commerce that uses social media and social networks.

Social Media: It refers to the internet technology that enables the creation and sharing of ideas and information and the building of virtual communities, networks, and relations.

Social Media Advertising: A kind of online advertising via social media.

Social Media Marketing: It refers to the process of marketing through the use of social media platforms.

This research was previously published in the Handbook of Research on Managerial Thinking in Global Business Economics; pages 318-335, copyright year 2019 by Business Science Reference (an imprint of IGI Global).

Chapter 51
Approach to Social Media Marketing Strategies in Different World Regions:
A Descriptive Study

Luis Matosas-López
iD https://orcid.org/0000-0001-7313-0146
Rey Juan Carlos University, Spain

Roberto Baelo Alvarez
iD https://orcid.org/0000-0003-1003-6739
University of León, Spain

ABSTRACT

The present study, using a sample of university organizations from different world regions, aims to provide an overview of social media marketing strategies used in different geographical locations. For this purpose, the authors conducted a descriptive study of the communication patterns implemented by university institutions in four regions: Africa and the Middle East, North America, Latin America, and Europe. The study, which adopts a comparative format, contrasts the findings obtained in each of the aforementioned regions, highlighting the existence of both similarities and differences in the social media marketing strategies of the organizations observed. In line with previous research, the authors took Twitter as the social media platform to be monitored.

INTRODUCTION

The development of Information and Communication Technologies (ICTs), in general, and the emergence of the Internet, in particular, has caused numerous social changes in the past decades (Cabero Almenara et al., 2007; Feng et al., 2019; García-Jiménez et al., 2013; García-Ruiz et al., 2015; García Galera et al., 2017; Gómez-García et al., 2020; Richter et al., 2011).

DOI: 10.4018/978-1-6684-6287-4.ch051

Access to the Internet among the citizenry has resulted in an increase in the use of social network services. By 2020, the number of Internet users worldwide reached 4.54 billion, being the average penetration of social media users 49% (Kemp, 2020). This average penetration in global terms obviously varies between countries. Thus, for example, the percentage in Ghana is 20%, in Egypt 41%, in Germany 45%, in Colombia 69%, in the US 70% and in South Korea 87% (Kemp, 2020).

The impact of these platforms over time is undeniable, and their integration into our daily life is a consummate reality (Piscitelli, 2010). The success of social media is caused by different factors, but among them stand out aspects such as the dynamism of the content, its collaborative utility, its intuitive use, its easy access and its interactive nature (Castaño et al., 2015).

Nevertheless, what is a social network service? Castañeda Quintero (2010) generically defines these platforms as those telematics tools organized around user profiles, personal or professional, that pursue the objective of connecting people with common interests.

The literature review by Almansa, Fonseca and Castillo (2013) differentiates three major topics of research in this field: (a) user representation and generation of links between users (Junco, 2012; McAndrew and Jeong, 2012); (b) structuring of the network around interests and motivations (Backstrom et al., 2006; Liu et al., 2006); and (c) privacy and risks of the media (Calvete et al., 2010; McBride, 2011).

The information stored on these platforms provides a vast record of thoughts and behaviors of individuals of all types and social conditions. In recent years, users' messages in social network services have been used around the world to explore social, economic, and cultural realities of various kinds. Examples of this are the analysis of the ideological polarization of political parties (Urman, 2020), the prediction of economic fluctuations in stock exchange markets (Li et al., 2016), the dissemination of hate messages after terrorist attacks (Bruns and Hanusch, 2017), the identification of environmental problems in certain areas (Chen et al., 2015) and the momentum of social activism movements (Matsilele and Ruhanya, 2020).

The widespread nature of the social media phenomena has transformed the way we communicate and interact with our environment to the point of making it necessary to create a descriptive term for the typical user of these platforms.

The academic community has recovered the term "prosumer", a term created during the 1970s (McLuhan & Nevitt, 1972; Toffler, 1980) to define the typical user of this media. Born from the union of the ideas of producer and consumer, "prosumer" serves to describe those individuals capable of consuming what they themselves produce. More recently, other authors have created from this concept the term "media prosumer" to refer to the user accustomed to the social media setting.

Sandoval Romero and Aguaded Gómez (2012), for example, describe the "media prosumer" as the subject able to take a leading role in the media, producing and consuming information to generate a culture of participation and interactivity. Sánchez Carrero and Contreras Pulido (2012), for instance, define the "media prosumer" as the user who actively assumes the role of the communication channel, becoming a recommender and opinion generator on a variety of topics.

However, the particularities and motivations of this "media prosumer" require an in-depth analysis. For this purpose, one of the approaches commonly employed by researchers is the so-called Uses and Gratifications Theory (U&G). Even though this approach has been applied in numerous studies on the use of social media in recent years (Chen, 2011; García-Ruiz et al., 2018; Matosas López, 2018; Raacke & Bonds-Raacke, 2008; Smock et al., 2011), U&G theory had been used previously to describe how audiences interact with other mass media such as radio, press or television (Katz et al., 1973, 1974; Ruggiero, 2000).

The conceptual framework defined by this theory explores how mass media is used to meet the needs of the individual. In accordance with Rubin (1994), U&G theory is based on five pillars: (1) the selection and use of the media have a goal; (2) the subject is the one who takes the initiative by selecting the media in order to satisfy an existing need; (3) the subject's behavior is conditioned by different social factors; (4) there are different media alternatives that compete with each other in terms of selection, use and needs satisfaction; and (5) the subject has a position of empowerment in the media.

The nature of the social media phenomena fits perfectly with the assumptions established by this theory. Users, having other possibilities, freely choose these platforms; they access them to obtain a reward; their communication is conditioned by social aspects; and they enjoy a position of privilege on the platform. The potential of social network services to propagate information to large audiences, as happens with other mass media (press, radio, or television), makes the U&G theory particularly suitable for contextualizing research in this field.

Chapter Objective and Structure

This chapter, using as a theoretical framework that of the U&G theory described above, aims to explore, from an international perspective, the social media digital marketing strategies carried out in different geographical locations around the world.

For this purpose, the authors conduct a descriptive study of communication patterns implemented in university organizations of four regions: Africa and the Middle East, North America, Latin America, and Europe.

The study adopts a comparative format, addressing the similarities and differences in the social media marketing strategies of the organizations subject to observation.

The chapter structure is organized as follow. Firstly, the chapter presents a Theoretical Background section in which the authors address, on the one hand, the importance of social media at university organizations and, on the other, the relevance of these techniques as marketing and communication tool in these institutions. Secondly, the Methodology is presented detailing all the information required within the subsections of: Sample Design, Data Extraction and Cleaning, and Data Analysis. Next, the authors show the main findings obtained in the Results section. To conclude, in the chapter's final part, the traditional sections of Discussion and Conclusions are presented, the last one including specifically subsections of Professional and Managerial Implications and Limitations and Future Research.

THEORETICAL BACKGROUND

Social Media at University Organizations

Within the university context, U&G theory is also used in numerous studies. In this regard, most authors who adopt U&G theory in their research examine the use patterns of these technologies among university students. Examples of this are the studies by Durán and Guerra (2015), García-Ruiz, Tirado and Hernando (2018), Florenthal (2015), and Doval-Avendaño et al. (2018).

Durán and Guerra (2015) explore the addictive behavior of students from different degree programs in the use of the extinct social network Tuenti. García-Ruiz, Tirado and Hernando (2018) examine the benefits that students find in the intensive use of Facebook, Instagram and YouTube. Likewise,

Florenthal (2015) discusses the motivations and barriers that business students identify for the use of LinkedIn. Finally, Doval-Avendaño et al. (2018) explore the reflections of a group of communication students after remaining deprived of access to their digital devices, and therefore their social profiles, over a 24 hour-period.

Another topic of study in the university context is the application of these technologies as a support for teaching. Notable in this regard are studies by Kabilan et al. (2010), Cabero and Marín (2014), Santoveña-Casal and Bernal-Bravo (2019), and Matosas-López and Romero-Luis (2019).

Kabilan et al. (2010) examine the possibilities of using Facebook as a learning environment in English language teaching. Similarly, the study developed by Cabero and Marín (2014) explores the instruction potential of different social networks (Twitter, Facebook, LinkedIn or Hi5) for collaborative purposes. The study conducted by Santoveña-Casal and Bernal-Bravo (2019) examines the use of Twitter as a motivational element in autonomous learning processes. Finally, the study by Matosas-López and Romero-Luis (2019), with Marketing students, explores the correlations between usage patterns on Facebook, Twitter and Instagram, and how students perceive the usefulness of certain digital learning resources.

Social Media in University Organizations as a Marketing and Communication Tool

University organizations, like any other type of organization, set their goals in the context in which they operate, to meet the needs of their target audiences. Although the target audience of any university, within its social purpose, consists of a wide range of entities (government agencies, companies, social agents, etc.), students in their broadest sense occupy a leading position. This category includes current students, future students, and alumni.

With regard to the student community, then, universities design and implement recruitment and loyalty plans in the same way that any company would do. Recruitment plans aim to reach as many subjects as possible, and loyalty plans build links with current students and with those who will become alumni after their graduation.

Within this context, examples of actions that could be part of recruitment plans are open days, participation in educational fairs or advertising in the press, radio, or television at the local level. As far as loyalty plans are concerned, we can point to discounts on subsidiary educational services, tuition funding, or the creation of postgraduate programs linked to student's undergraduate training.

These recruitment and loyalty plans are a good example of the type of actions that are framed in the marketing strategies of any university organization, whether public or private. However, all the foregoing actions are contextualized in an offline setting. In addition to this offline setting, there is also a wide range of potential actions within the digital sphere. Banners on educational portals, as a recruitment mechanism; or newsletters, as a loyalty tool, are just two examples. In this area of marketing strategies in digital environments, social network services are particularly relevant.

In recent years, these platforms have been used intensively by university organizations around the world. Nevertheless, different authors claim that there is still wide margin for improvement in exploiting these technologies as part of university marketing strategies. Casanoves Boix et al. (2018) point out that universities should invest in a greater and more professionalized presence on social media, in order to enhance their branding strategies. In the same line, Guzmán Duque et al. (2012) underline that these technologies should help universities to consolidate their corporate identity and to develop promotional and recruitment campaigns in the territories in which they operate.

Although social media marketing strategies still have a wide margin for improvement, numerous works have addressed this issue in recent years. Table 1 shows some of the studies conducted over the past ten years.

Laaser et al. (2012) use semi-structured interviews with management experts to analyze the use given to social network services such as Facebook, Twitter, LinkedIn and Google+. Concerning the use of these platforms, the authors reveal the existence of management problems, lack of strategic vision, and the need to define efficiency and reach indicators.

Kuzma and Wright (2013) study the role of Facebook, Twitter, LinkedIn and MySpace as a catalyst in the transformation of marketing strategies in the university context. According to these researchers, when such technologies are properly integrated into the organization's strategy, they not only create added value for the institution's audience and stakeholders, but also act as a recruitment instrument.

The study by Valerio Ureña et al. (2014), focusing on Facebook, examines the engagement between institution and target audience on this platform. The authors identify that time of publication impacts effectiveness in terms of likes, comments, and shared content; showing that the most successful publications occur outside the workday and usual office hours.

Bulbulia and Wassermann's research (2015) discusses the possibilities of using Twitter as a channel of interaction with the student community. In this work, the authors emphasize the possibilities of using social network services in the university context, and that the communication potential inherent to these technologies is not always exploited.

Túñez López et al. (2015) analyze the usefulness of Facebook and Twitter as digital communication tools in a sample of universities. In addition to showing that most publications were concentrated in the early and central part of the week, the authors point out that the content is fundamentally composed of images and links.

Similarly, Laudano et al. (2016) examine university libraries' use of the social network Twitter. Their findings reveal that although libraries use this platform to disseminate information about collections, services, or to promote activities, their use is generally diffuse and poorly planned from the strategic point of view.

The study conducted by López-Pérez and Olvera-Lobo (2016) explores the use of social networks for the dissemination of research results at the public university. The authors note that around 40% of the institutions examined use their corporate Facebook and Twitter accounts in the propagation of this type of content.

Puertas Hidalgo and Carpio Jiménez (2016) examine universities' use of Facebook, Twitter and Instagram platforms from a strategic perspective. The authors point out that the engagement generated throughout these social network services help the organization in achieving its strategic objectives.

Cabrera and Camarero's work (2016) analyses the communication channels used by universities for the dissemination of science and technology events. Among other findings, shows that 80% of students use Facebook, even above the university website, to be informed of their faculty events.

Peruta and Shields (2017) study how Facebook can improve engagement between university organizations and stakeholders. The authors demonstrate that aspects such as type of publication or publication frequency can contribute to improving both engagement with the audience and dissemination of the organization's content.

Table 1. Studies on the use of social media as a marketing and communication tool in the university context

Author/s	Platform considered	Region where the study was conducted
Laaser et al. (2012)	Facebook, Twitter, LinkedIn, and Google+	Latin America
Kuzma and Wright (2013)	Facebook, Twitter, LinkedIn and MySpace	Asia, Africa, and Europe
Valerio Ureña et al. (2014)	Facebook	Latin America
Bulbulia and Aquarius (2015)	Twitter	Africa
Tuñez López et al. (2015)	Facebook and Twitter	Europe and Latin America
Laudano et al. (2016)	Twitter	Latin America
López-Pérez and Olvera-Lobo (2016)	Facebook and Twitter	Europe
Puertas Hidalgo and Carpio Jiménez (2016)	Facebook, Twitter, Instagram, and Google+	Latin America
Cabrera and Waiter (2016)	Facebook	Latin America
Peruta and Shields (2017)	Facebook	North America
Bodunde et al. (2017)	Facebook and Twitter	Africa
Kimmons et al. (2017)	Twitter	North America
Quintana Pujalte et al. (2018)	Twitter	Europe
Wu et al. (2019)	Facebook	Asia
Matosas-Lopez and Romero-Ania (2020)	Twitter	Europe

Source: Self-elaboration

Likewise, Bodunde et al. (2017) compare the internal and external communication strategies of university organizations and banking companies. After exploring the uses given to Facebook and Twitter, among other marketing instruments, the authors emphasize that transparency and dialogue are key in the success of any organization, regardless of its nature.

Kimmons et al. (2017), analyzing a sample of 5.7 million Twitter messages from higher education institutions, underline that although social media has improved the reach of these organizations, their current reach is limited. The authors reveal that most of the messages from these institutions are one-way, lacked any feeling and focused on a very small variety of topics.

The work of Quintana Pujalte et al. (2018) explores the use of social media accounts to respond to situations of institutional crisis. The study reveals how the Twitter social profile can be used in such circumstances to redirect the flow of corporate communication, either to the official university website, or to press releases.

Wu et al. (2019) analyze the comments that publications from a sample of university institutions were able to generate on Facebook. The authors reveal that messages using a friendly tone receive a higher volume of comments than those using a direct, rigid tone.

Finally, the study by Matosas-López and Romero-Ania (2020) explores the variables that allow more efficient management of university organizations on Twitter. The authors reveal that the use of links, hashtags, messages in the early morning or publications on gender equality issues contribute to increase audience interaction with the institution.

All these works consider platforms such as Facebook, Twitter, Instagram, LinkedIn, Google+ or MySpace. However, these last two have gradually lost importance in favor of the former, just as did other platforms considered in previous investigations (Cabero-Almenara and Marín-Díaz, 2014; Durán and

Guerra, 2015; Espuny Vidal et al., 2011; Gómez-Aguilar et al., 2012; Laaser et al., 2012), for instance Hi5, MySpace, Tuenti, or Xing.

In addition, as can be seen in the third column of Table 1, the foregoing studies also show the variety of geographical locations considered in these investigations. Argentina, Ecuador, the United States, Spain, China, England, and Nigeria are just a few examples of countries whose university organizations have been the subject of study. In this regard, although Latin America and Europe are the regions where most studies have been carried out, we also find studies carried out in Africa, North America, and Asia.

Main Focus of the Chapter

The present study, using a sample of university organizations from different regions around the world, aims to provide an overview of the social media marketing strategies used in different geographical locations.

For this purpose, the authors conduct a descriptive study of communication patterns implemented in university institutions from four regions: Africa and the Middle East, North America, Latin America, and Europe.

The study, which adopts a comparative format, contrasts the findings obtained in each of the aforementioned regions, highlighting the existence of both similarities and differences in the social media marketing strategies of the organizations observed.

In line with previous research (Guzmán Duque et al., 2013; Kimmons et al., 2017; Laudano et al., 2016; Matosas-López and Romero-Ania, 2020), the authors took Twitter as the social media platform to be monitored.

The relevance of social media marketing strategies is beyond question. However, despite this fact, relevant evidence on the way to improve these strategies is still necessary. In this sense, the literature review carried out by Saura (2021) have recently underline the need to generate insights on these techniques in order to improve the strategies implemented in this field.

The originality and main value of this study lies in the analysis of social media marketing strategies from an international approach and perspective. This research reveal the similarities and divergences in social media marketing strategies in different geographical locations. Addressing that the general paradigms followed on the planning of these strategies, probably require reformulation when they have to be adapted to the specific realities of the geographical locations where they are implemented.

METHODOLOGY

Sample Design

The selection of sampling elements took into account two of the most recognized rankings for assessing the activity of university organizations worldwide: the Webometrics list (Marciniak, 2013) and the Academic Ranking of World Universities (ARWU), also known as the Shanghai ranking (Túñez López et al., 2015).

The Webometrics ranking was taken as the starting point in the selection of sampling elements. This ranking, developed by the Cybermetry Laboratory of the Higher Council for Scientific Research (CSIC) in Spain, not only measures the web presence and visibility of higher education institutions worldwide but also offers a categorization by geographical region that satisfies the comparative objective of the study (assessment criteria shown in Table 2).

Table 2. Webometrics ranking assessment criteria

Assessment criteria	Description	Criteria weight
Presence	Size (n° of pages) of the institution's main web domain. It includes all the subdomains that share the same main web domain.	5%
Visibility	N° of external networks (subnets) linking to the institution's web pages (normalized and then average value).	50%
Transparency or openness	N° of citations from top 210 authors.	10%
Excellence or scholarship	N° of papers amongst the top 10% most cited in one of the 26 disciplines of the full database.	35%
Total		**100%**

Source: Webometrics

The information extracted from the Webometrics ranking was then screened by the authors using the ARWU global ranking. This ranking of universities, designed by a group of experts from the Shanghai Jiao Tong University, lists the 1000 most reputable universities worldwide (assessment criteria shown in Table 3).

Table 3. ARWU ranking assessment criteria

Assessment criteria	Description	Criteria weight
Quality of education	Alumni of an institution winning Nobel Prizes and Fields Medals.	10%
Faculty quality I	Staff of an institution winning Nobel Prizes and Fields Medals.	20%
Faculty quality I	Highly Cited Researchers.	20%
Research output I	Papers published in Nature and Science.	20%
Research output I	Papers indexed in Science Citation Index-Expanded and Social Science Citation Index.	20%
Per capita performance	Per capita academic performance of an institution.	10%
Total		**100%**

Source: ARWU

Researchers began with universities in the top 50 of the Webometrics rankings in each region (Africa and the Middle East, North America, Latin America, and Europe). After that, the authors checked whether these institutions appeared also in the ARWU global ranking. After this verification, we took the first ten universities in each region that met the following two criteria: (1) among the top 50 of their regions in the Webometrics list, and (2) among the top 1000 in the world according to the ARWU ranking. The ten universities selected for each of the four regions examined are presented in Table 4.

For future investigations (after this work) only organizations that use English or Spanish to interact with their audiences were selected. This allows researchers to analyze text publications in the future. For the same reason, Asia, where university organizations tend to use the local language in their publications, was also eliminated for study purposes.

Table 4. Universities by region and country

Region / University	Country
Africa and the Middle East	
American University of Beirut	Lebanon
King Abdullah University of Science and Technology	Saudi Arabia
Stellenbosch University	South Africa
University of Cape Town	South Africa
University of Ibadan	Nigeria
University of Johannesburg	South Africa
University of KwaZulu-Natal	South Africa
University of Pretoria	South Africa
University of South Africa	South Africa
Wits University	South Africa
North America	
Columbia University	USA
Cornell University	USA
Harvard University	USA
Johns Hopkins University	USA
Massachusetts Institute of Technology (MIT)	USA
Stanford University	USA
University of California, Berkeley	USA
University of Michigan	USA
University of Pennsylvania	USA
University of Washington	USA
Latin America	
Catholic University	Chile
University of Buenos Aires	Argentina
University of Chile	Chile
Federal University of Minas Gerais	Brazil
Federal University of Rio de Janeiro	Brazil
Federal University of Rio Grande del Sur	Brazil
Federal University of Santa Catarina	Brazil
National Autonomous University of Mexico	Mexico
University of São Paulo	Brazil

continues on following page

Table 4. Continued

Region / University	Country
State University of Campinas	Brazil
Europe	
Cambridge University	England
ETH Zurich (Swiss Federal Institute of Technology Zurich)	Switzerland
Imperial College	England
King's College London	England
Oxford University	England
The University of Edinburgh	Scotland
The University of Manchester	England
University College of London	England
University of Copenhagen	Denmark
Utrecht University	Netherlands

Source: Self-elaboration

Data Extraction and Cleaning

Once the sampling elements were selected, researchers extracted from the Twitter platform all content published during 2019 by the official accounts of the forty institutions. Following the procedure of previous studies (Alkadri et al., 2015; Quintana Pujalte et al., 2018), the data were extracted through Twitter's API using the service provider Twitonomy.

This process allowed the authors to gather a total of 137,463 publications. Of these messages, 98,169 were tweets originally created and published by the university, 26,483 were retweets from the account to third-party publications, and 12,811 were replies from the organization when mentioned by another user of its audience.

The compiled dataset was stored for cleaning, extracting a total of thirty-two indicators organized into five categories: (a) Publication volumes, (b) Publication components, (c) Publications by day of the week, (d) Publications by time slot, and (e) Followership (see Table 5).

From the thirty-two indicators extracted, those corresponding to categories (a), (b), (c), and (d) served to examine social media marketing strategies in the regions analyzed in the study. Likewise, the eight indicators in category (e) served to obtain a first impression of the success of these strategies in each region.

Data Analysis

The authors, in line with similar research (Balan, 2017; Guzmán Duque et al., 2013; Matosas-Lopez, 2020; Valerio Ureña et al., 2014) in this field of study, applied descriptive analysis to the information collected.

The publications extracted for the selected sampling elements in each region were analyzed in an aggregated manner for the different areas (Africa and the Middle East, North America, Latin America, and Europe). All the analyses were conducted using the statistical software IBM SPSS in its version 26.

Table 5. Indicators extracted from the dataset

Category	Number of indicators	Indicator name
(a) Publication volumes	6	Tweets, Retweets, Replies, Daily Tweets, Daily Retweets, Daily Replies
(b) Publication Components	3	Mentions by post, Links by post, Hashtags by post
(c) Publications by day of the week	7	Post on Monday, Post on Tuesday, Post on Wednesday, Post on Thursday, Post on Friday, Post on Saturday, Post on Sunday
(d) Publications by time slot	8	Post 8:00 a.m. - 10:00 a.m., Post 11:00 a.m. - 13:00 p.m., Post 14:00 p.m. - 16:00 p.m., Post 17:00 p.m. - 19:00 p.m., Post 20:00 p.m. - 22:00 p.m., Post 23:00 p.m. - 1:00 a.m., Post 2:00 a.m. - 4:00 a.m., Post 5:00 a.m. - 7:00 a.m.
(e) Followership	8	Followers, Ratio followers / following, Tweets Retweeted, % of Tweets retweeted over total posts, Times each Tweet retweeted is retweeted, Tweets marked as favorite, % of Tweets marked as favorite over total posts, Times each Tweet marked as favorite is marked as favorite
Total	**32**	

Source: Self-elaboration

RESULTS

The results of the descriptive exploration of the 137,463 publications analyzed are presented following the categorization in Table 5: (a) Publication volumes, (b) Publication components, (c) Publications by day of the week, (d) Publications by time slot, and (e) Followership.

Within each category, findings are presented in a disaggregated manner for each of the four regions under observation: Africa and the Middle East, North America, Latin America, and Europe.

Publication Volumes

With regard to the publication volumes, results in Table 6 show that universities in North America and Latin America carry out more intense activity than institutions in Africa and the Middle East or Europe. Such a situation can be seen in the indicators of Tweets and Retweets.

Table 6. General publication volumes

Region	Tweets		Retweets		Replies	
	M	**SD**	**M**	**SD**	**M**	**SD**
Africa and Middle East	1655.50	1041.02	537.10	613.68	285.20	394.67
North America	2300.60	855.95	791.30	473.78	150.00	208.18
Latin America	2311.70	1119.97	381.80	458.06	222.20	330.36
Europe	1372.00	1070.01	323.70	207.72	333.30	513.42
Total sample	**1909.95**	**1069.65**	**508.45**	**480.28**	**247.67**	**369.88**

Source: Self-elaboration

Conversely, the response indicator presents values that invite reflection. The regions of North America and Latin America, the most active in terms of Tweets and Retweets, are the ones that show the lowest average of Replies. This fact points to the existence of one-way messages in these locations.

The exploration of this same information in daily terms corroborates what is shown in Table 6. The universities analyzed in North America and Latin America have the lowest daily response ratios, with averages of 0.41 and 0.60, respectively. By contrast, the institutions in Africa and the Middle East or Europe show average response rates of 0.78, in the first case, and 0.91, in the second.

Table 7. Daily publication volumes

Region	Daily tweets		Daily retweets		Daily replies	
	M	SD	M	SD	M	SD
Africa and Middle East	4.52	2.84	1.47	1.68	0.78	1.08
North America	6.28	2.33	2.16	1.29	0.41	0.57
Latin America	6.31	3.059	1.04	1.25	0.60	0.90
Europe	3.74	2.92	0.88	0.56	0.91	1.40
Total sample	**5.21**	**2.92**	**1.39**	**1.31**	**0.67**	**1.01**

Source: Self-elaboration

Publication Components

The information in Table 8 shows the degree to which the most characteristic components of Twitter publications are employed in each region.

As far as mentions are concerned, European universities make the most intensive use of this function with 0.86 mentions per publication. Additionally, links and hashtags reach their highest use levels in the case of Latin American universities, with averages of 0.73 and 0.71, respectively.

Table 8. Publication components

Region	Mentions by post		Links by post		Hashtags by post	
	M	SD	M	SD	M	SD
Africa and Middle East	0.33	0.26	0.39	0.20	0.65	0.81
North America	0.48	0.24	0.54	0.20	0.34	0.23
Latin America	0.45	0.37	0.73	0.19	0.71	0.92
Europe	0.86	0.46	0.46	0.16	0.64	0.38
Total sample	**0.53**	**0.39**	**0.53**	**0.22**	**0.58**	**0.64**

Source: Self-elaboration

These findings are in line with the results in Publication volumes' heading, at least as far as the European institutions are concerned. The organizations analyzed in Europe present the highest values in the response indicators, both in general terms and on a daily basis, a fact which indicates the existence of a dialogue between institution and target audience. In this regard, the mentions function, where European universities stand out, is also a mechanism of direct interaction between brand and audience.

Publications by Day of the Week

Table 9 shows, again, the intensity level in posting activity, in this case presenting the information by day of the week.

In the four regions, a clear cut between workdays and weekend days can be appreciated. This fact is reflected even in the institutions of Africa and the Middle East, areas where Muslim countries take, generally, their rest-day on Friday. Such would be the case in the organizations of Lebanon, Saudi Arabia and Nigeria listed in the sample. However, despite the above, there are no significant differences in this region, probably due to the international dimension of the institutions under observation.

Table 9. Average number of posts by day of the week

Region	Post on Monday	Post on Tuesday	Post on Wednesday	Post on Thursday	Post on Friday	Post on Saturday	Post on Sunday
Africa and Middle East	294.60	286.60	311.10	318.50	287.50	104.30	52.90
North America	341.00	385.60	393.90	404.50	388.7	221.90	165.00
Latin America	422.40	443.30	444.40	421.10	414.60	93.20	72.70
Europe	218.00	240.00	249.40	297.60	235.00	75.40	56.60
Total sample	**319.00**	**338.87**	**349.70**	**360.42**	**331.45**	**123.70**	**86.80**

Source: Self-elaboration

Regarding workdays, although it is true that no big variations between days were detected, there is a slight increase in the activity around the central part of the week (Wednesday and Thursday). This increase can be observed in all four regions under study.

Publications by Time Slot

Concerning the time of publication, Table 10 indicates similar patterns of action in all zones. In the four regions, the bulk of the activity is concentrated in the morning and afternoon slots, from 8 a.m. to 4 p.m.

On the opposite side, what we call peak-off hours, the activity drops substantially in the 8 p.m. to 10 p.m. time slot, and falls down drastically between 11 p.m. and 4 a.m. This situation is also homogeneous for all the locations examined.

The exception to the aforementioned homogeneity in peak hours and peak-off hours is detected in the time slot from 5 a.m. to 7 a.m. This period indicates that activity seems to start earlier in the regions of Africa and the Middle East and Latin America.

Table 10. Average posts by time slot

Region	Post 8:00 a.m. - 10:00 a.m.	Post 11:00 a.m. - 13:00 p.m.	Post 14:00 p.m. - 16:00 p.m.	Post 17:00 p.m. - 19:00 p.m.	Post 20:00 p.m. - 22:00 p.m.	Post 23:00 p.m. - 1:00 a.m.	Post 2:00 a.m. - 4:00 a.m.	Post 5:00 a.m. - 7:00 a.m.
Africa and Middle East	513.60	459.10	254.00	125.80	25.20	5.00	21.20	251.60
North America	506.40	610.40	533.70	365.10	169.80	24.20	1.60	89.40
Latin America	444.30	691.20	560.90	354.30	142.90	13.50	0.30	104.30
Europe	447.20	373.30	331.40	110.00	19.80	1.50	0.90	87.90
Total sample	**477.87**	**533.50**	**420.00**	**238.80**	**89.42**	**11.05**	**6.00**	**133.30**

Source: Self-elaboration

Followership

The fifth category of indicators includes those elements that can serve as a sign of the success obtained by the different social media marketing strategies in the regions analyzed. Table 11 provides an overview of the size of the organizations' target audiences in each zone. In this regard, universities in North America and Latin America seem to have significantly bigger target audiences than those observed for Africa and the Middle East or Europe. This fact can be seen not only in the average number of followers per account but also in the average ratio of followers / following per organization in each region.

Table 11. Followers per organization

Region	Average followers	Average ratio followers / following
Africa and the Middle East	120,198.40	358.14
North America	412,585.70	661.50
Latin America	393,387.50	989.06
Europe	151,049.80	187.50
Total sample	**269,305.35**	**549.05**

Source: Self-elaboration

Tables 12 and 13 present the recognition obtained by the publications of each institution in each region, on average. Table 12 displays acknowledgment obtained in terms of retweets, while Table 13 shows recognition achieved in terms of favorites.

The three retweet indicators are higher in North America and Latin America. In this point, perhaps the average percentage of Tweets that are retweeted over the total number of posts made by the university deserves special mention in Latin America. In this case, on average, 69.24% of posts are shared using the retweet function by members of the organization's audience.

Regarding the favorite indicators, once again, the recognition achieved by the universities analyzed in North America and Latin America stands out from the rest. Here, as it happens with the equivalent indicator in Table 12, it is worth mentioning the acknowledgment obtained by publications in Latin America. In this case, publications from the organizations examined in the region, on average, were marked as favorites in 82.61% of cases.

Table 12. Retweets obtained per organization

Region	Average Tweets retweeted	Average % of Tweets retweeted over total posts	Average n° of times each Tweet retweeted is retweeted
Africa and Middle East	776.80	55.05	97.64
North America	1313.80	57.29	158.90
Latin America	1535.20	69.24	158.20
Europe	765.00	51.57	112.10
Total sample	**1097.70**	**58.29**	**526.84**

Source: Self-elaboration

Table 13. Favorites obtained per organization

Region	Average Tweets marked as Favorite	Average % of Tweets marked as favorite over total posts	Average n° of times each Tweet marked as favorite is marked as favorite
Africa and Middle East	950.80	66.63	249.80
North America	1465.40	63.70	584.97
Latin America	1830.60	82.61	422.45
Europe	955.00	61.45	273.60
Total sample	**1300.45**	**68.60**	**1530.82**

Source: Self-elaboration

DISCUSSION

The importance of social network services in digital marketing strategies is undeniable. This fact is confirmed by the literature review on branding and marketing strategies in social media carried out by Cuevas-Molano et al. (2019). These authors examined articles indexed in the Web of Science (WOS) database over the previous fourteen years and underlined not only the existence of a mature and consolidated field of study, but also the relevance of a topic that concerns academics and professionals alike.

The dynamic and changing nature of these technologies forces brands and organizations to periodically analyze the data generated by these platforms, in order to extract the knowledge hidden therein. The millions of interactions that happen daily on social network services, between organizations and users, generate a huge volume of information that can be analyzed (Phillips et al., 2017).

In addition, social media marketing strategies are not homogeneous and universal, but depend on the market or sector, the target audience of the organization or the geographical area in which the actions are implemented (Matosas-Lopez, 2020). Thus, for example, a social media strategy can be efficient in one particular market and useless in a different sector. Similarly, a certain strategy can be appropriate in one geographical location and inadequate in another.

Different authors underline that social media marketing strategies, and media discourses, must be redefined and customized in accordance with the specific demands of markets or sectors, target audiences and geographical areas.

In this sense, Saura et al. (2021) emphasizes that organizations must personalize their publications based on the needs of their audiences. Scheffert (2011), for example, indicates that due to the digital revolution, marketing paradigms have drastically changed demanding higher leves sophistication and personalization in the relationship between audience and organization. Park et al. (2011) address that, in the management of social media strategies, factors such as the interaction or the customization have a direct influence on brand loyalty indicators. Likewise, Tong and Chan (2020) underline that, in the digital era, market-oriented approches are essential in the relationship with our target audience in social network services.

In addition, some studies suggest that these platforms require professionalized management systems and that their management cannot be left to non-specialized professionals (Casanoves Boix et al., 2018; Laaser et al., 2012). Other authors claim that organizations manage these technologies without a defined strategic vision (Laudano et al., 2016). In the same line, there are also studies which indicate that organizations should not settle for using their accounts to build their institutional image, but must also protect their reputation (Gureeva, 2018). Certain authors even assert that properly managed social media can become a powerful recruitment tool (Guzmán Duque et al., 2013).

The findings in this study provide academics and professionals with a good overview of social media marketing strategies that can be effective in different geographical locations around the world.

Publication Volumes

In terms of publication volumes, while strategies in North America and Latin America display the highest volume of Tweets and Retweets, the regions of Africa and the Middle East and Europe stand out for their response ratios.

These findings corroborate the results of Chen (2011) in his research on uses and perks on Twitter. Study in which the author points out that a high volume of posts acts as a motivating element that encourages the subject to interact with other users. Nevertheless, the low response rate in the American regions indicates more unidirectionality in the social media marketing strategies employed in these areas.

Publication Components

As far as publication components are concerned, European strategies emphasize the use of mentions, while Latin American universities accentuate the use of links and hashtags.

Authors such as Túñez López et al. (2015) and Guzmán Duque et al. (2013) have stressed the importance of links and hashtags in social media strategies. Examining the role of social networks as communication channels, they highlight the potential of these elements in facilitating promotion and projection of the organization in front of its target audiences.

However, Latin America's prioritization of link and hashtag use in preference to mentions' (traditional indicator of dialogue), seems to corroborate the previously mentioned unidirectionality of their social media marketing strategies.

Publications by Day of the Week

Day of publication, unlike the previous aspects of publication volume and publication components, does not show variations between regions. In all cases, the strategies applied concentrate the activity on workdays, in general, and on Wednesdays and Thursdays, in particular.

These results are in line with studies by Túñez López et al. (2015) and Valerio Ureña et al. (2014), where the authors emphasized the importance of publication frequency in the central part of the week. Nonetheless, these findings contradict the research of Hanifawati et al. (2019) on brand management in Facebook, where no significant differences were observed regarding day of publication, within workdays.

Publications by Time Slot

Concerning time of publication, just as with day of publication, there is also homogeneity between areas. In the four regions under study, most of the activity is concentrated in the morning and afternoon time slots, more specifically between 8 a.m. and 4 p.m.

These results are aligned with the findings of Hanifawati et al. (2019) and Valerio Ureña et al. (2014) mentioned above. These studies underline that strategies with high publication frequencies in the first part of the day tend to be positively perceived by the organization's target audience.

Followership

Finally, regarding audience response, the results show that in North America and Latin America not only did brands achieve greater followership on the platform, but also more user proactivity than in Africa and the Middle East or in Europe.

This fact confirms what has been stated by previous studies on marketing and communication-related strategies in Latin American university institutions (Cabrera and Camarero, 2016; Guzmán Duque et al., 2012; Laudano et al., 2016; Puertas Hidalgo and Carpio Jiménez, 2016). These studies always stress the importance and weight of social network services in institutional strategies.

CONCLUSION

Certain aspects of social media marketing strategies are universal and are managed similarly in different regions worldwide. Examples from our study were days of the week and times of publications. However, we can also identify aspects where important differences were detected, depending on the geographical area analyzed.

In this regard, it is worth mentioning that publication volumes were notably higher in North America and Latin America than in the locations of Africa and the Middle East, and Europe. Such a situation of heterogeneity in social media marketing strategies can also be seen in the publication components. While in Latin America the use of links and hashtags was prevalent, organizations in Europe put emphasis on the use of mentions. These nuances were also detected in the followership achieved by organizations, more intensive in North America and Latin America than in Africa and the Middle East, or in Europe.

The originality and main value of the present research lies in the international approach and perspective applied by the authors. The findings obtained in the present study lead us to reflect on differences in social media marketing strategies in different regions worldwide.

While strategies in social network services should be based generally on dialogue and interaction with the organization's target audience, this point can be more or less critical depending on the geographical region in which the brand operates. While Europe confers great importance on the organization's interaction with its audience (proof of this is the intensive use of replies and mentions), both North America and Latin America tolerate a greater degree of one-way communication. This is illustrated in that followership does not appear to be affected despite the lower degree of dialogue observed, according to the indicators analyzed during the study.

All the foregoing, then, leads to the conclusion that the paradigms governing the definition of social media marketing strategies at the global level, a priori universal, probably must be reformulated to fit on the particular realities of the regions where these strategies are applied.

Professional and Managerial Implications

In light of the findings obtained, the next professional-managerial implications can be pointed out for the design and implementation of social media marketing strategies.

In first place, the acceptance of our audience to a certain bulk of daily publications may differ considerably depending on the geographical location. Secondly, the volume of mentions, links, and hashtags per publication may have better or worse acceptance, depending on the region in which our organization operates. Consequently, each organization must identify the adequate management patterns in accordance whit its geographical location and its audience.

In conclusion, it can be said that management approaches in social media marketing strategies are influenced, among other variables, by the geographical area of the organization and its target audience. This situation forces marketing managers, in general, and social media managers and community managers, in particular, to develop a significant effort to adapt and customize their actions.

Limitations and Future Research

Finally, several limitations and prospects for future research can be addressed. Firstly, the investigation covers Africa and Middle East, North America, Latin America, and Europe; however, no geographical location is considered in Asia. Unfortunately, the platform monitored (has it happens whit other social network services) has a scarce presence in many of the territories of the Asian continent, which makes it impossible to carry out a comparative analysis under identical conditions. Future research should look for social media platforms with a minimal coverage in the Asia region, in order to expand this comparative analysis from an, even more, international perspective, if possible.

In second place, this research examines exclusively university organizations, ignoring other sorts of organizations. Therefore, future research should take into consideration, for instance, the analysis of social media marketing strategies in business organizations. This type of study would allow to expand the knowledge generated in the present study, revealing to what extent the findings obtained here can be extrapolated to other forms of organizations and target audiences.

Despite these limitations, the present study, in the authors' opinion, offers, academics and professionals, knowledge of relevance, addressing in addition new opportunities for future research.

ACKNOWLEDGMENT

This research received no specific grant from any funding agency in the public, commercial, or not-for-profit sectors.

REFERENCES

Alkadri, M.F., Istiani, N.F.F., & Yatmo, Y.A. (2015). Mapping Social Media Texts as the Basis of Place-Making Process. *Procedia - Social and Behavioral Sciences, 184*, 46–55. . doi:10.1016/j.sbspro.2015.05.052

Almansa, A., Fonseca, O., & Castillo, A. (2013). Redes sociales y jóvenes. Uso de Facebook en la juventud colombiana y española. *Comunicar, 20*(40), 127–135. doi:10.3916/C40-2013-03-03

Backstrom, L., Huttenlocher, D., & Kleinberg, J. (2006) Group formation in large social networks: Membership, growth, and evolution. In *Proceedings of 12th International Conference on Knowledge Discovery in Data Mining* (pp. 44–54). ACM Press. Available at: http://www.cs.cornell.edu/~lars/kdd06-comm.pdf

Balan, C. (2017) Nike on Instagram: themes of branded content and their engagement power. In *CBU International Conference* (pp. 13–18). Central Bohemia University. 10.12955/cbup.v5.894

Bodunde, H., Sotiloye, B., & Akeredolu-Ale, B. (2017) Comparative Analysis of Communication Strategies of two Selected Organizations in Nigeria. 5th international conference on management, leadership and governance (ICMLG 2017), 61–68.

Boyd, D., & Ellison, N. (2007). Social Network Sites: Definition, History, and Scholarship. Journal of Computer-Mediated Communication, 13(1). doi:10.1111/j.1083-6101.2007.00393.x

Bruns, A., & Hanusch, F. (2017). Conflict imagery in a connective environment: audiovisual content on Twitter following the 2015/2016 terror attacks in Paris and Brussels. *Media, Culture & Society, 39*(8), 1122–1141. . doi:10.1177/0163443717725574

Bulbulia, Z., & Wassermann, J. (2015). Rethinking the Usefulness of Twitter in Higher Education. *International Journal of Educational Sciences, 11*(1), 31–40. . doi:10.1080/09751122.2015.11890372

Cabero, J., & Marín, V. (2014). Posibilidades educativas de las redes sociales y el trabajo en grupo. Percepciones de los alumnos universitarios. *Comunicar, 21*(42), 165–172. doi:10.3916/C42-2014-16

Cabero Almenara,, J., Llorente Cejudo, M. del C., & Román Graván, P. (2007). La tecnología cambió los escenarios: El efecto Pigmalión se hizo realidad. *Comunicar, 15*(28), 167–175. doi:10.3916/C28-2007-16

Cabero-Almenara, J., & Marín-Díaz, V. (2014). Posibilidades educativas de las redes sociales y el trabajo en grupo. Percepciones de los alumnos universitarios. *Comunicar, 21*(42), 165–172. doi:10.3916/C42-2014-16

Cabrera, S. I., & Camarero, E. (2016). Comunicación de la ciencia y la tecnología en las universidades ecuatorianas: Estudio preliminar del impacto y percepción entre la población universitaria. *Revista de Comunicación de la SEECI, 40*(40), 27. doi:10.15198eeci.2016.40.27-47

Calvete, E., Orue, I., & Estévez, A. (2010). Cyberbullying in adolescents: Modalities and aggressors' profile. *Computers in Human Behavior, 26*(5), 1128–1135. . doi:10.1016/j.chb.2010.03.017

Casanoves Boix, J., Küster Boluda, I., & Vila López, N. (2018). ¿Por qué las instituciones de educación superior deben apostar por la marca? *Revista de Investigación Educacional, 37*(1), 111–127. doi:10.6018/rie.37.1.291191

Castaño, C., Maiz, I., & Garay, U. (2015). Redes sociales y aprendizaje cooperativo en un MOOC. *Revista Complutense de Educación, 26*(Especial), 119–139. . doi:10.5209/rev_RCED.2015.v26.46328

Chen, G.M. (2011). Tweet this: A uses and gratifications perspective on how active Twitter use gratifies a need to connect with others. *Computers in Human Behavior, 27*(2), 755–762. . doi:10.1016/j.chb.2010.10.023

Chen, J., Chen, H., & Hu, D. (2015). Smog disaster forecasting using social web data and physical sensor data. In *IEEE International Conference on Big Data, IEEE Big Data 2015* (pp. 991–998). Institute of Electrical and Electronics Engineers Inc. 10.1109/BigData.2015.7363850

Cuevas-Molano, E., Sánchez Cid, M., & Matosas-López, L. (2019). Bibliometric analysis of studies of brand content strategy within social media. *Comunicacion y Sociedad (Mexico), 2019*(0), 1–23. doi:10.32870/cys.v2019i0.7441

Doval-Avendaño, M., Domínguez Quintas, S., & Dans Álvarez, I. (2018). El uso ritual de las pantallas entre jóvenes universitarios/as. *Prisma Social, 21*(2), 480–499. https://revistaprismasocial.es/article/view/2323

Durán, M., & Guerra, J. M. (2015). Usos y tendencias adictivas de una muestra de estudiantes universitarios españoles a la red social Tuenti. *Anales de Psicología, 31*(1), 260–267. doi:10.6018/analesps.31.1.158301

Espuny Vidal, C., González Martínez, J., & Lleixà Fortuño, M. (2011). Actitudes y expectativas del uso educativo de las redes sociales en los alumnos universitarios. *RUSC. Universities and Knowledge Society Journal, 8*(1). Advance online publication. doi:10.7238/rusc.v8i1.839

Feng, S., Wong, Y.K., & Wong, L.Y. (2019). The Internet and Facebook Usage on Academic Distraction of College Students. *Computers & Education, 134*, 41–49. . doi:10.1016/j.compedu.2019.02.005

Florenthal, B. (2015). Applying uses and gratifications theory to students' LinkedIn usage. *Young Consumers, 16*(1), 17–35. . doi:10.1108/YC-12-2013-00416

García Galera, M. D. C., Fernández Muñoz, C., & Del Hoyo Hurtado, M. (2017). Ciudadanía informada, ciudadanía participativa. la movilización de los jóvenes en el entorno digital. *Prisma Social, 18*(1), 124–143. https://revistaprismasocial.es/article/view/1441/1659

García-Jiménez, A., López-de-Ayala, M. C., & Catalina-García, B. (2013). Hábitos de uso en Internet y en las redes sociales de los adolescentes españoles. *Comunicar, 21*(41), 1–9. doi:10.3916/C41-2013-19

García-Ruiz, R., Aguaded Gómez, J.I., & Caldeiro Pedreira, M.C. (2015). Alfabetización y responsabilidad social como base para el empoderamiento de los prosumidores en el entorno digital. *Media & Jornalismo*, 43–62.

García-Ruiz, R., Tirado, R., & Hernando, Á. (2018). Redes sociales y estudiantes : motivos de uso y gratificaciones . Evidencias para el aprendizaje. *Aula abierta, 47*(3), 291–298. DOI: . doi:10.17811/rifie.47.3.2018.291-298

Gómez-Aguilar, M., Roses-Campos, S., & Farias-Batlle, P. (2012). El uso académico de las redes sociales en universitarios. *Comunicar, 19*(38), 131–138. doi:10.3916/C38-2011-03-04

Gómez-García, M., Matosas-López, L., & Palmero-Ruiz, J. (2020). Social Networks Use Patterns among University Youth: The Validity and Reliability of an Updated Measurement Instrument. *Sustainability*, *12*(9), 3503. doi:10.3390u12093503

Gureeva, A. N. (2018). *Social Networks as a Media Communication Resource for Managing the Image of a Russian Higher Education Institution. Mediascope, 2(1)*. doi:10.30547/mediascope.2.2018.9

Guzmán Duque, A. P., Del Moral Pérez, M. E., & González Ladron de Guevara, F. (2012). Usos de Twitter en las universidades iberoamericanas. *Revista Latinoamericana de Tecnología Educativa – RELATEC, 11*(1), 27–39. Available at: https://mascvuex.unex.es/revistas/index.php/relatec/article/view/845

Guzmán Duque, A. P., del Moral Pérez, M. E., & González Ladrón de Guevara, F. (2013). Impacto de twitter en la comunicación y promoción institucional de las universidades. *Pixel-Bit. Revista de Medios y Educación*, *43*(Julio), 139–153. doi:10.12795/pixelbit.2013.i43.10

Hanifawati, T., Ritonga, U.S., & Puspitasari, E.E. (2019). Managing brands' popularity on Facebook: post time, content, and brand communication strategies. *Journal of Indonesian Economy and Business, 34*(2), 187–207. . doi:10.22146/jieb.45755

Junco, R. (2012). The relationship between frequency of Facebook use, participation in Facebook activities, and student engagement. *Computers & Education*, *58*(1), 162–171. doi:10.1016/j.compedu.2011.08.004

Kabilan, M.K., Ahmad, N., & Abidin, M.J.Z. (2010). Facebook: An online environment for learning of English in institutions of higher education? *The Internet and Higher Education, 13*(4), 179–187. . doi:10.1016/j.iheduc.2010.07.003

Katz, E., Blumler, J.G., & Gurevitch, M. (1974). Uses and Gratifications Research. *The Public Opinion Quarterly, 37*(4), 509–523. DOI: doi:10.2307/2747854

Katz, E., Haas, H., & Gurevitch, M. (1973). On the Use of the Mass Media for Important Things. *American Sociological Association, 164*(2), 164. Advance online publication. doi:10.2307/2094393

Kemp, S. (2020). *Digital 2020: Global Digital Overview. DIGITAL 2020. Global Digital Overview.* Available at: https://datareportal.com/reports/digital-2020-global-digital-overview

Kimmons, R., Veletsianos, G., & Woodward, S. (2017). Institutional Uses of Twitter in U.S. Higher Education. *Innovative Higher Education, 42*(2), 97–111. . doi:10.1007/s10755-016-9375-6

Kuzma, J.M., & Wright, W. (2013) Using social networks as a catalyst for change in global higher education marketing and recruiting. *International Journal of Continuing Engineering Education and Life-Long Learning, 23*(1), 53–66. . doi:10.1504/IJCEELL.2013.051766

Laaser, W., Brito, J. G., & Toloza, E. A. (2012). El uso de redes sociales por parte de las universidades a nivel institucional. Un estudio comparativo. *RED Revista de Educación a Distancia, 32*(3), 231–239. Available at: https://www.um.es/ead/red/32/

Laudano, C. N., Planas, J., & Kessler, M. I. (2016). Aproximaciones a los usos de twitter en bibliotecas universitarias de Argentina. *Anales de Documentacion*, *19*(2), 1–11. doi:10.6018/analesdoc.19.2.246291

Li, Q., Zhou, B., & Liu, Q. (2016). Can twitter posts predict stock behavior?: A study of stock market with twitter social emotion. In *IEEE International Conference on Cloud Computing and Big Data Analysis (ICCCBDA 2016)* (pp. 359–364). Institute of Electrical and Electronics Engineers Inc. 10.1109/ICCCBDA.2016.7529584

Liu, H., Maes, P., & Davenport, G. (2006). Unraveling the Taste Fabric of Social Networks. *International Journal on Semantic Web and Information Systems, 2*(1), 42–71. doi:10.4018/jswis.2006010102

López-Pérez, L., & Olvera-Lobo, M.-D. (2016). Comunicación pública de la ciencia a través de la web 2.0. El caso de los centros de investigación y universidades públicas de España. *El Profesional de la Información, 25*(3), 441. doi:10.3145/epi.2016.may.14

Marciniak, R. (2013). Propuesta metodológica para la aplicación del benchmarking internacional en la evaluación de la calidad de la educación superior virtual. *Revista de Universidad y Sociedad del Conocimiento, 12*(3), 46–61. doi:10.7238/rusc.v12i3.2163

Matosas López, L. (2018). Variables of twitter's brand activity that influence audience spreading behavior of branded content. *Esic Market Economics and Business Journal, 44*(3), 525–546. doi:10.7200/esicm.161.0491

Matosas-López, L. (2020) Cómo distintos tipos de organización gestionan su presencia en plataformas sociales. In *XX International Conference on Knowledge, Culture, and Change in Organizations.* University of Illinois.

Matosas-López, L., & Romero-Ania, A. (2020). The Efficiency of Social Network Services Management in Organizations. An In-Depth Analysis Applying Machine Learning Algorithms and Multiple Linear Regressions. *Applied Sciences (Basel, Switzerland), 10*(15), 5167. doi:10.3390/app10155167

Matosas-López, L., & Romero-Luis, J. (2019). Correlaciones entre redes sociales y recursos educativos digitales en estudiantes universitarios de Marketing en el EEES. In J. Sierra Sánchez (Ed.), *Contenidos Audiovisuales, Narrativas y Alfabetización Mediática* (pp. 393–402). McGraw Hill.

Matsilele, T., & Ruhanya, P. (2020). Social media dissidence and activist resistance in Zimbabwe. *Media, Culture & Society. SAGE Publications Ltd.* Advance online publication. doi:10.1177/0163443720957886

McAndrew, F.T., & Jeong, H.S. (2012). Who does what on Facebook? Age, sex, and relationship status as predictors of Facebook use. *Computers in Human Behavior, 28*(6). . doi:10.1016/j.chb.2012.07.007

McBride, D.L. (2011). Risks and benefits of social media for children and adolescents. *Journal of Pediatric Nursing: Nursing Care of Children and Families, 26*(5), 498–499. . doi:10.1016/j.pedn.2011.05.001

McLuhan, M., & Nevitt, B. (1972). *Take Today; the Executive as Dropout.* Harcourt Brace Jovanovich.

Park, J., Song, H., & Ko, E. (2011). The Effect of the Lifestyles of Social Networking Service Users on Luxury Brand Loyalty. *Journal of Global Scholars of Marketing Science, 21*(4), 182–192. doi:10.1080/21639159.2011.9726521

Peruta, A., & Shields, A.B. (2017). Social media in higher education: understanding how colleges and universities use Facebook. *Journal of Marketing for Higher Education, 27*(1), 131–143. . doi:10.1080/08841241.2016.1212451

Phillips, L., Dowling, C., & Shaffer, K. (2017) Using Social Media to Predict the Future: A Systematic Literature Review. *Computing Research Repository (CoRR)*. Available at: https://arxiv.org/abs/1706.06134

Piscitelli, A. (2010). El Proyecto Facebook y La Posuniversidad : Sistemas Operativos Sociales y Entornos Abiertos de Aprendizaje. Barcelona: Ariel.

Puertas Hidalgo, R., & Carpio Jiménez, L. (2016) Gestión de redes sociales por parte de las universidades categoría a en Ecuador. *Iberian Conference on Information Systems and Technologies, CISTI*. 10.1109/CISTI.2016.7521587

Quintana Pujalte, L., Sosa Valcarcel, A., & Castillo Esparcia, A. (2018). Acciones y estrategias de comunicación en plataformas digitales. El caso Cifuentes. *Prisma Social, 22*(3), 247–270. https://revistaprismasocial.es/article/view/2585

Raacke, J., & Bonds-Raacke, J. (2008). MySpace and Facebook: Applying the Uses and Gratifications Theory to Exploring Friend-Networking Sites. *CyberPsychology & Behavior, 11*(2), 169–174. . doi:10.1089/cpb.2007.0056

Richter, D., Riemer, K., & vom Brocke, J. (2011). Internet Social Networking. *Business & Information Systems Engineering, 3*(2), 89–101. . doi:10.1007/s12599-011-0151-y

Rubin, A. M. (1994). Media uses and effects: A uses-and-gratifications perspective. In Media Effects: Advances in Theory and Research. London: Lawrence Erlbaum Associates Inc.

Ruggiero, T.E. (2000). Uses and Gratifications Theory in the 21st Century. *Mass Communication and Society, 3*(1), 3–37. . doi:10.1207/S15327825MCS0301_02

Sánchez Carrero, J., & Contreras Pulido, P. (2012). De cara al prosumidor: producción y consumo empoderando a la ciudadanía 3.0. *ICONO14, 10*(3), 62–84. doi:10.7195/ri14.v10i3.210

Sandoval Romero, Y., & Aguaded Gómez, J.I. (2012). Nuevas audiencias, nuevas responsabilidades. La competencia mediática en la era de la convergencia digital. *ICONO14, 10*(3), 8–22. . doi:10.7195/ri14.v10i3.197

Santoveña-Casal, S., & Bernal-Bravo, C. (2019). Explorando la influencia del docente: Participación social en Twitter y percepción académica. *Comunicar, 27*(58), 75–84. https://orcid.org/0000-0002-2802-1618

Saura, J. R. (2021). Using Data Sciences in Digital Marketing: Framework, methods, and performance metrics. *Journal of Innovation and Knowledge, 6*(2), 92–102. doi:10.1016/j.jik.2020.08.001

Saura, J. R., Ribeiro-Soriano, D., & Palacios-Marqués, D. (2021). From user-generated data to data-driven innovation: A research agenda to understand user privacy in digital markets. *International Journal of Information Management, 102331*. Advance online publication. doi:10.1016/j.ijinfomgt.2021.102331

Scheffert, O. (2011). A Changing Paradigm in Marketing. Current Issues in Management of Business and Society Development, 643–649.

Smock, A.D., Ellison, N.B., & Lampe, C. (2011). Facebook as a toolkit: A uses and gratification approach to unbundling feature use. *Computers in Human Behavior, 27*(6), 2322–2329. . doi:10.1016/j.chb.2011.07.011

Toffler, A. (1980). *La Tercera Ola*. Plaza & Janés.

Tong, S. C., & Chan, F. F. Y. (2020). Exploring market-oriented relations in the digital era A study of public relations and marketing practitioners in Hong Kong. *Journal of Communication Management (London), 24*(1), 65–82. doi:10.1108/JCOM-10-2019-0133

Túñez López, M., Valdiviezo Abad, C., & Martínez Solana, Y. (2015). Las redes sociales en la gestión de la comunicación universitaria. *Opción, 6*, 852–874. https://dialnet.unirioja.es/servlet/articulo?codigo=5758749

Urman, A. (2020). Context matters: political polarization on Twitter from a comparative perspective. *Media, Culture & Society, 42*(6), 857–879. doi:10.1177/0163443719876541

Valerio Ureña, G., Herrera-Murillo, D. J., & Rodríguez-Martínez, M. D. C. (2014). Asociación entre el momento de publicación en las redes sociales y el engagement: Estudio de las universidades Mexicanas. *Palabra Clave (La Plata), 17*(3), 749–772. doi:10.5294/pacla.2014.17.3.8

Wu, J., Chen, J., Chen, H., Dou, W., & Shao, D. (2019). What to say on social media and how: Effects of communication style and function on online customer engagement in China. *Journal of Service Theory and Practice, 29*(5–6), 691–707. doi:10.1108/JSTP-11-2018-0243

ADDITIONAL READING

Carlson, J., Rahman, M., Voola, R., & De Vries, N. (2018). Customer engagement behaviours in social media: Capturing innovation opportunities. *Journal of Services Marketing, 32*(1), 83–94. doi:10.1108/JSM-02-2017-0059

Giakoumaki, C., & Krepapa, A. (2019). Brand engagement in self-concept and consumer engagement in social media: The role of the source. *Psychology and Marketing, 37*(3), 457–465. doi:10.1002/mar.21312

Majumdar, A., & Bose, I. (2019). Do tweets create value? A multi-period analysis of Twitter use and content of tweets for manufacturing firms. *International Journal of Production Economics, 216*, 1–11. doi:10.1016/j.ijpe.2019.04.008

Mariani, M. M., Mura, M., & Di Felice, M. (2018). The determinants of Facebook social engagement for National Tourism Organisations' Facebook pages: A quantitative approach. *Journal of Destination Marketing & Management, 8*, 312–325. doi:10.1016/j.jdmm.2017.06.003

Mukherjee, K., & Banerjee, N. (2019). Social networking sites and customers' attitude towards advertisements. *Journal of Research in Interactive Marketing, 13*(4), 477–491. doi:10.1108/JRIM-06-2018-0081

Oliva Marañón, C. (2012). Communication 2.0, visibility and interactivity: Fundaments of corporate image of Public Universities in Madrid on YouTube. *Fonseca. Journal of Communication, 5*, 117–139. https://dialnet.unirioja.es/servlet/articulo?codigo=4184587&info=resumen&idioma=ENG

Pansari, A., & Kumar, V. (2017). Customer engagement: The construct, antecedents, and consequences. *Journal of the Academy of Marketing Science, 45*(3), 294–311. doi:10.100711747-016-0485-6

Sabate, F., Berbegal-Mirabent, J., Cañabate, A., & Lebherz, P. R. (2014). Factors influencing popularity of branded content in Facebook fan pages. *European Management Journal*, *32*(6), 1001–1011. doi:10.1016/j.emj.2014.05.001

Saura, J. R., Herraez, B. R., & Reyes-Menendez, A. (2019). Comparing a traditional approach for financial brand communication analysis with a big data analytics technique. *IEEE Access: Practical Innovations, Open Solutions*, *7*, 37100–37108. doi:10.1109/ACCESS.2019.2905301

Tafesse, W. (2015). Content strategies and audience response on Facebook brand pages. *Marketing Intelligence & Planning*, *33*(6), 927–943. doi:10.1108/MIP-07-2014-0135

KEY TERMS AND DEFINITIONS

Engagement: Degree of emotional involvement that organization's followers have with the organization.

Followership: Intentional practice of someone in a subordinate role to enhance the synergetic interchange between the follower and the organization.

Hashtag: Word or phrase, preceded by a sign (#), used on social network services to identify digital content on a specific topic.

Media Prosumer: Term created to define the typical user of social network services.

Prosumer: Term created to define the typical user of mass media.

Target Audience: Group of subjects most likely to want a product or service, and therefore, the group of people who follow the organization.

Uses and Gratifications Theory (U&G): Conceptual framework used to describe how audiences interact with mass media.

Chapter 52
Playfulness in Online Marketing:
Challenges and Opportunities

Taina Vuorela
Oulu University of Applied Sciences, Oulu, Finland

Sari Alatalo
Oulu University of Applied Sciences, Oulu, Finland

Eeva-Liisa Oikarinen
University of Oulu, Oulu, Finland

ABSTRACT

This article explores different challenges and opportunities of using humour and playfulness in online marketing. Humour has been investigated intensively in marketing, especially in advertising, yet there is little knowledge of the challenges and opportunities in online marketing faced by practitioners. This study analyses key studies conducted in the context of a unique case: a Finnish research project exploring humour as a strategic tool for companies. These studies can provide emerging insights of humour in online marketing which are relevant for practitioners: humour as a transformational appeal, individual differences related to humour appreciation, role of storytelling and playfulness in blogging and challenges related to use of humour such as credibility.

INTRODUCTION

Advertising cannot be easily overlooked as it surrounds us. Humour and laughter are intimately connected with what it means to be a human being (Hietalahti, 2016) and thus, they are also important for marketing, the objective of which is to create relevant products and services and communicate of them in a relevant fashion. Not only does marketing shape what people want and thus how they spend their money, because of the trends and fashions it creates, but it also influences which businesses fail and which succeed (Cluley, 2017). The practices of marketing in general and those of advertising in particular should abide by common principles of appropriateness and good conduct. Ethical aspects of advertis-

DOI: 10.4018/978-1-6684-6287-4.ch052

ing and challenges related to legal regulations have attracted interest among researchers (Bjelica et al., 2016) and more recently also specific advertising issues in online environment, such as controversial advertising (Moraes & Michaelidou, 2017). Although the legislation seems clear, practices are at times unclear, as the line between proper and improper marketing and marketing communication is, at times, fine, and becomes even finer when customers travel to other countries, either as real or virtual shoppers. E.g. a tourist cannot help but wonder how some stores in the Canary Island of Fuerteventura are permanently going out of business and consequently advertise that they are selling all their goods at a discounted price. Clearly, when it comes to humour and play, what some people perceive appropriate in advertising, others find inappropriate. Thus, there are opportunities as well as challenges in the use of humour in marketing.

On the one hand, digital commerce is potentially immediately international – as soon as the e-retailer has set up a functional web shop in an international language. Language and related symbolic cues have been acknowledged as relevant issues in current international marketing, especially in online servicescape. In such a physical environment where services are provided, strategic choices of language are important so as to produce such messages for consumers from different cultural backgrounds that are consistent with brands and corporate values (Alcantara-Pilar et al., 2017). In addition, it can be assumed that consumers prefer to use their own language when operating in the global digital markets, and maybe they also look for online advertising to be easily understandable regardless of cultural backgrounds.

This is an interesting starting point for exploring the use of humour and playfulness in marketing and advertising. As Vuorela (2005) studied negotiation behaviour in international sales teams, a type of marketing communication as a genre as well, the following kinds of comments arose from the participants: "…there are no cultural differences here [in the negotiation process], as we are all engineers." But does culture then not play a role in the types of advertising styles that companies choose? Many companies opt for only 'serious' business-like communication as a safe solution, but are they losing or gaining business opportunities in doing so? Lidl is an interesting case in point: in Finland, the German grocery store is known for humorous, even daring advertising. To give an example, they sold lip gloss as a side product to customers during the doping scandal of a Norwegian skier who claimed that the anabolic steroids in her blood originated in lip gloss. Yet, the company is known for non-humorous advertising in Germany.

The aim of this paper is to gain more understanding on the challenges and opportunities of using humour and playfulness in online marketing. Many of the studies that were conducted within the context of a humour-related research project involved company interviews and gaining information of the insight that businesses have of using humour in their marketing practices. The objective of the present paper is to summarise such practitioner viewpoints of the functions of humour and playfulness in order to find new and relevant foci for a further scientific research agenda in the field of humour-based marketing.

BACKGROUND

Playfulness, and humour as a related sub-concept (Guitard et al., 2005), has been recognized by researchers to be a common practice in marketing; it has been studied especially in advertising (Eisend, 2009; Weinberger & Gulas, 1992) and service encounters (e.g., Bergeron & Vachon, 2008; Mathies et al., 2016; Söderlund & Oikarinen, 2018). Humour has also been discussed as a relevant advertising appeal particularly in online advertising, where it contributes to an ad becoming viral, that is spreading efficiently a company's message in social media (Oikarinen & Sinisalo, 2017; Porter & Golan, 2006).

However, it seems that humour has been less investigated in the online environment than other more traditional media.

Humour Definitions and Typologies

Humour is ubiquitous: it exists everywhere. It is possible to find humour in every country (Gulas & Weinberger, 2006, p. 54). However, humour is dependent on the context, time and place, and individuals have a bearing on what is considered humorous (Gulas & Weinberger, 2006; Hasset & Houlihan, 1979; Ruch et al., 1990). Playfulness can be described as a person's disposition, which is composed of sense of humour, spontaneity, curiosity and creativity (Guitard et al., 2005). According to scholars, humour should also be analysed as a cultural phenomenon (e.g., Biswas et al., 1992; Laroche et al., 2014). Besides, through humour, inhumane practices and tendencies can be criticised (cf. Hietalahti, 2016), and this can be relevant to marketing communication. Humour theories can be classified into congruence, relief and superiority theories; Beard (2005), in particular, has studied humour in advertising and the scholar has created a typology of humour used in advertising according to the theories under which they fall.

Besides Beard (2005), several scholars of advertising have made an effort to create humour typologies. Yet, there is a lack of agreement on typologies (see e.g., Catanescu & Tom, 2001; Spotts et al., 1997; Weinberger & Spotts, 1989). However, there is an agreement about three main humour theories; affective, cognitive and interpersonal humour (Meyer, 2000; Romero & Pescodolido, 2008; Morreall, 2014). Beyond this, a sense of humour can be defined (Ruch, 1996) and it has been shown to play an important role in buffering stress (Martin & Lefcourt, 1983). It may also help seeing issues from different angles, a feature which is successfully exploited e.g. by stand-up comedians. A further well-known typology of different humour types classifies them into self-enhancing/coping and affiliative humour as positive types, and self-defeating and aggressive humour types as negative ones (Martin et al., 2003; Mesmer-Magnus et al., 2012).

However, as humour in advertising is still most often approached as a stimulus in the ad (Warren & McGraw, 2016), and the humour typologies which emphasize the social aspect of interaction in humour seem to be less utilized. This is surprising, as the interaction between consumer and advertiser has become more interactive in nature, with consumers not only being passive receivers of ads (see Dahlén & Rosengren, 2016).

Challenges Related to Humour in Marketing

Based on the most recent definition of marketing by the American Marketing Association (2013), marketing comprises activities, institutions and processes that create, communicate, deliver and exchange offerings with value for various stakeholders, such as customers and society. This appears to be quite a wide view on marketing encompassing different aspects. Advertising, in turn, is seen as brand-initiated communication with an intent to influence people (Dahlén & Rosengren, 2016). Both of these definitions entail communication which is in some way relevant to the recipient of the communication. However, the latter one, advertising, seems to be a narrower concept, as it includes the idea of a brand being in the background of such communication.

What is then the difference between an advertisement and a news item or a piece of art work? They look similar – sometimes – and can be found in similar places (Cluley, 2017). Ads can be serious or funny, glamorous or mundane, memorable or annoying (ibid). Some are informative and explain about a product and how it functions, how much it costs, while others say nothing about a product (ibid). What unites different types of ads is not what they look like, but rather what they attempt to do: 'change demand through communication' (Cluley, 2017, p. 3). Advertising is not static but is constantly changing, because markets, cultures, media technologies and consumer behaviour, and hence also the theories through which they are discussed and analysed, change continuously (ibid). The above can be relevant to both online and offline advertising.

Generally, online marketing comprises three operational processes: customer acquisition, customer conversion as well as customer retention and growth (Chaffey, 2011). The aim of customer acquisition is to attract visitors to a website while the goal of customer conversion is to make these visitors behave the way the site owner wishes, e.g. to browse other content or to make a purchase. Furthermore, the idea of customer retention and growth is to encourage visitors to repeatedly use the digital channel and make more purchases. (ibid.) Playful marketing communication and advertising may be relevant to all of the above processes.

Earlier research suggests that humour has many benefits in advertising; it helps gain attention and create positive attitudes to the ad or advertiser (Weinberger & Gulas, 1992; Eisend, 2009), and it also helps create more positive brand attitudes and purchase intentions (Eisend, 2009). These are the kinds of reasons that may encourage companies to utilize humour in their communication. However, the pertinent question is how to make a decision on the type of humour to be used in order to gain such benefits.

In practice, humour types involving incongruity resolution are commonly used in advertising (Alden et al., 1993); e.g. word plays which may contain a surprise and require cognitive processing. Advertisers believe that humorous advertising is more suitable for consumer nondurables compared to company advertising (Madden & Weinberger, 1984). Humour also seem to be suitable in connection with low-involvement products (Chung & Zhao, 2003). Humour-based marketing does not seems to function well with products with high tech image, claim some scholars (e.g. Fugate, 1998), the potential reason being that their marketing requires strong argumentation. Yet, contrary business examples are plentiful, such as the timber harvester design and manufacturing company, PONSSE in Finland, which uses humour, not only for marketing purposes, but also as an inherent element in its company culture.

METHODOLOGY

This article is an overview of the most relevant topic-related studies conducted during the humour-oriented HURMOS Project. As there are several case studies overviewed, this study is related to a collective type of a case study. Based on Stake (1994, p. 237), when a number of cases are jointly studied to acquire information on a certain phenomenon, the study can be called a collective case study. This type of study is not of a collective kind but rather of an instrumental kind with the aim of gaining an insight into an issue through a case (ibid). Even though there are several researchers having independently conducted their studies, the studies can be grouped together as they attempted to shed light on the phenomenon of humour and play in marketing within the context of one particular project.

The data of the present paper consists of the studies conducted during the HURMOS project. The TEKES-funded (Finnish Funding Agency for Technology and Innovation) research project HURMOS 2014-2017 is globally a unique project. It has investigated the use of humour and playfulness in business and related marketing communication, with a special emphasis on digital marketing. The project aimed to increase awareness and competence of how to utilize humour strategically in Finnish companies with the aim of studying humour-related marketing and innovation in order to create and develop new practices and business opportunities with project partner companies, and thus promoting their growth and internationalization (HURMOS research plan, 2014). The research project explored how humour can create value in and around business organizations, through working in collaboration with customers, management and employees (ibid).

The studies were selected for the present paper on the basis of their foci and context: they represent studies on humour and playfulness in online marketing and marketing communication in the context and duration of the HURMOS project. This selection comprises theses by Bachelor and Master level students, articles by the project researchers, and presentations in a conference track organised by the HURMOS project. Altogether six studies were surveyed, of which three (3) are bachelor's theses, one (1) journal article, one (1) chapter in a book and one (1) conference presentation. The aim of the survey is to synthesise findings and clarify needs for further research.

FINDINGS

The theoretical and empirical results found in the studies on humour and playfulness in online advertising and marketing communication are presented next under key subthemes that emerged from the data during the study. Practice-based views discovered and reported in the studies are also included in the presentation of the findings below. The original sources of the theoretical and practice-based views drawn from the studies (see Table 1).

Humour as a Transformational Appeal: Culture, Time and Context Are Important

Using playfulness and humour in advertising is an efficient way to decrease the tension between the company and its customers. This is an interesting viewpoint that is taken up by a Managing Director (MD) of an advertising agency (Laiho, 2013, as cited in Immonen, 2016). Hence, according to the MD, when a company exploits humour in their advertising, customers laugh at the ad rather than the company. Successful humour in marketing communication may also increase the feeling of togetherness. The challenge is that customers may interpret the humour differently from its original intention, because people do not laugh at similar issues. How one understands humour is linked to e.g. gender, age and other contextual factors. (ibid.) There are also important cultural issues involved in how people respond to humour. Several studies corroborate some of the views by the above business practitioner (e.g. Hasset & Houlihan, 1979; Ruch et al., 1990; Martin et al., 2003). Consequently, it is important to pay close attention to the target group when planning an ad, so exploiting humour as part of an ad requires professionalism and customer understanding as it is expressed by Lou Dubois (2010) as cited in Immonen (2016). According to Juslen (2009) as cited in Immonen (2016), successful use of humour in an ad renders its text more human and personal. Humour in advertising should also be topical and related to current issues (Laiho, 2013, as cited in Immonen, 2016). Padley (2013) as cited in Pozdniakova (2015) states that brands should be careful not to overuse e.g. a recent meme, as they may become quickly outdated in online communication.

Humour enhances the attention the ad receives as it raises the viewer's emotional reaction (Unger, 1995, as cited in Lamberg, 2015). Humour in advertising produces transformational appeal (Kotler & Keller, 2009, p. 517 – 518, as cited in Lamberg, 2015): it gives the consumer an enjoyable experience and motivates purchase by inciting. Culture and time influence essentially the way humour can be used as well as the situations where it can be used (Martin, 2006, as cited in Lamberg, 2015). During the past century, the ways of viewing humour have changed: what used to be seen as socially inappropriate can now be viewed as positive and socially desirable (Martin, 2006, as cited in Lamberg, 2015). Moreover, companies should ensure that the humour they apply on their Facebook content is consistent with the company image (ibid).

Due to changes in society and due to increasing competition, humour is used more to obtain the consumer's attention (Beard, 2008). It can be claimed that on television in the USA, 20-25 per cent of commercials contain humour (Beard, 2008). Catanescu and Tom (2001), as cited in Lamberg (2015), estimate humour to occur in about 5 percent of journal advertisements and about 26 per cent of television advertising. The amount of humour in videobloing seems even more important. A successful blog offers its readers information, besides being entertaining and appealing to readers' emotions, e.g. via humour (Rissanen, 2014, as cited in Immonen, 2016). Humour is context specific; if the target audience of the joke is unknown, it is impossible to evaluate the outcome (Vaynerchuck, 2013, p. 17; Järvinen, 2013, p. 42, as cited in Pozdniakova, 2015). There are also cross-cultural differences in consumers' preferences: EU citizens from different countries continue to respond differently to marketing campaigns (see e.g. Kniel, 2002): e.g. the regulativeness of a particular society has a bearing on the preference for personal messages in advertising.

Unrelated Humour Attracts Attention but Does Not Necessarily Aid Selling Products

Humour can act as a tool for differentiating when developing a company's image. Social media marketing is inexpensive and helps companies to connect with their customers (Pozdniakova, 2015). In order to be authentic, marketers must prove that they are human, for example, by injecting some of their own personality into the Facebook content (ibid). Hence, online marketing is relatively inexpensive and facilitates maintaining customer relations, but marketers' personality needs to be visible there.

If the aim is to improve the recall of products by using humour, marketers should integrate humour as closely as possible within the information to be remembered, state Summerfelt et al. (2010) as cited in Lamberg (2015). It seems unlikely, however, that credibility is consistently enhanced when humour is used in marketing; on the contrary, there is evidence that humour may even harm company credibility in some cases (Gulas & Weinberger, 2006, p. 117, as cited in Lamberg, 2015). Humour may also decrease the strength of the claims in ads (Smith, 1993, p. 158, as cited in Lamberg, 2015) for some consumer groups. It is more likely that humour is effective in marketing when the brand is clearly identified and the humorous material does not weaken the particular message of the brand (Solomon et al., 2002, p. 175, as cited in Pozdniakova, 2015).

All in all, the use of humour in communication can be functional in marketing. However, it may have an adverse effect and decrease the credibility of the company and the strength of the message. In order to 'work' and be persuasive as planned, corporate communication should be authentic and humorousness in line with the company brand.

Individual Differences in Need for Humour: Customer Understanding Is Essential

There appear to be various factors influencing the way people respond to humorous messages in advertisements. How consumers react to humour in advertising depends not only on cultural, gender and age-related issues, but also on temperament (Hasset & Houlihan, 1979; Ruch et al., 1990; Martin et al., 2003). According to earlier research, even if some studies show mixed results, claims can be made about how temperament is connected with consumers' reactions to humour in advertisements. The influence of humour on attitudes towards the ad may depend on the individual's orientation for humour (Cline et al., 2003, as cited in Lamberg, 2015). Both a consumer's personality and the characteristics of an ad shape the consumer's response to the ad, but especially the individual's need for humour plays a role. Generally, individuals with high levels of need for humour respond more favourably to humorous ads. Knowledge of the common characteristics of a target group may suggest whether or not to use humour in advertising. (ibid.)

Companies will need to be aware of the risks involved in humour-based marketing: humour could have unwanted effects because of individual tastes, product category, or business circumstances. So, creating a humorous ad is not enough because humour is individual (Gulas & Weinberger, 2006, p. 118–119, as cited in Lamberg, 2015). When it comes to other individual characteristics, especially gender seems to be relevant; male customers seem to find ads humorous more often than females (Riecken & Hensel, 2012, p. 30, p. 34–35, as cited in Lamberg, 2015).

It seems that according to earlier research, there are at least some factors which have an effect on whether an advertisement is found humorous. People with a stronger need for humour and especially males respond favourably to humour in ads. Moreover, the nature of the ad and the product category as well as the business circumstance influence consumers' responses.

Storytelling and Playfulness are Important in Business Blogs and Video-Blogs

Business storytelling can be viewed similarly to traditional storytelling; it tells a story, but a special characteristic of a business story is the intention to engage an audience with the message (Dolan & Naidu, 2013, p. 1, 19, as cited in Lamberg, 2015) for transactional purposes. Emotions are important in business, and one of the ways emotions can be harnessed to work for business purposes is storytelling (ibid). Using intertextuality, i.e. exploiting the relationships between different types of texts, is an effective way of transferring wanted associations into products or services: through intertextuality the story may gain humoristic tones (Rope, 2005, as cited in Lamberg, 2015). The goal is to choose topics that are close to the customers' preferences and also related to the products or services a brand offers. Videos considered to be funny seem to be more likely to be shared than printed marketing material (ibid).

Blogging allows a new type of communication with customers (Kilpi 2006, p. 3, as cited in Immonen, 2016). Company blogs represent the company as well as the principles for blogging that are laid out by the company, and through blogging companies are more visible in social media (Kortesuo & Kurvinen, 2011, p. 171, as cited in Immonen, 2016). Social media is more prone to the use of humour as the style of communication is more casual. Versatile use of language and humoristic pieces of writing may have positive effects in a company's blog. In video material, humour also is acceptable and can be utilised more than in conventional media, claim business practitioners (MerjaHoo, 2014, as cited in Immonen,

2016). Such inbound marketing maintains customers' attention without being 'pushy' (Juslen, 2009, p. 205–207, as cited in Immonen, 2016).

Business practitioners view the use of humour as content marketing: the content is relevant to the customer segments who are drawn in without open selling attempts by the company, while the aim is profitable communication (Content Marketing Institute, 2014, as cited in Immonen, 2016). Via interesting content, the customer is given alternatives: reading a company's texts, watching their blogs, and then deciding whether they want to buy (Kortesuo, 2014, p. 94-96, as cited in Immonen, 2016). The practitioners find that the challenge of content marketing is retaining the customer's attention, and they find that this is where humour becomes relevant as a popular tool – customers have been found to spend ca. 2.7 minutes for viewing a video, but only 3-4 seconds for viewing web sites (Statistic Brain 25, 2015, as cited in Immonen, 2016).

Business practitioners find that producing emotional advertising content is close to traditional TV advertising as creating videos requires a large budget, a professional crew and a strong story (Kubo, Creative Agency, 2016, as cited in Immonen, 2016). A common way to create humorous content is through videos that are compiled from still images (ibid.). For many companies, the most popular blogs are video blogs, according to a survey conducted in 2015 (Manifesto, 2015, as cited in Immonen, 2016). It seems that the importance of humour in online and television marketing in particular has increased; advertising employs storytelling where playfulness and humour have an important role (Oikarinen, 2017).

An interesting case in point in the present data is the company Vincit (Borg & Heljakka, 2017) which uses playfulness in its company culture e.g. in the form of Vincent the Duck. Mascots are an important feature in the marketing efforts of many companies (see Terning, 2013), but Vincit is a special case, as Vincent the Duck functions as an organisational artefact which, besides being used in marketing, is also used to promote staff's innovation capabilities at work, in addition making everyday work life more enjoyable for them (see also Alatalo et al., 2018b). Table 1 summarises the results of the reviewed six studies.

Companies can use humour also to develop their ethical branding, which is the case with Varusteleka (see Alatalo et al., 2018a, in Table 1): the company in question exploits especially satirical humour in its communication with customers in Facebook, and playfulness in its marketing campaigns in its online shop. Borg and Heljakka (2017, see Table 1) have explored the use of playfulness and toys in creating a unique company culture. This attitude is also present on the company website (see vincit.com). The unique organisational culture extends to customers via their online marketing communication.

As a summary, it can be stated that social media has changed the nature of marketing, advertising included. Digital marketing communication allows for storytelling and this seems to inspire marketers to using more playful communication and humour in advertising. Even traditional technical and engineering companies can use humour in their corporate culture and marketing communication, e.g. PONSSE, which was one of the HURMOS partner companies.

Table 1. Examples of uses and functions of humour and play in marketing communication

Source	Examples of Use of Humour and Play	Functions of Humour and Play	Comments by Authors of the Original Texts
Lamberg, 2015	Linguistic ways to express humour or play built into text content as humorous story, happening; also via intertextuality with popular culture. If a company shows capability to laugh at itself on company website, it may appear more easily accessible.	Humour used to describe services or products in order to differentiate them and the company.	Incongruity, surprise, word play used the most commonly on the nine (9) HURMOS project partner company web sites, incl. high tech companies.
Pozdniakova, 2015	Relevance of the content: whether humour creates or interrupts entertainment is important. Highly humorous advertisements may harm product recall; this does not apply as much to social media marketing as to the older marketing channels.	Content considered to be funny was more likely to be shared than any other category, which makes humour a good aid to achieve virality. Humorous and casual content create, promote and sustain the company character; e.g. use of pop-culture to companies' advantage.	There is no detailed blueprint available on how to create effective/valuable humorous content; every company and product is different. Numerous factors affect the quality of content. Combining humour with pop-culture events can be risky, in case a large number of viewers is offended by the content. This is why research is crucial on the part of the companies.
Immonen, 2016	Humour is more acceptable in social media than in conventional marketing media. Humour is used in pictures and videos in the Zoo's blog posts. Incongruent humour entertains readers. Use of slow video in Ranua Zoo blogging: peaceful and atmospheric. Competitors also use emotional video material.	Ranua Zoo uses narrational humour that is accidentally produced by animals as a way to differentiate from competitors. Such content raises discussion among viewers.	Ranua Zoo could increase the use of humorous pictures in blogs. Surprise and incongruent humour could be used in a more planned fashion.
Borg & Heljakka, 2017	Vincent the Duck of Vincit, an IT company reinforces organisational culture and Vincit's way of working. Vincit's organisational culture is expressed in visible daily routines in a humorous/playful way that is unique. Vincit's culture is built around playful interaction: shared narratives, humorous communication, related characters and objects.	Vincent motivates and engages. It is part of the legitimization process of a unique organisational culture. It provides norms, standards, ideals, role models for the work tribe. Playful objects are used as artefacts: figurines and toys and their images as totems of organisational tribes. Vincent also acts as a marketing tool, online and offline.	Organisational artefacts make everyday work more enjoyable: reinforce playful communication at work and have a positive impact on group processes and groups' performance. IT field as a special case in point. Other fields e.g. sports teams could also be relevant. Organisational artefacts help make sense of organisational culture.
Alatalo, Oikarinen, Ahola & Järvinen, 2018a	Unconventional ethical branding via humour; incongruity is present in the vast majority of the Facebook posts by Varusteleka, its branding being innovative, experiment-oriented and resourceful. Responsibility and quality were the SME's core values conveyed through humour. The SME uses harsh disparagement humour which is rare in advertising.	Satirical humour in the data was generally more favoured by men than women. Seems that satirical tone and aggressive humour are becoming increasingly common as companies compete for customers' attention.	Ethical branding of the case company is characterized by its striving for responsibility and quality through the use of humour in its Facebook communication.
Oikarinen, 2017	Humour in recruitment advertising shows a tentative positive effect regarding the intention to share the ad: humour increases the likelihood of an ad becoming viral.	The effect of humour in online job recruitment ad had a negative effect on potential applicants' attitudes to the job ad and the advertiser.	There is a link between congruence of humour and fun job climate regarding the effectiveness of humour in online recruitment advertising. Humour should be used carefully in recruiting, as it did not increase candidates' interest in applying for the position.

CONCLUSION AND DISCUSSION

The objective of the present paper has been to share and summarise practitioners' views of the functions of humour and playfulness in order to find new and relevant foci for a further scientific research agenda in the field of humour-based marketing. The aim has also been to gain further understanding about the challenges and opportunities of using humour and playfulness in online marketing. Earlier studies on humour in marketing have been lacking in discussing online environments. Previous studies on humour in advertising have also been dominated by quantitative experimental studies (e.g. Eisend, 2009; Crawford & Gregory, 2015) and thus, the studies have lacked practitioners' views. This study is contributing to the research in the field by filling these research gaps.

The present paper has also attempted to provide an overview on the results of the studies conducted in the context of the HURMOS project that explored the strategic use of humour and playfulness in digital corporate communication. Although the collection of examples is small (six studies), it would seem that the importance of humour and the role of playfulness in business organisations and their communication with their customers is becoming increasingly important and taking different forms.

Humour and playfulness may not suit every field of business, nor every customer segment, but due to the transformational power of humour and playfulness in the experience and imagination economy of today, they are relevant tools and approaches in marketing and advertising both online and off-line and their power should not be overlooked. However, using them requires in-depth customer understanding and, especially in the case of video blogs and videos used in advertising, a professional media crew, although other online media may be more inexpensive to produce. Moreover, although corporate blogs, vlogs, and Facebook seem to allow for more playful and humorous online communication and advertising than is the case with traditional marketing media, whether this kind of advertising actually increases sales requires further research.

ACKNOWLEDGMENT

The authors gratefully acknowledge the funding provided by the Finnish Funding Agency for Technology and Innovation.

REFERENCES

Alatalo, S., Oikarinen, E.-L., Ahola, H., & Järvinen, M. (2018a). SMEs' ethical branding with humour on Facebook: a case study of a Finnish online army store. In E. Maon, A. Lindgren, J. Vanhamme, R. J. Angell, & J. Memery (Eds.), *Not All Claps and Cheers. Humour in Business and Society Relationships* (pp. 81–99). London, UK: Routledge.

Alatalo, S., Oikarinen, E.-L., Reiman, A., Ming Tan, T., Heikka, E.-L., Hurmelinna-Laukkanen, P., ... Vuorela, T. (2018b). Linking concepts of playfulness and well-being at work in the retail sector. *Journal of Retailing and Consumer Services*, *43*, 226–233. doi:10.1016/j.jretconser.2018.03.013

Alcántara-Pilar, J.M., Barrio-García, S.D., Porcu, L., & Crespo-Almendros, E. (2017). Language as a cultural vessel in online servicescapes: Its impact on consumers' perceived risk, attitudes, and behavioural intentions. *Journal of Consumer Behaviour, an international research review, 16*(6).

Alden, D. L., Hoyer, W. D., & Lee, C. (1993). Identifying global and culture-specific dimensions of humor in advertising: A multinational analysis. *Journal of Marketing, 57*(2), 64–75. doi:10.2307/1252027

American Marketing Association. (2013). Approved 2013 definition of marketing from the American Marketing Association. Retrieved from www.ama.org/AboutAMA/Pages/Definition-of-Marketing.aspx

Beard, F. K. (2005). Advertising and audience offense: The role of intentional humor. *Journal of Marketing Communications, 14*(1), 1–17. doi:10.1080/13527260701467760

Beard, F. K. (2008). *Humor in the advertising business. Theory, Practice and Wit*. Lanham, Maryland: Rowman & Littlefield Publishers, Inc.

Bergeron, J., & Vachon, M.-A. (2008). The effects of humour usage in financial advisors in sales encounters. *International Journal of Bank Marketing, 26*(6), 376–398. doi:10.1108/02652320810902424

Biswas, A., Olsen, J. E., & Carlet, V. (1992). A comparison of print advertisements from the United States and France. *Journal of Advertising, 21*(4), 73–81. doi:10.1080/00913367.1992.10673387

Bjelica, D., Gardasevic, J., Vasiljevic, I., & Popovic, S. (2016). Ethical dilemmas of sport advertising. *Sport Mont, 14*(3), 41–43.

Borg, K., & Heljakka, K. (2017, August). Playing with rubber ducks and manatees in the workplace: physical, playful artefacts as totems of organizational tribes. *Paper presented at the 24th Nordic Academy of Management Conference (NFF)*, Bodø, Norway, August 23-25.

Catanescu, C., & Tom, G. (2001). Types of humor in television and magazine advertising. *Review of Business, 22*(1/2), 92–95.

Chaffey, D. (2011). *E-business and e-commerce management. Strategy, implementation and practice* (5th ed.). Harley, England: Financial Times/Prentice Hall.

Chung, H., & Zhao, X. (2003). Humour effect on memory and attitude: Moderating role of product involvement. *International Journal of Advertising, 22*(1), 117–144. doi:10.1080/02650487.2003.11072842

Cline, T., Altsech, M., & Kellaris, J. (2003). When does humor enhance or inhibit ad responses? *Journal of Advertising, 32*(3), 31–45.

Cluley, R. (2017). *Essentials of advertising*. London: KoganPage.

Content Marketing Institute. (2014). What Is Content Marketing? Retrieved from http://contentmarketinginstitute.com/what-is-content-marketing/

Crawford, H. J., & Gregory, G. D. (2015). Humorous advertising that travels: A review and call for research. *Journal of Business Research, 68*(3), 569–577. doi:10.1016/j.jbusres.2014.09.005

Dahlén, M., & Rosengren, S. (2016). If advertising won't die, what will it be? Toward a working definition of advertising. *Journal of Advertising, 45*(3), 334–345. doi:10.1080/00913367.2016.1172387

Dolan, G., & Naidu, Y. (2013). *Hooked: How Leaders Inspire, Connect and Engage with Storytelling*. Somerset, CA: John Wiley & Sons.

Dubois, L. (2010). How to Use Humor in Advertising. Retrieved from http://www.inc.com/guides/2010/12/how-to-use-humor-in-advertising.html

Eisend, M. (2009). A meta-analysis of humor in advertising. *Academy of Marketing Science Journal, 37*(2), 191–203. doi:10.100711747-008-0096-y

Fugate, D. L. (1998). The advertising of services: What is an appropriate role for humor? *Journal of Services Marketing, 12*(6), 453–472. doi:10.1108/08876049810242731

Guitard, P., Ferland, F., & Dutil, E. (2005). Toward a better understanding of playfulness in adults. *OTJR: Occupation. Participation and Health, 25*(1), 9–22. doi:10.1177/153944920502500103

Gulas, C. S., & Weinberger, M. G. (2006). *Humor in advertising. A Comprehensive analysis*. Armonk, New York: M.E. Sharpe.

Hasset, J., & Houlihan, J. (1979). Different jokes for different folks. *Psychology Today, 12*(8), 64–71.

Hietalahti, J. (2016). *The Dynamic Concept of Humour. Erich Fromm and the Possibility of Humane Humour*. Jyväskylä: Jyväskylä University Printing House.

HURMOS Research Plan. (2014). (*Unpublished Project Plan*). Oulu, Finland: The University of Oulu and the Oulu University of Applied Sciences.

Immonen, P. (2016). *Humour in Ranua Zoo's blog marketing* [BA Thesis]. Oulu University of Applied Sciences, Oulu, Finland.

Järvinen, M. (2013). *Humor As a Marketing Communications Tool. Unpublished Bachelor's Thesis*. Oulu, Finland: Oulu University of Applied Sciences; Retrieved from www.theseus.fi

Juslen, J. (2009). *Netti mullistaa markkinoinnin*. Helsinki, Finland: Talentum.

Kilpi, T. (2006). Blogit ja bloggaaminen. Helsinki: Readme.fi.

Kniel, S. (2002). *Consumer preferences in a comparative European market research research study*. GRIN Verlag. Retrieved from https://www.grin.com/document/14294

Kortesuo, K. (2014). *Sano se someksi 2. Organisaation käsikirja sosiaaliseen mediaan*. Helsinki, Finland: Kauppakamari.

Kortesuo, K., & Kurvinen, J. (2011). *Blogimarkkinointi - Blogilla mainetta ja mammonaa*. Helsinki, Finland: Talentum.

Kotler, P., & Keller, K. L. (2009). *Marketing management* (13th ed.). New Jersey: Pearson Education Inc.

Kubo, Creative Agency. (2016). Videotrendit 2016 [Video Trends 2016]. Retrieved from http://www.kubo.fi/videotrendit-2016/

Laiho, T. (2013). Pelottava huumori. Markkinointi & Mainonta. Retrieved from http://www.marmai.fi/blogit/laihon_klinikka/pelottava-huumori-6269196

Lamberg, A. (2015). *Humour on the websites of the organisations participating in the HURMOS project* [BA Thesis]. Oulu University of Applied Sciences, Oulu, Finland.

Laroche, M., Nepomuceno, M. V., & Richard, M.-O. (2014). Congruency of humour and cultural values in print ads. Cross-cultural differences among the US, France and China. *International Journal of Advertising, 33*(4), 681–705. doi:10.2501/IJA-33-4-681-705

Madden, T. J., & Weinberger, M. G. (1984). Humor in advertising: A practitioner view. *Journal of Advertising Research, 24*(4), 23–29.

Manifesto. (2015). Blogibarometri 2015: Videoblogit ja sosiaalinen media muuttavat blogikenttää. Retrieved from http://www.manifesto.fi/fi/uutta/-blogibarometri-2015-videoblogit-ja-sosiaalinen-media-muuttavat-blogikenttaa

Martin, R. A. (2006). *Psychology of Humor: An Integrative Approach*. Burlington, MA: Academic Press.

Martin, R. A., & Lefcourt, H. M. (1983). Sense of humor as a moderator of the relation between stressors and moods. *Journal of Personality and Social Psychology, 45*(6), 1313–1324. doi:10.1037/0022-3514.45.6.1313

Martin, R. A., Puhlik-Doris, P., Larsen, G., Gray, J., & Weir, K. (2003). Individual differences in uses of humor and their relation to psychological well-being: Development of the humor styles questionnaire. *Journal of Research in Personality, 37*(1), 48–75. doi:10.1016/S0092-6566(02)00534-2

Mathies, C., Chiew, T. M., & Kleinaltenkamp, M. (2016). The antecedents and consequences of humour for service. *Journal of Service Theory and Practice, 26*(2), 137–162. doi:10.1108/JSTP-09-2014-0187

MerjaHoo. (2014). Yritysblogi – vai yritysvlogi? Retrieved from http://www.merjahoo.com/2014/10/yritysblogi-vai-yritysvlogi/

Mesmer-Magnus, J., Glew, D. J., & Viswesvaran, C. (2012). A meta-analysis of positive humor in the workplace. *Journal of Managerial Psychology, 27*(2), 155–190. doi:10.1108/02683941211199554

Meyer, J. F. (2000). Humor as a double-edged sword: Four functions of humor in communication. *Communication Theory, 3*(10), 310–331. doi:10.1111/j.1468-2885.2000.tb00194.x

Moraes, C., & Michaelidou, N. (2017). Introduction to the special thematic symposium on the ethics of controversial online advertising. *Journal of Business Ethics, 141*(2), 231–233. doi:10.100710551-015-2754-6

Morreall, J. (2014). Humor, philosophy and education. *Educational Philosophy and Theory, 46*(2), 120–131. doi:10.1080/00131857.2012.721735

Oikarinen, E.-L. (2017). The moderating role of congruence between humor and fun climate of the company on the effects of humor in Internet job ads. In G. Christodoulides, A. Stathopoulou, Anastasia, & M. Eisend (Eds.), Advances in Advertising Research Vol. VII: Bridging the Gap between Advertising Academia and Practice (pp. 167–181). European Advertising Academy. New York: Springer.

Oikarinen, E.-L., & Sinisalo, J. (2017). Personality or skill: A qualitative study of humorous recruitment advertising campaign on social media. *International Journal of Internet Marketing and Advertising*, *11*(1), 22–43. doi:10.1504/IJIMA.2017.082990

Padley, B. (2013). The Role of Humor in Social Media. Retrieved from http://www.socialmediatoday.com/content/role-humor-social-media

Porter, L., & Golan, G. (2006). From subservient chickens to brawny men: A comparison of viral advertising to television advertising. *Journal of Interactive Advertising*, *6*(2), 26–33.

Pozdniakova, N. (2015). *Creating valuable content on social media using humour* [BA Thesis]. Oulu University of Applied Sciences, Oulu, Finland.

Riecken, G., & Hensel, K. (2012). Using humor in Advertising: When does it work? *Southern Business Rewiev*, *37*(2), 27–37.

Rissanen, H. (2014). Mistä on hyvä yritysblogi tehty. Markkinointi & Mainonta. Retrieved from http://www.marmai.fi/blogit/mista+on+hyva+yritysblogi+tehty/a2230523

Romero, E., & Pescosolido, A. (2008). Humor and group effectiveness. *Human Relations*, *61*(3), 395–418. doi:10.1177/0018726708088999

Rope, T. (2005). *Markkinoinnilla menestykseen. Hehkeys- ja ilahduttamismarkkinointi*. Helsinki: Inforviestintä.

Ruch, W. (1996). Measurement approaches to the sense of humor: Introduction and overview. *Humor: International Journal of Humor Research*, *9*(3-4), 239–250. doi:10.1515/humr.1996.9.3-4.239

Ruch, W., McGhee, P. E., & Helh, F.-J. (1990). Age differences in the enjoyment of incongruity-resolution and nonsense humor during adulthood. *Psychology and Aging*, *5*(3), 348–355. doi:10.1037/0882-7974.5.3.348 PMID:2242239

Smith, S. M. (1993). Does Humor in Advertising Enhance Systematic Processing? *Advances in Consumer Research. Association for Consumer Research (U. S.)*, *20*(1), 155–158.

Söderlund, M., & Oikarinen, E.-L. (2018). Joking with customers in the service encounter has a negative impact on customer satisfaction: Replication and extension. *Journal of Retailing and Consumer Services*, *42*, 55–64. doi:10.1016/j.jretconser.2018.01.013

Solomon, M., Bamossy, G., & Askegaard, S. (2002). *Consumer behaviour: a European perspective*. Harlow, UK: Pearson Education Limited.

Spotts, H. E., Weinberger, M. G., & Parsons, A. L. (1997). Assessing the use and impact of humor on advertising effectiveness: A contingency approach. *Journal of Advertising*, *16*(3), 17–32. doi:10.1080/00913367.1997.10673526

Stake, R. E. (1994). Case Studies. In N. K. Denzin & Y. S. Lincoln (Eds.), *Handbook of Qualitative Research* (pp. 236–247). London: Sage Publications.

Statistic Brain. (2015). Attention Span Statistics. Retrieved from http://www.statisticbrain.com/attention-span-statistics/

Summerfelt, H., Lippman, L., & Hyman, I. E. (2010). The effect of Humor on Memory: Constrained by the Pun. *The Journal of General Psychology, 137*(4), 376–394.

Terning, M. (2013). *How companies use mascots in their digital marketing (Unpublished Bachelor's Thesis)*. Oulu, Finland: Oulu University of Applied Sciences; Retrieved from www.theseus.fi

Unger, L. S. (1995). Observations: A cross-cultural study on the affect-based model of humor in advertising. *Journal of Advertising Research, 35*(1), 66–71.

Vaynerchuk, G. (2013). *Jab, Jab, Jab, Right Hook*. New York: HarperCollins.

Vuorela, T. (2005). Laughing matters: A case study of humor in multicultural business negotiations. *Negotiation Journal, 21*(1), 105–130. doi:10.1111/j.1571-9979.2005.00049.x

Warren, C., & McGraw, A. P. (2016). When does humorous marketing hurt brands? *Journal of Marketing Behavior, 2*(1), 39–67. doi:10.1561/107.00000027

Weinberger, M. G., & Gulas, C. S. (1992). The impact of humor in advertising: A review. *Journal of Advertising, 21*(9), 35–59. doi:10.1080/00913367.1992.10673384

Weinberger, M. G., & Spotts, H. E. (1989). Humor in U.S versus U.K. TV commercials: A comparison. *Journal of Advertising, 18*(2), 39–44. doi:10.1080/00913367.1989.10673150

This research was previously published in the International Journal of Innovation in the Digital Economy (IJIDE), 10(3); pages 24-36, copyright year 2019 by IGI Publishing (an imprint of IGI Global).

Chapter 53
The Role of Social Media in Event Marketing:
Outcomes for Practitioners and Participants

Serap Serin Karacaer
Aksaray Universty Vocational School of Social Sciences, Turkey

ABSTRACT

Activities, which include events that are not all intangible, include large-scale service components, and hence, their marketing includes service marketing. From this point of view, it is possible to state that it is very difficult to market activities that the participants cannot take home and consume physically. In this context, it is very important that the event marketing activities convey the feeling to the target audience that they will have fun and be entertained. Therefore, social media is one of the most important tools used in the effective transfer of the organization to the target audience within the scope of event marketing activities. As the most effective current communication and interaction tool, social media has become the most important tool for event marketers who are trying to appeal to large audiences and promote a certain destination, product, or service.

INTRODUCTION

Events, whether they are public or private or organized for whatever reason such as commercial or aid, for celebration or commemoration, are organizations that bring people together to share an experience and achieve measurable results (Silvers, 2004). Furthermore, events that are organized for the protection and development of the social identity in the region where they are organized are also activities that are a tourist attraction for the destination (Derret, 2004: 39) have increased rapidly in number, variety and popularity in recent years. Therefore, the rapidly developing event industry is one of the industries with the biggest employment potential and positive economic impact in the world today (Theocharis, 2008). There is a multi-dimensional organizational network in direct proportion to the size of the event, such as

DOI: 10.4018/978-1-6684-6287-4.ch053

managing activities, managing financial affairs and staff, conducting public relations, ensuring security, advertising and promotion, decoration, organizing behind every event that is planned (Tassiopoulos, 2005). In this context, it is possible to provide this whole operation in a certain order with an organized event management and event marketing. Event management is the function of providing links between various sections of an event and organizing the flow of information between them (Bhe, Glasmacker, Meckwood, Pereira & Wallace, 2004). In other words, event management can be expressed as a way of dealing with the activities planned in an organization. Event marketing is the effort to coordinate the communication of an event. In other words, event marketing can be defined as an effort to coordinate communication around an event that occurs spontaneously or is organized by a professional sponsor (Behrer & Larsson, 1998). At this point, the purpose of organizing an event from the perspective of the sponsor is to announce the product to larger masses, to create an image and to increase participation (Lundmark, 1998).

Social media is one of the most important areas of communication, with its improved infrastructure facilities and its ever-increasing variety (Aktan & Çakmak, 2015). In today's internet age, social media has become a platform that allows people to turn themselves into "media" to collaborate and share information (Thevenot, 2007; Li & Wang, 2011). When evaluated from this point of view, it is possible to express social media as a communication tool that makes information sharing and communication very fast and easy (Koçyigit, 2015). However, the main strength of social media is its ability to enable two-way communication rather than information sharing (Chu & Kim, 2015). Furthermore, being mobile-based without time and space limitations, social media establishes a form of communication in which sharing, discussion and exchange of ideas is the main factor. Therefore, content sharing can take place instantly, quickly and easily, without the need for an intermediary, through social media (Vural & Bat, 2010) which consists of the dialogues and sharing that individuals have with each other on the internet (Kaynak & Koç, 2015). Hence, from this point of view, social media is seen as an important marketing tool to be used in event marketing.

Within the scope of the study, the concept of event marketing will be discussed in full detail, and the importance of social media will be emphasized in terms of the effective and efficient marketing of events. The role of social media in the promotion of events, enabling the participants to share their views with the target audience and receive feedback about events will be expressed in this context.

BACKGROUND

The Activity Concept

The concept of activity is a concept that can have different meanings depending on how it is defined. When the concept of activity is associated with the concept of "event", the meaning of the "event" concept also differs and is directly proportional to the purpose of each event (Eckerstein, 2002). In this context, in its most general form, an event can be expressed as bringing people together to influence them and create an experience for them (Silvers, 2004). From a wider perspective, an event is a series of activities that enable the revival of natural and physical resources in the cities or countries where it is organized, creating an image for that place and increasing the tourism attraction of the destination in question (Getz, 1997). The event concept, which expresses a unique time period (Berridge, 2007) apart from daily events, is also used to define activities designed for different purposes. These activities can be local involving art, sports, tourism and other social activities, but they can also be more formal and professional events organized by major organizers (Argan, 2007).

The reasons why people participate in activities can differ. Getz (1997) examined the incentive of individuals participating in activities by dividing them into three groups. Accordingly, individuals in the first group participated in activities in line with physical motives such as food, drink, exercise, relaxation and comfort. The incentives of the individuals in the second group participating in the activities were social and interpersonal motives such as socializing with family and friends, being included in groups, connections with cultural and ethnic origins, expressing feelings of socialism and nationalism, a desire to gain status and recognition. The third group participated in activities with personal motives such as seeking new experiences, information, a desire to be understood, and to realize their passions. Crompton and McKay (1997) addressed their study under six headings: innovation, cultural discovery, gaining balance, a desire to socialize as part of a certain group, the desire to socialize by interacting with other people, and family unity. One of the main motivating factors that affect individuals' participation in activities was the feeling of experiencing "a once in a lifetime" event. Neioretti et al. (2001) also concluded that the "once in a lifetime" experience was one of the main motives for individuals to participate in an event. Therefore, although the reasons for individuals to participate in events differ according to various motives, it is possible to state that these motives are also related to the personal characteristics of individuals (social, cultural, economic, etc.).

Numerous events are organized in different places and at different scales every year in the world to fulfill different purposes. In this context, two different classifications should be made regarding such events in terms of their scales as well as their form and content. Accordingly;

1. **Events by scale** vary according to criteria such as the number of participants, media influence, cost amount and benefits. However, there is a direct proportion between the size and scale of the event and its diversification. In other words, the higher the number of participants attending the event and the higher their spending, the greater the impact rate is and the classification according to scaling is made accordingly (Bowdin, G., Allen, J., O'Toole, W., Harris, R. & McDonnell, I., 2012: 16).

    a. **Mega events:** are those that have the highest number of participants in terms of event scales that generate the highest resonance and are the most talked about. Mega events require a more detailed planning and larger organization than others (Yürük, 2015: 12). Mega events are viewed as events that start with a cause-effect relationship, develop very rapidly, manifest their impact and results immediately, and show continuity (Hiller, 1998: 47). Global events such as the FIFA World Cup and the Olympic Games that have a strong global impact on society are examples of mega events (Arcodia & Robb, 2000: 156; Bowdin et al., 2006: 18).

    b. **Hallmark events:** Hallmark events can be defined as events planned to increase the attractiveness of a particular destination or region (Murphy & Carmichael, 1991: 32; Van der Wagen, 2005). The main purpose of holding Hallmark events is to increase awareness of the place where the event takes place and transform it into a special market (Derrett, 2011: 34). The most popular example that of such events is the Rio Carnival (Bowdin et al., 2006: 17). Other examples of hallmark events are the Kentucky Derby in America, the Chelsea Flower Show in Britain, Oktoberfest in Munich, the Edinburgh Festival in Scotland (Koh & Jackson, 2006: 21).

c. **Major events:** Major events are those that are smaller than mega and hallmark events with their scope and scale (Arcodia & Robb, 2000: 156). However, major events have cultural value as a result of the image effects they ensure for the host community or country (Richards & Wilson, 2004:1933). Formula 1 Grand Prix and Tennis Tournaments held in various cities or countries are examples of major events (Koh & Jackson, 2006: 21).

d. **Local events:** Local events that physically represent the narrowest geographic area can be defined as social and entertainment events organized for the local audience. Janiskee (1996: 404) defined local events as entertainment activities that are generated by institutions and organizations such as public institutions, non-governmental organizations, business associations utilizing public spaces such as streets, schools, parks where all the services are delivered voluntarily by the locals under the auspices and adopted by a certain host community. These events are events that evoke pride and strengthen the sense of belonging for the local community (Bowdin et al. 2012: 12).

2. **Events by format and content** are culture and festival-oriented events that have existed in many societies for years, have universal values and date back in history (Bowdin et al. 2012: 17).

    a. **Cultural events:** Society has a social role in these events which are organized to ensure that the profile and image of a city and society are different and unique. Festivals organized for socio-cultural activities such as music, art and science in a city or across the country are examples of cultural events. Festivals, which are the most well-known forms of cultural activities are described as events which are mainly attended by local people and develop rapidly (Arcodia & Whitford, 2006: 3). In other words, festivals are celebrations involving the participants' experience and emotions that the local community wants to share. The main feature that distinguishes festivals from other events is that they have emerged as a result of society and celebration. Another aim of festivals is to reach maximum numbers in terms of participants who undergo a major experience that differs from daily life (Arcodia & Robb, 2000: 156).

    b. **Sports events:** Involve sports activities that cover a full range of individual and multiple sports, such as the Olympic Games. These events benefit not only the management and sports organizers where the event is held, but also the players, coaches, officials, and viewers who come to enjoy and be entertained (Bowdin et al., 2006: 20).

    c. **Business and operation events:** Include events such as conferences, congresses, symposiums, panels, fairs, and exhibitions that are organized with a business content. These events, organized by countries or businesses with a work-related content, also play an important role in the development of the city where the event is organized (Mackellar, 2008: 47).

d. **Other events:** Recently, events organized in areas referred to as theme parks or amusement parks are also very popular. Theme parks, in particular, are a new concept established to attract tourists and create an impressive atmosphere in a place. The primary aim of these parks is to combine the structure of the organization with the physical condition, and present visitors with an experience. Disneyland, which opened in Anaheim, California in 1955 and adds a new dimension to entertainment, is one of the most well-known examples of theme parks (Milman, 2010: 221).

Attention should be paid to avoid overlooking the negative effects of the "event" phenomenon, which has become increasingly important recently throughout the country and sometimes in cities, for many reasons such as its economic return, advertisement and promotion opportunities, touristic attraction and appeal along with its positive effects. These effects can be listed as socio-cultural, tourism, economic, physical, environmental and political effects (Table 1). The many positive effects of events can be listed as the society having new experiences, learning and discovering new things (Delamere, Wankel & Hinch, 2001), creating a sense of togetherness in the host community (Arcodia & Whitford, 2006; Getz, 1993), contributing to the development of the city (Jeong & Faulkner, 1996), aiding in the promotion of attractions centers in the destination (Fredline & Faulkner, 2000) and enabling the exchange of thoughts and opinions between local people and visitors (Dwyer, Mellor, Mistilis & Mules, 2000).

On the other hand, events can have negative effects in a destination such as traffic congestion, crowds, increase in crime rate (Atci, Unur & Gursoy, 2016; Dwyer et al., 2000), destruction of natural, cultural and historical resources (Gursoy & Kendall, 2006), physical damage to the natural environment (Raj & Musgrave, 2009: 67), as well as a loss of identity that can be experienced in the society, as well as the deterioration of moral values (Leenders, Go & Bhansing, 2015).

Table 1. Positive and negative effects of events

Event Area	Positive Effects	Negative Effects
Socio-Cultural	· Sharing a common experience · Strengthening traditions · Enhancing social pride · Increased social participation · Introducing new and creative ideas · Expanding cultural perspectives	· Alienation of the society · Manipulating society · The formation of a negative social image · Negative behavior · Abuse of values · Change in the social structure · Loss of comfort
Physical and Environmental	· Displaying the environment · Presenting the best feasible models · Increasing environmental awareness · Infrastructure system to be inherited · Development of the transportation and communication system · Urban transformation and renovation	· Environmental destruction · Pollution · Damage to cultural heritage · Noise pollution · Traffic congestion
Tourism and Economy	· Promotion of the touristic area and increase in tourist numbers · Extention of their stay · Increase in income · Increase in tax revenues · Generating employment	· Resistance of society to tourism · Loss of originality · Damage to the image · Abuse by interest groups · Inflationary prices · Opportunity cost
Political	· International prestige · Advanced profile · Promotion of investments · Reciprocal social support · Development of administrative skills	· Risk of failure of the activity · Improper distribution of funds · Lack of responsibility in ownership and control · Legalization of ideologies

Source: (Mc Donnel, Allen & O'toole, 1998: 20)

MAIN FOCUS OF THE CHAPTER

Events designed for an audience and specially designed to enable people to interact with various goods and services are seen as an important market for many businesses today. Event marketing is a natural part of the marketing mix, and in fact, the concept of marketing has been around since its existence (Eriksson & Hjalmsson, 2000). The main theme of event marketing focuses on providing the audience with positive experiences about the event (Lundmark, 1998). The event is a formation that includes "participants". Therefore, conveying messages about the event to the participants in question and transferring the experiences they can experience is related to the function of event marketing. In this context, event marketing can be defined as an effort to coordinate communication around an event that occurs spontaneously or is organized by a professional sponsor (Behrer & Larsson, 1998). At this point, the purpose of organizing an event from the perspective of the sponsor is to announce the product to larger masses, create an image and increase the number of participants (Lundmark, 1998). Another definition of event marketing is to support a brand and organizational interests of a business by associating it with different, unique and special organizations (Martensen et al., 2007).

At the point of explaining the concept of marketing and how it works for businesses, it is possible to use a statement such as "meeting the demands and needs that are valuable for the customer by exchanging goods, services or ideas" (Bowdin et al., 2006: 180). Although the concept of event marketing has been used frequently in marketing literature recently, its explanation is not as easy as the concept of marketing. This is because event marketing is a combination of "opening, facilitating, accelarating and closing the sales business" during an event (Toner & Walker, 2014, p.32). In other words, what makes event marketing different is that event planners include media elements in this process and connect them together with all other elements before, during and after the event (Close et al., 2006, p. 422). Therefore, it is important for managers who carry out the activity business to know the factors that the event should include while marketing the events. These elements help define and facilitate the marketing process.

In this context, although the venue and purpose of each event is different, three basic elements should be taken into consideration in terms of marketing. These are (Hoyle, 2012; 1-2):

1. **Entertainment:** The dictionary defines entertainment as something which offers "a joyful and enjoyable time" (www.sozluk.gov.tr). Although the concept of entertainment exists in the daily lives of societies, it is an integral part of events. So much so that nobody wants to be part of a social event that does not offer entertainment. The main objective of event planners is to provide the participants with positive feelings and experiences during and after the event. Although the positive feeling in question varies depending on the motivating element of each of the participants, the desire to experience the feeling of "having fun" is the same in the event for almost all of the attending participants. Therefore, in terms of event marketing, it is important to present the correct format and activities that will entertain the target audience saturated with home entertainment such as television, computer, CD, DVDs. At this point, the success of event marketing is directly proportional to making the participant group, who is the target audience, feel that they will be offered a different, unique and tailor-made entertainment.

2. **Excitement:** Excitement is a concept that does not appear concretely, but it is known to exist in every person. However, excitement is also the key to making an event unforgettable. Excitement, which is an element of event marketing, should not be confused with entertainment. Excitement is an item offered to participants with activities such as a surprise party, uninterrupted music and dancing within the scope of an event. The realization of the phenomenon of excitement during the event, which is an important part of an effective event marketing, that was promised before the event is an important point in the success of the event marketing.

3. **Initiative:** The third element of event marketing which is initiative, is to create and present innovative and new approaches in partnerships and negotiations related to the activities to be carried out at the planned event. These initiatives should be designed in an exciting and desirable way by the

participating group. In other words, in event marketing, the initiative should be the element that keeps the activity fresh, and surprises and affects the participants with the innovations it offers.

Events can have many different purposes such as attracting attention, promoting a particular brand and creating an image, creating brand awareness, and increasing sales. Furthermore, the target group of event marketing can be a more comprehensive framework such as a business, the employees of a business, the customers that the business offers products to. Therefore, activities are carried out for a small number of people gathering for a small event or thousands of people are catered to for a large organization within the scope of event marketing activities (Behrer & Larsson, 1998). Another purpose of event marketing can be to provide information about any goods or services. In order to meet the goals of event marketing, elements included in the marketing karma such as the media, communication, sponsorship are utilized in addition to the event itself. Therefore, it is possible to say that event marketing is a part of marketing strategy (Eckerstein, 2002: 2).

The basic concepts of event marketing are messages, interaction and integration. The primary purpose of event marketing is to convey a message about a planned event. At this point, as is the case with other marketing tools, the aim is not to establish communication but to provide a communication that has value for the customer. A correct and effective message in event marketing ensures that the target group gets together at a certain place at a certain time. The second aim in event marketing is to ensure interaction between the target group and the event. The third objective is to ensure the integration of event marketing as part of marketing strategies. It is not possible for event marketing that is kept apart from general marketing or business strategies to be successful (Luttorp, 1997; Eckerstein, 2002: 2; Milgrom, 2002).

Any business should focus on four main decision areas before planning a marketing strategy. These decisions, known as product, price, place and promotion and expressed as 4P in marketing literature, form a marketing karma that every business should have (McCarthy, 1960: 45). Marketing karma elements known as 4P are also valid in event marketing. However, at the point of making event marketing different from other types of marketing, the "positioning" element should also be included and event marketing should be evaluated with the 5P. (Hoyle, 2012: 12). Accordingly, the **product** is the service offered by the event. The **Price** is the amount of money expected from the target group for the services provided within the event. The **Place** is the area prepared for presenting the event to the participants of the event. **Promotion** is the process of informing, persuading and influencing the target group regarding the event. **Positioning** is a necessary marketing karma element to fulfill the expectations of the participants at the event venue. The areas of interest of the consumers should be determined within the scope of positioning studies, which is a karma element related to the audience and therefore the target group of the event and the event should be designed accordingly (McCarthy, 1960: 45-47; Hoyle, 2012: 16-19).

The focus of event marketing is to convey various activities related to the event to be carried out to the target group. The mentioned event can involve different topics such as sports, entertainment, concerts, fairs, music. Therefore, it is important to analyze various demographic and psychographic characteristics of the target group well in order to determine what they are like, what they like, what they care about to market the event successfully (Saget, 2006). It should also be taken into account that a well-organized and executed event generates great value in the target group and leaves a long-lasting impression on the participants (Wood, 2009). The participants, who leave the event with positive impressions, share this situation with their social environments such as their families, friends and business circles. Therefore, the importance of event marketing is understood even better considering that different festivals and events are held in different places every year in the world and these events bring a competitive advantage and image to the host destination.

Social Media

There are different definitions in the literature regarding the concept of social media, which is one of the most powerful online tools of recent times, and which has been rapidly integrated into the social and economic life (Zeng & Gerritsen, 2014). Boyd and Ellison (2004: 211) have defined social media as "virtual environments where users create a profile which is wholly or partially open as well as a list of people they are in contact with, display and share with, and where they can observe the profiles and relationships of other users". According to Kaplan and Haenlein (2010: 61) social media is a "group of internet-based applications created by the user, enabling the production and sharing of content, built on the ideological and technological foundations of web 2.0". According to Kietzmann, Hermkens, Mc-Carthy and Silvestre (2011) social media is a highly interactive platform that uses mobile devices and other web-based technologies to facilitate individuals, groups and communities to develop, co-create, share, transform and discuss user-generated content. In the process, social media continued to develop and its usage areas expanded and hence its definitions changed and improved accordingly. In this context, Cohen (2011) gathered the important features and qualities of social media under three headings through his study which included nearly thirty social media definitions. Accordingly, (1) social media consists of online tools, applications, platforms and media and therefore depends on information technology; (2) the terminal-to-terminal communication channel using the social media web base enables interaction between various organizations, communities and individuals for information exchange, and brings significant and widespread changes in communication between those communities; (3) it is a tool that connects users to create a virtual community using social media cross platforms and therefore affects the behavior and real lives of people.

Nowadays social media is used for many different purposes. In other words, depending on the priorities of people, the utilization of social media differs from one person to another. Some people use this platform for entertainment, while others use it for organizational and business purposes. As a requirement of the current era, the popularity of social media is increasing day by day with the desire of people to stay in touch and interact with each other; it has become an excellent tool not only for entertainment purposes but also for businesses to realize their activities. Therefore, it is possible to state that the effective role of social media is active in all areas of life (Mangold & Faulds, 2009). One of these areas is marketing. In the field of marketing, social media is used as a great platform for customer orientation. Social media makes it easier for businesses to carry out their commercial activities and relieves their concerns about reaching customers (Wang, Carley, Zeng & Mao, 2007). However, the most important aspect of social media is that everything is related to people. Whether it is used for entertainment, mutual communication or commercial use, social media offers many possibilities such as the exchange of ideas, an energetic and dynamic discussion environment, perception of different thoughts, commercial coordination and cooperation on every platform (Bessenoff, 2006; Thompson, 2013). For all these reasons, the coverage of social media is expanding day by day and it is rapidly penetrating almost the whole world.

Social media tools such as Facebook, Instagram, Twitter, Youtube are the most widely known and recognized social media tools. While the common features of social media tools such as interaction, communication and sharing come to the fore in the conceptual definitions about social media, there are also some features that distinguish social media tools from each other. Although it does not seem possible to draw a systematic framework for the classification in question (Kaplan & Haenlein, 2010: 61; Fischer & Reuber 2011: 2-3), there are various classifications in the literature. Weinberg (2009: 9-11) classified social media in four groups, namely social news sites, social bookmarking sites, social networks and other social media sites. Kietzmann et al. (2011: 242) classified social media into seven groups as general mass sites, professional networks, media sharing sites, blogs, social news and bookmarking sites, microblogs, location-specific networks. Akar (2011: 25) classified social media blogs, microblogs as wikis, social networking sites, media sharing sites, social marking and tagging, podcasting and virtual worlds. While Fischer & Reuber (2011: 3) classified social media under eight different groups as social networks, social bookmarking, video sharing, photo sharing, professional networks, user forums, blogs and microblogs, Berthon et al. (2012: 263) distinguished them under five groups as blogs, microblogs, photo sharing sites, video sharing sites and social networks. An examination of the various classifications made in the literature reveals that the common denominator of social media tools appears to be social networks, blogs, microblogs and Wikis.

1. **Social networks:** According to Boyd and Ellison (2008: 211) social networks are internet-based services that allow people to create a public or semi-public profile within a limited system, to specify a clear list of other users with whom they share links, and reciprocally see the lists of others in the system and their activities". On the other, social networks are defined by Kaplan and Haenlein (2010: 63) as "Social networking sites are applications that create personal information profiles which can contain any kind of information such as photos, videos, audio files and blogs and invite friends and colleagues to access this profile, and send e-mails and exchange instant messages with each other, allowing users to connect with each other." Social networks have features that enable (1) user-owned profile pages and the sharing of text, video, music, (2) a higher user interaction than traditional media tools, (3) sharing that can be seen by all platform users at the request of the user, (4)) private messaging with other users and (5) is especially common among young internet users (Weinberg, 2009: 11; Kaplan & Haenlein, 2010: 63-64; Phua, Jin & Kim, 2017: 412-413).

2. **Blogs:** Blogs are a variant of websites with unique characteristics. Blogs are one of the first tools according to the chronological classification of social media. Blogs can be considered the equivalent of personal internet pages on social media (Kaplan & Haenlein, 2010: 63). Nardi, Schiano and Gumbrecht (2004: 222) have defined blogs as "websites that are usually sequenced in a reverse-chronological order, contain archived sharing series and are frequently updated". Akar (2011: 49) defines blogs as "a website, which is usually maintained by individuals or groups, recently by businesses which offers comments and ideas for a wide audience". Blogs include features such as (1) a reverse-chronological order in terms of sent content, (2) enabling interaction with readers, (3) frequently updated content, (4) it is comparable to a personal diary in terms of format, and (5) it is generally managed by a single person (Nardi et al., 2004: 222; Kaplan & Haenlein, 2010: 63).

3. **Microblogs:** Microblogs are smaller versions of social media compared to blogs. Berthon et al. (2012: 263) define microblogs as platforms where users exchange short text messages with character limitations. Microblogs are platforms that enable real-time updates (Kietzmann et al., 2011: 242), are faster to access and easier to use than blogs (Safko, 2012: 291). Features describing microblogs are indicated as (1) character limitation in the content sent, (2) posts are sorted in reverse chronological order, (3) users can establish friendships, (4) instantaneous news can be received, (5) messages, audio, images and files can be sent, and (6) they have features that enable product-service research and purchasing (Berthon et al., 2012: 263; Safko, 2012: 291).

4. **Wikis:** Wikis can be defined as internet-based information pages created and edited by users. Wikis are "Web sites that allow users to add, remove and modify text-based content" (Kaplan & Haenlein, 2010: 62). Wikis are noteworthy platforms in the context of users who connect to the internet with a decentralized system which generates results that are at least as good as those of an organization with a traditional hierarchical structure (Rigby, 2008: 11). Wikis are social media platforms (1) where their users can voluntarily add, remove or edit information-based content, (2) where the reliability of the content depends on the integrity of the contributors, and (3) that have an encyclopedic knowledge base (Rigby, 2008: 11; Kaplan & Haenlein, 2010: 62; Safko, 2012: 168).

Social media is a communication network that gives the opportunity to directly and precisely connect with many segments such as friends, family, relatives, acquaintances, colleagues, brand representatives, suppliers and customers (Gilbert and Karahalios, 2009). In recent years the importance of social media for businesses that have goods or services to offer in reaching and interacting with consumer masses is noteworthy (Hanna, Rohm and Crittenden, 2011). In this context, social media has become a prominent tool especially in the marketing activities of businesses. Marketing is a phenomenon that changes its rules and consequently its dimensions to develop according to constantly changing consumer expectations (Thackeray, Neiger, Hanson & McKenzie, 2008). Along with the globalization process ongoing throughout the world, the difference in the lifestyles of today's people compared to the previous generations has caused enterprises to turn to new searches in their marketing studies (Mulhern, 2009). Businesses, which have adopted many different marketing tools according to the periods they are in, have rapidly adapted to internet-based virtual usage that has developed with the advancement of technology in recent years. In this context, the increasing use of the internet, comfortable, fast and easy access to communication tools has also attracted marketers (Brown, Broderick & Lee, 2007; Saravanakumar & Suganthalakshmi, 2012). Therefore, today in many areas, social media is the focal point of individuals promoting and selling their products to giant multinational companies and corporate organizations.

Social Media in Event Marketing

Nowadays, it is possible to state that approximately half of the world's population, in other words, one out of every two people worldwide are social media users. It is possible to state that the main factor in increasing the use of social media in the world is that people have easier access to the internet. According to the January report of "2020 World Internet Usage and Social Media Statistics" published by "We Are Social", 59% of the world population (approximately 4.54 billion people) is internet, 49% (approximately 3.80 billion people) is an active social media user. Considering the previous year's data, the number of internet users in the world increased by 7% (298 million people) and the number of social media users increased by 9.2% (321 million people). When social media usage is ranked according to social media platforms, "Facebook" ranks first with its 2.49 billion users. "Youtube" with 2 billion users and "WhatsApp" with 1.6 billion users follow Facebook (Kemp, 2020). Therefore, from this point of view, it can be asserted that using social media is the fastest and most effective tool in the marketing studies of any product or a destination in the current world. In other words, social media is one of the platforms that are considered to be the most popular and fastest way of communicating and interacting with a large number of people (Evans, 2010).

Social media, which enables people to connect, interact and communicate with others virtually, provides these links with different social media tools and after a while the difference between virtual and real interaction decreases for people (Scott, 2009). From this point of view, the major and important role played by social media plays in the success of any event or activity is undeniable. Therefore, within the scope of the event marketing activities, the use of social media is very important in the process starting with the promotion activities of an event to the moment it starts and proceeds and subsequently to get feedback about the participant experiences. From this aspect, the basic elements of event marketing through social media need to be taken into account. These (Horo, 2015: 22-23):

1. **Provide Networking Opportunity:** Thanks to social media access, establishing potential connections with the event is enabled. These connections can be made before, during and even after the event. This will positively affect the course of the event and ensure a more efficient and productive process among the participants.
2. **Provide Informational Content:** Within the scope of marketing efforts for any event to be successful the preferences, tastes and similarities of the target audience must be analyzed well and planning should be done accordingly. At this point, social media tools (Facebook, Twitter, LinkedIn etc.) provide the advantage of following the likes and preferences of the target audience. Therefore, this advantage provides valuable information in creating the content of the event.
3. **Present Perfect Criticism:** Social media is a tool that encourages everyone to participate and be included in such an event. This does not only include the participants of the events, it includes a comprehensive range of speakers, staff, event planners and organizers. Therefore, all these participants will have a role in examining the event and presenting critical analysis. This will result in the participant groups undertaking the role of spreading the event all over the world via social media networks. An interaction of this size may also have disadvantages; however, it is a great opportunity for the event to be recognized and popular on a large scale. Furthermore, event organizers and planners will have the opportunity to carefully monitor participants' feedback and responses to be prepared for upcoming events.

Social media presents major advantages to enterprises practicing event marketing such as the opportunity to characterize the participants of the event, the potential of people to interact with each other by networking, and enabling the further dissemination of the effects related to the event even after its completion (Chalip, 2006; Williams & Chinn, 2010). The execution and success of an activity requires great effort. The success of an event is directly proportional to the number of participants as well as its attractiveness. Therefore, considering the potential of social media platforms to gather many people over network connections (Smith, 2006), its effectiveness in event marketing can be understood more clearly.

Mobile devices, which have emerged as a result of the rapid development of technology today, have also changed the dimensions of word of mouth marketing, one of the most common traditional marketing approaches. Word of mouth marketing is considered as one of the most effective, reliable and efficient marketing tools in the marketing literature. Nowadays, this category includes marketing with social media and social network usage. In fact, it can be argued that marketing activities through word-of-mouth communication are carried out on social media platforms (Williams & Chinn, 2010). This is accomplished by monitoring the sharing of different groups on social media sites, through social media, which plays an active role in determining the interests and expectations of businesses and event planners in the target market (Chalip, 2006). Sharing with mobile devices not only before the event but especially during the event increases the number of participants, and for those who cannot attend, it can create a feeling of following the event live and even being there. Therefore, the use of social media in event marketing is of great importance not only for the success of the event, but also for the reputation and brand awareness of the business organizer (Smith, 2006) as well as the event destination.

It is important that the studies on the use of social media tools in relation to event marketing are consistent with the studies on marketing activities with other communication channels. In other words, the content of the promotion, advertisement, informative activities carried out through various media such as television, posters and billboards related to the event and the content of the activities carried out on social networks such as Facebook, Instagram and Twitter should be similar. Messages with different contents to be given in different communication channels for any event may cause perception problems for the participants. However, the most important reason why social media tools are preferred more in event marketing is because while messages intended to attract the attention of participants in marketing studies conducted with traditional media wait for a reaction, transmissions made through social media tools generate value with instant participation and response (Gunelius, 2011: 11). In this context, there are clear differences between using social media in event marketing and using other marketing efforts such as continuous communication with the participants, involving the participants and, as a result, invoke a unique experience on the part of the participants (Kim & Ko, 2012: 1484). Some of the benefits of marketing efforts using social media can be listed as follows (Tuten, 2008: 19-20; Whiting & Deshpande, 2016: 84-85):

- As a result of the change which incurred in word of mouth communication with the development of the internet, the exchange of ideas about an event can spread very quickly.
- The interaction between event organizers and participants is strengthened.
- The message ensures that the target market is exposed longer to the message conveyed about the event.
- As a result, the target market, which is exposed to the message for a long time, is more likely to be involved in the event.
- Social media increases the internalization of the message about the event and strengthens the brand value.
- As a result of social media enabling closer and mutual communication with the participants, the expectations and desires of the target audience are understood more clearly and therefore the content of the event is shaped accordingly.
- Social media reduces the cost of communicating with the target market.
- Social media provides the opportunity to send personalized messages to the target audience.
- Social media offers the opportunity to reach a more specific target audience compared to other marketing tools.
- The positive impact of event marketing through social media lasts longer compared to other marketing tools.

SOLUTIONS AND RECOMMENDATIONS

In order to benefit effectively from the use of social media within the scope of event marketing activities, the elements of reading, creating, sharing and discussing that are important within the framework of the social media-based marketing approach should be taken into consideration. In this context, a detailed research should be carried out on social media on issues related to the activity planned as a priority. At this point, all posts, interactions, and conversations that might concern the event should be examined. While doing this, it should not be forgotten that social media is an active medium and the examinations in question should be continuous. Subsequently, content that might attract the attention of social media users and prepare the ground for their conversations should be created. Content related to the event to be organized and similar content related to the subject should be shared during the sharing process. Finally, it should not be forgotten that social media has a bi-directional communication network due to its dynamics and the comments on the posts should be taken seriously, answered if necessary, and the discussion environment should be kept robust by continuing the dialogue with the target audience.

FUTURE RESEARCH DIRECTIONS

Nowadays, it is possible to come across different studies in the literature regarding the activities realized with social media which is the fastest and most effective way of reaching large audiences and the participation of large masses. The role of social media in activity marketing studies has been discussed within the conceptual framework of the scope of the study. However, the subject of the study and similar issues has the potential to be a broader and more comprehensive field study. For researchers who want to work on a similar subject in the future, an efficient study result can be achieved by monitoring the process of a major event from the preparation stage to the feedback stage in the field. In addition, the effects of event marketing through social media on the awareness and image of the destination where the event is organized can be proposed as another subject to be studied.

CONCLUSION

Being involved in an event is invoked by the social aspects of people. Likewise, the essence of social media is about people being "social". Therefore, "social media", which is a social event, is also one of the most accurate tools that can be used for "event" activities, which are also social events. It is an accepted fact that social media enables people to connect and interact with each other and almost the whole world by using the innovations brought by technology. In this context, it can be said that businesses, organizations and agencies operating in all sectors, especially those that are involved in service marketing efforts, are very eager to use the communication and interaction power of social media. Consequently, the event industry, which has common characteristics regardless of type, purpose and scale, uses social media in almost every important step of their marketing activities such as promotion, advertising and publicity.

Reaching the target audience directly or indirectly is at the core of each event. In this context, the power of social media in reaching people directly, and especially the ability to get feedback from this outreach, makes this media indispensable in terms of event marketing activities. The fact that social media is a communication channel with the highest number of users in the world has made it an indispensable element of event marketing. Therefore, events that can act in integration with social media will benefit from all the technological opportunities offered by social networks. The activities and organizations related to an event activity reach large masses to be included in the event or to think about participating at a later time, talking about it to their inner circle such as friends, relatives, acquaintances through word of mouth and sharing their positive or negative opinions about the event with them as well as the event organizers makes social media the most effective tool in event marketing.

In conclusion, the reasons why social media is becoming a more and more indispensable element of human life with every passing day, the strengthening and increasing number of followers, and the opportunities enabled by technology which have started to offer limitless opportunities in social media in many areas have made social media an important channel for events as well. Whether it is a large mega event or a small local one, social media used in readying the groundwork for the preparation and presentation of practically every stage of events organized today motivates the participants of the event with its entertaining, informative, sharing, and interactive aspects and is also an important promotional tool for the brand or company and the destination where the event is organized.

REFERENCES

Akar, E. (2011). *Sosyal medya pazarlaması: Sosyal Web'te pazarlama stratejileri*. Efil Yayınevi.

Aktan, E., & Çakmak, V. (2015). Halkla ilişkiler öğrencilerinin sosyal medyadaki siber zorbalık duyarlılıklarını ölçmeye ilişkin bir araştırma. *Gümüşhane Üniversitesi İletişim Fakültesi Elektronik Dergisi*, *3*(2), 159–176.

Arcodia, C. & Robb, A. (2000). A future for event management: A taxonomy of event management terms. In J. Allen, R. Harris, L. K. Jago, & A. J. Veal (Eds.), *Events beyond 2000: Setting the agenda, proceedings of conference on event evaluation, research and education*. Sydney: Australian Centre for Event Management School of Leisure, Sport and Tourism, University of Technology.

Arcodia, C., & Whitford, M. (2006). Festival attendance and the development of social capital. *Journal of Convention & Event Tourism*, *8*(2), 1–18. doi:10.1300/J452v08n02_01

Argan, M. (2007). *Eglence pazarlamasi*. Detay Yayincilik.

Atçı, D., Unur, K., & Gürsoy, D. (2016). The impacts of hosting major sporting events: Resident's perceptions of the mediterranean games 2013 in Mersin. *International Review of Management and Marketing*, *6*(1), 139–145.

Behrer, M., & Larsson, A. (1998). *Event marketing att använda evenemang som strategisk resurs i marknadsföringen*. IHM Förlag AB.

Berridge, G. (2007). *Events design and experience, events management series* (1st ed.). Elsevier. doi:10.4324/9780080468112

Berthon, P. R., Pitt, L. F., Plangger, K., & Shapiro, D. (2012). Marketing meets web 2.0, social media, and creative consumers: Implications for international marketing strategy. *Business Horizons*, *55*(3), 261–271. doi:10.1016/j.bushor.2012.01.007

Bessenoff, G. R. (2006). Can the media affect us? Social comparison, self-discrepancy, and then ideal. *Psychology of Women Quarterly*, *30*(3), 239–251. doi:10.1111/j.1471-6402.2006.00292.x

Bhe, T., Glasmacker, P., Meckwood, J., Pereira, G. & Wallace, M. (2004). *Event management and best practices*. IBM.

Bowdin, G. A., Allen, J., O'Toole, W., Harris, R., & McDonell, I. (2006). *Events management* (2nd ed.). Publishing House Elsevier. doi:10.4324/9780080457154

Boyd, D. M., & Ellison, N. B. (2008). Social network sites: Definition, history, and scholarship. *Journal of Computer-Mediated Communication, 13*(1), 210–230. doi:10.1111/j.1083-6101.2007.00393.x

Brown, J., Broderick, A. J., & Lee, N. (2007). Word of mouth communication within online communities: Conceptualizing the online social network. *Journal of Interactive Marketing, 21*(3), 2–20. doi:10.1002/dir.20082

Chalip, L. (2006). Towards social leverage of sport events. *Journal of Sport & Tourism, 11*(2), 109–127. doi:10.1080/14775080601155126

Chu, S. C., & Kim, Y. (2017). The influence of perceived interactivity of social media advertising and voluntary self-disclosure on attitudes and intentions to pass-along. In Advertising and Branding: Concepts, Methodologies, Tools, and Applications (pp.1388-1405). IGI Global. doi:10.4018/978-1-5225-1793-1.ch064

Close, A. G., Finney, R. Z., Lacey, R. Z., & Sneath, J. Z. (2006). Engaging the consumer through event marketing: Linking attendees with the sponsor, community, and brand. *Journal Of Advertising Research, New York, 46*(4), 420–433. doi:10.2501/S0021849906060430

Cohen, H. (2011). *30 social media definitions. Posted by Heidi Cohen on May 9, 2011 in actionable marketing social media, 101.* http://heidicohen.com/ social-media-definition/

Crompton, J. L., & Stacey, L. (1997). Motives of visitors attending festival events. *Annals of Tourism Research, 24*(2), 425–439. doi:10.1016/S0160-7383(97)80010-2

Delamere, T. A., Wankel, L. M., & Hinch, T. D. (2001). Development of a scale to measure resident attitudes toward the social impacts of community festivals, part 1: Item generation and purification of the measure. *Event Management, 7*(1), 11–24. doi:10.3727/152599501108751443

Derret, R. (2011). Festivals, Events and The Destination. In *Festival and events management an international arts and cultural perspective*. Routledge Taylor&Francis Group.

Derrett, R. (2004). Making sense of how festivals demonstrate a community's sense of place. *Event Management, 8*(1), 49–58. doi:10.3727/152599503108751694

Dwyer, L., Mellor, R., Mistilis, N., & Mules, T. (2000). A framework for evaluating and forecasting the impacts of special events. In J. Allen, R. Harris, L. K. Jago, & A. J. Veal (Eds.), *Events beyond 2000: Setting the agenda* (pp. 31–45). Australian Centre for Event Management.

Eckerstein, A. (2002). *Evaluation of event marketing important indicators to consider when evaluating event marketing* (Master thesis). Graduate Business School School of Economics and Commercial Law, Göteborg University.

Evans, D. (2010). *Social media marketing: the next generation of business engagement*. John Wiley & Sons.

Fischer, E., & Reuber, A. R. (2011). Social interaction via new social media: (How) can interactions on twitter affect effectual thinking and behavior? *Journal of Business Venturing*, *26*(1), 1–18. doi:10.1016/j.jbusvent.2010.09.002

Fredline, E., & Faulker, B. (2000). Host community reactions a cluster analysis. *Annals of Tourism Research*, *27*(3), 763–784. doi:10.1016/S0160-7383(99)00103-6

Getz, D. (1993). Festivals and special events. In M. A. Khan, M. D. Olsen, & T. Var (Eds.), *Encyclopedia of hospitality and tourism* (pp. 789–810). Van Nostrand Reinhold.

Getz, D. (1997). *Event management and event tourism*. Cognizant Communication Corporation.

Gilbert, E., & Karahalios, K. (2009). Predicting tie strength with social media. In *Proceedings of the SIGCHI Conference on Human Factors in Computing Systems* (pp. 211-220). ACM.

Gunelius, S. (2011). *30-Minute social media marketing*. McGraw-Hill.

Gursoy, D., & Kendall, K. W. (2006). Hosting mega events-modelling locals' support. *Annals of Tourism Research*, *33*(3), 603–623. doi:10.1016/j.annals.2006.01.005

Hanna, R., Rohm, A., & Crittenden, V. L. (2011). We're all connected: The power of the social media ecosystem. *Business Horizons*, *54*(3), 265–273. doi:10.1016/j.bushor.2011.01.007

Hiller, H. H. (1998). Assessing the impact of mega-events: A linkage model. *Current Issues in Tourism*, *1*(1), 47–57. doi:10.1080/13683509808667832

Horo, S. (2015). *The Role of Social Media on Event Marketing* (Master's Thesis). The Republic of Turkey Bahcesehir University, Istanbul.

Hoyle, L. H. (2012). *How to successfully promote events, festivals, conventions, and expositions*. John Wiley & Sons.

Janiskee, R. L. (1996). Historic houses and special events. *Annals of Tourism Research*, *23*(2), 398–414. doi:10.1016/0160-7383(95)00069-0

Jeong, G. H., & Faulkner, B. (1996). Resident perceptions of mega-event impacts: The Taejon International Exposition Case. *Festival Management & Event Tourism*, *4*(1-2), 3–11. doi:10.3727/106527096792232388

Kaplan, A. M., & Haenlein, M. (2010). Users of the world, unite! The challenges and opportunities of social media. *Business Horizons*, *53*(1), 59–68. doi:10.1016/j.bushor.2009.09.003

Kaynak, S., & Koç, S. (2015). Telif hakları hukuku'nun yeni macerası: Sosyal medya. *Folklor/Edebiyat*, *21*(83), 389-410.

Kemp, S. (2020). *Digital 2020: 3.8 Billion People Use Social Media*. https://wearesocial.com/blog/2020/01/digital-2020-3-8-billion-people-use-social-media

Kietzmann, J. H., Hermkens, K., McCarthy, I. P., & Silvestre, B. S. (2011). Social media? Get serious! Understanding the functional building blocks of social media. *Business Horizons*, *54*(3), 241–251. doi:10.1016/j.bushor.2011.01.005

Kim, A. J., & Ko, E. (2010). Impacts of luxury fashion brand's social media marketing on customer relationship and purchase intention. *Journal of Global Fashion Marketing*, *1*(3), 164–171. doi:10.1080 /20932685.2010.10593068

Koçyiğit, M. (2015). *Sosyal ağ pazarlaması marka bağlılığı oluşturmada bir pazarlama stratejisi.* Eğitim Yayınevi.

Koh, K. Y., & Jackson, A. A. (2006). Special events marketing. *Journal of Convention & Event Tourism*, *8*(2), 19–44. doi:10.1300/J452v08n02_02

Leenders, M. A., Go, F. M., & Bhansing, P. V. (2015). The importance of the location in hosting a festival: A mapping approach. *Journal of Hospitality Marketing & Management*, *24*(7), 754–769. doi:10. 1080/19368623.2014.934981

Lundmark, M. (1998). Lys upp marknaden med Event Marketing. *Sälj och marknadsstrategi, 8*, 50-57.

Luttorp, E. (1997). Event marketing. *Ansikte Mot Ansikte Med Målgruppen,* 45-47.

Mackellar, J. (2008). Conventions, festivals and tourism. *Journal of Convention & Event Tourism*, *8*(2), 45–56. doi:10.1300/J452v08n02_03

Mangold, W. G., & Faulds, D. J. (2009). Social media: The new hybrid element of the promotion mix. *Business Horizons*, *52*(4), 357–365. doi:10.1016/j.bushor.2009.03.002

Martensen, A., Gronholdt, L., Bendtsen, L., & Jensen, M. J. (2007). Application of a model for the effectiveness of event marketing. *Journal of Advertising Research-New York*, *47*(3), 283–301. doi:10.2501/ S0021849907070316

McCarthy, E. J. (1960). *Basic marketing: A managerial approach.* R.D. Irwin, Indiana University.

McDonnel, I., Allen, J., & O'Toole, W. (1998). *Festival and special event management.* John Wiley & Sons.

Milgrom, J. (2002). *Two decades of event marketing and sponsorship, I have good and bad news. In Event Marketing Strategies.* EMS.

Milman, A. (2010). The global theme park industry. *Worldwide Hospitality and Tourism Themes*, *2*(3), 220–237. doi:10.1108/17554211011052177

Mulhern, F. (2009). Integrated marketing communications: From media channels to digital connectivity. *Journal of Marketing Communications*, *15*(2-3), 85–101. doi:10.1080/13527260902757506

Murphy, P. E., & Carmichael, B. A. (1991). Assesing the tourism benefits of an open access sports tournament: The 1989 B. C. Winter Games. *Journal of Travel Research*, *29*(32), 32–36. doi:10.1177/004728759102900305

Nardi, B. A., Schiano, D. J., & Gumbrecht, M. (2004). Blogging as social activity, or, would you let 900 million people read your diary? CSCW'04, 222-231.

Neirotti, L. D., Bosetti, H. A., & Teed, K. C. (2001). Motivation to attend the 1996 Summer Olympic Games. *Journal of Travel Research*, *39*(3), 327–331. doi:10.1177/004728750103900315

Phua, J., Jin, S. V., & Kim, J. (2017). Gratifications of using facebook, twitter, instagram, or snapchat to follow brands: The moderating effect of social comparison, trust, tie strength, and network homophily on brand identification, brand engagement, brand commitment, and membership intention. *Telematics and Informatics, 34*(1), 412–424. doi:10.1016/j.tele.2016.06.004

Raj, R., & Musgrave, J. (2009). *Event management and sustainability*. CABI. doi:10.1079/9781845935245.0000

Richards, G., & Wilson, J. (2004). The impact of cultural events on city image: Rotterdam, Cultural Capital of Europe 2001. *Urban Studies (Edinburgh, Scotland), 41*(10), 1931–1951. doi:10.1080/0042098042000256323

Rigby, B. (2008). *Mobilizing generation 2.0: A practical guide to using web 2.0 technologies to recruit, organize, and engage youth*. Jossey-Bass.

Safko, L. (2010). *The social media bible: tactics, tools, and strategies for business success*. John Wiley & Sons.

Saget, A. (2006). *The event marketing handbook: beyond logistics and planning*. Kaplan Publishing.

Saravanakumar, M., & Suganthalakshmi, T. (2012). Social media marketing. *Life Science Journal, 9*(4), 4444–4451.

Scott, D. M. (2009). *The new rules of marketing and PR: how to use social media, blogs, news releases, online video, and viral marketing to reach buyers directly*. John Wiley & Sons.

Silvers, J. R. (2004). *Professional event coordination*. John Wiley & Sons Inc.

Smith, W. A. (2006). Social marketing: An overview of approach and effects. *Injury Prevention, 12*(1, suppl_1), 38–43. doi:10.1136/ip.2006.012864 PMID:16788110

Tassiopoulos, D. (2005). *Event management: A professional and developmental approach* (2nd ed.). Juta Academic.

Thackeray, R., Neiger, B. L., Hanson, C. L., & McKenzie, J. F. (2008). Enhancing promotional strategies within social marketing programs: Use of Web 2.0 social media. *Health Promotion Practice, 9*(4), 338–343. doi:10.1177/1524839908325335 PMID:18936268

Theocharis, N. (2008). *Event Tourism: Examining the management of sports events from a physical approach*. Synenergy Forum, Athens.

Thevenot, G. (2007). Blogging as a social media. *Tourism and Hospitality Research, 7*(3/4), 287–289. doi:10.1057/palgrave.thr.6050062

Thompson, J. B. (2013). *Media and modernity: A social theory of the media*. John Wiley & Sons.

Toner, L. & Walker, M. (2014). *The new age of event marketing: Increase event attendance and engagment with an inbound marketing strategy*. Https://cdn2.hubspot.net/hub/53/file-1298172927pdf/The_New_Age_of_Event_Marketing.pdf

Tuten, T. L. (2008). *Advertising 2.0: Social media marketing in a web 2.0 world*. Praeger.

Van der Wagen, L. (2005). *Event management for tourism, cultural, business and sporting events* (2nd ed.). Pearson Education Australia.

Vural, Z. B., & Bat, M. (2010). Yeni bir iletişim ortamı olarak sosyal medya: Ege Üniversitesi İletişim Fakültesine yönelik bir araştırma. *Journal of Yasar University*, 5(20), 3348–3382.

Wang, F. Y., Carley, K. M., Zeng, D., & Mao, W. (2007). Social computing: From social informatics to social intelligence. *IEEE Intelligent Systems*, 22(2), 79–83. doi:10.1109/MIS.2007.41

Wang, W. T., & Li, H. M. (2012). Factors influencing mobile services adoption: A brand-equity perspective. *Internet Research*, 22(2), 142–179. doi:10.1108/10662241211214548

Weinberg, T. (2009). *The new community rules: Marketing on the social web*. O'Reilly Media.

Whiting, A., & Deshpande, A. (2016). Towards greater understanding of social media marketing: A review. *Journal of Applied Business and Economics*, 18(4), 82–91.

Williams, J., & Chinn, S. J. (2010). Meeting relationship-marketing goals through social media: A conceptual model for sport marketers. *International Journal of Sport Communication*, 3(4), 422–437. doi:10.1123/ijsc.3.4.422

Wood, E. H. (2009). Evaluating event marketing: Experience or outcome? *Journal of Promotion Management*, 15(1-2), 247–268. doi:10.1080/10496490902892580

Yürük, P. (2015). Etkinlik pazarlamasında sosyal etki algılamasının etkinliğe katılım, tatmin ve sadakat üzerine etkisi: Kırkpınar festivali örneği (Doktora tezi). Trakya Üniversitesi Sosyal Bilimler Enstitüsü, İşletme A.B.D., Edirne.

Zeng, B., & Gerritsen, R. (2014). What do we know about social media in tourism? A review. *Tourism Management Perspectives*, 10, 27–36. doi:10.1016/j.tmp.2014.01.001

ADDITIONAL READING

Chalip, L., & Green, B. C. (2001). Event marketing and destination image. In *American Marketing Association. Conference Proceedings*, 12, 346-351.

Kose, H., Argan, M. T., & Argan, M. (2011). Special event management and event marketing: A case study of TKBL all star 2011 in Turkey. *Journal of Management and Marketing Research*, 8, 1.

Leung, D., Law, R., Van Hoof, H., & Buhalis, D. (2013). Social media in tourism and hospitality: A literature review. *Journal of Travel & Tourism Marketing*, 30(1-2), 3–22. doi:10.1080/10548408.2013.750919

Wood, E. H., & Masterman, G. (2008, January). Event marketing: Measuring an experience. In *7th International Marketing Trends Congress*, Venice.

Zhang, J., & Wu, F. (2008). Mega-event marketing and urban growth coalitions: A case study of Nanjing Olympic New Town. *The Town Planning Review*, 79(2-3), 209–227. doi:10.3828/tpr.79.2-3.4

KEY TERMS AND DEFINITIONS

Event: Event is a series of activities that enable the revival of natural and physical resources in the cities or countries where it is organized, creating an image for that place and increasing the tourism attraction of the destination in question.

Event Marketing: The main theme of event marketing focuses on providing the audience with positive experiences about the event. The event is a formation that includes participants. Conveying messages about the event to the participants in question and transferring the experiences they can experience is related to the function of event marketing.

Social Media: Social media consists of online tools, applications, platforms and media and therefore depends on information technology; the terminal-to-terminal communication channel using the social media web base enables interaction between various organizations, communities and individuals for information exchange, and brings significant and widespread changes in communication between those communities; it is a tool that connects users to create a virtual community using social media cross platforms and therefore affects the behavior and real lives of people.

Social Media in Event Marketing: It is possible to state that the main factor in increasing the use of social media in the world is that people have easier access to the internet. Therefore, from this point of view, it can be asserted that using social media is the fastest and most effective tool in the marketing studies of any product or a destination in the current world. Therefore, within the scope of the event marketing activities, the use of social media is very important in the process starting with the promotion activities of an event to the moment it starts and proceeds and subsequently to get feedback about the participant experiences.

This research was previously published in Impact of ICTs on Event Management and Marketing; pages 262-281, copyright year 2021 by Business Science Reference (an imprint of IGI Global).

Index

T

U

V

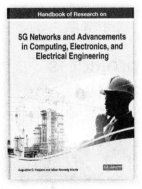
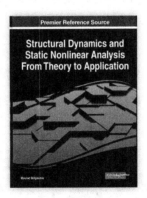

Ensure Quality Research is Introduced to the Academic Community

Become an Evaluator for IGI Global Authored Book Projects

Premier Reference Source

Stabilizing Currency and Preserving Economic Sovereignty Using the Grondona System

Patrick Collins

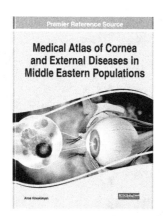

Premier Reference Source

Medical Atlas of Cornea and External Diseases in Middle Eastern Populations

Anna Hovakimyan

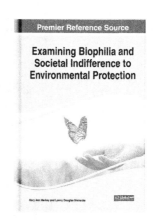

Premier Reference Source

Examining Biophilia and Societal Indifference to Environmental Protection

Mary Ann Markey and Lenny Douglas Meinecke

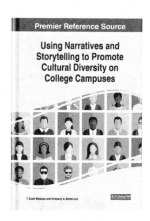

Premier Reference Source

Using Narratives and Storytelling to Promote Cultural Diversity on College Campuses

T. Scott Bledsoe and Kimberly A. Setterlund

The overall success of an authored book project is dependent on quality and timely manuscript evaluations.

Applications and Inquiries may be sent to:
development@igi-global.com

Applicants must have a doctorate (or equivalent degree) as well as publishing, research, and reviewing experience. Authored Book Evaluators are appointed for one-year terms and are expected to complete at least three evaluations per term. Upon successful completion of this term, evaluators can be considered for an additional term.

If you have a colleague that may be interested in this opportunity, we encourage you to share this information with them.

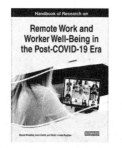

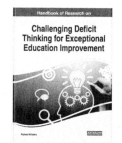

Printed in the United States
by Baker & Taylor Publisher Services